About the Authors

Wayne E. King is the Academic Dean at the Baltimore School for the Arts. He received his Bachelor of Science and Master of Science degrees from The Johns Hopkins University. He has taught American History and social studies at all educational levels. Mr. King has served as a consultant to schools, museums, and federal agencies and has lectured at national and international conferences on the teaching of American history and culture.

John L. Napp taught history for 30 years in both public and private schools. He also taught other social studies subjects, including political science, economics, and geography. He has been recognized for his excellence in teaching.

Photo credits for this textbook can be found on page 801.

The publisher wishes to thank the following people for their helpful comments during the review process for *United States History*. Their assistance has been invaluable.

Nelson Acevedo, Alternative Schools and Programs, Jamaica, NY; **Mary Ames**, Central Hardin High School, Cecilia, KY; **Ellen August**, City of Angels, Los Angeles, CA; **Stephen Baker**, Austwell-Tivoli High School, Tivoli, TX; **Phyllis Berman**, Scott School Assistance Center, Toledo Public Schools, Toledo, OH; **Gayle Boroughs**, Oak Ridge High School, Oak Ridge, TN; **Dr. Virginia Bryg**, Reading Consultant, Omaha Public Schools, Omaha, NE; **Sherryl Duff-Conrad**, Penn Hills Senior High School, Pittsburgh, PA; **Judy Faught**, Bowling Green High School, Bowling Green, KY; **Gustav Mark Gedatus**, Consulting Editor, Minneapolis, MN; **Jan Gleason**, Omaha Public Schools, Omaha, NE; **Gay Nita Grimm**, Emporia High School, Emporia, KS; **Debora J. Hartzell**, Lead Teacher, Special Education, East DeKalb Campus, Stone Mountain, GA; **Michael P. Hawkins**, SED Teacher, Brandon High School, Brandon, FL; **Dawn Holley**, Social Studies Teacher, Camden High School, Camden, NJ; **Janice Jones**, Curriculum Specialist/Special Education, Toledo Public Schools, Toledo, OH; **James John Kelly Jr.**, Social Studies Teacher, Camden High School, Camden, NJ; **Desi Kovacs**, Department Chair, Education Specialist, Canyon High School, Canyon Country, CA; **Gary Lussier**, Intern Assistant Principal, Barton Open Middle School, Minneapolis, MN; **Virginia Malling**, Oak Ridge High School, Oak Ridge, TN; **Laurence R. Manchester**, St. Paul School District, St. Paul, MN; **Anne Mandeville**, Santana High School, Rowland Heights, CA; **John Andrew O'Connor**, Accotink Academy, Springfield, VA; **Diane Odegard**, School District of Kansas City, Missouri, Kansas City, MO; **Debbie Persky**, City of Angels, Los Angeles, CA; **Lynn Pritchett**, Colquitt County High School, Moultrie, GA; **John W. Reiners**, Social Studies Teacher, Camden High School Camden, NJ; **Alice C. Richardson**, Central High School, Detroit, MI; **Christina Rivett**, Special Education Teacher, East Jackson High School, Coldwater, MI; **Dr. Clifford Watson**, Principal, Malcolm X Academy, Detroit, MI; **Cheryl Weglewski**, Wilmington High School, Wilmington, IL

Publisher's Project Staff

Vice President of Curriculum and Publisher: Sari Follansbee, Ed.D.; Director of Curriculum Development: Teri Mathews; Managing Editor: Patrick Keithahn; Senior Editor: Susan Weinlick; Development Assistant: Bev Johnson; Director of Creative Services: Nancy Condon; Senior Designer: Daren Hastings; Senior Production Coordinator/Designer: Laura Henrichsen; Purchasing Agent: Mary Kaye Kuzma; Product Manager: Brian Holl

© 2005 AGS Publishing
4201 Woodland Road
Circle Pines, MN 55014-1796
800-328-2560 • www.agsnet.com

Printed in the United States of America
ISBN 0-7854-3859-9
Product Number 94100
A 0 9 8 7 6

Contents

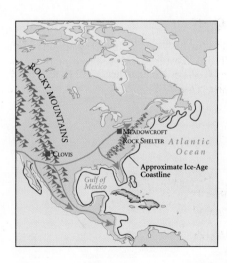

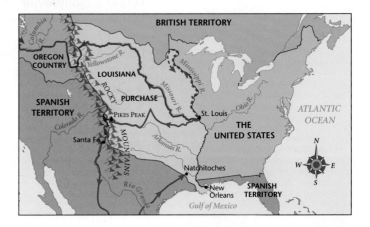

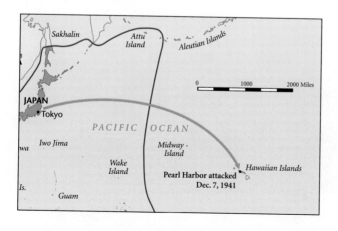

Biography

History in Your Life

Document-Based Reading

Civics Connection

Focus on Economics

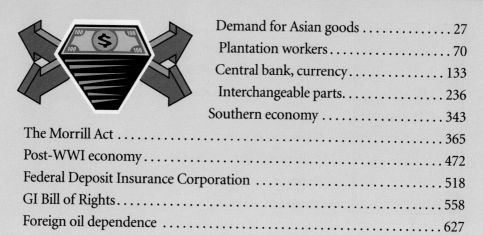

Technology Connection

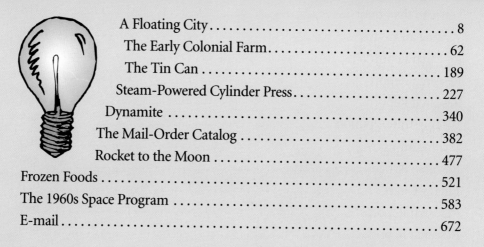

Skill Builder

Maps

Maps (continued)

Appendixes

How to Use This Book: A Study Guide

Welcome to the study of United States history. You may be asking yourself, "Why do I need to know about people, places, and events that happened a long time before I was even born?" When we study the past, we can have a better understanding of why some things happened the way they did. We can learn from the mistakes and the successes of the past.

This book is a story about the United States. As you read the units, chapters and lessons of this book, you will learn about the important people and events that shaped United States history.

Before you start to read this book, it is important that you understand how to use it. It is also important that you know how to be successful in this course. Information in this first section can help you achieve these things.

How to Study

These tips can help you study more effectively:

■ Plan a regular time to study.

■ Choose a desk or table in a quiet place where you will not be distracted. Find a spot that has good lighting.

■ Gather all the books, pencils, paper, and other equipment you will need to complete your assignments.

■ Decide on a goal. For example: "I will finish reading and taking notes on Chapter 1, Lesson 1, by 8:00."

■ Take a five- to ten-minute break every hour to keep alert.

■ If you start to feel sleepy, take a break and get some fresh air.

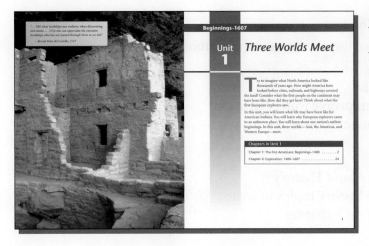

Before Beginning Each Unit

◆ Read the unit title and study the photograph. Do you recognize anything in the photo?

◆ Read the quotation. Try to connect the ideas to the picture.

◆ Read the opening paragraphs.

◆ Read the titles of the chapters in the unit.

◆ Read the Chapter Summary and Unit Summary to help you identify key ideas.

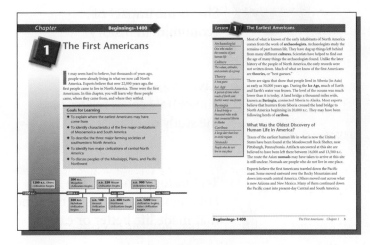

Before Beginning Each Chapter

◆ Read the chapter title and dates.

◆ Read the opening paragraphs.

◆ Study the Goals for Learning. The Chapter Review and tests will ask questions related to these goals.

◆ Study the timeline. Timelines help you see the order in which key events occurred. The timeline covers the years in the chapter title.

◆ Read the Chapter Summaries to help you identify key issues.

◆ Look at the Chapter Review. The questions cover the most important information in the chapter.

Note These Features

You can find complete listings of these features in this textbook's table of contents.

 Biography
Highlights people who have made
contributions to America

 **Writing About History**
Provides history topics to write
about in each chapter

History in Your Life
Relates history to the modern world

 **Focus on Economics**
Shows the impact of
economics in history

 Civics Connection
Shows how civics relates to
the study of history

 Technology Connection
Highlights inventions at the time
that made life better or easier

 Document-Based Reading
Presents primary- and secondary-source
documents related to each chapter

 Skill Builder
Focuses on social studies skills

Before Beginning Each Lesson

Read the lesson title and restate it in the form of a question. For example, write: *Where did the earliest Americans come from?*

Look over the entire lesson, noting the following:

◆ bold words
◆ text organization
◆ photos
◆ maps
◆ graphs and charts
◆ Lesson Review questions

Lesson 1 The Earliest Americans

Archaeologist
One who studies the remains of past human life

Culture
The values, attitudes, and customs of a group

Theory
A best guess

Ice Age
A period of time when much of Earth and Earth's water was frozen

Beringia
A land bridge a thousand miles wide that connected Siberia to Alaska

Caribou
A large deer that lives in arctic regions

Nomads
People who do not live in one place

Most of what is known of the early inhabitants of North America comes from the work of **archaeologists**. Archaeologists study the remains of past human life. They have dug up things left behind from many different **cultures**. Scientists have helped to find out the age of many things the archaeologists found. Unlike the later history of the people of North America, the early records were not written down. Much of what we know of the first Americans are **theories**, or "best guesses."

There are signs that show that people lived in Siberia (in Asia) as early as 30,000 years ago. During the **Ice Age**, much of Earth and Earth's water was frozen. The level of the oceans was much lower than it is today. A land bridge a thousand miles wide, known as **Beringia**, connected Siberia to Alaska. Most experts believe that hunters from Siberia crossed the land bridge to North America beginning in 20,000 B.C. They may have been following herds of **caribou**.

What Was the Oldest Discovery of Human Life in America?

Traces of the earliest human life in what is now the United States have been found at the Meadowcroft Rock Shelter, near Pittsburgh, Pennsylvania. Artifacts uncovered at this site are believed to have been left there between 16,000 and 13,500 B.C. The route the Asian **nomads** may have taken to arrive at this site is still unclear. Nomads are people who do not live in one place.

Experts believe the first Americans traveled down the Pacific coast. Some moved eastward over the Rocky Mountains and down into south central America. Others moved east across what is now Arizona and New Mexico. Many of them continued down the Pacific coast into present-day Central and South America.

Beginnings–1400   *The First Americans Chapter 1*   **3**

As You Read the Lesson

◆ Read the major headings.
◆ Read the subheads and paragraphs that follow.
◆ Study the maps, graphs, and charts.
◆ Before moving on to the next lesson, see if you understand the concepts you read. If you do not, reread the lesson. If you are still unsure, ask for help.
◆ Practice what you have learned by completing the Lesson Reviews.

Using the Bold Words

Bold type

Words seen for the first time will appear in bold type

Glossary

Words listed in this column are also found in the glossary

Knowing the meaning of all the boxed words in the left column will help you understand what you read.

These words appear in **bold type** the first time they appear in the text and are often defined in the paragraph.

Archaeologists study the remains of past human life.

All of the words in the left column are also defined in the **Glossary**.

Archaeologist (är kē ol´ ə jist) A person who studies the remains of past human life (p. 3)

Word Study Tips

◆ Start a vocabulary file with index cards to use for review.

◆ Write one term on the front of each card. Write the chapter number, lesson number, and definition on the back.

◆ You can use these cards as flash cards by yourself or with a study partner to test your knowledge.

> Archaeologist
>
> Chapter 1, Lesson 1
>
> A person who studies the remains of past human life

Taking Notes in Class

◆ Outline each lesson using the subheads as the main points.

◆ Always write the main ideas and supporting details.

◆ Keep your notes brief.

◆ Write down important information only.

◆ Use your own words.

◆ Do not be concerned about writing in complete sentences. Use phrases.

◆ Do not try to write everything the teacher says.

◆ Use the same method all the time. Then when you study for a test, you will know where to go to find the information you need to review.

◆ Review your notes to fill in possible gaps as soon as you can after class.

Using the Summaries

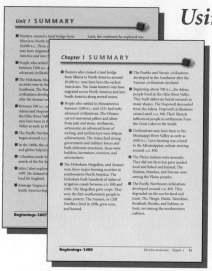

◆ Read each Chapter Summary to be sure you understand the chapter's main ideas.

◆ Review your notes and test yourself on vocabulary words and key ideas.

◆ Practice writing about some of the main events from the chapter.

◆ At the end of each unit, read the Unit Summary to be sure you understand the unit's main ideas.

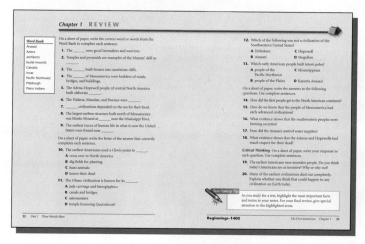

Using the Reviews

◆ Answer the questions in the Lesson Reviews.

◆ In the Chapter Reviews, answer each fill-in-the-blank, multiple choice, and short-answer question.

◆ Review the Test-Taking Tips.

Preparing for Tests

◆ Complete the Lesson Reviews and Chapter Reviews. Make up similar questions to practice what you have learned. You may want to do this with a classmate and share your questions.

◆ Review your answers to Lesson Reviews and Chapter Reviews.

◆ Reread the Chapter Summaries.

◆ Test yourself on vocabulary words and key ideas.

"... Oh! what hardships one endures, when discovering new lands.... [N]o one can appreciate the excessive hardships who has not passed through them as we did."

~ *Bernal Diaz del Castillo, 1517*

Unit 1

Three Worlds Meet

Try to imagine what North America looked like thousands of years ago. How might America have looked before cities, railroads, and highways covered the land? Consider what the first people on the continent may have been like. How did they get here? Think about what the first European explorers saw.

In this unit, you will learn what life may have been like for American Indians. You will learn why European explorers came to an unknown place. You will learn about our nation's earliest beginnings. In this unit, three worlds— Asia, the Americas, and Western Europe—meet.

Chapters in Unit 1

1

The First Americans

I t may seem hard to believe, but thousands of years ago, people were already living in what we now call North America. Experts believe that over 22,000 years ago, the first people came to live in North America. These were the first Americans. In this chapter, you will learn why these people came, where they came from, and where they settled.

Goals for Learning

◆ To explain where the earliest Americans may have come from

◆ To identify characteristics of the five major civilizations of Mesoamerica and South America

◆ To describe the three major farming societies of southwestern North America

◆ To identify two major civilizations of central North America

◆ To discuss peoples of the Mississippi, Plains, and Pacific Northwest

1200 B.C. Olmec civilization begins

200 B.C. Mogollon civilization begins

A.D. 250 Mayan civilization begins

A.D. 900 Toltec civilization begins

1200 B.C. | 400 B.C. | A.D. 400 | A.D. 1400

300 B.C. Hohokam civilization begins

A.D. 100 Anasazi civilization begins

A.D. 400 Pacific Northwest civilizations begin

A.D. 1200 Inca civilization begins, Aztec civilization begins

Archaeologist

One who studies the remains of past human life

Culture

The values, attitudes, and customs of a group

Theory

A best guess

Ice Age

A period of time when much of Earth and Earth's water was frozen

Beringia

A land bridge a thousand miles wide that connected Siberia to Alaska

Caribou

A large deer that lives in arctic regions

Nomads

People who do not live in one place

Most of what is known of the early inhabitants of North America comes from the work of **archaeologists.** Archaeologists study the remains of past human life. They have dug up things left behind from many different **cultures.** Scientists have helped to find out the age of many things the archaeologists found. Unlike the later history of the people of North America, the early records were not written down. Much of what we know of the first Americans are **theories,** or "best guesses."

There are signs that show that people lived in Siberia (in Asia) as early as 30,000 years ago. During the **Ice Age,** much of Earth and Earth's water was frozen. The level of the oceans was much lower than it is today. A land bridge a thousand miles wide, known as **Beringia,** connected Siberia to Alaska. Most experts believe that hunters from Siberia crossed the land bridge to North America beginning in 20,000 B.C. They may have been following herds of **caribou.**

What Was the Oldest Discovery of Human Life in America?

Traces of the earliest human life in what is now the United States have been found at the Meadowcroft Rock Shelter, near Pittsburgh, Pennsylvania. Artifacts uncovered at this site are believed to have been left there between 16,000 and 13,500 B.C. The route the Asian **nomads** may have taken to arrive at this site is still unclear. Nomads are people who do not live in one place.

Experts believe the first Americans traveled down the Pacific coast. Some moved eastward over the Rocky Mountains and down into south central America. Others moved east across what is now Arizona and New Mexico. Many of them continued down the Pacific coast into present-day Central and South America.

Migration Routes into the Americas

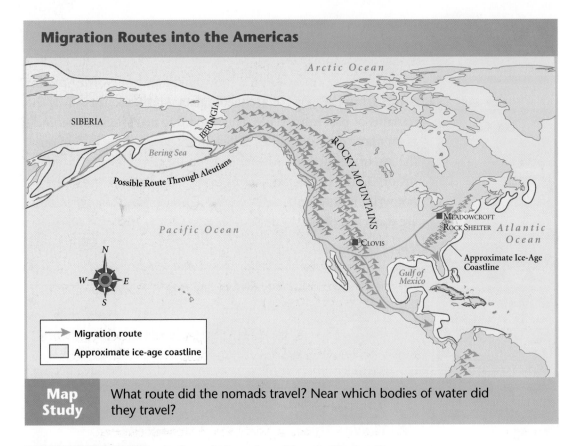

Map Study What route did the nomads travel? Near which bodies of water did they travel?

What Was the Clovis Point?

Clovis point
A finely flaked stone spearhead

Glacier
A large body of ice

Early American hunters began using spear points for hunting tools about 11,000 B.C. Named for the area of New Mexico in which it was found, the **Clovis point** was a finely flaked stone spearhead. When attached to a wooden pole, the Clovis point was a powerful tool for killing animals. It was also used for gathering and building. Clovis points have been found near bones of mammoths or bison.

What Happened to the Land Bridge?

By 18,000 B.C., the gradual melting of **glaciers**—large bodies of ice—caused the seas to start rising. The land bridge from Asia to North America was covered with water. People could no longer travel to North America on foot. At this time, however, hunters had already spread to the southern tip of South America.

The remains of Meadowcroft Rock Shelter include traces of the earliest human life in North America.

Lesson 1 Review On a sheet of paper, write the correct word or words from the Word Bank to complete each sentence.

1. _____ was a land bridge a thousand miles wide, that connected Siberia to Alaska.

2. The _____ was a finely flaked stone spearhead.

3. _____ are people who do not live in one place.

4. _____ study the remains of past human life.

5. Much of the earth and the earth's water was frozen during the _____.

What do you think ?

What can be learned from studying ancient cultures?

Mesoamerica

The area of land that includes what is now Mexico and other countries south through Costa Rica

Civilization

A high level of cultural development

Cultivate

To grow crops

Settlement

A place or region newly settled

Hieroglyphic

A system of writing that uses picture-like symbols

Astronomy

The study of space and the planets

Architect

A person skilled in designing buildings

Many of the first people in the Americas settled in **Mesoamerica** and South America. Mesoamerica includes what is now Mexico and other countries south through Costa Rica. Based on the findings of archaeologists, the people in this region had the earliest advanced **civilizations.** Civilization is a high level of cultural development. Archaeologists believe that the first corn was **cultivated,** or grown, in Mexico as early as 5000 B.C. There were five main civilizations of Mesoamerica.

Who Were the Olmecs?

The strongest **settlement** of early Americans was established in Mexico by the Olmecs between 1200 B.C. and A.D. 600. A settlement is a place or region newly settled. Archaeologists have learned a good deal about the Olmecs from digs in La Venta and San Lorenzo, two of their cities near the Gulf of Mexico.

The Olmecs carved in jade and stone. The remains of their world include pillars, stone heads, figurines, and pottery. An Olmec **hieroglyphic** slab, with a date matching 31 B.C., is thought to be the oldest piece of writing in North America. A hieroglyphic is a system of writing that uses picturelike symbols.

Where Did the Mayans Live?

From about A.D. 250, the Mayans built a huge civilization in Mesoamerica. It covered the area which is now Belize and parts of Guatemala, Honduras, El Salvador, and Mexico. For at least 600 years, the Mayans were a major force in Mesoamerica.

The Mayans were masters of **astronomy**—the study of space and the planets—and of arithmetic. They were the first people in the Americas to develop an advanced form of writing. The ruins of their great cities also show us that they were skilled **architects** and artists. An architect is a person skilled in designing buildings. Long after the fall of the Mayans, the ruins of their temples and pyramids remained as examples of some of the finest building in Mesoamerica.

The people of Mesoamerica built large civilizations such as this one in Monte Alban, Mexico.

What Happened to the Toltecs?

Beginning in A.D. 900, the Toltecs ruled a strong civilization in the Mexican highlands. The ruins of their main city, Tula, includes remains of several temples. One of these temples honored Quetzalcoatl, a great feathered serpent, who the Toltecs believed had founded the city. Experts believe that nomads took over the Toltecs about 1200. They went on to form the Aztec civilization.

Then and Now

Long ago, when people built their own houses and grew their own crops, they did not need money. As time passed, people began to trade goods and services. Goods are the things that people buy. Services are work done for other people for a fee. This exchange is called barter. For bartering to work, people must agree on the value of what is traded. Eventually, people began to use certain items as money. Early people used beads, shells, and even cacao beans as money, or wampum.

Today, we still have a barter economy. If you have a job, you exchange your labor for money. However, buying and paying for goods and services has become more complex. While many consumers pay for goods and services with currency, or cash, some people write checks to buy things. A check tells a bank to pay a certain amount of money to a person or a company. People also use credit cards to pay for items. Credit cards allow consumers to buy now and pay later.

Who Were the Aztecs?

The Aztec civilization took shape about 1200. It is thought to be the result of 3,000 years of improvements and growth by the people in Mesoamerica. From their main city of Tenochtitlán (now Mexico City), the Aztecs ruled a large kingdom in much of central and southern Mexico. By the time of the fall of the Aztecs in 1521, 100,000 people were living in Tenochtitlán.

The government and **military** forces of the Aztecs were strong and well run. They built roads, **canals,** bridges, and many buildings. A canal is a waterway made by humans. People worked as farmers, weavers, or **artisans.** An artisan is a skilled worker. The Aztecs worshiped gods of the sun, the rain, and the wind as well as Quetzalcoatl.

Civilizations of Mesoamerica

Civilization	Location	Date Started
Olmecs	Mexico	1200 B.C.
Mayans	Central America, Mexico	A.D. 250
Toltecs	Mexico	A.D. 900
Aztecs	Central and southern Mexico	A.D. 1200
Incas	Peru	A.D. 1200

Technology Connection

A Floating City

The land where the Aztecs settled was mostly swamp. To gain more usable land, the Aztecs built "islands" in the swamp. They wove giant mats from reeds and attached the mats to stumps or posts. Then they piled mud from the swamp bottom onto the mats. These islands seemed to float but were really held in place by plant roots. The artificial islands were called chinampas. The soil on the chinampas was very rich, so the Aztecs raised crops on them.

The Aztecs built their great city, Tenochtitlán, on chinampas. They removed mud from the canals to form chinampas. They also built bridges from the floating city to dry land.

Juanita, the Maiden of Ampato: c. 1400s

Juanita was a 12- to 14-year-old Inca girl whose body was found in the Peruvian Andes in 1995. Researchers found her perfectly frozen body near the heart of the ancient Inca Empire. The researchers nicknamed her "Juanita." Her body was refrigerated to prevent decay and for further study. By studying her remains, researchers have learned about the ancestry, health, lifestyle, and diet of the ancient Incas. She was surrounded by small statues, corn, and leaves of the coca plant. Researchers believe Juanita was sacrificed to a mountain god in the 1400s. She had long black hair and perfect teeth. She was dressed in fine, colorful wool garments and leather slippers. She most likely wore a plumed headdress. The researchers hope to learn more about the lives of the Incas through further respectful study of Juanita.

Who Were the Incas?

About 1200, the Incas started a kingdom in southern Peru in South America. The Incas were very good builders, lawmakers, and warriors. They learned about astronomy. Within 200 years, the Incan civilization had grown to include all of present-day Peru. It also included parts of Ecuador on the north and Chile and Argentina on the south.

> **What do you think** ?
>
> What might lead you to believe that the civilizations of Mesoamerica were advanced?

Lesson 2 Review Choose the name in parentheses that best completes each sentence. Write your answers on a sheet of paper.

1. The (Toltecs, Olmecs, Incas) worked with hieroglyphics.

2. The (Mayans, Aztecs, Incas) were the first people in the Americas to develop an advanced form of writing.

3. The (Mayans, Olmecs, Incas) started a kingdom in southern Peru.

4. A major city of the (Olmecs, Toltecs, Aztecs) was Tenochtitlán.

5. The (Olmec, Toltec, Incan) city of Tula includes remains of several temples.

Three farming societies started to develop in what is now the southwestern United States. The Hohokam lived in what is now Arizona. The Mogollon built their civilization in southeastern Arizona and southern New Mexico. The Anasazi built where Arizona, New Mexico, Utah, and Colorado meet. They also built along the Rio Grande and upper Pecos valleys of New Mexico.

Irrigation

A system of watering crops that uses canals or ditches of water

Ritual

An action that takes place during a ceremony

Mesa

A flat-topped height

Kiva

A large underground room used for ceremonies

What Did the Hohokam Build?

Archaeologists believe that the Hohokam developed from local peoples and from Mesoamericans who had moved northward. Their civilization began about 300 B.C. The Hohokam were farmers. They were skilled at controlling the land. From A.D. 800 until 1000, the Hohokam built hundreds of miles of **irrigation** canals for watering crops.

Snaketown was a major Hohokam civilization. This city was one of a few large cities that ruled smaller villages, largely through control of the canals. The Hohokam built ball courts in their villages. These were used for sport and for **rituals.** Mounds found within the remains of Hohokam villages may have been dance platforms or places on which their leaders' homes were built. Hohokam people weaved cotton goods. Cotton is a plant used to make cloth. By about 1450, most people had abandoned the Hohokam area. This most likely was because of a lack of water and a failed irrigation system.

Who Were the Mogollon?

The Mogollon area was larger than that of the Hohokam. This group is believed to have begun about 200 B.C. The Mogollon were farmers. They built small villages of about 20 houses on bluffs, **mesas,** or on other high grounds. Their communities included underground "pit houses" believed to be the earliest southwestern **kivas.** Kivas were large underground rooms used for ceremonies.

The Anasazi built dwellings in cliffs.

The Mogollon were the first southwestern people to make pottery. Using ways of painting learned from the Anasazi, the Mogollon created their own designs. Their pottery was used throughout their lives and for **burial** offerings to cover the heads of the dead.

Geography Note

The Anasazi ruins in Chaco Canyon show a settlement with a network of roads. The roads connected this settlement to about 80 other communities. They allowed for trade and distribution of food. The roads made it possible for the communities to help meet each other's needs.

What Did the Chaco Canyon Anasazi Build?

The Anasazi civilization began around A.D. 100. They grew corn and hunted. By A.D. 900, the main settlement of the Anasazi was Chaco Canyon in what is now north central New Mexico. The Anasazi were called "Cliff Dwellers" because they built houses into cliffs. The **dwellings** were made of the same copper-colored sandstone of the cliffs. The largest dwelling had more than 600 rooms.

The Anasazi farmers relied on rainfall and their system of catching water runoff from the cliffs. They also kept a calendar by watching the sun and moon. The Anasazi sun priests were able to plan for planting cycles and **religious** ceremonies.

The period of the Chacoan Anasazi lasted fewer than 300 years. From 1130 to 1180, a drought forced people to leave. The Anasazi continued to live at Cliff Palace and Spruce Tree House at Mesa Verde in Colorado and at Keet Seel in Arizona.

Where Did the Mesa Verde Anasazi Live?

The Mesa Verde Anasazi lived on the sides of high mesas in southwestern Colorado and southeastern Utah. About A.D. 700, they moved from their pit houses to dwellings aboveground. They built thousands of dams on small streams. On Chapin Mesa, the Anasazi built a stone-lined **reservoir** that could hold almost two million gallons of water. A reservoir is a large place used to store water.

Who Were the Kayenta Anasazi?

Another group of Anasazi known as the Kayenta lived from 1100 to 1300 in small villages in northeastern Arizona. They were masters of pottery making and weaving.

Around 1250, the Kayenta Anasazi began building larger cliff dwellings. Experts believe that the move was made for protection from enemies. Just before 1300, the Anasazi left the Southwest completely. There was warfare among Anasazi groups. A drought and lack of good land for farming caused the wars. Some of the Anasazi moved down into the Rio Grande area where many of their **descendants,** the Pueblos, live today.

During the time when the Pueblo culture was formed, Navajos moved near the Pueblos from Canada and Alaska. The Navajos learned farming from the Pueblos. One group of today's Pueblos, the Hopi of northeastern Arizona, are known for their **kachina** rituals. Kachinas are spirits of ancestors. Today, Pueblo men act and dress like kachinas in rituals to bring success to the Pueblo people.

Southwestern Civilizations

Civilization	Location	Date Started
Hohokam	Arizona	300 B.C.
Mogollon	Arizona, New Mexico	200 B.C.
Anasazi	Arizona, Colorado, New Mexico, Utah	A.D. 100

History in Your Life

Architecture from the Anasazi

Anasazi people built large homes on ridges of river canyon walls or the sides of mesas. Many families lived in buildings made up of dozens of cubelike apartments.

Anasazi farmed the flat land below their homes. The Pueblos, Anasazi descendants, continued to live in this manner until the 1500s. Then Navajos took over the Pueblo land and dwellings.

The unique architecture and placement of the Anasazi rock and clay dwellings made them durable. Many are still fairly complete. You can see them in Mesa Verde National Park in southwestern Colorado. These remnants of an ancient American Indian culture have influenced southwestern architecture.

Word Bank

Anasazi

Hohokam

Hopi

Mogollon

Navajos

Lesson 3 Review On a sheet of paper, write the correct word from the Word Bank to complete each sentence.

1. The _____ built irrigation canals to water crops.

2. The _____ were farmers who lived on mesas.

3. The _____ are called Cliff Dwellers because they built their houses in cliffs.

4. The _____ are Pueblos known for their kachina rituals.

5. The _____ learned farming from the Pueblos.

What do you think ?

What seemed to be the most difficult problem facing the southwestern peoples?

Tobacco

A plant that some people smoke or chew

About 700 B.C., one group of American Indians began building burial mounds in the Ohio River Valley to honor their dead. These people are known today as the Adena. Many of the burial mounds were as large as 300 feet across. With great respect, the Adena put the dead in small log rooms. The rooms were filled with stone tablets, **tobacco,** and pipes for smoking the tobacco.

Who Were the Hopewell?

The Hopewell peoples were direct descendants of the Adena. They thrived for several hundred years until about A.D. 300. Unlike many other people who lived during this time, the Hopewell never built great cities. Their largest settlements had fewer than 400 people. Instead, they built mounds of far greater detail than those the Adena built.

The Hopewell people often built mounds in the shape of animals. Serpent Mound near present-day Hillsboro, Ohio, is a perfectly preserved example of a Hopewell mound. It is a huge mound shaped like a snake.

The Hopewell were known to build mounds in the shapes of lizards, birds, panthers, and even human beings. They held burial services and spent much time honoring their dead.

The Hopewell made stone figures. The figure above is a Hopewell medicine man.

Serpent Mound (right) near present-day Hillsboro, Ohio, is an example of a Hopewell mound.

However, many experts believe that the Hopewell were more concerned with celebrating life, nature, and rebirth.

Many Hopewell began to trade with settlements throughout the areas east of the Mississippi River. Other peoples adopted Hopewell customs and rituals. The Hopewell respect for rebirth and nature became a part of the beliefs of people from the Great Lakes to the deep South. Some groups of Hopewell continued to live throughout these areas for many years. The original Ohio settlement fell around A.D. 300.

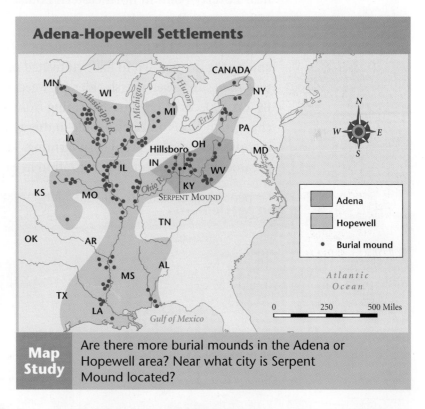

Adena-Hopewell Settlements

Map Study Are there more burial mounds in the Adena or Hopewell area? Near what city is Serpent Mound located?

What do you think?

Why did the Hopewell build mounds in the shape of people and animals?

Lesson 4 Review On a sheet of paper, write the answers to the following questions. Use complete sentences.

1. What did the Adena build?

2. What were Hopewell settlements like?

3. What is Serpent Mound?

4. What did the Hopewell celebrate?

5. Who did the Hopewell begin to trade with?

Researchers have found burial grounds in the lower Mississippi River Valley. The grounds are believed to have been built as early as 4500 B.C. Between 1500 and 1000 B.C., one of the earliest civilizations in North America developed in this area. It was formed in parts of present-day Mississippi, Louisiana, and Arkansas. Several different peoples formed a civilization near Poverty Point in northeastern Louisiana. Sometime after 1000 B.C., the Poverty Point civilization died out.

People who lived in the lower Mississippi River Valley were among the first known to have cultivated plants. For example, they used sunflower, marsh elder, pigweed, and barley for food. By A.D. 800, corn and squash farming from Mesoamerica changed the lives of many people in this area. Populations increased as people started corn farming. The Mississippians became the most advanced civilization in eastern North America.

Main Mississippian Settlements

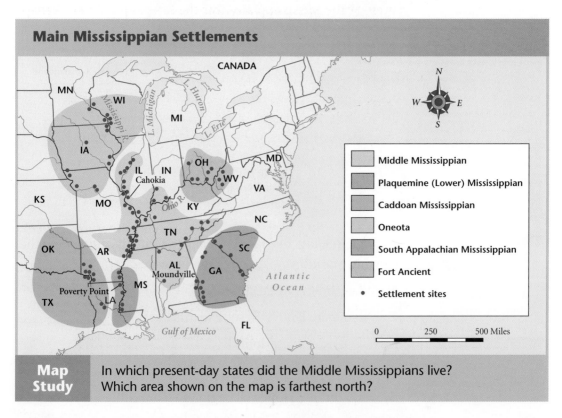

Legend:
- Middle Mississippian
- Plaquemine (Lower) Mississippian
- Caddoan Mississippian
- Oneota
- South Appalachian Mississippian
- Fort Ancient
- • Settlement sites

0   250   500 Miles

Map Study   In which present-day states did the Middle Mississippians live?
Which area shown on the map is farthest north?

The Cahokia Mounds State Historic Site preserves the burial mounds of an Indian civilization which inhabited the area from A.D. 900 to 1500.

What Were Cahokia and Moundville?

Near present-day Collinsville in western Illinois, Middle Mississippians built Monks Mound at Cahokia. This mound, 100 feet high, covered 16 acres of land. It is the largest object built of earth north of Mesoamerica. Cahokia was a major trade center for the Mississippians near the Mississippi River. Perhaps as many as 40,000 people lived there at one time. By 1500, Cahokia was completely abandoned.

Moundville, Alabama, was built about 1050 by Middle Mississippians in the southern region. It was the largest settlement in the Eastern Woodlands. By the middle of the 1500s, however, only small groups of people remained in Moundville and in the other settlements.

Who Are Descendants of the Mississippians?

Many present-day peoples such as the Cherokees are descendants of the Mississippians. Although they adopted many European customs, they still keep some traditions of their ancestors from Moundville. For example, every year the Cherokees celebrate the Green Corn Ceremony in honor of the people of Moundville.

The Iroquois also are believed to have descended from Mississippian roots. Northern Iroquois lived in what is now upper New York state. Six tribes—the Oneida, Mohawk, Onondaga, Cayuga, Seneca, and Tuscarora—later joined

Writing About History

Research a group of people from this chapter. In your notebook, write a report about the people. Include information you find from your research.

together. They formed a group that stretched 200 miles across New York state. Several families lived together in one house. Although they never numbered more than about 22,000, the Iroquois were the strongest force north of Mesoamerica when the Europeans arrived.

Today, other descendants of the Mississippians such as the Mohawks, the Ojibway, and the Natchez carry on the ways of these earliest ancestors.

Who Were the Plains Indians?

The Plains Indians have been called nomadic peoples. However, they developed villages too. Beginning about 250 B.C., traders carried stones and metals back to the Hopewell centers. Hopewell ideas caught on with the Plains people. They began making pottery, building burial mounds, taking part in long-range trade, and growing corn.

The Hidatsa and Mandan of North Dakota grew some food. They also fished and hunted. Along the Knife River, 13 or 14 villages have been found. Each one is believed to have had between 2,000 and 3,000 people living there. Villages were set four to six miles apart so that they could keep track of one another. If an enemy burned a village, the people in the neighboring village saw the smoke and prepared to defend themselves.

Mississippi, Plains, and Northwestern Civilizations

Civilization	Location	Date Started
Mississippian	Mississippi River Valley	4500 B.C.
Plains Indians	North American Plains	250 B.C.
Pacific Northwest	Northwestern America, Canada, Alaska	A.D. 400

Totem pole

A tall, colorful carved object with a certain religious meaning

Totem poles had religious meaning for some Pacific Northwest people.

What do you think ❓

Why do you think burial mounds were so important to the first Americans?

Pawnee people living in what is now the midwestern United States keep and practice some beliefs of their Mississippian ancestors. For example, the Pawnees believe that the use of ceremonial bundles filled with objects from nature can bring good luck to a village. As with many other tribes, the Pawnees today are connected to the religious and cultural ways of the Southwest and of Mesoamerica.

Who Were the Peoples of the Pacific Northwest?

By A.D. 400, the Pacific Northwest civilizations began. These peoples include the Tlingit, Haida, Tsimshian, Kwakiutl, and Nootka. In most cases, they built shoreline villages. They depended heavily on the sea for their food and trade. The Nootka, for example, were whalers. Some carved **totem poles**. These tall, colorful objects had a religious meaning to some of these people.

North of the Pacific Northwest civilizations lived the Eskimo, or Inuit as they are called today. These people are believed to have come from Asia. They settled near the Bering Sea coast in what is now Alaska and along the coasts of Canada and Greenland. They got clothing, food, oil, and tools from sea mammals, fish, and caribou. Today, about 63,000 Inuit still live in America and Canada.

Lesson 5 Review Choose the term in parentheses that best completes each sentence. Write your answers on a sheet of paper.

1. Cahokia was a major trade center for the (Hidatsa, Iroquois, Mississippians).

2. Moundville was the largest settlement in (the Eastern Woodlands, the Plains, Mesoamerica).

3. The Hidatsa and Mandan were mainly fishers and (whalers, hunters, farmers).

4. The (Haida, Inuit, Tlingit) lived north of the Pacific Northwest region civilization.

5. Some Nootka built (burial mounds, Monks Mound, totem poles).

An Osage Belief

The Osage are a people who once roamed freely in Missouri, Arkansas, and Oklahoma. Now most of them live on a reservation in Oklahoma. Like the Mayans of Mesoamerica, the Osage believe that their people were descended from the sun and the moon. This passage is an explanation of how Osage people came to live on the earth.

Way beyond, a part of the Osage lived in the sky. They desired to know their origin, the source from which they came into existence. They went to the sun. He told them that they were his children. Then they wandered still farther and came to the moon. She told them that she gave birth to them, and that the sun was their father. She told them that they must leave their present abode and go down to the earth and dwell there. They came to the earth, but found that it was covered with water. They could not return to the place they had left, so they wept, but no answer came to them from anywhere. They floated about in the air, seeking in every direction for help from some god; but they found none. The animals were with them, and of all these the elk was the finest and most stately, and inspired all the creatures with confidence; so they appealed to the elk for help. He dropped into the water and began to sink. Then he called to the winds, and the winds came from all quarters and blew until the waters went upward as in a mist.

At first rocks only were exposed, and the people traveled on the rocky places that produced no plants, and there was nothing to eat. Then the waters began to go down until the soft earth was exposed. When this happened, the elk in his joy rolled over and over on the soft earth, and all his loose hairs clung to the soil. The hairs grew, and from them sprang beans, corn, potatoes, and wild turnips, and then all the grasses and trees.

Document-Based Questions

1. Where did the Osage live at first?

2. What relation to the Osage were the sun and the moon?

3. Whom did the Osage appeal to for help?

4. When the waters went down, how did vegetables, grasses, and trees begin to grow?

5. Which part of the Osage legend do you like the best? Explain your answer.

Source: The Omaha Tribe, *translated by Alice Fletcher and Francis La Flesche, 1905–1906.*

Chapter 1 SUMMARY

- Hunters who crossed a land bridge from Siberia to North America around 20,000 B.C. may have been the earliest Americans. The Asian hunters may have migrated across North America and into South America along several routes.

- People who settled in Mesoamerica between 1200 B.C. and 1521 had early advanced civilizations. The Olmecs carved enormous pillars and altars from jade and stone. Arithmetic, astronomy, an advanced form of writing, and architecture were Mayan achievements. The Aztecs had strong government and military forces and built elaborate structures. Incas were builders, lawmakers, warriors, and astronomers.

- The Hohokam, Mogollon, and Anasazi were three major farming societies in southwestern North America. The Hohokam built hundreds of miles of irrigation canals between A.D. 800 and 1000. The Mogollon grew crops. They were the first southwestern people to make pottery. The Anasazi, or Cliff Dwellers, lived in cliffs, grew corn, and hunted.

- The Pueblo and Navajo civilizations developed in the Southwest after the Anasazi civilizations declined.

- Beginning about 700 B.C., the Adena people lived in the Ohio River Valley. They built elaborate burial mounds in many shapes. The Hopewell descended from the Adena. Hopewell civilizations existed until A.D. 300. Their lifestyle influenced people in settlements from the Great Lakes to the South.

- Civilizations may have been in the Mississippi River Valley as early as 4500 B.C. Corn farming was central to the Mississippian culture starting around A.D. 800.

- The Plains Indians were nomadic. They did not farm but grew needed food and fished and hunted. The Hidatsa, Mandan, and Pawnee were among the Plains peoples.

- The Pacific Northwest civilizations developed around A.D. 400. They depended on the sea for food and trade. The Tlingit, Haida, Tsimshian, Kwakiutl, Nootka, and Eskimo, or Inuit, are among the northwestern cultures.

Chapter 1 REVIEW

Word Bank

Anasazi

Aztecs

architects

burial mounds

Cahokia

Incas

Pacific Northwest

Pittsburgh

Plains Indians

On a sheet of paper, write the correct word or words from the Word Bank to complete each sentence.

1. The _____ were good lawmakers and warriors.

2. Temples and pyramids are examples of the Mayans' skill as _____.

3. The _____ built houses into sandstone cliffs.

4. The _____ of Mesoamerica were builders of roads, bridges, and buildings.

5. The Adena-Hopewell people of central North America built elaborate _____.

6. The Hidatsa, Mandan, and Pawnee were _____.

7. _____ civilizations depended on the sea for their food.

8. The largest earthen structure built north of Mesoamerica was Monks Mound at _____ near the Mississippi River.

9. The earliest traces of human life in what is now the United States were found near _____.

On a sheet of paper, write the letter of the answer that correctly completes each sentence.

10. The earliest Americans used a Clovis point to _____.

   A cross over to North America

   B dig fields for planting

   C hunt animals

   D honor their dead

11. The Olmec civilization is known for its _____.

   A jade carvings and hieroglyphics

   B canals and bridges

   C astronomers

   D temple honoring Quetzalcoatl

12. Which of the following was not a civilization of the Southwestern United States?

   A Hohokam   **C** Hopewell

   B Anasazi   **D** Mogollon

13. Which early American people built totem poles?

   A people of the   **C** Mississippians
      Pacific Northwest

   B people of the Plains   **D** Kayenta Anasazi

On a sheet of paper, write the answers to the following questions. Use complete sentences.

14. How did the first people get to the North American continent?

15. How do we know that the people of Mesoamerica had early advanced civilizations?

16. What evidence shows that the southwestern peoples were farming societies?

17. How did the Anasazi control water supplies?

18. What evidence shows that the Adenas and Hopewells had much respect for their dead?

Critical Thinking On a sheet of paper, write your response to each question. Use complete sentences.

19. The earliest Americans were inventive people. Do you think today's Americans are as inventive? Why or why not?

20. Many of the earliest civilizations died out completely. Explain whether you think that could happen to any civilization on Earth today.

Test-Taking Tip

As you study for a test, highlight the most important facts and terms in your notes. For your final review, give special attention to the highlighted areas.

2

Exploration

For many years, people in Europe knew of a distant land to the east called Asia, or the Far East. They wanted to explore routes to the Far East. In this chapter, you will learn about these explorations and how they affected world history.

Goals for Learning

◆ To describe the importance of new technology in early navigation and exploration

◆ To identify the major European explorers and the areas they explored

◆ To describe how England's and Spain's power in Europe changed after the Spanish Armada was defeated

◆ To identify the first European colonies and who started them

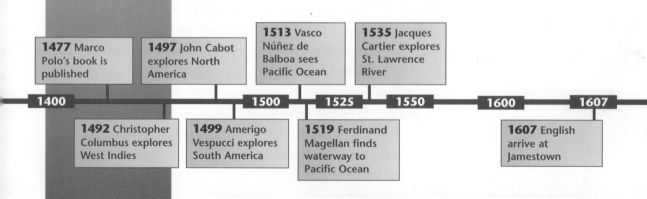

1477 Marco Polo's book is published

1492 Christopher Columbus explores West Indies

1497 John Cabot explores North America

1499 Amerigo Vespucci explores South America

1513 Vasco Núñez de Balboa sees Pacific Ocean

1519 Ferdinand Magellan finds waterway to Pacific Ocean

1535 Jacques Cartier explores St. Lawrence River

1607 English arrive at Jamestown

1400   1500   1525   1550   1600   1607

Merchant

A buyer and seller of goods

Monarch

A person who rules a kingdom or territory

Territory

Land belonging to a country or government

Noble

Someone who is part of a society's upper or ruling class

Compass

A device used to show direction

Globe

A model of the earth

Publish

To print something, such as a book, newspaper, or magazine

For many years, Arab traders brought jewels, fine silks, perfumes, and spices by land from the Far East. These goods were sold to **merchants** in Italy who then carried them along the Mediterranean Sea to other Europeans. **Monarchs,** people who rule kingdoms or **territories,** and **nobles,** people of the upper class, were eager to buy these goods. The routes traders used were long and dangerous. People soon began to think about finding a route to the Far East by sea.

How Did Exploration Begin?

During the 1400s, several events had a great effect on exploration. One event was the development of the **compass**. The compass had markings and a pointer that showed the direction of north. The compass helped sailors to know what direction they were going. Water travel became much safer.

The second great development was in mapmaking. Maps were being drawn more correctly. Maps helped people to accept that the earth was round.

A third event was the production of an improved **globe**. A globe is a model of the earth. Unfortunately, early globes showed only one ocean separating Europe from Asia. They also did not show North America. At that time, people believed that the world was much smaller than it really is.

In 1477, a book was **published** about the experiences of Marco Polo, who had explored the Far East during the 1200s. The book described China as a land of great wealth. This excited the people in Europe. They began to dream of finding a safer and shorter route to Asia and its riches. The lands in Asia were given the name "Indies" because they included India, China, and the Spice Islands.

History in Your Life

Mariner's Astrolabe

Today's travelers have many choices for finding their way. Modern vehicles have built-in compasses to point the direction. The global positioning system uses space-based satellites to find a location anywhere on Earth.

Finding their way was more difficult for sailors of the 1400s and 1500s. One instrument that allowed ships to sail unknown waters was the mariner's astrolabe. This device was a brass ring divided into degrees, along with a sight that allowed a ship's navigator to determine how far above the horizon the sun was. The navigator sighted on the sun at noon and could then determine his latitude north or south of the equator. Spanish and Portuguese ships of the 1400s relied heavily on the astrolabe. Columbus used astrolabes on his voyages, but he also observed the signs in nature to find his way.

Who Explored the West Indies?

A man from Italy named Christopher Columbus wanted to find an all-water route to the Indies. He was one of many who believed that since the earth was round, he could reach the Indies by sailing west.

Queen Isabella of Spain agreed to pay for Columbus's voyage. He explained his plan to Isabella and her Royal Court before she agreed.

Columbus did not have enough money to make his dream come true. He tried to get help from the kings of Portugal and England, but they both turned him down. The king and queen of Spain also refused to help at first. Finally, just as he was about to give up hope of making his journey, Queen Isabella of Spain agreed to pay for his **voyage**. He set sail in August 1492 with three small ships—the *Niña*, the *Pinta,* and the *Santa María.*

Continent

A large land mass on Earth; for example, North America or Africa

Focus on Economics

The desire for wealth drove the exploration of the Americas. By the 1400s, wealthy Europeans were eager to purchase Asian goods. They wanted silks, jewels, and spices from the East. Muslims controlled the land and sea trade routes to the East, but Europeans wanted to gain control of this trade. European explorers sailed west to find their own route to the East.

The Continents Between Europe and Asia

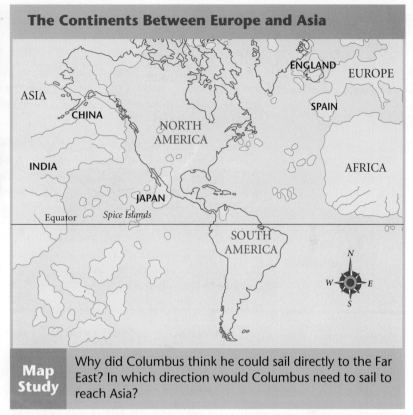

Map Study Why did Columbus think he could sail directly to the Far East? In which direction would Columbus need to sail to reach Asia?

Columbus did not know that between Europe and Asia lay two great **continents,** or masses of land. When his crew sighted land on October 12, 1492, he thought he had reached the Indies. He called the natives he found on the island "Indios." This word later became "Indians" in English.

Columbus made three more voyages across the Atlantic Ocean. He explored other islands, still believing them to be the East Indies. Because of his mistake, this group of islands is now called the West Indies.

Columbus started the first Spanish colony at Hispaniola in 1493. Soon there were many Spanish settlements on the islands of Hispaniola, Cuba, and Puerto Rico.

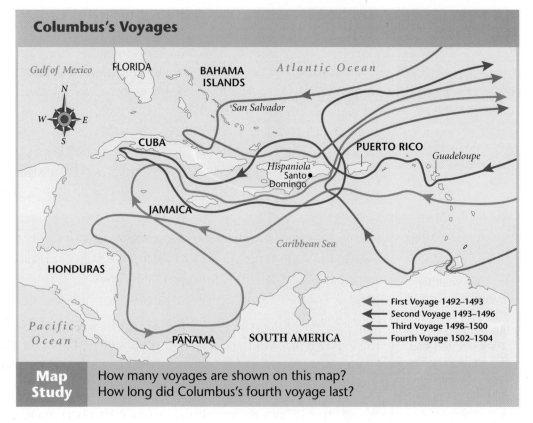

Columbus's Voyages

Gulf of Mexico
FLORIDA
BAHAMA ISLANDS
Atlantic Ocean
San Salvador
CUBA
PUERTO RICO
Guadeloupe
Hispaniola
Santo Domingo
JAMAICA
HONDURAS
Caribbean Sea
Pacific Ocean
PANAMA
SOUTH AMERICA

First Voyage 1492–1493
Second Voyage 1493–1496
Third Voyage 1498–1500
Fourth Voyage 1502–1504

Map Study How many voyages are shown on this map?
How long did Columbus's fourth voyage last?

Lesson 1 Review On a sheet of paper, write the answers to the following questions. Use complete sentences.

1. Why did Europeans want to find a water route to the Far East?

2. Who paid for the first journey of Christopher Columbus?

3. How did the compass aid in exploration?

4. What effect did the development of maps have on most people?

5. How were goods from the Far East brought to Europe?

What do you think ?

There were many reasons why the Europeans wanted to find a water route to the Far East. What do you think was the main reason? Why?

Mainland
The main part of
a continent

Other countries soon learned of Columbus and his voyages. In 1497, England sent John Cabot to explore. Cabot was an Italian from Venice who lived in England and had taken an English name. Like Columbus, Cabot thought he could reach the East Indies by sailing west. Cabot set sail farther north. He had one small ship and a crew of 18 sailors. Cabot reached what is now Newfoundland after one month. He claimed much land for England.

Cabot made a second trip to explore the east and northeast coasts of North America. He was disappointed he had not found the rich cities of China. He still believed he had been just off the coast of the Asian continent.

The mystery of the two continents that lay between Europe and the Far East had not been solved. Columbus and Cabot were sure they had reached Asia. The map on page 32 clearly shows that Cabot was no closer than Columbus.

AMERICUS VESPUTIUS

America got its name from the Italian explorer Amerigo Vespucci.

In 1497, an Italian named Amerigo Vespucci made several voyages to explore the northeastern coast of what is now South America. Vespucci's letters and records described what he found. He called it a new land. People in Europe were so impressed with his descriptions that they named the continent "America." People also called it the "New World."

Who Explored on Land?

One of the first Spanish explorers to go to the New World after Columbus was Juan Ponce de León. In 1513, he led a group in search of gold and the "Fountain of Youth." According to legend, water from the Fountain of Youth made people young again. Ponce de León reached the southeastern tip of the **mainland,** or main part of the continent. He named the place "Florida," the Spanish word for flower.

Also in 1513, Vasco Núñez de Balboa led a group of men in search of gold and silver. They became the first Europeans to see the Pacific Ocean from its eastern shore. One of the men with Balboa was Francisco Pizarro. Pizarro heard about the rich **empire** of the Incas. An empire is a large amount of territory under one ruler. Pizarro was determined to **conquer** the Incas and take their land and riches for Spain.

By 1533, the Incas had been defeated and forced into **slavery**. Their rights were taken away and they were forced to work for the Spanish. Slaves removed huge amounts of gold and silver from mines in the Andes Mountains and shipped it to Spain. Pizarro was killed in Lima, Peru, in 1541.

What Did Ferdinand Magellan Do?

Ferdinand Magellan, a Portuguese captain, was **commissioned** to sail in search of the Far East in 1519. He crossed the Atlantic Ocean and reached the coast of South America. He then journeyed south to the southern tip of South America. The stormy waters led from the Atlantic to the Pacific Ocean. Magellan had found the water route around the New World.

Magellan never completed his journey to the Far East. He was killed in the Philippines. Only one of his five ships and 18 of his

men finally reached the Far East before returning to Spain. It took them three years to complete the trip around the world.

Magellan's voyage was very important. It proved the earth really was round and provided Europeans with valuable information about the great land that separated Europe and Asia.

Ferdinand Magellan

In the 1530s, French explorer Jacques Cartier helped establish French settlements along the St. Lawrence River. From bases at Quebec City and Montreal, the French were able to reach deep into North America. The St. Lawrence became the main route for settlement and for furs and other goods coming from Canada. Today, the river remains Canada's most important commercial waterway.

Who Was Hernando Cortés?

Also in 1519, Spanish explorer Hernando Cortés landed on the coast of what is now Mexico. He was searching for gold and silver. Two years later, his army was equipped with cannons, armor, and 16 horses. They defeated the Aztec king, Montezuma, and captured his empire in central Mexico.

What Was the Northwest Passage?

An Italian by the name of Giovanni da Verrazano set sail from France in 1524. Some people in Europe believed there was a northern route to the Far East.

This became known as the Northwest Passage. Verrazano carried the French flag to the New World in search of the Northwest Passage. After a stormy voyage of some 50 days, Verrazano reached the American coast of what is now North Carolina. From North Carolina, he sailed north to Newfoundland. His records of the voyage greatly added to Europe's growing knowledge of this new continent.

In 1534, France sent Jacques Cartier in search of the Northwest Passage. He explored the St. Lawrence River in Canada. He thought this great river was the true way to the East. After three voyages to its shores, he finally realized he was mistaken. Cartier was very disappointed with his failure to find the waterway. The lands he claimed for France would later be of great value.

Then and Now

Have you seen a photograph of Earth from space? You can see the world is round. Europeans in the early 1400s could not even imagine a photograph, much less one taken from space. Many of them still believed that the world was flat. They did not know the Western Hemisphere existed. Ferdinand Magellan's trip in 1519 proved that the world is round. Still, many areas of the world were unknown to Europeans. Their maps and globes were far from complete. Now every area of Earth has been explored. You can find a map for any part of it.

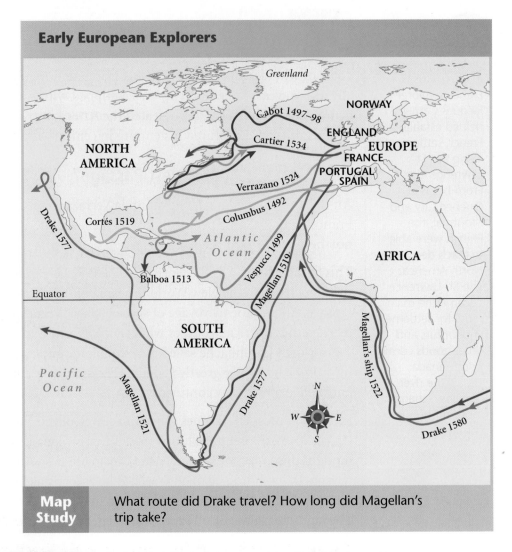

Early European Explorers

Greenland

NORWAY

Cabot 1497–98

ENGLAND

NORTH
AMERICA

Cartier 1534

EUROPE
FRANCE

PORTUGAL
SPAIN

Verrazano 1524

Columbus 1492

Cortés 1519

*Atlantic
Ocean*

AFRICA

Drake 1577

Vespucci 1499

Magellan 1519

Balboa 1513

Equator

Magellan's ship 1522

SOUTH
AMERICA

*Pacific
Ocean*

Magellan 1521

Drake 1577

N
W   E
S

Drake 1580

Map Study	What route did Drake travel? How long did Magellan's trip take?

What Did Sir Francis Drake Explore?

Expedition

A journey made by a person or group for a certain purpose

Sir Francis Drake of England was also an important explorer. His **expedition,** or journey, began in 1577. Drake sailed to the New World and around the southern tip of South America. He traveled up the Pacific coast as far as what is now the state of Washington. Then he crossed the Pacific Ocean and returned to England by 1580. His expedition was the second to sail around the world.

Civics Connection

Explorers in the New World

Christopher Columbus claimed American lands for the king and queen of Spain. Spain and other European countries wanted to increase their wealth and power. One way of doing so was by conquering other lands. This was a common way for countries to make their kingdoms larger.

Throughout the late-1400s and 1500s, European explorers claimed more and more lands in the Americas. The people already living there had their own cultures. However, Europeans did not think about the lives of these people. The explorers felt they had a right to the land.

Today, taking land that belongs to others is not acceptable. Democratic countries value the rights of all people, no matter where they live. The United Nations, an international organization, tries to stop human rights abuses.

1. What might the explorers have done if the native people had not allowed them to land?

2. Find out about actions the United Nations has taken recently. How has this organization protected the rights of people in other nations?

Lesson 2 Review On a sheet of paper, write the answers to the following questions. Use complete sentences.

1. How did America get its name?

2. What was Ponce de León searching for in the New World?

3. List the countries that sent explorers to the New World.

4. Where did Magellan find the water route around the New World?

5. Who searched for the Northwest Passage?

What do you think ?

Many early explorers fought with or conquered native peoples. Why do you think the explorers did this? What more peaceful actions could the explorers have taken?

Loot

To take or damage things by use of force

Armada

A fleet of warships

Charter

A written agreement granting power in the name of a state or country

Colony

A group of people living in a new area under rule of their native land

Spain began to benefit from the great treasures of the New World. Other countries grew jealous of these treasures. French, Dutch, and English ships began seizing Spanish ships on the high seas and **looting** Spanish towns along the coast of America. King Philip II of Spain was very angry with England for these attacks. He sent a fleet of ships in 1588 to crush the English and overthrow Queen Elizabeth I of England. Much to his disappointment, however, the more skilled English sailors defeated this fleet, called the Spanish **Armada**. Spain's power began to weaken after this defeat. England's power increased.

What Was Roanoke?

In 1578, Queen Elizabeth granted an agreement, or **charter,** to Sir Humphrey Gilbert to begin a **colony**. A colony is a group of people living in a new area. Gilbert wanted to establish a colony in the New World. However, Gilbert died during his second attempt at establishing a colony. Sir Walter Raleigh, Gilbert's half brother, received the charter.

English ships defeated the Spanish Armada in the English Channel.

Permanent

Meant to last for
a long time

Sir Walter Raleigh

Sir Walter Raleigh was determined to establish a **permanent** colony. He wanted to claim North America for England. Between 1584 and 1587, Raleigh sent three different expeditions to the New World. The first group was sent to explore and set up a base to supply English warships. The second group was sent to live in the new colony. The colony did not do very well, and many people died. Others returned to England.

Raleigh would not give up his plan to start a colony. He asked John White to lead a third and final group. They settled on Roanoke Island off the coast of North Carolina. White returned to England in 1587 to get more supplies. He was unable to return to Roanoke until 1590. No trace could be found of the settlers when he returned. The group had simply disappeared.

What Became of the Lost Colony?

Perhaps some colonists starved. Others may have been killed by Indians. England's war with Spain, which lasted until 1604, may have been part of the reason the colony did not survive. England was preparing for the invasion by the Spanish Armada and could not send help to the new colony. For that reason it is called the "Lost Colony." The only clues were the letters "CRO" carved on one tree and the word "CROATOAN" carved on another. No one knew what the word meant. White's daughter and granddaughter, Virginia Dare, were among the missing. Virginia Dare was the first English child born in America.

Writing About History

What do you think may have happened to people at the Roanoke colony? In your journal or notebook, write two or three paragraphs explaining what you think could have happened to the colony.

Where Were Other Colonies Started?

The French had shown some earlier interest in starting colonies in America, but little came of it. Seventy years had passed since Cartier discovered the St. Lawrence River and claimed much of Canada for France. The first French colony was started on the St. Lawrence River in the early 1600s. The leader of this small colony, Samuel de Champlain, named the settlement Quebec.

France's territories in America were later called New France. This colony spread and eventually covered a large area, from Hudson Bay to the Gulf of Mexico. New France never attracted many settlers. The population remained very small for over 100 years. Although Spain, Portugal, and France had claimed large areas of land, only a few scattered colonies were successful.

King James I of England

What Other Colonies Did England Start?

Major changes took place when King James I took the English throne in 1603. He had strict religious rules. He had little patience with those who disagreed with him. English people started to look for a new place to live. The faraway lands of the New World were appealing. These people were looking for religious and **political** freedom.

Two groups of wealthy nobles and merchants formed the Virginia Company of London. They were interested in making money from trade. King James granted them a charter for land within the region of Virginia in 1606. A second charter was granted in the same year to the Plymouth Company. It included land farther to the north in what is now New England.

Three small ships and about 100 men reached the shores of Virginia in April 1607. The place where they landed was named Jamestown in honor of their king.

Montezuma II: c. 1466–1520

Montezuma II was the king of the Aztec Empire. The empire stretched from the Gulf of Mexico to the Pacific Ocean in present-day Mexico. Like earlier kings, Montezuma expanded the kingdom. The capital of the empire, Tenochtitlán, was set on an island in the middle of a lake. In 1519, the Spanish explorer Hernando Cortés marched on Tenochtitlán, the present Mexico City. Montezuma thought that Cortés was a god who had been expected to return to Earth. Because of that, Montezuma sent Cortés rich gifts. Cortés wanted more treasure, however, so he attacked Tenochtitlán. Montezuma died from wounds he received during the attack.

Lesson 3 Review On a sheet of paper, write the answers to the following questions. Use complete sentences.

1. Which country defeated the Spanish Armada?

2. What was the name of the first English colony?

3. What happened to the Roanoke colony?

4. Where was the first French colony started? Who was its leader?

5. Why did the people of England dislike the way King James I ruled?

What do you think ?

What did the defeat of the Spanish Armada do to England's and Spain's power in Europe? Why do you think this was important?

Cabeza de Vaca's Journal

In 1527, Spanish explorer Álvar Núñez Cabeza de Vaca set out to colonize what is now Florida. In 1528 after shipwrecking off the Texas coast, he and his crew explored Mexico and what is now the southwestern United States. They traveled over American Indian trails and had much contact with Indians. Here is part of Cabeza de Vaca's journal.

I ordered . . . our strongest man to . . . find any worn trails. . . . We had begun to worry what . . . happened to him, so I detailed another two men to check. They met him shortly and saw three Indians with bows and arrows following him. . . . Later 100 bowmen . . . reinforced the first three. . . . They looked like giants to us in our fright. . . . We gave them beads and bells, and each . . . gave us an arrow as a pledge of friendship. . . .

The next morning, the Indians [brought] . . . fish and . . . roots. . . . Provided with what we needed, we . . . embark[ed] again. . . . We had rowed . . . from shore

when a wave . . . capsized the boat. . . . We lost everything. . . .

At sunset the Indians, not knowing we had tried to leave, came again with food. When they saw us looking so strangely . . . I explained . . . that our barge had sunk and three . . . drowned. . . . The Indians, understanding our full plight, sat down and [wailed] . . . When the cries died down, I conferred . . . about asking the Indians to take us to their homes. Some . . . who had been to New Spain warned that the Indians would sacrifice us. . . . But . . . I . . . beseeched the Indians. They were delighted. . . .

In the morning, they brought us fish and roots and acted in every way hospitably. We . . . somewhat lost our anxiety. . . .

Document-Based Questions

1. Why were Cabeza de Vaca and his men frightened of the Indians?

2. What were some kindnesses the Indians showed the explorers?

3. What caused the American Indians to sit down and wail?

4. Why did the explorers ask to go to the Indians' homes, even though they thought they might be killed?

5. How did you react to the way the Indians treated Cabeza de Vaca and his men?

Source: Álvar Núñez Cabeza de Vaca's Journal *in* Adventures in the Unknown Interior of America, *translated by Cyclone Covey.*

Chapter 2 SUMMARY

- In the 1400s, the development of the compass and improvements in mapmaking and globes helped exploration.

- In 1477, Marco Polo's book describing the Far East excited the people of Europe and encouraged exploration.

- Christopher Columbus made his first voyage in search of the Far East in 1492. He explored what was later called the West Indies.

- John Cabot explored North America in 1497. He claimed much of northeastern North America for England.

- Amerigo Vespucci made several voyages to South America beginning in 1499. Later, the continent he explored was named America after him.

- Juan Ponce de León searched for gold and the Fountain of Youth in 1513. He named the land he explored Florida.

- Vasco Núñez de Balboa led a voyage in 1513 in search of gold and silver. He and his crew were the first Europeans to see the Pacific Ocean.

- Ferdinand Magellan led a voyage around the world in 1519.

- Hernando Cortés conquered the Aztecs in 1521.

- Giovanni da Verrazano searched for the Northwest Passage in 1524. He later reached North Carolina and Newfoundland. Jacques Cartier searched for the Northwest Passage in 1534. He explored the St. Lawrence River in Canada.

- Sir Francis Drake led the second expedition around the world between 1577 and 1580.

- The English defeated the Spanish Armada in 1588.

- Sir Walter Raleigh organized three expeditions to the New World between 1584 and 1587. Under Raleigh, John White formed a colony in Roanoke, North Carolina. The colony, Roanoke, later disappeared.

- The first French colony was started on the St. Lawrence River in the early 1600s.

- In 1606, King James I granted charters for land in the New World. The Virginia Company settled a colony in Jamestown, Virginia, in 1607.

Chapter 2   REVIEW

Word Bank

Amerigo Vespucci

Christopher
   Columbus

Ferdinand
   Magellan

Francis Drake

Francisco Pizarro

Hernando Cortés

Jacques Cartier

Vasco Núñez
   de Balboa

Match each sentence below with an explorer from the Word
Bank. Write your answers on a sheet of paper.

1. He explored the West Indies.

2. He led the second expedition around the world.

3. He led an expedition that became the first group of
   Europeans to see the Pacific Ocean.

4. He explored the St. Lawrence River.

5. He defeated the Aztecs.

6. His expedition was the first to sail around the world,
   though he was killed during the journey.

7. America is named after him.

8. He worked for Vasco Núñez de Balboa before becoming
   interested in conquering the Incas.

On a sheet of paper, write the letter of the answer that correctly
answers each question.

9. What desire led to the wave of world exploration in the
   1400s and 1500s?

   A to trade with wealthy Asian nations

   B to see the unknown

   C to conquer native peoples

   D to claim new lands for Europe

10. What was most important about Ferdinand Magellan's
    voyage?

    A Magellan was killed in the Philippines.

    B It proved the earth was round.

    C It proved there was a Northwest passage.

    D It made Portugal a rich nation.

11. Which explorer reached Newfoundland when England sent him to look for the East Indies?

A Hernando Cortés   **C** Ponce de León

B Giovanni da Verrazano   **D** John Cabot

On a sheet of paper, write the answers to the following questions. Use complete sentences.

12. How did the globe, compass, and map improve exploration?

13. What happened when other countries became jealous of Spain's discoveries in the New World?

14. Why was defeating the Spanish Armada important for the English?

15. What was Roanoke colony? Who started it?

16. What was the first French colony? Who started it?

17. Why did many people want to leave England when James I became king?

Critical Thinking On a sheet of paper, write your response to each question. Use complete sentences.

18. Do you think the Europeans would have found the New World as quickly if Columbus had not made his voyages? Why or why not?

19. Who do you think was the most important explorer? Explain.

20. Many people left England because they were searching for political or religious freedom. Do you think these rights are important in the United States today? Explain.

Test-Taking Tip

When studying for a test, review the topics in the chapter. The titles and headings will help you recall the information you learned.

Timelines

Timelines display dates and events on a line. They may show key events for a region. They also may list events during an individual's life. Timelines can span thousands of years or cover only a few months.

Timelines show time relationships between events. Timelines help you think of events in the order they occurred. They show when an event occurred. They also show what took place before and after the event.

Always look at the beginning and ending dates to understand the time period.

Each chapter in this book begins with a timeline. These timelines will help you focus on key events and ideas from the chapter. Remember, creating your own timeline of events as you read a chapter can help you study.

This timeline gives important dates in the life of explorer Hernando Cortés. Study it. Then answer the questions.

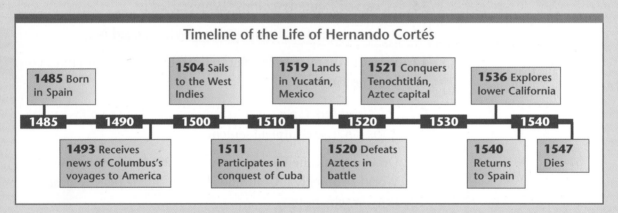

Timeline of the Life of Hernando Cortés

- **1485** Born in Spain
- **1504** Sails to the West Indies
- **1519** Lands in Yucatán, Mexico
- **1521** Conquers Tenochtitlán, Aztec capital
- **1536** Explores lower California

1485 — 1490 — 1500 — 1510 — 1520 — 1530 — 1540

- **1493** Receives news of Columbus's voyages to America
- **1511** Participates in conquest of Cuba
- **1520** Defeats Aztecs in battle
- **1540** Returns to Spain
- **1547** Dies

1. What are the timeline's beginning and ending dates?

2. In what year was Hernando Cortés born?

3. About how old was Cortés when Christopher Columbus first landed in America?

4. What was Cortés doing in 1505?

5. Where was Cortés in 1511?

6. In what year did Cortés land on the Yucatán Peninsula of Mexico?

7. Ferdinand Magellan sailed around the tip of South America in 1520. What was Cortés doing when this happened?

8. How many years after Cortés defeated the Aztecs did he conquer their capital city?

9. How old was Cortés when he died?

10. Create a timeline showing key events in your life during the last school year.

Unit 1 SUMMARY

- Hunters crossed a land bridge from Siberia to North America about 20,000 B.C. These earliest Americans may have migrated across North America and into South America.

- People who settled in Mesoamerica between 1200 B.C. and 1521 had early advanced civilizations.

- The Hohokam, Mogollon, and Anasazi societies were in the North American Southwest. The Pueblo and Navajo civilizations developed in the Southwest after the Anasazi societies declined.

- Between 700 B.C. and A.D. 300, the Adena and Hopewell people lived in the Ohio River Valley. Civilizations may have been in the Mississippi River Valley as early as 4500 B.C.

- The Pacific Northwest civilizations began around A.D. 400.

- In the 1400s, the compass, mapmaking, and globes helped exploration.

- Columbus made his first voyage in search of the Far East in 1492.

- John Cabot explored North America in 1497. He claimed much northeastern land for England.

- Amerigo Vespucci made voyages to South America beginning in 1499.

Later, the continent he explored was named America after him.

- In 1513, Vasco Núñez de Balboa and his crew were the first Europeans to see the Pacific Ocean.

- In 1519, Ferdinand Magellan led a voyage around the world.

- Hernando Cortés conquered the Aztecs in 1521.

- Giovanni da Verrazano searched for the Northwest Passage in 1524. Jacques Cartier searched for the Northwest Passage in 1534.

- Sir Francis Drake led the second expedition around the world between 1577 and 1580.

- The English defeated the Spanish Armada in 1588.

- Sir Walter Raleigh organized three expeditions to North America between 1584 and 1587.

- The first French colony was started on the St. Lawrence River in the early 1600s.

- In 1606, King James I granted charters to the Virginia Company of London and the Plymouth Company. The Virginia Company settled in Jamestown in 1607.

"Many noble persons . . . have resolved to send an expedition to Virginia as soon as possible. . . . This notice is published to announce the expedition to all workmen— blacksmiths, carpenters, barrel-makers, ship builders, wood workers . . . architects, bakers, weavers, shoemakers . . . both men and women, of any occupation—who wish to join this voyage for colonizing the country. . . ."

~ *Virginia Company Broadside, ca. 1614*

Unit 2

Colonization and Settlement

Think of yourself as a European living in the 1600s. You are unhappy with the way your government rules. You are unhappy about being unable to worship as you choose. You have heard about a "new land" across a wide sea. Will you be among those who choose to leave home for the new land? Will you be brave enough to sail for three or four months to get to an unknown place? How will you want your government and religion to be different in a new country? Will you be able to brave many hardships to have a better life?

In this unit, you will learn why the first European settlers came here and how they made a life. You will learn which countries established settlements and claimed land. You will learn about their very first struggles for freedom.

Chapters in Unit 2

3 English Colonies Are Created

Early exploration paved the way for colonization in the New World. Many people in England and other parts of Europe considered leaving their homelands. Businesses were eager to take advantage of what the New World had to offer. In this chapter, you will learn how the first English colonies were established.

Goals for Learning

◆ To describe how the Jamestown colony became a successful settlement

◆ To identify the Pilgrims and the Puritans and where they settled

◆ To explain how each English colony came into being

◆ To describe what life was like in colonial times

◆ To recognize which colonies made up the New England, middle, and southern regions

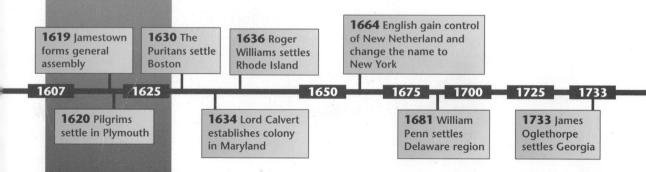

1619 Jamestown forms general assembly

1630 The Puritans settle Boston

1636 Roger Williams settles Rhode Island

1664 English gain control of New Netherland and change the name to New York

1607   1625   1650   1675   1700   1725   1733

1620 Pilgrims settle in Plymouth

1634 Lord Calvert establishes colony in Maryland

1681 William Penn settles Delaware region

1733 James Oglethorpe settles Georgia

Geography Note

The swampy ground along the James River provided a poor location for Jamestown. Ocean tides made the water salty and undrinkable. English foods grew poorly nearby, so the colonists did not have enough food. Mosquitoes carried malaria and other diseases. These diseases and malnutrition killed many settlers.

It took English settlers four months to make the trip from England to Virginia. English settlers arrived in Virginia in April 1607. They explored the region for one month to find a proper place for a colony. Jamestown was established in May 1607.

The colonists spent a lot of time searching for gold and silver. The settlers wanted to find the route to the Far East. Thus, they paid little attention to growing crops. Poor leadership and disease were taking a toll. The region was swampy and did not have good drinking water. Steadily, the number of colonists decreased to nearly half the original number. Because they had come for adventure or gold, some of the men did not want to work. The food supply got smaller as winter approached. There were also many American Indian attacks.

How Did Conditions at Jamestown Improve?

Changes needed to be made quickly if the colony was to succeed. The settlers had to find a leader. Fortunately, among the settlers was an experienced military man named Captain John Smith. The settlers made Captain Smith the new leader. He set up a rule that every person had to work.

Jamestown was established in 1607. Conditions were difficult for these colonists at first.

If a person did not work, then he or she would get no food. Smith tried to get along with the Powhatan tribe. He also ordered a **blockhouse,** or fort, to be built for better protection of the settlement. The Powhatans supplied corn to the starving colonists and proved to be helpful. In spite of this and all of Captain Smith's efforts, the situation was very difficult. Captain Smith was hurt in a gunpowder explosion and had to return to England for proper care. Without him as leader, the colony was in even more trouble.

An English ship arrived at Jamestown in 1610. Conditions had become so bad that the settlers decided to abandon Jamestown. They wanted to go back to England. The settlers went on board, and the ship set sail for open waters. Just as the vessel neared the mouth of the James River, three more English ships came into sight. They were coming to Jamestown. They carried new supplies and about 150 more men. This gave the colony new hope. The settlers turned around and went back to Jamestown.

What Happened When the Settlers Returned?

Three important events took place after the settlers returned to Jamestown. First, Lord Delaware was made **governor** of the colony. This noble proved to be a strong and fair leader. Second, John Rolfe planted tobacco. Jamestown now had a crop of value. Third, Rolfe married a young American Indian woman named Pocahontas. She was the daughter of Powhatan, the chief of the Powhatan tribe. This further improved the colonists' relationship with the Powhatans. In a few years the colony was well on its way to becoming a growing and lasting settlement.

Tobacco became very popular in Europe. Colonists needed more land to keep up with the demand for tobacco. The Virginia Company gave the colonists more land. Colonists built large farms called **plantations**. The farmers soon needed more land. They began to use American Indian land for their crops.

Several things affected Jamestown in 1619. The Virginia Company gave settlers permission to form a **general assembly**. This group was known as the House of Burgesses. It met with the governor to make laws for the colony. The settlers chose their own **representatives** to serve in the House of Burgesses. This was the beginning of a representative government in America.

The Virginia Company also realized many of the men wanted to leave Jamestown after they made their fortune. This would have hurt the tobacco farming. The Virginia Company would lose money. To prevent this, they brought 90 single women to Jamestown to marry and settle in this new land. During this same year, the captain of a Dutch ship sold 20 Africans to the colonists. These African slaves worked in the tobacco fields.

Word Bank

blockhouse
general assembly
governor
representatives
tobacco

Lesson 1 Review On a sheet of paper, write the correct word or words from the Word Bank to complete each sentence.

1. John Smith ordered the colonists to build a _____ for defense.

2. John Rolfe planted _____.

3. Lord Delaware became _____ of Jamestown in 1610.

4. A _____ was formed in Jamestown in 1619.

5. The Jamestown colonists elected _____ to serve in the House of Burgesses.

What do you think ?

Why was forming a general assembly an important step for the Jamestown colonists?

A kind of company called a **stock company** helped colonization. These companies were owned by people who owned **shares** of the company's stock. Shares are parts of a company. Stock companies were interested in trade and profit. They rewarded **investors** for the risks involved in settling a new colony. People who invested their money hoped to earn a profit. However, they could also lose money.

The Plymouth Company was a stock company. Its charter granted the company the rights to settle in Virginia. However, they settled in what is now called New England. The company's first attempt to establish a colony was a disaster. Poor planning and the cold winter forced the colonists to return to England.

Who Were the Pilgrims?

Religious problems increased in England under the rule of James I. The king was very unhappy with the group of people who did not share his religious ideas. Members of this group were known as Separatists, or Pilgrims. They wanted to break away from the Church of England completely. James I did not accept this group and treated them very harshly. Many of them fled to Holland in Western Europe. Holland, or the Netherlands, as it is called today, was Dutch. The Pilgrims were not comfortable in this setting. The Dutch people had a different language and way of life. Many Pilgrims thought about going to the New World, but they did not know how to get there. Ships and supplies were expensive, and they could not afford them.

What Plan Did the Pilgrims Make?

A determined group of Pilgrims formed a stock company and bought as many shares as they could. Much more money was needed. The Pilgrims were able to get the additional money from wealthy investors of the London Company. Many members of the London Company were interested in setting up a new colony.

Destination

A place where one is going

Majority

A number greater than half of the total

Democratic

A government in which the power is held by the people

The investors were willing to pay for the ships and all the supplies. However, the Pilgrims had to agree to certain conditions:

- The Pilgrims could settle on land that belonged to the London Company in Virginia.
- The settlers would have to work for seven years and give all the profits back to the investors.
- After the seven-year period was over, the settlers would be on their own and free to do as they wished.

The small group of Pilgrims, plus a large number of other people, set sail on the *Mayflower*. After a 64-day voyage across the Atlantic Ocean, the small crowded vessel reached the shore of what is now Cape Cod in 1620. The ship had blown off course. Scouts were sent out to explore the region. A month later, the Pilgrims sailed to their new site, which they called Plymouth.

The Mayflower *was blown off its original course. It eventually anchored off Cape Cod.*

What Was the Mayflower Compact?

While the *Mayflower* was anchored in the water off of Cape Cod, the Pilgrims held a meeting in the cabin of the ship. They had landed outside of their chartered **destination**. They were not bound to their charter this far north. They seized the opportunity to set up their own rules of government.

The group elected John Carver as its first leader. William Bradford was elected after Carver died. Bradford was leader for most of the next 30 years. Choosing a leader was very important. The passengers agreed that laws passed by the **majority** of the group would be obeyed. They wrote the Mayflower Compact in 1620 to represent this idea. Rule by majority is still a main part of our **democratic** government, which is a government ruled by the people.

Signing the Mayflower Compact was the beginning of democracy in America.

Parliament

A group in England that makes laws

A great historical event had taken place. This was the first time European Americans had set up their own government. They agreed to obey the laws that the majority made.

The Mayflower Compact could not solve all the problems of the colony. The poor soil, cold winters, heavy debt, and strict religious practices were difficult problems. Because of their strong religious views, the Pilgrims were not able to attract more settlers. However, in time, the settlement was a success.

Who Were the Puritans?

The Puritans were a religious group. Like the Pilgrims, they were unhappy with the way the king treated them. When Charles I became king in 1625, problems increased. He did not approve of their religious ideas. It was difficult for the king to deal with the Puritans. There were many of them in **Parliament,** and they were well educated. Parliament is a group in England that makes laws.

Charles I took strong measures to keep the Parliament under control. Officials were removed from government positions, and ministers were not allowed to be part of the Church. Many Puritans were put into prison.

In 1629, some wealthy Puritans decided to go to America. They obtained a charter in the name of the Massachusetts Bay Colony. The 1,000 colonists included teachers, doctors, lawyers, ministers, merchants, and well-to-do country gentlemen. The Puritans spent a great deal of time planning, organizing, and gathering **provisions**. They were well aware of the dangers and problems that lay ahead.

The group of Puritans set out for America with a fleet of 15 ships. They landed in Boston, Massachusetts, in 1630. John Winthrop became the governor of the new settlement. Within a few years, nearly 10,000 colonists came to this settlement. Because the expedition was well managed, it was a success.

The Puritans also had very strong religious ideas. They had journeyed a great distance to worship as they pleased. Because they had suffered under a cruel king, it was very important for them to have religious freedom. However, they did not grant this freedom to others.

All laws dealing with religion, trade, business, and government were made according to the Puritans' beliefs. Every colonist was expected to follow these laws. Stern measures were taken to make sure people would obey.

The Pilgrams formed a successful settlement in Plymouth, Massachusetts.

Lesson 2 Review Decide whether each statement below tells about the Pilgrims or the Puritans. Write *Pilgrims* or *Puritans* beside each number on a sheet of paper.

1. A religious group that formed a new colony in Boston.

2. A religious group that formed a new colony in Plymouth.

3. They wrote an agreement called the Mayflower Compact.

4. John Winthrop became governor of their settlement.

5. They elected John Carver as their leader.

What do you think

Why do you think the Puritans wanted religious freedom but did not want to grant that freedom to others?

History in Your Life

The Earliest Bowling

Our modern bowling began in Europe during the Middle Ages. German players rolled or threw a ball at nine wooden clubs that stood upright. The clubs were weapons commonly carried for protection. The game was called "ninepins."

During the 1600s, Dutch settlers played ninepins on a green in New Amsterdam. New Amsterdam was later named New York. The green where the Dutch played this game was called the "bowling green," as that area of New York is still called. When bowling attracted gamblers in America, some states made "bowling at ninepins" illegal. In the 1840s, clever bowlers added a tenth pin to get around the ruling. Since then, bowling has become one of America's most popular sports.

Boundary

A real or imaginary marker that shows what land a person owns

Proprietor

One who owns a colony

Equality

Having the same rights as others

Clergy

A person given the power by the church to perform religious tasks

Guidance

Direction or leading

Pastor

A member of the clergy

A new kind of colony was started under Charles I. A wealthy noble could receive a charter with clearly defined **boundaries**. The landowners, called **proprietors,** would have the right to govern their colonies as they wished.

The first such colony was Maryland. King Charles I made George Calvert the proprietor of the Maryland colony in 1632. Calvert died before the charter became official. His son, Cecilius Calvert, received the charter in his place and became proprietor. A colony was established in what is now St. Marys City, on the shores of the Chesapeake Bay, in 1634. Although Lord Calvert was a Roman Catholic, he wanted all religious groups to worship as they wished. Maryland passed the Toleration Act in 1649. The law allowed everyone to enjoy religious freedom. The act was very important. It established an **equality** of rights for people of all religions.

When Were Rhode Island and Connecticut Settled?

The strict policies of the Puritans soon brought about problems. Roger Williams, a member of the **clergy,** spoke out against the policies. He fled from the colony in order to avoid prison. Williams made his way to what is now Rhode Island. The Narragansett tribe helped him. He called his settlement Providence, which meant "God's **guidance**." Soon, some of his followers came to the new settlement. A true democratic colony was formed for the first time in 1636. Roger Williams went to England and got a charter to protect the settlement. He established complete freedom of religion in Rhode Island.

Another group of people was interested in migrating west to the Connecticut Valley. The valley had rich farmland. Thomas Hooker, a **pastor,** was the leader. He was also a member of the clergy. Hooker started a settlement in Connecticut in 1636. Two years later, Puritans founded New Haven. Each group drew up a written constitution in 1639. These documents were the Fundamental Orders of Connecticut and of New Haven. They are called the first written constitution in the New World.

How Were Other Colonies Settled?

The region that extended south of Virginia to Florida was available for colonies. It was possible that the Spanish in Florida would move northward. This would be a serious problem for English settlements in that area.

Carolina

In 1663, several English nobles approached Charles II, then king of England, and requested a charter to settle that region. The king recognized the advantages of settling in this area. Different crops could be grown in the warmer climate. The charter was granted. The region was called Carolina. As settlers arrived, Charleston, named in honor of Charles II, became an important port.

Political quarrels developed in Carolina. They were continually a source of trouble. The proprietors finally gave up and sold their interest to the British government. They in turn divided Carolina into North Carolina and South Carolina in 1729.

New York

New York's original name was New Netherland. It began in 1609 as a Dutch colony. The colony grew very slowly because of its strict land-ownership **policy**. The Dutch landlords, or **patroons,** kept a tight hold on available lands for settlers. The English were uncomfortable with this Dutch settlement. King Charles II declared that all lands of the region belonged to his brother, James, Duke of York. An English fleet forced the Dutch governor, Peter Stuyvesant, to give up the Dutch claim. The English took over the colony in 1664 and renamed it New York.

New Hampshire

Another colony was New Hampshire. This colony was part of Massachusetts for 39 years. New Hampshire was sold to the king of England in 1679. The king made New Hampshire a royal colony. It did not have an elected government. The king chose the governor.

Pennsylvania

Access

The ability to obtain or make use of something

William Penn was granted a charter for the land between New York and Maryland in 1681. King Charles II was in debt to William Penn's father. The king had borrowed a large amount of money. The charter was given as payment for what the king owed.

William Penn was a Quaker. He believed in the equality of all people. He gave the colonists of Pennsylvania two important individual rights: freedom of religion and the right to elect public officials. Philadelphia, a city in Pennsylvania, later came to be known as the City of Brotherly Love.

Delaware

In 1682, the Duke of York granted William Penn a region known today as Delaware. This gave Pennsylvania **access** to the Atlantic Ocean. Dutch, Swedes, and Finns settled in that area. The region was controlled by Pennsylvania and divided into three separate areas. This area was called the "Three Lower Counties." It became one colony—Delaware—in 1704.

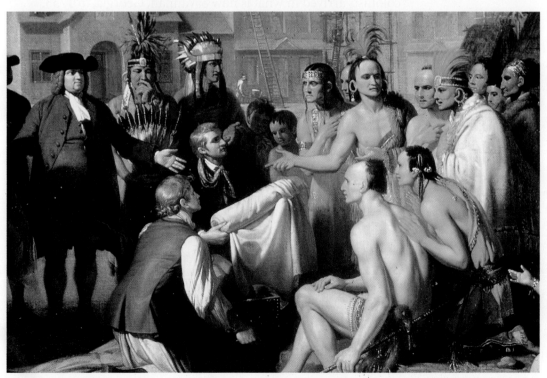

William Penn (left) founded Pennsylvania and established good relations with the Delaware Indians.

New Jersey

Part of the land claimed by the Duke of York was a region called New Jersey. Two nobles, friends of the duke, were interested in the region. East Jersey and West Jersey were established to please these friends. For many years, problems related to the government of the regions continued. Finally, in 1702, the two regions were made into one single colony called New Jersey.

Georgia

Conditions in England grew worse under the strict rule of King George II. People were sent to overcrowded prisons for minor crimes. James Oglethorpe, a wealthy businessman, asked for a colony where the poor and unfortunate could settle when they left prison. He was given the land between South Carolina and Florida. The British were worried that the Spanish in Florida would move northward. This could cause serious problems for the British. The land given to Oglethorpe would prevent the Spanish from moving northward. This area was named Georgia. The colonists arrived in what is now Savannah, Georgia, in 1733.

 Biography

Margaret Brent: 1600–1671

Margaret Brent has been called one of America's first promoters of women's rights. She came to the Maryland colony from England in 1638. She became a landowner at a time when few women had that privilege. Brent did well, becoming one of the largest landowners in her state.

Shortly after hiring soldiers to fight a Protestant uprising, Lord Calvert died in 1647. Margaret Brent managed his estate after his death. Unpaid and hungry, the troops threatened trouble. Brent acted quickly. She sold Lord Calvert's estate to pay the soldiers and imported corn to feed them. The Maryland Assembly later praised Brent, saying that the colony was safe in her hands.

Then and Now

Importing clothes or fabrics into the American colonies from Europe was expensive. To save the expense, nearly all colonists made their own clothing. Linen was a common fabric. It came from a plant called flax by a process of rotting, beating, and spinning into thread and then cloth. Wool was another common material. It came from sheared sheep by a process of sorting, washing, beating, drying, and spinning. Linen and wool fibers were sometimes combined into a fabric called linsey-woolsey. In remote areas, people used leather clothes made from animal skins. Blue and red were popular dye colors. Many people also wore black or brown clothes.

Today, machines in huge factories make rainbows of colorful cloth. Plants and animals still provide some fabrics. But scientists also create new fabrics through chemistry. The clothes we wear often combine many different materials.

Lesson 3 Review Choose the word in parentheses that best completes each sentence. Write your answers on a sheet of paper.

1. Lord Calvert set up a colony in (Georgia, Maryland, New York).

2. (Roger Williams, James Oglethorpe, Thomas Hooker) settled Connecticut.

3. Carolina was divided into North Carolina and South Carolina in (1609, 1663, 1729).

4. An owner of a colony was called a (governor, king, proprietor).

5. Pennsylvania was settled by (George Calvert, William Penn, James Oglethorpe).

What do you think ?

Do you think most Maryland colonists liked the Toleration Act? Explain your answer.

Expansion

Spreading out or increasing in size

Estimate

To make a guess based on some facts

Emigrate

To leave for another place or country

Refuge

Protection or shelter

Minority

A group of people that is a smaller part of a population

Settlement of the 13 colonies took place between 1607 and 1733. The number of colonists coming to America was slowly increasing. Poor traveling conditions and concern about the American Indians slowed **expansion**. Population by the late 1600s is **estimated** to have been between 200,000 and 300,000.

At first, most of the colonists were English. Other Europeans began to **emigrate,** or move to America because of religious and political problems in their countries. America was becoming known as a place of safety and **refuge**. Germans, Irish, Dutch, French, Swedes, and Scotch-Irish were among the growing population. The English majority was rapidly becoming a **minority**. The desire for freedom brought many people to America.

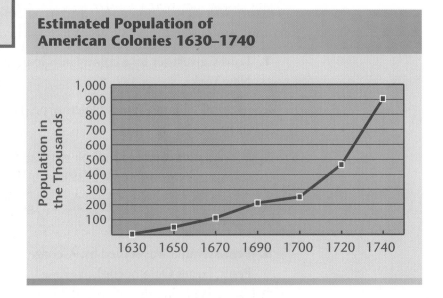

Estimated Population of American Colonies 1630–1740

Indentured servant

A person who came to the colonies under a contract to work without pay for a certain time

Chattel slavery

Slavery in which the enslaved person was legally owned by his or her master

Epidemic

An outbreak of disease

American life was taking shape. Farmers cleared the land and planted crops. Merchants sold and shipped goods. The early colonial society had a wealthy class, a middle class, and a lower class. The wealthy class was merchants or large planters. Farmers, shopkeepers, artisans, and teachers were the middle class. The lower class was unskilled workers, **indentured servants** (someone who works as part of a contract), or slaves.

Indentured service was a common form of labor in colonial times. In the 1600s, there were more indentured servants than slaves in the southern colonies.

An indentured servant would come to the colonies from Europe. To pay for the trip, a servant would work for someone in the colonies. Most indentured servants had to work anywhere from four to seven years. Servants had harsh working conditions. Many Europeans were forced to be indentured servants. People were sometimes kidnapped and sold as servants. Indentured service was different from **chattel slavery,** in which the enslaved persons were legally owned by their masters. Chattel slavery started becoming more common later in the 1700s.

During this time period, houses were usually wood. A fireplace provided warmth, and people used it for cooking. Sparks from the fireplace or chimney could cause a fire that might destroy the house. Furnishings were plain and sturdy. Mattresses were canvas bags filled with straw. Homemade candles provided light. The food was rather simple. Corn was often used to make bread. Meat or wild game was cooked with vegetables in a large iron pot. With no refrigeration, food could not be stored very long. Meat was salted or smoked to preserve it. Vegetables could be dried or pickled. Some fruits could be stored in cool, dry cellars.

Generally, the health of the early colonists was poor. Little was known about the cause and treatment of diseases. Sometimes an **epidemic,** or an outbreak of widespread disease, would occur.

What Were the Three Colonial Regions?

The northern or New England colonies included New Hampshire, Massachusetts, Rhode Island, and Connecticut. Farms were small in the New England colonies. This was because of the rocky soil and long, cold winters. Clusters of small towns were established as interest in certain jobs grew. Shipbuilding, lumbering, fishing, trading, and ironworks grew steadily.

The southern colonies were Maryland, North Carolina, South Carolina, Georgia, and Virginia. These colonies had broad lowlands, fertile farmlands, and a much warmer climate. The southern settlers were spread out over a large area. Plantations produced "money crops" such as rice, tobacco, and **indigo,** which was a plant used to make dye. Slave labor was introduced and used by wealthy plantation owners.

The middle colonies included New York, New Jersey, Pennsylvania, and Delaware. The climate was a mixture of both the northern and southern conditions. The colonies in the central part of colonial America served as the link between the northern and southern regions. Grains such as corn and wheat soon became important crops. The middle colonies were called the "bread colonies" because they produced large amounts of grain.

Technology Connection

The Early Colonial Farm

Early colonists brought European ideas and tools for farming to the Americas. In the 1600s, European farmers used big, clumsy wooden plows pulled by oxen. Most colonists did not have plows at first. They used hoes to prepare fields. They seeded by hand. They used scythes to cut the grain. A scythe had a long, curved blade attached to a wood handle.

Even with a plow and oxen, farming was hard, slow work. It took two farmers all day to plow an acre or two. At the most, a farmer could harvest about an acre of grain in one day.

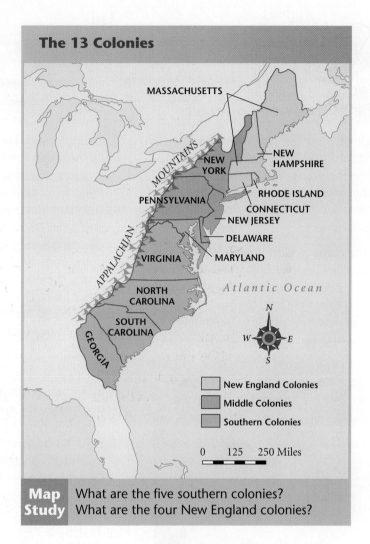

The 13 Colonies

MASSACHUSETTS

NEW HAMPSHIRE

NEW YORK

RHODE ISLAND

CONNECTICUT

NEW JERSEY

PENNSYLVANIA

DELAWARE

VIRGINIA

MARYLAND

NORTH CAROLINA

Atlantic Ocean

SOUTH CAROLINA

GEORGIA

APPALACHIAN MOUNTAINS

New England Colonies
Middle Colonies
Southern Colonies

0   125   250 Miles

N W E S

Map Study What are the five southern colonies?
What are the four New England colonies?

What do you think ?

What do you think would be the most difficult part about being a colonist? Explain why.

Lesson 4 Review Finish each sentence. Write the entire sentence on a sheet of paper.

1. The American colonies were established over a period of . . .

2. Farms were small in New England because . . .

3. Crops in the South included . . .

4. Plantation owners encouraged the use of . . .

5. The middle colonies could be described as . . .

The Mayflower Compact

Pilgrims wrote the Mayflower Compact on board ship on November 11, 1620. It is recognized as the first agreement for self-government ever composed and signed in America. Forty-one male adults signed the document.

In the name of God, Amen. We whose names are underwritten, the Loyal Subjects of our dread Sovereign Lord, King James, by the Grace of God, of Great Britain, France and Ireland, King, Defender of the Faith, & so on.

Having undertaken, for the Glory of God, and the Advancement of the Christian Faith, and the Honor of our King and

Country, a voyage to plant the first colony in the northern Parts of Virginia; do by these Presents, solemnly and mutually in the Presence of God and of one another, covenant and combine ourselves together into a civil Body Politic, for our better Ordering and Preservation, and Furtherance of the Ends aforesaid; And by virtue hereof to enact, constitute, and frame, such just and equal Laws, Ordinances, Acts, Constitutions and Offices, from time to time, as shall be thought most meet and convenient for the General good of the Colony; unto which we promise all due Submission and Obedience.

In Witness whereof we hereunto subscribed our names at Cape Cod the eleventh of November, in the reign of our Sovereign Lord, King James of England, France and Ireland . . . and of Scotland . . . . Anno Domini, 1620.

Document-Based Questions

1. The Pilgrims ended up in New England. Where had they planned to go?

2. Over what countries did King James rule?

3. What was the purpose of this agreement?

4. What kinds of laws did the Pilgrims want to make?

5. What was the importance of this document for future government of America?

Source: The Mayflower Compact, November 11, 1620.

- Jamestown colony was established in May 1607. The colony formed a general assembly, named the House of Burgesses, in 1619.

- The Pilgrims reached the shore of what is now Cape Cod in 1620. There they wrote the Mayflower Compact. It stated that the Pilgrims agreed to obey laws created by the majority. They later formed a settlement in Plymouth.

- The Puritans landed in Boston in 1620. Within a few years, nearly 10,000 colonists came to this settlement.

- Lord Calvert established a colony in what is now St. Marys City, Maryland, on the shores of the Chesapeake Bay, in 1634.

- Roger Williams settled Providence, Rhode Island, in 1636.

- Thomas Hooker started a settlement in Connecticut in 1636.

- English nobles, under a charter from King Charles II, settled Carolina in 1663. Carolina was divided into North Carolina and South Carolina in 1729.

- The English took over a Dutch colony in 1664 and renamed it New York in honor of the Duke of York.

- New Hampshire, formerly part of Massachusetts, was sold to the king of England in 1679. The king made New Hampshire a royal colony.

- William Penn was granted a charter for the land between New York and Maryland in 1681. The colony was called Pennsylvania.

- In 1682, the Duke of York granted William Penn a region known today as Delaware. The region, controlled by Pennsylvania, was divided into three counties. These became Delaware in 1704.

- East Jersey and West Jersey united into New Jersey in 1702.

- James Oglethorpe settled a colony in what is now Savannah, Georgia, in 1733.

- The early colonial society was made up of a wealthy class, a middle class, and a lower class.

- The colonies included three regions—the northern or New England colonies, the southern colonies, and the middle colonies.

Chapter 3 REVIEW

Word Bank

Connecticut

Georgia

Maryland

New Hampshire

New York

North Carolina

Pennsylvania

Rhode Island

South Carolina

Virginia

On a sheet of paper, write the correct state name from the Word Bank to complete each sentence.

1. Thomas Hooker started a settlement in _____.

2. _____ began as a Dutch colony.

3. Lord Calvert set up a colony in _____ in 1634.

4. Carolina became _____ and _____.

5. King Charles II gave William Penn a charter for _____ in 1681.

6. Colonists settled in what is now Savannah, _____, in 1733.

7. Roger Williams settled Providence, _____, in 1636.

8. The Jamestown Colony was located in _____.

9. _____ was sold to the king of England in 1679.

On a sheet of paper, write the letter of the answer that correctly completes each sentence.

10. English settlers set up the Jamestown Colony in _____.

  A 1590

  B 1607

  C 1619

  D 1629

11. The colonists who signed the Mayflower Compact to set up a government were the _____.

  A Pilgrims

  B Jamestown settlers

  C Puritans

  D group led by William Penn

12. In colonial times, farmers, shopkeepers, artisans, and teachers formed the _____.

   A wealthy class

   B middle class

   C lower class

   D servant class

On a sheet of paper, write the answers to the following questions. Use complete sentences.

13. What two problems did the Jamestown colonists face when they first started the colony?

14. What three things affected Jamestown in 1619?

15. Who were the Pilgrims? Where did they settle?

16. Who were the Puritans? Where did they settle?

17. Which were the middle colonies? The southern? The northern?

18. How did many of the colonists make a living?

Critical Thinking On a sheet of paper, write your response to each question. Use complete sentences.

19. The Pilgrims' Mayflower Compact represented rule by majority. Do you think rule by majority works? Why or why not?

20. Do you think you would have liked living in colonial times? Why or why not?

Test-Taking Tip

Before you begin taking a test, look it over. See how many parts it has. Notice what each part requires you to do. Then plan your time accordingly.

4   A Struggle for Power

The 1700s in America involved more change for the colonists and Great Britain. The colonists began to appreciate doing things for themselves even though Great Britain wanted to control the colonies. At the same time, problems developed with the American Indians and the French over land to the west. In this chapter, you will learn about these struggles for power.

Goals for Learning

◆ To describe colonial trade practices

◆ To describe triangular trade

◆ To identify the problems over land that led to war between the French and British

◆ To identify the major battles of the French and Indian War

◆ To explain how the French and Indian War affected control of land and power in the colonies

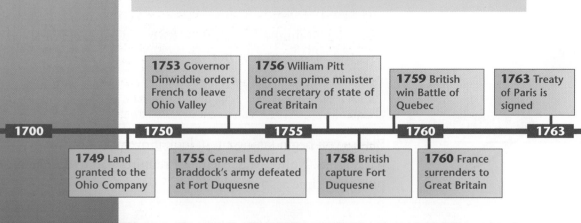

1749 Land granted to the Ohio Company

1753 Governor Dinwiddie orders French to leave Ohio Valley

1755 General Edward Braddock's army defeated at Fort Duquesne

1756 William Pitt becomes prime minister and secretary of state of Great Britain

1758 British capture Fort Duquesne

1759 British win Battle of Quebec

1760 France surrenders to Great Britain

1763 Treaty of Paris is signed

1700   1750   1755   1760   1763

Independence

Ability to take care of oneself

Responsibility

The need to complete duties or tasks

Delegate

A person elected to serve in government

Legislature

A group of people elected to make laws

Cultural

Having to do with the arts

Colonists took pride in what they did. Clearing the land, building homes, and producing goods were important developments. Farming became people's main work. Families raised crops and animals for their food. Most farm families made their own clothes, furniture, and tools. The colonists were showing their ability to take care of themselves, or **independence**. With independence came a love of freedom and a strong sense of **responsibility**.

As more and larger towns were built among the farms, colonists started sharing news and ideas with their neighbors. They held town meetings to pass laws, to set taxes to help their schools, and to select **delegates**. A delegate serves in the **legislature**. A legislature is a group of people elected to make laws. The legislature worked together to provide goods and services. Libraries and newspapers were started. Colonial writers, painters, and musicians added to the **cultural** life of the people. The colonists became aware of their own progress, which was separate from the advances of the countries from which they had come. However, they soon realized that in order to grow, they needed to trade beyond the shores of America.

It Happened in History

John Peter Zenger and Freedom of the Press

In 1734, John Peter Zenger was the publisher of a weekly newspaper in New York. Some writers didn't like the royal governor, William Cosby. They asked Zenger to publish their articles criticizing Cosby. The articles accused Cosby of being dishonest. No one had ever criticized the government like this in a newspaper.

Governor Cosby declared that the articles were untrue and had Zenger arrested. Zenger was tried and found not guilty because he was telling the truth. This was an important case that established the idea of freedom of the press in America. In 1791, the first amendment to the Constitution guaranteed freedom of the press.

What Was Mercantilism?

As the lives of the colonists became more **complex,** their need to trade with other countries increased. However, Great Britain would not allow the colonies to trade with whomever they wished. Laws had been passed to control colonial trade.

The practice of **regulating** colonial trade for the profit of the home country was called **mercantilism.** Great Britain was not the only country that practiced mercantilism. France, the Netherlands, Spain, and Austria also used this policy to profit from their settlements in America. Great Britain intended to make a profit from the trading the American colonies did. The American colonies did not want controls that would benefit the British. They looked for ways to trade on their own.

The shipping business was an important part of colonial trade.

Focus on Economics

In the southern colonies, the economy was based on plantations. These large farms raised tobacco, cotton, indigo, and rice. Plantation owners made a living by selling the crops. To have a strong economy, landowners of these large farms needed more and more workers. Because of this, demand for slave labor was high.

Civics Connection

Free Trade Versus Regulated Trade

Great Britain did not allow free trade. The colonies were allowed to trade only with Great Britain. In the colonies, the British sold their goods for a profit. They bought American goods at prices the British set. This gave Great Britain control of all colonial trade. The colonists thought Britain was being unfair.

Today, the United States buys and sells goods all over the world. Billions of dollars flow into and out of the nation through trade. However, the United States still has laws that govern trade. The government tries to set up agreements for free trade with other countries. It passes laws that favor the sale of American goods to other countries. It also puts taxes on some goods brought in from other countries.

The United States is a member of the World Trade Organization (WTO). This international organization deals with the rules of trade among nations.

1. Do you agree with the colonists that Great Britain's trade rules were unfair? Explain.

2. Why do you think the U.S. government taxes goods from other countries? Explain.

Lesson 1 Review On a sheet of paper, write the answers to the following questions. Use complete sentences.

1. How did farm families get their food, clothing, furniture, and tools?

2. How did the colonists exchange news and ideas?

3. Why did the colonists need to trade with other countries?

4. What is mercantilism?

5. Which countries practiced mercantilism?

What do you think ?

Why do you think freedom and independence were so important to the colonists?

Triangular trade

Trade between Africa, the West Indies, and New England

Enforce

To make sure something is done according to a law

Unite

To join together as a single unit

New England, Africa, and the West Indies formed a trade triangle. This **triangular trade** was outside of British control, so it made more money for the colonials. Trade continued until Great Britain began to **enforce** the laws for colonial trade.

The increasing colonial businesses and trade gave more jobs and opportunities to the settlers. A spirit of independence was growing. Many colonists lost the feeling that they were living in British colonies. People from different countries—Sweden, the Netherlands, Germany, and Ireland—were increasing in number. They felt no need to be led by Great Britain. Freedom provided a better life and a desire for more independence.

Who Were the Victims of Triangular Trade?

Countless American Indians were victims of Europeans who claimed tribal lands and forced them from their homes. With the growth of the colonies, the Indians were pushed farther and farther west.

The other group harmed for the gain of the European colonists was Africans. As part of the triangular trade involving Africa, people from that continent were treated as property, not as human beings. Millions of Africans were captured from their native lands and brought to America. Many colonists who needed free labor for their farms and plantations did not allow these people any rights. Millions of Africans died as a result of triangular trade. It would be many years before enslaved Africans could **unite** and move toward justice.

What Were the Navigation Acts?

Great Britain decided to start enforcing the Navigation Acts that were passed between 1651 and 1673. The purpose of the acts was to regulate colonial trade. Problems developed as the settlers refused to accept Great Britain's strict control.

Writing About History

Imagine that you are a colonist living in America in the 1700s. In your notebook, write a personal letter to a family member who lives in Europe. Explain what your daily routine is like and whether you like your life as a colonist.

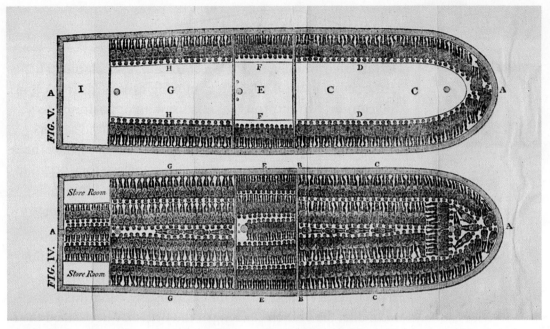

This diagram shows the crowded conditions enslaved Africans faced on ships bound for America.

Rebellion

A group fighting another group that is in power

Most American merchants continued to trade with other countries. British officials in the colonies were often paid to look the other way. More new laws were passed, including the Woolens Act in 1699, the Hat Act in 1732, and the Iron Act in 1750. The Molasses Act, passed in 1733, was Great Britain's direct response to triangular trade. This law added a tax to items such as molasses that were imported from the West Indies. The threat of fighting back, or **rebellion,** and the hope for freedom were growing.

Lesson 2 Review On a sheet of paper, write the answers to the following questions. Use complete sentences.

What do you think

Why do you think Europeans treated the American Indians and African slaves so poorly?

1. What was triangular trade?

2. How did triangular trade affect American Indians?

3. How did triangular trade affect Africans?

4. What were the Navigation Acts?

5. How did Americans react to the Navigation Acts?

Frontier

A region with little population

Despite their problems with Great Britain, the colonies continued to grow. Settlers were moving westward, developing the **frontier**. Adventurous colonists saw an opportunity to go beyond the Appalachian Mountains. Westbound settlers faced danger because the region was already occupied by the American Indians and the French. Nevertheless, they began to go west in great numbers. The fertile land in the Ohio Valley was perfect for farming. The French, however, refused to give up the vast area claimed by their forefathers.

Both France and Great Britain had made claims to the Ohio Valley. In 1749, King George II of Great Britain granted 200,000 acres of land to the Ohio Company. After this grant was made, the French challenged the British. They staked their claims with lead markers. King Louis XV of France ordered forts built along the rivers to protect these claims.

Then and Now

At this time in history, if you had a toothache your only way to get rid of the pain was to have the tooth pulled. Nothing was available to relieve your toothache or the pain when your tooth was pulled. In colonial America, a wigmaker might have pulled your tooth with some fierce-looking instrument. After your tooth was gone, you would remain toothless. There was no way to replace lost teeth then.

Today, you and your dentist have choices. Cavities can be filled or caps or crowns can be put on teeth. Nerves in a painful tooth can be removed without pulling the tooth. Now dentists avoid pulling teeth unless absolutely necessary. If you must have a tooth pulled, it can be replaced with a bridge, dentures, or implants. You can have pain relief during any of these processes.

Geography Note

The Ohio River gets its name from an Iroquois Indian phrase meaning "great river." This wide river was easy to navigate. It provided a highway into North America. Both sides of the river were heavily forested with many rivers, fish, and game animals. These conditions attracted American settlers to the region. Conflicts increased between Indians and settlers as Americans entered the territory.

What Problems Did Land Claims Cause?

The issue of land ownership still had not been resolved. In 1753, Governor Dinwiddie of Virginia sent a message to the French. He ordered them to leave the Ohio Valley and to recognize the British claim to the land. George Washington carried the message. He was a 21-year-old major in the Virginian Army. The French received him with proper respect, but they did not accept the British order to leave.

Washington was sent into the Ohio Valley again in 1754. This time, he commanded a troop of soldiers. He had orders to drive the French away from one of their forts—Fort Duquesne. The French, however, had increased the number of soldiers in their army. They greatly outnumbered Washington's force. Shots were exchanged, and the young leader had no choice but to retreat. In that brief battle, Washington showed his courage and leadership ability. The French were determined to keep control of the region.

What Was the Albany Plan of Union?

The colonists knew that the problems with land ownership could start a war between France and Great Britain. Delegates from seven colonies met in Albany, New York. The purpose of the Albany Congress was to secure an **alliance** with the Iroquois. An alliance is an agreement that joins groups of people or countries together. The other purpose was to discuss a plan to form a **union**. A union is a group of territories joining together under one government. Delegate Benjamin Franklin proposed a plan modeled after the Iroquois League. The union could create and collect taxes, maintain an army, control trade with the American Indians, and pass other laws.

The plan was turned down. Even the threat of a war did not convince the delegates the union was a good idea. They feared their individual freedoms would be lost. Though this first attempt to create a colonial government was unsuccessful, it was still important. Franklin's Albany Plan of Union had set the stage for great things to come in the future.

Recruit
───────
To get new members
for a group

How Did the British and the French Match Up?

The threat of a war between Great Britain and France still existed. If a war broke out, each of the two countries would have certain advantages and disadvantages.

Great Britain had the advantage of more people. About 2 million colonists had settled the new land. Great Britain could use the colonies for support and to **recruit** men to fight the war. Unfortunately, the British colonies were not politically united. Therefore, Great Britain would have to deal with each of the 13 colonies individually.

Benjamin Franklin

France's main disadvantage was that it had fewer people. About 65,000 French colonists were widely scattered over a large area. France's major settlements were Montreal and Quebec in what is now Canada. A big advantage, however, was that French colonies had only one controlling government. The colonists were expected to obey the decisions of the king of France, including an order to fight the war.

The French were familiar with the hard life on the Ohio Valley frontier. They enjoyed a good relationship with the American Indians developed through years of fur trading. French men married American Indian women and adopted their way of life. Many French soldiers also learned frontier warfare from the American Indians.

History in Your Life

The Inventions of Benjamin Franklin

Benjamin Franklin was among the first to suggest the idea of daylight saving time. He invented bifocals—eyeglasses that have lenses with parts for reading and for distance. He invented a stove that improved home heating while using less fuel than other stoves did. In one experiment, he attached a metal key to a kite that he flew during a thunderstorm. The experiment demonstrated the electrical nature of lightning. Soon thereafter Franklin invented the lightning rod, which helps prevent fires started by lightning strikes. Many of his scientific inventions and ideas are still a part of our everyday lives.

Appoint
To name or choose a person to do something

Regiment
A large group of soldiers

In 1754, Major General Edward Braddock was **appointed** commander in chief of the British army in America. He was chosen for this position because he was one of Great Britain's finest officers. Soon after his arrival, Great Britain sent two new **regiments** of soldiers to join him. The British expected that war would break out at any moment. The fight would later be known as the French and Indian War or the Seven Years' War. The American Indians and the French were allies in this war. They fought together against the British.

Lesson 3 Review Decide whether each statement below tells about the British or the French. Write *British* or *French* beside each number on a sheet of paper.

What do you think

Who do you think was better prepared for a war—the French or the British? Why?

1. They granted 200,000 acres of land in the Ohio Valley to the Ohio Company.

2. This group forced George Washington to retreat from Fort Duquesne.

3. These people lived among the American Indians.

4. They had about 2 million colonists.

5. They had fewer settlers.

It Happened in History

The Enlightenment

The word *enlighten* means to educate or inform. The Enlightenment was a movement that started in Europe during the 1700s. It was the awakening of science, arts, theater, medicine, and so much more. The movement spread to America in the middle 1700s.

Enlightenment ideas helped establish the identity of the United States in the Western world. To many people in the 1700s, Benjamin Franklin represented the creative spirit of America. He was greatly influenced by ideas from the Enlightenment. Franklin was a man of many talents. He was philosopher, inventor, diplomat, scientist, and journalist. He was an important contributor to the successful formation of the United States. His newspaper, the *Pennsylvania Gazette,* played a role in the pursuit of independence.

General Braddock had very little respect for American Indians as warriors. George Washington was serving under Braddock. He suggested that General Braddock prepare for a very different kind of battle. He would not listen to advice about wilderness military action.

Fort Duquesne was an important French fort. The British needed to capture the fort in order to drive the French out of the Ohio Valley.

Braddock led his army of British and colonial troops toward Fort Duquesne in 1755. However, hiding behind rocks and trees were French, Canadians, and American Indians. As British soldiers marched forward, the French, Canadians, and Indians found the bright scarlet and blue coats easy targets. Braddock and several officers were killed. Washington gathered the **survivors** and struggled back to safety. This was a crushing blow for the British and the American colonials.

Biography

Auguste Chouteau: 1749–1829

Auguste Chouteau was born in New Orleans. His stepfather was Pierre Laclède Liguest, the head of the Louisiana Fur Trade Company. In 1763, the two men traveled to the area where the Mississippi and Missouri Rivers meet. Laclède wanted to build a fur-trading post there. Chouteau, who was 13 years old, served as his stepfather's assistant and helped him build the trading post. The site of the trading post soon became the city of St. Louis.

When Laclède died in 1778, Chouteau inherited his business. Chouteau later became a judge and a colonel in the militia. He worked out peace treaties with the Sioux, Iowa, Sauk, and Fox Indians. A St. Louis historian wrote, "Laclède founded, and Auguste Chouteau built, St. Louis."

The British went on to lose battles at Fort Oswego and Fort William Henry in New York. They lost many men in failed attacks on Crown Point and Fort Ticonderoga. They failed, too, at an attempt to capture Louisbourg, a French naval base in Nova Scotia. The colonists, upon seeing many of their friends die at the hands of the French, lost confidence in the proud British army. Many of them wanted to fight their own war, without the British to give the orders.

What Did William Pitt Do?

King George II was aware that France could win the war. If this happened, France would claim all the land to the Mississippi River. He needed to make some changes. In 1756, King George appointed William Pitt as prime minister and secretary of state of Great Britain.

Pitt offered words of encouragement to the colonists. This brought him greater cooperation from colonial legislatures. He sent troops and supplies from Great Britain, and he appointed only the finest officers. Together, Great Britain and the colonies formed an army of 50,000. This new army had more soldiers than all the French soldiers in the New World. The colonists gained confidence in the British leadership. They were prepared to fight the enemy and win the war.

Lesson 4 Review On a sheet of paper, write the correct words from the Word Bank to complete each sentence.

1. _____ told General Braddock that he needed a new fighting style against the American Indians.

2. General Braddock was killed in a battle at _____.

3. Losing the war would mean France would claim land as far as the _____.

4. _____ was made prime minister of Great Britain in 1758.

5. The colonists had confidence in Pitt because he sent troops and supplies from _____.

Word Bank

Fort Duquesne

Great Britain

Mississippi River

William Pitt

George Washington

What do you think ?

Why do you think General Braddock was defeated by the American Indians and the French?

Reinforcements

Additional soldiers used to back up an army

Stronghold

A place, such as a military base, that is well protected from attack

Treaty

An agreement to end fighting

The British colonial army returned to Louisbourg and defeated the French. General John Forbes also led several thousand colonial soldiers against Fort Duquesne in 1758. Upon seeing this army approach, the French set the fort afire and fled. The capture of Fort Duquesne was an important turning point in the war.

What Were the Final Stages of the War?

The British, under James Wolfe, destroyed a French fleet of **reinforcements** about to leave France. Reinforcements are additional soldiers. Sir William Johnson and some Iroquois captured Fort Niagara for the British. General Amherst captured two French forts, Carillon and St. Frederick, and renamed them Fort Ticonderoga and Crown Point.

James Wolfe and his fleet of ships traveled up the St. Lawrence River to attack Quebec.

The British needed one major victory to force the French to surrender. The **stronghold** of the French was Quebec, Canada. A stronghold is a place that is well protected from attack. General Louis Montcalm, the French leader, was sure his position was protected by its high cliffs.

Wolfe led a fleet of ships up the St. Lawrence River to Quebec. He discovered a path that led up the cliffs to the plains above. They fought the battle on September 13, 1759. The British won. Montcalm and Wolfe were both killed. France surrendered in 1760.

What Happened After the War?

The Treaty of Paris was signed in 1763. A **treaty** is an agreement to end fighting. France gave Great Britain the land east of the Mississippi River, except New Orleans. The area of Louisiana west of the Mississippi and New Orleans, which France had claimed, went to its ally, Spain. Great Britain got the territory of Florida from Spain in exchange for Cuba. France kept two islands south of Newfoundland and some islands off the West Indies.

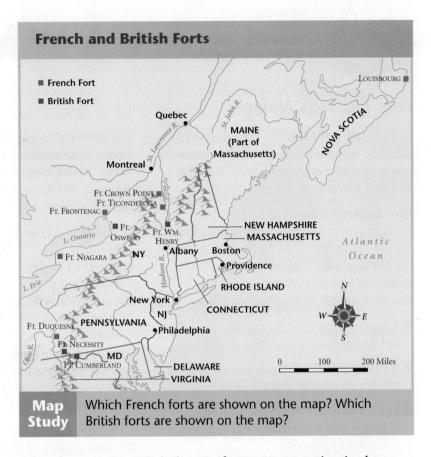

French and British Forts

■ French Fort
■ British Fort

LOUISBOURG

Quebec

MAINE
(Part of
Massachusetts)

NOVA SCOTIA

Montreal

St. Lawrence R.

St. John R.

FT. CROWN POINT
FT. TICONDEROGA
FT. FRONTENAC

FT. OSWEGO

FT. WM. HENRY

L. Ontario

FT. NIAGARA

NY

Albany

NEW HAMPSHIRE

MASSACHUSETTS

Boston

Atlantic
Ocean

Hudson R.

Providence

L. Erie

RHODE ISLAND

New York

NJ

CONNECTICUT

N
W   E
S

FT. DUQUESNE

PENNSYLVANIA

Philadelphia

Ohio R.

FT. NECESSITY

MD

FT. CUMBERLAND

DELAWARE

VIRGINIA

0   100   200 Miles

Map Study Which French forts are shown on the map? Which British forts are shown on the map?

After the war, Great Britain was the strongest nation in the world. It would have to look to the colonies for higher taxes to pay for the war. Now that the French were no longer a threat to them, however, the colonists would not have to depend on Great Britain for protection.

Lesson 5 Review On a sheet of paper, write the answers to the following questions. Use complete sentences.

1. What did the French do to Fort Duquesne?

2. Why were the British victories at Fort Duquesne and Quebec important?

3. How did General Wolfe attack Quebec?

4. What was the Treaty of Paris?

5. What land did Britain gain after the war?

What do you think ?

How might the United States be different today if the British had lost the French and Indian War?

Chapter 4   R E V I E W

Word Bank

Battle of Quebec

Fort Duquesne

George
   Washington

mercantilism

Navigation Acts

Ohio Valley

Treaty of Paris

triangular trade

William Pitt

On a sheet of paper, write the correct word or words from the Word Bank that match each sentence.

1. This fort was captured by the British in 1758.

2. He became prime minister and secretary of state of Great Britain in 1758.

3. He was sent to drive the French away from Fort Duquesne in 1754.

4. This land caused disputes between the French and British.

5. This was signed after the French and Indian War.

6. This was the battle that forced France to surrender.

7. Trade between Africa, the West Indies, and New England was called this.

8. These were British laws to regulate trade between the colonies and other countries.

9. This was the practice of regulating colonial trade for the profit of the home country.

On a sheet of paper, write the letter of the answer that correctly completes each sentence.

10. Most of all, Great Britain wanted the colonies to be _____.

   A free and independent   **C** cultural centers

   B profitable trade centers   **D** self-governing states

11. The French and Indian War was fought over the right to _____.

   A settle the Ohio Valley

   B trade with Indians

   C trade in American seaports

   D ship enslaved Africans to the Americas

12. During the war, one advantage of the British was their
_____.

   A good relationship with the Indians

   B large population in America

   C politically united government

   D good fighting techniques

13. The British leader who succeeded in winning the war
was _____.

   A General Amherst   **C** General Braddock

   B General Louis Montcalm   **D** James Wolfe

On a sheet of paper, write the answers to the following
questions. Use complete sentences.

14. How well were the British prepared for war?

15. How well were the French prepared for war?

16. Why was the Battle of Quebec important?

17. Who gained what land from the Treaty of Paris?

18. How did Great Britain's power change after the war?

Critical Thinking On a sheet of paper, write your response to
each question. Use complete sentences.

19. Though they had not achieved complete independence,
the colonists began to like feeling free to do things without
outside controls. How are people independent today?

20. The French and Indian War was fought mostly because of
land rights. What other things do you think cause war?

Test-Taking Tip

Prepare for a test with several short study sessions rather
than one long one. The week before a test, review your notes
and the text for a little while each evening.

Unit 2

Skill Builder

Maps

To read a map, you need to understand its symbols. Most maps have a key, or legend, that explains the symbols.

☐ New England Colonies
☐ Middle Colonies
☐ Southern Colonies

Some maps are drawn exactly to scale. You can use the scale to find the actual distances on a map.

0   100   200   300 Miles

Most maps show direction. A compass rose shows at least the four major directions—north, east, west, and south. Some compass roses also show northeast, southeast, northwest, and southwest. Some maps show direction only by using an arrow with the letter N to show the direction of north.

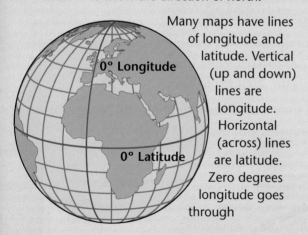

Many maps have lines of longitude and latitude. Vertical (up and down) lines are longitude. Horizontal (across) lines are latitude. Zero degrees longitude goes through Greenwich, England. Zero degrees latitude is at the equator—the widest part of the globe.

There are many different kinds of maps. Each kind of map provides a different kind of information. Here are some examples of maps and what they show:

Physical map—Shows the roughness of Earth's surface, including mountains, rivers, and plains

Elevation map—Shows different heights of land above the level of the sea

Political map—Shows borders between countries and states or states and counties

Climate map—Shows different kinds of climates, including hot, dry, cold, and wet

Natural resources map—Shows where natural resources such as minerals, oil, and natural gas are in an area

Choose the kind of map you would use to answer each question.

1. Which states have a hot, dry climate?

2. What country shares the northern border of the United States?

3. Where is the Charles River located?

4. Where is the most oil in the United States located?

5. Does North Carolina include any land at an elevation of 5,000 or more feet?

Unit 2 SUMMARY

- Jamestown colony was established in May 1607.

- The Pilgrims formed a settlement in Plymouth in 1620.

- The Puritans landed in 1620.

- Lord Calvert established a colony in 1634.

- Roger Williams settled Providence, Rhode Island, in 1636.

- Thomas Hooker started a settlement in Connecticut in 1636.

- English nobles settled Carolina in 1663.

- The English renamed a Dutch colony New York in 1664.

- New Hampshire became a colony in 1679.

- William Penn was granted a charter for the land between New York and Maryland in 1681. The colony was called Pennsylvania. In 1682, the Duke of York granted Penn a region known today as Delaware.

- East Jersey and West Jersey united into New Jersey in 1702.

- James Oglethorpe settled a colony in what is now Georgia in 1733.

- Colonists showed independence and responsibility in the 1700s.

- Enslaved Africans and American Indians suffered from triangular trading.

- American merchants ignored Great Britain's trade laws. As a result, the British passed more laws to control trade in the colonies.

- Problems developed in 1749 between Great Britain and France.

- The French and Indian War took place between 1755 and 1763.

- France surrendered to the British in 1760.

- The Treaty of Paris was signed in 1763. Land was divided among Great Britain, Spain, and France.

"It is yet to be decided whether the Revolution must ultimately be considered as a blessing or a curse . . . not to the present age alone, for with our fate will the destiny of unborn millions be involved."

~ *George Washington, Circular to the States, 1783*

Unit 3

Revolution and the New Nation

Facing challenges often is easier when people work together. If you were a colonist in the struggling new nation, you would need to cooperate with other colonists. How would you work together to protect your new nation's freedom against threats from other nations? How would you band together to establish your government? How would you unite to defend your nation in wars?

In this unit, you will learn about many challenges facing the young nation. You will learn how colonists fought for the nation's independence and how they united to form a government. You also will learn how the United States defended itself against other nations after it gained independence.

Chapters in Unit 3

5

A New Nation Begins to Grow

After the French and Indian War, Great Britain tightened its control over the colonies. The British began a series of actions against the colonies that the colonists did not welcome. In this chapter, you will learn what the British did to the colonists and how the colonists reacted.

Goals for Learning

◆ To explain the purpose of the Proclamation of 1763

◆ To identify the taxes the British placed on the colonists and how the colonists protested them

◆ To explain what caused the Boston Tea Party

◆ To describe the actions taken by the First Continental Congress

◆ To explain what occurred at Lexington and Concord

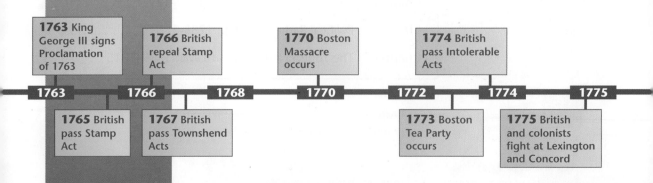

1763 King George III signs Proclamation of 1763

1766 British repeal Stamp Act

1770 Boston Massacre occurs

1774 British pass Intolerable Acts

| 1763 | 1766 | 1768 | 1770 | 1772 | 1774 | 1775 |

1765 British pass Stamp Act

1767 British pass Townshend Acts

1773 Boston Tea Party occurs

1775 British and colonists fight at Lexington and Concord

Relationship

Two or more things or groups connected in some way

British control of America was firmly established with the 1763 Treaty of Paris. However, the real hold that Great Britain had on the colonies was weak. New and different laws were passed in an effort to control trade. Colonial merchants and shippers found other ways of getting around those laws. Then new events affected the **relationship** between Great Britain and the colonies.

What Was the Proclamation of 1763?

The first problem was caused by an event that took place in the spring of 1763. Great numbers of colonists settled in the Ohio Valley, west of the Appalachian Mountains. An Ottawa chief, Pontiac, knew that more American Indian land was in danger of being lost to British settlers. Chief Pontiac organized several Indian nations and attacked colonial forts with some success.

Great Britain now had control of the territory east of the Mississippi River, including the Ohio Valley. The American Indians who lived in the Ohio Valley were afraid that they would be driven even farther west by English colonists. To ease the fears of the Indians, England issued the Proclamation of 1763. It ordered colonists to leave the Ohio Valley. It did not allow any more people to make new settlements west of the Appalachians. It said that no traders could enter the area without approval of the king.

The colonists were opposed to the new law. They had fought in the long French and Indian War. Now the law was saying that no one could go west. Many colonists felt that the king didn't really care about protecting them from the American Indians. They felt its real purpose was to prevent them from developing the new land.

Chief Pontiac led a rebellion of American Indians against colonial forts beginning in 1763.

They also felt that they could fight their own battles with the Indians. The Proclamation of 1763 was the first of several new controls to be forced on the colonies.

What Was Taxation Without Representation?

The British debt from the French and Indian War was another problem. Supplies, ships, and soldiers had been very expensive. Some money had been raised by increasing taxes of people in Great Britain. The government had to find a way to pay off the debt without taxing the British taxpayers too much. In 1764, Parliament, the government of Great Britain, agreed that it had the right to tax the colonies in exchange for protection from all enemies. The colonists disagreed with this policy, saying they did not need the British to help them protect themselves. As subjects of Great Britain, the colonists had no right to object to its rulings. Nevertheless, many felt this **taxation** without colonial agreement, or "taxation without representation," could not be **tolerated.** The colonists began talking about a war over taxation.

What New British Policies Were Started?

George Grenville became prime minister of Great Britain in 1763. He decided it was necessary to get more money from the American colonies. The Sugar Act was passed in 1764. This act raised the tax on sugar, cloth goods, and other articles from countries except Great Britain. The Currency Act, also passed in 1764, made it illegal for the colonies to print their own money. The Quartering Act was passed in 1765. This act demanded that the colonies provide housing and goods for all British soldiers in America. The Stamp Act was passed in 1765. The purpose of the act was to enable the government to tax **legal** and business papers used in America. It also taxed such items as playing cards and dice. Special stamp agents were appointed to sell the stamps and collect the taxes.

The colonists protested the Stamp Act. One way they protested was to **tar and feather** tax collectors. They covered the tax collectors with tar and then with feathers. Colonists burned legal papers and refused to pay the taxes. They **boycotted** all goods from Great Britain.

Taxation

The act of taxing, or charging people for public and government services

Tolerate ·

To allow something to happen

Legal

Having to do with law

Tar and feather

To cover persons with tar and then with feathers in order to punish them

Boycott

To refuse to have dealings with a person, country, or group

A boycott occurs when a person, country, or group refuses to deal with another person, country, or group. Parliament decided to remove, or **repeal,** the tax in 1766.

The repeal of the Stamp Act pleased the colonists. The good feeling, however, did not last long. Shortly thereafter, Parliament passed the Declaratory Act. This act stated that Great Britain had control over the colonies in all cases.

These people are marching to protest the Stamp Act.

Lesson 1 Review On a sheet of paper, write the answers to the following questions. Use complete sentences.

1. Why did the British decide to tax the colonists?

2. Why did the colonists protest the Proclamation of 1763?

3. What was the attitude of the king toward the colonists?

4. Why did the colonists feel that taxation was unfair?

5. What was the Stamp Act and when was it passed?

Finance

Having to do
with money

Revenue

Money gained
from something

**Geography
Note**

**The Mason-
Dixon Line**

In 1750, there was
a disagreement
about the
boundary dividing
Maryland and
Pennsylvania.
Two men,
Charles Mason
and Jeremiah
Dixon, set up
the boundary
between 1763
and 1767. This
boundary is called
the Mason-Dixon
Line. It became a
symbol of the
division between
the North and
the South.

Charles Townshend was appointed minister of **finance** in 1766. This put him in charge of finance for Great Britain. Like others before him, Townshend had little interest in the colonies. However, he saw them as a good source of **revenue** for Great Britain. Townshend was responsible for a new set of tax laws.

The Townshend Acts were passed in 1767. These acts reduced the colonists' freedom to govern themselves. New taxes were placed on many items important to the colonists, including glass, paper, and tea. Protests became stronger than before. The colonists agreed to boycott British goods. Trade soon slowed down greatly.

The boycott hurt the British. It also caused serious problems for the colonial merchants. Many people lost their jobs in American ports where trade was important. For many people, it became harder to make a living and easier to be angry at the British.

What Fight Did Samuel Adams Lead?

Boston, the largest city in New England, soon became the center of action against this new British taxation policy. Samuel Adams, a member of the Massachusetts legislature, organized town meetings in Boston. A group called the Sons of Liberty, first set up in 1765 to protest the Stamp Act, took charge of the city. Great Britain sent extra regiments of troops to Boston to protect tax collectors. Fights broke out between soldiers and townspeople. By the beginning of 1770, about 4,000 British soldiers were in Boston. The soldiers were in daily contact with 16,000 Bostonians under Samuel Adams.

What Was the Boston Massacre?

One evening early in March 1770, a crowd gathered near a group of British soldiers. The crowd began throwing stones and snowballs at the soldiers. The soldiers then fired a round of shots into the crowd. The first to fall was a free African, Crispus Attucks. A few colonists were killed, and several were wounded.

The BLOODY MASSACRE perpetrated in King—Street BOSTON on March 5th 1770 by a party of the 29th REGt.

BUTCHERS HALL

Engrav'd Printed & Sold by PAUL REVERE BOSTON

Unhappy Boston! see thy Sons deplore,
Thy hallow'd Walks besmear'd with guiltless Gore:
While faithless P—n and his savage Bands,
With murd'rous Rancour stretch their bloody Hands;
Like fierce Barbarians grinning o'er their Prey,
Approve the Carnage and enjoy the Day.

If scalding drops from Rage from Anguish Wrung
If speechless Sorrows lab'ring for a Tongue,
Or if a weeping World can ought appease
The plaintive Ghosts of Victims such as these;
The Patriot's copious Tears for each are shed,
A glorious Tribute which embalms the Dead.

But know Fate summons to that awful Goal,
Where Justice strips the Murd'rer of his Soul.
Should venal C—ts the scandal of the Land,
Snatch the relentless Villain from her Hand,
Keen Execrations on this Plate inscrib'd,
Shall reach a Judge who never can be brib'd.

The unhappy Sufferers were Messrs Saml Gray Saml Maverick, Jams Caldwell, Crispus Attucks & Patr Carr
Killed. Six wounded; two of them (Christr Monk & John Clark) Mortally

This engraving by Paul Revere shows what the Boston Massacre may have looked like.

Massacre

The act of killing a large number of people in a cruel way.

News of the Boston **Massacre,** as it was called, spread throughout the colonies. A massacre is the act of killing a large number of people in a cruel way. The people of Boston demanded that the British soldiers be removed from the city. The governor of Massachusetts agreed to remove the soldiers to prevent more trouble. In April 1770, all of the Townshend taxes were repealed except for the tax on tea. Great Britain had lost a good deal of money due to the boycotts. It was believed that the tax on tea was kept mainly as a symbol of the British right to rule.

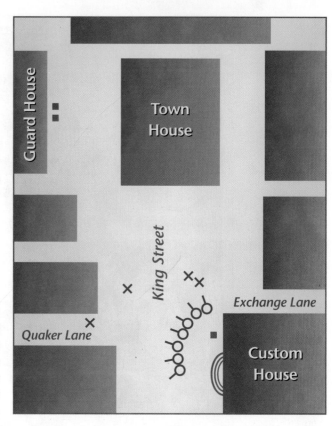

Guard House

Town House

King Street

Exchange Lane

Quaker Lane

Custom House

This diagram shows the area where the Boston Massacre took place. It shows the British soldiers (near the Custom House) and the places where four of the five killed colonists fell.

Writing About History

Research the Boston Massacre. Then write a first person account in your notebook about what happened at the Boston Massacre as if you were really there. Talk about how the event changed you as a person.

How Did the Colonists Organize and Protest?

The colonies steadily lost much of their earlier freedom. British governors, chosen by the king, could do as they pleased. They became very strict. Samuel Adams encouraged the leaders of cities to meet and talk about what to do about the British.

The committees wrote strong statements of American rights and complaints. The statements were given out all over the colonies. This helped to bring the colonists together in opposing their common enemy, the British.

Neither King George III nor Parliament took the colonists seriously. The king looked upon the colonies as weak. He thought they were no match for the mighty British army and navy.

Biography

Phillis Wheatley: 1753–1784

Phillis Wheatley was the first acknowledged African poet in America. A native of Africa, she was born around 1753. At age eight, she was kidnapped and taken on a slave ship to Boston. There she was purchased by a wealthy tailor as a servant for his wife. Unlike most slaves, Wheatley was allowed to learn to read and write English. She studied Greek, Latin, and history. At age 13 she wrote her first poems, including "To the University of Cambridge in New England." Her first book was published when she was 20. Despite her early reputation, she was very poor and practically unknown when she died at only age 30.

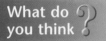
What do you think

Do you think Samuel Adams was right to organize protests that often ended up in fights? Explain your answer.

Lesson 2 Review Match each name in Part 1 with a description in Part 2. Write the letter of the correct description on a sheet of paper.

Part 1

1. Charles Townshend

2. Samuel Adams

3. Boston Massacre

4. George III

5. Crispus Attucks

Part 2

A killed in Boston Massacre

B minister of finance for Great Britain

C British soldiers shot into a crowd of colonists

D Great Britain's king

E led protests in Boston

Duty

A tax placed on goods brought into a certain place

Competitor

A company that sells or buys the same goods or services as another company

Impose

To establish a rule or law, such as a tax, on a group with less power

Cargo

Objects or goods carried in a ship or some other form of transportation

The British-controlled East India Trading Company sold tea. The company had to pay a tax to Great Britain on the tea before shipping it to other places. It could not afford to pay the tax, yet it would be ruined if it did not sell the tea.

What Was the British Tea Tax?

Frederick North, Great Britain's prime minister, came up with a plan. He wanted to ship the tea to America and then force the colonies to pay a **duty.** A duty is a tax placed on goods brought into a certain country or region. Lord North expected his plan to save the East India Trading Company from financial disaster and to bring in more revenue for Great Britain.

The colonists refused to pay this tax. They were afraid that soon all British merchants would pay no tax. As a result, the American **competitors** would go out of business. Samuel Adams organized the tea merchants who agreed to cancel all orders for tea. The colonists wanted to keep the tea from being unloaded to make sure that no tax would be paid.

Lord North and the king had clearly underestimated the strong feelings of the colonists. Adams made it clear the colonists would not accept a tax **imposed** without colonial consent.

What Was the Boston Tea Party?

A ship carrying tea arrived in Boston's harbor in late November 1773. The British governor of Boston was determined to have the tea unloaded and to collect the taxes. Adams was equally determined to keep the tea from being unloaded. A group of colonists dressed as Mohawk Indians boarded the ship on the night of December 16, 1773. They promised not to harm the ship if the **cargo** was made available to them. The captain agreed, and the Boston Tea Party began.

More than 300 chests containing British tea were dumped into the harbor. Similar incidents took place in other cities. In Charleston, South Carolina, the tea was allowed to rot in damp cellars. In Annapolis, Maryland, the ship carrying tea was burned. The colonial **resistance** to British taxation had spread throughout the colonies.

The Boston Tea Party was a protest against the British Tea Tax.

How Did the British React to the Tea Party?

Some colonists did not agree with the actions taken in Boston, Charleston, and Annapolis. Many felt that dumping tea, burning a ship, and allowing tea to rot were not proper ways to protest. Some merchants even offered to pay for the tea that had been destroyed. **Outraged** by the events, the king and Parliament paid no attention to these loyal colonists.

The British **responded** to the colonists' actions by passing the Intolerable Acts in 1774. These acts allowed Great Britain to close the port of Boston to all trade, **ban** town meetings, and house British troops in people's homes.

Resistance

The act of opposing something

Outrage

Anger

Respond

To do or say something in return

Ban

To disallow something

A New Nation Begins to Grow Chapter 5

Province

A part of a country or region

The acts said that British soldiers accused of breaking the law would be tried in Great Britain. Parliament also passed the Quebec Act. This act extended the Canadian **province** of Quebec into the Ohio Valley. A province is a part of a country or region. The act forced the colonists to stay to the east. The British intended to test how badly the colonists wanted to govern themselves.

Then and Now

If you were a man in colonial times, you might go to a local tavern for business, social, or political gatherings. As a woman then, however, you might be a tavern keeper but not a customer. As a colonial traveler, you would get on or off stagecoaches at taverns. On a journey, you could get a good meal and lodging at a tavern. You might share a room and even a bed with more than one stranger. Sharing a bed in winter was practical because it kept you warm after the fire went out. You could expect an uncomfortable bed. Today, you expect a comfortable bed and fresh sheets and towels daily. You expect a private room in a motel or hotel. You don't expect the owner to assign two or more strangers to the same room.

What do you think

Why do you think the Intolerable Acts said that British soldiers accused of crimes would be tried in Great Britain and not in the colonies?

Lesson 3 Review On a sheet of paper, write answers to the following questions. Use complete sentences.

1. What plan did Frederick North have?

2. Why did the colonists object to Frederick North's plan?

3. When and why did the Boston Tea Party take place?

4. Did all of the colonists approve of what happened at the Tea Party? Why?

5. How did the British respond to the Tea Party?

Unify

To join together as a group or whole

Convention

A formal meeting called for a special purpose

Patriot

Someone who loves his or her own country

Debate

An argument or discussion among persons or a group

Submission

The act of giving up on something

The British actions against Boston increased the colonists' need to be more **unified** against the king. Samuel Adams wanted to find ways to bring about more changes. Earlier protests had brought changes. He decided that a meeting, or congress, of representatives from all the colonies should be held.

Why Did the First Continental Congress Meet?

Adams invited all the colonies to a **convention** in Philadelphia. A convention is a formal meeting called for a special purpose. This Continental Congress would help to bring about a better understanding of possible actions against the king. The meeting was called a Continental Congress because the British referred to Americans as Continentals.

All of the colonies except Georgia elected delegates to the Congress. Fifty-six important men attended, including George Washington, Patrick Henry, Samuel Adams, John Adams, and John Jay. These **patriots** were well educated and were leaders in their colonies. A patriot is someone who loves his or her own country.

The Continental Congress was held in Carpenter's Hall in Philadelphia in September 1774. The delegates **debated** important issues for seven weeks. They agreed that a Declaration of Rights should be adopted and sent to the king. The Declaration made it clear that taxation by the British would be unacceptable to the colonies. The Congress also agreed to boycott British goods. This boycott was to be strictly enforced by select committees. Another Continental Congress would be held in May 1775 if the king rejected the Declaration of Rights.

The king and Parliament became furious when they received this declaration. They replied that the colonists, should they resist, would be crushed into **submission.** A few British leaders warned Parliament that changes needed to be made. The king and Parliament refused to listen to these men.

What Happened at Lexington and Concord?

American leaders Samuel Adams, John Hancock, and Patrick Henry were sure that the colonists would have to fight for freedom. A group of men had to be trained to be soldiers since the colonists had no organized army. They were called **minutemen** because they agreed to gather at a minute's notice and become soldiers.

General Gage, the military governor of Massachusetts, became aware of the military supplies stored at Concord. He had ordered a regiment under Major Pitcairn to seize all the supplies, including a gunpowder supply, stored at Concord. They had also been instructed to travel to Lexington and capture the rebel leaders.

Colonial minutemen were called to battle when word got out that British soldiers were coming.

The patriots learned about the British plans. Paul Revere and William Dawes warned the colonists of their attack by riding through Massachusetts on horseback.

The British reached Lexington first. Even though British troops later fought minutemen at Concord, most of the fighting took place at Lexington.

Revere was captured by the British, and Dawes was forced to flee toward Lexington. However, Samuel Prescott, a third rider, continued the journey to Concord. He warned colonists that the British were approaching. The colonists rushed to meet the British at Lexington.

Major Pitcairn reached Lexington on April 19, 1775. He was surprised to find about 70 armed minutemen waiting for him. Both sides fired shots and a number of people were injured or killed. These shots were later described as "the shots heard 'round the world." The war with Great Britain was about to begin.

What do you think

Do you think the colonists or the British were better prepared for war? Explain your answer.

Lesson 4 Review On a sheet of paper, write the answers to the following questions. Use complete sentences.

1. What was the purpose of the First Continental Congress?

2. How could the delegates at the Congress best be described?

3. What action did the Continental Congress take?

4. Who were minutemen?

5. What did Paul Revere, William Dawes, and Samuel Prescott do?

History in Your Life

The First Permanent Theater in America

Pennsylvania was one of the 13 British colonies when David Douglass built the Southwark Theatre in 1766. It was the first permanent theater in America. Located in Philadelphia, the Southwark was constructed of brick and wood. Oil lamps lighted its earliest productions. On April 24, 1767, Douglass presented the first professionally produced play by an American-born playwright. The play was Thomas Godfrey's *The Prince of Parthia.*

When the Revolutionary War ended, Congress passed laws against "play acting." Theater director Lewis Hallam got past the laws by presenting what he called "moral lectures." The Southwark's American Company of Comedians dominated American theater until it was disbanded in 1805. The Southwark closed in 1817 and was torn down in 1912. Still, it had started a tradition of regional and local theater throughout America that continues today.

The Stamp Act

The road toward independence in the United States was long. As the colonies grew in size and economic power, they became more valuable to England. The British passed many acts to control trade with the colonies. These acts made the colonists increasingly angry. The colonists rebelled when the Stamp Act was passed in 1765. They refused to pay the tax. The colonists were unified in their outrage, and they reacted in violent opposition.

For every skin or piece of vellum or parchment, or sheet or piece of paper, on which shall be engrossed, written or printed, any declaration, plea, replication, rejoinder, demurrer, or other pleading, or any copy thereof, in any court of law within the British colonies and plantations in America, a stamp duty of three pence.

. . . And for and upon every pack of playing cards, and all dice, which shall be sold or used . . . the several stamp duties following (that is to say)

For every pack of such cards, the sum of one shilling.

And for every pair of such dice, the sum of ten shillings.

For every such pamphlet and paper being larger than half a sheet, and not exceeding one whole sheet . . . a stamp duty of one penny, for every printed copy thereof.

For every almanack or calendar, for any one particular year, or for any time less than a year, which shall be written or printed on one side only of any one sheet, skin, or piece of paper parchment, or vellum . . . a stamp duty of two pence.

Document-Based Questions

1. Why did England want to hold on to the American colonies?

2. Why was the Stamp Act passed?

3. In your judgment, which of the taxed items listed would disturb the colonists the most?

4. The Stamp Act was removed in 1766. Why was this a great victory for the colonists?

5. How would you feel about the Stamp Act if you were a colonist at this time?

Source: The Stamp Act, 1765.

- King George III signed the Proclamation of 1763, which ordered all settlers to leave the Ohio Valley. The colonists were strongly opposed to the new law.

- In 1764, the British Parliament agreed that it had the right to tax the colonies in exchange for protection from all enemies. The colonists disagreed with this policy.

- The British passed the Stamp Act in 1765. This enabled the British government to tax items including all legal and business papers used in America. The colonists protested the Stamp Act. Parliament repealed it in 1766.

- The British passed the Townshend Acts in 1767. These acts reduced the colonists' freedom to govern themselves. The acts included new taxes on many items important to the colonists, including glass, paper, and tea. The colonists agreed to boycott British goods.

- In 1770, a crowd of people threw stones and snowballs at a group of British soldiers. The soldiers shot into the crowd, killing and wounding several colonists. This became known as the Boston Massacre. Crispus Attucks, an African, was the first person killed in the event.

- A group of colonists dressed as Mohawk Indians boarded a ship carrying tea on the night of December 16, 1773. They dumped more than 300 chests of British tea into Boston Harbor. This became known as the Boston Tea Party. Similar incidents took place in other cities.

- The king and Parliament passed the Intolerable Acts in 1774. These acts allowed Great Britain to close the port of Boston to all trade, ban town meetings, and house British troops in people's homes. They also said that British soldiers accused of breaking the law would be tried in Great Britain.

- The First Continental Congress met in 1774 and wrote the Declaration of Rights. It agreed to meet in 1775 if Great Britain rejected the declaration.

- The British fought a small group of American minutemen at Lexington and Concord in 1775. Many people were injured or killed.

Chapter 5   R E V I E W

Word Bank

Currency Act

Declaration of Rights

Declaratory Act

Intolerable Acts

Proclamation of 1763

Quebec Act

Stamp Act

Sugar Act

Townshend Acts

On a sheet of paper, write the correct word or words from the Word Bank to complete each sentence.

1. The _____ ordered all settlers to leave the Ohio Valley and return to the established colonies.

2. The _____ raised the tax on sugar and cloth goods.

3. The _____ enabled the British government to tax legal and business papers used in America.

4. The _____ stated that the British had control over the colonies in all cases.

5. The _____ placed new taxes on many items important to the colonists, including glass, paper, and tea.

6. The _____ extended the Canadian province of Quebec into the Ohio Valley.

7. The _____ made it illegal for the colonies to print their own money.

8. The _____ allowed Great Britain to close the port of Boston to all trade, ban town meetings, and house British troops in people's homes. It also required that British soldiers accused of any unlawful act be tried in Great Britain.

9. The First Continental Congress wrote the _____.

On a sheet of paper, write the letter of the answer that correctly completes each sentence.

10. British troops fired on a crowd of colonists in Boston because _____.

   A the colonists fired on them first

   B the colonists tried to tar and feather them

   C the colonists threw stones at them

   D they had orders to start a battle

11. A group of colonists threw unwanted tea into Boston harbor in a protest called the _____.

A Boston Tea Party   **C** Continental Congress

B Declaratory Act   **D** Proclamation of 1763

12. The battles at Lexington and Concord were most important because _____.

A the minutemen's gunpowder was saved

B Paul Revere was arrested

C they signaled war was about to begin

D the British lost the battles

On a sheet of paper, write the answers to the following questions. Use complete sentences.

13. What did Chief Pontiac do in 1763?

14. What was the purpose of the Proclamation of 1763?

15. What caused the Boston Tea Party?

16. What action did the First Continental Congress take?

17. Who were minutemen?

18. What happened at Lexington and Concord?

Critical Thinking On a sheet of paper, write your response to each question. Use complete sentences.

19. The colonists showed many ways to protest against the British. Some ways were violent and some were nonviolent. What are some nonviolent ways to protest that are used today? Which one do you think is most effective? Why?

20. How could a country fight for freedom yet enslave others?

Test-Taking Tip

As you read directions on a test, restate them in your own words. Explain what you are expected to do. This will help you give complete, correct answers.

6 The American Revolution

Lexington and Concord were the first of many battles between the colonists and the British. The colonists were determined to win their independence. The British were just as determined to keep the colonies under their control. The result was war—the American Revolutionary War—which lasted for more than eight years. In this chapter, you will learn about what happened in that war.

Goals for Learning

◆ To explain what events immediately followed Lexington and Concord

◆ To identify what actions the Second Continental Congress took

◆ To explain why the Declaration of Independence was written

◆ To identify the strengths and weaknesses of the colonists and the British

◆ To explain why the Battle of Saratoga was a turning point in the war

◆ To describe how the colonists won the war

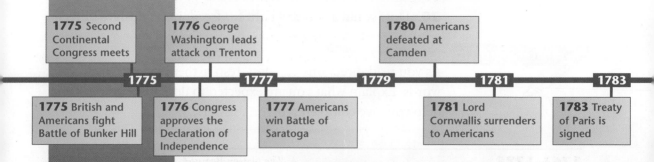

1775 Second Continental Congress meets

1776 George Washington leads attack on Trenton

1780 Americans defeated at Camden

1775   1777   1779   1781   1783

1775 British and Americans fight Battle of Bunker Hill

1776 Congress approves the Declaration of Independence

1777 Americans win Battle of Saratoga

1781 Lord Cornwallis surrenders to Americans

1783 Treaty of Paris is signed

Disarm

To take weapons away from someone

Militia

An organized group of citizens who serve as soldiers in times of war

News of the Lexington and Concord incidents spread rapidly throughout the colonies. The colonists became upset when they heard that British soldiers burned houses and fired upon innocent people. They were proud of the courage the minutemen showed in trying to prevent the British from reaching Lexington and Concord. The British did not capture Samuel Adams or John Hancock. The colonists had proved they were equal to the British and could fight for their rights.

Meanwhile, the British had seized a store of gunpowder in Virginia. Colonists were sure the British intended to **disarm** them completely. They knew they couldn't let that happen. Thus, the colonists prepared for possible attacks. They seized military supplies in New York intended for British soldiers. They prevented ships from trading with Great Britain or any of its colonies. New Jersey, Pennsylvania, the Carolinas, and Maryland worked to increase their **militia**. A militia is an organized group of citizens who serve as soldiers in times of war. The colonies were working together for a common cause—freedom.

Which British Forts Did the Americans Seize?

Massachusetts was the first colony to take military action. The leaders wanted to protect their own people. Beyond that, they thought they must take control of two major British strongholds—Fort Ticonderoga and Fort Crown Point. These forts, at the entrance to Canada, contained a large amount of military supplies.

Ethan Allen and his Green Mountain Boys were a militia from Vermont. Along with Colonel Benedict Arnold, they seized both forts without a shot being fired. The British, who were not prepared to fight, surrendered quickly. In this important victory, the colonists obtained badly needed cannons and a huge supply of ammunition.

When Did the Second Continental Congress Meet?

Resign

To give up an office or job

Petition

A written paper asking for a right or benefit from someone in power

On May 10, 1775—the same day that Fort Ticonderoga was seized—the Second Continental Congress began in Philadelphia. A new delegate named John Hancock was chosen as its president. The only other new delegates were Thomas Jefferson of Virginia and Benjamin Franklin of Pennsylvania. Franklin had just returned from Great Britain after **resigning** his duties as colonial agent there.

Many colonists who wanted some peaceful way to settle the problem sent a **petition** to the king. A petition is a written paper asking for a right or benefit from someone in power. Their petition stated that they were still loyal to the king but would not accept unfair British laws. But the king did not change any policies.

The Americans now had to choose between giving in to the king and fighting a war for freedom. As they had shown at Boston, Lexington, and Concord, they were not afraid to stand up to the British.

Lesson 1 Review On a sheet of paper, write the answers to the following questions. Use complete sentences.

1. How did the colonists react to Lexington and Concord?

2. How did the colonists prove they were equal to the British army?

3. What did the colonists do to prevent being disarmed?

4. Why was capturing Fort Ticonderoga and Fort Crown Point important for the colonists?

5. What peaceful way to solve the problem with the British did some colonists try?

What do you think ?

Why do you think the king did not do anything in response to petitions from the colonists?

Interfere

To enter into or take part in other people's business

Commander

Someone who controls an army or some other military group

Plea

An urgent request

Postmaster

A person who runs the post office

Pardon

An official statement forgiving someone of something

Loyalty

The act of being faithful to someone

Congress knew it would have to create some form of central government. After many days of debate, the delegates agreed that Congress had the power to do certain things. Congress had the power to provide for protection against future British attacks. It could declare war. It would not **interfere** in the private matters of the colonies. Each colony wanted to protect the personal freedoms of its people.

The delegates moved to organize an army. Several leaders were considered as the possible chief **commander**. A commander is a leader of a military group. One member of Congress stood out as the best choice. A vote was taken, and George Washington was officially made commander in chief of the American army. They sent out a **plea** to the colonies for troops and money to pay for the war effort.

While the war itself was beginning, Congress took other steps as a central, unified governing body. It set up a colonial post office, naming Benjamin Franklin as its **postmaster**. A postmaster runs the post office. Congress sent agents to other countries to ask for their help. It organized a navy to attack approaching British ships. It reopened ports to trading with any country except Great Britain.

How Was Boston Recovered?

After the fighting at Lexington and Concord, thousands of minutemen were waiting in camps around Boston. The governor of Boston, General Gage, issued an order that put Boston under complete control of the British army. Gage also offered **pardons** to all colonists who would pledge their **loyalty** to the king. A pardon is an official statement forgiving someone of something. The pardon did not apply to John Hancock or Samuel Adams. No one came forward to accept a pardon.

General Gage knew he had to protect the area in Boston known as Dorchester Heights. He planned to arm Bunker Hill and Breed's Hill against colonial attack. The colonists learned of Gage's plan and quickly responded. American soldiers worked all through the night to make Breed's Hill stronger. The hill became the Americans' first line of defense.

On June 17, 1775, British warships in Boston Harbor opened an attack on Breed's Hill and Bunker Hill. The British expected an easy victory. The colonial soldiers held their ground.

British General William Howe led another attack. With little gunpowder, the Americans held their fire until the British were very close. The British suffered great losses and retreated. There

was another British attack, and then the colonials retreated. The British captured Breed's Hill and Bunker Hill. The losses were heavy on both sides, including several British officers. After the battle, General Gage said, "One more victory like that will destroy us."

Colonial and British losses were heavy at the Battle of Bunker Hill.

Then and Now

Did you know that the first known wartime submarine attack occurred during the Revolutionary War? David Bushnell, a college student at Yale, had designed a one-person submarine. It was powered by a handheld propeller. As you might expect, when Bushnell tried to sink a British warship in New York Harbor in 1776, his mission failed.

U.S. Navy submarines today are very different from Bushnell's. They are at least 300 feet long and require about 130 crew members. They have atomic-powered engines and carry torpedoes and guided missiles. Today, submarines find their targets by sending out sound waves that bounce off enemy ships.

Two weeks after this battle, called the Battle of Bunker Hill, General Washington reorganized and drilled the troops. The following spring, the Americans seized Dorchester Heights.

The Americans brought in cannons captured at Fort Ticonderoga. Now they could control the harbor below. General Howe viewed his position as hopeless. Quietly the British army and many people loyal to the British made their way to Halifax, Nova Scotia. They left Boston to the Americans.

It Happened in History

Help from Europe

At the beginning of the Revolutionary War, the colonists needed help from European countries. They wanted the countries to support their cause. France and Spain, in particular, did not like the British. The colonists also needed to get guns and ammunition to fight the war. Congress decided to send Benjamin Franklin to Paris to work out a treaty. Meanwhile, John Jay went to Spain and John Adams to the Netherlands (Holland) to arrange to get war supplies.

Supplies sent by France, Spain, and the Netherlands were very important to the colonial war effort. At first, the foreign aid was done secretly. As the war progressed, the European nations more openly supported the Americans. France did sign a treaty, but neither Spain nor the Netherlands declared their support of the war against the British.

What do you think ?

What did General Gage mean when he said after Bunker Hill, "One more victory like that will destroy us"?

Lesson 2 Review On a sheet of paper, write the answers to the following questions. Use complete sentences.

1. What task did Congress give to George Washington?

2. What task did Congress give to Benjamin Franklin?

3. Why did Congress send out a plea to the colonists?

4. What did General Gage offer to colonists who pledged loyalty to the king?

5. Why did the colonists fortify Breed's Hill?

Invade

To attack or take over something

Location

The place where something is positioned

Loyalist

An American who supported the king of Great Britain

Orator

One who is good at public speaking

Statesman

Someone who knows and practices government ideas

Congress learned in late 1775 that the British were forming an army in Canada. They became concerned that the British could **invade** New York from the North. Congress agreed to a plan to capture Montreal and Quebec. They hoped that American troops would receive help from the French colonists in Quebec.

General Richard Montgomery led the march to Montreal and captured the city. From Montreal, he led troops to Quebec, meeting Colonel Benedict Arnold and more troops along the way. Because of its **location**, Quebec was not an easy city to capture. The Americans lost the battle. General Montgomery was killed, and Colonel Arnold was severely wounded.

The failed attack on Canada was offset by a victory in North Carolina. Americans defeated British **loyalists** at Moore's Creek, North Carolina, in February 1776. Loyalists were Americans who supported the king. The victory was important for two reasons. First, it greatly decreased the loyalists' desire to fight. Also, the good news of victory raised the spirits of the Americans. Not long after that victory, the Americans were successful in turning back a naval attack on Charleston, South Carolina.

What Was the Declaration of Independence?

Richard Henry Lee of Virginia made a speech to Congress in June 1776. He stated, "these United Colonies are, and of right ought to be free and independent states." Separating from Great Britain was a big step for the colonists to take. Many still hoped that Great Britain would cooperate. Samuel Adams of Massachusetts and Patrick Henry of Virginia knew the British would not change their policy of strict colonial control. Henry was an **orator** and **statesman**. A statesman is someone who knows and practices government ideas. To both men, the war had already started. Henry voiced his opinion loud and clear: "Separate and fight! The war has already begun!"

Patrick Henry, addressing the Virginia Assembly, called for war.

A committee was formed to write a formal letter to announce the decision that Congress reached. Thomas Jefferson wrote the **document** and presented it to Congress in late June 1776. After some debate and a few changes, the Declaration of Independence was approved. Jefferson considered many facts when writing the Declaration. Even though Jefferson owned African slaves, one point he wanted to include was the end to the slave trade. However, some southern and northern delegates disagreed. They refused to sign the Declaration if the slave **clause** remained. To save the Declaration, Jefferson removed the clause.

As of July 4, 1776, the 13 colonies considered themselves to be free states. Next, the states would have to unite and form a government in order to fight the British. The Declaration of Independence can be found in Appendix A of this textbook.

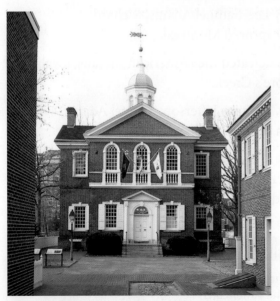

The Declaration of Independence was signed in this building—Carpenter's Hall—in Philadelphia, Pennsylvania.

It Happened in History

A Push Toward Freedom

In January 1776, Thomas Paine wrote a pamphlet titled "Common Sense." Paine had recently left Great Britain to come to the colonies. In the pamphlet, he pointed out how foolish it was for a small island 3,000 miles away to be controlling an entire continent. For one thing, the process of making decisions took a long time. People and messages had to travel back and forth across the Atlantic Ocean. To Paine, independence for the colonies was just "common sense."

Many people read the pamphlet. Paine's ideas helped start the push for independence in the colonies.

Lesson 3 Review Choose the word or name in parentheses that best completes each sentence. Write your answers on a sheet of paper.

1. Congress was concerned that the British could invade (New York, Montreal, Quebec) from the North.

2. (Richard Henry Lee, Samuel Adams, Richard Montgomery) captured Montreal.

3. The Americans defeated the (American Indians, loyalists, British) at Moore's Creek.

4. (Patrick Henry, Thomas Jefferson, Samuel Adams) wrote the Declaration of Independence.

5. Some delegates refused to sign the Declaration of Independence if the (slave, freedom, independence) clause remained.

What do you think ?

Why do you think the Declaration of Independence was an important step for the Americans?

Revolution

The act of overthrowing and replacing a government

At the beginning of the **Revolutionary** War, there were clear differences between the British and colonial forces. Key strengths and weaknesses helped decide the outcome of the war.

How Did the British Take New York City?

George Washington moved several thousand American soldiers to New York. He was sure the British would try to take control of the New York harbor. If the British were successful, the colonies would be split into two parts and greatly weakened.

British general William Howe and his brother, Admiral Richard Howe, arrived on Staten Island in the New York harbor in July 1776. General Washington had been correct, and he was prepared to defend the city. Meanwhile, King George III offered one last chance for peace.

General Howe announced that all crimes against Great Britain would be pardoned if the people would surrender. The king's offer angered the Americans.

General Howe prepared his large army for battle. They attacked with full force. The Americans were driven off Long Island.

Colonial Strengths and Weaknesses

Strengths	Weaknesses
• Had a strong leader in George Washington	• Had little money and depended on other countries for supplies
• Were used to frontier life and using firearms	• One-third of Americans were British loyalists
• Had military experience from the French and Indian War	• Had a weak navy
• Were fighting for their independence on their own soil	

British Strengths and Weaknesses

Strengths	Weaknesses
• Had well-trained soldiers, expert leaders, and the finest equipment	• Were not used to frontier style of American warfare
• Had a powerful navy	• Had to fight far from home
• Could pay other countries to fight for them	• Were fighting other wars with France, Spain, and the Netherlands at the same time
• Had help from British loyalists in America	

Nathan Hale was a young former teacher who had proved himself at Boston and now in this **siege** at New York. A siege is when an army prevents people in a fort or city from leaving. This is done in an attempt to capture the fort or city. Hale offered to go behind the enemy lines on Long Island to gain information for General Washington. Unfortunately, he was caught and ordered by General Howe to be hanged. According to legend, as he was about to die, he said, "I only regret that I have but one life to lose for my country."

The Americans were forced beyond New York City. George Washington realized that he could not win the battle. He led a retreat across the Hudson River. This prevented the remaining members of his army from being captured or killed.

Washington led a surprise attack on Trenton, New Jersey, on December 25, 1776. He guided his troops through a blinding storm across the ice-clogged Delaware River. He defeated the **Hessians**. The Hessians were soldiers from Hesse, Germany. They were hired by the British to fight the Americans.

Washington and his men then went on toward Princeton, New Jersey. One week later, they defeated three enemy regiments at Princeton. At this time when Americans needed hope, the two victories were of great importance.

Biography

Sybil Ludington: 1761–1839

Sybil Ludington was 16 years old when her father, Colonel Henry Ludington, led the militia in Fredericksburg, New York. On April 26, 1777, Colonel Ludington received bad news. The British were attacking Danbury, Connecticut, which was only 25 miles away. Troops were needed to fight the British.

Colonel Ludington's troops were at home on their farms. He had to figure out how to gather them quickly to fight the British. Sybil offered to help. On her horse, Star, she rode 40 miles and awakened troops along the way. The troops gathered and attacked the British returning to their ships. Today, Sybil Ludington is remembered as a hero. The path of her late-night ride is marked in Putnam County, New York. There is also a statue of Sybil on her horse.

History in Your Life

The Nail-Making Machine

Researchers believe that the first nails were made in the Middle East about 5,000 years ago. Nail making was a slow process for hundreds of years. The handmade nails had squared, tapered sides. They often split the wood pieces they were to hold together. Nails were also expensive. To avoid using nails, carpenters used wooden pegs or pieces that locked together.

In the 1700s, American inventors worked on a nail-making machine. Ezekiel Reed patented the first one in 1786. His machine made better nails than those hammered by hand or cut from large sheets of iron. Unfortunately, his nails were too expensive for wide use. Within a decade, Jacob Perkins improved on Reed's invention. Perkins's machine cut and put heads on nails in one operation. Soon the price of nails dropped from 25 cents to 8 cents per pound. Nails are now a common item in our everyday life.

Word Bank

General William Howe

New York Harbor

Trenton

Princeton

Nathan Hale

Hessians

Lesson 4 Review On a sheet of paper, write the correct word or words from the Word Bank to complete each sentence.

1. General Washington was sure the British would try to take _____.

2. Americans were driven off Long Island by the British army, led by _____.

3. General Howe ordered the hanging of _____ for spying.

4. The British paid soldiers called _____ to fight the Americans.

5. Americans won two important victories at _____ and _____, New Jersey.

What do you think ?

Why do you think the British paid the Hessians to fight rather than use their own soldiers?

Isolate

To set apart from others

Three-pronged attack

An attack in three separate places against an enemy

Proposal

A suggestion for others to consider

Compromise

A settlement of differences in which each side gives up some of its demands

Writing About History

Find information about a battle in the Revolutionary War. Then imagine you are a newspaper journalist. Write an article in your notebook about the battle. Explain who fought the battle, where it was fought, and why it was significant.

The British wanted to **isolate**, or set apart, New England from the other colonies. If the British controlled New York, this could be done. General Howe planned a **three-pronged attack** in October 1777. A three-pronged attack is an attack in three separate places against an enemy. The plan was carefully laid out: General John Burgoyne would march from Canada. Colonel Barry St. Leger would attack from the west. General Howe would reinforce from the south. The British intended to destroy the American army once and for all.

This plan, however, proved to be a total failure. Colonel St. Leger was met with great resistance and could not make much progress. General Howe did not send reinforcements as planned. Instead, he sent his army to attack Philadelphia. At Saratoga, the Americans met General Burgoyne and defeated his army. He surrendered to Horatio Gates, the American general.

News of the Saratoga defeat shocked the British. They wondered what they could do to make peace with the colonists. The king's earlier **proposal** to pardon and forgive the New York colonists had not been accepted. The Americans were demanding complete self-government. A peaceful **compromise** was no longer possible.

The British defeat at Saratoga caused a debate in France. Benjamin Franklin had asked the French for both military help and money. The French were not willing to provide aid. They thought the American army was weak and would lose to the British. After the American victory at Saratoga, however, the French decided to help the colonies.

Evacuate

To move away from a dangerous area

What Happened at Valley Forge?

Washington tried to keep Howe's army from taking Philadelphia. However, Washington was badly defeated at Brandywine. When Howe's men moved into Philadelphia, Washington struck again. This time the Americans were stopped at Germantown. Washington retreated with his surviving men, setting up winter quarters at Valley Forge.

It was a bitter winter. The troops suffered many hardships such as poor shelter, no warm clothes, small amounts of food, and irregular pay. Despite the situation, Washington was able to keep his troops together.

General Howe was called to Great Britain in the spring of 1778 to explain why he had not won the war. Meanwhile, Howe's replacement, Henry Clinton, was on his way to Philadelphia. Upon arriving, he immediately **evacuated** the troops. France was sending a fleet of ships to aid the Americans.

Conditions were difficult for the American army at Valley Forge.

What Victories Did the Americans Win?

Wanting to concentrate British strength in one area, Clinton moved his troops on to New York. Washington and his men left Valley Forge to follow the British army. In a battle at Monmouth, the Americans almost succeeded in defeating the British. Clinton's army managed to escape to New York. There, Washington and his men contained the British for most of the rest of the war.

Meanwhile, the British had persuaded the American Indians to attack American settlements on the western frontier. In response, Virginia Governor Patrick Henry sent George Rogers Clark into the Ohio Valley to stop these raids. Clark was an experienced frontiersman who knew the region well. He marched his soldiers through the wilderness. Clark captured the British forts at Kaskaskia, Cahokia, and Vincennes. His outstanding leadership and courage helped the Americans control the West.

Word Bank
Clinton
Howe
Saratoga
Valley Forge
Vincennes

Lesson 5 Review On a sheet of paper, write the correct word or words from the Word Bank to complete each sentence.

1. General Washington set up winter quarters at _____.

2. General _____ planned a three-pronged attack.

3. The Americans defeated the British at _____.

4. General _____ led the British army at Monmouth.

5. The Americans captured a British fort at _____.

What do you think ?

Why do you think General Howe's three-pronged attack failed?

Convict

To find someone guilty of a crime

Traitor

Someone who turns against his or her own country

Before the French fleet came to America's aid, the colonists had only a few warships. They had a few small merchant vessels that had been fitted with guns. The French ships brought military supplies from Europe. They attacked British ships on their way to the colonies. By the end of the war, they had captured or destroyed over 700 British vessels.

American Captain John Paul Jones became a naval hero. He successfully raided many towns along the coast of Great Britain. He also scored a naval victory in a battle with the British warship *Serapis* in September 1779. Jones's ship was sinking, and the British ordered him to surrender. His reply was, "I have not yet begun to fight!" He captured the *Serapis* and sailed it to safety. This victory still stands as an example for the present-day United States Navy.

What Did Benedict Arnold Do?

Benedict Arnold had fought in the battles of Quebec and Saratoga. He had shown strong military ability and courage. General Washington appointed him to command West Point, the strongest and most important fort in America. However, Arnold probably felt that he was not getting enough credit. He plotted to turn West Point over to Great Britain. In return, he was promised a high British army rank.

Plans for the takeover were to be delivered to Arnold by John André, a major in the British army. On the way, Major André was stopped by three men and searched. They found the plans he had hidden in his boots. Major André was tried, **convicted** as a spy, and hanged. Benedict Arnold escaped to Great Britain, where he spent his remaining years in shame as an American **traitor**. A traitor is someone who turns against his or her own country.

How Were the British Defeated?

Sharpshooting

The ability to shoot a gun with great success

Lure

To draw in someone or something by hinting of gain

Inland

A region of land that is far away from the coast

Occupy

To take control of a place

Redeem

To release from blame for something by doing something else better

Prime Minister

The main official in some countries, such as Great Britain and Canada.

The British captured the ports of Savannah and Charleston. In 1780, an American army fell to these determined British at Camden, South Carolina. However, a force of militiamen skilled at frontier **sharpshooting** beat the British back at Kings Mountain, North Carolina. Sharpshooting is the ability to shoot a gun with great success.

General Nathaniel Greene **lured** the British army, led by Lord Cornwallis, **inland** in North Carolina. Greene's army weakened the British army. Greene then recaptured most of the inland positions previously **occupied** by the British.

Lord Cornwallis invaded Virginia in an effort to **redeem** himself. However, the Americans pushed him back. Cornwallis moved his men north to Yorktown, Virginia. There he hoped the British navy would provide him with supplies and protect his position.

Washington decided to move to the south for a surprise attack. Count François Joseph Paul de Grasse intended to move his French fleet up into the Chesapeake Bay. With Count de Grasse controlling the bay and Washington attacking from the North, Cornwallis had no way to escape.

Cornwallis tried to retreat to the West. There he was cut off by a young French naval officer, Marquis de Lafayette. The British fought hard, but they had too few men. On October 19, 1781, Cornwallis surrendered.

When Great Britain's **prime minister,** Lord North, heard of the defeat of Cornwallis, he reportedly said, "It is all over." Lord North then resigned. The new British government was prepared to make peace and give in to the Americans' demands for independence. The war had come to an end.

Major Battles of the Revolutionary War

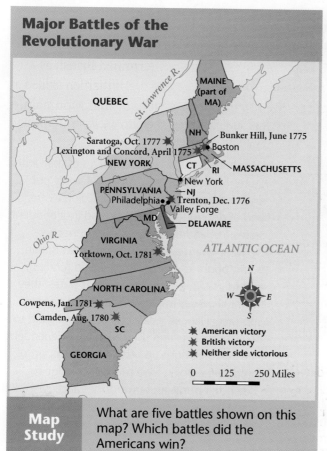

Map Study What are five battles shown on this map? Which battles did the Americans win?

What Was the 1783 Treaty of Paris?

Great Britain's control of America had been made stronger by the Treaty of Paris in 1763. Great Britain recognized America's independence with the signing of another Treaty of Paris on September 3, 1783. This treaty established the new nation's boundaries—Canada on the north, the Mississippi River on the west, and Florida on the south. Great Britain was forced to return Florida to Spain. France gained nothing.

What do you think ?

Which American leader do you think did the most to win the Revolutionary War? Why?

Lesson 6 Review Choose the name in parentheses that best completes each sentence. Write your answers on a sheet of paper.

1. John Paul Jones was a(n) (British, American, French) sea captain.

2. (John Paul Jones, Benedict Arnold, Nathaniel Greene) was a traitor.

3. The British captured (North Carolina, Savannah, Kings Mountain).

4. Lord Cornwallis surrendered at (Charleston, Camden, Yorktown).

5. The Treaty of Paris set the American boundary to the west as (the Mississippi River, Canada, Florida).

Unalienable Rights

The Declaration of Independence is one of the most important documents in United States history. Its writer, Thomas Jefferson, wrote that the British king had taken away some of the colonists' rights. He believed these unalienable rights were given by God and could not be taken away. The signers of the Declaration of Independence would do whatever was needed to give these rights back to the people. The excerpt below is from the Declaration of Independence.

We hold these truths to be self-evident, that all men are created equal, that they are endowed by their creator with certain unalienable rights, that among these are life, liberty and the pursuit of happiness. That to secure these rights, governments are instituted [set up] among men, deriving their just powers from the consent of the governed. That whenever any form of government becomes destructive of these ends, it is the right of the people to alter or to abolish it, and to institute new government, laying its foundation on such principles and organizing its powers in such form, as to them shall seem most likely to effect their safety and happiness. . . . governments long established should not be changed for light and transient [brief] causes; . . . But when a long train of abuses . . . evinces [proves] a design to reduce them under absolute despotism [dictatorship], it is their right, it is their duty, to throw off such government, and to provide new guards for their future security.

Such has been the patient sufferance of these colonies; and such is now the necessity which constrains [forces] them to alter their former systems of government. . . .

We, therefore, the representatives of the United States of America, . . . do, . . . solemnly publish and declare, that these United Colonies are, and of right ought to be free and independent states; . . . and that all political connection between them and the state of Great Britain, is and ought to be totally dissolved [ended]; and that as free and independent states, they have full power to levy war, conclude peace, contract alliances, establish commerce, and to do all other acts and things which independent states may of right do. And for the support of this declaration, . . . we mutually pledge to each other our lives, our fortunes and our sacred honor.

Document-Based Questions

1. What are the unalienable rights mentioned in the Declaration of Independence?

2. What does the Declaration of Independence say should happen if a government no longer allows these rights?

3. How do you think the unalienable rights affect your life today?

4. How do you know that the signers of the Declaration strongly believed in the document? Give an example from the reading.

5. Do you think the words of the Declaration of Independence influenced how the U.S. government was set up? Explain your answer.

Source: The Declaration of Independence, 1776.

Chapter 6 SUMMARY

- On May 10, 1775, the Second Continental Congress met in Philadelphia. John Hancock was chosen as its president. Congress decided it could declare war and that it would not interfere in the private matters of the colonies. Congress chose George Washington as commander in chief of the American army.

- On June 17, 1775, British warships in Boston Harbor opened an attack on Breed's Hill and Bunker Hill. The British later won the battle, but only after heavy losses. The battle was called the Battle of Bunker Hill. The next spring, the Americans captured Dorchester Heights above Boston, forcing the British to leave Boston to the Americans.

- In late 1775, General Richard Montgomery captured Montreal. From Montreal, he led troops to Quebec, meeting Colonel Benedict Arnold and more troops along the way. The Americans lost at Quebec. General Montgomery was killed.

- The Americans defeated British loyalists at Moore's Creek, North Carolina, in February 1776.

- Thomas Jefferson wrote the Declaration of Independence and presented it to Congress in 1776. Congress approved it after removing a slavery clause.

- The British drove the American army from New York in July 1776. General Washington then led a surprise attack on Trenton, New Jersey, on December 25, 1776. He guided his troops through a storm across the Delaware River and defeated Hessian soldiers.

- General Howe planned a three-pronged attack in October 1777. The plan was intended to defeat the Americans all at once. The plan failed. The Americans defeated the British at Saratoga.

- After being pushed back by the Americans at Virginia, Britain's Lord Cornwallis moved his army to Yorktown. After heavy fighting, the British surrendered on October 19, 1781.

- Great Britain signed the Treaty of Paris on September 3, 1783. The treaty established the new nation's boundaries—Canada on the north, the Mississippi River on the west, and Florida on the south. Great Britain was forced to return Florida to Spain. France gained nothing.

Chapter 6 REVIEW

Word Bank

commander

Hessians

loyalist

militia

pardon

petition

postmaster

statesman

traitor

On a sheet of paper, write the correct word from the Word Bank to complete each sentence.

1. A _____ is a group of citizens who serve as soldiers in times of war.

2. An official statement forgiving someone of something is called a _____.

3. A written paper asking for a right or benefit from someone in power is called a _____.

4. The Second Continental Congress chose George Washington to be _____ of the American army.

5. The Second Continental Congress made Benjamin Franklin the _____.

6. The British hired _____ to fight against the Americans.

7. A _____ was an American who supported the king of Great Britain.

8. Benedict Arnold was a _____.

9. Someone who practices government ideas is a _____.

On a sheet of paper, write the letter of the answer that correctly completes each sentence.

10. Commander George Washington's colonial army had an important victory after a surprise attack on _____.

   A Bunker Hill   **C** Valley Forge

   B New York harbor   **D** Trenton, New Jersey

11. On the western frontier, George Rogers Clark helped to stop _____.

   A attacks by American Indians

   B attacks by French frontiersmen

   C attacks by loyalist settlers

   D British trade with American Indians

12. The American Revolution ended in 1781 with the surrender of _____.

   A Lord North in Great Britain
   B Marquis de Lafayette at Saratoga
   C Lord Cornwallis at Yorktown
   D General Howe at New York City

On a sheet of paper, write the answers to the following questions. Use complete sentences.

13. What events immediately followed Lexington and Concord?

14. Why did the Congress write the Declaration of Independence?

15. What strengths did the Americans have during the Revolutionary War?

16. What strengths did the British have during the Revolutionary War?

17. Why was the Battle of Saratoga a turning point of the war?

18. What finally won the war for the Americans?

Critical Thinking On a sheet of paper, write your response to each question. Use complete sentences.

19. How do you think the Revolutionary War was different from the French and Indian War?

20. The French got nothing from the war. Why do you think they helped the Americans?

Test-Taking Tip

When preparing for a test, review any earlier quizzes or tests that cover the same information.

7 A Government Is Formed

A new nation was born when the Treaty of Paris was signed in 1783. British control was no longer a problem, for America had won its independence. Now America had to form a government that would act as a unit for all of the states. Forming this new government of many different types of people would not be a simple task. In this chapter, you will learn how the government was formed.

Goals for Learning

◆ To explain the Articles of Confederation and the problems it caused

◆ To explain what happened at the Constitutional Convention

◆ To identify the differences between the New Jersey Plan and the Virginia Plan

◆ To identify the three branches of government

◆ To describe the purpose of the Bill of Rights

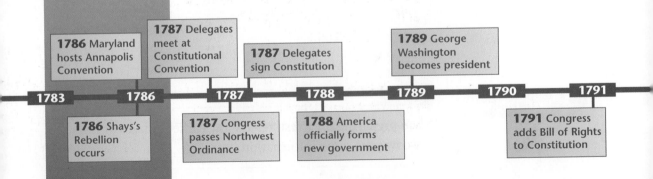

1786 Maryland hosts Annapolis Convention

1787 Delegates meet at Constitutional Convention

1787 Delegates sign Constitution

1789 George Washington becomes president

| 1783 | 1786 | 1787 | 1788 | 1789 | 1790 | 1791 |

1786 Shays's Rebellion occurs

1787 Congress passes Northwest Ordinance

1788 America officially forms new government

1791 Congress adds Bill of Rights to Constitution

During the Revolutionary War in 1781, the states adopted the Articles of Confederation. The articles set up a government with limited power over each state. During the war, the states had been willing to unite against the British. After the war, the Articles of Confederation caused problems.

What Problems Developed in the Western Lands?

Pioneers had begun to settle in the West long before the war started. A pioneer is one of the first persons to settle in a territory. They ignored the fact that the land already belonged to American Indians. Sometimes, two states claimed the same area. This made it difficult for settlers to get help fighting the Indians or Spanish in the southern regions. Steps to solve the problem of overlapping claims included a workable system of land **ownership.** In 1784, Thomas Jefferson developed a plan for a **temporary** government of western lands. This plan would later lead to the Northwest Ordinance of 1787.

Pioneer

One of the first persons to settle in a territory

Ownership

The act of owning something, such as land or a house

Temporary

Lasting only a short time

Biography

Benjamin Banneker: 1731–1806

Benjamin Banneker was a free African who became an internationally famous mathematician and astronomer. With little schooling, he taught himself mathematics while working on his family farm in Maryland. He invented his own difficult math problems and then solved them. In his 50s, Banneker began making astronomical calculations for local almanacs. He accurately forecast that a solar eclipse would occur in the spring of 1789. Banneker began publishing his own almanac in 1792. Thomas Jefferson and members of the Academy of Sciences in Paris highly praised Banneker for the almanac. Banneker came to be known in Europe as America's "African astronomer." He was named to the commission that made the original survey of Washington, D.C. Banneker spoke out against the injustice of slavery in a famous letter to Jefferson.

What Trade Problems Did the Americans Face?

Americans had depended upon trade with Great Britain for many years. After the war, Great Britain closed its ports to American shippers. British merchants, though, continued to send their goods to the United States. They could sell the goods for less than the American **manufacturers** could. Americans had to find new trading partners to survive.

What Problems Developed with the Spanish?

The Spanish controlled Florida, New Orleans, and the land west of the Mississippi River. They did not take the Treaty of Paris seriously. Americans were not welcome in the southern region. Spain would not permit them to ship goods from New Orleans. Because they could not use New Orleans, western settlers had to travel by land. The route was slow and costly. The United States was too weak to force the Spanish to change their policy.

How Was the Government Out of Control?

The government of the 13 states was weak and ineffective under the Articles of Confederation. Nine of the 13 states, each having one vote, had to give their **approval** before Congress could act. If a change in the articles was proposed, all 13 states had to agree on it. Each state, no matter how large its population, had only one vote in Congress. Larger states felt that this practice was unfair.

Congress had no power to create and collect taxes or place duties on **imports.** An import is a good brought in from a foreign country. Congress had to ask the states to give it money. Less and less money was coming in, but the debt was increasing.

To add to the problem, states were printing their own money. Paper money often lost its value. Sometimes it would not be accepted either within the state or between states. Some people thought that if more money was printed, the problem would be solved. Without gold to back it, though, the money would be worthless.

Manufacturer

A company that makes something to sell to the public or to other companies

Approval

An acceptance or agreement

Import

A good brought in from a foreign country

Geography Note

After the Revolutionary War, the U.S. government sold land northwest of the Ohio River. The Ordinance of 1785 ordered the land surveyed into plots of 36 square miles (93 square kilometers). These squares, called townships, held 36 sections of 640 acres (259 hectares). The ordinance set the pattern for settling much of the rest of the United States.

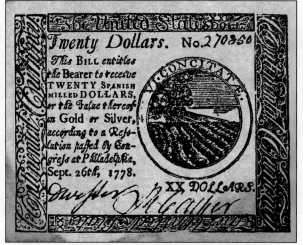

This is what a $20 banknote looked like in 1778.

Congress also lacked the power to regulate trade among states. States began to treat each other as separate countries. They added **tariffs**—a tax on goods leaving or entering some place—to keep out other states' goods. The tariffs caused a decrease in **interstate** trade. This encouraged Americans to buy British goods instead of American goods.

There were also no national courts. State courts could not settle **disputes** among states. All of these were serious problems that the central government was unable to solve.

 Focus on Economics

The Revolutionary War left the United States in debt. At this time, each state had its own form of money, or currency. Some states could not pay their bills, so they printed more money. This created a huge problem. Alexander Hamilton of New York suggested a central bank. The bank would handle the war debt and print a standard currency.

In 1791, Congress created the First Bank of the United States. The bank issued paper money for the new country. It could set and collect taxes, pay debts, and borrow money for Congress. The Bank was strong because it had $10 million to hold up the value of the paper money. The bank operated successfully for 20 years, and it helped the nation succeed.

Articles of
  Confederation

disputes

Great Britain

import

tariff

Lesson 1 Review On a sheet of paper, write the correct word or words from the Word Bank to complete each sentence.

1. A(n) _____ is a tax on goods leaving or entering some place.

2. The _____ set up a government with limited power over each state.

3. Americans had depended upon trade with _____ before the Revolutionary War.

4. A(n) _____ is a good brought in from a foreign country.

5. National courts were needed to settle _____ among states.

What do you think ?

What do you think was the most difficult problem facing the Americans after the Revolutionary War? Why?

Then and Now

Handwriting in the 1700s was quite different from most handwriting today. Look at this part of a letter written by Abigail Adams to her husband, John Adams. Notice the way she formed an s. Some of her s's look like a modern f. See how her d slants to the left. At that time, many common nouns were capitalized. Today we do not capitalize such words.

Commercial

Something linked to business or buying and selling

Not everyone agreed with the Articles of Confederation. Business owners, merchants, shippers, manufacturers, and bankers wanted a stronger government. They could not protect themselves from the practices of stronger foreign countries and from unfair laws that Great Britain passed. The weak American government could do nothing to help these groups. Constant disputes among the states only increased the difficulties.

Why Was the Annapolis Convention Held?

Maryland and Virginia were having a dispute over **commercial** rights on the Potomac River. Delegates from these two states met at George Washington's home in Mount Vernon and worked out many of the problems.

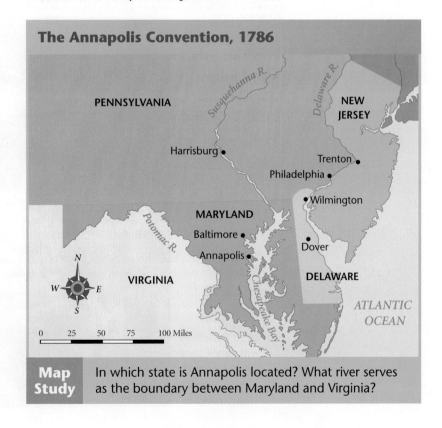

The Annapolis Convention, 1786

Map Study   In which state is Annapolis located? What river serves as the boundary between Maryland and Virginia?

Due to the success of the Mount Vernon Conference, James Madison proposed having another convention in 1786. Delegates from all the states would be invited. However, the Annapolis Convention was not successful because only five states sent delegates. Even Maryland, the **host** state, did not send a representative. Alexander Hamilton of New York proposed a convention for 1787. The main business would be forming a stronger government.

Host

A person or group who provides a place for guests to do something

What Was Shays's Rebellion?

Any doubt about the need for a strong central government ended after a rebellion against the government of Massachusetts in the winter of 1786. Farmers were upset by low farm prices and high state taxes. Many of them were afraid they would lose their farms. They gathered under former army captain Daniel Shays. Shays's Rebellion closed courthouses and almost captured a storehouse of weapons. The group grew to include over 2,000 farmers. The rebellion lasted for several months.

Shays's Rebellion was proof that a strong central government was needed.

What Happened at the Constitutional Convention?

The Articles of Confederation had succeeded in doing some good things. It had led the Americans through the war and the signing of the Treaty of Paris. It had kept the 13 states together during a difficult time, and it provided for the peaceful settlement of western land. Now, however, it was time to create a stronger, more forceful government.

The delegates met in May 1787 at Independence Hall in Philadelphia. All states except Rhode Island were represented at this meeting. The meeting was called the Constitutional Convention. Fifty-five of the most respected Americans were present. Among these were George Washington, James Madison, and Edmund Randolph of Virginia; John Dickinson of Delaware; Benjamin Franklin of Pennsylvania; Alexander Hamilton of New York; and William Paterson of New Jersey. Both Thomas Jefferson and John Adams were in Europe at the time and were absent from the convention. Most of the delegates were lawyers, while some were farmers and merchants.

At the start of the convention, it was decided that all the **sessions** were to be held in **secrecy.** The delegates wanted to be able to debate freely. They could even change their minds about some very serious subjects. The delegates felt that their heated debates need not be shared with the public.

The delegates chose George Washington to lead the convention. He was recognized as an intelligent, well-educated person and a great military leader. The delegates also greatly respected him. The delegates' choice proved to be a wise one because the convention needed a strong leader.

Civics Connection

Shays's Rebellion

After the Revolutionary War, times were difficult for Americans. Many people could not pay their debts. The laws seemed unfair to farmers and other workers. People could not vote if they could not afford to pay a polling tax. The court system sent people who owed money to prison.

A group of angry farmers from Massachusetts asked for help. They wanted lower taxes, paper money backed by gold, and a fair court system. When the reforms were not made, the farmers rebelled. The rebellion became known as Shays's Rebellion. Leaders were arrested and sentenced to death for trying to overthrow the government. However, the governor of Massachusetts, John Hancock, gave them their freedom.

Today, the Constitution protects citizens from unfair practices and abuses. But the government is also a strong central power. People may protest by picketing and boycotting, but not by violence.

1. Do you think the rebelling farmers should have been punished? Explain your answer.

2. Why do you think the Constitution allows United States citizens to protest? Explain your answer.

What do you think?

What problems do you think occur when a government is weak?

Lesson 2 Review On a sheet of paper, write the answers to the following questions. Use complete sentences.

1. What was wrong with the Articles of Confederation?

2. Why was the Annapolis Convention a failure?

3. Why did the delegates meet at the Constitutional Convention?

4. Why were the Constitutional Convention meetings held in secrecy?

5. Why did the delegates choose George Washington to lead the Constitutional Convention?

Guarantee

An agreement to protect something, such as property

Congress

The body of government that makes laws, consisting of the House of Representatives and the Senate

Exist

To be in place or operating

The original purpose of the Constitutional Convention was to adjust the Articles of Confederation. However, there were too many details to be worked out. It soon became clear that the delegates needed to develop a completely different system of government.

What Were the Virginia and New Jersey Plans?

One plan for a new government was presented by Edmund Randolph of Virginia. His plan included a much stronger central government and greater control by the larger states. The proposal became known as the "large-state plan," or Virginia Plan. It called for representatives based on population.

The plan was to establish a congress to make laws, a separate government branch to enforce the laws, and a court system to **guarantee** justice under the law. **Congress,** the lawmaking branch, was to be divided into two parts. Legislators in the lower house would be elected by the people. Members of the upper house would be chosen by the members of the lower house. The Virginia Plan, as Randolph saw it, was very democratic. It provided for government by the people.

After two weeks of heated discussion of the Virginia Plan, William Paterson of New Jersey presented another plan. The New Jersey Plan, or "small-state plan," provided for a system of government much like the one that already **existed.** Under this plan, each state was to have an equal vote in the government. The states would have much more control of the government.

Why Was a Compromise Needed?

The delegates examined each plan and expressed their points of view. As the summer temperatures soared, so did the tempers of the delegates. The debate became so strong that at times some delegates were ready to quit and call the convention a failure.

Wise old Benjamin Franklin, at age 81, calmed everyone down. The much younger delegates respected him and listened to his humorous but intelligent remarks. Washington's strong sense of reason encouraged the delegates to be willing to compromise.

The **deadlock** between the larger states and smaller states dragged on. The key issue was the amount of power the central government should have and how much power large and small states would continue to hold. A special committee was formed to try to work out a compromise.

Lesson 3 Review Decide if each description tells about the New Jersey Plan or the Virginia Plan. Write *New Jersey Plan* or *Virginia Plan* beside each number on a sheet of paper.

1. Presented by Edmund Randolph

2. States had equal votes

3. Congress was to make laws

4. Presented by William Paterson

5. Stronger central government

What do you think ?

Why do you think the amount of power state and central governments should hold caused such a debate?

Legislative branch

The branch of government that makes laws

Bill

A proposal for a new law

Runaway

Someone who is trying to escape

The Compromise Committee proposed a **legislative branch** made up of two houses—the House of Representatives and the Senate. These groups would form Congress, which would make laws. The committee proposed that the House of Representatives would be made up according to the population of each state. The states with more people would have more representatives. This pleased the members who supported the Virginia Plan. The committee suggested the Senate have two representatives from each state, regardless of its population. This pleased the delegates who supported the New Jersey Plan. Each house would be equal except that all **bills** dealing with money would be started in the House of Representatives. A bill is a proposal for a new law. The delegates accepted the plan, called the "Great Compromise," on July 16, 1787. Roger Sherman of Connecticut is credited with suggesting the Great Compromise.

What Other Compromises Were Made?

Other problems needed to be worked out. Southern states wanted slaves to be represented in the population count but not in taxation. Northern states protested. A compromise permitted three out of every five slaves to be included in the population and taxation count of the southern states. This plan is known as the Three-Fifths Compromise.

Other problems for the southern states involving slaves included **runaway** slaves. The committee proposed that all slaves who had run away be returned to their owners. Many in the South feared that Congress would try to control the number of slaves brought into the South. The committee ruled, however, that Congress could not affect the slave market until the year 1808.

Trade was of great concern to all states. The Compromise Committee recommended that Congress regulate trade between states and foreign countries. Duties would not be allowed between states. Tariffs would be permitted on goods coming to the United States from foreign countries.

Southern farmers were pleased. Under this plan, their **exports** to foreign countries would not be taxed. An export is a good sent to another country. Another very important part of the rulings was that states would not be allowed to print their own money. The ruling called for the central government to print money.

What Are the Executive and Judicial Branches?

The delegates decided that a president would be elected as the head of the executive branch of the government. The **executive branch** would enforce the laws. The president would serve a four-year term and would be responsible for choosing a group of **advisers.** An adviser is a person who gives information, advice, or help.

The Supreme Court would serve as the highest court in the country. The Supreme Court and lower courts would be part of the **judicial branch.** This branch would **interpret** the laws.

The Supreme Court has eight judges, called **justices.** Justices hear court cases from lower courts. The Supreme Court also has a chief justice who leads the other justices. John Jay of New York became the first chief justice in 1789.

The United States Federal Government

Legislative Branch—makes laws

House of Representatives:	Senate:	
Made up according to the population of each state	Two representatives from each state, regardless of its population	

Judicial Branch—interprets laws

Supreme Court:	Other courts:	
Highest court in the country	Hear most court cases	

Executive Branch—enforces laws

President:	Advisers:	
Head of the executive branch	Give information, advice, or help to the president	

The delegates signed the Constitution in 1787. George Washington, leader of the convention, is standing by the flags.

Federal government

A government that is divided between central and state governments

The three branches of government set up by the Constitution—the executive, legislative, and judicial branches—are still in place today. The delegates felt the branches provided for a separation of powers. The power would not rest in any one branch. The power is given to the **federal government** by the states. A federal government is one that is divided between central and state governments.

Who Signed the Constitution?

The Constitution did not please all of the delegates, even though many felt the Compromise Committee had done a good job. On September 17, 1787, the delegates signed the Constitution with the hope that the states would approve it. The delegates' work was done. It was up to the states to decide if the Constitution was acceptable as the law of the land.

What Was the Northwest Ordinance?

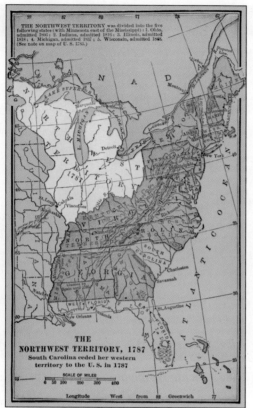

THE NORTHWEST TERRITORY was divided into the five following states (with Minnesota east of the Mississippi): 1. Ohio, admitted 1803; 2. Indiana, admitted 1816; 3. Illinois, admitted 1818; 4. Michigan, admitted 1837; 5. Wisconsin, admitted 1848. (See note on map of U. S. 1783.)

THE
NORTHWEST TERRITORY, 1787.
South Carolina ceded her western
territory to the U. S. in 1787

SCALE OF MILES
0   50   100   200   300   400

Longitude   West   from   Greenwich

This map shows the Northwest Territory in 1787.

During the debate over the Constitution, one important law was created. For many years, control of land east of the Mississippi River and north of the Ohio River had caused serious problems among the states. Based on Thomas Jefferson's plan of 1784, Congress passed the Northwest Ordinance in 1787. This law stated that the area would become three to five new states as soon as the population became large enough. The Northwest Territory is highlighted in yellow on the map to the left. This area became the states of Wisconsin, Michigan, Illinois, Indiana, and Ohio.

Word Bank

bill
executive
federal
judicial
legislative

Lesson 4 Review On a sheet of paper, write the correct word from the Word Bank to complete each sentence.

1. The _____ branch interprets laws.

2. A(n) _____ government is divided between central and state governments.

3. The _____ branch enforces the laws.

4. A(n) _____ is a proposal for a new law.

5. The _____ branch makes the laws.

What do you think ?

Is it necessary or important to have three branches of government? Why or why not?

Ratify

To approve something

Supreme

To the highest degree

Federalist

One who supported the Constitution

Anti-Federalist

One who felt that the Constitution gave the central government too much power

Essay

A piece of writing addressing a subject from a personal point of view

Circulate

To pass something from person to person or place to place

The people needed to decide if they would accept the Constitution. Each of the 13 states elected delegates to debate the issues and decide whether to approve the Constitution. When 9 of the 13 states approved, or **ratified,** the Constitution, it would become the **supreme** law of the land.

Not everyone supported the Constitution. Under the new plan, the power of the central government would increase. There was concern that the government would be too strong and would take away some of the freedoms that people enjoyed. People did not quite know what the Constitution could do, or how it could be enforced.

Who Were the Federalists and Anti-Federalists?

As the discussions continued in the states, two groups developed. Those who supported the Constitution were called **Federalists.** Those who felt that the Constitution gave the central government too much power were called **Anti-Federalists.** They feared that state governments would be destroyed and taxes would be increased. Farmers felt the Constitution favored other businesses. The Anti-Federalists thought that the Constitution did not provide for protection of personal freedoms.

The approval of the Constitution seemed unlikely. The Federalists—led by Alexander Hamilton, James Madison, and John Jay—fought hard for its ratification. The three men published a series of **essays** called the *Federalist Papers.* They explained what the Constitution really meant. The papers were **circulated** throughout the states. Support for the Constitution increased when George Washington agreed to serve as the first president if he was called upon to do so. The Constitution would probably not have been approved without the outstanding leadership of Hamilton, Madison, Jay, and Washington.

History in Your Life

The U.S. Census

After the Constitution was ratified, an accurate measure of the country's population was needed. The number of seats for a state in the House of Representatives was to be proportionate to its population. The government planned for a census. It would be taken to measure the United States population every 10 years. The first census was taken in 1790, counting 3.9 million people. At that time, the Constitution provided that only three-fifths of the slave count be used to give seats for Congress.

In 1902 the U.S. Bureau of the Census was formed. The Bureau has counted the population every 10 years since then. The 22nd census in 2000 counted more than 281 million Americans. The bureau now gathers information on race, gender, age, religion, occupation, and more. Census figures are still used to allot seats in Congress. They are also used to allot funds for social service and other government programs.

How Was the Constitution Ratified?

The first state to ratify was Delaware in 1787, followed by Pennsylvania and New Jersey. In 1788, Georgia and Connecticut ratified the Constitution. Massachusetts ratified it in February 1788 with the support of John Hancock. Maryland and South Carolina followed. New Hampshire was the ninth state to approve the Constitution. When that state ratified in June 1788, the United States officially had a new government. Without the support of New York and Virginia, however, the government would be at a serious disadvantage.

James Madison and John Marshall led the Federalists at the Virginia convention. Patrick Henry and George Mason led the Anti-Federalists. On June 25, 1788, Virginia ratified the Constitution.

Writing About History

Which right in the Bill of Rights benefits you most as a citizen of the United States? Write an essay in your notebook explaining why a certain part of the Bill of Rights is most important to you.

Alexander Hamilton led the Federalists in New York. The news that Virginia had ratified the Constitution helped Hamilton. On July 26, 1788, by a vote of 30 to 27, New York became the 11th state to approve the Constitution.

The last two states to ratify were North Carolina and Rhode Island. On November 21, 1789, North Carolina voted to approve the Constitution. It was not until May 29, 1790, that Rhode Island gave its approval. All 13 states had democratically approved the new form of government.

The new government began to take shape even before some states had ratified the Constitution. George Washington was elected president in February 1789 by **unanimous** consent. He took office in April 1789. John Adams, who had received the second largest number of votes, became vice president.

Why Was the Bill of Rights Added to the Constitution?

Some states did not like the Constitution because it did not clearly spell out personal freedoms. In 1789, it was suggested that provisions for such freedoms be added to the original document. In 1791, Congress adopted 10 **amendments**, or changes, to the Constitution. The first 10 amendments are described on page 148. These became known as the Bill of Rights. The amendments provided for personal freedoms.

Amendments 11 through 27 are also described on page 148. These 17 amendments have been added since the original Bill of Rights. You will learn more about these amendments in later chapters. The Constitution can be found in Appendix B of this textbook. The Bill of Rights and the amendments can also be found in Appendix C.

Bill of Rights

- **1st Amendment**
  Americans' rights to practice any religion, to express themselves in speech or writing, to give opinions in newspapers, books, and other printed materials, to **assemble** peacefully in public places, and to petition the government

- **2nd Amendment**
  The right to bear arms

- **3rd Amendment**
  Protection from having to house soldiers

- **4th Amendment**
  Protection from having your home searched

- **5th Amendment**
  Provides that certain steps be taken if someone is charged with a crime

- **6th Amendment**
  The right to a fair trial

- **7th Amendment**
  Civil lawsuits, court cases involving private rights, may be brought to a jury trial if it involves a sum of $20 or more

- **8th Amendment**
  The right to fair punishment

- **9th Amendment**
  The rights maintained by the people

- **10th Amendment**
  The rights maintained by the states and the people

Amendments 11–27

- **11th Amendment (1795)**
  Only citizens of the United States can use the courts

- **12th Amendment (1804)**
  Covers rules of the election of the president and vice president

- **13th Amendment (1865)**
  Slavery is abolished, or gotten rid of

- **14th Amendment (1868)**
  Civil rights of citizens; numbers of representatives in each state; qualifications to hold government offices; U.S. debt

- **15th Amendment (1870)**
  Male citizens, regardless of race or color, can vote in elections

- **16th Amendment (1913)**
  Congress has the power to collect income taxes

- **17th Amendment (1913)**
  The direct election of senators

- **18th Amendment (1919)**
  Making or selling liquor is against the law

- **19th Amendment (1920)**
  Women are given the right to vote

- **20th Amendment (1933)**
  Number of terms the president and members of Congress can serve

- **21st Amendment (1933)**
  Repeals, or gets rid of, the 18th Amendment

- **22nd Amendment (1951)**
  A person can be elected president for no more than two terms

- **23rd Amendment (1961)**
  Voting in the District of Columbia (Washington, D.C.)

- **24th Amendment (1964)**
  States cannot make people pay a tax in order to vote

- **25th Amendment (1967)**
  Says what happens if a president dies

- **26th Amendment (1971)**
  Citizens who are 18 years old can now vote

- **27th Amendment (1992)**
  Pay raises for members of Congress

Assemble
To gather together

Civil lawsuit
A court case involving private rights

Lesson 5 Review On a sheet of paper, write the letter of the description in Part 2 that matches the term in Part 1.

Part 1

1. Federalists
2. Anti-Federalists
3. Bill of Rights
4. amendment
5. Constitution

Part 2

A A change

B Supreme law of the land

C Supported the Constitution

D Felt the Constitution gave the central government too much power

E The first 10 amendments to the Constitution

What do you think?

How fair do you think the original Constitution was to women and groups such as enslaved Africans?

The Northwest Ordinance

In 1784, Thomas Jefferson wrote an early draft of what became the Northwest Ordinance. The Northwest Ordinance was enacted in 1787. It set forth the rules for the development of the area north of the Ohio River and east of the Mississippi. It was one of the most important parts of the Articles of Confederation. It clarified the way in which territories could become states. A map of the Northwest Territory appears on page 144. Here are some paragraphs from the Ordinance.

Be it ordained by the United States in Congress assembled, that the said territory, for the purposes of temporary government, be one district, subject, however, to be divided into two districts, as future circumstances may . . . make it expedient . . . .

Be it ordained . . . that there shall be appointed . . . by Congress, a governor for a term of three years . . . [and] . . . a secretary for a term of four years. . . . There shall also be appointed a court to consist of three judges.

The governor and judges . . . shall adopt . . . laws of the original States . . . .

The following articles shall be [a] compact between the original States and . . . the . . . territory . . . .

Art. 2 The inhabitants of the . . . territory shall be entitled to . . . a trial by jury, a proportionate representation . . . in the legislature, and of judicial proceedings according to . . . common law. . . . No cruel or unusual punishments shall be inflicted.

Art. 3 Schools and the means of education shall forever be encouraged. . . . The utmost good faith shall always be observed toward the Indians; their lands and property shall not be taken without their consent. . . .

Art. 5 There shall be formed in the . . . territory, not less than three nor more than five states; [and the boundaries of said States shall be fixed by federal guidelines] . . . . Whenever any of the said states have sixty thousand free inhabitants, it shall be . . . admitted to the Congress . . . on an equal footing with the original States in all respects.

Art. 6 There shall neither be slavery nor involuntary servitude in said territory.

Document-Based Questions

1. Congress appointed five people for the territory. What were their positions?

2. In what ways did the Northwest Ordinance protect the rights of citizens in the territory?

3. What did the Ordinance say about Indians and their land and property?

4. How many inhabitants did a territorial state need before it could be admitted to Congress?

5. How did the Northwest Ordinance control the spread of slavery?

Source: The Northwest Ordinance, by Thomas Jefferson, 1787.

- After the Revolutionary War, Americans had trouble settling to the West, experienced difficulties with trade, and had problems with the Spanish. The government under the Articles of Confederation was out of control.

- Delegates met in Annapolis, Maryland, in 1786 to work out some of the problems. The convention was a failure because so few delegates attended.

- In 1786, Daniel Shays led a rebellion to protest low farm prices and high state taxes. The rebellion, called Shays's Rebellion, lasted for several months.

- Delegates met at the Constitutional Convention in Philadelphia in 1787 to create a plan for a stronger central government. Two plans were discussed: The Virginia Plan favored a strong central government and more power to the larger states. The New Jersey Plan favored equal power between the states. The delegates agreed on a compromise.

- The delegates decided that three out of every five slaves would be included in the population and taxation count of the southern states. This plan is known as the Three-Fifths Compromise.

- They also agreed that Congress could not change the slave market until 1808.

- The Constitution set up three branches of government: the executive, legislative, and judicial.

- Congress passed the Northwest Ordinance in 1787. This law stated that the area east of the Mississippi River and north of the Ohio River would become three to five new states as soon as the population became large enough.

- The delegates signed the Constitution on September 17, 1787. Those who supported the Constitution were called Federalists. Anti-Federalists were those who felt that the Constitution gave the central government too much power. America officially had a new government by 1788.

- George Washington was elected the first president in 1789.

- Congress added the Bill of Rights to the Constitution in 1791. These are the first 10 amendments to the Constitution. They protect individual rights.

Chapter 7 REVIEW

Word Bank

Anti-Federalist

bill

executive branch

export

Federalist

import

judicial branch

legislative branch

pioneer

tariff

On a sheet of paper, write the correct word or words from the Word Bank to complete each sentence.

1. A tax on goods leaving or entering a place is called a(n) _____.

2. A good sent to another country is called a(n) _____.

3. The president belongs to the _____.

4. The Senate and House of Representatives belong to the _____.

5. A(n) _____ felt that the Constitution gave the central government too much power.

6. A(n) _____ is a good brought in from a foreign country.

7. A person who supported the Constitution was a(n) _____.

8. The Supreme Court belongs to the _____.

9. A(n) _____ settles land that has not been settled before.

10. A(n) _____ is a proposal for a new law.

On a sheet of paper, write the letter of the answer that correctly completes each sentence.

11. Anti-Federalists did not support the new Constitution because it gave _____.

   A too much power to states

   B too much power to central government

   C too little freedom to people

   D the South more voice than the North

12. The _____ provided for an equal voice for every state and state control of the federal government.

   A Virginia Plan   **C** Bill of Rights

   B New Jersey Plan   **D** Three-Fifths Compromise

13. The delegates wanted the federal government to have three branches so that _____.

   A each region would have its own branch

   B it could meet all needs

   C no branch would have too much power

   D the law would guarantee justice

On a sheet of paper, write the answers to the following questions. Use complete sentences.

14. What were the Articles of Confederation?

15. What powers did the government lack under the Articles of Confederation?

16. What was the purpose of the Constitutional Convention?

17. What was the Three-Fifths Compromise?

18. What was the purpose of the Bill of Rights?

Critical Thinking On a sheet of paper, write your response to each question. Use complete sentences.

19. It took a long time for the Constitution to be created and ratified. Why do you think it needed to take so long?

20. What do you think would have happened if the Federalists had not worked so hard to support the Constitution? Why?

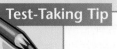

Test-Taking Tip

When choosing the correct term to complete a sentence, try each choice in the blank. Then choose the answer that best completes the statement.

8

Political Parties Develop

The United States was well on its way to a lasting government when the states ratified the Constitution. The next 20 years saw the first three presidents take office. The American political system also came to be during this period. In this chapter, you will learn about the first three presidents and the first political systems.

Goals for Learning

◆ To list the parts of Alexander Hamilton's financial plan

◆ To explain what Washington accomplished as president

◆ To describe what happened during President Adams's term

◆ To explain what happened in the election of 1800

◆ To describe what Jefferson accomplished as president

◆ To describe the Louisiana Purchase and why it was significant

◆ To describe some important Supreme Court cases

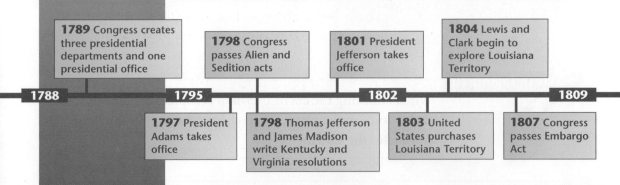

1789 Congress creates three presidential departments and one presidential office

1798 Congress passes Alien and Sedition acts

1801 President Jefferson takes office

1804 Lewis and Clark begin to explore Louisiana Territory

1788   1795   1802   1809

1797 President Adams takes office

1798 Thomas Jefferson and James Madison write Kentucky and Virginia resolutions

1803 United States purchases Louisiana Territory

1807 Congress passes Embargo Act

Cabinet

A group of advisers to the president

Treasury

A place where money is stored; the government department that handles money

The Constitution became law on June 21, 1788. It did not provide for a body of presidential advisers. Congress created three departments and one office in 1789. The heads of each department would help the president make decisions.

President Washington appointed four advisers: Thomas Jefferson from Virginia was named secretary of state; Alexander Hamilton from New York, secretary of the treasury; Henry Knox from Massachusetts, secretary of war; and Edmund Randolph from Virginia, attorney general. This group was called the **Cabinet.** A Cabinet is a group of advisers to the president. It was established as a permanent part of the American government. Washington's early decision to form a Cabinet shows how he thought a democratic government should work. He chose people whom he knew and trusted to be members of his Cabinet.

The first Cabinet was (from left) Henry Knox, Thomas Jefferson, Edmund Randolph, Alexander Hamilton, and President Washington.

What Was Alexander Hamilton's Financial Plan?

The United States was in debt because of the long, costly war and the weakness of the Articles of Confederation. This weakness was a result of conflict among the states. The **treasury,** a place where money is stored, was empty. Congress had passed the Tariff Act of 1789, but the money collected was not enough to pay the amount owed. The states also had large debts. To gain the respect of nations across the ocean, the United States would have to pay off this debt. In addition, the treasury needed money to run the government.

The task of getting the country out of debt was put into the hands of Alexander Hamilton, secretary of the treasury. Hamilton recommended that several important financial measures be taken.

Bond

A document that is proof of money owed

Interest

Money paid to someone who lends money

Details of Hamilton's financial plan include:

- Pay the $10 million owed to foreign nations.
- Pay the $40 million owed to people who had lent money to the government during the war.
- Have the central government take on the debts that the states were left with from the war.

Hamilton's plan was not popular with many in Congress. The idea of paying off the debts of the states was especially unpopular with southern states. These states had paid off most of their debts, while the northern states still had large amounts of unsettled debts. Jefferson and Madison did not agree with Hamilton's plan. However, they agreed to help him gain the support of Congress. In exchange, they wanted Hamilton to do them a favor. Hamilton was to try to obtain a southern location as the nation's capital instead of New York. Hamilton agreed. With the help of Jefferson and Madison, Hamilton's plan passed in Congress. The District of Columbia, now our nation's capital, was established.

FEDERAL HALL

In order to decrease the debt to people who had lent money to the government, Hamilton suggested giving them **bonds** that would pay **interest** over a period of time. A bond is a document that is proof of money owed. Interest is money paid to someone who lends money.

George Washington was officially made president in this building, Federal Hall, in New York City. This was the nation's capital at the time. The capital later became the District of Columbia.

Industry
Related to business and manufacturing

Hamilton also helped organize the First Bank of the United States as a safe place for funds collected as taxes. He set up the United States mint where the first American coins were put into use. Hamilton gave the country a sound financial plan.

Under Hamilton's plan, the government was able to pay off its debts. Taxes raised enough money to keep the government working. Trade increased and **industry** grew. The people of other countries, as well as Americans, gained a greater respect for the United States government.

Lesson 1 Review On a sheet of paper, write the correct word or words from the Word Bank to complete each sentence.

Word Bank

Alexander Hamilton

bonds

Cabinet

northern

southern

treasury

1. The president's team of close advisers is called the _____.

2. In 1788, the United States had many large debts and an empty _____.

3. As secretary of the treasury, _____ developed a financial plan.

4. The _____ states did not want the country to pay off the debts of the _____ states.

5. Part of the plan was to give _____ to people owed money by the government.

What do you think

What do you think may have happened if the United States had not paid off its debt?

Biography

Mother Elizabeth Seton: 1774–1821

Mother Elizabeth Seton was the first native-born American to be declared a saint. Born Elizabeth Ann Bayley, she married William M. Seton in New York in 1794. The couple had five children. After her husband died in 1803, Elizabeth became a nun. Called Mother Seton, she founded the Daughters of Charity in 1809. She started the first private religious school and the first Roman Catholic orphanage in the United States. On September 14, 1975, the Roman Catholic Church made her Saint Elizabeth Ann Seton. Her feast day is celebrated on January 4.

Political party

A group that represents a certain political belief

Affairs

The day-to-day business of a person or group

Disagreement

A quarrel over something

Neutral

Not siding with any particular person or group

Alexander Hamilton's financial plan played a large part in the development of **political parties.** A political party is a group that represents a certain political belief. Those who supported his plans formed the Federalist Party. Thomas Jefferson and James Madison were among those who felt that states should have more power to run their own **affairs,** or day-to-day business. These men helped form the Democratic-Republican Party. The new party supported stronger state government. The Federalist Party wanted a much stronger central government.

The Federalists generally received their strongest support from wealthy merchants and bankers. Farmers, laborers, and small shopkeepers usually backed the Democratic-Republicans. Many people thought Washington was a Federalist, although he never sided with either party. He often warned that having opposing parties could lead to further **disagreement.** Most of the leaders during Washington's presidency and that of the next president, John Adams, were Federalists.

Alexander Hamilton

Why Did Washington Want Neutrality?

President Washington had other concerns besides the nation's debt and the newly formed political parties. France declared war against Great Britain in 1793. Because the French had helped the Americans during the Revolutionary War, they expected some help in return. The United States was in no condition to fight another war so soon. The military was very weak and the country was far in debt. Washington felt it was unwise to plunge into another war, and Hamilton agreed with him. Jefferson felt that the Americans should help France. After careful thought, the president chose to remain **neutral** and not help either country. The needs of the United States had to come first.

Navigation

Travel by water

Public service

Any job or effort done for the good of the people, such as a government job

What Problems Developed in the Western Lands?

Great Britain and Spain continued to interfere with Americans as they moved westward. The British sold firearms and whiskey to the American Indians in the north. The Indians were fighting to protect their land, which the settlers also claimed. War was likely if the British continued to cause trouble.

President Washington could not risk a war with the British and the American Indians. He sent John Jay to London in 1794 to discuss a treaty. Jay got the British to agree to leave their American forts. Americans would pay their debts to Britain. The British would repay American shippers for cargo they had seized.

Jay's Treaty, as it was called, was not very popular with Congress. It did not protect American ships bound for France from being seized by the British. However, President Washington urged its approval in order to maintain peace with Britain.

What Agreement Did Spain and America Reach?

After Jay's Treaty had been approved, the president needed to act on the problem with Spain. The Spanish controlled the Mississippi River as well as New Orleans, which the Americans needed for a trade route. Spain also controlled a section of Florida that Americans occupied. Surprisingly, Spain agreed to permit free **navigation** on the Mississippi in 1795. This opened the port of New Orleans. In addition, the disputed west Florida territory was turned over to the United States.

How Did Washington Contribute to America?

President Washington's health was failing after so many years of **public service.** Public service is any job or effort done for the good of the people. The country, however, still needed him as its leader. He agreed to a second term.

As differences in political ideas **emerged** near the end of Washington's second term, two separate political parties were taking shape. Washington was unsure how to handle the increasing arguments about how the government should be run. Tired and longing for his Virginia home, he refused to serve a third term. Washington died two years later at the age of 67.

The **contributions** George Washington made to the United States were many. As the first president of a new nation, he had no example to follow. Everywhere, there were problems that needed his guidance. He chose excellent advisers and put the country on its feet financially and politically. Washington kept the young country out of European wars. He is called the "Father of His Country" because of these contributions.

Lesson 2 Review On a sheet of paper, write the answers to the following questions. Use complete sentences.

1. Why did George Washington want to stay out of the war?

2. Why did American settlers in western lands call for action against the British?

3. Why did Americans need to use the Mississippi River and New Orleans?

4. What did John Jay's treaty do?

5. Why is George Washington called the "Father of His Country"?

What do you think

Which one of George Washington's contributions do you think was most important? Explain your answer.

History in Your Life

A Smallpox Vaccine

In 1796, English physician Edward Jenner discovered a way to prevent smallpox. In America, outbreaks of smallpox had been destructive, especially among American Indians, to whom the disease was previously unknown. In 1799, Harvard medical professor Benjamin Waterhouse read about Jenner's discovery. Within a year, Waterhouse gave the first U.S. vaccinations. Today, smallpox has been wiped out in the United States. Medical researchers now have developed other vaccines to protect people from diseases such as measles and polio.

Candidate

A person who has been selected to run for a political office

Electoral vote

A ballot cast by a person who is chosen to vote for the president and vice president

John Adams had served for eight years as vice president. The Federalists chose him to be their **candidate** for the next president. A candidate is a person who has been selected to run for a political office. Adams was well educated and experienced in government. He had been present at the First and Second Continental Congress, and he was a signer of the Declaration of Independence. He had helped achieve peace with Britain through the Treaty of Paris in 1783. Like Washington, he was strongly against any change in the power of the central government. He was known to be a stubborn man with very strong opinions.

Democratic-Republicans backed Thomas Jefferson of Virginia in his bid for the presidency. When the election of 1796 was held, Adams won, but not by much. Adams received 71 **electoral votes.** With 68 electoral votes, Thomas Jefferson became vice president. This put Adams in a difficult position. He, as president, was a loyal Federalist. He favored a strong central government, whereas his vice president was a supporter of strong state governments.

What Was the XYZ Affair?

Several European countries were at war with France when John Adams took office in 1797. The American policy of neutrality angered the French. Also, the signing of Jay's Treaty had led France to think that America was allied with Great Britain. The French began to seize American ships that carried supplies to the British.

President Adams wanted to avoid a war. He sent a group to work out a deal with France. Three secret French agents known as X, Y, and Z refused to cooperate with the delegates unless the United States gave them a large amount of money. The delegates rejected the demands for money and reported the demands to Congress. This became known as the XYZ Affair.

In preparation for war with France, Congress set up the Department of the Navy. During the next two years, the U.S. Navy fought several battles against France, capturing 80 French ships while losing only one of their own. Finally, in 1800, the French signed an agreement to stop interfering with American merchant ships. However, France refused to pay any earlier shipping losses. Many Americans wanted the government to take much stronger action.

John Adams was not a popular president. He was an honest man and a loyal American, but he was also considered to be **arrogant** and narrow minded. He would not compromise on issues. There was evidence of his unpopularity. For example, newspapers often did not support his policies. In addition, many foreigners coming to the United States joined the opposing party.

What Roles and Rights Did Women Have?

Before the Revolutionary War, the role of most married women was to take care of the home and do what their husband told them to do. The women had to make most household items such as clothing, prepare meals, and take care of the children. They had few legal rights and could not own property. If the family lived on a farm, women also had to help with the farm chores. During the war, some poor women traveled with their husbands from camp to camp, cooking meals and helping the soldiers.

First Lady Abigail Adams supported women's rights. She wanted her husband, John Adams, to press for more freedom for women in America. He would not.

By the end of the Revolutionary War, women's roles had changed somewhat. Some of the work that women had done was now being done in factories.

This gave women more free time. It became more acceptable for women to work outside the home, but only in jobs such as teaching.

After the Revolutionary War, women who lived in New Jersey could vote if they owned property. However, this right was taken away from them in 1807. It would be many more years before women won **suffrage,** or the right to vote.

What Did the Alien and Sedition Acts Do?

The Federalists decided to take action to preserve their control. Congress, controlled by the Federalists, passed a series of harsh laws called the Alien and Sedition acts in 1798. Under the Alien Act, **immigrants** had to wait 14 years before they could become United States citizens. An immigrant is a person who comes to live in a new country. Before the Alien Act, the waiting period had been five years. In addition, **aliens** could be **deported,** or put into prison, if they were judged to be dangerous. An alien is someone who lives in one country but is a citizen of another. To deport means to send someone away from a country.

The Sedition Act made it a crime for anyone to speak out, write, or print articles against the government. Those who did and were convicted had to pay a fine of $5,000 and serve up to five years in prison.

The Federalists' actions caused great excitement and became a major issue in the election of 1800. Immigrants feared they might be deported. Democratic-Republican writers were fined for their comments. Many people thought these laws went against the Constitution. The Constitution provided for freedom of the press and freedom of speech. The Federalists were trying to become more powerful by weakening those who disagreed.

Why Were the Kentucky and Virginia Resolutions Written?

Thomas Jefferson and James Madison, in response to the Alien and Sedition acts, wrote the Kentucky and Virginia **resolutions** in 1798. A resolution is an expression of opinion or intent voted on by a group. The legislatures of those two states passed the resolutions. The writers stated that the Alien and Sedition Acts were not **constitutional**—the acts did not follow what was set forth in the Constitution. The states had created the national government and limited its powers to those written in the Constitution. States did not have to obey acts that were not constitutional.

What Happened in the Election of 1800?

The election of 1800 was the first real contest between Democratic-Republicans and Federalists. Although the Democratic-Republican Party was formed before the election of 1796, its competition with the Federalist Party did not develop until 1800.

The Federalists supported John Adams. Adams selected Charles Pinckney to be his **running mate** for vice president. A running mate is a candidate who runs for office with another candidate who is running for a different position. Thomas Jefferson was

the Democratic-Republican candidate for president. His ideas appealed to farmers, small business owners, and ordinary workers. The Democratic-Republicans chose Aaron Burr of New York as Jefferson's running mate. Jefferson did not like Burr, but Burr was popular in New York. Jefferson felt Burr could help win votes in the North.

Aaron Burr

An unusual problem came up with this election. The Constitution called for an **electoral college.** This was a group of people called **electors** who were chosen to elect the president and vice president. The Constitution stated that each elector was to vote for any two candidates. When the votes were counted, Thomas Jefferson and Aaron Burr had 73 electoral votes each. Adams had 65 votes, and Pinckney had 64. The Constitution said the person with the highest number of votes would become the president. The person with the second highest number of votes would become vice president. Because the vote was tied, the House of Representatives then had to decide the election.

How Did Hamilton Influence Congress?

Congress found it difficult to choose between Jefferson and Burr. The Federalists wanted to elect Burr. His political views were closer to the Federalists than those of Thomas Jefferson. Alexander Hamilton, a Federalist, helped come up with the final outcome of the election. Hamilton had very little regard for Jefferson's political ideas, but he thought even less of Burr. In Hamilton's opinion, Burr could not be trusted. Hamilton was able to swing the vote in Jefferson's favor. Thomas Jefferson became president, and Aaron Burr became vice president. The Democratic-Republicans had gained control of both the executive and the legislative branches of the government.

To prevent such a tie from happening in the future, Congress passed the 12th Amendment to the Constitution in 1804. This stated that electors would vote separately for president and vice president.

What Did the Federalists Accomplish?

Although the Federalist Party was defeated in the election of 1800, members of this party had helped establish the country. They had put the Constitution into effect and helped the country recover from debt. They had helped build trade with other countries and kept America out of war with France and Great Britain.

Then and Now

Would you be surprised to know that the first political parties in the United States developed over a disagreement? They differed over how much power the federal government should have. Federalists wanted to increase the government's power. Anti-Federalists wanted to weaken the government's power.

Did you know that today's two major political parties developed from these first parties? Under Thomas Jefferson, the Anti-Federalists became the Republican Party. They emphasized the democratic process. Later they became the Democratic-Republican Party and finally were called the Democratic Party.

Many Federalists became National Republicans. Later they became Whigs. The Whig Party split when members could not agree on issues. A part of the Whig Party developed into today's Republican Party.

Word Bank

Alexander Hamilton

Alien Act

electoral votes

freedom of speech

freedom of the press

John Adams

Lesson 3 Review On a sheet of paper, write the correct words from the Word Bank to complete each sentence.

1. In 1796, _____, a Federalist, became president of the United States.

2. The _____ forced immigrants to wait 14 years before they could become citizens.

3. The Sedition Act went against the Constitution's rights of _____ and _____.

4. In the election of 1800, both Thomas Jefferson and Aaron Burr received 73 _____.

5. Because he did not trust Aaron Burr, _____ helped Thomas Jefferson become president.

What do you think ?

Why do you think the Federalists passed some unconstitutional laws?

Thomas Jefferson was a rich landowner from Virginia. Despite his wealth, he did not dress in fancy clothes. Many thought he was untidy and not very friendly. He had been the author of the Declaration of Independence. He had a different **philosophy** of government. Philosophy is a person's beliefs or way of understanding something. Jefferson believed that the government could do only what the Constitution allowed.

Philosophy

A person's beliefs or way of understanding something

Inaugurate

To swear someone into office

Inaugural address

A speech a president gives to accept the presidency

What Did Jefferson Do as President?

Jefferson was sworn in as president, or **inaugurated,** in the District of Columbia in 1801. In his speech to accept the presidency, called an **inaugural address,** he strongly urged all political parties to join together for the good of the country. Jefferson knew that progress would continue only if the people were united.

Other events during Jefferson's term include:

- The Alien and Sedition acts ended. People imprisoned under those acts were released, and charges against them were removed from the records.
- The time a person needed to live in America before becoming a citizen was lowered to five years.
- The remaining federal debt was lowered.
- The United States Military Academy at West Point was established.
- Slaves could no longer be imported into the United States (although approximately 25,000 more Africans who became enslaved were imported illegally by 1860).
- America bought the Louisiana Territory.

Geography Note

The Louisiana Purchase stretched to the Rocky Mountains west from the Mississippi River, and northwest from New Orleans. Rich farmlands and towering mountains were part of the purchase. It was rich in oil, forests, and gold and other minerals. These resources attracted settlers to the west.

What Was the Louisiana Purchase?

After the French and Indian War, France had surrendered some land west of the Mississippi River to Spain. In 1800, Spain had been forced to return the land, known as Louisiana, to France. Jefferson was troubled by the move. New Orleans was an important port for international trade. America had an agreement with Spain that it could bring in goods to New Orleans. Two years after Napoleon Bonaparte, emperor of France, took control of the region, this agreement was withdrawn. This prevented eastern trade.

President Jefferson sent James Monroe to Paris, France, in 1803 to buy as much of Florida and New Orleans as he could for $10 million. Robert Livingston, American **ambassador** to France, was already **negotiating** with Napoleon in Paris. An ambassador is a representative from a country who works out problems with another country. Napoleon offered to sell the Louisiana region for $15 million. America would **acquire** 828,000 square miles of land for roughly three cents an acre. Jefferson turned to Congress for approval of the purchase. Congress approved, and the Louisiana Territory became part of America on December 20, 1803. This is known as the Louisiana Purchase.

The election of Jefferson, a Democratic-Republican, had caused a sharp division between the Democratic-Republicans and the Federalists. The Federalists opposed the purchase of the Louisiana Territory. They thought the land was worthless and did not share Jefferson's support for western expansion. They feared that the new region would be divided into many new states. New England states had many Federalists. Adding western and southern states would reduce the power of the Federalists. Federalists also argued that the purchase was unconstitutional.

The Federalists gained little support for their view, however. A new spirit of unity emerged in the West. Jefferson had once been viewed as a threat to organized government. But he had become a very popular president. Even New England supported President Jefferson.

With the addition of the Louisiana Territory, westward expansion would certainly continue. The obvious problem was the spread of slavery. The fertile land and mild climate would be ideal for slave-labor crops. The balance of political power would surface between slave states and non-slave states. In addition to the political considerations, the economic and social issues added to the tension.

Why Was the Louisiana Purchase Important?

The Louisiana Territory doubled the size of America. Now America controlled the entire Mississippi River and could use the port of New Orleans. America had gained **resources** in the fertile Louisiana land. In time, the Louisiana Territory would be divided into all or parts of 15 additional states: Louisiana, Arkansas, Missouri, Iowa, Minnesota, North and South Dakota, Nebraska, Kansas, Oklahoma, Colorado, Wyoming, Texas, New Mexico, and Montana.

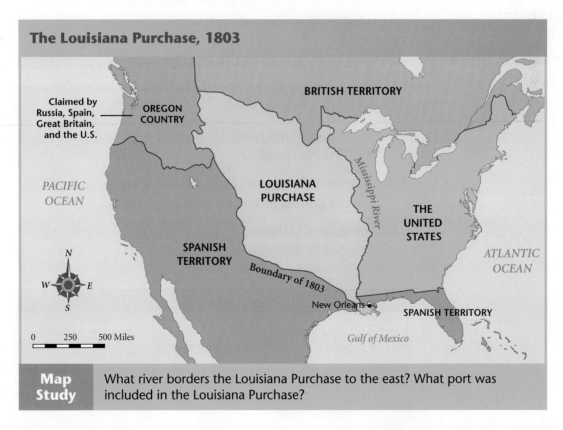

The Louisiana Purchase, 1803

Claimed by Russia, Spain, Great Britain, and the U.S.

OREGON COUNTRY

BRITISH TERRITORY

PACIFIC OCEAN

LOUISIANA PURCHASE

Mississippi River

THE UNITED STATES

ATLANTIC OCEAN

SPANISH TERRITORY

Boundary of 1803

New Orleans

SPANISH TERRITORY

Gulf of Mexico

0   250   500 Miles

Map Study What river borders the Louisiana Purchase to the east? What port was included in the Louisiana Purchase?

It Happened in History

Toussaint L'Ouverture was a former slave. He became an important leader in the 1791 revolution of slaves against the French on the island of Haiti. By 1801, he had established himself as governor of the entire island.

Napoleon had planned to establish a naval base in Haiti to protect his New World empire. He sent a large military force to gain control of the island. Toussaint resisted but was arrested and exiled to France. General Jean-Jacques Dessalines assumed the leadership of the rebels. Yellow fever weakened the French military to the point that it was defeated in 1803. On January 1, 1804, the French colony became the independent black nation of Haiti. As of 1804, there were two independent nations in the Western world—the United States and Haiti.

Lesson 4 Review Choose the word or words in parentheses that best complete each sentence. Write your answers on a sheet of paper.

1. (John Adams, Thomas Jefferson, James Monroe) was inaugurated as president in 1801.

2. In 1800, Spain was forced to return the land west of the Mississippi, known as Louisiana, to (Great Britain, France, the United States).

3. The United States bought the Louisiana Territory for ($20, $10, $15) million.

4. (Napoleon Bonaparte, Great Britain, James Monroe) sold the Louisiana Territory to the United States.

5. The state of (Missouri, Florida, Montana) was not included in the Louisiana Purchase.

What do you think ?

In his acceptance speech, Jefferson called for all political parties to work together. Why do you think he said this?

Sacajawea with Lewis and Clark

Jefferson wanted to know as much as possible about what the United States had gained in the Louisiana Purchase. In 1804, he sent Meriwether Lewis and William Clark to explore the unknown northern regions.

Beginning at St. Louis, they journeyed northwest to the source of the Missouri River. They crossed the Rocky Mountains into Oregon Country, where they followed the Columbia River to the Pacific Ocean. They were guided by a Shoshone woman, Sacajawea.

Lewis and Clark brought back information to Jefferson about the peoples, wildlife, and lands of Oregon Country. Many years later, the findings of Lewis and Clark would help America make a claim to that area.

Louisiana Purchase Explorations

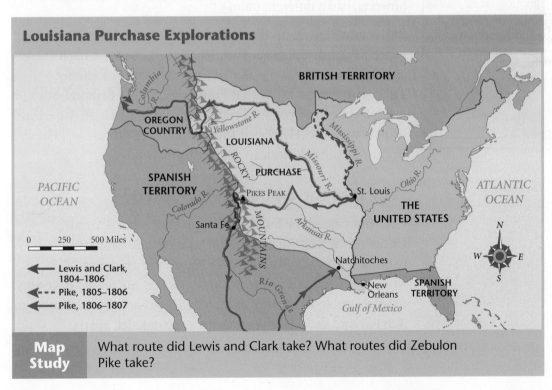

BRITISH TERRITORY

OREGON COUNTRY

Columbia R.

Yellowstone R.

LOUISIANA

Mississippi R.

PACIFIC OCEAN

SPANISH TERRITORY

Colorado R.

ROCKY

PURCHASE

Missouri R.

PIKES PEAK

Ohio R.

St. Louis

THE UNITED STATES

ATLANTIC OCEAN

Santa Fe

MOUNTAINS

Arkansas R.

N
W   E
S

0   250   500 Miles

← Lewis and Clark, 1804–1806
◄--- Pike, 1805–1806
← Pike, 1806–1807

Rio Grande

Natchitoches

New Orleans

SPANISH TERRITORY

Gulf of Mexico

Map Study	What route did Lewis and Clark take? What routes did Zebulon Pike take?

Writing About History

Write a speech to Americans as if you are President Jefferson. Explain the difficult problems the nation faces and offer some suggestions for solving them. Include an introduction, body, and conclusion in your speech.

In 1805 and 1806, Zebulon Pike explored the northern regions of the Louisiana Purchase. He was seeking the source of the Mississippi River. In 1806 and 1807, he led an expedition to the Southwest. He followed the Arkansas River to the Rockies, and reached a mountain he would name Pikes Peak in Colorado. However, this expedition was cut short when he traveled into Spanish territory where he was jailed for a time in what is now New Mexico.

How Did Jefferson Avoid War?

During Jefferson's second term as president, Great Britain and France were again at war. Napoleon's army was in full force and had conquered all his enemies except Great Britain. The United States was neutral and traded freely with France and Great Britain. American businesses **prospered** as ships carried supplies to both countries. Neither France nor Great Britain looked favorably upon America trading with its enemy. Jefferson believed the oceans were neutral and that ships could move freely. The British and French, however, had a different point of view.

Both countries set up **blockades.** A blockade is something that prevents goods or people from entering a country. Each country forbade other countries to trade with its enemy. Thomas Jefferson knew that France and Great Britain both needed supplies from America. He proposed that all American ships stay home. He hoped this would force France and Great Britain to allow American ships into their ports.

Why Was the Embargo Act Passed?

Congress passed the Embargo Act on December 22, 1807. Under this act, no American ships could trade with foreign nations. Jefferson called this act a "peaceable **coercion.**" If it worked, it would show the world that war is not always necessary to solve problems. American merchants did not like the Embargo Act. For one and a half years, American trade fell apart.

Many shippers chose to disobey the law. Jefferson realized that the Embargo Act had been a failure. President Jefferson signed a law repealing the Embargo Act in March of 1809, only a few days before he left office.

Who Was John Marshall?

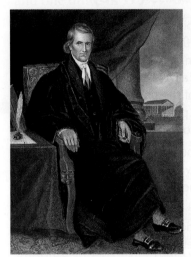

John Marshall

The 1789 Judiciary Act had set up the Supreme Court. President John Adams named John Marshall chief justice of the Supreme Court in 1801. Marshall was mainly self-educated, with little law school experience. He was a wealthy Virginia Federalist who had served at Valley Forge during the American Revolutionary War.

Under Justice Marshall, the Supreme Court tried a number of important cases. The cases strengthened the "checks and balances" among the three branches of the federal government. The landmark case of *Marbury v. Madison* in 1803 was very important. It clearly established that it was the responsibility of the judicial department to explain the law. Chief Justice Marshall heard many other cases as well. These included *Fletcher v. Peck,* 1810, and *McCulloch v. Maryland,* 1819. The Fletcher case was especially important. It established the right of the Supreme Court to strike down state laws that disagreed with the federal Constitution.

John Marshall was chief justice from 1801 to 1835. During that time, he helped make the Constitution a document that could meet the changing needs of the nation.

Lesson 5 Review On a sheet of paper, write the answers to the following questions. Use complete sentences.

1. What did Lewis and Clark do?

2. What did Zebulon Pike do?

3. What did President Jefferson do to avoid war?

4. What was the Embargo Act?

5. What did John Marshall do?

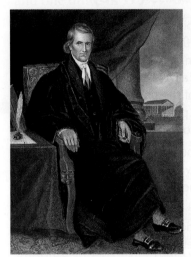

What do you think

In addition to the Embargo Act, what do you think could have been done to avoid war with France and Great Britain?

Chapter 8 REVIEW

Word Bank

Alien Act

Cabinet

elector

electoral college

Embargo Act

Jay's Treaty

political party

Sedition Act

XYZ Affair

On a sheet of paper, write the correct word or words from the Word Bank to complete each sentence.

1. _____ got the British to leave their forts that were built on American soil.

2. The _____ involved three secret French agents who refused to cooperate with American delegates unless the United States gave them money.

3. The group of advisers who help the president is called a(n) _____.

4. The _____ is a group of people chosen to elect the president and vice president.

5. Immigrants had to wait 14 years before they could become United States citizens under the _____.

6. The _____ made it a crime for anyone to speak out, write, or print articles against the government.

7. A person who is chosen to vote for the president and vice president is called a(n) _____.

8. A(n) _____ is a group that represents a certain political belief.

9. Under the _____, no American ships could trade with foreign nations.

On a sheet of paper, write the letter of the answer that correctly answers each question.

10. Who chose Thomas Jefferson as president in 1800?

   A the electoral college

   B the majority of citizens who voted

   C both houses of Congress

   D the House of Representatives

11. What was not constitutional according to the Virginia and Kentucky resolutions?

    A the election of 1800   **C** the XYZ Affair

    B the Alien and Sedition acts   **D** immigration

12. Who led the expedition to explore the Louisiana Purchase?

    A Meriwether Lewis and William Clark

    B James Monroe and Robert Livingston

    C Sacajawea

    D Zebulon Pike

On a sheet of paper, write the answers to the following questions. Use complete sentences.

13. List three things Washington accomplished as president.

14. Which debts were to be paid off through Alexander Hamilton's financial plan?

15. What two events happened during President Adams's term?

16. Why was the election of 1800 unlike other elections?

17. List three events that happened during Jefferson's term.

18. What was the Louisiana Purchase? How did the United States benefit from it?

Critical Thinking On a sheet of paper, write your response to each question. Use complete sentences.

19. What makes the job of president of the United States so difficult?

20. American Indians were left out of negotiating the Louisiana Purchase. Why do you think that was so?

Test-Taking Tip

Answer all test questions as completely as you can. When you are asked to explain an answer, write complete sentences.

9 The Young Nation Goes to War

The first three U.S. presidents made it clear that the nation was not ready for another war. However, the troubles with France and Great Britain continued. Something had to be done to solve the problems. President James Madison was next in line to try to find a solution. In the end, the young country was forced into another war—the War of 1812. In this chapter, you will learn what caused this war and its outcome.

Goals for Learning

♦ To describe President Madison and his policies

♦ To list the causes of the War of 1812

♦ To identify the battles fought during the War of 1812

♦ To describe the outcome of the War of 1812

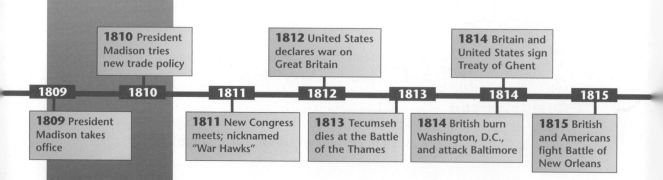

1810 President Madison tries new trade policy

1812 United States declares war on Great Britain

1814 Britain and United States sign Treaty of Ghent

1809 | 1810 | 1811 | 1812 | 1813 | 1814 | 1815

1809 President Madison takes office

1811 New Congress meets; nicknamed "War Hawks"

1813 Tecumseh dies at the Battle of the Thames

1814 British burn Washington, D.C., and attack Baltimore

1815 British and Americans fight Battle of New Orleans

James Madison, the Democratic-Republican candidate from Virginia, became the fourth president in 1809. Madison was a quiet, intelligent man. He had many years of political experience. He became president just after the Embargo Act was repealed. He faced the challenge of finding a new policy for peace.

Restriction

An act of limiting or preventing something

Aggressive

Forceful

Influence

The ability to convince someone of something

Conflict

A fight, battle, or war

What New Policy Did Madison Propose?

President Madison tried to continue the neutral policy of Jefferson. In 1810, Madison proposed a new policy that permitted foreign trade. Madison wanted to bring back trade lost under the Embargo Act. His policy called for either France or Great Britain to stop its **restrictions** against American ships. If they did, America would refuse to trade with the other country.

Napoleon of France took advantage of Madison's proposal. He planned to use the United States against his British enemy. Britain's revenues would be greatly decreased with American ports closed to British goods. In August 1810, Napoleon stated that France would accept American trade and would not seize American ships on the high seas.

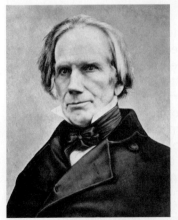

Henry Clay helped push the United States into the War of 1812.

What Brought America Closer to War?

Important changes took place in 1811. The new 12th Congress included young, **aggressive** members. They wanted changes in policy. They did not like the way Great Britain was treating the United States. They became known as the "War Hawks."

Henry Clay was a member of Congress from Kentucky and a good speaker. Clay was chosen to lead the House of Representatives. Clay was only 34 years of age, but he had great **influence.** He and his followers were tired of American Indian raids on the frontier and blamed the British. The War Hawks wanted to put an end to the Indian **conflict.** They also wanted to make sure there was freedom on the seas.

War would result if other countries denied America that right. Meanwhile, the British continued to seize American ships and sailors as before. The British took nearly 1,000 vessels, and the French captured more than 500 American ships. At that time, both Great Britain and France were enemies of the United States.

Anti-British feelings had existed since colonial days. Americans did not have these feelings toward the French. France had helped America during the Revolutionary War. Jefferson and Madison looked upon France as a friend. Unfortunately, Madison trusted Napoleon. He did not know that Napoleon only wanted to use America in his war against the British.

What do you think

Do you think the War Hawks were right or wrong to feel the way they did toward Britain? Explain your answer.

Lesson 1 Review On a sheet of paper, write the answers to the following questions. Use complete sentences.

1. What was the trade policy that President Madison proposed?

2. How did Napoleon use the United States?

3. Who were the War Hawks?

4. What changes did the War Hawks want to make?

5. What did the Americans think of the British?

History in Your Life

Robert Fulton's Steamboat

In 1807, Robert Fulton built the first steamboat that could be used to transport goods. He used a steam-powered engine made in England and an unusual set of wheel-shaped paddles from another American inventor. On August 17, 1807, his new ship—the *Clermont*—sailed the Hudson River from New York to Albany in 32 hours. It was the first of many commercial steamboats. Those boats carried grain from western farms down the Ohio and Mississippi rivers to the Gulf of Mexico. From the Gulf, the grain could easily be shipped to large ports on the east coast and in Europe. These ships helped to open up America's newly acquired western territories, enabling settlements there to thrive.

Cash crop

A crop that can be sold

Speaker of the House

Leader of the House of Representatives

Geography Note

A port is a protected stretch of water where ships can load and unload cargo and passengers. Ports may be natural or artificial. They may lie on a seacoast for easy access to the ocean. Inland ports need a wide, deep river that large ships can navigate. Military, fishing, and oil ports are all important for a country's economy and defense.

The first three presidents—Washington, Adams, and Jefferson—had kept the country out of war. Each was certain that a war would destroy the young nation. By the time Madison became president, 20 years had passed since the Constitution established the new government. America was a new land with bold ideas.

The country's population had grown from about four million to more than seven million by 1810. The area of the United States had doubled in size. New England was rapidly developing industries, southern states were producing valuable **cash crops,** and slavery was increasing. A cash crop is a crop that can be sold. The frontier was being pushed farther west.

The new breed of Americans had only faint memories of colonial America. They may have felt the time had come for the United States to take action, and the War Hawks led the way. At the same time, Great Britain agreed to Madison's earlier offer to reopen trade between the two countries. Unfortunately, Madison was unaware of this decision.

What Were People's Attitudes Toward the War?

Henry Clay led the House of Representatives as **Speaker of the House.** He and John C. Calhoun of South Carolina saw British-owned Canada as an easy target. They thought that Canada could be defeated in just a few weeks. The War Hawks continued to stir up public opinion so that President Madison would have no choice but to declare war on Great Britain. With all the war talk, it was difficult to work toward a peaceful settlement.

The northern states, led by the Federalists, strongly opposed a war with Great Britain. But others saw several reasons for war against the British. The British had seized American ships and sailors, interfered with trade, and closed their ports to American goods.

Tecumseh tried to start a confederacy against settlers.

Tecumseh, chief of the Shawnees, tried to **organize** an American Indian **confederacy** against western settlers. A confederacy is a group that has formed an alliance. Many Americans were certain that the British would supply the Indians with weapons from Canada.

Why Was the United States Not Prepared for War?

The **regular army** of the United States was poorly trained and very small. This was the nation's permanent army. It had fewer than 10,000 soldiers. The generals were old and had little or no experience in real war situations. Over the 30-year period since the Revolutionary War, the army had become less and less important. The country could not pay for a big, well-trained army because it had no money to support it.

America's navy was also not in shape for war. It had only 16 warships. The United States would be no match for the powerful Great Britain, which had the largest navy in the world. Even with these disadvantages, talk of war still continued.

At the same time, America's foreign trade had almost come to a complete standstill. Trade brought in money for the government through tariffs. Now, without the revenue from tariffs, America had no money to fight a war.

Elbridge Gerry: 1744–1814

Elbridge Gerry was active in early American politics. He signed the Declaration of Independence. He refused to sign the Constitution because he said it gave too much power to the national government. Gerry served in the House of Representatives, and he was James Madison's vice president from 1813 to 1814.

But Gerry is not best remembered for these activities. In 1812, he was governor of Massachusetts. He signed a law that set up new voting districts in the state. The districts were divided to favor Federalists. Some people thought one district looked like a salamander. They began calling it a "gerrymander" after Governor Gerry. Since then, dividing a voting district to favor one group over another has been known as gerrymandering.

Word Bank

confederacy

industry

seven million

16

War Hawks

Lesson 2 Review On a sheet of paper, write the word or number from the Word Bank that best completes each sentence.

1. By 1810, the country's population had doubled in size to _____.

2. New England's economy developed around _____. while the South's economy developed around cash crops.

3. The _____ wanted a war with Great Britain.

4. Tecumseh tried to organize a _____ to fight western settlers.

5. The U.S. navy had only _____ warships.

What do you think ?

Why do you think the United States was not ready for a war?

President Madison asked Congress to declare war against Great Britain on June 1, 1812. Both the House of Representatives and the Senate approved the request. Both votes were very close. Madison did not have the popular support he needed to fight a war. However, Congress declared war on June 18, 1812. They were unaware that Britain had decided to reopen trade with the United States.

The presidential election of 1812 was a contest between the War Hawks and those for peace. The War Hawks supported Madison, and those for peace supported DeWitt Clinton of New York. The vote was close, but Madison's re-election was clearly a victory for those who favored the war with Great Britain. Many well-off shippers thought the United States should wait it out with Britain rather than participate in what they called "Mr. Madison's War."

The American warship Constitution *defeated the British warship* Guerrière *in 1812. After this battle,* Constitution *was nicknamed "Old Ironsides."*

Which Early Battles Were Fought?

On land, American soldiers had very little success. Each of the three attempts in 1812 to invade Canada resulted in defeats. One defeat was at Detroit, where the Northwest Indians under Tecumseh joined the British. The following year a group invaded York (now Toronto), but held it for only a short time. A later attempt at taking Montreal was also a failure. The War Hawks' earlier claims of an easy victory in Canada had been wrong.

In the first year of the war, the American warship *Constitution* captured British ships along the Atlantic coast. After one

Outmaneuver

To move more quickly or better than an enemy

battle, the ship earned the nickname "Old Ironsides" because cannonballs bounced off its sides. The American navy destroyed 1,500 British merchant ships during the early days of the war. In time, however, the larger British navy brought America under control by sea. It created a blockade, which stopped all shipping to and from the United States.

Which Battles Did the Americans Win?

In 1813, the Americans under Captain Oliver Hazard Perry built a fleet of small ships with timbers from a Pennsylvania forest. Then, in a fierce battle, they defeated a British naval fleet on Lake Erie. The victory was important because it stopped a possible British invasion of the Ohio Valley and gave Americans control of Lake Erie.

Two other American victories were of special importance following Perry's naval triumph in 1813. General William Henry Harrison defeated a British and American Indian force in the Battle of the Thames in Canada. Tecumseh, the Shawnee leader, was killed in that battle. The death of Tecumseh put an end to his plans to organize the American Indians against the settlers. It also put an end to the cooperation between the American Indians and the British. General Harrison became famous from this battle.

During the War of 1812, members of the Creek tribe fought with the British against American troops. Andrew Jackson defeated the Creeks at Horseshoe Bend early in 1814. General Jackson's victory forced the American Indians to sign a treaty giving up about 20 million acres of land. This opened up Georgia and present-day Alabama to American settlers. Jackson had become a hero, but his fame was just beginning to grow.

When 11,000 British troops invaded New York in 1814, they were sure that the Americans would be no match for them. However, in the Battle of Lake Champlain, the tiny American fleet **outmaneuvered** the heavily armed British ships and defeated them completely. The British returned to Canada after giving up hope of capturing New York.

What Happened at Washington, D.C., and Baltimore?

In August 1814, a British fleet landed about 4,000 soldiers close to Washington, D.C. The well-trained soldiers marched on to the capital. In a few hours, the capitol building and the president's home, called the White House by some, were set on fire. Other buildings were also burned. It was a crushing loss for the Americans.

The British navy sailed northward and shelled Fort McHenry in an attempt to capture Baltimore, Maryland. Fort McHenry guarded the entrance into Baltimore's harbor. Shells exploded all through the night.

The British attacked Washington, D.C., in 1814. They burned the capitol building and the White House.

Then and Now

After the battle in Baltimore's harbor during the War of 1812, Francis Scott Key saw the U.S. flag still flying over Fort McHenry. The flag was a visible symbol of U.S. independence. Key, a Washington lawyer, expressed his national pride by writing the poem "The Star-Spangled Banner."

In 1916, President Wilson named "The Star-Spangled Banner" the national **anthem.** Soldiers sang the anthem while raising and lowering the flag. During the 1930s, the poem officially became the U.S. national anthem. Today, the song is commonly sung before American sporting events and for Americans who win events during the Olympic Games.

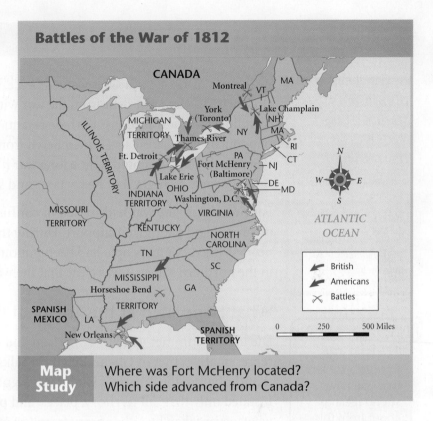

Battles of the War of 1812

Map Study: Where was Fort McHenry located? Which side advanced from Canada?

What do you think ❓

Why do you think the American Indians were willing to fight on the side of the British?

Lesson 3 Review Choose the name in parentheses that best completes each sentence. Write your answers on a sheet of paper.

1. (Oliver Hazard Perry, William Henry Harrison, Tecumseh) defeated a British naval fleet on Lake Erie.

2. (Francis Scott Key, Andrew Jackson, DeWitt Clinton) defeated the Creeks at Horseshoe Bend.

3. (Andrew Jackson, Oliver Hazard Perry, Tecumseh) was killed at the Battle of the Thames.

4. The War Hawks supported (President Madison, DeWitt Clinton, Oliver Hazard Perry) for president in the 1812 election.

5. A lawyer named (DeWitt Clinton, Andrew Jackson, Francis Scott Key) wrote the "Star-Spangled Banner."

Vocabulary

Confusion

The state of being mixed up

Possession

An object belonging to someone

Restore

To put something back or give something back to its owner

By the end of 1814, both sides wanted peace. Great Britain already had a large war debt from the war with France. Increased spending and continued loss of trade revenues made the war very unpopular. The British also remembered from the Revolutionary War that Americans could fight a long war if necessary. The British people were tired of heavy taxes and so many wars.

For Americans, the war had started in **confusion.** It was poorly organized and had mixed support. During the war, trade was nearly ruined. Many people had been put out of work, especially in the northern states. It was clear that the war had failed.

What Happened at the Treaty of Ghent?

During the summer of 1814, American and British representatives met in Ghent, Belgium. Talks went on for months before the Treaty of Ghent was signed in December. It stated only that "all territory, places, and **possessions** whatsoever taken by either party from the other during the war . . . shall be **restored.**" The war was declared a tie.

What Happened at the Battle of New Orleans?

American and British troops fought a battle in New Orleans in 1815. News of the Treaty of Ghent had not yet reached them. The American troops in the New Orleans area were led by Andrew Jackson. His small frontier army faced 8,000 of Britain's best soldiers. When the fighting ended, almost 2,000 British soldiers had been killed or wounded. American losses were fewer than 100. The victory was celebrated as "the surrender of the British." Jackson's fame and popularity spread throughout the land.

> **Writing About History**
>
> Choose a subject that you have strong feelings about from this chapter. In your notebook, write a letter to the editor of an imaginary newspaper. Explain how you feel about this subject.

War of 1812 Statistics

Began: June 18, 1812   **Americans wounded:** 4,505
Ended: January 14, 1815   **Cost for Americans:** $89 million
American deaths: 2,260

The War of 1812 is often called the Second Revolutionary War. Though America had declared its independence in 1776, British feelings toward their former colony had remained unchanged until the War of 1812. America's strong showing in the war had helped it win the respect of the British and countries around the world.

The war gave more Americans a sense of **nationalism,** or a sense of loyalty to their country. Americans wanted to make the nation grow and prosper. During the war, manufacturing in America was given a boost as the need to be **self-sufficient** had grown.

The possibilities for safe westward expansion were improved because of forced movements of the American Indians.

Technology Connection

The Tin Can

In 1810, Peter Durand of England received a patent for preserving food in "vessels of glass, pottery, tin, or other metals. . . ." Durand did not do any canning himself, but others used his design. Soon, tins of food were being sent to the British army and navy. In 1812, Thomas Kensett set up a factory in New York. There he sealed oysters, meat, fruits, and vegetables in metal containers.

Early cans had thick walls, and they had to be hammered open. They did not break, and they kept food from spoiling. Cans provided a safe food source for settlers, explorers, and military troops.

What do you think

Do you think the War of 1812 was necessary for the United States?

Lesson 4 Review On a sheet of paper, write the answers to the following questions. Use complete sentences.

1. Why did the United States want to see an end to the war?

2. Why did Great Britain want to see an end to the war?

3. Who won the War of 1812?

4. What did the Treaty of Ghent state?

5. How did the United States benefit from the war?

Speech by Tecumseh

Shawnee Chief Tecumseh worked to unite American Indians against white settlers. Settlers were rapidly taking land and forcing Indians out. Unless Indians united, they would have no land of their own. Americans respected Tecumseh. He was an excellent speaker. Tecumseh gave this speech in 1810 in a meeting with Indiana Governor Harrison.

I am a Shawnee. My forefathers were warriors. Their son is a warrior. From them I take only my existence; from my tribe I take nothing. . . . I would not . . . ask [Governor Harrison] to tear the treaty . . . but I would say to him: Sir, you have the liberty to return to your own country. . . . The being within . . . tells me that once . . . there was no white man on this continent. That it then all belonged to red men, children of the same parents, placed on it by the Great Spirit that made them, to keep it, to traverse it, to enjoy its productions, and to fill it with the same race, once a happy race, since made miserable by the white people who are never contented, but always encroaching. The . . . only way . . . to stop this evil, is for all the red men to unite in claiming a common and equal right in the land, as it was at first . . . for it never was divided, but belongs to all for the use of each. . . .

The white people have no right to take the land from the Indians, because they had it first; it is theirs. . . . All red men have equal rights to the unoccupied land. . . . There cannot be two occupations in the same place. The first excludes all others. It is not so in hunting or traveling; for there the same ground will serve many . . . but the camp is stationary, and that is occupancy. It belongs to the first who sits down on his blanket or skins which he has thrown upon the ground; and till he leaves it no other has a right.

Document-Based Questions

1. Who was Tecumseh and what did he try to do?

2. What did Tecumseh say Governor Harrison was free to do?

3. Whom did Tecumseh blame for American Indians no longer being a happy race?

4. Why did Tecumseh say that white people had no right to take American Indians' land?

5. Tecumseh did not object to white people hunting and traveling over the land. What did he say was a problem?

Source: Speech by Tecumseh to Governor Harrison, August 12, 1810.

■ James Madison became the fourth president in 1809. He started a new trade policy in 1810 with France and Great Britain. The policy said if either country stopped its trade restrictions against the United States, America would refuse to trade with the other country.

■ The 12th Congress met in 1811. Many members of Congress wanted to put an end to the American Indian conflict and wanted freedom on the seas. This group was nicknamed the "War Hawks."

■ The War Hawks, Henry Clay, and John C. Calhoun began to persuade the public that war with Britain was necessary.

■ Federalists in the northern states opposed a war. The United States military was not prepared for a war.

■ Congress declared war on Britain on June 18, 1812.

■ The 1812 presidential election was a contest between the War Hawks and those wanting peace. The War Hawks supported Madison, who was re-elected.

■ The Americans won battles at Lake Erie, the Thames, and Horseshoe Bend in 1813. Tecumseh, an American Indian leader who had organized a confederacy, was killed at the Battle of the Thames.

■ The War Hawks thought they would have no trouble defeating Canada. They were wrong.

■ The British attacked and burned Washington, D.C., and then attacked Baltimore, Maryland.

■ Andrew Jackson gained fame for winning battles during the War.

■ By 1814, both sides wanted peace. They signed the Treaty of Ghent to end the war. However, news of the treaty had not reached New Orleans, where one final battle was fought and won by the Americans. The war was declared a tie.

■ The United States benefited from the war because it won the country the respect of other countries. The war increased feelings of nationalism, and cleared the way for westward expansion.

Chapter 9   REVIEW

Word Bank

Andrew Jackson

Battle of Lake Champlain

Battle of the Thames

Constitution

Francis Scott Key

James Madison

Oliver Hazard Perry

Tecumseh

War Hawks

William Henry Harrison

On a sheet of paper, write the correct word or name from the Word Bank to complete each sentence.

1. The fourth president of the United States was _____.

2. The _____ were members of Congress who wanted changes in policy.

3. A small American fleet outmaneuvered heavily armed British ships at the _____.

4. A Shawnee chief named _____ organized an American Indian confederacy.

5. The Creeks were defeated by _____ at Horseshoe Bend.

6. A general named _____ defeated an American Indian and British force at the Battle of the Thames.

7. An American warship called the _____ was nicknamed "Old Ironsides."

8. A lawyer named _____ wrote the "Star-Spangled Banner."

9. A captain named _____ defeated a British naval fleet on Lake Erie.

10. Tecumseh was killed at the _____.

On a sheet of paper, write the letter of the correct answer.

11. Who led the House of Representatives to push for war with Britain in 1811?

    A Henry Clay   **C** William Henry Harrison

    B Tecumseh   **D** Andrew Jackson

12. Where did the Americans suffer a crushing loss in the War of 1812?

    A on Lake Erie in 1813

    B at Horseshoe Bend in 1814

    C at Lake Champlain in 1814

    D at Washington, D.C., in 1814

13. Why did Americans go to war with the British?

   A Britain seized American ships and sailors.

   B Britain had won the Revolutionary War.

   C Britain wanted more trade with America.

   D Americans wanted Canada.

14. What was the outcome of the Treaty of Ghent?

   A New Orleans was defeated.

   B The British were clear winners.

   C The war was declared a tie.

   D The Americans were clear winners.

On a sheet of paper, write answers to the following questions. Use complete sentences.

15. What kind of person was President Madison? What trade policy did he introduce?

16. What were three causes of the War of 1812?

17. Why was 1812 a poor time for the United States to go to war?

18. What did the War of 1812 do for the United States?

Critical Thinking On a sheet of paper, write your response to each question. Use complete sentences.

19. The War of 1812 shows Congress's power to declare war. Do you think it is right for Congress to have this power?

20. How do you think the War of 1812 was different from the Revolutionary War?

Test-Taking Tip

Working with a partner can help you study for a test. Each of you can write test items and then take each other's tests. Check your answers together.

Unit 3

Skill Builder

Graphs and Charts

A graph is a figure that shows relationships between numbers. Types of graphs are bar, line, and circle graphs. **Use a graph to compare numbers and percents.**

Here are examples of a simple bar graph and a simple circle graph. Each compares the number of Revolutionary War battles won by the Patriots and the Redcoats in 1777.

Revolutionary War Battles Won in 1777

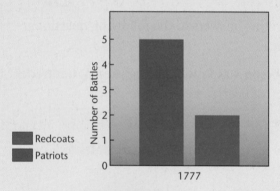

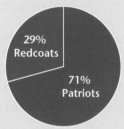

A chart is a way to put information together so it is clear. The information can be put in rows (across) and columns (up and down). **Use a chart to organize information.**

The chart in the next column gives more information about major Revolutionary War battles in 1777.

Major Revolutionary War Battles of 1777			
Name of Battle	Place of Battle	Winner Patriots	Redcoats
Bennington	Vermont	X	
Brandywine	Pennsylvania		X
Freeman's Farm (1st Battle)	New York	X	
Freeman's Farm (2nd Battle)	New York	X	
Germantown	Pennsylvania		X
Princeton	New Jersey	X	
Saratoga	New York	X	

The first column names the battles. The second column tells where the battles were fought. The Xs in the third or fourth column tell which side won each battle. Read across the row for information on a particular battle. Study the chart to answer the questions.

1. How many major battles were fought in 1777?

2. In which state did the most battles occur?

3. Which two battles were fought in the same location?

4. Which side won the most battles?

5. Read the information below. Use it to make a chart showing which states were added between 1791 and 1814.

By 1790, all 13 of the original colonies had signed the U.S. Constitution. They became the first 13 states. Five states were added within the next 25 years. Vermont was added in 1791, Kentucky in 1792, and Tennessee in 1796. Ohio became a state in 1803, and Louisiana was admitted in 1812.

Unit 3 SUMMARY

- In 1764, the British Parliament agreed to tax the colonies. The colonists protested.

- The Boston Massacre occurred in 1770.

- Colonists dumped tea into Boston Harbor on December 16, 1773.

- The First Continental Congress met in 1774.

- On May 10, 1775, the Second Continental Congress decided it could declare war.

- Colonists had several battles with the British in 1775 and early 1776.

- Congress approved the Declaration of Independence on July 4, 1776.

- The Revolutionary War ended at Yorktown, Virginia, on October 19, 1781.

- The states adopted the Articles of Confederation in 1781.

- In 1783, the Treaty of Paris established the new nation's boundaries.

- The Constitutional Convention created a plan for a stronger central government in 1787.

- George Washington was elected the first president and took office in 1789.

- Congress added the Bill of Rights to the Constitution in 1791.

- Alexander Hamilton's successful financial plan helped form political parties.

- France declared war against England in 1793. The United States stayed neutral.

- John Adams became president in 1797, and Thomas Jefferson became president in 1801.

- France sold the Louisiana Territory to the United States for $15 million.

- James Madison became president in 1809.

- Congress declared war on Britain on June 18, 1812, to end the American Indian conflict. The Treaty of Ghent ended the war.

"Cautiously I slipped from under the buffalo hide, got up on my knees and peered over the side of the wagon. There seemed to be nothing to see; no fences, no creeks or trees, no hills or fields. If there was a road, I could not make it out in the faint starlight. There was nothing but land: not a country at all, but the material out of which countries are made."

~ *Willa Cather*, My Antonia, *1918*

Unit 4

Expansion and Reform

Have you heard the expression "growing pains"? America was feeling growing pains between 1816 and 1850. The population was increasing. Industries were growing and multiplying. Disagreements over issues were more numerous. Slavery especially was becoming an issue that divided people. Americans had to adapt to many changes as the nation experienced the pain of growth.

In this unit, you will learn about westward growth of the United States. You will learn about growing industries, new inventions, and border disputes. You will learn about disagreements and the changing political scene in the first half of the 1800s.

10 A New Spirit of Expansion

With the War of 1812 behind it, the United States was on its way to expansion. At the same time, industry and farming began to thrive in the North and the South. The country also began to address the issue of slavery and problems with bordering European colonies. James Monroe was chosen to lead the way as the next president. In this chapter, you will learn about westward expansion, problems of slavery, and some of the issues facing President Monroe.

Goals for Learning

◆ To identify how settlers moved west and the problems they faced

◆ To explain which industries developed in the North and in the South

◆ To describe the Era of Good Feelings

◆ To describe how the issue of slavery caused problems

◆ To explain the Missouri Compromise

◆ To describe the Monroe Doctrine

◆ To explain what happened in the election of 1824

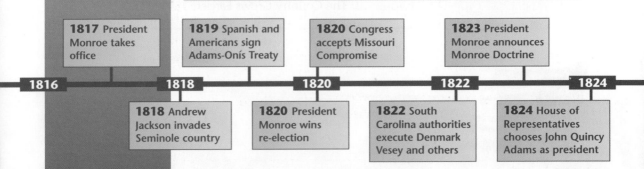

1817 President Monroe takes office

1819 Spanish and Americans sign Adams-Onís Treaty

1820 Congress accepts Missouri Compromise

1823 President Monroe announces Monroe Doctrine

1816   1818   1820   1822   1824

1818 Andrew Jackson invades Seminole country

1820 President Monroe wins re-election

1822 South Carolina authorities execute Denmark Vesey and others

1824 House of Representatives chooses John Quincy Adams as president

James Monroe, a Democratic-Republican, was elected president by an electoral vote of 183 to 34 in 1816. He was helped by the fact that President Madison, also a Democratic-Republican, was more popular at the end of his second term than he had been earlier. Now, after so many victories by the Democratic-Republicans, the Federalists were finished as a political party. President Monroe took office in 1817.

How Was the Country Expanding?

Between 1790 and 1820, the population of the United States increased from about 4 million to nearly 10 million. In the western states, the number of persons grew from 100,000 to well over 2 million during that time. The country was rapidly expanding. Its shape was changing too. The western state of Indiana was admitted to the Union in 1816. Mississippi became a state in 1817, Illinois in 1818, and Alabama in 1819. At that point, the United States had 22 states, an increase of 9 since the Constitution was ratified by the 13 original states.

Many settlers moved westward in covered wagons along the Ohio River route to Indiana, Illinois, northern Kentucky, and western Tennessee. The government built the Cumberland Road leading from Maryland through Virginia in 1818. This popular route was later extended across Ohio into Indiana and Illinois. When the Erie Canal was completed in New York in 1825, New Englanders could choose yet another all-water path toward the West. This water route and the many rivers leading west became regular paths for almost 70 steamboats in common use by 1820.

U.S. Population Growth, 1790–1820

Population in Millions: 0–10

1790   1800   1810   1820

What does this graph show? About how much did the population increase from 1790 to 1820?

How Were Westerners Different?

Settlers of the western states were not like the earlier American colonists. The western frontier was both lonely and dangerous. It was necessary for settlers to help and protect one another. Everyone was equal. The way of life on the frontier was difficult and required hard work. Westerners were fiercely independent. Many of them had been dissatisfied with their lives on the East Coast. Some were new immigrants from Europe who wanted a fresh, independent start. Love of freedom and pride in the United States were most important to them.

This new American spirit of nationalism grew in the frontier states. Henry Clay of Kentucky brought that new spirit to the United States Congress. Politically, the frontier reflected much of the independent character of the rugged pioneer. In the frontier states, women would win the right to vote more easily than in northern and southern states.

There were four problems that the western states had to face: more roads were needed to improve transportation; land prices had to be inexpensive and regulated by the central government; **loans** from banks had to be available to farmers; and markets for farm goods had to be protected by the government.

Why Was Farming Ideal in the South?

In the early 1800s, most Americans were farmers. They found conditions in the South to be ideal for farming. They took advantage of the long **growing season,** plenty of rainfall, and broad, fertile **lowlands.** The South produced crops that could be sold to other states and European countries.

Little manufacturing was done in the South. Most of the products needed by the southern states had to be bought from European countries. Tariffs added to European products resulted in higher prices for goods that the South needed.

Why Was Cotton Important in the South?

Eli Whitney invented the cotton gin in 1793. The "gin," as it was called, separated the seeds from cotton by machine rather than by hand. Cotton was not **profitable** before the gin because of the labor involved to remove the seeds.

Cotton production was less than 100,000 bales in 1799. The amount had grown to nearly 350,000 bales by 1820. The crop became known as "King Cotton," or white gold. Cotton became so profitable that cotton growing spread westward. More land was being used to raise more cotton. The number of African slaves also increased.

This poster (left) announced the sale of African slaves in the 1800s. The number of African slaves increased after the cotton gin (above) was invented.

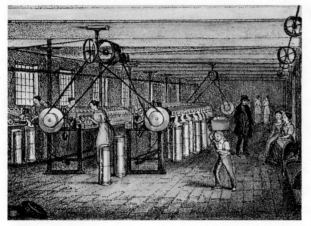

This picture shows one of the many textile mills in New England in the early 1800s.

Which Industries Developed in the North?

The industrial development of the northern states began early in colonial days. Fishing, shipbuilding, trading, and ironworks were all important to the northern states. There was little farming because of the cold winters and rocky land. Manufacturers in the Northeast wanted the government to keep European products out of the country as American industries grew. They were concerned that they wouldn't be able to compete against British products, which were less expensive.

The North did benefit from the success of the cotton crop in the South. Cotton mills in the North turned the raw cotton into thread. One Massachusetts merchant, Francis Lowell, built a new type of water-powered spinning machine and loom. The cotton thread was made into cloth and the cloth into articles of clothing. These factories, as well as factories making countless other items, grew throughout the northern states. Knowledge of manufacturing brought to America from Europe was helping create better products in a shorter amount of time.

Different political points of view were being developed as three separate regions took shape—the western frontier states, the southern states, and the northern states.

What do you think

Why do you think people living on the frontier needed to be independent?

Lesson 1 Review On a sheet of paper, write the answers to the following questions. Use complete sentences.

1. What special problems did the western states face?

2. How were westerners different?

3. Why was farming good for the southern states?

4. How did the cotton gin increase cotton production?

5. How did the North benefit from cotton?

Sectional

Related to the interests of a region

James Monroe was very much aware of the growing **sectional** differences within the country. He kept these differences in mind when he chose his Cabinet. His choice for secretary of state was John Quincy Adams, the son of John Adams, from Massachusetts. The choice greatly pleased New Englanders. John C. Calhoun of South Carolina was appointed secretary of war. William Crawford of Georgia was named secretary of the treasury. Monroe had considered Henry Clay of Kentucky for a Cabinet position. Clay refused, however, because he wanted to remain as Speaker of the House of Representatives. President Monroe's selections resulted in a well-balanced Cabinet that represented all sections of the nation.

What Was the Era of Good Feelings?

James Monroe's two terms were called the "Era of Good Feelings." In the election of 1816, the Democratic-Republicans defeated the Federalists with very little trouble. The electoral vote was 183 to 34. In 1820, Monroe won all the electoral votes except one. Some believe William Plumer of New Hampshire voted for John Quincy Adams so that George Washington would be the only president elected unanimously. There was no party to go against the Democratic-Republicans in the election of 1820. This was one sign of the unity found during the Era of Good Feelings.

What Problems Did America Have with Spanish Florida?

Trouble along the Georgia-Florida boundary had increased over the years. Plantation owners in Georgia complained that the Seminole Indians crossed the border and attacked American families. According to some Georgians, the Seminoles captured slaves and took them to Spanish Florida. Others complained that Spanish officials encouraged slaves to escape across the border.

Geography Note

The border along Florida and Georgia is generally rough and wild. Starting at the Atlantic coast, marshy grasslands extend far inland. The heart of these marshy areas is the Okefenokee Swamp. For many years, these marshy areas hid Indian nations from the U.S. government.

Because of the border problems, Andrew Jackson was ordered into the area. In early 1818, General Jackson gathered a fighting force of 1,000 troops. He led an invasion into Seminole country and Spanish Florida. Jackson and the troops easily took over the Spanish stronghold at St. Marks. They then captured the Spanish post in Pensacola, Florida. The Spanish protested Jackson's use of strong military force.

In 1819, the Adams-Onís Treaty was signed. Under the terms of the treaty, the Spanish gave all of Florida and other claims east of the Mississippi to the United States in exchange for $5 million, which was used to pay a debt to American citizens. The United States gave up its claim to Spanish Texas. Once again, General Andrew Jackson was the hero of the nation.

Biography

John Ross: 1790–1866

Cherokee leader John Ross was born of a Scottish father and a mother who was Scottish and Cherokee. He was called Koowescoowe, or "the egret," in Cherokee. Well educated and well spoken, he spent his life trying to resolve the deep conflicts between American Indians and the colonists. Ross worked for the U.S. government as a young man. He fought alongside Andrew Jackson in the Creek War during the War of 1812. Later, as a Cherokee chief, he opposed the U.S. government. He won a U.S. court case against the state of Georgia, which tried to seize Cherokee land. The court's decision was ignored. After a hard struggle to keep their land, Ross had to give up and lead the Cherokee people to Oklahoma. This journey was known as the "Trail of Tears." He helped to write a constitution for a united Cherokee nation. Ross was elected chief of the new nation, but the Cherokees never achieved the unity he had hoped for.

How Did Slavery Become an Issue?

Slave state

A state that allowed the practice of slavery

Free state

A state that did not allow the practice of slavery

Movement

A series of actions carried out to work toward a certain goal

Missouri was located in the cotton-growing region and wanted to be admitted as a **slave state**. A slave state was one that could practice slavery. As of 1819, there were 11 slave states and 11 **free states**. Free states could not practice slavery. Power in the Senate was balanced between the North and the South. The addition of Missouri as the 12th slave state would upset the balance of power. Congress had to consider this problem before deciding whether to let Missouri enter the Union as a state that allowed slavery. Also, the legislators would have to decide whether to allow slavery in new western states as far north as Missouri.

Missouri would be the first slave state west of the Mississippi River. Northerners feared slavery would spread throughout the entire Louisiana region. They thought if Missouri joined the Union as a slave state, more would follow. Congress would be unable to stop the spread of slavery.

Southern states had a different point of view. If Missouri was admitted as a free state, Congress would be able to destroy the slave system in all the states. Northerners spoke out strongly against slavery. The antislavery **movement** was of great concern to owners of cotton plantations in the South. The Missouri problem was beginning to heat up, as two sections with strong views debated the issue. Control of the Senate by northern or southern states would determine future government policies.

Cotton plantations such as this one thrived in the South.

How Did Maine and Missouri Become States?

The debate went on for several months. Then, by chance, Maine asked to be admitted to the Union in December 1819. Its constitution contained a clause that did not allow slavery. There was no question that Maine would be a free state. Maine's admission provided a possible solution to the problem. During these debates, Henry Clay of Kentucky was the Speaker of the House of Representatives. Clay, a strong leader who came to be known as the "Great Compromiser," had to satisfy both sides.

A compromise was proposed. First, the requests for becoming a state, or **statehood,** by Maine and Missouri were combined. Missouri was to be allowed to enter the Union as a slave state. Maine would join as a free state. With 12 slave states and 12 free states, there would still be a balance of power in the Senate. In addition, slavery would not be allowed in any new states north of 36 degrees 30 minutes north latitude in the Louisiana Territory. Missouri was the only state to which this law did not apply.

This Missouri Compromise, as it was called, was approved by Congress on March 3, 1820. Henry Clay's influence had made the approval possible. The issue of slave states and free states was worked out for the time being.

The Missouri Compromise had made southern plantation owners think that slavery was "safe" in the South. Then one of many damaging events took place in Charleston, South Carolina, in 1822. Having heard of a possible **revolt** by the slaves of that city, the **authorities** prepared for trouble. A group of 9,000 people, led by freed slave Denmark Vesey, had planned to attack several South Carolina cities. However, Vesey and 35 other people were **executed** before any revolt could take place. This event led to stronger laws to control the movement and education of freedmen and slaves.

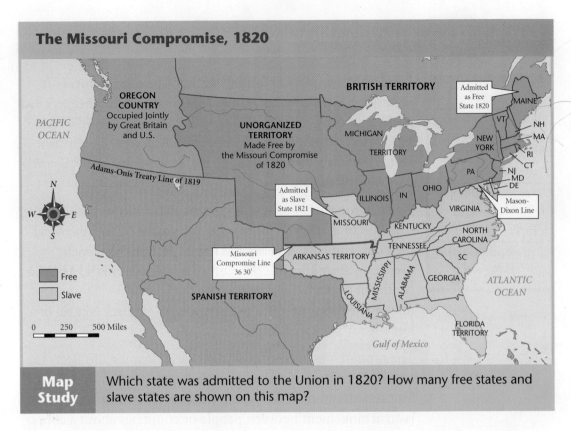

The Missouri Compromise, 1820

OREGON COUNTRY
Occupied Jointly by Great Britain and U.S.

PACIFIC OCEAN

BRITISH TERRITORY

Admitted as Free State 1820

MAINE

UNORGANIZED TERRITORY
Made Free by the Missouri Compromise of 1820

MICHIGAN TERRITORY

VT
NH
MA
RI
CT

NEW YORK

Adams-Onis Treaty Line of 1819

N
W E
S

Admitted as Slave State 1821

MISSOURI

ILLINOIS
IN
OHIO
PA
NJ
MD
DE

Mason-Dixon Line

KENTUCKY
VIRGINIA

NORTH CAROLINA

Missouri Compromise Line 36 30'

ARKANSAS TERRITORY

TENNESSEE

SC

Free
Slave

SPANISH TERRITORY

LOUISIANA
MISSISSIPPI
ALABAMA
GEORGIA

ATLANTIC OCEAN

0   250   500 Miles

FLORIDA TERRITORY

Gulf of Mexico

Map Study Which state was admitted to the Union in 1820? How many free states and slave states are shown on this map?

Word Bank

Democratic-Republican

Denmark Vesey

Seminoles

slave

Spain

Lesson 2 Review On a sheet of paper, write the correct word or words from the Word Bank to complete each sentence.

1. James Monroe's political party was the _____ Party.

2. In 1818, _____ owned Florida.

3. Andrew Jackson led an invasion into Florida to attack the _____ and the Spanish posts there.

4. As part of the Missouri Compromise, Missouri entered the Union as a _____ state in 1821.

5. A slave revolt in South Carolina was prevented when freed slave _____ and his followers were executed.

What do you think ?

Why do you think different ideas about slavery were beginning to cause problems in the United States?

Agreement

An arrangement between people or countries as to a course of action

Joint declaration

To declare something as a group

Doctrine

A statement of a certain government policy

Besides the trouble in Florida and the issue of Missouri's admission as a slave state, James Monroe faced another serious problem during his presidency. At that time, there still were European colonies in North and South America. The British, Dutch, Spanish, and Russians all had land claims from the early days of exploration.

These European colonies saw what revolutions could do. They could become free and independent countries by overthrowing their governments. America did it in 1776, and the French overthrew their king in 1789. European colonies on the American continent began to rebel against their governments. European monarchies now had to calm the revolts to get back control or lose their American colonies.

The monarchies agreed to send powerful armies and fleets to take back control of the colonies in North and South America. The British did not take part in the **agreement.** An agreement is an arrangement between people or countries about a course of action. Trade with those colonies was very profitable for the British. Any change would mean less trade. The United States, as well, desired to protect those markets because of the profits of trade.

What Proposal Did the British Make?

The British foreign secretary suggested that the United States and Great Britain make a **joint declaration.** It would warn all European monarchies to keep out of the affairs of Latin America. President Monroe discussed the matter with Thomas Jefferson and James Madison. Both agreed that the proposal was a good one. John Quincy Adams, secretary of state, did not agree. He was able to show Monroe that the United States should act alone. The president took his advice and created the statement of policy that became known as the Monroe **Doctrine.** A doctrine is a statement of a certain government policy.

What Was the Monroe Doctrine?

James Monroe announced his famous doctrine in his yearly message to Congress in December 1823. He said that any attempt by a European power to extend its influence in any part of the **Western Hemisphere** would be considered dangerous to the peace and safety of the United States.

The Monroe Doctrine received widespread approval by Americans. The British, however, were not pleased with it

Elizabeth Monroe, wife of President James Monroe, brought a stiff, orderly manner to the White House.

because it was not a joint declaration. Other countries in Europe did not consider the **proclamation** to be important. The doctrine, adopted in 1823, would not be tested for many years to come. The main point, however, is that when that time came, the Monroe Doctrine could be used.

History in Your Life

Sequoyah and a Different Form of Writing

Sequoyah was a Cherokee scholar. He invented a new writing system for the Cherokee language around 1821. His system was comprised of 86 symbols. Some symbols were English letters but without the same English sounds. Sequoyah's symbols represented all the Cherokee sounds. Thus, Sequoyah helped Cherokees become the first American Indian tribe to read and write in their own tongue. He taught many Cherokees to read and write. Parts of the Bible and the first American Indian newspaper, the *Cherokee Phoenix,* were printed in Cherokee. Sequoyah's accomplishment helped unite Cherokees and made them leaders among other tribes. His intelligence and pride in his culture were inspiring.

Agricultural	
Having to do with raising crops or animals for food or profit	
Qualified	
Fit for a given purpose	

The United States had become three distinct regions—the freedom-loving West, the increasingly industrial North, and the **agricultural** South. Each region had a different political point of view, representing different needs. By 1824, sectional politics had produced four presidential candidates. The influence of the South was declining. The West and the North were becoming more and more influential.

The New England states nominated John Quincy Adams of Massachusetts. He was serving as secretary of state under President Monroe. Adams, whose father was the second president of the United States, had a broad background in politics. John Q. Adams was clearly a **qualified** candidate.

The West nominated Henry Clay of Kentucky and Andrew Jackson of Tennessee. Clay had experience in government and had been Speaker of the House of Representatives. Clay appeared to have an excellent chance to win. No man since George Washington was as popular as Jackson. His military successes in Louisiana, Tennessee, and Florida made Americans proud. He was also a strong candidate.

The South supported William Crawford of Georgia. All four men were well known as strong nationalists. They were loyal to the country and had similar views about what direction the growing country should take.

None of the four candidates received a majority of the votes, however. According to the 12th Amendment to the Constitution, the House of Representatives had to choose a president from the three who had the most votes. Henry Clay did not want Andrew Jackson to win. He did not like Jackson's political ideas. He strongly believed that John Q. Adams would be a better choice. Clay persuaded members of the House of Representatives to support Adams, and Adams was chosen president.

A few days later, President Adams announced that Henry Clay would serve as his secretary of state. It seemed that Adams and Clay had made an agreement. Jackson was angry. He felt that he should have been president.

Then and Now

If you were a pioneer woman at this time in history, you might have done hard work. While men saw to the outside chores, women were expected to cook, care for children, and clean. The saying "Man works from sun to sun, but woman's work is never done" shows how difficult a woman's life was. It could even be dangerous—many pioneer women died during childbirth.

Women now have many more life choices than pioneer women had. Modern women no longer have to sew all the clothing for their families or cook all the meals from scratch. They may choose to work outside the home or attend college. They are represented in every occupation. Modern medicine has made childbirth much safer. In the 1800s, only about 15 percent of people, men or women, lived beyond their 50th birthday. Today, the life expectancy for American women is almost 80 years.

Lesson 3 Review On a sheet of paper, write the answers to the following questions. Use complete sentences.

1. What was the purpose of the Monroe Doctrine?

2. Why were the European monarchies concerned about their colonies in North and South America?

3. What were the three regions of the United States?

4. Why did the House of Representatives have to choose the president in 1824?

5. How did Henry Clay help to determine the final outcome of the election of 1824?

What do you think ?

Why do you think the Monroe Doctrine was important?

The Monroe Doctrine

President James Monroe saw signs of possible trouble as European colonies in the Americas moved toward independence. The stronger European countries might try to use force and interfere in the Western Hemisphere. In 1823, President Monroe set forth the Monroe Doctrine. Although the doctrine was not regarded as important then, it served our country well over the years that followed.

The American continents, by the free and independent condition which they have assumed and maintain, are henceforth not to be considered as subjects for future colonization by any European powers. . . .

In the wars of the European powers in matters relating to themselves we have never taken any part. . . . It is only when our rights are invaded or seriously menaced that we resent injuries or make preparation for our defense.

We owe it therefore, to candor [honesty] and to the amicable [friendly] relations existing between the United States and those powers to declare that we should consider any attempt on their part to extend their system to any portion of this hemisphere as dangerous to our peace and safety.

With the existing colonies or dependencies of any European power we have not interfered and shall not interfere. But with the Governments who have declared their independence and maintained it, and whose independence we have, on great consideration and on just principles, acknowledged, we could not view any interposition [interference] for the purpose of oppressing them, or controlling in any other manner their destiny, by any European power in any other light than as the manifestation of an unfriendly disposition toward the United States.

Our policy in regard to Europe . . . is not to interfere in the internal concerns of any of its powers. . . .

Document-Based Questions

1. Why did President Monroe say that future European colonies would no longer be possible in the Americas?

2. The United States did not interfere in European affairs. In return, what did President Monroe expect European countries to do?

3. When would it be necessary for the United States to take action against a European power?

4. Write one statement from the doctrine that shows President Monroe wanted the United States and European countries to continue to be friendly.

5. The Monroe Doctrine pointed out that any act of force in the Western Hemisphere by a European power would be considered a threat to the security of the United States. Why is that a special point to make?

Source: The Monroe Doctrine, 1823.

Chapter 10 SUMMARY

- President Monroe took office in 1817. His election victory finished the Federalists as a political party.

- Between 1790 and 1820, the population of the United States increased by almost six million people. Much of this population increase was on the frontier. Settlers moved west on wagons and by water routes. These people were very independent and had a strong sense of nationalism. However, they wanted more roads, better land prices, loans for farmers, and protection of markets for farm goods.

- Farming, especially cotton farming, thrived in the South. Industries such as shipbuilding, trading, and ironworks thrived in the North.

- The Era of Good Feelings was used to describe President Monroe's two terms. However, America experienced problems with Spanish Florida, as Seminoles attacked Americans. Andrew Jackson led troops into Spanish Florida in 1818 and captured St. Marks and Pensacola. This led to the Adams-Onís Treaty in 1819, which gave Florida to America. The United States gave up Spanish Texas.

- Slavery became an issue in 1819 when Missouri tried to enter the Union. This would have upset the balance of power between free states and slave states in Congress. In 1820, the Missouri Compromise solved the problem by letting both Maine, a free state, and Missouri, a slave state, enter the Union. However, slavery was still a problem. Several people, including a freed slave named Denmark Vesey, were executed in South Carolina for planning a slave revolt.

- President Monroe announced the Monroe Doctrine in 1823. This policy stated that any attempt by a European power to extend its influence in any part of the Western Hemisphere would be considered a threat to the peace and safety of the United States.

- John Quincy Adams became president in the election of 1824. The House of Representatives chose him because none of the candidates received a majority vote.

Chapter 10 REVIEW

Word Bank
Andrew Jackson

cotton gin

Denmark Vesey

doctrine

free state

Henry Clay

James Monroe

John Quincy Adams

proclamation

slave state

On a sheet of paper, write the correct word or name from the Word Bank to complete each sentence.

1. A _____ is an official public announcement.

2. The _____ was used to separate cotton seeds.

3. A _____ does not practice slavery.

4. A _____ practices slavery.

5. _____ led troops into Seminole country in 1818.

6. A freed slave named _____ was executed for planning a revolt in South Carolina.

7. A statement of a certain government policy is called a _____.

8. _____ took office as president in 1817.

9. _____ was known as "The Great Compromiser."

10. The House of Representatives chose _____ as president in 1824.

On a sheet of paper, write the letter of the answer that correctly answers each question.

11. What candidate did the South support in the election of 1824?

    A Henry Clay   **C** William Crawford

    B Andrew Jackson   **D** John Q. Adams

12. The Missouri Compromise was an agreement between the North and South members of Congress. What problem did it solve?

    A attacks on Florida

    B attacks by foreign powers

    C balance of free and slave states

    D who would be president

13. What statement said that attempts by European powers to influence the Western Hemisphere would be seen as a threat to the United States?

   A Monroe Doctrine   **C** Missouri Compromise

   B Adams-Onís Treaty   **D** Era of Good Feelings

14. To what does the Era of Good Feelings refer?

   A westward expansion

   B progress in the United States

   C industrial development

   D James Monroe's two terms in office

15. From 1790 to 1820, how much did the U.S. population grow?

   A from 1 million to 4 million   **C** it doubled

   B from 4 million to 10 million   **D** it tripled

On a sheet of paper, write the answers to the following questions. Use complete sentences.

16. What problems did the western settlers face?

17. Which industries developed in the North and in the South?

Critical Thinking On a sheet of paper, write your response to each question. Use complete sentences.

18. What problems did slavery cause in this time period?

19. Do you think the Missouri Compromise was a good compromise? Explain your answer.

20. Of the three sections of the United States—North, South, or West—which one would you have chosen to live in? Why?

Test-Taking Tip

Some test questions call for more than one answer. Be sure to read questions carefully.

11 Political Changes Take Place

The United States saw many political changes with the next three presidents—John Quincy Adams, Andrew Jackson, and Martin Van Buren. New political parties were formed. People in the nation's three regions became more divided on their government needs. In this chapter, you will learn about these political changes in the United States.

Goals for Learning

◆ To explain why the Tariff of 1828 caused problems for the federal government

◆ To describe the ways in which Andrew Jackson was different from presidents before him

◆ To describe the rebellion led by Nat Turner and explain its importance

◆ To explain why the American Indian relocation west of the Mississippi is known as the "Trail of Tears"

◆ To describe major events in the struggle for Texas independence

◆ To explain the election of 1836 and the Panic of 1837

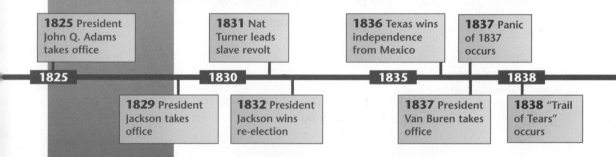

1825 President John Q. Adams takes office

1831 Nat Turner leads slave revolt

1836 Texas wins independence from Mexico

1837 Panic of 1837 occurs

1825   **1830**   **1835**   **1838**

1829 President Jackson takes office

1832 President Jackson wins re-election

1837 President Van Buren takes office

1838 "Trail of Tears" occurs

Capable

Having the ability for a task

Domestic

Related to one's own country

Campaign

A group of activities connected to getting elected to office

John Quincy Adams got off to a bad start as president when he took office in 1825. Many people felt that Adams had made a deal in order to win the election. Adams was **capable** and experienced in government, but he was not a popular president.

By 1824, the three regions of the country had become even more different. President Adams did not consider the three parts separately. He believed that the job of the central government was to lead the country as a whole.

Why Was the Tariff of 1828 Passed?

A bill passed in 1828 imposed tariffs on imported goods to protect American industries. The tariff was intended to raise prices of products made in foreign countries. Foreign products would be more expensive than **domestic** items. Americans would be more likely to buy cheaper U.S. goods.

The South did not like the tariffs. Southerners were farmers, not manufacturers. The tariffs raised the cost of the products they needed. Northerners depended on industry and wanted even higher taxes on imported goods. As a result of the bill Adams became more disliked, while Andrew Jackson gained popularity.

Who Won the Election of 1828?

As early as 1825, Andrew Jackson began his election **campaign.** A campaign is a group of activities connected to getting elected to office. Jackson, Senator Martin Van Buren of New York, and other members of Congress separated from the Democratic-Republican Party and formed the Democratic Party. Members of Adams's party became the National Republicans.

This cartoon, titled "King Andrew the First," made fun of President Jackson. Some people felt his style as president was like that of a powerful king.

The National Republican Party chose, or **nominated,** John Q. Adams for a second term. The Democratic Party nominated Jackson. Jackson won the election. Westerners were excited by his victory. Thousands of Americans attended Jackson's inauguration.

What Was the Spoils System?

When Jackson took office in 1829, he believed that government work required no special experience. The person needed only to support the proper American ideas and be a loyal supporter of the party. Some government workers who had not supported Jackson were fired. Jackson gave government jobs to loyal supporters. This practice became known as the **spoils system.**

How Did Jackson Set Up His Cabinet?

"Old Hickory," as President Jackson was called, was a man of the average people. Instead of turning to his Cabinet for advice, he called upon his friends. These unofficial advisers became known as Jackson's "Kitchen Cabinet."

Jackson considered it his duty to carry out the wishes of the people. Most of the American people trusted him.

Word Bank

campaign

Democrat

Kitchen Cabinet

spoils system

tariffs

Lesson 1 Review On a sheet of paper, write the correct word or words from the Word Bank to complete each sentence.

1. In 1828, northerners liked the _____ on imported goods because they protected American industries.

2. In 1825, Andrew Jackson began his _____ for the 1828 presidential election.

3. In the election of 1828, Andrew Jackson ran as a _____.

4. President Jackson's unofficial advisers were called the _____.

5. Giving political jobs to supporters, as Andrew Jackson did, is called the _____.

What do you think

Do you think the spoils system is a good system? Why or why not?

Oppression

Unfair or cruel actions by one group against another group with less power

In 1831, an enslaved African from Virginia named Nat Turner set out to free all slaves in America. His master had allowed Turner to learn to read. Having become a preacher at an early age, Turner wanted to end slavery. He and a group of his followers killed about 60 slave owners and their families across Virginia. When they were stopped, Turner and about 20 of the others were hanged. After the revolt, however, more than 100 innocent slaves were killed by fearful masters.

The revolt led by Nat Turner was the most serious slave revolt in American history. The white southerners realized more than ever that the Africans were not about to remain enslaved without a fight. For the slaves, the name Nat Turner came to represent the courage to fight **oppression** by whatever means necessary. Oppression is unfair or cruel actions by one group against another group with less power.

Nat Turner and his confederates planned a revolt against slave owners.

What Problems Developed over Tariffs?

The South and the West had strongly opposed the tariff act passed under Adams in 1828. It raised the prices of the manufactured goods they needed. Northerners, however, wanted even higher taxes on imports so their goods would cost less than imports. A new tariff act that lowered some of the tariffs was passed in 1832. Neither the North nor the South was pleased.

The protective tariff continued to cause problems during Jackson's term. Vice President John C. Calhoun, a southerner, found himself in a difficult position. He depended upon the political support of plantation owners, yet he disliked speaking against the president. He proposed that a state be able to decide whether a law was acceptable. The state could turn down a law it thought to be unfair. The South Carolina legislature, in turn, passed the Ordinance of Nullification. In this act, the people of this state declared that the tariff laws did not apply to them. They said that federal officials would not get the duties from their state, and forced collection would cause South Carolina to withdraw from the Union.

Jackson was a strong supporter of states' rights. He also loved his country. Jackson sent a message to South Carolina, making his position clear. All states would have to obey the laws if the country were to remain a Union. No one state would be permitted to challenge the unity of the country.

History in Your Life

Spirituals

Originally, spirituals were part of African American worship in the South. During early slavery days, African slaves often worshipped in the fields as they worked. They blended Psalms and hymns their masters sang with music many had learned in Africa. Their singing style was very much their own. In 1801, Richard Allen compiled *A Collection of Spiritual Songs and Hymns* for the black church. He was the first African American to present a collection of these songs. By the early 1800s, jubilant "call and response" songs were common. In these, one singer calls out short phrases and everyone answers. Other spirituals were slow "sorrow songs." Examples are "Nobody Knows the Trouble I've Seen," "Were You There?" and "Sometimes I Feel Like a Motherless Child." Today spirituals can be heard in concert halls and in worship of many faiths.

Lesson 2 Review On a sheet of paper, write the answers to the following questions. Use complete sentences.

1. What did Nat Turner do?

2. What is oppression?

3. Why did northerners want higher taxes on imports?

4. What was the Ordinance of Nullification?

5. What position did President Jackson take with South Carolina?

What do you think ?

Do you think Nat Turner's revolt helped or hurt the antislavery movement? Explain your answer.

Renew

To make something new again, such as a charter that has come to an end

Expire

To come to an end

Veto

The power given to the president to turn down a bill

Andrew Jackson stood up for the common people. He believed that all male citizens should have the right to vote. Also, he was in favor of improving schools, working conditions, and the treatment of prisoners. President Jackson wanted Americans to have more influence on government and an improved quality of life. However, he also supported the interests of slave owners. His plan for moving American Indians caused tremendous hardships and suffering for the Indians.

The Bank of the United States had a 20-year charter that had been granted by Congress and signed by President James Madison in 1816. In 1832, the president of the Bank asked for the charter to be **renewed.** This date was four years before the charter **expired.** Congress passed the bill granting the new charter to the Bank of the United States.

President Jackson did not like the Bank and did not want to renew its charter. The Bank of the United States and other banks were governed by a wealthy few. Jackson thought the Bank favored the rich and powerful people. He felt the Bank was not democratic and should be destroyed. President Jackson **vetoed** the bill when it was presented to him. A veto is the power given to the president to turn down a bill.

Presidents before Jackson had rarely used the veto. They let Congress decide the issues. As president, Jackson believed he should make the important decisions. He used the veto to control Congress. Jackson set an example for presidents who followed him. They appreciated the value of the veto power.

The First Bank of the United States was in Philadelphia, Pennsylvania.

In 1831, Henry Clay was nominated as the National Republican candidate for president. Clay had supported the renewal of the charter for the Bank of the United States in 1832. He made the Bank veto into an election **issue.** Clay was confident he would win the election.

Jackson continued to speak out against the Bank during his campaign. Jackson won the election by a large number of votes. Jackson received 219 electoral votes, and Clay got 49. It was a crushing defeat for Clay.

President Jackson took his re-election as public approval of this Bank policy. He continued to destroy the Bank by removing all government funds from it. He **deposited** the money into smaller banks. Jackson's enemies called these banks "pet banks." Jackson was successful in reducing the power of the Bank of the United States.

What Was the Trail of Tears?

Writing About History

Imagine you are an American Indian. You are being forced to give up your home and move far away. In your notebook, write a paragraph about this. Explain how you feel.

Jackson went to Congress for help to decrease the fighting among settlers and American Indians. He asked that land west of the Mississippi be set aside for the Indians. The Indian Removal Act of 1830 provided for moving Indian peoples remaining east of the Mississippi to this land.

The "Trail of Tears" was the forced removal of thousands of American Indians.

At this time, American Indians had not yet been granted citizenship. Many groups of Indians were forced to give up their **homeland.** The largest movement took place in 1838. It included the Choctaws, Cherokees, Chickasaws, Creeks, and Seminoles. So many of these people died during the difficult trip that the journey became known as the "Trail of Tears." Very few Indians remained east of the Mississippi River. Some Seminoles were still in Florida, and the Sauk and Fox people were in the upper Northwest Territory.

Word Bank

Andrew Jackson

Henry Clay

Bank of the United States

Trail of Tears

veto

Lesson 3 Review On a sheet of paper, write the correct word or words from the Word Bank to complete each sentence.

1. President Jackson did not like the _____ and did not want to renew its charter.

2. A _____ is the power of the president to turn down a bill.

3. In 1831, _____ was nominated as the National Republican candidate for president.

4. _____ believed that all citizens should have the right to vote and that working conditions should be improved.

5. Many American Indians died during the _____.

Then and Now

If you were a student in 1825, you probably would have gone to school only through eighth grade. You would have studied only the three Rs—reading, writing, and 'rithmetic. Most schools were only a one-room building then. Many families could send children to school for only a few weeks a year. Your family might have needed your help in a factory or the fields. If your parents wanted you to have more schooling, you might have attended a private academy.

You can thank Horace Mann, the father of modern education, for a free high school education for everyone. Owing to his efforts, free high schools were a national law by 1875. Today students in most states must attend school nine months a year through age 16. Most Americans now receive a high school education.

Dictator

A person ruling a country with total control

Mission

A church

Geography Note

After independence from Spain in 1821, Mexico was eager to settle its northern territories. Very few people lived in Texas at that time, so the Mexican government encouraged Americans to settle in Texas. By 1830, Americans far outnumbered Mexicans. Today, the Texas population density of about 80 people per square mile is still low compared with, for example, New Jersey's 1,135 people per square mile.

Back in the middle of the 1820s, President John Quincy Adams was willing to pay $1 million for the Mexican territory that is now Texas. A few years later, President Jackson offered to pay $5 million for the land. In both cases, Mexico refused to sell.

Mexicans encouraged Americans to move into the territory. The area was well suited to cotton growing, so many planters brought their slaves to establish large cotton plantations. By 1835, about 20,000 Americans were living there. The Mexicans asked only that these people obey their laws.

In time, the Texans, as they called themselves, refused to obey the laws of Mexico. Texans declared their territory independent of Mexico. They appointed Sam Houston as commander-in-chief of the Texan army.

What Happened at the Alamo and Goliad?

Antonio López de Santa Anna was president and **dictator** of Mexico. A dictator is a person ruling a country with total control. He organized 4,000 men and led them to San Antonio in February

The Texans lost the battle at the Alamo in 1836.

1836. Santa Anna was met by a small army of Texans, led by Colonel William Travis. Santa Anna ordered the colonel to surrender. Instead, Colonel Travis moved his men into the Alamo, a rebuilt **mission.** They used the Alamo as a fort. After many days of fighting, the Texans in the Alamo were defeated. Santa Anna made sure that every one of the Texans was killed. Among the dead were two famous westerners, Jim Bowie and Davy Crockett.

The Republic of Texas, 1836

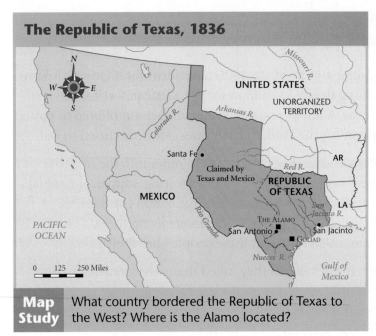

UNITED STATES

UNORGANIZED TERRITORY

Santa Fe

Claimed by Texas and Mexico

REPUBLIC OF TEXAS

MEXICO

AR

LA

PACIFIC OCEAN

THE ALAMO
San Antonio
San Jacinto
GOLIAD

Missouri R.
Arkansas R.
Colorado R.
Red R.
Rio Grande
San Jacinto R.
Nueces R.

Gulf of Mexico

0   125   250 Miles

Map Study What country bordered the Republic of Texas to the West? Where is the Alamo located?

Santa Anna then moved his army to the town of Goliad. The Texans were defeated again. Santa Anna had lost many soldiers in the two battles. Nevertheless, he intended to defeat Sam Houston and win the war.

How Did Texas Win Its Independence?

Sam Houston ordered his Texan army to retreat slowly as Santa Anna pushed forward to the San Jacinto River. "Remember the Alamo!" and "Remember Goliad!" were the battle cries of the Texans as they attacked and defeated the Mexican army. Santa Anna, who had been taken prisoner, agreed to give Texas its independence. In October 1836, the new nation elected Sam Houston as its first president. Texas became the Republic of Texas.

Lesson 4 Review On a sheet of paper, write the correct name from the Word Bank to complete each sentence.

Word Bank

Davy Crockett

Colonel William Travis

John Quincy Adams

Sam Houston

Santa Anna

1. _____ was willing to pay $1 million for Texas.

2. The leader of the Texans at the Alamo was _____.

3. The leader of the Texan army that defeated Santa Anna was _____.

4. _____ was the president and dictator of Mexico.

5. _____ was a famous westerner killed in the Alamo.

What do you think ?

Why do you think the Texan army used the battle cries "Remember the Alamo" and "Remember Goliad"?

Jackson's second term as president was ending. He persuaded the Democratic Party to nominate his vice president, Martin Van Buren, for president. Van Buren was an experienced, well-educated political figure.

During the eight years of Jackson's presidency, the National Republicans joined other groups to form the Whig Party. Led by Henry Clay and Daniel Webster, the Whigs's strongest support came from the manufacturers and shippers in the Northeast. They favored the renewal of the Bank of the United States charter, keeping high tariffs, and a strong central government.

During the 1830s, the Whigs resisted many of Jackson's policies. They didn't want the American Indians to be moved west of the Mississippi River. The Whigs thought that removal was unnecessary and unconstitutional. Despite the Whigs's opposition, Jackson removed the Cherokee and other nations from Georgia, South Carolina, and other southeastern states.

Van Buren told voters that he would follow the same approach that Jackson had used to govern the country. A vote for Van Buren was a vote for Jackson. Van Buren won the election. He had the largest popular vote. Van Buren had 170 electoral votes, and three Whig candidates had a total of 113.

Technology Connection

Steam-Powered Cylinder Press

Until 1833, generally only the rich read newspapers. At six cents a copy, they were expensive. But in 1833, Benjamin Day found a way to print 4,000 copies of a newspaper in an hour. To do this, Day used a new steam-powered cylinder press.

People did most of the work to run early presses. A person moved a lever and pushed a printing plate onto paper in a flat bed. The presses had springs. These made lifting easier for the printer. But printing was still slow and difficult work.

The steam-powered press used steam, not people, to move the lever and flat bed. Then the press design changed. Paper on a revolving cylinder was pressed against a flat printing form. These improvements greatly increased production of printed matter. Newspapers and books could be printed faster. They became much cheaper. This meant many people could now afford to buy them.

What Caused the Panic of 1837?

Trouble was waiting for President Van Buren when he took office in 1837. The United States entered a **depression,** called the Panic of 1837. A depression is a period of financial difficulties experienced by an entire country. Many of the smaller banks that Jackson had favored over the Bank of the United States had become careless. They had used paper money that was not backed by gold or silver. Some had given loans to people who never paid them back. When word of the problems got out, people rushed to the banks to take out money deposited before the panic. However, there was no money in those banks.

Many banks failed as a result of this panic. Prices on farm products and manufactured goods fell. Factories and mills closed. New work on roads and canals came to a halt. **Unemployment** spread, especially in the Northeast. This depression lasted for several years. Van Buren was unable to solve most of the problems it created.

Biography

Sarah Grimké: 1792–1873
Angelina Grimké: 1805–1879

The Grimké sisters were daughters of a judge from Charleston, South Carolina. They became outspoken about ending slavery, and they favored women's rights. After they moved to Philadelphia and became Quakers, they began publishing antislavery papers. They later gave public lectures against slavery. Some other antislavery people thought that women should not give lectures. The Grimkés responded by publishing essays calling for equal rights for women and enslaved people. The sisters remained committed to the antislavery and women's rights movements, which both blossomed during their lifetimes. They insisted that their parents leave them equal shares of the family's slaves, whom they freed as soon as possible. In New Jersey, they helped found and taught at schools with Angelina's husband, Theodore Weld.

It Happened in History

The Second Great Awakening

By the late 1700s, many people in the United States had lost interest in religion. In response to this, in the early 1800s, there was a rebirth of American religious feeling. This was called the Second Great Awakening, and it had a big influence on American society. The movement broke with past beliefs by talking more about the actions of people and less about the decisions of God. People began to feel closer to God.

Charles Grandison Finney started the revival, or renewal, in 1821 in western New York. At camp meetings, a preacher would set up a tent and talk, sometimes for days, to large crowds. Tent revivals in remote rural areas became common. They were combined religious services and social events.

The Second Great Awakening also contributed to many social reforms. Movements began against slavery and public drinking, and for women's suffrage and public education. Many women were attracted to the movement, which encouraged their participation.

Lesson 5 Review On a sheet of paper, write the answers to the following questions. Use complete sentences.

1. Where did the Whigs's strongest support come from?

2. What did Martin Van Buren tell voters?

3. What problem did President Van Buren face when he took office?

4. What is a depression?

5. What happened as a result of the Panic of 1837?

What do you think ?

How do you think you would feel if you were living during a depression? Why?

A Message from the Alamo

On February 24, 1836, Texas was fighting for independence from Mexico. Texans tried to stop the Mexican army under President Antonio López de Santa Anna at San Antonio. At the Alamo, a tiny mission, fewer than 200 Texans fought 4,000 Mexican soldiers. In this letter, Colonel William Barrett Travis sent word to his fellow citizens.

Fellow Citizens and Compatriots:

I am besieged by a thousand or more Mexicans under Santa Anna. I have sustained a continued bombardment for 24 hours and have not lost a man. The enemy have demanded a surrender at discretion; otherwise the garrison is to be put to the sword if the place is taken. I have answered the summons with a cannon shot and our flag still waves proudly from the walls.

I shall never surrender or retreat.

Then, I call on you in the name of liberty, or patriotism, and of everything dear to the American character to come to our aid with all dispatch. The enemy are receiving reinforcements daily and will no doubt increase to three or four thousand in four or five days. Though this call may be neglected, I am determined to sustain myself as long as possible and die like a soldier who never forgets what is due to his own honor and that of his country. Victory or death!

Document-Based Questions

1. On what date was the letter written?

2. After a nonstop day-long attack, how many men had Travis lost?

3. Under what circumstances was Travis willing to surrender?

4. What did Travis call on in his appeal for help?

5. Why do you think Travis said "this call may be neglected"?

Source: Colonel William Barrett Travis, February 24, 1836.

- John Quincy Adams was not a popular president. He did not consider the differences between various parts of the country in his decisions.

- The country had developed into three distinct regions—the western frontier, New England, and the South. Each region had its own interests.

- The Tariff of 1828 imposed a tax on imported goods. The country was split in its opinion of this tariff. Northern industrialists favored the tax, while farmers in the South felt the taxes hurt them.

- Andrew Jackson, known as "Old Hickory," was a popular president elected in 1828. Jackson was a "common person" and a defender of states' rights.

- Jackson supported a system of giving favors and jobs to political friends. This was known as the "spoils system."

- Nat Turner, an African slave from Virginia, led a slave revolt in 1831. This uprising resulted in the deaths of many slave owners as well as slaves. Turner became a hero to African slaves.

- The South Carolina Ordinance of Nullification was an early sign of a separation between southern states and the Union. South Carolina declared that it would not obey the tariff laws.

- President Jackson used his veto power to help control the actions of Congress. His veto helped destroy the Bank of the United States. His policy toward the Bank helped him win re-election in 1832.

- Jackson asked Congress to set aside the land west of the Mississippi for the American Indians. The Choctaws, Cherokees, Creeks, and Seminoles were among the people who were relocated. Their journey westward became known as the "Trail of Tears."

- Many Americans began to settle in the Texas territory, which was owned by Mexico. The settlers refused to obey Mexican laws. Mexico sent an army to Texas and many battles were fought, including the Battle of the Alamo. Sam Houston led the Texans to independence in 1836.

- In 1837, Martin Van Buren took office as president.

- The country entered a depression that began with the Panic of 1837. Many banks failed during this depression.

Chapter 11 REVIEW

Word Bank

Andrew Jackson

Bank of the
 United States

John Quincy
 Adams

North

Panic of 1837

Sam Houston

South

Tariff of 1828

Whig

On a sheet of paper, write the correct word or words from the Word Bank to complete each sentence.

1. _____ was not a popular president because he didn't understand regional differences.

2. The _____ imposed taxes on imported goods in order to protect American industries.

3. Farming was the major industry in the _____.

4. President _____ supported the common person.

5. The people in the _____ supported the Tariff of 1828 because they believed it protected their industries.

6. The _____ led to an economic depression for the country.

7. Jackson vetoed the charter for the _____ because he believed it favored rich and powerful people.

8. _____ helped Texans fight for independence from Mexico.

9. _____ was the name of the party formed during Jackson's presidency.

On a sheet of paper, write the letter of the answer that correctly answers each question.

10. Andrew Jackson rewarded his supporters with government jobs. What did this practice become known as?

    A the spoils system

    B the tariff system

    C the Kitchen Cabinet

    D the independence movement

11. Who led a revolt of slaves in 1831?

    A Martin Van Buren

    B Santa Anna

    C Nat Turner

    D the Grimké sisters

12. Why were many Americans living in the Mexican territory of Texas by 1835?

    A Mexico encouraged them to move into the territory.

    B They wanted to be ready for war.

    C They would not have to obey laws.

    D They organized to defeat Santa Anna.

On a sheet of paper, write the answer to each question. Use complete sentences.

13. Why were southern slave owners concerned about Nat Turner's rebellion, even though it lasted less than a week?

14. What problems did the tariff of 1828 cause the federal government?

15. How was President Jackson different from earlier presidents?

16. What were the three regions of the United States in the early 1800s, and what were their main interests?

17. Why did Jackson force American Indians to move west?

18. Why did the American Indian relocation become known as the "Trail of Tears"?

Critical Thinking On a sheet of paper, write your response to each question. Use complete sentences.

19. The tariff of 1828 affected different sections of the country differently. If you were a farmer in the South, how would you convince the government that the tariff was unfair?

20. Why do you think that Nat Turner led a rebellion even though the army and militia were against him?

Test-Taking Tip

Make a timeline as a study tool. It can help you remember the order of events.

12 America Becomes More Democratic

The last chapter explained how the U.S. political system changed in the early 1800s. However, many other things changed the nation in the early to middle 1800s. This was a time of growth in industry. Many inventions changed the way Americans did things. Immigrants came to America to seek a better way of life. Education and literature helped to shape the nation's culture. In this chapter, you will learn how inventions, education, literature, and the growth of industry changed the nation.

Goals for Learning

◆ To identify major inventions and how they contributed to the growth of industry

◆ To describe early labor unions

◆ To describe developments in transportation

◆ To list some major developments in communication

◆ To describe how immigration contributed to population growth and affected cities

◆ To identify the contributions of some early American educators

◆ To identify several early American writers and their contributions to American literature

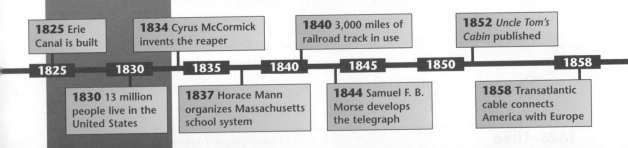

1825 Erie Canal is built

1834 Cyrus McCormick invents the reaper

1840 3,000 miles of railroad track in use

1852 *Uncle Tom's Cabin* published

1825   1830   1835   1840   1845   1850   1858

1830 13 million people live in the United States

1837 Horace Mann organizes Massachusetts school system

1844 Samuel F. B. Morse develops the telegraph

1858 Transatlantic cable connects America with Europe

Rural

Relating to places well outside of cities

Labor union

A group of workers trying to bring about change in working conditions

The growth of industry in the United States was slow. There was not a good market for manufactured items. Between 1790 and 1840, about 90 percent of the American people lived in **rural** regions. Farmers had little money to spend and did not need most manufactured goods. Merchants made few sales to farmers.

Iron manufacturing and shipbuilding were two important industries in the United States. But for many other goods, American manufacturers could not compete with British industry. Great Britain had many more years' experience at producing most goods. British items were easy to obtain at good prices. In addition, American cities did not have enough workers.

Money for starting a factory was difficult to get. Bankers were not eager to lend money to would-be manufacturers because the risk of failure was so high. Without a loan, most people could not afford to buy equipment or materials.

What Are Labor Unions?

Beginning in the early 1800s, there were attempts to organize unions. A **labor union** is a group of workers trying to bring about change in working conditions. Workers demanded better pay, shorter workdays, and a cleaner environment. Long hours and low wages made it difficult for workers to support their families. But only property owners could vote. Without political influence, workers could do little to make changes.

A number of factors weakened the growth and influence of unions. The flood of immigrants looking for employment found the wages to be more than they had been able to earn in Europe. Cultural differences and the language barrier did not help. The crushing blow to the growth of unions was the depression of 1837. The enormous loss of jobs made workers desperate. They were eager to work for lower wages and longer hours. Gradually, when good times returned in the 1850s, labor unions regained their strength.

How Did Industries Begin to Grow?

Mechanic

Someone skilled in working with machines

Textile

Fabric or cloth

Memorize

To remember what has been learned

Interchangeable parts

Parts of a machine that can be used with other machines

Mass-produce

To make great amounts of product very fast

The United States had begun to change into an important industrial country in 1790. The roots of this change go back to Samuel Slater, a skilled **mechanic** in Great Britain. He decided to travel to America in 1789, hoping to make a fortune in the new **textile** industry there. Textile is fabric or cloth. British law, however, would not permit machinery to leave the country. The British didn't want designs for their machinery to leave the country, either. So Slater **memorized** the parts of a machine he was using in a cotton factory in Great Britain. Later, in Rhode Island, Slater was able to build a textile machine from memory.

With the aid of this machine, along with Eli Whitney's cotton gin, the textile industry began to grow. Americans were able to produce a good product faster and cheaper than ever before. They could begin to compete with other industrial nations. Because of the machinery he built, Samuel Slater is known as "The Father of American Industry."

In addition to inventing the cotton gin, Eli Whitney helped develop the idea of using **interchangeable parts** in manufacturing. In the early 1900s, manufacturer John Hall would use many of Whitney's ideas to **mass-produce** rifles. To mass-produce means to make great amounts of a product very fast.

A method of burning coal as a fuel in making iron was developed in the 1830s. Demand for iron in manufacturing was very high. As American industry became able to make its own iron, industries that made machines, farm tools, rails, and parts of railroad cars grew very quickly.

Focus on Economics

By 1820, the way goods were made had changed. Goods could be made with parts that were standardized, or made to be exactly the same. This change in the way goods were produced was important in the further development of industry. A broken part in one machine could now be replaced with the same part from a different machine. Farm equipment could be made to last longer and work better. Textile factories and clock makers starting using interchangeable parts. Soon manufacturers of such things as sewing machines and typewriters used interchangeable parts. America was on its way to becoming an industrial leader.

Early farming equipment was very simple and crude. Plows were made out of wood and could break easily. Every step in the crop-growing process was done by hand. In 1834, Cyrus McCormick invented a machine that could harvest grain. His new machine—the reaper—made farming possible on a much bigger scale. Shortly thereafter, John Deere invented the steel plow, which helped farmers to convert the hard prairie **sod** into usable farm land. Many machines and processes were invented during this time. With improved transportation, canal building, and the use of water power, America would rapidly become an industrial nation.

Cyrus McCormick's reaper improved farming in the 1830s.

What do you think

How do inventions improve life? Explain.

Lesson 1 Review On a sheet of paper, write the answers to the following questions. Use complete sentences.

1. Why was industry slow to get started?

2. Why were factories slow to get started?

3. How was Samuel Slater able to build his textile machine?

4. How did Slater's machine change the textile industry?

5. What did Cyrus McCormick's reaper do?

Biography

Margaret Knight: 1838–1914

Margaret (Mattie) Knight grew up in Manchester, New Hampshire. Like many children in 1850, Knight went to work in a cotton factory. She saw several young people get hurt on the job. Every time a thread broke on a loom, the machinery would slip, and someone was injured. Knight wanted to make looms safer. She drew pictures and made models. At age 12, she invented a new machine part. It would stop a loom after a thread broke so the moving machine would not hurt the worker. Amoskeag Mills in New Hampshire used Knight's invention on its looms. Mattie Knight kept inventing things throughout her life. She became known for 26 inventions. The photo above shows one of her inventions, a machine that folds paper bags.

Turnpike

A road that travelers pay to use

Early land transportation was slow and expensive. Raw materials had to be sent to factories, yet high shipping costs made the factories' products too expensive to buy. In the 1790s, a **turnpike** was built in Pennsylvania to improve transportation. A turnpike is a road that travelers pay to use. The Cumberland Road was a turnpike in use since 1811. It now spread to the west for nearly 600 miles. Wagons and stagecoaches could travel along this road at speeds of about 10 miles per hour.

The Cumberland Road and the Wilderness Road

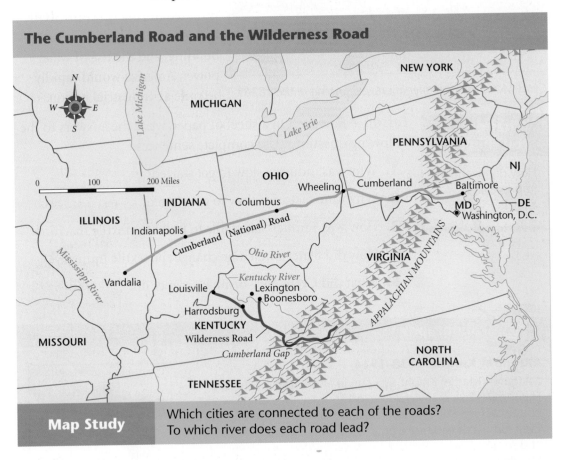

Map Study — Which cities are connected to each of the roads? To which river does each road lead?

Natural barriers affected early American transportation. Rivers acted as "highways" into the North American interior. But mountains, lakes, and forests often hindered travel. For years, the Appalachian Mountains, for example, blocked westward canals, roads, and rail travel. Rivers themselves, so friendly to boats, could stall the building of roads until engineers learned how to cross them.

What Water Transportation Developed?

Transporting goods by water was slow, backbreaking, and expensive. Men using long poles could push a boat at the rate of one mile per hour.

Robert Fulton traveled from New York City to Albany, New York, in a steam-powered boat in 1807. His small ship, the *Clermont*, covered 150 miles in 32 hours—about four and a half miles per hour. The steam engine was fueled by burning wood. Many people laughed at him and called his boat "Fulton's Folly." But his steamboat made faster water transportation possible. By 1820, almost 70 steamboats were carrying people up and down the Mississippi and the rivers joining it. Water transportation became the least expensive way to travel and ship goods. By 1837, hundreds of steamboats carried passengers from port cities of Pittsburgh, Pennsylvania; Cincinnati, Ohio; St. Louis, Missouri; and Vicksburg and Natchez, Mississippi.

Why Were Canals Built?

The first major canal was the Erie Canal. In 1816, the idea of a canal from Albany, New York, to Buffalo, New York, was proposed. The project was sometimes referred to as "Clinton's Big Ditch." Governor De Witt Clinton led the canal project. Many people made fun of the Big Ditch, but Governor Clinton was determined to build it. Waterways from New York City to Lake Erie would connect the Atlantic Ocean with the West.

The Erie Canal was finished by 1825. Boats could move through it at speeds of up to five miles per hour. Shipping times and costs were greatly decreased. A trip that once took three weeks to complete could now be made in one week. Shipping costs for a ton of grain dropped from $100 to $10. New York became the strongest shipping and trading center in the country.

The success of the Erie Canal led to the construction of many more canals. In fact, by 1840, 3,000 miles of canal had been built. The Great Lakes were connected by canal to many rivers in the Northeast.

Early locomotives were simple. They became more advanced as the popularity of railroads increased.

How Did Railroads Change the Nation?

Steamboats, roads, and canals improved transportation, but not as much as the railroads did. The first railroad in America to carry passengers was the Baltimore and Ohio Railroad. It ran a distance of 13 miles. At first, horse-drawn cars were used on the tracks. Soon, **locomotives** replaced the horses, beginning with Peter Cooper's *Tom Thumb*. A locomotive is a vehicle that rides on rails and has an engine for pulling railroad cars. Gradually, more railroads were built. Better tracks were developed. Railroads were far better than any other kind of transportation. People and freight could now travel by land in all directions. Though trains were uncomfortable and not very safe, they were faster than anything else. By 1840, 3,000 miles of railroad track were in use on various lines.

How Did Communication Improve?

There was a growing need for better, faster means of **communication**. In 1844, Samuel F. B. Morse developed the **telegraph**, the first of many important improvements in communication. The telegraph used coded signals to send communications over a wire. This invention brought about major changes for industry, transportation, and **commerce**.

Cyrus Field successfully laid an underwater telegraph cable from Newfoundland to Ireland in 1858. The cable was placed on the floor of the Atlantic Ocean. The cable stretched a distance of about 1,900 miles. This **transatlantic** cable connected America with Europe. Several years passed before it worked right, but the cable improved communication.

Locomotive

A vehicle that rides on rails and has an engine for pulling railroad cars

Communication

The act of sending and receiving information

Telegraph

A device that uses coded signals to send communications over a wire

Commerce

Having to do with buying or selling goods

Transatlantic

Crossing the Atlantic Ocean

What Was the Pony Express?

The pony express also improved communication. Mail took weeks to get across the country before this postal system was started. Horse-drawn stagecoaches ran regularly, but they were unable to go very fast. The pony express could run mail from St. Joseph, Missouri, to Sacramento, California, in just 10 days.

Pony express riders carried mail from Missouri to Sacramento.

The distance was about 2,000 miles. Lightweight, young riders rode their horses as fast as they could go. Every 10 miles or so, a fresh horse was ready. Despite all kinds of weather and danger from attacks by American Indians and bandits, the riders raced across the country. This postal system was used for only 18 months. The pony express came to an end when the telegraph was introduced to California in 1861.

Writing About History

Imagine you are a rider on the pony express. Write a news story about a typical day. Explain some of the dangers you face as you ride across the country.

Then and Now

In 1840, you would have traveled from New York to Illinois by stagecoach. You would have traveled on narrow, muddy, unpaved roads. You might have held your breath when the horses and coach crossed bridges. Many bridges were mere planks and poles laid across the water. After only five miles, you would stop at a tavern for lunch. After another five miles, you would have to stop for supper and a night's lodging. Your trip from New York to Illinois by stagecoach would have taken about 20 days in summer, and longer in winter.

One way you can make that trip today is by car. You can travel at 65 miles per hour on paved four-lane interstate highways. You might stop to buy gas and eat lunch in a restaurant. At night, you might stay in a motel. Traveling about eight hours a day, you can make the trip in about two days. If you need to get there quickly, you can arrive in about two hours on a jet.

The U.S. Postal Service

The United States Postal Service began in 1775 with Benjamin Franklin as the first postmaster general. The Postal Service helps people share ideas and information through the mail. As transportation improved, so did mail service. From its beginning, the Postal Service helped develop new transportation methods. It bought stagecoaches to deliver mail over roads. It also encouraged new stagecoach designs to make travel and mail delivery safer.

The Postal Service used steamboats to carry mail over water. By the 1830s, it began to use railroads to carry mail short distances. The Postal Service also looked for new ways to collect and deliver mail. It worked hard to find ways to carry mail more quickly and less expensively.

Today, the Postal Service continues to change. It runs like a big business. It meets its customers' needs as a big business does. It tries to provide the best service at low costs.

1. Why do you think the Postal Service used new methods of transportation before most Americans did?

2. Citizens may not interfere with the mail service. They may not open other people's mail. Why are these rules necessary?

Word Bank

Cumberland Road

Erie Canal

railroad track

steamboat

telegraph

What do you think ?

Why do you think many people laughed at Robert Fulton's steam-powered boat?

Lesson 2 Review On a sheet of paper, write the correct word or words from the Word Bank to complete each sentence.

1. The _____ was a turnpike on which people could travel west for almost 600 miles.

2. Robert Fulton's _____ made water transportation of goods and people practical.

3. The _____ was built to improve transportation by water between New York and the Great Lakes.

4. By 1840, there were 3,000 miles of _____ that were used for land transportation.

5. The pony express and the _____ improved communication in the United States.

In 1790, the U.S. population was nearly four million. By 1820, it had more than doubled. In 1830, almost 13 million people were living in the United States. Immigrants contributed to the growth of the nation during that 40-year period. Most of the population growth, though, was due to the high birthrate in America at that time.

Where Did Early Immigrants Come From?

Aware of the great risks and high death rate, many people hesitated to make the long voyage across the Atlantic Ocean. However, about 10,000 immigrants arrived in the United States each year from 1790 to 1820. Most of these immigrants came from England, Ireland, Wales, and Scotland. The desire for a better life overcame any fears they may have had about the long three-month journey to America.

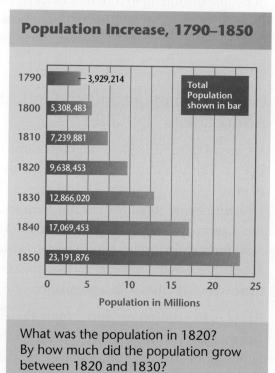

Population Increase, 1790–1850

Year	Total Population (shown in bar)
1790	3,929,214
1800	5,308,483
1810	7,239,881
1820	9,638,453
1830	12,866,020
1840	17,069,453
1850	23,191,876

Population in Millions

What was the population in 1820? By how much did the population grow between 1820 and 1830?

By 1830, newer and faster sailing ships were being used. The transatlantic trip now took two weeks instead of two to three months. Even though the trip was still dangerous and uncomfortable, the cost was much lower. More people could now afford to go to America. The Irish and Germans, especially, had reasons for leaving their countries.

Starvation

Suffering from lack of food

Melting pot

A nation where several groups of people belonging to different races or cultures live together

Urbanization

The process of taking on the ways of city life

The potato crop in Ireland was destroyed by disease in 1846. Most of the Irish depended on potatoes as their major source of food. Hunger and **starvation** spread throughout Ireland. Many Irish people had no choice. They had to leave their homeland. By 1850, about one million Irish people were living in the United States.

People from Germany also sought refuge in America. They left their country to escape unpleasant political conditions. Germany also had a crop failure, though it was not as serious as the one in Ireland. Many Germans made the journey across the Atlantic Ocean. By the year 1850, about four million German people had come to the United States.

The Irish and the Germans were the first to come to the United States in large numbers. Later, people from every part of the world found their way to this country. With so many different cultures, the United States became known as the **melting pot** of the world. A melting pot is a nation where several groups of people belonging to different races or cultures live together. Problems developed because of differences in language and customs. As time passed, however, the immigrants were able to make a new home for themselves in the United States.

How Did Immigration and Industrialization Affect Life in the Cities?

Between 1820 and 1860, immigrants came mostly from Northern Europe. Hardships in Ireland and Germany forced thousands to leave in hope of a better life in America. The population in 1800 numbered about five million, with only six cities with a population of 8,000. The cities were Baltimore, Maryland; New York; Philadelphia, Pennsylvania; Boston, Massachusetts; Charleston, South Carolina; and Salem, Massachusetts. In 1860, there were 141 cities with a population of 8,000.

Rapid **urbanization** produced more than its share of problems. Urbanization is the process of taking on the ways of city life. Slums, poor street lighting and garbage disposal, rodents, and dirty water all had an impact on early city life.

Nativist

A person who believes that people born in a country should have more rights than immigrants

Violence

Rough or harmful action

As industries expanded and the flood of immigrants sought employment, competition rapidly developed. The willingness of the newcomers, who had no money, to work longer hours for lower wages led to conflict with the earlier immigrants. Urban life was made more dangerous by friction among religious groups who had different opinions about slavery.

Between 1845 and 1855, a wave of immigrants sought a new life in America. This sudden surge of foreigners alarmed **nativists,** Americans who had been in the country longer. New immigrants would work for lower wages and longer hours. They lived together in large cities and spoke foreign languages. A downturn in the economy only made matters worse. People blamed the immigrants. **Violence** targeting the newly arrived foreigners broke out in the 1840s. Violence is rough or harmful action.

The Know-Nothing Party gained support against the rapid increase in the number of immigrants flooding into the country. The official name of the party was the American Party. The Know-Nothing Party had some success in electing party members to state legislatures, governors, and even Congress. But their poor showing in the election of 1856 meant the end of the American Party.

What do you think

Why do you think a country that is a melting pot can have problems?

Lesson 3 Review Choose the word in parentheses that best completes each sentence. Write your answers on a sheet of paper.

1. In (1790, 1820, 1830), nearly 13 million people were living in the United States.

2. The (Irish, British, Scottish) depended on potatoes for food.

3. The (Irish, British, Germans) left their country because of unpleasant political conditions.

4. By 1850, (two, four, eight) million Germans had come to the United States.

5. A melting pot is a nation of several races and (cultures, countries, states).

Tutor

A person who has been paid to teach another person

Standards

Guidelines that a person or group must follow

Not every child in the new nation had an opportunity to attend school. Many people believed that education was intended only for those who could pay for it. Wealthy families paid private **tutors** to teach their young children. Academies and colleges were established for educating older children.

Public education was not a popular idea. Children of working-class families were needed at home. They had many chores to do. Before the 1800s, a few public schools did exist, but the quality of education was poor. Schools were small, and children of all ages were grouped together in the same class. Teachers, in general, were not well educated. They could read and write, but they had no special training.

During the presidency of Andrew Jackson, more people had gained the power to vote in national elections. More Americans were coming to realize that education was important so that people could vote wisely. Many states began to adopt **standards** for school systems. Training schools for teachers were established, and money was provided for better books and school buildings.

What Educational Changes Began?

Working-class people in New England became aware of the importance of education. Their children needed to go to school if they were to have a better life. Much earlier, Thomas Jefferson had said that a democracy calls for an educated people. Andrew Jackson had also favored education for all children.

Country schoolhouses like this one were common in the 1800s.

Horace Mann reorganized the Massachusetts school system in 1837. Schools were placed under state control to be supported by taxes. All children had to attend. Mann, who was in charge of education for the state, said that all schools had to have the same program of studies. The subjects taught were on a higher level than those in the early schools. Teachers had to be trained before they could teach. Similar plans were introduced in Rhode Island and Connecticut.

Another member of the Massachusetts school system, Noah Webster, wrote a series of readers, spellers, and grammar books. These books provided a standard of learning for American schoolchildren. His two-volume **reference book,** *An American Dictionary of the English Language,* was first published in 1828. It became widely used in schools across the country. Despite the efforts of Mann, Webster, and other educators, however, only about half of all white children attended a public school in 1850.

Lesson 4 Review On a sheet of paper, write the answers to the following questions. Use complete sentences.

1. Why did not every child have an opportunity to attend school?

2. Why was the quality of education poor before the 1800s?

3. Why did people begin to feel that education was important?

4. What did Horace Mann do?

5. Why were Noah Webster's books important for education?

McGuffey's Readers were used in schools beginning in 1836. They were used to educate thousands of students.

What do you think ?

How do you think education has changed since the 1800s?

At first, colonists lived in America much as they had in Great Britain. They held on to the old customs that they had brought from their homeland. The South, the western frontier, and New England were all different from Great Britain. Unlike the original colonists, many Americans did not care about the Great Britain of the past. During the 200 years between the settling of Jamestown and the election of President Jefferson, the nation had found its own culture. Writers and artists of that time period recorded life in America.

Which Writers Contributed to American Literature?

Before this time, Benjamin Franklin was one of the few American writers whose works were popularly read. However, between 1815 and 1860, many writers described the America they knew in books, stories, and poems. Tales of adventure and **bravery** in the growing country became **classics**. A classic is a book that has lasting value or meaning. People all over the world began to take an interest in the spirit of this bold new land.

James Fenimore Cooper wrote about the American Revolution and the French and Indian War. He also wrote about adventures on the high seas, the frontiers, and the plains. His best-known novels are the five *Leatherstocking Tales*. Some of these are *The Last of the Mohicans* (1826), *The Pioneers* (1823), and *The Deerslayer* (1841).

Novelist James Fenimore Cooper, the first great American novelist, wrote tales of adventure.

One early American writer, Washington Irving, was successful with tales such as "The Legend of Sleepy Hollow" and "Rip Van Winkle." In 1851, Herman Melville wrote *Moby Dick.* Nathaniel Hawthorne published *The Scarlet Letter,* set in colonial times in 1850. Edgar Allan Poe wrote several frightening stories, including "The Fall of the House of Usher" in 1839 and "The Murders in the Rue Morgue" in 1841. Poe also wrote a number of poems such as "The Raven."

Some American poets wrote about the vast opportunity in America, while many attacked the serious problems in the country. Henry David Thoreau focused on the peace and beauty in nature. Walt Whitman wrote about freedom and those who fought for it.

Henry Wadsworth Longfellow wrote poetry and **prose,** including works such as "Paul Revere's Ride" and "Poems on Slavery" that looked at history and current events. Ralph Waldo Emerson wrote about life and what it meant to be a human being. During this period, he became very active in the antislavery campaign.

History in Your Life

Edgar Allan Poe

Many regard Edgar Allan Poe (1809–1849) as one of the most brilliant, original writers in American literature. Poe struggled to make a living during the 1830s and 1840s. He published his writings and worked as a magazine editor and critic. A complicated, troubled man, Poe is remembered for such eerie poems as "The Raven" and "Annabel Lee." He is also remembered for short stories like "The Fall of the House of Usher." Poe established a tradition of American horror stories. Filmmakers and writers like Stephen King carry on that tradition today. Poe is also considered one of the creators of the modern detective story. Examples of his detective stories are "The Murders in the Rue Morgue" and "The Masque of the Red Death." Poe never enjoyed much commercial success from his writing. However, millions of people today enjoy reading his work.

Abolitionist

A person who wanted slavery stopped

John Greenleaf Whittier had become an established writer. Mobs often attacked him because he was one of the people who started the American Anti-Slavery Society. Writers such as James Russell Lowell and Oliver Wendell Holmes also used their poetry to attack slavery, which they considered to be an evil practice.

Which Other Writers Attacked Slavery?

Several other writers helped to bring attention to the slavery issue during this time. Harriet Beecher Stowe of New England wrote a book called *Uncle Tom's Cabin* in 1852. She described the terrible conditions under which slaves had to live. Thousands of copies of the book were sold in the United States and in Europe. *Uncle Tom's Cabin* added to the movement to abolish slavery.

In 1857, poor southerner Hinton R. Helper wrote *The Impending Crisis of the South*. This book carried the message that the evil of slavery was ruining the South. He described the South as poor, especially due to its lack of industry. Its people were not educated and were far behind the rest of the country. This book upset a lot of people, especially those in the South.

In 1831, William Lloyd Garrison published a newspaper called *The Liberator*. His point of view was clear: slavery must be stopped. Garrison was liked by some people, but others thought him to be much too violent. Equally important were the contributions made by an ex-slave, Frederick Douglass. Douglass bought his freedom after escaping from Maryland.

Douglass was self-taught and became an excellent speaker and writer. When he settled in Rochester, New York, Douglass published an antislavery newspaper called *The North Star*. Douglass tried to help in the fight against slavery through his speeches and writings. Both Garrison and Douglass were **abolitionists**. An abolitionist was a person who wanted slavery stopped, or abolished.

How Did Other Countries View American Literature?

For many years after America was established, the Europeans did not view the nation as being well developed. European nations thought that the younger country could produce no great literature. However, by the middle of the 1800s, Americans were proving that their stories were rich and exciting. The United States was becoming a storyteller to the world.

Lesson 5 Review On a sheet of paper, write the correct name from the Word Bank to complete each sentence below.

Word Bank

Frederick Douglass

Harriet Beecher Stowe

Henry David Thoreau

Herman Melville

William Lloyd Garrison

1. *Moby Dick* was written by _____.

2. _____ wrote about peace and beauty in nature.

3. _____ wrote *Uncle Tom's Cabin*.

4. A newspaper called *The Liberator* was published by _____.

5. _____ published an antislavery newspaper called *The North Star*.

What do you think ?

Why do you think American literature is important? Explain.

It Happened in History

Transcendentalism

Transcendentalism was an important movement in the United States during the mid-1800s to the early 1900s. Transcendentalists believed God was present in nature. They also believed that people could save themselves without organized religion. Leading Transcendentalist Ralph Waldo Emerson taught that people should learn directly from life and inner reflection. The search for inner truth emphasized individual responsibility and self-reliance. Emerson and one of his students, Henry David Thoreau, spread their Transcendental philosophy through their writings. Emerson strongly opposed slavery. Thoreau refused to pay taxes used for the Mexican War and was briefly sent to jail. Another Transcendentalist, Margaret Fuller, is sometimes called America's first feminist.

"Slavery As It Is"

As a student in 1834, Theodore Dwight Weld organized abolitionists in Cincinnati, Ohio. Weld married Angelina Grimké, another abolitionist, in 1838.

In 1839, he published American Slavery As It Is. *The pamphlet documented the evils of slavery based on testimony of such witnesses as Frederick Douglass. Harriet Beecher Stowe partly based* Uncle Tom's Cabin *on the pamphlet. Weld's pamphlet is considered second only to Stowe's book in its influence on the antislavery movement. By the time of his death in the late 1800s, Weld had become known as "the greatest Abolitionist."*

This passage is from the introduction to American Slavery As It Is.

We will prove that the slaves in the United States are treated with barbarous inhumanity; that they are overworked, underfed, wretchedly clad and lodged, and have insufficient sleep; that they are often made to wear round their necks iron collars armed with prongs, to drag heavy chains and weights at their feet while working in the field, and to wear yokes, and bells, and iron horns . . . that they are often hunted with bloodhounds and shot down like beasts . . . that they are whipped and beaten till they faint, . . . and sometimes until they die . . . that they are maimed, mutilated, and burned to death. . . . All these things, and more, and worse, we shall prove. Reader, we know whereof we affirm, we have weighed it well; more and worse WE WILL PROVE.

Document-Based Questions

1. What word did Weld use to describe how slaves were housed?

2. What were two things slaves were made to wear?

3. What were two things Weld claimed was done to slaves?

4. How did Weld intend to prove the things he said?

5. Weld was a white man. Why do you think he fought so hard on behalf of the slaves?

Source: American Slavery As It Is, *1839, by Theodore Weld.*

- Workers started to organize early in the colonies.

- Samuel Slater brought designs for British textile machines to America. He built new machines in America and contributed to the growth of the textile industry in New England.

- Eli Whitney invented the cotton gin, which contributed to the growth of the textile industry. Whitney also helped develop the idea of interchangeable parts in manufacturing and the concept of mass production.

- Cyrus McCormick and John Deere invented machines that had major effects on farming.

- The Cumberland Road, originally built in 1811, led to a system of roads and highways that spread westward for nearly 600 miles.

- In 1807, Robert Fulton's steamboat made water transportation faster. By 1837, there were hundreds of steamboats carrying passengers and cargo on the Mississippi River and the rivers that joined it.

- Canals allowed goods to be shipped quickly and cheaply. By 1840, the Northeast had a network of thousands of miles of canals and rivers.

- Railroads began to provide another means of transportation. Steam locomotives could move people and freight faster than any other transportation. By 1840, there were over 3,000 miles of railroad lines in the United States.

- Samuel F. B. Morse developed the telegraph in 1844. In 1858, Cyrus Field laid a transatlantic telegraph cable that connected North America with Europe.

- The pony express carried the mail from St. Joseph, Missouri, to Sacramento, California.

- From 1790 to 1830, the U.S. population grew from 4 million to 13 million people.

- Early immigrants to America came from Great Britain, Wales, Scotland, and Ireland. The second wave of immigrants came from Ireland and Germany.

- The wave of immigrants in the mid-1800s caused cities to grow rapidly. Poor housing and dirty conditions were often the result.

- Public education grew in the 1800s. Horace Mann did much to reform the Massachusetts school system.

- Washington Irving, Edgar Allan Poe, and Harriet Beecher Stowe were among many writers who contributed to American literature.

Chapter 12 REVIEW

Word Bank

education

Erie Canal

grain

John Deere

Noah Webster

pony express

potato

The Scarlet Letter

steamboat

telegraph

On a sheet of paper, write the correct word or name from the Word Bank to complete each sentence.

1. The steel plow, which allowed hard prairie sod to be farmed, was invented by _____.

2. The _____ ran from St. Joseph, Missouri, to Sacramento, California, in about 10 days.

3. Cyrus McCormick invented a mechanical reaper to harvest _____.

4. The first dictionary of American English was written by _____.

5. In 1825, the _____ ran from Albany, New York, to Buffalo, New York.

6. Samuel F. B. Morse developed the _____, which made communication possible over long distances.

7. Nathaniel Hawthorne's famous book _____ was set in colonial times.

8. Horace Mann tried to make people understand the importance of _____ for all children.

9. A failed _____ crop caused many immigrants to come to the United States from Ireland.

10. Robert Fulton's _____ was known as "Fulton's Folly."

On a sheet of paper, write the letter of the answer that correctly answers each question.

11. Which writer was very active in the antislavery campaign?

    A Washington Irving   **C** Henry Wadsworth Longfellow

    B John Greenleaf Whittier   **D** Herman Melville

12. Which form of transportation improved transportation in the United States the most?

    A steamboats   **C** canals

    B roads   **D** railroads

13. Political unrest in which country led many of its citizens to immigrate to America?

A Ireland   **C** Germany

B Great Britain   **D** Mexico

On a sheet of paper, write the answers to the following questions. Use complete sentences.

14. Why did Governor De Witt Clinton want the Erie Canal to be built?

15. Why was making iron important to American industry?

16. What background did Frederick Douglass have that made him such a powerful speaker on the evils of slavery?

17. Why were some people unhappy about the large numbers of new immigrants?

Critical Thinking On a sheet of paper, write your response to each question. Use complete sentences.

18. Of all the inventions that you studied in this chapter, which one do you think was the most important? Explain your answer.

19. Fewer than one out of every six children went to school in 1820. Today almost all children go to school. Why is going to school important?

20. Explain the route you would have taken from Philadelphia to St. Louis in 1837. Tell which means of transportation you would take on each section of the trip. Describe what the trip would be like.

Test-Taking Tip

To learn vocabulary, write each term on one side of an index card. Write the meaning on the other side. Practice with a partner, testing how well you know the words.

13 The Country Grows Larger

The country became much larger in the 1840s. This was the result of compromises with other countries over territory. It was also the result of a war with Mexico. Yet another cause of this expansion was the discovery of gold in California. Presidential elections were also changing. In this chapter, you will learn about these and other changes in the United States in the 1840s.

Goals for Learning

◆ To identify ways that presidential campaigns changed

◆ To discuss the concept of Manifest Destiny

◆ To describe the boundary conflicts with Great Britain over Maine and the Oregon Country

◆ To explain the reasons for the Mexican War

◆ To describe the election of 1848

◆ To describe events of the California gold rush

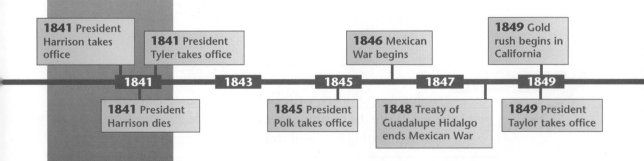

1841 President Harrison takes office

1841 President Tyler takes office

1846 Mexican War begins

1849 Gold rush begins in California

1841   1843   1845   1847   1849

1841 President Harrison dies

1845 President Polk takes office

1848 Treaty of Guadalupe Hidalgo ends Mexican War

1849 President Taylor takes office

Recall from Chapter 11 that Martin Van Buren became president in 1837. President Van Buren ran for re-election in 1840. The Whigs, needing a national hero, nominated William Henry Harrison as their candidate. At age 68, Harrison was still remembered for his great victory against the American Indians at Tippecanoe in 1811. The Whigs chose John Tyler as their candidate for vice president. They hoped Tyler would appeal to voters from the South. "Tippecanoe and Tyler, too!" became the **slogan** of the Whig Party.

What New Election Methods Were Used?

The Democrats made fun of William Henry Harrison. They said he lived in a log cabin and sat on the porch all day drinking hard cider, a kind of alcohol. Actually, Harrison lived in a very large house on 3,000 acres of land.

The Whigs decided to use the log cabin and hard cider story to help their candidate win the election. They held big parades with a log cabin mounted on a wagon. They passed out leaflets describing Harrison as a man of the people, an old fighter, and a great hero. In addition, they organized political meetings and painted large **billboards** with pictures of Harrison and Tyler. This was the first election campaign to use these new ways of winning votes. These ways worked, for Harrison easily won the election. In addition, the Whig Party gained control of the Congress.

Whigs used posters such as this one to win votes for William Henry Harrison and to announce rallies, or meetings.

What Happened to President Harrison?

Harrison took office in 1841. Weary and worn out from the election, Harrison came down with a cold. His condition grew worse, and on April 4, 1841, he died. He had been the president for only one month. Harrison was the first president to die in office. Vice President John Tyler then became president.

Formerly a U.S. Senator, Tyler had been a faithful Democrat. Although he had switched to the Whig Party, he held on to his belief in states' rights and a weak central government. As a result, he often came into conflict with Congress during his presidency.

 **History in Your Life**

John James Audubon

Our knowledge of birds owes much to one man, John James Audubon. His hobby since boyhood was observing and sketching birds. Audubon later pursued his hobby full time. In 1828, he displayed drawings entitled "The Birds of America" in Scotland. Audiences loved them, and Audubon quickly became known internationally. His pictures showed birds in great detail in their natural environment. Over 12 years, he created 435 hand-colored, full-page illustrations. Publishers printed his drawings with text he wrote with William MacGillivray. Some of the species he illustrated have become extinct, which means that there are no longer any of these birds alive in the world today. His drawings are now the best record of those species. The National Audubon Society publishes field guides and sponsors wildlife preservation projects.

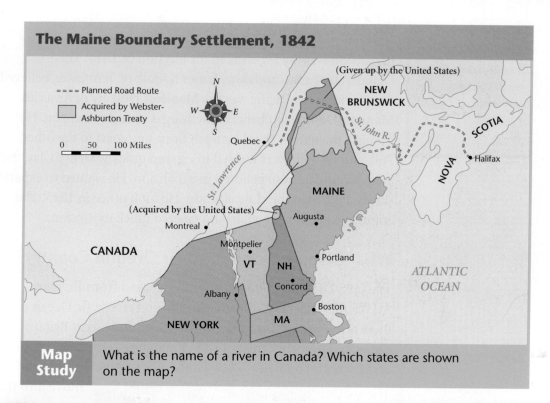

The Maine Boundary Settlement, 1842

==== Planned Road Route

☐ Acquired by Webster-
Ashburton Treaty

0   50   100 Miles

(Given up by the United States)

NEW BRUNSWICK

NOVA SCOTIA

St. John R.

Halifax

Quebec

St. Lawrence

MAINE

(Acquired by the United States)

Augusta

Montreal

Montpelier

CANADA

VT

NH

Portland

Albany

Concord

ATLANTIC OCEAN

Boston

NEW YORK

MA

Map Study	What is the name of a river in Canada? Which states are shown on the map?

Geography Note

Northern Maine pushes into Canada like a thumb. Along the thumb's western edge run the rugged White Mountains, part of the Appalachian Mountains. Farther north, the entire border region, which is about the size of Vermont and New Hampshire combined, is heavily forested. Rivers crisscross the region.

How Were Canadian Boundaries Still a Dispute?

The United States and Great Britain were still disputing the location of the boundary between Maine and Canada. By 1842, the disagreement nearly turned into a war. British ambassador Lord Ashburton met with Secretary of State Daniel Webster to try to work out a compromise.

The land in question covered 12,000 square miles. Both countries wanted the whole area. However, after many talks, a compromise was reached. Lord Ashburton said he would accept 5,000 square miles if the boundary did not block a road planned to go from Halifax, Nova Scotia, to Quebec. The United States received a large part of land, which included the fertile Aroostook Valley. Then, as a part of the same agreement, the British adjusted the boundary of what is now northeastern Minnesota. The United States gained control over an area that was later found to contain rich iron ore on the Mesabi Range in Minnesota.

What Was Manifest Destiny?

Expansion was the big issue in the election of 1844. The Democratic Party candidate, James K. Polk of Tennessee, believed expansion to the Pacific was the **Manifest Destiny** of America. Manifest Destiny is a belief something is meant to happen. He thought the nation should stretch from one coast to the other. Polk and his followers wanted to expand quickly. Henry Clay, the Whig candidate, also believed in expansion. He wanted to expand slowly. Polk won the close election. He took office in 1845. The country had chosen a man who favored quick expansion.

What Dispute Occurred over Oregon Country?

The area known as Oregon Country spread from Russian Alaska to Mexican California, and from the Pacific Ocean to the Rocky Mountains. The United States and Great Britain signed a temporary treaty in 1818 allowing settlement of the area by both countries. Then land-hungry Americans began to move into the region. Many of them had packed all of their belongings into crowded covered wagons in hope of a better life on the fertile Oregon land.

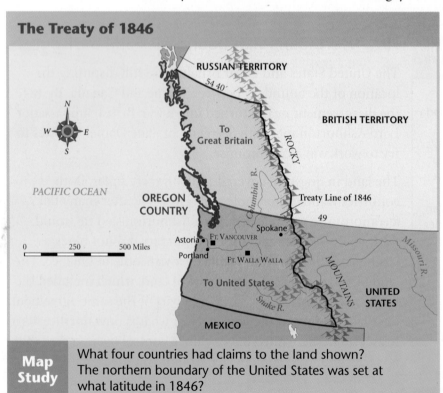

The Treaty of 1846

RUSSIAN TERRITORY
54 40'
To Great Britain
BRITISH TERRITORY
ROCKY
PACIFIC OCEAN
OREGON COUNTRY
Columbia R.
Treaty Line of 1846
49
Spokane
Astoria Ft. Vancouver
Portland Ft. Walla Walla
Missouri R.
0   250   500 Miles
To United States
MOUNTAINS
Snake R.
UNITED STATES
MEXICO

Map Study
What four countries had claims to the land shown? The northern boundary of the United States was set at what latitude in 1846?

As the American population of Oregon Country grew, America and Great Britain disputed the boundary of American Oregon. In his election speech, President Polk had promised to take American Oregon as far north as 54 degrees 40 minutes north latitude. He used the slogan "54–40 or fight." After the two sides debated the issue, the British agreed to 49 degrees north latitude as the northern boundary of America. President Polk felt this was a fair compromise, and he wanted to keep America out of yet another war with Great Britain. In the Treaty of 1846, the United States accepted the southern part of Oregon Country. Great Britain took the northern part, with 49 degrees north latitude as the boundary.

What do you think ?

Why do you think Americans felt it was so important to expand U.S. territory?

Lesson 1 Review On a sheet of paper, write the answers to the following questions. Use complete sentences.

1. How was the election of 1840 different from other elections?

2. What happened to President Harrison?

3. How did Britain and America settle boundary disputes over the Maine and Canadian boundary?

4. What is Manifest Destiny?

5. What was Oregon Country?

Biography

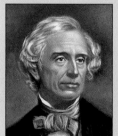

Samuel F. B. Morse: 1791–1872
Samuel F. B. Morse was first recognized as a painter and a founder of the National Academy of Design. He is better known today, however, as the inventor of the first successful electric telegraph. In effect, the telegraph made electricity visible. It also made immediate communication of messages over long distances possible. With his Morse code—an alphabet of dots and dashes—messages could be sent by telegraph. The first telegraphic message was sent by Morse in 1844 from Washington, D.C., to Baltimore, Maryland. It was the famous greeting, "What hath God wrought!" Later he experimented with underwater cable telegraphy. He was also involved in introducing the daguerreotype, an early type of photograph, in the United States.

Insult

An action that upsets others

When Santa Anna surrendered to Sam Houston in the War of Texas Independence in 1836, he had agreed that the Rio Grande River was the boundary between Mexico and Texas. Later, he said the boundary was the Nueces River, which gave Texans far less territory. Texans would not accept the new Mexican boundary.

The Republic of Texas became part of the United States in 1845. Texas was the 28th state to join the Union. Slavery was allowed in Texas. Many Americans were against the state joining the Union because of this slavery issue. However, the border dispute was a more pressing problem. After Texas joined the Union, some people feared there would be a war with Mexico.

President Polk was eager to settle the Texas boundary dispute with Mexico. At the same time, he wanted to see if that country would sell California to America. He thought that Mexico, which needed money, would be willing to sell the land. The president sent John Slidell to Mexico City in 1845. As Polk's personal representative, Slidell could offer up to $25 million as payment for California. The Mexican officials refused to see him. President Polk did not take this **insult** to the United States lightly.

It Happened in History

Pioneers in Women's Rights

On page 268 you will read about the Seneca Falls Declaration of Sentiments of 1848. It was one of the first documents relating to women's rights. Elizabeth Cady Stanton was at the Seneca Falls Convention. When she met Susan B. Anthony in 1851, they became partners in a long effort to win the right of women to vote. They did not live to see their dream come true. Stanton died in 1902 and Anthony in 1906. It was not until 1920 that the 19th Amendment granted women the right to vote—more than 70 years after the Seneca Falls Convention.

Susan B. Anthony, left, and Elizabeth Cady Stanton

What Was the Mexican War?

Polk ordered General Zachary Taylor to advance his army beyond the Nueces River toward the Rio Grande in January 1846. The Mexican army remained quiet. February and March passed; there was still no action. Finally, on April 25, 1846, Mexican troops crossed the Rio Grande and killed many of General Taylor's soldiers. The United States, in turn, declared war with its southern neighbor on May 13, 1846. This was the beginning of the Mexican War.

Polk still wanted to extend the United States to the Pacific coast. He ordered American troops to invade California. The troops were led by Stephen W. Kearny, John D. Sloat, and John C. Frémont. They had very little trouble defeating the Mexicans. Meanwhile, Zachary Taylor fought his way into Mexico. "Old Rough and Ready," as he was called, won a major victory for the Americans at Buena Vista.

General Winfield Scott was known as "Old Fuss and Feathers."

In early 1847, General Winfield Scott led a charge on Mexico City. Scott was an expert in preparing for battles. Because of his complete attention to every last detail, he was known as "Old Fuss and Feathers." At that time, many believed he was the country's most capable general. In September, Scott and his troops captured Mexico City.

How Did the Mexican War End?

Mexico, which had a new government, finally was ready to make peace. President Polk had sent Nicholas P. Trist to negotiate a treaty. In 1848, the Treaty of Guadalupe Hidalgo was presented to Congress. In the treaty, Mexico would turn over California and all the land between Texas and California. Mexico also agreed that the Rio Grande was the southern boundary of Texas. The United States paid Mexico $15 million for the land. Polk suggested that the treaty be accepted. Congress agreed to the treaty in 1848. The United States now stretched from coast to coast.

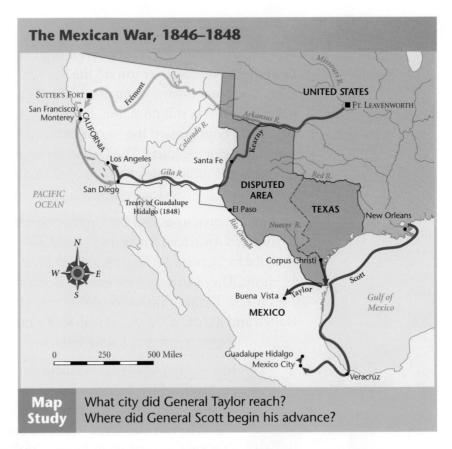

The Mexican War, 1846–1848

Map Study

What city did General Taylor reach?
Where did General Scott begin his advance?

What do you think ?

Do you think all of Mexico should have been turned over to America after the war? Explain your answer.

Lesson 2 Review Choose the name in parentheses that best completes each sentence. Write your answers on a sheet of paper.

1. (President Polk, Zachary Taylor, Winfield Scott) wanted to settle the border dispute with Mexico.

2. President Polk sent (Sam Houston, Winfield Scott, John Slidell) to Mexico to offer payment for California.

3. (Santa Anna, Zachary Taylor, Winfield Scott) won a major victory for the Americans at Buena Vista.

4. (Zachary Taylor, Winfield Scott, Sam Houston) captured Mexico City.

5. (Winfield Scott, Zachary Taylor, President Polk) was known as "Old Rough and Ready."

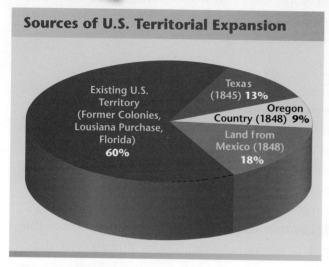

Sources of U.S. Territorial Expansion

- Existing U.S. Territory (Former Colonies, Lousiana Purchase, Florida) **60%**
- Texas (1845) **13%**
- Oregon Country (1848) **9%**
- Land from Mexico (1848) **18%**

What percentage of U.S. land came from Oregon Country? What percentage of U.S. land came from Mexico in 1848?

In addition to the expansion of the United States, President Polk had other goals for the future of the country. He wanted to lower tariffs and acquire California from Mexico. During his four-year term as president, Polk got what he wanted. Between 1845 and 1848, the United States added more than 800,000 square miles of land. Also, tariffs were lowered, and there was less government spending. However, even with his successes in office, President Polk refused to run for a second term.

What Happened in the Election of 1848?

Americans were excited about the victory over Mexico and about the land that had been added. New land, however, meant new problems. The biggest problem was the possible spread of slavery into the western region.

Slavery was the most important issue in the election of 1848. However, the Whigs and the Democrats took limited stands on it. Both parties were unsure how such a stand would affect the success of their candidates in the election.

The Whigs nominated General Zachary Taylor. Taylor was a hero, having won an important victory at Buena Vista during the Mexican War. Taylor was a southerner and would get strong support from slave states. The Democrats nominated Lewis Cass, a northerner from Michigan.

Many Democrats who did not want Cass broke away and formed the Free Soil Party. The Free Soilers chose Martin Van Buren as their candidate for president. The new party favored free speech, free labor, and free men.

Zachary Taylor won the election. He received 163 electoral votes; Cass had 127. The Democrats lost the popular vote too. The Free Soilers took votes that would have gone to Cass. The issue of slavery decided the election by splitting the Democratic Party. Taylor took office in 1849.

How Did California Become Important?

Before the 1840s, most inhabitants of California were Spaniards and American Indians. Swiss-American settler John A. Sutter was one of the first to gain success in California. He owned a large amount of land in a valley north of San Francisco. He built a big fort that travelers used on their way into California. Sutter also grew wheat and corn and had large numbers of cattle, sheep, and horses. He had this "kingdom" all to himself for most of the 1840s. However, his way of life changed a lot after an event that took place in 1848.

One day, a man who worked for Sutter collected a small sack of nuggets and dust he believed was gold. He showed the sack to Sutter. They intended to keep the find a secret. However, by 1849, the message had spread throughout the land, and people came from every direction.

Miners, or Forty-Niners, labored over the California land in search of gold. Most of them ended up with nothing.

Towns were formed as laborers, miners, farmers, merchants, **professional** people, and other **fortune seekers** rushed to California. The Forty-Niners, named for the year of the gold rush, used every means of transportation possible to reach the gold country. Prices for supplies and services greatly increased. Crime also increased. The output of gold rose to $10 million in 1849.

California's population increased from about 15,000 to more than 100,000. Some of those who joined the rush struck it rich, but most of them ended up with nothing.

In only slightly more than a year's time, the population of California had increased by nearly 10 times. Cities had sprung up in many regions of the western land. Almost overnight, it had grown to look like a part of the United States. Then, in 1850, it became the 31st state.

Word Bank

President Polk

slavery

state

John Sutter

Zachary Taylor

Lesson 3 Review On a sheet of paper, write the correct word or words from the Word Bank to complete each sentence.

1. Between 1845 and 1848, _____ raised government spending, lowered tariffs, and added land to the nation.

2. The election of 1848 was decided by the issue of _____, which split the Democratic ticket.

3. In 1849, _____, a Whig, took office as president.

4. In 1848, gold was found on land in California owned by _____.

5. In 1850, California entered the Union as the 31st _____.

What do you think ?

Why do you think the gold rush brought so many people to California?

Then and Now

What conditions did immigrants face? In 1850, for example, Irish immigrants faced difficult times. Without money to travel west, they settled in New York slums. As Catholics, they were not welcomed by Protestant Americans. They took low-paying jobs in factories or as housekeepers. Still, many Irish were able to send money to poor family members in Ireland.

In 1850, most immigrants came to the United States from Europe. Today, most immigrants come from Asia or Mexico. In 1850, any healthy European was welcome. Today, immigration is strictly controlled. Immigrants must be accepted before coming. Then they must go through several steps before becoming U.S. citizens.

Seneca Falls Declaration of Sentiments

In 1848, the Seneca Falls Convention was held in New York. It was led by Elizabeth Cady Stanton and Lucretia Mott. Delegates adopted the Declaration of Sentiments and Resolutions. It is considered to be one of the first documents calling for equal rights for women.

When, in the course of human events, it becomes necessary for one portion of the family of man to assume among the people of the earth a position different from that which they have hitherto occupied, but one to which the laws of nature and of nature's God entitle them, a decent respect to the opinions of mankind requires that they should declare the causes that impel them to such a course.

We hold these truths to be self-evident: that all men and women are created equal. . . .

The history of mankind is a history of repeated injuries and usurpations [taking over] on the part of man toward woman, having in direct object the establishment of an absolute tyranny over her. To prove this, let facts be submitted to a candid world. . . .

Now, in view of this entire disenfranchisement of one-half of the people of this country, their social and religious degradation, in view of the unjust laws above mentioned, and

because women do feel themselves aggrieved, oppressed, and fraudulently [by cheating] deprived of their most sacred rights, we insist that they have immediate admission to all the rights and privileges which belong to them as citizens of the United States. . . .

Resolved, therefore, that being invested by the Creator with the same capabilities and the same consciousness of responsibility for their exercise . . . and this being a self-evident truth growing out of the divinely implanted truth of human nature, any custom or authority adverse to it, whether modern or wearing the hoary [old] sanction of antiquity, is to be regarded as a self-evident falsehood, and at war with mankind.

Document-Based Questions

1. What does this declaration say women are entitled to?

2. The second paragraph is similar to the beginning of the Declaration of Independence. What words have been added to make it different?

3. What does the third paragraph say about the history of men's treatment of women?

4. The last paragraph says a truth of human nature is that women are invested with the same capabilities and responsibilities as men. What does it say about any authority that disagrees with that?

5. How wise do you think it was for these women to make this declaration?

Source: The Declaration of Sentiments and Resolutions, Elizabeth Cady Stanton, 1848.

- William Henry Harrison ran for president and used new campaign methods, including leaflets, billboards, and the slogan "Tippecanoe and Tyler, too!" Harrison died one month after he became president. He was the first president to die while in office.

- A dispute arose between Great Britain and America over the northern boundary of Maine. Great Britain and America reached a compromise that gave land to both countries.

- President Polk promoted the idea of Manifest Destiny. He said that the United States was meant to control the lands and people from the Atlantic Coast to the Pacific Coast.

- Great Britain and America disagreed about the boundaries for Oregon Country in the Northwest. America wanted the boundary to be at 54 degrees 40 minutes north latitude. A compromise reached in 1846 set the boundary at 49 degrees north latitude.

- Texas became a state in 1845, but there were questions about the border between Texas and Mexico. Polk ordered American troops to advance to the Rio Grande River. The United States declared war on Mexico in May 1846.

- After American troops captured Mexico City, the Mexicans made peace with the United States. The Treaty of Guadalupe Hidalgo in 1848 ended the Mexican War and gave America the California territory.

- President Polk accomplished his goal of Manifest Destiny and added more than 800,000 square miles of land to the United States during the four years he was president.

- Slavery was the biggest issue of the 1848 presidential election. Zachary Taylor, a southerner and hero of the Mexican War, won the election.

- In 1848, gold was discovered on land in California owned by John Sutter. The discovery led to the largest movement of people in U.S. history.

- During the gold rush of 1849, the population of California increased from about 15,000 to more than 100,000. Many people grew rich by mining gold. But many more grew rich by selling supplies to the Forty-Niners, the people who came to California to search for gold.

- In 1850, California applied for statehood and became the 31st state.

Chapter 13 REVIEW

Word Bank

California

"54–40 or fight"

John Sutter

John Tyler

Manifest Destiny

Minnesota

Texas

"Tippecanoe and Tyler, too!"

William Henry Harrison

Zachary Taylor

On a sheet of paper, write the correct word or words from the Word Bank to complete each sentence.

1. _____ was a phrase used by President James Polk to encourage the United States to expand from coast to coast.

2. President _____ was known as "Old Rough and Ready" because of his leadership in the Mexican War.

3. Gold was discovered on land owned by _____ in California.

4. The first president to die in office was _____.

5. The Forty-Niners helped increase the population of _____.

6. _____ was a very strong supporter of states' rights.

7. The slogan _____ was about a dispute over the borders of Oregon Country.

8. Harrison's campaign slogan was _____.

9. Settlers in _____ decided to give up their independence and become a state in 1845.

10. The United States gave up part of Maine, but gained a portion of what is now _____.

On a sheet of paper, write the letter of the answer that correctly answers each question.

11. What was the outcome of the Mexican War?

   A The United States received California and other land in exchange for money.

   B Texas became the 28th state.

   C Mexican officials insulted President Polk.

   D Texas became smaller.

12. Why did so many people rush to California in 1849?

  A Gold was discovered.

  B They fought in the war.

  C The cities had job openings.

  D A cross-country railroad was finished.

13. What territory became the 31st state in 1850?

  A Texas   **B** California   **C** Oregon   **D** Iowa

14. Which president died one month after taking office?

  A James Monroe   **C** Zachary Taylor

  B William Henry Harrison **D** James Polk

On a sheet of paper, write the answer to each question. Use complete sentences.

15. Why did Great Britain dispute Maine's northern boundary?

16. How did President Polk fulfill his dream of Manifest Destiny?

17. What were two main reasons for the Mexican War?

18. How far south into Mexico did the United States army go during the Mexican War?

Critical Thinking On a sheet of paper, write your response to each question. Use complete sentences.

19. Harrison's presidential campaign used slogans and billboards to tell people about him. How important is advertising in today's presidential races?

20. Many people sold everything they owned so that they could go to California to search for gold. Do you think these people made good decisions? Why or why not?

Test-Taking Tip

To get ready for a test, review your notes. Use a marker to highlight key words and important ideas. Make up test questions involving these parts.

Unit 4

Skill Builder

Fact and Opinion

As you study history, you will read many facts. Sometimes people write books about history in which they state their opinions. You need to be able to tell the difference between fact and opinion.

A fact can be proven true or false.

> The Cumberland Road stretched from Cumberland to Vandalia.

An opinion is someone's judgment, belief, or way of thinking about something. Look for words that tell how someone felt.

> Travel on the Cumberland Road was difficult.
>
> Travel on the Cumberland Road was easy.

Decide which of the two sentences in items 1–4 is fact and which is opinion. Explain your answers. Then write your own fact and opinion statements for item 5.

1. The cotton gin was the best invention of the 1800s.

   The cotton gin enabled cotton production to increase.

2. A poll is an organized method of asking people what they think about a candidate.

   Polls are not always correct.

3. Between 1790 and 1810, the population of the United States nearly doubled.

   Immigrants to the United States faced many hardships.

4. Because Mexico needed money, it would be willing to sell California to the United States.

   Mexican officials refused to meet with President Polk's personal representative.

5. Write a statement of fact and a statement of opinion about slavery.

- James Monroe became president in 1817.

- Between 1790 and 1820, the U.S. population increased by six million.

- Farming thrived in the South. Industry thrived in the North.

- The Adams-Onís Treaty gave Florida to America in 1819.

- Slavery became an issue in the 1800s.

- President Monroe announced the Monroe Doctrine in 1823.

- Congress chose John Quincy Adams as president in 1825.

- The country was split on the Tariff of 1828.

- Andrew Jackson became president in 1829.

- Nat Turner led a slave revolt in 1831.

- Jackson asked Congress to set aside land for American Indians.

- Texans won independence from Mexico in 1836.

- Martin Van Buren became president in 1837.

- The Panic of 1837 resulted in a depression and many bank failures.

- Many machines helped industry and farming grow.

- By 1837, hundreds of steamboats provided transportation on rivers.

- The Erie Canal opened in 1825.

- Railroads became the fastest means of transportation.

- The telegraph expanded communication.

- By 1830, the U.S. population grew to 13 million.

- The second wave of immigrants came from Ireland and Germany.

- Public education grew in the 1800s.

- President William Henry Harrison died in office.

- The United States declared war on Mexico in 1846.

- President James Polk's Manifest Destiny added land to the United States.

- Slavery was the big issue in the 1848 election.

- In 1848, gold was discovered in California.

"I can anticipate no greater calamity for the country than the dissolution of the Union. It would be an accumulation of all the evils we complain of, and I am willing to sacrifice everything but honor for its preservation."

~ *General Robert E. Lee, from a letter to his son, January 23, 1861*

Unit 5

Civil War and Reconstruction

D ifferences over slavery and states' rights were growing strong in the United States around 1850. Divisions between the North and the South grew until the country split apart. The split caused the country to enter a four-year civil war. Even individual families were sometimes divided, with members fighting against each other on opposite sides. When the war ended, the country had to bind up its wounds, heal its divisions, and rebuild.

In this unit, you will learn about many differences over the issue of slavery. You will learn about events that led the United States into a war within itself. You will learn about the damage the war did to individuals, families, and the nation. You will learn what the nation did to reunite and rebuild.

Chapters in Unit 5

14 The Slavery Problem Grows

Slavery in the United States continued to cause many problems. The North and the South, and now the newly created West, debated the issue around the nation and in Congress. Short-term solutions began to appear. However, people were beginning to see that the issue was dividing the nation. In this chapter, you will learn how the issue of slavery became the main concern of the nation.

Goals for Learning

◆ To describe the various issues faced by the North and the South concerning slavery

◆ To explain the significance of the Compromise of 1850

◆ To explain the Fugitive Slave Law

◆ To describe the Underground Railroad and how it worked

◆ To explain the importance of cotton to the United States

◆ To describe the Kansas-Nebraska Act

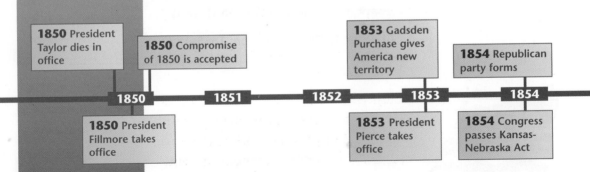

1850 President Taylor dies in office

1850 Compromise of 1850 is accepted

1853 Gadsden Purchase gives America new territory

1854 Republican party forms

1850   1851   1852   1853   1854

1850 President Fillmore takes office

1853 President Pierce takes office

1854 Congress passes Kansas-Nebraska Act

Exaggerate
To overstate the truth

Since the 1830s, abolitionists had campaigned against slavery. Leaders such as William Lloyd Garrison used antislavery newspapers to try to sway opinion in the country. Theodore Weld and his wife, Angelina Grimké, traveled all over the country speaking and organizing new abolitionist groups. Countless others helped slaves escape to freedom.

Southerners felt the abolitionists were trying to harm their way of life. The white people of the South believed they needed slave labor for their plantations and businesses. They felt the abolitionists were unfairly **exaggerating** how poorly the slaves were treated. Southern writers wrote that free Africans in the North were treated worse than enslaved Africans in the South who worked on the plantations. They claimed that free Africans had no political rights, low-level jobs, and poor living conditions. Enslaved Africans, on the other hand, were given food, clothing, and shelter by their owners.

Many Northerners needed goods from Southern businesses. They felt the abolitionists caused problems for them in their dealings with the South. Even those who may have opposed slavery believed that the abolitionists did more to harm the country than to improve it. Despite these difficulties, by 1850 more than 200,000 Americans were members of abolitionist groups throughout the Northern states.

What New Debate Started in Congress?

Between 1836 and 1848, six new states had been added to the Union, bringing the total number of states to 30. The balance of free states to slave states was at 15 each. However, when California sought admission to the Union as a free state, tempers once again flared.

Southerners were certain that the antislavery states in the North would gain control of the country. Southern leaders wanted to protect their rights. They felt that the South should not have to change. The Southern economy depended on slavery.

What Compromise Helped the Slavery Issue?

Three of America's most experienced leaders helped to bring a temporary settlement to the slavery issue. Daniel Webster, Henry Clay, and John C. Calhoun had spent many years in public service. All of them were well-respected leaders.

Webster and Calhoun debated the slavery issue in Congress. Webster wanted the country to stay united. Calhoun was from South Carolina. He felt slavery should be allowed to continue, yet he didn't want it to destroy the country.

Henry Clay proposed a compromise. President Taylor, who opposed the spread of slavery, would not permit any compromise. The situation changed, though, when Taylor suddenly became ill and died in July 1850. He had been in office only 16 months.

Vice President Millard Fillmore became president. Unlike Taylor, he favored a compromise. He believed that an agreement could be worked out. After eight months of debate, the Compromise of 1850 was accepted by the North and the South. The compromise was much better for the North than for the South.

What Was the Compromise of 1850?

The compromise agreed to:

- allow California to become a free state.
- allow additional western territories such as Utah and New Mexico to decide for themselves if they wanted to allow slavery when they joined the Union.
- abolish slave trade in the District of Columbia.
- allow Texas to sell its claim on New Mexico for $10 million.
- create a new law, called the **Fugitive** Slave Law, to help slave owners recapture their runaway slaves.

Then and Now

The word *abolish* means to end something. As far back as the early 1800s, people called abolitionists worked hard to end slavery in the United States. In 1833, the American Anti-Slavery Society was founded in Philadelphia. Slavery was not ended until the passage of the 13th Amendment to the Constitution in 1865. However, for years afterward, African Americans often were treated unfairly.

In the mid-1900s, several brave leaders emerged to work for permanent civil rights for all Americans. New laws helped end segregation and gain new rights for African Americans. Today, African Americans have made progress, but the effects of slavery continue. Poverty hits minority groups harder than whites. Courts have ended some systems that help minority groups attend college, get a job, or buy a house.

What do you think ?

Do you agree that the North benefited more by the Compromise of 1850? Explain.

Lesson 1 Review On a sheet of paper, write the letter of the answer that correctly completes each sentence.

1. Since the 1830s, _____ had campaigned against slavery.
   A slaves
   B abolitionists
   C Southerners
   D plantation owners

2. California wanted admission to the Union as a _____.
   A slave state
   B free state
   C neutral state
   D Southern state

3. The South feared that the antislavery states would _____.
   A gain control of the country
   B leave the Union
   C stop trading with the South
   D divide the nation

4. In 1850, the slavery debate was settled in Congress by _____.
   A a debate
   B President Taylor
   C the Compromise of 1850
   D the Supreme Court

5. The part of the compromise that favored the South was the _____.
   A end of slave trade in the District of Columbia
   B admission of California as a free state
   C sale of Texas claims to New Mexico
   D passage of the Fugitive Slave Law

Writing About History

Research one stop on the Underground Railroad. In your notebook, write a report explaining where it was and how it hid and moved slaves. Include diagrams to show the way of hiding.

Under the Fugitive Slave Law, the federal government could be called upon to settle fugitive slave cases. People in the North had to return runaway slaves to owners. Anyone caught helping slaves would be fined. Sometimes these people were put in prison. According to the law, the owner had to provide proof of ownership to a judge. That's all that was needed to prove an African was enslaved. Clearly, this law challenged any African's right to freedom.

Slave owners thought this law was fair. Northerners, though, chose to ignore the law completely. Abolitionist efforts to help slaves to escape were not slowed down.

How Did the Underground Railroad Help Slaves?

The Underground Railroad developed to help slaves escape slavery. The Underground Railroad was not really a railroad at all. It was a secret escape route to help slaves reach free states.

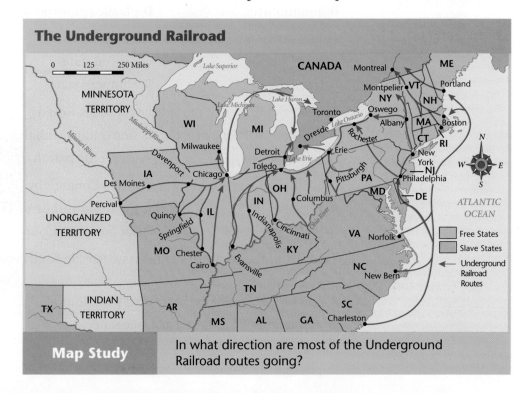

The Underground Railroad

Map Study In what direction are most of the Underground Railroad routes going?

It was very dangerous for both the slaves and those who helped them. Antislavery **conductors** were people who helped to hide slaves as they moved from station to station. "Stations" were homes of people who hid the slaves during the day and sent them to other homes at night. This secret **network** went from the South to the North and into Canada. Former slaves Frederick Douglass, Sojourner Truth, and Harriet Tubman spoke out against slavery. They helped many people take advantage of the Underground Railroad.

Sojourner Truth

Frederick Douglass

How Did Cotton Control the Nation?

After the invention of the cotton gin, Southern plantation owners began to receive large profits. Cotton was sold both in the United States and to other countries. It was an important raw material for the textile industry in the North. Cotton made up more than half of the total exported products of the United States. Cotton was not just another crop; it was the big moneymaker of the country.

The Underground Railroad helped many slaves escape slavery.

Unfortunately, the South had made little progress over the years. The rich plantation owners prevented changes by controlling the state governments. Southerners closed themselves off to the major changes that came to the rest of the country. They got angry when people spoke out against slavery. They felt that their way of life was being threatened.

The majority of Southerners did not own slaves. Most of the people in the South were farmers who did all of their own work. Many Southerners did not think that slavery was wrong. They considered the practice to be good for both the slaves and the plantation owners.

What Did Franklin Pierce Do as President?

Franklin Pierce, a Democrat from New Hampshire, became president in 1853. Pierce was not against slavery, even though he was from a northern state. He chose Jefferson Davis to be his secretary of war. Davis had served in the House of Representatives and the Senate.

Under President Pierce, Davis sent James Gadsden, the United States minister to Mexico, to work out the purchase of land in the Southwest in 1853. A strip of land that now makes up part of New Mexico and Arizona cost $10 million. With this purchase, called the Gadsden Purchase, the United States was free to build a railroad to Southern California. The permanent southwest boundary between the United States and Mexico was set.

Word Bank

Franklin Pierce

Fugitive Slave Law

Gadsden Purchase

Sojourner Truth

Underground Railroad

What do you think

Most Southerners who did not own slaves did not think slavery was wrong. Why do you think they thought this?

Lesson 2 Review On a sheet of paper, write the correct words from the Word Bank to complete each sentence.

1. The _____ made Northerners return runaway slaves.

2. The _____ helped free slaves.

3. _____ was a former slave who spoke out against slavery.

4. _____ became president in 1853.

5. The _____ was the purchase of land that set the boundary between the United States and Mexico.

Produce
Fruits or vegetables

Geography Note

In 1853, President Pierce wanted to build a railroad to the West Coast. That was the reason for the Gadsden Purchase. It would be easier to build a railroad in this region, which is now part of New Mexico and Arizona, than in the North. The railroad was completed in 1882.

The population of California was growing well beyond the 100,000 who lived there at the time it became a state. Each month, thousands more people were making their way to the West. Travel by covered wagon often took months. Sailing around South America was long and dangerous. Something had to be done to make the trip easier and faster.

Many towns and cities throughout the East were connected by railroads. Farmers used the railroad to bring their **produce** to market. Businesses used the railroads to ship their goods. People traveled safely and quickly by railcar. If the country was going to grow, a railroad from coast to coast was necessary.

Congress discussed possible routes for the railroad. The railroad could go:

• from Chicago to the Oregon coast,

• from Chicago to St. Louis to San Francisco,

• from New Orleans to San Diego, or

• from Memphis to a point east of Los Angeles.

Congress could not agree on a route. Southerners wanted to build a railroad from New Orleans to San Diego. Northerners were against a Southern route. They feared Southerners would move west and take their slaves with them.

What Did Stephen Douglas Do?

The Northerners, led by Senator Stephen Douglas, wanted to build a railroad from St. Louis or Chicago to California. This route, however, would go through Nebraska. Nebraska was not an organized territory.

"The Little Giant," as Douglas was called, introduced a bill to allow Nebraska to become a territory. This action brought up the slave state issue. According to the Missouri Compromise of 1820, Nebraska would organize as a free territory. The boundary line for free states was at 36 degrees 30 minutes north latitude.

Popular sovereignty

The power of the people to decide something, especially whether to become a free state or a slave state

Tension

Uncomfortable feelings toward another person or group

Stephen Douglas and others suggested a compromise. Douglas wanted to repeal the 1820 law. He wanted to organize the territories of Kansas and Nebraska. His bill also allowed the voters in the territories to decide whether each would become a free state or a slave state. This was called **popular sovereignty**.

Congress passed the Kansas-Nebraska Act in 1854. This bill caused many conflicts between political parties. **Tension** between the slave states and free states was at an all-time high. The slavery issue was hurting the country.

How Did the Republican Party Form?

A group of Free Soilers, Northern Whigs, and Democrats met in 1854 and formed the Republican Party. Their main problem with the existing parties was that they did not take a clear stand on slavery. Gaining most support from the North, the new party wished to repeal the Kansas-Nebraska Act and the Fugitive Slave Law.

History in Your Life

The Sewing Machine

American Walter Hunt invented the "practical lock stitch" sewing machine in 1832. Many tailors and seamstresses feared they would lose their living if the machines became popular. People who sewed by hand reacted so negatively that it failed. In the 1840s in Boston, Elias Howe developed an improved lock stitch machine. However, he was unable to sell his machine in America or England. Finally, in 1852, using Howe's needle design, Isaac Merrit Singer developed and successfully marketed a sewing machine. The key to his success was selling the machines on installment, or credit, plans. By 1860, the Singer Manufacturing Company was the world's largest producer of sewing machines. Singer sewing machines are still made today.

Lesson 3 Review On a sheet of paper, write the answers to the following questions. Use complete sentences.

1. Why were railroads needed for travel to the West?

2. Which routes for a railroad were discussed?

3. Which railroad route did the Northerners favor?

4. Which railroad route did the Southerners favor?

5. Which groups formed the Republican Party?

What do you think ?

Which railroad route would you choose if it were up to you? Why?

Biography

Harriet Tubman: c. 1820–1913

Harriet Tubman was an African American and a bold abolitionist. Born into slavery in Maryland around 1820, she worked as a field hand. She never learned to read or write. In 1849, she escaped to Philadelphia. From there, she made many dangerous rescue missions into the South. She eventually led more than 300 other slaves to freedom through the Underground Railroad. During the Civil War, Tubman served the Union Army in South Carolina as a nurse, a scout, and a spy. Sarah Bradford wrote the story of Tubman's life and work in her book *Scenes in the Life of Harriet Tubman.*

Daniel Webster's Speech to the Senate

After serving as an outspoken member of Congress during the 1820s, Daniel Webster became the leader of the Whig party. He served as Secretary of State under Presidents Harrison, Tyler, and Fillmore. Webster believed that the unity of the country was more important than the abolition of slavery. After a return to the Senate in the mid-1840s, he went on to endorse the Compromise of 1850. As a result, he lost the support of many party members who strongly opposed slavery. The following passage is from one of Webster's speeches to the Senate in 1850.

Secession [leaving]! Peaceable secession! Sir, your eyes and mine are never destined to see that miracle. The dismemberment of this vast country without convulsion! The breaking up of the fountains of the great deep without ruffling the surface! Who is so foolish—I beg everybody's pardon—as to expect to see any such thing? . . .

Is the great Constitution under which we live here—covering this whole country—is it to be thawed and melted away by secession as the snows on the mountain melt under the influence of a vernal [spring] sun—disappear almost unobserved and die off? No, sir! No sir! . . . . I see it as plainly as I see the sun in heaven—I see that disruption must produce such a war as I will not describe, in its twofold characters.

Peaceable secession! Peaceable secession! The concurrent agreement of all the members of this great republic to separate! . . . Where is the line to be drawn? What states are to secede? What is to remain American? What am I to be? An American no longer? Where is the flag of the republic to remain? Where is the eagle still to tower? Or is he to cower, and shrink, and fall to the ground?

Document-Based Questions

1. To what does Webster compare the Constitution?

2. Why do you think Webster repeated the phrase "peaceable secession" so often?

3. Why did Webster think that a war over secession was inevitable?

4. Webster named two main issues on which Congress was unlikely to agree regarding secession. What was one of them?

5. Do you agree with Webster's method of speaking? Explain your answer.

Source: Daniel Webster's Speech to the Senate, 1850.

Chapter 14 SUMMARY

- The abolitionist movement continued to grow.

- Many Southerners believed that the end of slavery would mean the end of their way of life. The South's economy depended on the free labor of slaves.

- As new states were added to the United States, Congress had to decide whether they would be free states or slave states. Many Northerners did not want slavery to spread and opposed adding new slave states. Southerners believed that there should be an equal number of slave and free states.

- The Compromise of 1850 was the most important act of Congress in this period. The compromise allowed California to enter the Union as a free state. It also set out rules for the addition of future free and slave states, abolished slave trade in the District of Columbia, and established the Fugitive Slave Law.

- The Fugitive Slave Law stated that Northerners had to return runaway slaves to their Southern owners. The law challenged the right to freedom of almost all African slaves and freemen.

- The Underground Railroad was a secret escape route for slaves who were seeking freedom. People helped the runaways by hiding them from authorities. The routes ran northward to Canada.

- Many former slaves were active in the abolitionist movement and with the Underground Railroad. Among the most famous were Sojourner Truth, Frederick Douglass, and Harriet Tubman.

- Manufacturing textiles involved both the North and the South. Cotton from the South was the raw material for the mills of the North. Cotton and fabrics were the largest export of the United States.

- In 1853, the Gadsden Purchase added the final piece of land to the United States. America purchased the strip of land, which is now in New Mexico and Arizona, for $10 million.

- The country needed to establish a railroad route from the East Coast to the West Coast. Choosing a route for the railroad caused new problems between free and slave states.

- The Kansas-Nebraska Act allowed voters in the territories to decide if they would be admitted to the United States as a free state or a slave state.

Chapter 14 REVIEW

Word Bank

abolitionists

Compromise of 1850

free states

Gadsden Purchase

Harriet Tubman

Kansas-Nebraska Act

slave states

textiles

Underground Railroad

William Lloyd Garrison

On a sheet of paper, write the correct word or words from the Word Bank to complete each sentence.

1. Many senior statesmen, including Henry Clay and John C. Calhoun, worked on the _____.

2. _____ published an abolitionist newspaper.

3. The _____ was used to help slaves escape to freedom.

4. _____ was a famous "conductor" on the Underground Railroad.

5. People who actively worked to end slavery were called _____.

6. California was admitted to the Union as one of the _____.

7. The _____ were concerned that abolitionists wanted to ruin their way of life.

8. Crops from the South provided the raw materials to make _____ in the North.

9. The _____, proposed by Stephen Douglas, was very unpopular with slave states.

10. A piece of land in the Southwest became U.S. territory with the _____.

On a sheet of paper, write the letter of the answer that correctly answers each question.

11. What helped ease the conflict over slavery for a time?

    A Underground Railroad   C Kansas-Nebraska Act

    B Compromise of 1850   D formation of the Republican Party

12. What made the most money for the United States in the 1850s?

    A slavery   C cotton

    B railroads   D the slave tax

13. Which of the following was guaranteed by the Compromise of 1850?

  A California became a slave state.

  B The Fugitive Slave Law was repealed.

  C Slave trade was abolished in the District of Columbia.

  D Nebraska became a territory.

On a sheet of paper, write the answers to the following questions. Use complete sentences.

14. Why was cotton so important for both the South and the North?

15. What impact did the railroad have on the Kansas-Nebraska Act?

16. Which part of the Compromise of 1850 affected California the most?

17. Why did Southerners feel that abolitionists were wrong?

18. What was the purpose of the Fugitive Slave Law?

Critical Thinking On a sheet of paper, write your response to each question. Use complete sentences.

19. Do you think the Compromise of 1850 was fair to both free and slave states? Explain the reasons for your answer.

20. Both sides felt very strongly about the slavery issue and had a difficult time compromising. Think of an issue that divides people today. Compare this issue to the abolitionist movement. How are they alike? How are they different?

Test-Taking Tip

After you finish a test, reread the questions and your answers. Ask yourself, "Did I answer the question that was asked? Does this answer show that I understood the question?"

15 The Country Separates

T he issue of slavery was still not solved. It continued to cause problems. People began to use violence to try to settle their disagreements about slavery. The nation was entering a very difficult period of time. Eventually, a presidential election caused the country to separate. In this chapter, you will learn the reasons why several states left the Union.

Goals for Learning

◆ To explain why the statehood of Kansas was an issue for proslavery and antislavery forces

◆ To identify the importance of the Dred Scott Case

◆ To explain the importance of the Lincoln-Douglas debates

◆ To describe John Brown's raid on Harpers Ferry

◆ To explain the importance of the election of 1860

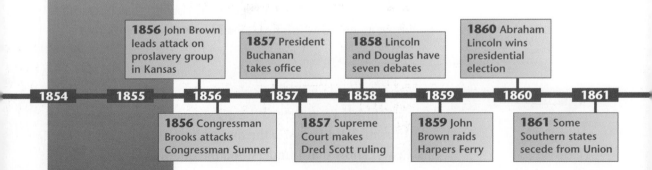

1856 John Brown leads attack on proslavery group in Kansas

1857 President Buchanan takes office

1858 Lincoln and Douglas have seven debates

1860 Abraham Lincoln wins presidential election

1854   1855   1856   1857   1858   1859   1860   1861

1856 Congressman Brooks attacks Congressman Sumner

1857 Supreme Court makes Dred Scott ruling

1859 John Brown raids Harpers Ferry

1861 Some Southern states secede from Union

Radical

Very great; more than usual

Geography Note

To grow properly, cotton needs a sunny and warm to hot climate. Cotton also needs productive, well-drained soil. It needs certain nutrients in the ground. These nutrients provide energy for growth. They may come from chemical fertilizer or from animal manure. The South has the best climate for growing cotton.

Nebraska's long, cold winters did not appeal to proslavery plantation owners. The climate was not good for growing cotton. Kansas, on the other hand, was farther south and was the target of settlers who favored slavery.

What Caused Fighting in Kansas?

Proslavery and antislavery supporters wanted to claim land in Kansas before it was admitted to the Union. People from New England moved to Kansas with the help of the New England Emigrant Aid Society. They brought with them boxes of guns disguised as boxes of Bibles. Southerners came from Alabama, Georgia, and North Carolina. They were also prepared to fight. Kansas became a battleground for the two groups. The territory became known as "Bleeding Kansas."

The time came to organize a territorial government in Kansas. An election was to be held; the settlers would vote for legislators. Just before the election, Missouri's senator, David R. Atchison, led a group of people into Kansas to vote for proslavery candidates.

Proslavery candidates won the election. They quickly formed a government and wrote a constitution. Antislavery people were angry with the outcome. They formed their own government. Kansas now had two governments, each claiming to be the legal government.

A group of proslavery men raided Lawrence, Kansas. Many people who were against slavery lived in Lawrence. The invaders burned buildings and one man was killed. In response to this action, **radical** abolitionist John Brown and a small band of men attacked a proslavery group at Pottawatamie Creek in 1856, killing five proslavery settlers. These and other attacks caused 200 deaths and over $2 million in property damage by the end of that same year. It was unlikely that the slavery issue would be settled peacefully.

Biography

Lucy Stone: 1818–1893

Lucy Stone was a reformer. She worked for women's rights and the end of slavery. She taught school to pay for her own way through college. She was one of the first women of Massachusetts to earn a degree. In 1847, she started speaking for Massachusetts Anti-Slavery Society. She also spoke widely on women's rights. In the 1850s, she helped put together conventions on women's rights. In 1855, Stone married abolitionist Henry Blackwell. She kept her own name. She may have been the first American woman to do so. Stone and Blackwell set up the American Woman Suffrage Association in 1869. A year later, they began producing the Women's Journal. This magazine promoted women's right to vote.

Lesson 1 Review Write the answers to the following questions on a sheet of paper. Use complete sentences.

1. Why was Nebraska not good for plantations?

2. Why did proslavery and antislavery supporters want to claim land in Kansas?

3. What did antislavery people do when proslavery people formed a government in Kansas?

4. What act of violence did the proslavery people commit?

5. What act of violence did the antislavery people commit?

What do you think ?

Why do you think control over the state of Kansas was so important?

Belittling
Insulting

An unusual event took place in May 1856. Senator Charles Sumner of Massachusetts made a speech against slavery. In his speech, he insulted Senator Andrew Butler of South Carolina. Sumner also made several **belittling** remarks about the state of South Carolina. His name-calling brought applause from the Northern senators.

SOUTHERN CHIVALRY — ARGUMENT versus CLUB'S.

Congressman Preston Brooks struck Senator Charles Sumner several times with a cane in 1856.

Sumner's remarks upset Senator Butler's nephew, Preston Brooks. Brooks was a member of the House of Representatives. A few days later, Brooks walked up to Sumner's desk and struck the senator several times with a cane. Sumner was seriously hurt by the hard blows to his head. It took him almost three years to recover enough to return to his place in the Senate. Even intelligent leaders were turning to violence and were unable to use common sense when dealing with the slavery problem.

History in Your Life

Otis and the Elevator

In 1852, Elisha G. Otis invented a safety device to prevent the fall of an elevator car if its support cable broke. In 1854, the daring Otis demonstrated his new device. He stood in an elevator car while its cable was chopped with an ax. Before this, elevators had been fairly unfamiliar devices. They were used only in factories to lift heavy objects one floor at a time. Otis had demonstrated that elevators could be made safe enough to lift people. Thus, he began what became a large industry. He patented the first passenger elevator in 1857 and a steam-powered elevator in 1861. His new elevators paved the way for a new era in architecture. The Otis safety elevator made possible the modern skyscrapers that now define skylines of cities worldwide. The Otis Elevator Company is still a large elevator manufacturer.

Who Won the Election of 1856?

Optimistic

Having good feelings toward what may happen in the future

Resolve

To settle a difference

Ruling

The decision of a court case

Slavery was the major issue of the election of 1856. There was still trouble in Kansas, and the country seemed to be slowly heading toward war.

The Democrats nominated James "Old Buck" Buchanan of Pennsylvania. Buchanan had not been involved in the Kansas dispute. The Democrats considered Old Buck to be a safe choice.

The Republicans chose John C. Frémont of California. Frémont had been an army leader during the Mexican War. He also was a well-known explorer.

Writing About History

Imaging you are a Supreme Court justice ruling on the Dred Scott case. In your notebook, explain your decision.

The number of immigrants in the United States had increased between the years 1820 and 1850, as more people looked to America as a land of new hope. Many people feared that foreigners would take over the country. They had formed the American Party, or Know-Nothing Party, to stop the wave of new immigrants. Millard Fillmore was their candidate in 1856.

James Buchanan won the election. He received 174 electoral votes to Frémont's 114. Only eight electoral votes went to Fillmore. Even though the Republicans lost the election, they showed strength. The Republicans were **optimistic** about the 1860 election. President Buchanan took office in 1857.

How Did the Dred Scott Case Affect Slavery?

Dred Scott

President Buchanan hoped the slavery issue would finally be **resolved**. However, two days after Buchanan took office in 1857, the Supreme Court made a **ruling** that heated the issue. A ruling is a decision of a court case. This ruling was about the freedom of an African slave named Dred Scott. It would be of great importance in the election of 1860.

Dred Scott had been enslaved in Missouri. His master took him to live in the free state of Illinois, and then to Wisconsin, which was a free territory. Then they returned to Missouri, where his master died five years later. Scott **sued** for his freedom on grounds that he had lived in a free territory. To sue is to bring legal action against a person to settle a difference. Scott claimed he was **entitled** to be a free man.

The case reached the Supreme Court. Chief Justice Roger Taney of Maryland gave the Supreme Court's decision. You can read part of his statement on page 302. According to Taney, a majority of the justices had ruled that Scott had no right to sue for his freedom—he was a slave and not a citizen. Scott's freedom was denied because he was now enslaved in a slave state. The Supreme Court declared that the Missouri Compromise violated the Constitution and therefore was not legal. Taney said that slaves were property and could be taken anywhere. The court's decision made it possible to extend slavery into all territories. The decision shocked the country. Northerners feared that it opened the door to the spread of slavery throughout the entire nation.

Word Bank

Charles Sumner

Dred Scott

James Buchanan

Preston Brooks

Roger Taney

Lesson 2 Review On a sheet of paper, write the correct name from the Word Bank to complete each sentence.

1. A former slave from Missouri named _____ was the subject of a Supreme Court case in 1857.

2. _____ struck Charles Sumner several times with a cane.

3. The Supreme Court justice who gave the Dred Scott ruling was _____.

4. _____ insulted Senator Andrew Butler of South Carolina.

5. The winner of the election of 1856 was _____.

What do you think ?

How do you think it was possible for two members of Congress, Preston Brooks and Charles Sumner, to be involved in such an act of violence?

Vow

To promise to do something

Opponent

A person who takes an opposite position in an event such as a debate or contest

Forbid

To use power to prevent something from occurring

In 1854 in Peoria, Illinois, former U.S. Representative Abraham Lincoln gave a speech in response to the Kansas-Nebraska Act. He spoke out against slavery and the act itself. He **vowed** to return to politics to see what could be done to end slavery once and for all.

In 1858, Abraham Lincoln ran for the U.S. Senate. His **opponent** was Stephen Douglas. Douglas was thought to be unbeatable, but Lincoln did not think so. Although Lincoln had served two years as a U.S. Representative, he was not well known. He challenged Douglas to a series of seven debates.

Douglas welcomed the opportunity to debate Lincoln. Douglas was an excellent speaker. Lincoln was not a good speaker. The two men were different in another way. Douglas was very short—barely over five feet tall. Lincoln was six feet, four inches tall.

Abe Lincoln's popularity increased during the Lincoln-Douglas debates of 1858.

During the debates, Lincoln reminded Douglas that the policy of popular sovereignty permitted a territory to **forbid** slavery. The Dred Scott decision, however, stated that a territory could not ban slavery. Which, Lincoln asked, did Douglas prefer? Douglas said that the people in a given state should be able to forbid slavery in spite of the Dred Scott decision. Douglas's response made many Southerners angry.

Lincoln had a way of saying things that made people listen. During the seven debates, Lincoln did very well against Douglas. Lincoln lost the Senate election to Douglas, but his popularity increased. People began to call him "Honest Abe." Douglas realized that debating Lincoln had been a mistake.

What Happened at Harpers Ferry?

Arsenal

A place used to make or store military weapons

Ammunition

Bullets, gunpowder, and other things used with guns or other weapons

John Brown took action again as disputes over slavery continued. Brown believed that slaves must be freed, even if violence was necessary. He had a plan to seize the U.S. **arsenal** at Harpers Ferry, Virginia (now in West Virginia), and take the guns and **ammunition**. An arsenal is a place used to make or store military weapons. He hoped to arm the slaves and lead them in a revolt against their masters.

John Brown is shown here kissing a child before being hanged.

Then and Now

Politicians today reach voters through debates and ads on television and radio and in newspapers. In the 1850s, politicians did not have radio or television. Congressional candidates traveled throughout their state. They gave what became known as stump speeches, because they often stood on tree stumps to address the people. Universities or towns hosted the seven Lincoln-Douglas debates. Each debate included hour-long speeches by both men. Ninety-minute replies followed the speeches. Each candidate ended with a 30-minute summary. Since 1988, the Commission on Presidential Debates has hosted the debates. Now debates usually last about 90 minutes and are shown on many television networks.

Brown captured the arsenal in 1859. Colonel Robert E. Lee was sent with marines to stop Brown. The marines captured Brown. He was tried for **treason** and found guilty. Treason is a crime involving an attempt to overthrow the government. He was hanged at Charlestown, Virginia (now in West Virginia), in December 1859. Before his death, he wrote, "I, John Brown, am now quite certain that the crimes of this guilty land will never be purged away but with blood. I had, as I now think, mainly flattered myself that without very much bloodshed it might be done."

The raid at Harpers Ferry increased the tension between the North and the South. Northerners were shocked by the violence. Southerners believed there would be more bloodshed by abolitionists.

It Happened in History

A Journalist and a Politician

Journalist Horace Greeley wrote passionately about what he believed in. He stood behind every word he wrote. He believed that honesty was the best policy. He did not talk down to the common person.

His paper, the *Log Cabin*, contributed to the election of William Henry Harrison in 1840. He later started the *New York Tribune*, which printed lots of political opinion articles. There he wrote articles against slavery. He supported many political reforms, such as women's rights. He worked for the rights of workers to be paid a fair wage. He supported westward expansion and encouraged people to seek a new life on the frontier.

He helped to organize the Republican Party and elect Abraham Lincoln president in 1860. Later Greeley himself ran unsuccessfully for president. Historians believe he was too much a person of principle to be a politician. People either loved him or hated him—but everyone respected him.

Lesson 3 Review On a sheet of paper, write the letter of the answer that best completes each sentence.

1. In 1858, Abraham Lincoln challenged Stephen Douglas
   _____.

   A in the U.S. Senate

   B to a series of seven debates

   C to forbid slavery in new states

   D to pass the Kansas-Nebraska Act

2. Lincoln lost the senate election because _____.

   A Lincoln was not well known

   B Lincoln was too tall

   C Lincoln debated poorly

   D Douglas made Southerners angry

3. Lincoln benefited from the debates because he _____.

   A showed he favored slavery

   B was amusing

   C became more popular

   D attracted Southern voters

4. John Brown planned to _____ at the arsenal in Harpers
   Ferry, Virginia.

   A steal the ammunition

   B make a speech

   C prevent the outbreak of war

   D prevent a slave revolt

5. John Brown was captured, tried, and hanged for _____.

   A treason   **C** stealing

   B mutiny   **D** rioting

What do you think ?

Why do you think people liked Abe Lincoln?

The election of 1860 offered four new presidential candidates. Their campaigns reflected the bitter divisions of the country.

Platform

A statement of ideas, policies, and beliefs of a political party in an election

Why Did the Democratic Party Split?

The Democratic Party could not agree on issues and on a presidential candidate. They split into two groups. The Northern delegates chose Stephen Douglas as their candidate. He supported popular sovereignty. The Southern delegates selected John C. Breckinridge of Kentucky, a supporter of slavery.

What Issues Did the Republicans Support?

The Republican Party nominated Abraham Lincoln as the presidential candidate. The Republican **platform,** which is a statement of ideas, policies, and beliefs of a political party in an election, stated:

- Slavery would not be allowed in new territories.
- Slave states could make decisions about slavery within their own borders.
- Free land would be available for farming in the territories.
- Higher tariffs would be imposed.
- No state would be permitted to leave the Union.

What New Political Party Was Formed?

Another group, called the Constitutional Union Party, also nominated a candidate for president. This new party was made up of former Whig and American Party members. They believed that the nation would be kept at peace if everyone cooperated. John Bell of Tennessee was chosen as their candidate.

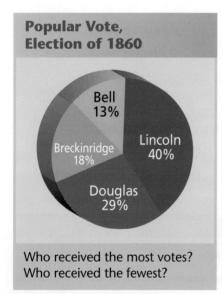

Popular Vote, Election of 1860

Bell 13%

Breckinridge 18%

Lincoln 40%

Douglas 29%

Who received the most votes? Who received the fewest?

Secede

To leave a group or organization

Lincoln won the election by nearly 500,000 votes. Before the election, some Southern states had decided to leave the Union if Lincoln won. By February 1, 1861, South Carolina, Mississippi, Florida, Alabama, Georgia, Texas, and Louisiana had voted to **secede,** or leave the Union.

The Secession of the Southern States

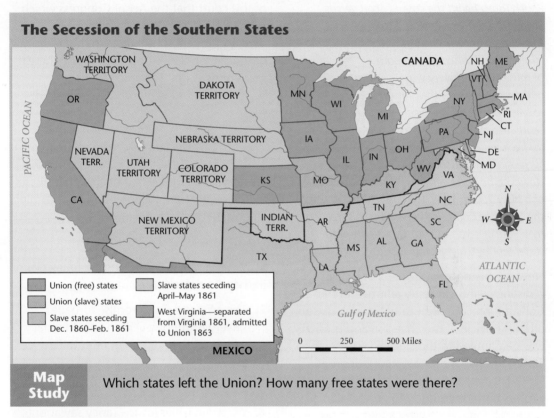

Legend:
- Union (free) states
- Union (slave) states
- Slave states seceding Dec. 1860–Feb. 1861
- Slave states seceding April–May 1861
- West Virginia—separated from Virginia 1861, admitted to Union 1863

0   250   500 Miles

Map Study Which states left the Union? How many free states were there?

What do you think?

Why do you think the Republican Party did not want any state to leave the Union?

Lesson 4 Review On a sheet of paper, write answers to the following questions. Use complete sentences.

1. What caused the Democratic Party to split in 1860?
2. Who was the Republican candidate for president?
3. What was the position of the Republican Party on slavery?
4. What belief united the Constitutional Union Party?
5. What happened by February 1861 because Lincoln won the election?

The Dred Scott Decision

In 1857, Chief Justice of the Supreme Court Roger Taney heard the case of Scott versus Stanford. Scott was enslaved to a Missouri doctor who had moved to Illinois and Wisconsin. In both of those states, slavery was outlawed. Following their return to Missouri, his owner died. Scott sued the doctor's widow for his freedom. Scott was successful in a Missouri court. However, he had been claimed as the property of a New Yorker. Thus, the case ended up before the Supreme Court. He was denied his freedom by a vote of seven to two. This is part of the statement by Chief Justice Taney.

Now . . . the right of property in a slave is distinctly and expressly affirmed in the Constitution. The right to traffic in it, like an ordinary article of merchandise and property, was guaranteed to the citizens of the United States, in every State that might desire it, for twenty years. And the Government in express terms is pledged to protect it in all future time, if the slave escapes from his owner. . . . And no word can be found in the Constitution which gives Congress a greater power over slave property or which entitles property of that kind to less protection than property of any other description. The only power conferred is the power coupled with the duty of guarding and protecting the owner in his rights.

Upon these considerations it is the opinion of this court that the Act of Congress which prohibited a citizen from holding and owning property of this kind in the territory of the United States north of the line therein mentioned is not warranted by the Constitution, and is therefore void; and that neither Scott himself, nor any of his family, were made free by being carried into this territory; even if they had been carried there by the owner with the intention of becoming a permanent resident. . . .

Document-Based Questions

1. What rights did Chief Justice Taney claim he was defending?

2. The Missouri Compromise forbade slavery north of a certain line. In what way does this statement refer to it?

3. What responsibility did the federal government have to the slaves?

4. What did Chief Justice Taney say about Scott's freedom?

5. How fair do you think Chief Justice Taney's decision was?

Source: The Dred Scott Decision, *Chief Justice Roger Taney, 1857.*

Chapter 15 SUMMARY

- As Kansas moved toward statehood, it was unclear if it would be a slave state or a free state. The residents of the territory were to vote one way or the other.

- People from both sides of the slavery issue moved to Kansas to help swing the vote their way. The proslavery people won the election and violence broke out.

- By the election of 1856, the country was becoming more separated by the issue of slavery.

- James Buchanan of Pennsylvania won the election for president. He had not been involved in the Kansas dispute.

- The Supreme Court made an important ruling concerning slavery in the Dred Scott Case. Dred Scott was a slave who filed a suit that said he should be free because he had lived in a free state. The court said that slaves were property and could be taken anywhere.

- Abraham Lincoln ran for the U.S. Senate in 1858. He ran against the popular Stephen Douglas.

- Lincoln and Douglas held a series of debates in which Lincoln showed his great wisdom and leadership style. Although he lost the election for Senate, Lincoln's popularity grew.

- A radical abolitionist, John Brown, attacked an army arsenal at Harpers Ferry, Virginia. Brown wanted to arm slaves and lead them in a revolt.

- John Brown was captured and hanged for treason. His actions and death increased the tensions between the North and the South.

- The Democratic Party split into two separate parties. The issue that divided them was slavery.

- Lincoln ran for president in 1860 as the Republican candidate. The Republican platform stressed opposition to slavery and said that no state could leave the Union.

- Soon after Lincoln won the election, several Southern states voted to leave the Union and form a new country.

Chapter 15 REVIEW

Word Bank

Abraham Lincoln

Bibles

Dred Scott

"Honest Abe"

James Buchanan

John Brown

property

Robert E. Lee

Stephen Douglas

Union

On a sheet of paper, write the correct word or words from the Word Bank to complete each sentence.

1. After his debates, Lincoln became known as _____.

2. _____ was an abolitionist who believed only violence could end slavery.

3. The winner of the 1856 election was _____.

4. _____ was a slave who sued for his freedom because he had lived in free states.

5. The Republican candidate for president in 1860 was _____.

6. Lincoln debated with _____ in the 1856 Senate race.

7. The Supreme Court ruled in the Dred Scott Case that slaves were _____ and could be taken anywhere and still remain enslaved.

8. _____ led the marines who captured John Brown during his raid on Harpers Ferry.

9. Abolitionists brought guns into Kansas in boxes that said they were boxes of _____.

10. After Lincoln was elected president, several states voted to leave the _____.

On a sheet of paper, write the letter of the answer that correctly completes each sentence.

11. _____ led people from Missouri into Kansas to vote illegally for proslavery candidates.

   A David Atchison   **C** Charles Sumner

   B John Brown   **D** Preston Brooks

12. In its Dred Scott ruling, the Supreme Court found that slaves _____.

   A could sue for freedom   **C** were property, not citizens

   B were free in free states   **D** could not be freed in slave states

13. The Kansas Territory was nicknamed "Bleeding Kansas" because _____.

A it had many slaves

B it had conflicts over political parties

C proslavery and antislavery forces clashed there

D the Harpers Ferry raid took place there

14. John Brown was hanged because he _____.

A blew up an arsenal

B was found guilty of treason

C led a slave revolt

D helped runaway slaves

On a sheet of paper, write the answer to each question. Use complete sentences.

15. Why was the election in Kansas so important?

16. How did Lincoln make himself look so good in the debates with Douglas?

17. Why did John Brown attack people at Pottawatamie Creek in Kansas?

18. What was a major issue in the election of 1860?

Critical Thinking On a sheet of paper, write your response to each question. Use complete sentences.

19. Why do you think the Supreme Court decided against Dred Scott?

20. How important are the debates between candidates before presidential elections?

Test-Taking Tip

When you take a matching test, first answer the items you know. Cross those choices out. It will be easier to try to match the remaining items.

16 The Civil War

After several states left the Union, it was clear that the nation was in trouble. Very little could be done to prevent a war. Though President Lincoln tried to avoid war when he took office, the Civil War began in 1861. In this chapter, you will learn how the war started, which battles were fought, and how it came to an end.

Goals for Learning

- ◆ To explain the events leading to the Civil War
- ◆ To describe the preparations and plans of the North and the South
- ◆ To describe the major events and identify important people in the Civil War
- ◆ To explain the Emancipation Proclamation and some important battles of the Civil War
- ◆ To explain how the war ended
- ◆ To describe the losses from the Civil War

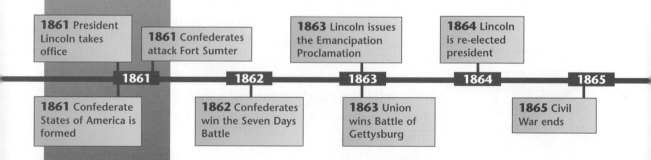

1861 President Lincoln takes office

1861 Confederates attack Fort Sumter

1863 Lincoln issues the Emancipation Proclamation

1864 Lincoln is re-elected president

| 1861 | 1862 | 1863 | 1864 | 1865 |

1861 Confederate States of America is formed

1862 Confederates win the Seven Days Battle

1863 Union wins Battle of Gettysburg

1865 Civil War ends

During Buchanan's last four months as president, seven states left the Union. Buchanan did nothing to stop them. Although he was a Northerner, he agreed with the Southern states. He maintained that the North had caused the problems that led to secession. He proposed that the North should return all runaway slaves, while all the new territories should be opened to slavery. Buchanan thought the Southern states would then rejoin the Union.

Senator John Crittenden of Kentucky offered a compromise. He suggested that the Constitution be changed to allow slavery in all new territories. He also suggested that any state north of 36 degrees 30 minutes north latitude could vote to enslave people or not. This boundary was an imaginary line that divided the Louisiana Territory into two areas, north and south. Crittenden thought the Southern states would be pleased with this plan and return to the Union. He hoped the slavery issue would finally be settled.

Members of the Senate discussed the compromise, but they reached no agreement. Abraham Lincoln, leader of the Republican Party, felt that slavery must be stopped forever. Senator Crittenden's plan for compromise was turned down.

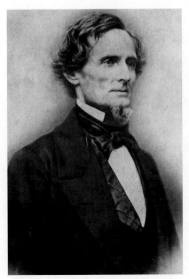

What New Government Did the Southern States Form?

In February 1861, the Southern states met in Montgomery, Alabama. They formed the government of the Confederate States of America, or the Confederacy. They drew up a constitution that said each state would be independent, slavery would be protected, and Confederate states would pay no federal tariffs. Jefferson Davis was chosen to serve as president of the Confederacy. Montgomery was its first capital. Davis had fought in the Mexican War and served as a senator and a secretary of war.

Jefferson Davis

What Did the Seceded States Do?

Near the end of Buchanan's presidency, the seceded states took over most of the federal properties inside their borders. These included forts and arsenals filled with large supplies of weapons. The South claimed many post offices and **customhouses,** as well as the large supply of coins at the New Orleans Mint.

Fort Sumter in South Carolina was commanded by Major Robert Anderson. The newly formed Southern government expected the North to turn the fort over to the South. President Buchanan did not agree with South Carolina's **request.** Instead, he sent a ship of supplies and food to troops at the fort. Confederates fired upon the vessel, forcing it to turn back. Afterward, Buchanan did nothing more to help the troops in Fort Sumter or in any other federal properties in the South.

Abraham Lincoln

What Happened When President Lincoln Took Office?

On March 4, 1861, Lincoln became president. He faced a very serious situation. No state had the right to leave the Union and form a separate government. Lincoln's first challenge as president was to bring the South back into the Union peacefully.

When Lincoln was sworn in as president, his inaugural address was about peace. He stressed that he did not intend to stop slavery in states where it was already in use. However, he wanted to see all federal properties in the South returned to Union control and all tariffs paid.

Lincoln wanted the Union to be preserved. He appealed to the Southern states to return to the Union without bloodshed. Lincoln made it clear, though, that any warlike action the South took would lead to a **civil war.** A civil war is a war between groups within the same country.

Biography

Susie King Taylor 1848–1912

Susie King Taylor grew up in slavery. She had been enslaved on an island off the coast of Georgia. But unlike most slaves, she had the chance to learn to read and write. During the Civil War, she joined the Union army. She was only 14 years old. At first, Taylor washed clothes for the soldiers. Later she became the army's first African American nurse.

Although she left the army at age 18, Taylor continued serving others. She helped start a branch of the Women's Relief Corps. She also began a school for freed slaves. The army awarded Taylor the Women's Relief Corps Medal. Her autobiography, *Reminiscence of My Life in Camp: A Black Woman's Civil War Memoirs,* told about her work. She wrote, "My hands have never left undone anything they could do toward aid and comfort."

Word Bank

Abraham Lincoln

Jefferson Davis

John Crittenden

President Buchanan

Robert Anderson

Lesson 1 Review On a sheet of paper, write the correct name from the Word Bank to complete each sentence.

1. _____ thought the Southern states would rejoin the Union if the North returned all runaway slaves.

2. Fort Sumter was commanded by _____.

3. _____ proposed a compromise that would have allowed slavery in new territories.

4. The Confederacy chose _____ as its president.

5. The first challenge facing _____ was to get the Union back together.

What do you think ?

Do you think Lincoln's policy toward the Confederacy was good? Why or why not?

Defense

Protection against attack

President Lincoln received a message from Fort Sumter in March 1861. Food and supplies were running out. More men were needed too. Major Anderson would have to surrender the fort unless immediate action was taken. President Lincoln would not let Fort Sumter surrender to South Carolina.

In early April, President Lincoln sent a message to the governor of South Carolina. He told him that a ship was being sent to the fort. Jefferson Davis told General Beauregard, the Confederate commander in South Carolina, to order Major Anderson to

surrender the fort. Major Anderson refused to surrender. On April 12, 1861, Confederates attacked Fort Sumter. Major Anderson and his men fought for nearly two days before they were forced to surrender.

Confederates attacked Fort Sumter in 1861. This was the first battle of the Civil War.

The news of the attack on Fort Sumter spread quickly. Thousands joined the Union army when Lincoln called for volunteers. Four more states, Virginia, North Carolina, Arkansas, and Tennessee, joined the Confederacy. A total of 11 states had left the Union and now formed the Confederacy.

Richmond, Virginia, became the new Confederate capital. Virginia organized a large, well-trained army led by good generals. Virginia would serve as a solid line of **defense** for the rest of the Confederacy. The states farthest north in the Confederacy were much stronger and better prepared for war than those in the deep South. The Confederate attack on Fort Sumter was the beginning of a bloody civil war.

What Advantages Did Each Side Have?

With 23 states, the Union had a larger population than the Confederacy. Only 11 states were in the Confederacy. Nearly three times as many people lived in the North as in the South. The North had most of the country's factories and industrial labor force. In addition, the North had more money to pay for a war.

The Confederates were united against those who wanted to destroy their way of life. Southerners were fighting to defend their land and their rights. The Confederacy had some excellent military leaders, including General Robert E. Lee. The Southern men were more familiar than the Northerners with firearms, the outdoors, and horses. Also, the fighting broke out on Southern soil. In 1861, as the war began, the South had a definite military advantage.

Confederate General Robert E. Lee

What Was the North's Plan?

The war was expected to last only a few months. General Winfield Scott, "Old Fuss and Feathers" of the Mexican War, was the commander of the Union army. Scott was still thought to be an excellent leader. He called his plan for winning the war the "Anaconda Plan." An anaconda is a large snake that crushes its prey to death. Scott planned to crush the enemy. His plan called for:

- a blockade of the South to stop all imports and exports,
- capturing Richmond, Virginia, the new capital of the Confederacy, and
- stopping all shipping on the Mississippi River.

If the plan was successful, the South would be defeated and forced to surrender. Many looked upon the plan as too slow and not forceful enough.

Writing About History

Write a short story or poem about the Civil War. Describe how a person not fighting in the war would be affected by the war, how a slave might view the war, or a similar topic. Write the story or poem in your notebook.

President Lincoln ordered a blockade of all the Southern states that had seceded. He cut off the seaports of the South. The Confederates were unable to ship cotton from their harbors. They needed to trade cotton for guns and ammunition from Europe. The blockade decreased the amount of supplies coming into the South.

The blockade was an important part of the Union's war plan. Some people said that with trade cut off, the South would choke to death. The South had very little industry and could not produce the materials needed to fight a war.

What Was the South's Plan?

The Southerners took a different approach. They planned to let the North come to them. In addition, the South counted on the North losing interest in the war. Many Southerners also thought that at some point Europe would break the Union blockade to get the cotton that it needed.

What do you think

Who do you think was more prepared for the Civil War— the North or the South? Why?

Lesson 2 Review On a sheet of paper, write the answers to the following questions. Use complete sentences.

1. What did the attack on Fort Sumter cause?
2. What happened in Virginia after the attack on Fort Sumter?
3. What were two advantages the North had during the war?
4. What were two advantages the South had during the war?
5. Why did the North form a blockade of the South?

Then and Now

Today we usually think of hot-air balloon rides as recreation. Did you know that hot-air balloons were used during the Civil War? The Union army sent men up in hot-air balloons to observe Confederate troop movements. The men signaled information to officers on the ground. Officers used this information to direct Union troop movement and cannon fire.

Today, the United States detects military activities from satellites revolving around Earth in space. Directed from control centers in the United States, the satellites gather information. With special cameras, the satellites photograph a target on Earth. Then they send images back to Earth. These images show whether countries are building or disarming weapons according to treaties.

The new recruits for the Union army were in Washington, D.C., being trained. Scott ordered General Irvin McDowell to lead about 35,000 of these inexperienced soldiers. He led them 25 miles to Manassas Junction, near a stream called Bull Run in northern Virginia. Despite their inexperience in battle, Northerners were certain that their soldiers would defeat the Southern "rebels," as they were called. They were so certain that many people traveled down from Washington to watch the battle.

Camped on the banks of Bull Run, the Confederates were ready for the attack. On July 21, 1861, the battle began. At first, the Union army seemed to be winning. However, troops under General Thomas "Stonewall" Jackson held off many attacks. Then Confederate troops under General Joseph Johnston arrived. The Union army was defeated. They fled back to Washington in panic.

The defeat shocked the North. They realized that the war would be a long one. Northerners were eager for a victory. They urged another attack. Northern newspapers had headlines that read, "Forward to Richmond!"

It Happened in History

Stonewall Jackson

When the Union seemed to be winning the first Battle of Manassas, a Confederate general, trying to get his men to fight on, pointed to General Thomas J. Jackson. "There is Jackson standing like a stone wall. Rally behind the Virginians!" This is how Jackson came to be known as "Stonewall."

Who Became the New Union Leader?

In November 1861, General Winfield Scott retired. He was 75 years old. It was time for a younger general to take charge. President Lincoln chose General George B. McClellan as chief of the Union armies. McClellan was 35 years old and a **veteran** of the Mexican War. A veteran is an experienced or former member of the armed forces. He graduated second in his class at West Point, a military school in New York.

McClellan was good at organizing an army and training new soldiers for battle, but he was a very cautious leader. Before going into another battle, McClellan drilled his men over and over. Finally, in the spring of 1862, McClellan was ready to face the Confederate troops in Richmond.

What Happened in the Western Campaign?

The Confederate forts in western Tennessee were important in the Union plan to defeat the South. In February 1862, Union General Ulysses S. Grant and the navy's **gunboats,** or armed ships used for battle, captured Fort Henry. This was the Confederate stronghold on the Tennessee River. Grant continued up the Cumberland River to capture Fort Donelson near Nashville. Under the direction of Admiral David G. Farragut, the Union also gained control of most of the Mississippi Valley. However, the Union needed complete control in order to stop the Confederacy from using the river.

What Happened Between the *Monitor* and the *Merrimac?*

In 1861, the Confederates raised a sunken Union ship, the USS *Merrimac,* and renamed it *Virginia.* The Confederates then covered the vessel with iron plates so it could not be damaged by cannonballs. This kind of ship was called an **ironclad.** The North also had an ironclad ship, called the *Monitor.*

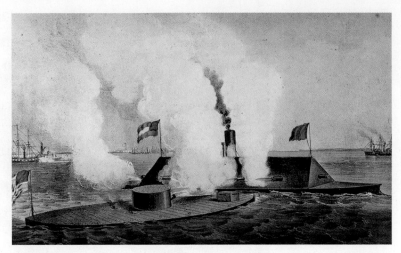

The Monitor *and the* Merrimac (Virginia) *battled at Hampton Roads channel in Virginia.*

The two ships had a battle in March 1862. The Confederates wanted to break the Northern blockade. Neither ship won the battle. The Confederates, however, did use the *Merrimac* to prevent McClellan's army from approaching Richmond on the James River. The Confederates later destroyed the *Merrimac* to keep it from falling into the hands of the North. The *Monitor* sank off the coast of North Carolina. The *Merrimac* and the *Monitor* were the first ironclad ships to be used in battle.

Who Won the Seven Days' Battle?

McClellan led his troops toward Virginia. The Confederates were ready for the attack on Richmond. They let McClellan get within a few miles of Richmond before attacking. There was heavy fighting at many different locations for seven days. For this reason, the battle was called the Seven Days' Battle. From time to time, each side seemed to be winning. However, thinking his army was **outnumbered,** McClellan retreated after the seven days.

Fallen soldiers were a common sight on September 17, 1862. Over 4,800 soldiers died that day during the Battle of Antietam.

Who Won Battles at Manassas, Antietam, and Fredericksburg?

In late August 1862, a second battle was fought at Manassas (Bull Run). The Confederate army again defeated the Union soldiers.

General Lee changed his plan from defense to offense. He prepared to attack Northern states. Confederate soldiers marched into Maryland. On September 17, 1862, General McClellan and his Union army of the Potomac blocked Lee at Sharpsburg, Maryland, on Antietam Creek. The Battle of Antietam turned out to be one of the bloodiest battles of the war. At the end of the fighting, Lee was forced to retreat. McClellan did not follow Lee into Virginia. For this reason Lincoln removed McClellan as the Union leader, replacing him with General Ambrose Burnside.

General Burnside took the Union army to Fredericksburg, Virginia. Positioned on a line of hills, the Confederates defended the city. The Union army made a strong attempt to charge the hills, but their efforts failed. More than 12,000 Union soldiers were killed. General Burnside resigned. General Joseph Hooker replaced him.

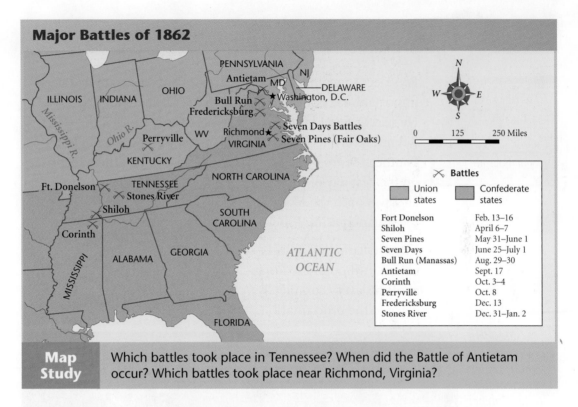

Major Battles of 1862

Fort Donelson — Feb. 13–16
Shiloh — April 6–7
Seven Pines — May 31–June 1
Seven Days — June 25–July 1
Bull Run (Manassas) — Aug. 29–30
Antietam — Sept. 17
Corinth — Oct. 3–4
Perryville — Oct. 8
Fredericksburg — Dec. 13
Stones River — Dec. 31–Jan. 2

Map Study Which battles took place in Tennessee? When did the Battle of Antietam occur? Which battles took place near Richmond, Virginia?

Lesson 3 Review On a sheet of paper, write the correct word from the Word Bank to complete each sentence.

Word Bank

confederate

gunboats

Monitor

Union

Virginia

1. The _____ army won both of the battles at Bull Run, or Manassas.

2. In February 1862, Ulysses Grant and navy _____ captured Fort Henry on the Tennessee River.

3. The South renamed the USS *Merrimac* the _____.

4. The _____ and the *Merrimac* were the first ironclad ships to be used in battle.

5. General Burnside resigned after the _____ loss at Fredericksburg.

What do you think ?

How does the battle of the *Monitor* and the *Merrimac* show that the Civil War was a different kind of war from wars in the past?

Emancipate

To release

Enlist

To join the armed forces

President Lincoln knew that the victory at Antietam had been important. He issued a warning to the Confederate states. He said he would free all the slaves in those states if the states did not return to the Union by January 1, 1863. The fighting Southern states did not think he would do it. To their surprise, on the first day of January 1863, President Lincoln declared that all slaves in the states that had seceded were free. This was called the **Emancipation** Proclamation.

The proclamation applied only to those states that had left the Union. Although the Emancipation Proclamation did not abolish slavery completely, it was a major step. Northerners cheered the proclamation.

President Lincoln read the Emancipation Proclamation to his Cabinet in 1862.

What Did Many Runaway Slaves Do?

Many slaves had run away and joined the Union army even before the Emancipation Proclamation. By the end of the war, nearly 180,000 former slaves had **enlisted** in the army and fought against the Confederacy. To enlist means to join the armed forces.

Twenty-three African American soldiers won the Medal of Honor for bravery. Several regiments of Africans were formed. They took part in many major battles. The first African group from a free state was called the 54th Massachusetts Volunteers.

The Fourth Colored Infantry was one of many African regiments to serve in the Civil War.

What Happened at Chancellorsville and Gettysburg?

General Joseph Hooker had intended to keep an army at Fredericksburg to keep General Lee busy. He hoped to attack Chancellorsville at the same time. Meanwhile, General Lee had heard of the planned attack. He left a small army at Fredericksburg, and went on to surprise Hooker at Chancellorsville. Lee's and General Jackson's soldiers easily defeated a much larger Union army. During the battle, Stonewall Jackson was accidentally shot and wounded by his own men. He died eight days later. Lee had lost his most important general.

General Lee's original plan had been to fight a defensive war. He would wait and be ready. Now, though, the war was not going well for the South in the western states. Lee thought about sending soldiers to win back the West. On the other hand, he felt one major victory in the North would bring an end to the war.

Lee decided to attack the North. He made his way into Pennsylvania with an army of about 65,000 well-trained soldiers. General George G. Meade's Union army in Pennsylvania numbered almost 85,000. The two armies prepared for battle near the quiet town of Gettysburg.

On July 1, 1863, Lee attacked. The battle continued for three days, with each side having the advantage from time to time. Lee made a desperate strike on the third day. He sent General George Pickett with 13,000 soldiers to charge the Union line. The line moved back, but it did not break. Slowly, Meade's army forced the Confederates back.

The South lost the battle, and Lee retreated to the Potomac River. The losses on both sides had been very heavy. Gettysburg was the turning point of the war. Although the South continued to fight after this battle, it had little possibility of winning.

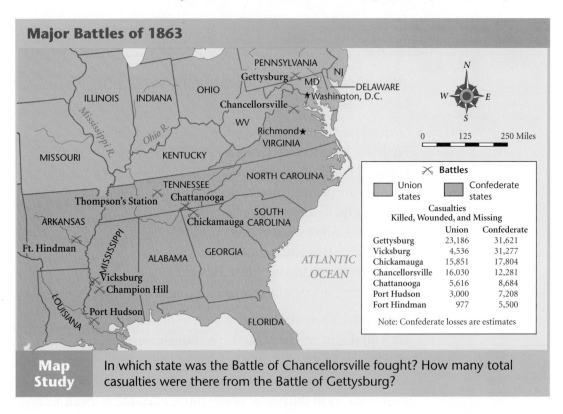

Major Battles of 1863

Casualties Killed, Wounded, and Missing		
	Union	Confederate
Gettysburg	23,186	31,621
Vicksburg	4,536	31,277
Chickamauga	15,851	17,804
Chancellorsville	16,030	12,281
Chattanooga	5,616	8,684
Port Hudson	3,000	7,208
Fort Hindman	977	5,500

Note: Confederate losses are estimates

Map Study In which state was the Battle of Chancellorsville fought? How many total casualties were there from the Battle of Gettysburg?

The Union won the Battle of Gettysburg in 1863.

What Was the Gettysburg Address?

Four months after the Battle of Gettysburg, President Lincoln **dedicated** a national cemetery for those who died there. His dedication speech, known as the Gettysburg Address, was short but effective. The speech told of the grief President Lincoln felt for the soldiers who died there. It also expressed his feeling that the men fighting in the Civil War were fighting for a good cause—to protect the nation and democracy.

A famous line from the address explains this idea: "... that this nation, under God, shall have a new birth of freedom—and that government of the people, by the people, for the people, shall not perish from the earth."

What Did Women Do During the War?

Northern and Southern women provided for their households and took on other responsibilities usually done by men. They also became involved as nurses, caring for wounded soldiers. In some cases, the women fought side by side with the men.

With so many men in the Confederate army, women in the South took on even more. They did field work, gathered food from the wilderness, and made do without many items needed for daily life. Some went to work in factories to support the war effort. Facing the sadness and suffering of war was frightening, and the women of the South struggled to survive.

What do you think ?

Why do you think so many Africans were willing to fight in the Civil War?

Lesson 4 Review Choose the word or words in parentheses that best complete each sentence. Write your answers on a sheet of paper.

1. The (Gettysburg Address, Emancipation Proclamation, Medal of Honor) declared that slaves were free in the states that had seceded.

2. General (Robert E. Lee, Stonewall Jackson, Joseph Hooker) wanted to keep an army at Fredericksburg and attack Chancellorsville.

3. General (George G. Meade, Robert E. Lee, Stonewall Jackson) was wounded at a battle fought at Chancellorsville.

4. General (George G. Meade, Robert E. Lee, Joseph Hooker) forced the Confederates back at Gettysburg.

5. The Union army won a battle at (Fredericksburg, Chancellorsville, Gettysburg).

History in Your Life

Civil War Music

Music was very important to the soldiers during the Civil War. Union and Confederate army bands played loud marching and battle tunes to encourage the soldiers. Trumpets, piccolos, and drums could often be heard above the noise of battle. These instruments were sometimes used to communicate commands. The bands were often called upon to entertain the soldiers in quiet times between battles. They also played patriotic songs in parades and small towns.

The songs spilled into everyday use in the North and South. In rural areas during the same period, folk music was played on banjos, fiddles, and other stringed instruments. Several kinds of music were popular. Songs like "My Old Kentucky Home" fought soldiers' homesickness. "When Johnny Comes Marching Home" and similar songs helped civilians remember their loved ones at war. "Swing Low Sweet Chariot" and other spirituals originated in African American communities. In time, this music became an influence on the jazz and folk music we know today.

Admiral David Farragut and the Union navy had attacked New Orleans, at the mouth of the Mississippi. They forced the Confederacy to surrender there. General Grant, under General Halleck of the army in the West, had scored many victories in the Mississippi River valley. These victories included Shiloh, Perryville, and Murfreesboro in Tennessee.

Admiral David Farragut's Union navy allowed Union forces to capture New Orleans.

As Lee retreated from the Battle of Gettysburg, he learned that Vicksburg, Mississippi, also had been captured by General Grant. The loss of Vicksburg meant that the entire Mississippi River was controlled by the Union army. As Grant moved eastward, the North took all the Confederate states except Georgia, North Carolina, South Carolina, and Virginia.

Lincoln appointed Grant as commander in chief of all the Union armies. On May 4, 1864, he forced his way toward Richmond. Even though his losses were heavy, he pressed on. Grant wanted to destroy the South so it could no longer fight. This would include destroying the cotton industry, railroads for transporting goods, and seaports for receiving goods from Europe.

Lee realized that he was fighting a Union general who would not retreat, despite his losses. Lee's army was getting smaller with each battle. There was still hope for the South, though. President Lincoln was seeking re-election, and his defeat could lead to a settlement.

Who Won the Election of 1864?

In 1864, the Republicans nominated Lincoln for a second term. Civil War veteran George McClellan was the Democrats' choice for president. His party stood for bringing an end to the war. Before the election, the Union scored victories on land and sea. The sudden change in events ruined the chances for the Democrats. Lincoln won easily.

How Did General Sherman Advance His Army?

Under General Grant's orders, General William Sherman led an army of 100,000 men into Atlanta, Georgia. Confederate General John Hood tried to stop the Union troops, but he was forced to retreat. On September 2, 1864, General Sherman captured Atlanta. He continued his march to Savannah and then on to the sea.

General Sherman and about 60,000 Union troops set out from Atlanta. They had only the supplies each soldier could carry. Sherman commanded his troops to destroy everything in sight. His army cut a path 50 miles wide through Georgia. Sherman's troops destroyed bridges, barns, **livestock,** railroads, and crops. On December 21, 1864, the Union army captured Savannah.

General Sherman's army destroyed everything that could be used by the Confederacy in Georgia.

General Sherman marched northward to join General Grant at Richmond in the spring of 1865. Phillip Sheridan, another Union general, was closing in quickly from the West. General Lee was in a difficult situation. In one last desperate move, the Confederate leader marched his men westward. Sheridan's troops surrounded Lee near Appomattox Court House in Virginia. Lee asked for the terms of surrender, to avoid even more losses on both sides.

How Did the War End?

General Lee met General Grant to discuss the terms of surrender on April 9, 1865. General Lee knew he must agree with Grant's conditions. If not, his army would be attacked. Grant respected General Lee as a military leader. He knew that Lee had fought bravely.

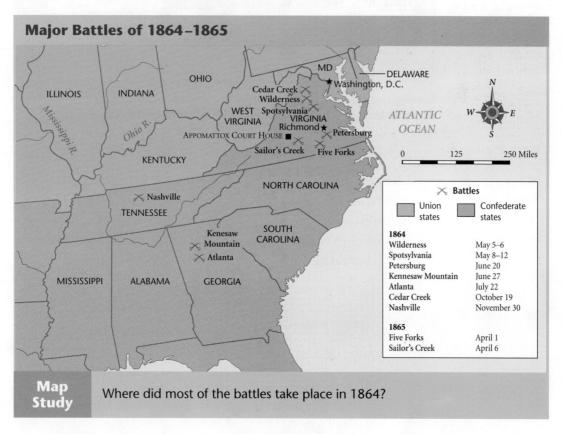

Major Battles of 1864–1865

Battles	
Union states	Confederate states

1864

Wilderness	May 5–6
Spotsylvania	May 8–12
Petersburg	June 20
Kennesaw Mountain	June 27
Atlanta	July 22
Cedar Creek	October 19
Nashville	November 30

1865

Five Forks	April 1
Sailor's Creek	April 6

Map Study Where did most of the battles take place in 1864?

Rebuild

To build something again

Grant's terms of surrender were generous. The Confederate soldiers would be allowed to keep their horses and mules. Officers could also keep their pistols. All other military guns and supplies were to be turned over to the Union. General Lee was pleased with the terms and agreed to them. The war was over. Confederate President Jefferson Davis was later arrested and placed in prison for two years. The Union had been saved, and the slavery question was finally settled.

General Grant and his officers met with General Lee at a house in Appomattox Court House, Virginia. General Lee agreed to surrender.

What Were the Losses from the War?

The losses from the war were very high. It claimed more American lives than any other war before it or after it. The fighting damaged property too. Sherman's march alone was estimated to have caused over $100 million in damages. The South would need a **rebuilding** program.

Civil War Statistics		
	Union	**Confederacy**
Soldiers served	2,213,400	1,003,600
Battle deaths	110,000	94,000
Wounded	275,000	226,000
Deaths by disease	224,000	60,000

Note: Confederate losses are estimates

The McLean House

General Lee and General Grant ended the Civil War by meeting in a house owned by Wilmer McLean, a farmer. McLean had offered his own house as the meeting site. A reproduction of the house still stands today at the Appomattox Court House National Historic Park in Virginia.

Lesson 5 Review On a sheet of paper, write the answers to the following questions. Use complete sentences.

1. How was the loss at Vicksburg harmful to the Confederacy?

2. What was Grant's plan for winning the war?

3. Why was the election of 1864 important?

4. How did General Sherman's army destroy the South?

5. Why was General Lee forced to surrender?

What do you think ?

The Civil War resulted in a huge loss of life and damage to property. What other things do you think the war affected?

General Robert E. Lee's Farewell

On April 9, 1865, Confederate General Robert E. Lee surrendered to Lt. General Ulysses S. Grant, head of the Union Army. This surrender would end the Civil War. Many of Lee's soldiers were angry and distressed at this action. Lee was concerned that his soldiers would not stop fighting. The next day, General Lee issued this farewell to his army.

I need not tell the brave survivors of so many hard fought battles, who have remained steadfast [loyal] to the last, that I have consented to this result from no distrust of them; but feeling that valor [bravery] and devotion could accomplish nothing that could compensate for the loss that must have attended the continuance of the contest, I determined to avoid the useless sacrifice of those whose past services have endeared them to their countrymen.

By the terms of the agreement, officers and men can return to their homes and remain until exchanged. You will take with you the satisfaction that proceeds from the consciousness of duty faithfully performed . . . . With an unceasing admiration of your . . . devotion to your Country, and a grateful remembrance of your kind and generous consideration for myself, I bid you all an affectionate [kind] farewell.

Document-Based Questions

1. Why did Lee feel he needed to write this address?

2. What did Lee give as his reason for surrendering?

3. How did Lee's soldiers feel about the surrender?

4. How did Lee say the soldiers should feel about what they had done?

5. What did you learn about General Lee's relationship with his army by reading this passage?

Source: General Orders No. 9, General Robert E. Lee's Farewell to the Army of Northern Virginia, April 10, 1865.

- The Confederate States of America was formed in February 1861 after 7 states left the Union. Later, 4 more states joined the Confederacy.

- Abraham Lincoln became president on March 4, 1861. He wanted to unite the country again.

- Fort Sumter, a Union fort in South Carolina, was captured by the Confederacy in April 1861. This action was the beginning of the Civil War.

- The Union established a blockade to prevent the South from selling cotton to European customers. Money from cotton would have gone toward buying military supplies.

- The Union had a larger population, more factories and workers, and more money to pay for supplies. However, not everyone was committed to the war.

- The Confederacy had strong military leaders and people were fighting to maintain their way of life.

- Lincoln appointed George McClellan as the commander of the Union army. Robert E. Lee led the Confederate army.

- The Confederate army won many of the major battles in the early part of the war.

- After the bloody Battle of Antietam, Lincoln removed General McClellan. Lincoln appointed Ambrose Burnside as the head of the Union army in 1862.

- Lincoln issued a warning to the Confederate States. He said that if they did not return to the Union, he would free slaves in those states. Lincoln issued the Emancipation Proclamation on January 1, 1863.

- The Battle of Gettysburg was fought in July 1863. It was the worst battle of the war and lasted three days. Won by the Union, it was the turning point of the war.

- General Grant became the head of the Union army in 1864.

- President Lincoln was re-elected in 1864.

- In 1864, General William Sherman led Union soldiers on a march through Georgia, destroying everything along the way.

- Lee surrendered to Grant on April 9, 1865, ending the Civil War.

Chapter 16 REVIEW

Word Bank

Antietam

Appomattox
Court House

Emancipation
Proclamation

Fort Sumter

Gettysburg

Gettysburg
Address

John Hood

Stonewall Jackson

Vicksburg

William Sherman

On a sheet of paper, write the correct word or words from the Word Bank to complete each sentence.

1. _____ was the Confederate general whose troops tried to defend Atlanta from Union attack.

2. The battle at _____ lasted for three days and was the turning point of the war.

3. One of the bloodiest battles of the war was fought in Maryland on _____ Creek.

4. The troops of _____ cut a path of destruction 50 miles wide through Georgia.

5. After General Grant captured _____, the Union controlled the entire Mississippi River.

6. The Civil War began with the attack on _____.

7. _____ and his troops helped the Confederacy to win the Battle of Manassas in July 1861.

8. President Lincoln gave the _____ at the dedication of a national cemetery.

9. The _____ freed enslaved people in the Confederate States on January 1, 1863.

10. Lee signed the surrender to Grant in Virginia at _____.

On a sheet of paper, write the letter of the answer that correctly answers each question.

11. Who was the commander of the Confederate army?

    A George Pickett   C Ulysses S. Grant

    B Stonewall Jackson   D Robert E. Lee

12. With what strategy did Grant plan to defeat the Confederacy?

    A destroy their economy   C choke off their supply routes

    B destroy their cavalry   D start slave revolts

13. Who replaced McClellan as commander of the Union forces?

    A William Sherman   **C** Ambrose Burnside

    B Ulysses S. Grant   **D** Joseph Hooker

14. Who was the President of the Confederate States of America?

    A Abraham Lincoln   **C** Ulysses S. Grant

    B David Farragut   **D** Jefferson Davis

On a sheet of paper, write the answers to the following questions. Use complete sentences.

15. What was the purpose of the Union blockade?

16. What happened that helped Lincoln win re-election in 1864?

17. What were the terms of Lee's surrender to Grant?

18. What was no longer an issue after the Civil War was over?

Critical Thinking On a sheet of paper, write your response to each question. Use complete sentences.

19. Many of the soldiers who fought in the Civil War were teenagers. What do you think of the idea of teenagers fighting in a war?

20. Lee considered Grant's terms of surrender to be generous. If you had been Grant, what would your terms of surrender have been?

Test-Taking Tip

If you cannot answer a question, mark it and continue to the next question. When you have answered all the questions you know, return to the items you marked and try to answer them.

17

Reconstruction

The bloody war between the North and South had ended. Slavery was over once and for all. The nation needed to heal its wounds. Both the North and the South had changed during the war. The South lay in ruin and had to be rebuilt. The period of Reconstruction, or rebuilding, was a time of political unrest. Some members of Congress tried to punish the South. Former slaves fought to keep their freedom. They became voters and landholders. By the end of Reconstruction, however, much of their freedom became limited. In this chapter, you will learn about Reconstruction in the South.

Goals for Learning

◆ To describe the assassination of Abraham Lincoln, problems in the South after the Civil War, and the 13th Amendment

◆ To explain the 14th Amendment, Andrew Johnson's conflicts with Congress and his impeachment, and the effects of Reconstruction on the American Indians

◆ To explain social and economic changes in the South, and changes in the status of women

◆ To explain the 15th Amendment, the problems in Grant's administration, and the end of Reconstruction

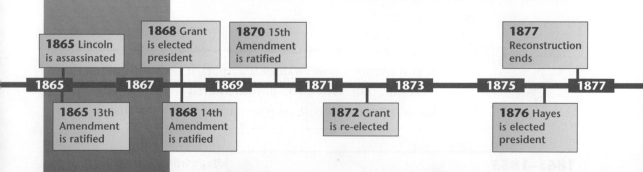

1865 Lincoln is assassinated

1868 Grant is elected president

1870 15th Amendment is ratified

1877 Reconstruction ends

1865   1867   1869   1871   1873   1875   1877

1865 13th Amendment is ratified

1868 14th Amendment is ratified

1872 Grant is re-elected

1876 Hayes is elected president

Oath

A pledge that promises loyalty to a government or other cause

Amnesty

A pardon granted by the government

Assassination

The killing of a politically important person

Abraham Lincoln began his second term as president as the war was ending. In his inaugural address, Lincoln expressed his hopes for rebuilding the Union. He wanted all Americans to forget the war as soon as possible. He put together a plan to rebuild the nation.

The president's plan said a state could rejoin the Union when 10 percent of its voters took an **oath,** or promised, to support the Union. He offered **amnesty,** or a pardon, to Southerners. This would allow the states to rejoin the Union as quickly as possible. New state governments could be formed, but they would have to obey the ban on slavery. Lincoln knew that many in Congress did not agree with his plan. However, Lincoln felt that he had the power to proceed without the approval of Congress.

On the evening of April 14, 1865, Lincoln attended a play at Ford's Theater in Washington, D.C. John Wilkes Booth went to the box where Lincoln was sitting and shot the president in the back of the head. Booth had supported the Southern cause. Lincoln died the next morning. A few days after the **assassination,** soldiers killed Booth. President Lincoln did not live to see his plans carried out. His death delayed rebuilding in the South.

John Wilkes Booth assassinated President Lincoln at Ford's Theater.

What Were the Problems in the South?

Reconstruction

Rebuilding of the South after the Civil War

In the South, the damage from the war had been great. Countless farms and large plantations were ruined. Confederate money was worthless. As a result, many formerly wealthy people had no funds. They could not rebuild. Most banks, also victims of the failed Confederate cause, had closed. Roads throughout many Southern states had become blocked with rubble from the war. Many bridges had been destroyed. Even the railroad tracks had been damaged during efforts to slow down shipments of troops and supplies.

The South had few police, no judges, and no courts. Some groups of desperate people tried to take the law into their own hands. None of the Southern states had an established government to help people during the hard times that lay ahead.

Richmond, Virginia, was one of many areas in the South ruined by the Civil War.

Among the homeless and the unemployed were the former slaves, who had to find a way to support themselves.

What Was Reconstruction?

Reconstruction—the rebuilding of the South—was now in the hands of the new president, Andrew Johnson. Although he had served as vice president to Lincoln, Johnson was not well liked by many members of Congress. Johnson was a Democrat, former governor of Tennessee, and representative in Congress. He had been a senator at the outbreak of the war. He had remained loyal to the Union even though he had strong ties to the South.

President Johnson tried to follow Lincoln's Reconstruction plan. He pardoned most Southerners who took an oath. He appointed temporary governors in many states to help them reform their governments and elect new representatives to Congress.

Within a few months, most of these states had reorganized and ratified the 13th Amendment, which abolished slavery. By the end of 1865, Johnson announced that all of the Southern states but Texas were readmitted to the Union. Congress did not agree.

Congress met in December 1865. Members of Congress called the "Radical Republicans" opposed the Reconstruction plan. The Radical Republicans wanted to punish the former Confederate States for the trouble they caused the nation. The Radicals refused to recognize the newly formed Southern governments or the recently elected representatives from them. They did not accept the states back into the Union.

Some newly established state governments in the South had adopted **"Black Codes."** These laws only applied to African Americans. Under the Black Codes, former slaves, now called **freedmen,** were restricted from voting, owning certain kinds of land, and working certain skilled jobs. Many members of Congress felt that the Black Codes proved that the Southern states did not intend to end slavery.

Lesson 1 Review Write the answers to these questions on a sheet of paper. Use complete sentences.

1. Under Lincoln's plan, how could states come back into the Union?

2. Who assassinated Abraham Lincoln?

3. What was the South like after the Civil War?

4. What was the importance of the 13th Amendment?

5. What was the name of the group that was against Reconstruction?

What do you think?

Do you think African Americans were really free in the South? Explain your answer.

Lawsuit

A case brought before a court of law

Due process

The formal process of justice carried out in a court of law

Agency

An organization set up by the federal government

Geography Note

Secretary of State William Seward learned that Russia wanted to sell its Alaska territory. He planned to buy this land. Most Americans laughed at the idea. They called Alaska "Seward's Icebox" because it was so cold. On March 30, 1867, Seward signed a treaty that gave Alaska to the United States. The purchase price was $7.2 million, which is about two cents an acre!

In readmitting states to the Union, Johnson allowed voting rights to white men in the South. He made no effort to give such rights to the freedmen. Southern whites, who blamed Republicans for the war, were strongly Democratic. The freedmen, on the other hand, were pro-Republican, because President Lincoln had helped them gain their freedom. Republicans in Congress were eager to win the votes of African Americans. Northern business leaders were happily back into successful business deals. They did not want a Democratic South to start lowering tariffs again.

Congress began to put its own Reconstruction plan into effect by passing the Civil Rights Act of 1866. Put into effect over President Johnson's veto, this act was intended to reverse the Black Codes. Under this law, African Americans were allowed to own property, to bring **lawsuits,** and to marry legally. A lawsuit is a case brought before a court of law. Shortly afterward, Congress proposed the 14th Amendment. The amendment made the Bill of Rights cover all Americans, including whites and African Americans. It said that no state shall "deprive any person of life, liberty, or property without **due process** of law; nor deny to any person . . . equal protection of the laws." Due process is the formal process of justice carried out in a court of law. The 14th Amendment did not apply to American Indians.

Tennessee was the only Southern state that accepted the 14th Amendment and was readmitted to the Union. The other Confederate States rejected the amendment and were not readmitted.

What Was the Freedmen's Bureau?

Congress had started the Freedmen's Bureau in 1865 as a temporary **agency** to help former slaves and some white Southerners. One of the first programs of the Freedmen's Bureau was to establish hospitals to aid Southern African Americans injured in the war.

In 1866, with the Freedmen's Bureau Bill, Congress enlarged the agency. It was extended to give freedmen food, clothing, and shelter until they found jobs. Freedmen and their children were given opportunities to go to school. Agents of the Freedmen's Bureau tried to help protect the **civil rights** of the African Americans. Civil rights are basic human rights belonging to all people.

What Was the Second Great Indian Removal?

In the 1830s, the United States government had forcibly removed Indians from the Southeast to an area in present-day Oklahoma. When the Civil War began, many of these Indians supported the Confederacy. With the defeat of the Confederacy, the Reconstruction Treaties of 1866 forced these tribes to give up the western part of their Indian Territory. They were also forced to allow railroads to cross their land. The federal government used the western half of this territory to resettle Indians from other areas. The government moved eastern tribes such as the Delaware and Shawnee to this area. Tribes were also relocated from Kansas. Plains Indians were forced onto reservations too, even though they put up strong resistance. This relocation is known as the "Second Great Removal."

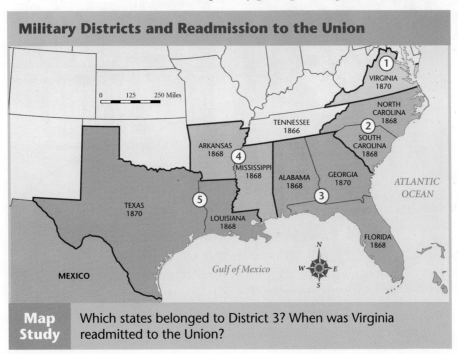

Military Districts and Readmission to the Union

0   125   250 Miles

VIRGINIA
1870

NORTH CAROLINA
1868

TENNESSEE
1866

SOUTH CAROLINA
1868

ARKANSAS
1868

MISSISSIPPI
1868

ALABAMA
1868

GEORGIA
1870

ATLANTIC OCEAN

TEXAS
1870

LOUISIANA
1868

FLORIDA
1868

MEXICO

Gulf of Mexico

N W E S

Map Study Which states belonged to District 3? When was Virginia readmitted to the Union?

What Was the Reconstruction Act of 1867?

Override

To reject or not accept

In March 1867, Congress passed the first of four Reconstruction acts over the veto of the president. The first act stated that the 10 states that had not returned to the Union would be put under military rule by the federal government. The South was then divided into five sections. In order to be readmitted to the Union, states had to hold constitutional conventions with delegates elected by all men—white and African American. Congress had to approve a state's constitution and the state had to accept the 14th Amendment before it could rejoin the Union. By 1870, all 10 Southern states were readmitted to the Union.

Why Did Congress Try to Impeach Johnson?

Johnson tried to veto a number of bills passed by Radicals in Congress. Congress was able to **override** his veto. In 1867, Congress passed the Tenure of Office Act. This act required approval from the Senate before the president could fire an appointee. Believing that the act limited the president, Johnson vetoed it. Congress overrode the veto.

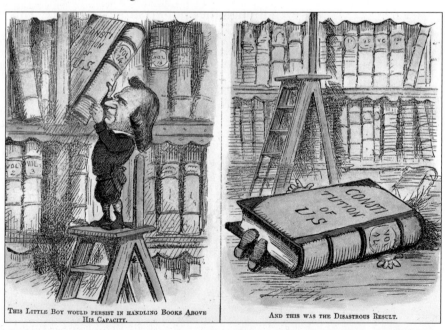

THIS LITTLE BOY WOULD PERSIST IN HANDLING BOOKS ABOVE HIS CAPACITY.

AND THIS WAS THE DISASTROUS RESULT.

This cartoon from 1868 makes fun of President Andrew Johnson. It shows what happened to Johnson—the "Little Boy"—when he broke a law.

Writing About History

Write a song about this time period. The song could focus on a certain event covered in the chapter or on a feeling people had at that time. Write the song in your notebook.

President Johnson then fired one of his Cabinet members, Edwin Stanton. Stanton disagreed with Johnson's Reconstruction policy. Some powerful senators were very upset. They wanted to **impeach** Johnson, which means that he would be charged with **misconduct.** The House of Representatives did impeach Johnson. The Senate then had to decide if he should be removed from office.

A trial was held in the Senate. In order to reach a decision, two-thirds, or 36, of the senators had to agree. The vote was 35 for impeachment and 19 against. The Radical Republicans failed to remove President Johnson by only one vote.

Unfortunately, Johnson had lost much support during these problems. For the remainder of his presidency he was unable to do anything further to promote the Reconstruction efforts he favored.

 Civics Connection

Impeachment

The Constitution gives Congress the right to remove high government officials from office for wrongdoing. First, Congress must find the official guilty of "treason, bribery, or other high crimes and misdemeanors." The House of Representatives and the Senate each have a role in impeachment. The House charges an official with wrongdoing. This is called impeachment. Then the Senate holds a trial. If two-thirds of the Senate agrees that the official is guilty, the official is removed from office.

The Constitution says that the three branches of government are separate and independent. Impeachment gives Congress power over the president. The writers of the Constitution wanted a way to remove a guilty official from office. However, they did not want impeachment to be easy. They did not want Congress to remove someone for political reasons.

Congress has never removed a president from office. In 1867, Congress tried to impeach President Johnson. Charges also were brought against President Richard Nixon in 1974. Nixon resigned before the House voted on the charges. In 1999, the Senate found President Bill Clinton not guilty at his impeachment trial.

1. Do you think the meaning of "high crimes and misdemeanors" should be made clearer? Explain your answer.
2. Do you think the impeachment process seems fair? Explain your answer.

Who Won the Election of 1868?

In 1868, the Republicans chose General Ulysses S. Grant to be their candidate. Grant had no political experience, yet he was well known for leading the Union army in the Civil War. The Democrats chose former New York Governor Horatio Seymour as their candidate. Many felt that Grant had saved the Union, so now he would save the country. Grant won the election in a very close popular vote. About 450,000 African Americans had voted for Grant. Political parties became aware that African Americans were important to the outcome of an election.

Word Bank

Andrew Johnson

Democrats

14th Amendment

Radical
   Republicans

Ulysses S. Grant

Lesson 2 Review On a sheet of paper, write the correct word or words from the Word Bank to complete each sentence.

1. The House of Representatives voted to impeach _____.

2. The _____ said that African Americans had "equal protection of the laws."

3. Most of the Southern whites were _____.

4. _____ created their own Reconstruction plan.

5. _____ was elected president in 1868.

What do you think ?

What sorts of things would a president have to do for you to vote for impeachment?

Technology Connection

Dynamite

As the nation grew, builders sometimes had to remove rock or tear down buildings. For example, to tunnel through a mountain, workers had to remove many tons of rock. Drilling and digging by hand took a lot of time. An explosive could remove the rock more quickly, but explosives were dangerous. Some, like nitroglycerine, could explode without warning. Alfred Nobel, a Swedish inventor, worked to make nitroglycerine safe to use.

In the 1860s, Nobel found that nitroglycerine could be mixed with silica. He could handle the resulting substance safely. He shaped it into rods. Workers could place the rods into drilled holes. Then they used a blasting cap to explode the mixture at the right time. Nobel called his invention dynamite. It made construction work easier and much less costly. It allowed for faster growth and change than ever before.

The Reconstruction acts provided for political reorganization of the South. Under the acts, the right to hold office was taken away from men who had been political leaders of the Confederacy. Other Southerners, however, were allowed to be legislators. During the 13 years that followed, a total of 16 African Americans served in Congress.

Scalawag

A white Southerner who controlled the new politicians who had little government knowledge

Corruption

Using wrong or unlawful ways for financial gain

Carpetbagger

A Northerner elected to political office in the South who took advantage of people; carried belongings in carpetbags

Who Were the Scalawags and Carpetbaggers?

In some states, such as South Carolina, white Southerners put African Americans in state offices. In general, former slaves had little knowledge of government. They did what they were told to do. White Southerners who controlled the new politicians were called **scalawags.**

Some Northerners traveled to the Southern states looking for jobs. Others from the North wanted to help the cause of the freedmen, as either teachers or school administrators. Still other Northerners were elected to political office in the South. Some took advantage of the people and made money through **corruption.** Many of these Northerners carried their belongings in bags made from carpet material. They became known as **carpetbaggers.**

THE MAN WITH THE (CARPET) BAGS.
The bag in front of him, filled with others' faults, he always sees. The one behind him, filled with his own faults, he never sees.

Some carpetbaggers took advantage of people and carried belongings in bags made of carpet material.

What Happened to the Plantations?

The Civil War brought many changes to the South, particularly to the old plantation system. Plantations could no longer use slave labor. Large plantation owners now paid wages to their former slaves. Even though the wages were low, they decreased the profits of the plantation owners.

Many of the large plantations were divided into smaller pieces of land for **tenant farmers.** In this situation, landowners rented their land to owners of small farms. Usually, the tenant farmers paid a set amount of rent. They sold their crops to pay the landowner. Sometimes they might use crops to pay their rent. No matter how they paid it, the farmer ended up with less than the landowner.

Some large landowners let former slaves have land to farm. In return, the owner would get a large share of the crop. The owner provided the seed, tools, food, and general supplies to the farmer. The crop was payment for the supplies the farmer had received. These farmers were known as **sharecroppers.** Slavery had ended, but sharecropping was not much better. The owner sold the crops at a high price and paid the sharecropper a lower price. The sharecropper never stopped owing money. The sharecropper's debt got bigger and bigger. A new form of slavery had begun.

In sharecropping and tenant farming, the freedmen had a place to live and a chance to do the work they knew. Neither practice was good for the farmer. Even though they worked hard, the farmer and the farmer's family remained poor.

History in Your Life

The Works of Mark Twain

"Mark Twain" was a humorous author and lecturer in the late 1800s. Born Samuel Clemens, he found his pen name while working as a Mississippi riverboat pilot. The call "Mark twain!" meant the water was two fathoms deep and thus safe to travel on. Twain's first notable tale was "The Celebrated Jumping Frog of Calaveras County." He wrote many other short stories and novels. His most famous novels are *The Adventures of Tom Sawyer* (1876) and *The Adventures of Huckleberry Finn* (1884). Twain created memorable characters in American literature and realistic portraits of life in the 1800s. Twain's later works are gloomier than his early works. His writing sometimes reflected the prejudice of his time. As a result, many people today are uncomfortable with his work. Nonetheless, his books have been loved for their colorful pictures of childhood and humorous insight into human folly.

Cotton remained a major crop throughout the South, as did tobacco and rice. After the war, pecans, peanuts, corn, wheat, fruits, and vegetables were planted. This gave the South several different kinds of crops. They no longer had to depend on just cotton, tobacco, and rice.

How Did the Civil War Change the Status of Women?

The roles of women changed a great deal during and after the Civil War. The role of the traditional European woman began to fade as women of the frontier encountered the hardships of pioneer living. Strong women emerged. They demanded rights that had been denied to them since colonial times.

During the war, some women worked as nurses, taking care of the sick and wounded. Some women joined the fighting. Some even disguised themselves as men and fought along with the other soldiers. In both the North and the South, women formed aid societies. The women in these groups collected food and supplies for the soldiers. Sometimes they sewed clothing and blankets.

The rapid expansion of industries in the North during and after the Civil War encouraged women to seek employment. Greater financial independence and the suffrage movement added to the importance of women in the workplace and in politics.

Focus on Economics

Southern plantation owners no longer had free labor. Much of the South lay in ruins, and the economy had been destroyed. Farmers did not have money to buy farm equipment such as reapers. Sharecropping did not help renters or landowners. Sharecroppers rarely got out of debt. Landowners lost their lands because they could not pay debts or taxes. Landowners insisted on planting cotton although the demand for it had dropped. The Southern economy would not recover for many decades.

What Were Other Changes in the South?

People discovered iron ore, coal, and limestone in various parts of the South. This led to the creation of a strong iron and steel industry. Birmingham, Alabama, became a major steel-producing center. In other cities, lumber mills provided a good deal of the nation's building material. Mills to produce cotton cloth were built. Railroads, roads, and new industries spread throughout the South. Towns and cities got larger. Progress was beginning to shape the once-rural South.

Before the war, the South had paid little attention to public education. Those who could afford it sent their children to private schools. During Reconstruction, states began to require public education for children. Schools were **segregated,** which meant white and African American children attended separate schools. This practice of segregation continued for many years.

Biography

P. B. S. Pinchback: c. 1837–1921

Captain Pinckney B. S. Pinchback fought for the Union in the Civil War. He served as a member of General Richard Butler's Corps d'Afrique. During Reconstruction, he became lieutenant governor of Louisiana. Governor Henry C. Warmouth was impeached in 1872. Pinchback thus became the first African American governor. He served only one month in that position. Within the next year, he was elected as both a Republican representative and senator to Congress. However, opposing Democrats feared his outspoken fight for African American rights. Some claimed he broke laws to become elected. As a result, Pinchback was never seated as a representative or senator. In the years that followed, he published a weekly newspaper. He also kept fighting to end segregation and violence against African Americans.

What do you think

Would you choose to be a tenant farmer or a sharecropper? Explain your answer.

Lesson 3 Review On a sheet of paper, write the answers to the following questions. Use complete sentences.

1. What was the purpose of the Reconstruction acts?

2. Who were the scalawags?

3. What did carpetbaggers do?

4. What was the difference between a tenant farmer and a sharecropper?

5. How did public schools in the South become segregated?

It Happened in History

African Americans Leave the South

The Civil War left many African Americans poor and without a home or an education. There were few opportunities for African Americans, and some states would not allow them to own land. Many whites were uneasy with African Americans who were no longer slaves. Between 1870 and 1880, thousands of African Americans left the South, convinced that this was the only way they could gain true freedom. A few set sail for Africa. Many moved west hoping to start a new life. During this time, thousands of African Americans, called Exodusters, looked for a better life in northern and western parts of the United States. The photo shows a group of Exodusters waiting for the boat that will carry them westward.

Kansas became a popular western destination. By about 1880, thousands of former slaves had settled there. They were able to own their own land in Kansas. Some became cowhands and others worked as prairie farmers. Some settled in cities, and some worked in mines. Gradually they became more successful. They had the right to vote and hold political office.

Grandfather clause

A clause that stated that any adult African American male could vote if his grandfather was a registered voter on January 1, 1867

In February 1870, the 15th Amendment gave African American men the right to vote. Regardless of race, color, or previous slavery, every male citizen could vote. Suffrage, or the right to vote, had been given to all citizens except women. Southerners opposed the new amendment. They were concerned that African Americans could decide the outcome of an election. Most Northerners were not concerned because the African American population was small.

Some Southern states prevented African Americans from voting. African Americans were told that they could not vote because they could not read or did not understand the Constitution. Voting laws were passed that contained a **grandfather clause.** Any adult male could vote if his grandfather was a registered voter on January 1, 1867. Because no African American was allowed to vote before that date, all freedmen were prevented from voting. By the end of the 1800s, most African Americans had lost the right to vote in the ex-Confederate Southern states.

The 15th Amendment gave African American men the right to vote for the first time in history.

These Ku Klux Klan members were captured during an uprising in 1868.

African Americans faced other problems. Whites organized secret groups such as the **Ku Klux Klan.** The Klan wanted to keep African Americans from voting, to punish the scalawags, and to make the carpetbaggers leave the South. They used violence to scare their victims. Sometimes the violence led to murder. African Americans were most often the target of their attacks.

What Problems Did Grant Have?

President Grant had very little training in political matters. He found that being president was very different from serving as a general. He appointed his friends to government jobs and trusted that they would be honest. Although Grant was an honest man, many of his friends were not.

His **administration** was hurt by several **scandals.** Grant's friends tried to get rich by using the power of their government offices. In 1872, Grant was elected for a second term.

Shortly after President Grant began his second term, the country went into a depression. Businesses and factories began to shut down. Thousands of workers lost their jobs. Many families had no money to buy food. This depression lasted for more than five years. During this time the Republicans lost many seats in Congress. President Grant was a Republican. The country's problems were getting worse, and people blamed the Republicans.

How Did Reconstruction End?

Northerners had grown tired of high taxes. They wondered how much longer Reconstruction could go on. Ten years had passed. Many Northerners had lost interest in the problems of the South. They felt it was time to forget about the war. Grant's two terms had been full of corruption. The election of 1876 called for a president who could restore the people's trust in the government.

Centennial

A 100th year celebration

The Republicans chose Rutherford B. Hayes, the governor of Ohio, as their candidate. He was an honest man. The Democrats chose Samuel J. Tilden, the governor of New York, as their candidate. Tilden won the popular vote, but neither candidate won a majority of electoral votes. An Electoral Commission decided the election. Twenty electoral votes were in dispute.

Hayes made a political deal. He told Southern Democratic leaders that he would end Reconstruction if they would support him. This deal was called the Compromise of 1877. With Southern support, the House of Representatives agreed with the Electoral Commission's decision to make Hayes president. Hayes took office in March 1877. Within a few months all federal troops left the Southern states. Reconstruction had come to an end.

The country celebrated its **centennial** in 1876. A centennial is a 100th year celebration. A Centennial Exposition was held in Philadelphia to show the achievements of the young nation. Americans were becoming masters of science and industrial development. A great nation had risen from the wilderness. It was strong and ready to face the next 100 years.

Then and Now

Think what a subway ride was like in 1870 when Alfred Beach built America's first subway. It ran under Broadway in New York City and extended only 312 feet. The luxurious car held about 20 passengers and was "shot" through a tunnel like a cannonball. The tunnel was decorated with wall paintings. This was intended only as a demonstration subway. When Beach was unable to get city approval to expand the system, it failed.

Have you ridden on today's subways? Many large cities have them. New York City's subway is about 230 miles long— the second longest system after London's. Opened in 1904, New York's subway is powered by electricity. About 3.5 million people ride the New York subway every day.

The country still had social and political problems. Sometimes white Americans and African Americans did not get along. Freedmen continued to fight for the rights they felt they deserved. African American voters helped elect two African American senators and 15 African American representatives between 1865 and 1877. Both senators were from Mississippi. Those members of Congress proved to be good politicians.

After Reconstruction, Southern state governments began denying African Americans social equality and the right to vote. The gains achieved during Reconstruction quickly vanished. In some states, conditions for African Americans were not much better than they had been before the Civil War.

What do you think ?

Grant chose friends to fill important government posts. If you were president, how would you choose people to fill posts?

Lesson 4 Review Choose the word or words in parentheses that best complete each sentence. Write your answers on a sheet of paper.

1. A secret society called the (Ku Klux Klan, Scalawags, Radical Republicans) used violence to prevent African Americans from voting.

2. The presidency of (Hayes, Grant, Tilden) was marked by corruption.

3. After Reconstruction, most African Americans (lost, gave up, gained) most of their rights.

4. The United States celebrated its centennial in (1865, 1867, 1876).

5. When federal (leaders, carpetbaggers, troops) left the South, Reconstruction ended.

Advice to African American Students

W. E. B. Du Bois lived from 1868 to 1963. He argued that African Americans need good schools and a good education. In a letter, he once advised a student not to leave school.

There are in the United States today tens of thousands of [young African-American women] who would be happy beyond measure to have the chance of educating themselves that you are neglecting. If you train yourself as you easily can, there are wonderful chances of usefulness before you: you can join the ranks of 15,000 Negro women teachers, of hundreds of nurses and physicians, of the growing number of clerks and stenographers, and above all the host of homemakers.

Ignorance is a cure for nothing. Get the very best training possible and the doors of opportunity will fly open before you as they are flying before thousands of your fellows.

On the other hand every time a colored person neglects an opportunity, it makes it more difficult for others of the race to get such an opportunity. Do you want to cut off the chances of the boys and girls of tomorrow?

Document-Based Questions

1. Why does Du Bois urge the student to stay in school?

2. What does Du Bois say happens to African Americans who neglect to get a good education?

3. What do you think Du Bois meant when he said that "ignorance is a cure for nothing?" Do you agree? Why?

4. Du Bois warned the student about neglecting the opportunity for education. He said that neglecting the opportunity would "cut off the chances of the boys and girls of tomorrow." What do you think he meant by that?

5. Du Bois named some careers that were open to African American women at that time. How do you think careers have opened up for all women since then?

Source: A Documentary History of the Negro People in the United States, *by Herbert Aptheker, 1989.*

- John Wilkes Booth assassinated Abraham Lincoln on April 14, 1865, at Ford's Theater in Washington, D.C. Andrew Johnson became president.

- The war ruined the former Confederate States. Plantations, roads, bridges, and railways were destroyed. President Johnson appointed temporary governors in many Southern states to help them form new governments.

- Some Northerners punished the former Confederate States by refusing to recognize newly elected officials.

- Congress set up the Freedmen's Bureau in 1865 to help former slaves and some white Southerners find jobs and to provide medical help, clothing, food, and shelter.

- Some Southern governments adopted "Black Codes" that prevented freedmen from owning certain kinds of land, voting, and working certain skilled jobs. The Civil Rights Act of 1866 allowed freedmen to own property, marry, and bring lawsuits.

- The 14th Amendment to the Constitution, which gave African Americans equal protection under the law, was ratified in 1868. The 15th Amendment, ratified in 1870, gave African American men the right to vote.

- In 1867, Congress passed the first of four such Reconstruction acts. It divided the South into five sections and put them under military rule. It also required the Southern states to create new constitutions that had to be approved by Congress.

- Because of a dispute over the powers of the president, Congress impeached Andrew Johnson but failed to remove him from office.

- Scalawags were white Southerners who controlled new politicians, particularly African American politicians. Carpetbaggers were Northerners who traveled to the South and sometimes took advantage of people.

- Most Southern plantations were divided into smaller pieces of land. Landowners farmed their land using tenant farmers and sharecroppers.

- Ulysses S. Grant was elected president in 1868. His two terms as president were marked with corruption and problems.

- Rutherford B. Hayes became president in 1877. Hayes made a deal with Southern congressmen that he would end Reconstruction and remove federal troops from the South.

Chapter 17 REVIEW

Word Bank

Andrew Johnson

Civil Rights Act
of 1866

15th Amendment

14th Amendment

Freedmen's Bureau

impeachment

John Wilkes Booth

Reconstruction

tenant farmers

Ulysses S. Grant

On a sheet of paper, write the correct word or words from the Word Bank to complete each sentence.

1. The _____ to the United States Constitution gave African American men the right to vote in elections.

2. The first _____ act divided the South into five regions and placed federal troops there to maintain order.

3. _____ was Lincoln's vice president and became president after Lincoln died.

4. The _____ was an agency that was supposed to help former slaves and some white Southerners find jobs.

5. African Americans were given equal protection under law by the _____.

6. The Congress tried to get rid of President Johnson by holding hearings on _____.

7. Abraham Lincoln was shot to death by _____, who supported the Southern cause.

8. Congress passed the _____ before the 14th Amendment was ratified.

9. _____ was elected president because people thought that he had saved the Union during the Civil War.

10. _____ rented their farms from landowners.

On a sheet of paper, write the letter of the answer that correctly completes each sentence.

11. Former slaves who gave most of their crops to a landowner were _____.

   A freedmen   **C** tenant farmers

   B sharecroppers   **D** carpetbaggers

12. The violent organization of whites called the _____ attacked African Americans.

   A scalawags   **C** Ku Klux Klan

   B freedmen   **D** carpetbaggers

13. The Centennial Exposition was held to _____.

   A show the achievements of the United States

   B fight for the rights of African Americans

   C reorganize the South

   D educate the public about voting laws

On a sheet of paper, write the answer to each question. Use complete sentences.

14. What was the South like right after the Civil War ended?

15. What did "Radical Republicans" in Congress want to do to the South? Why?

16. Why did Congress establish the Freedmen's Bureau?

17. How did the plantation system change after the Civil War?

18. What were some of the problems that Grant faced as president?

Critical Thinking On a sheet of paper, write your response to each question. Use complete sentences.

19. Ulysses S. Grant had been a capable general during the Civil War and was a hero of the North. Grant was not a very good president. Do you think that it is a mistake to elect military heroes to be president? Why or why not?

20. Do you think the Freedmen's Bureau was a good idea? Why or why not?

Test-Taking Tip

Read test directions more than once. Underline key words. These words may tell you how many examples to give and what kind of information is needed.

Cause and Effect

Looking for causes and effects will help you better understand what you read. An effect is something that happens as a result of a cause. One cause may have several effects. To determine causes and effects, ask these questions:

> Why did the event happen? (cause)
>
> What made the event happen? (cause)
>
> What happened as a result of the event? (effect)
>
> What cause triggered an event?
>
> What is the effect of that event?

Here is an example of one cause and effect that led to the Civil War:

Cause: Political parties and other groups disagreed over states' rights.

Effect: Southern states seceded from the Union.

Here are more causes and effects that led to the Civil War. Read each pair of sentences. Decide which statement is the cause and which is the effect. Rewrite each sentence on your paper. Label it with *cause* or *effect*.

1. A depression occurred in 1857, with a sharp decline in prices.

   Economic differences between the North and the South widened.

2. The proslavery principle expanded in the South.

   Chief Justice Roger Taney's decision denied Dred Scott his freedom.

3. The tragedy of "bleeding Kansas" opened sectional divisions in the country that could not be resolved.

   The Kansas-Nebraska Act was passed.

4. The Democratic Party was split in its views on slavery.

   Abraham Lincoln was elected president.

5. Extremist politicians, editors, and reformers created divisions between the North and South primarily through the slavery issue.

   Divisions between the North and South deepened until they burst into war.

- Congress had to decide whether new states would be free or slave states.

- The Compromise of 1850 settled some slavery issues. The Fugitive Slave Law challenged the right to freedom of almost all slaves and free Africans.

- The Gadsden Purchase set the boundary between Mexico and the United States.

- Choosing a railroad route from coast to coast caused problems between free and slave states.

- The Kansas-Nebraska Act allowed territorial voters to decide if their state would be free or slave. Proslavery people won in Kansas Territory, and violence began.

- In the Dred Scott case, the Supreme Court ruled that slaves were property no matter where they were taken.

- Abolitionist John Brown's actions increased tensions between North and South.

- The Democratic Party split over slavery. The Republican platform opposed slavery and secession. Republican presidential candidate Abraham Lincoln won in 1860.

- Several Southern states left the Union and formed the Confederate States of America in February 1861.

- The Confederacy captured Fort Sumter, a Union fort, in April 1861. This capture began the Civil War.

- Robert E. Lee led the Confederate Army. It won many early battles.

- In 1863, Lincoln freed the slaves with the Emancipation Proclamation.

- The largest battle was at Gettysburg in July 1863. The Union won. It became the turning point of the war.

- Lincoln was re-elected in 1864. Lee surrendered to Ulysses S. Grant on April 9, 1865.

- Lincoln was assassinated on April 14, 1865.

- The war ruined the South.

- Congress set up the Freedmen's Bureau in 1865.

- The 14th Amendment gave former slaves equal protection under the law. The 15th Amendment gave African American men voting rights.

- The Reconstruction Act of 1867 placed the South under military rule and required that new constitutions be written.

- Grant became president in 1868. Rutherford B. Hayes became president in 1877 and ended Reconstruction.

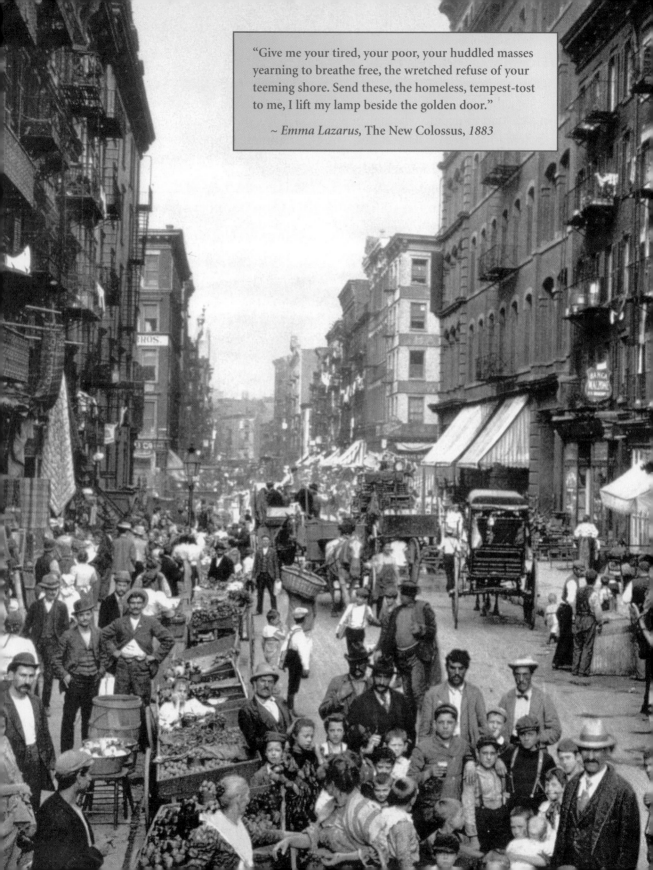

"Give me your tired, your poor, your huddled masses yearning to breathe free, the wretched refuse of your teeming shore. Send these, the homeless, tempest-tost to me, I lift my lamp beside the golden door."

~ *Emma Lazarus*, The New Colossus, *1883*

Unit 6

Development of Industrial America

America has been a land of frontiers. During the last part of the 1800s, America expanded on many frontiers. Settlers headed to the western frontier, claiming lands of American Indians and their ancestors. On the industrial frontier, huge and powerful industries developed. On the frontier of cities, populations grew at an astounding rate with millions of immigrants. And with all this growth came more new problems to solve.

In this unit, you will learn about the western frontier and what happened to American Indians. You will learn about rapid growth of industries and inventions. You will learn how cities grew with waves of immigrants. You will learn how this growth brought about labor and political reforms.

Chapters in Unit 6

18 Settling the Western Frontier

The end of the Civil War turned more attention toward the West. The "last frontier," as it was called, was a land of freedom and adventure. It was a place where pioneers could find an opportunity for a better life. From 1862 to 1890, settlers took up the challenge to tame the nation's last frontier. In this chapter, you will learn how the United States expanded westward.

Goals for Learning

◆ To explain how pioneers traveled in the West and how the transcontinental railroad was built

◆ To describe what kinds of people lived on the frontier and what life was like for them

◆ To explain how the westward movement affected the American Indians in the West

◆ To describe the help that Congress gave the Indians and the end of the frontier

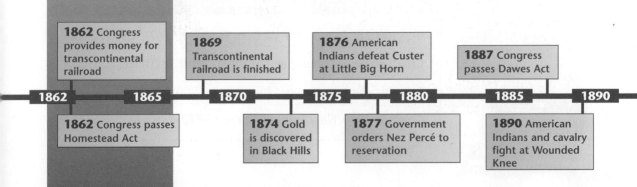

1862 Congress provides money for transcontinental railroad

1869 Transcontinental railroad is finished

1876 American Indians defeat Custer at Little Big Horn

1887 Congress passes Dawes Act

1862   1865   1870   1875   1880   1885   1890

1862 Congress passes Homestead Act

1874 Gold is discovered in Black Hills

1877 Government orders Nez Percé to reservation

1890 American Indians and cavalry fight at Wounded Knee

Stagecoach

A horse-drawn coach that was used for transporting people or mail

Wagon train

A large number of wagons traveling together

Transcontinental

Extending across a continent

The Great Plains is a vast stretch of land between the Missouri River and the Rocky Mountains. During the 1840s and 1850s, European settlers passed up this area on their way to the rich lands of Oregon and the gold in California. The flat, dry Great Plains seemed useless to them.

Beginning in 1858, many Americans traveled westward by **stagecoach** from St. Louis, Missouri. A stagecoach is a horse-drawn coach that was used for transporting people or mail. St. Louis was the western end of the railroad at that time. The three-week journey over mountains and deserts was a difficult one. Travelers were under constant danger of attack by robbers or American Indians. The Indians often saw the settlers as invaders. At the same time, most shipments of supplies from the East traveled by long, ox-drawn **wagon trains.** A wagon train is a large number of wagons traveling together. Communication improved in 1861, with the completion of the telegraph. The appeal of the western frontier grew stronger to many Americans in the East.

European and Chinese immigrants were hired to help build the transcontinental railroad.

How Was the Transcontinental Railroad Built?

In 1862, Congress provided money for the construction of the **transcontinental** railroad. The time had come to link the far western parts of the country to the East. Two companies were chosen to build the railroad. The Central Pacific Railroad started in the West at Sacramento, California, and was built eastward. The Union Pacific Railroad started at Omaha, Nebraska, and was built westward.

Work on the railroad increased after the Civil War ended in 1865. The Union Pacific Railroad hired thousands of war veterans, many of whom were Irish.

Early American explorers called the Great Plains the "Great American Desert." Senator Daniel Webster said, "To what use could we ever hope to put [them] . . . ?" Such descriptions kept white settlers away from the area for years. Not until the 1840s could settlers see that the area might be farmed successfully.

The work was hard and dangerous. Many workers were killed in accidents and American Indian raids. Because of difficult working conditions and the loss of workers, only a few miles of track were laid each day.

Chinese immigrants on the West Coast worked for the Central Pacific Railroad. They worked very hard, but progress was very slow because the land was so mountainous. The workers had to blast tunnels. Sometimes it took all day to go just a few feet.

In May 1869, the two railroads met at Promontory Point, Utah. The Central Pacific Railroad had laid about 700 miles of track. The Union Pacific had laid more than 1,000 miles of track. A golden spike was driven into the final link of the track. The news of the completed transcontinental railroad went out on the telegraph to the country. Now, settling the Great Plains was more appealing to many Americans.

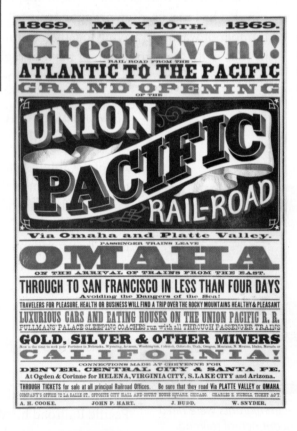

This poster announces the opening of the Union Pacific Railroad in 1869.

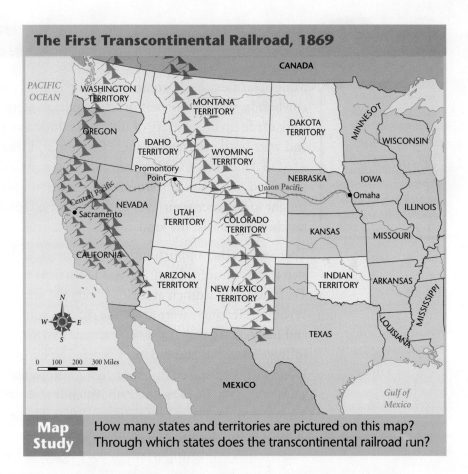

The First Transcontinental Railroad, 1869

Map Study How many states and territories are pictured on this map? Through which states does the transcontinental railroad run?

Word Bank

Central Pacific

Great Plains

St. Louis

Union Pacific

Utah

Lesson 1 Review On a sheet of paper, write the correct word or words from the Word Bank to complete each sentence.

1. The _____ was land between the Missouri River and the Rocky Mountains.

2. The _____ Railroad started at Omaha, Nebraska, and was built westward.

3. The _____ Railroad started in the West at Sacramento, California, and was built eastward.

4. The Union Pacific and Central Pacific railroads met at Promontory Point, _____.

5. The western end of the railroad in 1858 was _____.

What do you think ?

Why do you think many immigrants were willing to work on the railroad?

Cowhand

A person who tends cattle

Prospector

A person who searches an area for gold, silver, or other minerals

Miners, farmers, and people who tended cattle, called **cowhands,** were important in settling the western frontier. They were made up of a variety of different ethnic and racial groups and were both men and women. Chinese and Irish miners, African American and Hispanic cowboys, and German farmers all looked to the western frontier as a place of opportunity. Each sought to enhance their lives as they searched for gold, ran cattle ranches, or farmed the land.

There were other opportunities for women too. The first major step toward universal suffrage was taken in Wyoming in 1869. That was when women at least 21 years old and living in Wyoming Territory were given the right to vote. Colorado, Utah, and Idaho had granted women suffrage by 1896. By 1914, women suffrage had been granted in 11 states. The effort of women in World War I advanced the campaign for universal suffrage for women. Finally, in 1919, the 19th Amendment was ratified by a narrow margin. It went into effect in 1920. This amendment granted voting rights to all women. Very early successes in the western states were important to the passage of this amendment.

How Did Mining Start in the West?

Gold was discovered near Pikes Peak, Colorado, just before the start of the Civil War. Silver and gold were found in Nevada. Miners and **prospectors** traveled many miles to these places. A prospector is a person who searches an area for gold, silver, or other minerals. During the 1860s, gold was also discovered in Montana, Idaho, and Wyoming. The mining boom throughout this Rocky Mountain region was similar in many ways to the California gold rush of 1849.

Most miners never became rich. Individual prospectors could not do as much as large mining companies that brought special equipment to the mountains. These machines were faster than the pick, pan, and shovel methods that individual miners used.

Many of those who had traveled westward in search of gold settled down as farmers or ranchers. Others became loggers, taking advantage of the rich timber resources.

The lack of law and order in many mountain areas during this gold rush was similar to that in California in 1849. Many former miners grouped together to form city governments. They elected sheriffs to help provide them and their families with some law and order. As their lives became more civilized, the settlers in cities on the former frontier developed some pride in their new homes.

What Was Cattle Country?

Settlers in Texas discovered that large herds of longhorn cattle were running wild. This kind of cattle had been brought to America many years earlier by Spanish settlers. The Texans rounded up the cattle and raised the animals for beef, hides, and other goods. Texas became an important ranching area. Cattle were easy to raise in the grasslands of the Great Plains.

Ranchers wanted to bring their cattle to Chicago, Illinois, and many eastern cities. They could make more money if the cattle were sold in these areas. The ranchers' main problem was a lack of transportation. However, this problem was solved with the development of the railroad system. The railroads linked the grasslands to America's major cities.

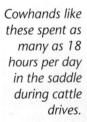

Cowhands like these spent as many as 18 hours per day in the saddle during cattle drives.

Cowhands guided cattle to the holding pens near railroads. Before moving the cattle, every calf was branded with the special mark of its owner. Some cattle were moved over 1,000 miles. The Chisholm Trail was a widely used route. This trail stretched from San Antonio in southern Texas to Abilene in east central Kansas.

The herd traveled 10 to 15 miles a day. A cattle drive took more than two months. During that time, cowhands usually spent as many as 18 hours a day in the saddle. The cowhands' main jobs were to prevent a **stampede** and to protect the cattle from thieves. A stampede is a wild rush of animals.

Cow towns were a welcome sight to tired cowhands. Cow towns had many **saloons** and gambling houses. A saloon was a public building where people gathered to drink or gamble. The only law in cow towns was provided by U. S. marshals such as Wild Bill Hickock. It was a difficult job, for a marshal had to cover a large territory. Law and order developed as the frontier became more settled.

History in Your Life

Barbed Wire

After the Civil War, pioneers moved rapidly into the West. Farmers claimed land and raised crops. Cowhands drove huge herds of cattle onto open range to graze. Farmers soon found that they needed practical fencing to keep cattle from trampling their crops. In 1867, Lucien Smith patented an artificial thorn hedge. This was wire with short metal spikes, or barbs, twisted onto it and stretched between posts. In 1868, a twisted double-strand wire was invented to hold the barbs. In 1874, an improved production process locked the barbs into place. At first, the barbed wire did not prevent all problems. Sometimes cowhands cut farmers' fences so cattle could graze freely or blocked cattle trails so other herds couldn't use them. However, the fences did keep cattle off railroad tracks. The fences made expansions of railroads to the West easier.

What Was the Homestead Act?

In 1862, Congress passed the Homestead Act. This act made it very easy for pioneers to own land. Settlers were given 160 acres of land provided they agreed to live on it for five years. This offer brought many farmers, factory workers, and immigrants to the Great Plains.

Focus on Economics

In 1862, Congress passed the Homestead Act, which gave land to settlers. The same year, Congress also passed another important act called the Morrill Act. The Morrill Act was the first time the federal government provided money for higher education. It gave every state in the Union 30,000 acres of land for each member of Congress. The smallest amount of land a state could receive was 90,000 acres. States were supposed to sell the land and use the money to create colleges that focused on agriculture, engineering, and military science. Over 70 "land grant" colleges were established under the Morrill Act.

What Problems Did Plains Farmers Face?

Pioneers who owned land under the Homestead Act were called **homesteaders.** These people faced difficulties that were unknown to the farmers east of the Mississippi River. Eastern farmers were used to good land, plentiful water, and good supplies of wood. The plains farmers found the ground hard to plow, and there was little rain. In many areas, trees for building materials and fuel could be found only on the riverbanks.

Farmers soon learned that sod, which is thickly matted grass and roots, could be used in place of wood as building material. Brick-like chunks of sod were cut from the ground. They were piled one on top of the other to build the walls of a house. Trees from riverbanks formed the roof, which was then covered with sod. A sod house kept a farm family cool in the summer and warm in the winter.

Windmill

A wind-powered device used to pump water from a well

There was enough water on the plains for farming, but it was underground. New inventions made it possible to drill deep wells into the earth. Farmers then pumped water to the surface by using wind-powered devices called **windmills.** Farmers also used a dry farming method. Part of the land remained unplanted each year so that the area could absorb rainwater.

Lesson 2 Review On a sheet of paper, write the answers to the following questions. Use complete sentences.

1. What did many of the people who set out to search for gold end up doing?

2. Why did ranchers want to bring their cattle to Chicago and eastern cities?

3. What were cow towns like?

4. What was the Homestead Act?

5. How did farmers build their houses?

What do you think

Do you think being a cowhand was really like it seems on television and in books? Explain.

Then and Now

Early colonists used horse-drawn wood plows to turn the soil for planting. This was hard work and took a long time. Farmers could plant and harvest only a small field. In 1797, the first cast-iron plow received a patent. This made plowing faster and easier. After 1830, farmers wanted to settle the Great Plains, but the heavy roots prevented even iron plow blades from working.

In 1837, the first steel plows, called "grasshopper plows," were introduced. These plows easily sliced and turned the tough grasses, opening the plains to widespread farming. By 1850, farmers needed about 80 hours of labor to produce 100 bushels of corn in a field. Now farmers use huge, modern tractors to pull giant plows. They need less than 3 hours of labor to produce 100 bushels of corn.

The Cheyenne, Comanche, Blackfeet, and the tribes of the Sioux Nation lived on the open plains. They were called the Plains Indians. Their way of life depended on the buffalo. The Plains Indians were hunters and nomads. They followed the constantly moving buffalo herds. They ate the meat, used the hides for clothing and shelter, and made the bones into tools.

How Were American Indian Ways Destroyed?

Some army and government officials wanted to kill all the buffalo. That way the American Indians could no longer follow the herds and would settle in one place. Farmers and ranchers wanted the buffalo out of their way. Others killed the buffalo so that they could sell the hides. Between 1865 and 1875, millions of buffalo were killed. William F. Cody got the name "Buffalo Bill" after he killed more than 4,000 buffalo in 18 months.

Buffalo hides were very valuable for making high-quality leather products. Buffalo robes were popular in winter. By 1889, only 541 buffalo survived in the United States. As the buffalo herds disappeared, the Plains Indians lost their independence. They were forced to find another way to live.

Lacrosse, similar to soccer, came from American Indian ways. Indians like this group of Sioux played the game.

Why Were American Indians Moved to Reservations?

The settlers and the U.S. government thought that the American Indians were in the path of progress. Government officials had little understanding of the Indians. They thought that the tribes should settle in one place.

The government signed treaties with the Indians. According to these treaties, the Indians would stay within certain boundaries. The remaining land would be used for the European settlers and railroads. In return, the government would teach the Indians to become farmers. Most Indian nations, feeling that they had little choice, moved to a government **reservation**. A reservation is land set aside by the government for the Indians. Some Indians, however, chose to fight.

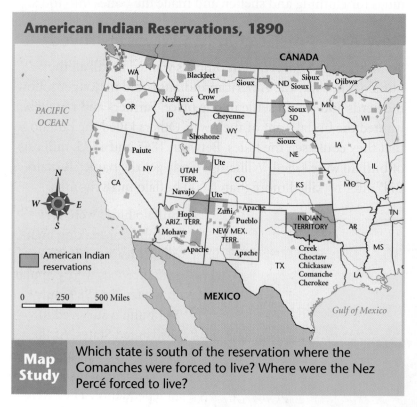

American Indian Reservations, 1890

Map Study Which state is south of the reservation where the Comanches were forced to live? Where were the Nez Percé forced to live?

By the mid-1870s, after many battles and much bloodshed, most American Indians agreed to live on reservations. These reservations were in New Mexico, Arizona, and the territories of Dakota and Wyoming. By 1890, there were reservations in many more states, as shown on this map. The government told the Indians that their way of life would be protected.

What Happened When Gold Was Discovered?

The government's reservation policy was tested in 1874. That's when gold was discovered in the Black Hills of what is now South Dakota. This land was holy to the Sioux. They believed the Great Spirit was present in these hills. The United States government had promised that the Black Hills would belong to the Sioux forever.

Government troops tried to protect these hills for the American Indians. But the number of prospectors who wanted gold was too great. It was clear that the government could not keep its word. Chiefs Sitting Bull and Crazy Horse gathered more than 2,000 Sioux and Cheyenne warriors together. They decided to defend their lands.

Colonel George Armstrong Custer and his Seventh Cavalry met this force. It happened at the Little Big Horn River in Montana on June 25, 1876. Custer and about 210 of his troops were killed. The only survivor was an officer's horse named Comanche.

The defeat of Custer shocked the country. The American Indians had won a great victory. However, Custer's Last Stand, as it was called, would be the last big victory for the Plains Indians. They eventually surrendered to government troops because of lack of food and ammunition.

Chief Joseph

In response to Custer's defeat, the government decided to move all American Indians onto reservations. In the summer of 1877, the government ordered the Nez Percé to a small reservation in Idaho. Settlers took their horses when the Nez Percé were leaving their homes. Angry warriors raided European settlers. The Nez Percé tried to escape to Canada to avoid any more bloodshed.

About 750 Nez Percé fled. Chief Joseph led them. They traveled 1,500 miles in 75 days. The weather was cold, and they did not have blankets. Little food was available. Many died along the way.

The Nez Percé were about 30 miles from the Canadian border when Chief Joseph urged his people to surrender. He told them he was tired of fighting. "Hear me, my chiefs," he said. "I am tired; my heart is sick and sad. From where the sun now stands I will fight no more forever."

Misunderstanding
Failure to understand

In 1870, Chief Red Cloud of the Oglala Sioux wanted to inform the government officials of the problems of the Plains Indians. He spoke at a meeting in Washington, D.C. He told the audience about broken treaties, dishonest government agents, fear, and **misunderstanding.** Red Cloud wanted the president of the United States, whom he called the Great Father, to understand that he wanted peace.

What do you think

What do you think Chief Joseph meant when he said, "I will fight no more forever"?

Lesson 3 Review Choose the word or name in parentheses that best completes each sentence. Write your answers on a sheet of paper.

1. (Colonel Custer, Buffalo Bill, Red Cloud) was defeated at Little Big Horn.

2. The Nez Percé were led by Chief (Sitting Bull, Joseph, Red Cloud).

3. In 1877, the U.S. government ordered the (Cheyenne, Sioux, Nez Percé) to a reservation.

4. Chief (Crazy Horse, Joseph, Red Cloud) spoke at a meeting in Washington, D.C.

5. Gold was discovered in (the Black Hills, Montana, Canada) in 1874.

Biography

Cochise: 1815–1874

A chief of the friendly Chiricahua Apaches, Cochise was falsely accused of seizing a rancher's child in 1861. Cochise declared he was innocent, but the U.S. Army arrested him. He escaped, and fighting followed. Thus the Apache Wars began. Cochise led his band of Apaches on raids against American troops and European settlers. The raids nearly drove the settlers from Arizona. In 1871, General George Crook forced Cochise to surrender. With a peace treaty in 1872, Cochise agreed to live peaceably on a reservation. He lived on the reservation along Apache Pass until his death in 1874.

(Cochise's picture was never taken for religious reasons. Therefore, no picture appears with his biography.)

Writing About History

Imagine that you are an American Indian Chief. Write a speech in your notebook to your people. Talk about a problem your people face, such as being forced to live on a reservation or losing the buffalo herd.

The American people became aware of what had happened to the American Indians living on the western frontier. In 1881, Helen Hunt Jackson published *A Century of Dishonor*, a detailed history of how the Indians were mistreated. Her book was sent to every member of Congress.

Why Was the Dawes Severalty Act Passed?

Congress passed the Dawes Severalty Act in 1887. *Severalty* means separateness. The purpose of the law was to turn the American Indians into independent farmers. Their lands were divided into family-size farms. Any Indians who accepted land would be made citizens of the United States. They could not sell their land for 25 years. The Dawes Act attempted to protect the Indians from being cheated. In many cases, however, the Indians were cheated by land-hungry European settlers. In some cases, even government agents took advantage of them. It was not until 1924 that all Indians were made citizens.

What Happened at Wounded Knee?

In the late 1800s, some American Indian tribes practiced a religion called the Ghost Dance. The Indians wore special clothing during the dance. They believed this clothing would protect them from soldiers' bullets. They also hoped to bring back the buffalo herds, remove settlers from their lands, and bring back their old way of life.

The Seventh Cavalry killed hundreds of Sioux on this site at Wounded Knee, South Dakota.

The Ghost Dance frightened the settlers. They thought it might be a war dance. An army was sent to prevent violence. The Seventh Cavalry arrived to arrest and disarm several hundred Ghost Dance followers at Wounded Knee, South Dakota, on December 28, 1890.

The next day, the cavalry tried to disarm the Ghost Dance followers. Someone fired a shot. It is not known who fired. The soldiers turned their guns on the Indians and killed or wounded about 290 men, women, and children. Twenty-five soldiers were also killed. This massacre at Wounded Knee ended the fighting between the United States government and the American Indians of the western plains.

It Happened in History

George Catlin, Painter of American Indians

Much of what we know about different American Indian cultures during this time comes from the work of George Catlin. George Catlin was a painter who dedicated himself to painting pictures of American Indians. Beginning in 1830, he lived among them and learned their languages. Catlin made more than 500 paintings of people from 50 different tribes. He continued to paint and write almost until his death in 1872. His paintings and the books he wrote about his experiences recorded many sides off the daily lives of the Indians. Today, most of his paintings are in a special wing of the National Museum of American Art in Washington D.C.

George Catlin

This George Catlin painting shows a Mandan Bull Dance.

Western States Admitted to the Union, 1864–1912

Year	State	Year	State
1864	Nevada	1890	Idaho
1867	Nebraska	1890	Wyoming
1876	Colorado	1896	Utah
1889	North Dakota	1907	Oklahoma
1889	South Dakota	1912	New Mexico
1889	Montana	1912	Arizona
1889	Washington		

Which Western Lands Became States?

Settlers had moved into most areas of the western frontier. By 1890, for the first time in American history, there was no frontier line. The frontier had been conquered. Between 1864 and 1912, the United States created 13 states from these western lands.

Word Bank

American Indians

citizens

farmers

Ghost Dance

13

Lesson 4 Review Choose the word or words from the Word Bank that best complete each sentence. Write your answer on a sheet of paper.

1. Helen Hunt Jackson's book *A Century of Dishonor* described how _____ were mistreated.

2. The purpose of the Dawes Severalty Act was to make American Indians into independent _____.

3. Beside granting them farmland, the Dawes Severalty Act made Indians who accepted the farmland _____.

4. In 1890, the cavalry killed 290 American Indians who were attending a _____ at Wounded Knee.

5. The western lands were made into _____ states between 1864 and 1912.

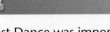

What do you think ?

Why do you think the Ghost Dance was important to American Indian people?

"The Laws"

In the late 1800s, thousands immigrated to America from Europe and Asia. Chinese American writer Maxine Hong Kingston has examined immigrants' right to belong in America. In her book China Men, *Kingston included laws against Chinese immigration.*

The United States . . . and . . . China . . . recognize the . . . right of man to change his home and allegiance, and . . . the advantage of free . . . emigration of their citizens . . . from the one country to the other. . . . Article V of the Burlingame Treaty, signed in Washington, D.C., July 28, 1868. . . .

1868: . . . the year 40,000 miners of Chinese ancestry were Driven Out. The Fourteenth Amendment, adopted in that same year, said that naturalized Americans have the same rights as native-born Americans, but in 1870 the Nationality Act specified that only 'free white' and 'African aliens' were allowed to apply for naturalization. Chinese were not white. . . .

1878: California . . . prohibited Chinese from entering. . . . New state laws empowered cities . . . to confine them . . . or to throw them out. Shipowners . . . were to be fined for . . . transporting them. . . . [Chinese] were barred from attending public schools. The only California fishermen forced to pay fishing and shellfish taxes were the Chinese . . . they were prohibited from owning . . . real estate. They could not apply for business licenses. Employers could be fined . . . for hiring them. No Chinese could be hired by . . . governments. . . . No Chinese . . . could testify in court 'either for or against a white man' . . . . Federal courts declared some of the state and city laws unconstitutional. . . . The . . . laws were reenacted in another form.

1880: The Burlingame Treaty was modified . . . . the immigration of Chinese laborers to the United States would be 'reasonably limited.' In return . . . the American government promised to protect Chinese from lynchings.

1881: The Burlingame Treaty was suspended for . . . twenty years. . . . In protest . . . China ordered scholars studying in the United States to return home. . . .

Document-Based Questions

1. What did the Nationality Act of 1870 say?

2. How did the U.S. government offer to protect the Chinese?

3. The Burlingame Treaty was suspended for 20 years. How did the Chinese respond?

4. How did the United States never really abide by the original Burlingame Treaty?

5. Which do you think was the most unreasonable law or event in the passage? Why?

Source: China Men, *by Maxine Hong Kingston, 1980.*

- The Great Plains stretched between the Missouri River and the Rocky Mountains.

- In 1862, Congress provided money for the transcontinental railroad. The railroad was finished in 1869. It was built by two companies—the Union Pacific Railroad and the Central Pacific Railroad.

- Miners, farmers, and cowhands were the first Europeans to settle the West. Miners were drawn to gold discoveries in Nevada, Montana, Idaho, Wyoming, and Colorado. Cowhands and cattle ranchers raised cattle for beef, hides, and other goods. The Homestead Act of 1862 encouraged farmers and homesteaders to settle land in the West.

- The Plains Indians were nomads. Their way of life was changed forever when farmers, ranchers, and others killed off the buffalo herds. Many American Indians were moved to reservations. The U.S. government promised the Indians that their way of life would be protected.

- When gold was discovered in 1874 in the Black Hills of South Dakota, the government's policy to protect the American Indians was tested. Gold prospectors wanted to make claims on the land, a holy land for the Sioux.

- Government troops tried but could not protect the Black Hills region for the American Indians. In the end, the Indians chose to protect their land. Colonel Custer and about 210 members of the U.S. Cavalry fought and lost a battle against the Sioux and the Cheyenne at Little Big Horn in 1876.

- Congress passed the Dawes Severalty Act in 1887. This act tried to protect American Indians. However, settlers still cheated the Indians.

- In 1890, the Seventh Cavalry was sent to prevent violence between settlers and American Indians because of the Ghost Dance. The soldiers ended up killing or wounding about 290 men, women, and children at Wounded Knee.

- Between 1864 and 1912, 13 states were added to the United States.

Chapter 18 REVIEW

Word Bank

Black Hills

Central Pacific

Colonel Custer

Dawes
  Severalty Act

Ghost Dance

Great Plains

Homestead Act

prospector

Union Pacific

Wounded Knee

On a sheet of paper, write the correct word or words from the Word Bank to complete each sentence.

1. The _____ Railroad laid over 1,000 miles of railroad track.

2. Chinese immigrants worked for the _____ Railroad.

3. Gold discovered in the _____ region tested the government's reservation policy.

4. The _____ was land between the Missouri River and the Rocky Mountains.

5. The _____ was passed to turn the American Indians into farmers.

6. A _____ is a person who searches for gold, silver, or other minerals.

7. The _____ made it easier for pioneers to settle land.

8. Some American Indians believed in a religious movement known as the _____.

9. _____ was defeated at Little Big Horn.

10. U.S. soldiers killed or wounded about 290 men, women, and children at _____.

On a sheet of paper, write the letter of the answer that correctly completes each sentence.

11. The transcontinental railroad was completed in 1869 at _____.

    A Sacramento, California   C Promontory Point, Utah

    B Omaha, Nebraska   D St. Louis, Missouri

12. A problem for ranchers that the railroad helped solve was _____.

    A lack of transportation   C lack of law and order

    B herding cattle   D Indian attacks

13. _____ led the Nez Percé to the Canadian border before surrendering.

  A Red Cloud   **C** Crazy Horse

  B Sitting Bull   **D** Chief Joseph

On a sheet of paper, write the answers to the following questions. Use complete sentences.

14. Where in the West did pioneers travel? How did they get there?

15. Why was the transcontinental railroad built?

16. What three kinds of people lived on the frontier? What did each do?

17. How was the Plains Indians' way of life destroyed?

18. During what time period did many western states enter the Union? How many western states entered the Union during this time?

Critical Thinking On a sheet of paper, write your response to each question. Use complete sentences.

19. What do you think would be a good title for a book describing what happened to the Plains Indians? Why?

20. Do you think you would have liked living on the frontier? Why or why not?

Test-Taking Tip

Studying together in small groups and asking questions of one another is one way to review material for tests.

19 Becoming an Industrial Giant

I n the early 1800s, most Americans were farmers or shop owners. Manufacturing in small factories was done mostly in areas of the Northeast. During the Civil War, the need for war supplies, farm equipment, and machines of all types increased. Following the completion of the railroads after the war, the transportation of people and materials between the two coasts made manufacturing in all parts of the country easier. Tariffs on imports made products from other countries more expensive. Americans wanted products that had been made in America. As the population continued to grow, so did the demand for more and better products. Industry became common. In this chapter, you will learn more about how industry increased in the United States.

Goals for Learning

◆ To describe the development of the steel industry

◆ To describe the development of the petroleum industry and the new ways in which businesses were organized

◆ To list new industries and inventions that changed the world

1870 John D. Rockefeller starts Standard Oil Company of Ohio

1876 Thomas Edison starts lab in Menlo Park

1877 Thomas Edison invents phonograph

| 1870 | 1872 | 1874 | 1876 | 1878 | 1880 | 1882 | 1900 |

1873 Andrew Carnegie enters steel industry

1876 Alexander Graham Bell invents telephone

1883 Brooklyn Bridge opens

Petroleum

A liquid that can be made into fuel

Entrepreneur

A person who starts and organizes a business

Purify

To make something pure

Flexible

Able to move or twist easily

Method

A way of doing something

People all over America began discovering and using the country's many natural resources—coal, iron, lumber, and **petroleum**. Petroleum is a liquid that can be made into fuel. As ways of doing things were improved and machines were invented, new industries were formed. A large flow of immigrants gave these industries an eager labor force.

Strong business leaders helped American industries grow. Andrew Carnegie and John D. Rockefeller were **entrepreneurs**. An entrepreneur is a person who starts and organizes a business. They used the opportunities of this new industrial age. These men played an important part in starting the nation's steel and oil industries.

How Did Andrew Carnegie Develop the Steel Industry?

Andrew Carnegie

Andrew Carnegie realized that most bridges in the country were made from wood. One day he saw men building a bridge out of iron instead of wood. He soon organized the Keystone Bridge Company to build iron bridges for railroad companies.

Carnegie began to realize that iron was not the best product with which to build bridges. Iron would rust, and it was not very strong. It cracked and broke when bent. He needed to find another material to make bridges. He knew steel, which is **purified** iron, was very strong and **flexible**. However, steel was expensive to produce in large amounts.

Back in the 1850s, two men had developed an inexpensive way of making large amounts of steel. William Kelly, an American, discovered a **method** of making iron into steel. Meanwhile, in England, Henry Bessemer had developed a similar method. They had both discovered that the impurities in iron could be "burned off" by blowing cold air through heated iron.

Suspension bridge

A large bridge supported by wires or chains attached to tall towers

Engineering

Using science and math to design and construct buildings or other objects

Skyscraper

A tall building

While visiting England, Carnegie learned about how this method worked. He returned to America and entered the new steel industry in 1873. Carnegie's company made steel for railroad tracks that cost half as much as iron tracks and were much stronger.

How Did Steel Become an Important Building Material?

Inexpensive steel rapidly changed America. The longest **suspension bridge** in the world at the time, the Brooklyn Bridge in New York, was opened in 1883. A suspension bridge is a large bridge supported by wires or chains attached to tall towers. It was a wonderful example of modern **engineering**. Tall buildings built on steel supports began to appear. They rose 10 to 20 stories high. This height seemed so great that people called them **skyscrapers**. Soon steel was used to make such things as pins, nails, washtubs, and barbed wire for fences.

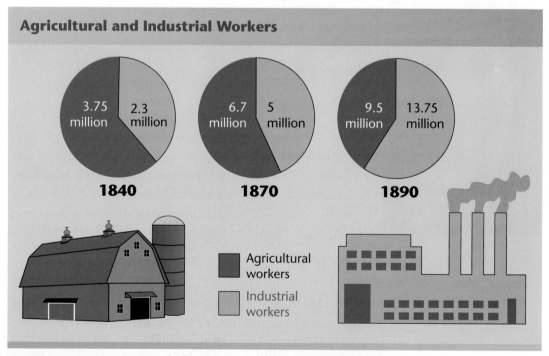

Agricultural and Industrial Workers

1840	1870	1890
3.75 million / 2.3 million	6.7 million / 5 million	9.5 million / 13.75 million

Agricultural workers

Industrial workers

By how much did the number of industrial workers increase between 1840 and 1890? How many agricultural workers were there in 1870?

New York's Brooklyn Bridge opened in 1883. The bridge is a national historic site today.

Carnegie's steel company produced most of the steel in the United States. He retired a very rich man in 1901. He was generous with his money. Carnegie funded libraries, colleges, medical research, and many other projects. He gave away more than $350 million in his lifetime.

 **History in Your Life**

The Brooklyn Bridge

Until the 1880s, New Yorkers used a ferry to cross the East River from Manhattan to Brooklyn. In 1867, a bridge was designed and a company was hired to build it. John A. Roebling, a pioneer in suspension bridge design, created the Brooklyn Bridge plan. He died before the bridge was built. Roebling's son, Washington, supervised construction, which began in 1869. In 1872, Washington Roebling became ill and could not leave his bed. His wife, Emily, managed the rest of the construction.

When the bridge opened on May 24, 1883, it was hailed as the "eighth wonder of the world." With a main span of 1,595 feet, it was the world's longest bridge. It also was the first suspension bridge to use steel wire cables. Four main cables nearly 16 inches thick are hung from two massive 275-foot granite towers. Foundations 78 feet below water level support the towers. The bridge cost $15 million. In 1964, the Brooklyn Bridge was declared a national historic site. Its six traffic lanes and its sidewalks make crossing the East River easy.

Technology Connection

The Mail-Order Catalog

In 1870, the majority of Americans lived on farms. They had to go to town to buy goods. Usually, this meant a long trip. Once the farmer arrived in town, the store might have only a few goods that the farmer needed.

In 1872, A. Montgomery Ward helped change how farmers bought goods. He set up a mail-order company in Chicago, Illinois. It sold many kinds of goods to farmers. The idea caught on quickly. Soon, many farmers were ordering from catalogs.

In the 1880s, Richard W. Sears began selling watches by mail. Before long, he and a partner set up a mail-order company for general goods. They sold tools, clothes, and things for the home. They published their first catalog in 1888. By 1900, Sears and his partner were selling about $10 million in merchandise per year.

Farm families could now order products in the latest styles and models. The prices were lower than those at local stores. The buyer did not have to pay delivery charges for the goods. Mail order greatly improved the lives of American farmers.

Word Bank

Andrew Carnegie

Brooklyn

entrepreneur

skyscraper

William Kelly

Lesson 1 Review On a sheet of paper, write the correct word or words from the Word Bank to complete each sentence.

1. A(n) _____ is a person who starts a business.

2. The longest suspension bridge in the world at the time it opened was the _____ Bridge.

3. A(n) _____ is a tall building.

4. _____ built the first steel plant in the country.

5. _____ discovered a way to make iron into steel.

What do you think ?

How is steel still important today?

Refinery

A place where a good is made pure or made into other products

Geography Note

Oil fields dot the United States. When people think of oil, they often think of Oklahoma. Oklahoma's oil reserves are among the largest in the United States. Oil wells and their towers appeared all around the state. Today, visitors can view oil pumps on the dusty plains. The pumps duck up and down, like giant insects sucking their black riches from the ground.

A stream called Oil Creek flowed through the village of Titusville, about 100 miles north of Pittsburgh, Pennsylvania. It was called Oil Creek because of the black, sticky oil that came up to the surface from below the ground. Most people believed that oil was not very valuable. Then, in 1855, a scientist reported that half of the petroleum or "rock oil" could be made into a product that could be burned in lamps.

This report caught the attention of Edwin Drake, who traveled to the small village of Titusville, Pennsylvania. After one unsuccessful attempt, Drake drilled a hole in the ground using pipes to keep the sides from falling in. From 69 feet in the earth, oil began running through the pipe. This happened in August 1859. This first oil well turned out to be the beginning of America's giant oil industry.

Soon, Titusville was filled with "oil prospectors" in search of "black gold." Oil wells appeared all along Oil Creek and areas of southwestern New York. Railroad tank cars and large pipes called pipelines were built to carry the oil to **refineries**. Oil was made into different products at these refineries. Titusville became a place where fortunes could be made overnight.

Edwin Drake (right front) built this oil well in Titusville, Pennsylvania.

What Business Did Rockefeller Start?

John D. Rockefeller traveled from Cleveland, Ohio, to Titusville to see how he and his partners could make money from the new oil business. Rockefeller decided that he was not interested in drilling for oil because it was too risky. He believed that he could make more money refining it.

Rockefeller organized and became the president of a new company, the Standard Oil Company of Ohio, in 1870. Within 10 years, the company became the most powerful company in its field. The company controlled the production and price of oil throughout the country.

In the early years, most oil was refined into a fuel called **kerosene** that was used for lamps. The need for these lamps ended about 1900, after the electric light was invented. However, the widespread popularity of the motor car in the 1900s created a new use for an oil product—gasoline.

How Did Business Change?

Before the Civil War, most businesses were owned by one person or a group of partners. These businesses usually employed a few workers. They sold their goods to local customers. This simple organization worked well for small businesses. After the Civil War, as businesses grew larger, many organized into **corporations**. These are large companies owned by shareholders.

John D. Rockefeller

Andrew Carnegie, John D. Rockefeller, and other business leaders were **criticized** for forming large companies. The critics believed that big businesses were too powerful. They felt it was impossible for smaller businesses to compete with them. Large corporations that have little competition are called **monopolies**. Without competition from other companies selling the same product, a monopoly can charge higher prices for poorer quality products. The buyer, with no other company to turn to, has little choice but to pay that price or do without the product.

How Were Corporations Important to Business Growth?

Corporations are usually a safe form of business organization. Individuals invest money into corporations. They are protected if the corporation fails. A person who invests in a corporation has limited risk, or **liability**, for the company's debts.

Money used for investment is called **capital**. A corporation allows thousands of people to invest in a business by buying shares of stock. People who own stock can make money on their investment if the company is profitable. Corporations like Carnegie Steel and Standard Oil raised millions of dollars by selling stock.

How Did Companies Become Larger?

Business leaders searched for new ways to organize their companies. Andrew Carnegie did not want to depend on other companies to produce his product. He relied on mining and railroad companies. He found a new, simple solution. He bought mining and transportation companies and combined them into one large company. This allowed Andrew Carnegie to control each step in making steel. This type of new business organization became known as **vertical combination**.

John D. Rockefeller was also concerned with control. He decided to get rid of competition by buying other oil refining companies. This type of organization is known as **horizontal combination**. Standard Oil Corporation became more powerful each time Rockefeller bought a new refinery.

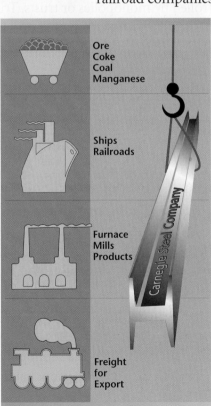

Ore
Coke
Coal
Manganese

Ships
Railroads

Furnace
Mills
Products

Freight
for
Export

Carnegie Steel Company

Vertical combination allowed Carnegie to control each step in steel production.

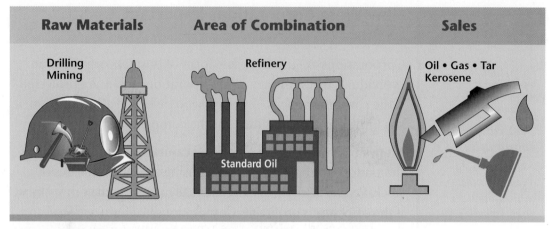

Raw Materials	Area of Combination	Sales
Drilling Mining	Refinery	Oil • Gas • Tar Kerosene
	Standard Oil	

Horizontal combination allowed Rockefeller to eliminate competition.

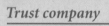

Trust company

A large, powerful company that often is a monopoly

Each of these types of businesses took away competition. Carnegie Steel and Standard Oil became monopolies. They were called **trust companies**. Many kinds of trust companies developed. A trust company became a popular tool for businesses to increase their wealth. Sugar, copper, railroad, and tobacco companies were all controlled by monopolies or trusts. Trust companies could employ thousands of workers. They became giant industries that were very powerful. This changed America into an industrial nation.

What do you think ?

How is oil still important today?

Lesson 2 Review Choose the best word or name in parentheses to complete each sentence. Write your answers on a sheet of paper.

1. The first oil well was built in (New York, Pennsylvania, Ohio).

2. (Andrew Carnegie, John D. Rockefeller, Edwin Drake) organized Standard Oil Company.

3. A (monopoly, liability, refinery) is a company that has little competition.

4. A kind of business organization that controls each step in making something is called a (trust company, horizontal combination, vertical combination).

5. A large, powerful company that often is a monopoly is called a (trust company, vertical combination, liability).

Lesson 3 — Other Major U.S. Industries

Slaughter
To kill animals for food and other products

By-product
Something produced in the process of making something else

As the railroads were built across the nation, they helped provide the key to the success of cattle ranching. The ranchers shipped their cattle to large midwestern cities such as Chicago. In these cities, the meatpacking industry, as developed by Philip Armour, Gustavus Swift, and Nelson Morris, began to do well in the late 1890s. Cattle and hogs were **slaughtered** for meats and meat **by-products**. These products were transported to all parts of the country in refrigerated railroad cars.

Leaders in the construction of new railroad lines in the late 1800s included Cornelius Vanderbilt and James J. Hill. Vanderbilt linked a number of short railroads in the Northeast, creating America's first great railroad system—the New York Central. His system was the first to use steel rails, steel bridges, and double tracks. James J. Hill, who became known as "The Empire Builder," developed the Great Northern Railway System to the Northwest. He encouraged immigrants to settle in that region by teaching them the newest farming methods. He founded schools and helped to start businesses that could provide different types of employment and services.

Cornelius Vanderbilt

How Did Inventions Change American Society?

Americans have always been proud of their ability to invent new machines and tools. This sense of pride was never higher than after the Civil War. These were exciting years for American inventors. Some of the most important inventions used in America today were produced during this time. Many were made by Thomas Alva Edison.

Edison was known as "The Wizard of Menlo Park." A wizard is someone who is supposed to have magical powers. Edison, who never claimed to have any special powers, said his success was due to hard work.

Thomas Edison invented the phonograph.

In 1876, Edison started a research laboratory in Menlo Park, New Jersey. He brought scientists, engineers, machinists, and even clock makers together in this one place. He organized them into a team to produce things that businesses and the public could use. Edison said that his "invention factory" could turn out a minor invention every 10 days and a major one every six months.

The indoor electric lightbulb was one of Edison's finest inventions. For several years, outdoor electric lights had been used in a few cities. Up until Edison's time, however, oil and gas lamps provided the only indoor lighting. After searching for two years, Edison found the solution for safe indoor electric lighting.

Reproduce
To copy or duplicate

Phonograph
A machine used to reproduce sound

The first words **reproduced** by a machine were "Mary had a little lamb." Edison spoke this line from a children's poem into his **phonograph** in 1877. Phonographs were used to reproduce sound. His improvements to Alexander Graham Bell's telephone allowed people to speak naturally instead of shouting, as was necessary with Bell's early telephone. Edison invented a successful motion picture machine. He later added sound by joining it with his phonograph.

It Happened in History

George Washington Carver

The work of an African American scientist, George Washington Carver, changed farming in the South. Carver was born near the end of the Civil War. His family was enslaved. He graduated from Iowa State Agricultural College in 1894. Booker T. Washington, an African American leader, asked Carver to join the Tuskegee Institute in Alabama two years later. At Tuskegee, Carver taught and did research. He developed many new products from pecans, peanuts, and sweet potatoes. Because of his work, southern farmers had other cash crops to grow besides cotton.

What Were Other Important Inventions?

Typesetting

The methods used to prepare type to be printed

Many important inventions came out of the 1870s and 1880s. Bell invented the telephone in 1876. George Eastman simplified the Kodak camera in 1880 so that more people could take photographs. Ottmar Mergenthaler invented a machine in 1884 that would make **typesetting** much easier for newspaper and book publishers all over the country. Typesetting is the method used to prepare type to be printed. Elisha Otis invented the elevator, which made the construction of skyscrapers more appealing. The first electric elevator was installed in 1889.

Alexander Graham Bell made the first long-distance call with his telephone in 1892.

Other inventors followed. Henry Ford experimented with gasoline-powered automobile engines. He developed an assembly line method for building cars cheaply. Shortly into the next century, Ford would make it possible for the average American to own an automobile.

Each of these inventors did more than create a new machine. Each invention created a new industry. These industries created new jobs for the American worker and a brighter future for the country.

How Did Industrial Development Affect the Environment?

Industrial development created new industries, new jobs, and new wealth. But it changed the nation in another way too. There was an **environmental** cost to this development. The air near factories grew more **polluted**. Waste products from factories and mines caused water pollution.

Starting in the 1890s, concern about the environment gradually became more common. Laws were passed to help protect forests, rivers, and wildlife. National parks were created, such as California's Yosemite National Park in 1890. The Sierra Club started in 1892, one of many groups and clubs that came together to promote **conservation** of **natural resources**. Theodore Roosevelt, who would become president in 1901, started many important conservation programs.

Then and Now

How do you think the Wright brothers' airplane compares with a modern jet? It was the Wrights who completed the first successful flight in 1903. Look at this table to compare the two planes.

Description	Wright's Flyer	A Boeing 747
Materials	Wood and cloth	Metal
Weight	750 pounds	775,000 pounds
Wing span	40.5 feet	196 feet
Length	21 feet	231 feet
Flight distance	120 feet	6,000 miles
Time in flight	12 seconds	15 hours
Altitude	40 feet	40,000 feet
Passengers held	1 person	400 people
Speed capacity	30 mph	600+ mph
Power source	Two propellers	Turbojet engine
Fuel storage	Less than 1 gallon	47,000 gallons

Writing About History

Research an invention that was developed between 1870 and 1900. Then write a paragraph in your notebook describing what it is used for and how it works.

Lesson 3 Review On a sheet of paper, write the answers to the following questions. Use complete sentences.

1. How were railroads the key to success for cattle ranchers?

2. Why is James J. Hill called "The Empire Builder"?

3. What are some of the inventions that Thomas Edison and his team at Menlo Park produced?

4. What contribution did Alexander Graham Bell make?

5. How did Henry Ford make automobiles cheap and affordable?

What do you think

Which of the inventions mentioned in this lesson do you think had the most impact on society today? Why?

Biography

Horatio Alger: 1834–1899

Horatio Alger wrote more than 100 books about poor young boys who became rich and successful through honesty and hard work. His popular "rags-to-riches" stories were meant to inspire and teach young people. He also wanted to educate adults about the horrible conditions in which some children lived. An activist, Alger helped to inspire new laws against child labor.

Alger disappointed his father—a Unitarian minister—when he abandoned a career as a minister and became a writer. Alger moved to New York City, where he befriended many homeless orphan children. The children had come to the city after the Civil War. He often based characters in his books on children he knew.

Queen Liliuokalani's Statement on Hawaii

With the help of U.S. Marines, American business leaders attempted to take over the government of Hawaii in 1891. Queen Liliuokalani of Hawaii was unwilling to surrender the government. Still, she did not want to see any battle. She issued this statement to American authorities on January 17, 1893.

I Liliuokalani, by the Grace of God and under the Constitution of the Hawaiian Kingdom, Queen, do hereby solemnly protest against any and all acts done against myself and the Constitutional Government of the Hawaiian Kingdom by certain persons claiming to have established a Provisional Government of and for this Kingdom.

That I yield to the superior force of the United States of America, whose minister. . . His Excellency John L. Stevens, has caused the United States troops to be landed at Honolulu and declared that he would support the Provisional Government.

Now to avoid any collision of armed forces, and perhaps the loss of life, I do this under protest and impelled by said force yield my authority until such time as the Government of the United States shall, upon the facts being presented to it, undo the action of its representatives and reinstate me in the authority which I claim as the Constitutional Sovereign of the Hawaiian Islands.

Document-Based Questions

1. What did Queen Liliuokalani say the business leaders had established?

2. What did John L. Stevens do and say about the Hawaiian situation?

3. Why was Queen Liliuokalani giving up control of Hawaii?

4. For how long was she giving up control of Hawaii?

5. Do you think that Queen Liliuokalani's response was a wise one? Why or why not?

Source: History of the Later Years of the Hawaiian Monarchy, *by W. D. Alexander, 1896.*

Chapter 19 SUMMARY

■ In the second half of the 1800s, the United States began to develop new industries. Before this time, most Americans were farmers or shopkeepers.

■ Andrew Carnegie began a business that built iron bridges. Carnegie's factories used an inexpensive method of converting iron into steel.

■ Carnegie dominated the steel industry. He became a very wealthy man and contributed to many charities.

■ Edwin Drake drilled the first oil well near Titusville, Pennsylvania. "Black gold" brought many people to Titusville to search for their fortunes.

■ John D. Rockefeller formed a corporation, the Standard Oil Company of Ohio, to refine crude petroleum into usable oil. Rockefeller's company became the most powerful in the oil business.

■ Early oil companies refined kerosene for lamps. Later they produced gasoline to be used in cars.

■ After the Civil War, companies became much larger. Large companies called corporations were started. They were owned by many investors who bought stock in the corporation and earned money from their investments.

■ Carnegie bought mining and railroad companies and combined them into one large corporation. Rockefeller tried to eliminate competition by buying other oil refining companies. These large companies were monopolies, since they had little competition.

■ Cornelius Vanderbilt and James J. Hill made fortunes by constructing and running railroad systems. Railroads were important for the meatpacking industry.

■ Many inventions changed peoples' lives during this period. The inventions included Thomas Edison's indoor electric lightbulb and phonograph, Alexander Graham Bell's telephone, George Eastman's Kodak camera, and Henry Ford's assembly line.

Chapter 19 REVIEW

Word Bank

Andrew Carnegie

"The Empire Builder"

engine

George Eastman

meatpacking

monopoly

natural resources

phonograph

railroads

Standard Oil Company

On a sheet of paper, write the correct word or name from the Word Bank to complete each sentence.

1. James J. Hill built the Great Northern Railway System and was known as _____.

2. _____ gave millions of dollars to fund libraries, colleges, and medical research.

3. Rockefeller's _____ refined crude petroleum into oil and kerosene.

4. A large company or corporation that has little or no competition is called a(n) _____.

5. Railroads helped people like Philip Armour and Gustavus Swift develop the _____ industry.

6. Thomas Edison recited "Mary had a little lamb" on the _____, one of his inventions.

7. _____ simplified the Kodak camera, making it possible for thousands of people to take photographs.

8. Henry Ford helped develop a gasoline powered _____. that would later be used in automobiles.

9. Cornelius Vanderbilt made his fortune building _____.

10. _____ such as coal, iron, and petroleum helped the United States to become an industrial giant.

On a sheet of paper, write the letter of the answer that correctly completes each sentence.

11. The manufacture of _____ made it possible to build strong railroad tracks, skyscrapers, and bridges.

    A automobiles **B** steel **C** telephones **D** electricity

12. To control their markets, business owners bought competing companies. This strategy is called _____.

    A horizontal combination   **C** capital growth

    B vertical combination   **D** shares of stock

13. Indoor electric lighting was invented by _____.

    A Alexander Graham Bell   **C** Cornelius Vanderbilt

    B Elisha Otis   **D** Thomas Edison

On a sheet of paper, write the answers to the following questions. Use complete sentences.

14. How did Andrew Carnegie's steel company become so successful?

15. How did James J. Hill bring people to the Northwest?

16. How is a corporation organized?

17. What was Rockefeller's contribution to the oil industry?

18. How did Edison create so many inventions at his Menlo Park laboratory?

Critical Thinking On a sheet of paper, write your response to each question. Use complete sentences.

19. What are some of the problems with becoming an industrial society?

20. Oil is one of the most highly used natural resources today. How do you think the world would be a different place today without oil?

Test-Taking Tip

When studying for a test, practice writing or saying the material out loud. Have a partner listen to check if you are right.

20 A Nation of Cities

As industry grew in the United States, so did the nation's cities. Immigrant groups and other people began to live in cities because they wanted to be close to factories. Though city life had much to offer, people living in cities faced tough working and living conditions. Many people faced discrimination. In this chapter, you will learn what it was like to live in the nation's cities.

Goals for Learning

◆ To identify reasons for the growth of cities

◆ To describe working conditions in factories

◆ To explain the reasons for different immigrant groups coming to the United States

◆ To explain how immigrants and African Americans faced discrimination

◆ To describe some of the developments that made city living interesting

◆ To explain why cities had social problems

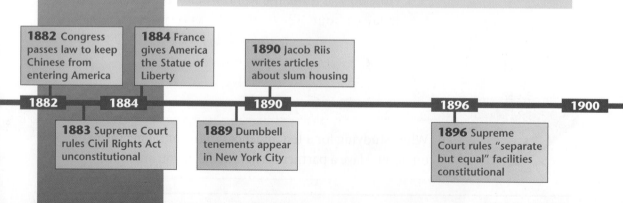

1882 Congress passes law to keep Chinese from entering America

1884 France gives America the Statue of Liberty

1890 Jacob Riis writes articles about slum housing

1882   1884   1890   1896   1900

1883 Supreme Court rules Civil Rights Act unconstitutional

1889 Dumbbell tenements appear in New York City

1896 Supreme Court rules "separate but equal" facilities constitutional

Dweller
A person who lives in a place

Specialize
To make and sell goods or services in one or two areas of business

Urban
Related to the city

By 1850, more than 23 million people lived in the United States. Twenty million of them lived on farms, in towns, and in areas smaller than towns called villages. Three and a half million (or 15 percent) of the American people lived in cities. By 1900, this percentage of city **dwellers** had increased to 40 percent.

People were drawn to cities for many reasons. Cities had exciting events. Cities had many different things to do and places to go. The main reason people moved to cities was because they could find jobs. American industry grew as more and more factories were opened in or near cities. Factories were usually built near railroad lines or a good seaport. Large factories needed many workers.

American cities usually **specialized** in one or two industries. Pittsburgh, Pennsylvania, became the nation's center for making steel. Cleveland, Ohio, became an important oil-refining city. Chicago, Illinois, grew because of the meatpacking business. Other cities like Salt Lake City, Utah; Kansas City, Missouri; and San Francisco, California, grew with the arrival of the railroad.

Railroads were a good way to move products and people from one end of the country to the other. Cities were no longer isolated from one another. Raw materials and products in one city could be shipped easily and cheaply to other cities around the nation.

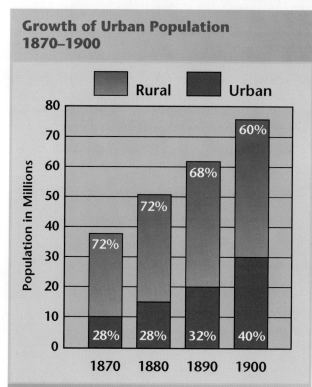

Growth of Urban Population 1870–1900

Rural   Urban

Population in Millions

Year	Urban	Rural
1870	28%	72%
1880	28%	72%
1890	32%	68%
1900	40%	60%

Employer

A person or company that pays workers for their services

Immigrants moved to cities because that's where the factories were. Factories meant jobs. They were usually built near seaports and rivers that made moving products easier, because boats and barges could be used. Sometimes factories and mills used waterwheels, which used energy from flowing water in rivers.

How Were American Workers Treated?

America's new industries needed workers. Large factories and industrial plants employed hundreds or even thousands of workers. Mass production lowered the cost of products. The success of one industry often led to other new industries. Each new industry meant more jobs.

Competition for these jobs was great. **Employers** did not have to pay high wages because so many workers were available. Many workers earned less than $10.00 for a 60-hour workweek, including only one day off.

Poor working conditions were also a problem. Powerful machines were dangerous. Most employers believed that it was the workers' responsibility to protect themselves from dangerous or unsafe working conditions. Workers who were hurt on the job received no help from the employer. Many children also worked in the factories.

Workers like these often worked long hours in poor working conditions.

If you were a child in the 1800s, you might have had to work. No laws restricted child labor at that time. Some poor children did not go to school and instead went to work. Children as young as seven or eight years old helped to make cloth in textile mills. They started by sweeping floors. Later they removed lint or mended broken thread. Barefoot boys under age 10 climbed onto running machines. They removed empty bobbins of thread and

replaced them with filled bobbins. Child laborers worked 12 to 15 hours per day every day but Sunday. They made only a few cents per day.

Today, U.S. laws prevent employers from hiring children under 16 years old. However, child labor still exists in some developing countries. American children are required to attend school until they are 16 years old. If you have a job, your working conditions are a lot different from those in the 1800s.

Word Bank

dwellers

employers

jobs

steel

wages

Lesson 1 Review On a sheet of paper, write the correct word from the Word Bank to complete each sentence.

1. By 1900, city _____ made up 40 percent of the American people.

2. People moved to the cities mainly because they could find _____.

3. Pittsburgh, Pennsylvania, was a city that specialized in making _____.

4. Many workers took factory jobs that paid low _____.

5. Workers who were hurt on the job did not get help from their _____.

What do you think ❓

Many children were forced to work in factories. Why was this unfair?

Steerage

A part of a ship for passengers paying the lowest fare

The Statue of Liberty, an 1884 gift to the United States from France, stands in the harbor of New York City. The huge copper lady holds a golden torch high above her head. She provided a first look at America for millions of immigrants. They had come to America seeking liberty, jobs, and an opportunity for a better life. Ellis Island is also in New York Harbor. There the immigrants faced medical inspections and questions about legal status. Some were turned away. The main building is now a museum.

Getting to the United States was very difficult for most immigrants. A ticket on a steamship often cost an immigrant family all of their savings. Most immigrants bought a ticket in **steerage**. Steerage had the lowest fare. Its passengers had to ride in the dirtiest and noisiest part of the ship in the lowest decks near the engines. The conditions were unhealthy in steerage. The air was stale, and the area was crowded. There was little food, and people often became ill. Immigrants were willing to put up with the conditions to get to America.

Most of the immigrants before the 1880s came from England, Ireland, Germany, Sweden, and Norway. These people were known as "old immigrants." During the 1880s, more than 500,000 "new immigrants" came from Italy, Russia, Poland, and Greece.

The first thing many immigrants to America saw was the Statue of Liberty.

Immigrants came to the United States for many reasons. Many were farmers. Others came to America to escape laws that were unfair. Some came for religious freedom. Almost half of the people who came from Poland and Russia were Jewish.

The Homestead Act of 1862 offered cheap, fertile land to immigrants. American railroad companies **advertised** in Europe to attract immigrants to the American West. However, by the time most immigrants arrived in America, the best land had already been taken. Unable to move on to the western farmlands, most immigrants stayed in America's eastern and midwestern cities.

More than 12 million immigrants passed through Ellis Island between 1892 and 1954.

What Problems Did Immigrants Face?

Few immigrants could speak English. Many were very poor. They had to work hard jobs. Men paved or cleaned streets. Many helped build new skyscrapers. Women found work in clothing factories. Many of these immigrants experienced **discrimination**. Discrimination is treating people unfairly because of their race, sex, religion, or age.

Immigrants from Asia had settled on the West Coast, yet many were denied jobs. Much of the hard work on the transcontinental railroad had been done by the Chinese. In 1882, Congress passed a law saying that no more Chinese could come to the United States.

The largest group of new immigrants came from Italy. Most of the immigrants were men. They planned to work in America for only a few years. They hoped to save their money and then return home to Italy and their families. Jewish immigrants from eastern Europe were the next largest group. Many left Europe to escape religious **prejudice**. Prejudice is a belief or action against someone because of race, sex, religion, or age. Unlike the Italians, Jewish immigrants from Russia and Poland did not plan to return to their homeland. Entire families of Jewish people had moved to America.

Some Americans did not like the new immigrants. They feared that immigrants might take jobs that Americans needed, or work at a lower wage. They disliked dealing with people who were not comfortable speaking the English language. Unfortunately, too many people had forgotten that many of their American ancestors had come to the United States as immigrants too.

What Other Groups Faced Discrimination?

Immigrants were not the only people to experience discrimination at this time. The Civil Rights Act of 1875 had made segregation in public places against the law. However, in 1883, the Supreme Court said the Civil Rights Act was unconstitutional. This cleared the way for more laws against African Americans.

The **Jim Crow Laws** were passed in the 1880s and 1890s. These laws separated African Americans and whites in public places. Signs saying "White Ladies Only" and drinking containers marked "White Water" and "Colored Water" began to appear in restaurants, theaters, and railroad cars. The goal of segregation was to develop "separate but equal" African American and white communities. The laws achieved the goal of separating the races. However, African Americans were never treated as equal to whites.

The only hope of ending Jim Crow Laws was the United States Supreme Court. The 14th Amendment, adopted in 1868, said the Bill of Rights applied to African Americans as well as whites. However, the court ruled that this Amendment applied only to state government and not to individuals. Therefore, store owners, railroad companies, and other private businesses could discriminate against African Americans or anyone else. Following this ruling, segregation in the South became even greater. This continued until segregation in the South was again outlawed after World War II.

Civics Connection

From Immigrants to Citizens

Immigrants came to the United States for a better life. They wanted to become citizens. They also wanted to become part of the American culture. This was not an easy task.

After 1860, many immigrants entered the country. Some Americans became uneasy. They feared that these newcomers threatened the nation's unity. Most Americans had ancestors who had come to the United States from other countries, yet they did not like the new immigrants. These newcomers did not look like them or share their culture.

The government put limits on immigration. People from northern Europe were allowed to come to the United States. Jewish, Catholic, Italian, and Asian immigrants faced prejudice. For a time, the law said some ethnic groups, such as the Chinese, could not settle in America.

Yet all of the immigrants helped make America strong. They contributed to the economy and culture.

Today, to become a citizen, an immigrant must:

• live in the United States for 5 years;

• be at least 18 years old;

• be able to read, write, and speak English;

• show an understanding of American history and government;

• take an examination for citizenship;

• make an oath, or promise, of loyalty to the United States in court and in front of a judge.

1. Do you think the government should limit immigration? Explain.

2. Which requirement for citizenship do you think is most important? Explain.

Writing About History

Write a dialogue between an immigrant to the United States and an American-born citizen. Express each person's worries and hopes for the future. Include each person's feelings about immigration.

What Was *Plessy v. Ferguson?*

Louisiana passed a law in 1890 requiring railroad companies to provide "separate but equal facilities" for African American and white passengers. Homer Plessy tested this law in 1892. This African American refused to move from the "white only" car in which he was riding. Plessy's purpose was to challenge the "separate but equal" law. He was arrested and brought before a judge named Ferguson. Plessy was found guilty.

Plessy appealed his case to the United States Supreme Court. He argued that the Louisiana law was unconstitutional. He said the 14th Amendment forbids state laws that discriminate against African Americans. The Supreme Court disagreed. In 1896, the Supreme Court upheld the Louisiana law and wrote that "separate but equal" facilities were constitutional. This was a major setback for African Americans and their struggle for equal treatment before the law. This law stood until the Supreme Court overturned the Plessy ruling in 1954. That is when segregation in public schools was determined to be unconstitutional.

Lesson 2 Review Choose the correct word in parentheses to complete each sentence. Write your answers on a sheet of paper.

1. The Statue of Liberty was a gift from (Sweden, France, Ireland).

2. Immigrants after the 1880s were called (old immigrants, new immigrants, late immigrants).

3. The largest group of new immigrants came from (Italy, Ireland, Germany).

4. Jim Crow Laws segregated (African Americans, immigrants, American Indians) from white people.

5. (Discrimination, Steerage, Prejudice) is treating people unfairly because of their race, sex, religion, or age.

What do you think ?

How do you think most African Americans felt about segregation?

Most cities provided **leisure** and entertainment. Theaters, roller skating rinks, and dance and music halls became popular. **Retail** areas included convenient stores, restaurants, and service shops. Public libraries offered all people the opportunity to escape their cares and read.

What Forms of Transportation Improved City Life?

People traveled around the city by foot or in private coaches until horse-drawn **trolleys** were invented. The trolleys carried 10 to 15 people. Horses pulled the trolleys along steel rails set into the street. Americans called them **streetcars**.

Transportation improved when Thomas Edison invented a system for sending electricity in the early 1880s. The electric motor made the electric streetcar possible. Electric streetcars carried about 45 people. They received electricity from overhead wires. Electric streetcars were faster than trolleys.

Streetcar routes affected the way a city grew. The routes fanned out from the center of the city like the spokes of a wheel. Housing and businesses developed along these routes. Streetcars ran on a time schedule and were inexpensive to ride. Workers could live several miles from where they worked. Streetcars allowed people to travel easily around the city.

Leisure
Something that is done for amusement

Retail
Relating to the buying and selling of goods

Trolley
A carriage that rides on rails and is used for transportation

Streetcar
A horse-drawn or electric carriage that rides on rails and is used for transportation

In the late 1800s, streetcars helped people get around the city. The streetcars ran on rails and were pulled by horses.

How Did Department Stores Begin?

At first, stores were small and specialized in a few products. Shoppers went from one store to another. Business owners later thought of putting all of these small stores into one building. It was called a department store. The new department store had hundreds of goods in one large building. Department stores became very popular. Soon every major American city had at least one department store.

F. W. Woolworth created a department store that sold many different products for a **fixed price**. A fixed price is a set price for a product or service. Most of the products sold in his store cost no more than 5 or 10 cents. Woolworth's "5 and 10 Cents" store became very popular with people who had a limited **income**. He eventually built the Woolworth Building in New York City. It was the tallest building in the world for a time.

What Other Leisure Activities Were Popular?

Cities became centers for the arts. Communities in Pittsburgh, Philadelphia, Chicago, and New York built opera houses and started symphony orchestras. New museums collected paintings and sculptures. Americans could listen to the music of the great composers and see works of art from around the world.

Sporting events also became popular. Professional sports teams developed. Baseball became the nation's first **spectator** sport. The National League was organized in 1876. However, baseball was a summer sport. In 1891, James Naismith of Springfield, Massachusetts, created a new indoor winter sport known as "basketball."

Lesson 3 Review On a sheet of paper, write the answers to the following questions. Use complete sentences.

1. What forms of transportation were used in cities?
2. What was the purpose of department stores?
3. What is a fixed price?
4. What kinds of places promoted the arts in cities?
5. Which spectator sports were started at this time?

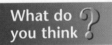

What do you think

Why do you think spectator sports were and still are important for American cities?

Sanitation

The act of disposing of waste and keeping areas clean

Tenement

A cheaply made building divided into apartments

Slum

A run-down urban area often without electricity or indoor plumbing

Although America's growing cities were exciting places to live, they did have many problems. Most cities had grown rapidly. Housing and **sanitation** were not very good. Living conditions became worse as more people moved into the cities.

In an attempt to create more housing, landlords in Philadelphia, New York, and Boston, Massachusetts, built special kinds of housing. They were called **tenements**. Tenements were cheaply made buildings divided into apartments. Many people lived in the small apartments in these buildings.

By 1889, dumbbell tenements appeared in New York City. As many as 32 families lived in one of these five- or six-story brick buildings that were shaped like dumbbells. Dumbbells are narrow in the middle and larger at both ends. They were miserable places to live. People began to call these and other poor areas **slums**.

Immigrant families like this often lived in tenements. Tenements were crowded and noisy.

In the late 1870s, Jacob Riis, a New York newspaper reporter, began to write articles about the lives of people living in "slum housing." His book, *How the Other Half Lives,* told the story of the lives of new immigrant families. He described buildings with dark halls that served as playgrounds for children in winter. Many tenements did not have good **ventilation**. The air was stale in the winter and very hot in the summer. Because of the large numbers of people living so close together, the buildings were very noisy. Worst of all, many of these buildings had no fire escapes. This made them dangerous places to live.

Ventilation

The process of circulating fresh air in an enclosed area

How Were Cities Governed?

City governments were not prepared to deal with the problems of slums. Before the Civil War, people living in cities needed few services from the government. They got their water from a city spring or private well. Volunteer fire companies provided fire protection. People disposed of their own garbage. However, in the larger cities a different kind of organization was needed. City governments needed a lot of practice to successfully manage these large communities.

City, or urban, problems increased during the 1880s. City officials did not know how to deal with them. Little was known about the people who lived in slums. People believed that those living in slums were poor because they had no skills or they were lazy. Religious leaders began to question this belief. They knew that something had to be done to improve the living conditions. Many religious groups were set up to help the urban poor. Examples are the Salvation Army, the Young Men's Christian Association (YMCA), and Young Women's Christian Association (YWCA).

Word Bank
city officials
slums
tenement
urban
YMCA

Lesson 4 Review On a sheet of paper, write the word or words from the Word Bank to complete each sentence.

1. A(n) _____ is a five- or six-story building that houses 8 to 10 families.

2. The _____ was set up to help the urban poor.

3. Areas with poor living conditions were called _____.

4. If something is related to the city or city life, it is _____.

5. _____ did not know how to solve city problems in the 1880s.

What do you think ?

Many city dwellers did not have good places to live. How can this cause problems for people?

Biography

Elizabeth Jane Cochrane (Nellie Bly): c. 1864–1922

In 1885, young Elizabeth Jane Cochrane answered an article in the *Pittsburgh Dispatch*. A newspaper writer had said that women belonged at home. They should not be a part of the workforce. Cochrane was angry. She described women who had little money and needed jobs. Her letter landed her a job at the newspaper, where she took the pen name Nellie Bly.

Soon Bly became a reporter for the *New York World*. She wrote about young women who worked in factories. She wrote about people who had difficult lives. She even went undercover in a hospital. There she learned how people with mental illnesses were treated.

In 1889, Bly traveled around the world. She hoped to beat the time of the fictional hero in *Around the World in Eighty Days*. Bly made the trip in 72 days. Because of this, she became famous. She captured people's attention as she told about wrongdoings in America and around the world.

Blanche Bruce's Speech to the Senate

Born into an enslaved family in Virginia, Blanche Bruce received his early education from his owner's son. During the Civil War, he left his master and opened a school for African Americans in Missouri. In the early years of Reconstruction, he held various Mississippi state offices. He was elected to the U.S. Senate in 1874. He held many other political appointments into the late 1800s. The passage below is from a speech Bruce made to the Senate in 1876.

We want peace and good order at the South; but it can only come by the fullest resignation of the rights of all classes. The opposition must concede the necessity of change, not only in the temper but in the philosophy of their party organization and management. The sober American judgment must obtain in the South as elsewhere in the republic, that the only distinctions upon which parties can be safely organized and in harmony with our institutions are differences of opinions relative to principles and policies of government, and that differences of religion, nationality, or race can neither with safety nor propriety be permitted for a moment to enter into the party contests of the day.

The unanimity with which the colored voters act with a party is not referable to [caused by] any race prejudice on their part. On the contrary, they invite the political cooperation of their white brethren, and vote as a unit because proscribed [limited] as such. They deprecate [criticize] the establishment of the color line by the opposition, not only because the act is unwise and wrong in principle but because it isolates them from the white men of the South, and forces them, in sheer self-protection and against their inclination, to act seemingly upon the basis of a race prejudice that they neither respect nor entertain. . . .

When we can entertain opinions and select party affiliations without proscriptions, and cast our ballots as other citizens and without jeopardy to person or privilege, we can safely afford to be governed by the considerations that ordinarily determine the political action of American citizens.

Document-Based Questions

1. According to Senator Bruce, what things should determine a person's political party affiliation?

2. In the second paragraph, Senator Bruce refers to a color line established by the "opposition." Who were the opposition?

3. Why did Bruce say African Americans disapproved of the color line?

4. Senator Bruce suggests that African Americans were being encouraged to show prejudice. How?

5. Do you think Senator Bruce was speaking more to African Americans or to European Americans? Explain your reason.

Source: Blanche Bruce, Speech to the Senate, 1876.

- Between 1850 and 1900, the percent of the population living in cities grew from 15 percent to 40 percent.

- Many people moved to cities to find work in industry and manufacturing.

- Working conditions in most factories were poor. Workers were paid low wages for long hours of work. Employers showed little concern for the safety of their workers.

- In 1884, France gave the Statue of Liberty as a gift to the United States. It was placed in New York's harbor, where it welcomed millions of immigrants.

- In the second half of the 1800s, a majority of the immigrants came from Italy, Russia, Poland, and Greece.

- Some immigrants came to seek their fortunes. Others, such as Jewish immigrants from eastern Europe, came to find religious freedom.

- Many immigrants faced prejudice because they had different customs, languages, and religious values.

- As cities grew, new developments helped people live better lives. Public transportation systems helped people get around. Department stores offered many different items in one location. Museums, concert halls, and sporting events provided leisure activities.

- Because cities grew so rapidly, there was not enough housing. Lack of sanitation became a major problem.

- Most city governments were not able to deal with the problems, so religious organizations such as the YMCA, YWCA, and Salvation Army were set up to help the poor.

Chapter 20 REVIEW

Word Bank

department stores
mass production
oil-refining
safety
sanitation
spectator
steerage
streetcars
wages
working
  conditions

On a sheet of paper, write the correct word or words from the Word Bank to complete each sentence.

1. _____ in most factories were very bad because of long hours, poor air quality, and dangerous machines.

2. F. W. Woolworth founded one of the first _____ in the country.

3. Cities had poor _____, which caused health problems for everyone.

4. Workers would receive as little as $10.00 in _____ for a 60-hour week of back-breaking work.

5. Public transportation often took the form of _____ pulled by horses and later powered by electricity.

6. Many employers were not concerned with _____, because they believed it was the workers' problem.

7. Cleveland, Ohio, became known as a center for the _____ industry.

8. Baseball was the nation's first _____ sport.

9. Large quantities of items were made in factories using a process known as _____.

10. Immigrant families traveled to the United States in the _____ section of steamships.

On a sheet of paper, write the letter of the answer that correctly completes each sentence.

11. Most immigrants to the United States settled in eastern and midwestern cities because _____.

  A the best lands of the West were taken

  B the best jobs were there

  C they preferred city life

  D there was less prejudice there

12. The Jim Crow Laws of the 1880s and 1890s attempted to
_____.

A destroy big-business monopolies

B separate African Americans and whites

C discriminate against immigrants

D increase immigration

13. The *Plessy v. Ferguson* case caused a setback for _____.

A Asian immigrants in the West

B workers' rights

C African American civil rights

D Jewish immigrants in the East

On a sheet of paper, write the answers to the following
questions. Use complete sentences.

14. What are two reasons immigrants came to the United States?

15. What problems did African Americans face?

16. Why were city governments unable to deal with the
problems that population growth created?

17. Why were tenement buildings needed?

18. What was the advantage of shopping at a department store?

Critical Thinking On a sheet of paper, write your response to
each question. Use complete sentences.

19. If you had been living in Europe in the late 1800s, would you
have immigrated to the United States? Why or why not?

20. Compare life in cities today with life in cities in the 1890s.
How is it the same? How is it different?

Test-Taking Tip

An essay question may ask you to compare and contrast things.
Be sure to tell how the things are alike and how they are different.

21 A New Spirit of Reform

During the late 1800s, the United States was a modern nation filled with opportunity. The changes at this time improved the lives of many Americans. As communication, transportation, industry, and science advanced, so did American citizens. But problems remained. There was still political corruption. Working conditions remained poor. Beginning in the 1870s, people began to do something about these problems. In this chapter, you will learn how the nation worked on these reforms.

Goals for Learning

◆ To explain why reforms were needed

◆ To describe the major reforms that occurred during the period

◆ To explain how labor unions helped workers

◆ To explain the purpose of the Sherman Antitrust Act

◆ To describe the Populist movement

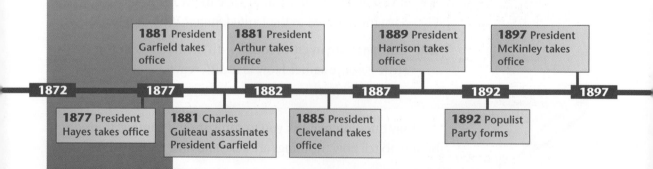

1881 President Garfield takes office

1881 President Arthur takes office

1889 President Harrison takes office

1897 President McKinley takes office

1872 1877 1882 1887 1892 1897

1877 President Hayes takes office

1881 Charles Guiteau assassinates President Garfield

1885 President Cleveland takes office

1892 Populist Party forms

Author Mark Twain called the 1870s the "**Gilded** Age." He thought that American society was like a gilded piece of metal. Something that is gilded is covered with a thin coating of gold. Gilding covers up the original object. Twain thought many poor and powerless Americans were hidden under the control of the nation's wealthy few.

Many average American workers, certain that industrial America was hurting them, wanted change. A new spirit of **reform** began. Reform is a change intended to make something better. The people leading reform movements thought that many industrial leaders had corrupted the national and local governments for their own gain. They were becoming rich while common people suffered.

Gilded

Covered with a thin coating of gold

Reform

A change intended to make something better

Contract

A work agreement between at least two groups

What Was the Crédit Mobilier Scandal?

The *New York Sun* newspaper published an article about the Union Pacific Railroad in 1872. The Union Pacific was one of the companies that helped build the transcontinental railroad. The article accused Union Pacific officials of making money illegally from the government through a construction company called Crédit Mobilier of America. Union Pacific had purchased the Crédit Mobilier Company. Then it gave the company **contracts** to lay railroad tracks for the federal government. Union Pacific overpaid Crédit Mobilier $50 million for laying the tracks. This way the company's records looked successful and the stock became very valuable.

RESIGNATION UNDER TRYING CIRCUMSTANCES.

President Ulysses S. Grant thinks how it would be if all the corrupt people quit at once.

1872–1897

People began to question the relationship between Union Pacific and Crédit Mobilier. The head of the company, Oakes Ames, was also a congressman. He gave company stock to members of Congress to try to prevent them from **investigating**. However, Congress still investigated and found that many politicians took part in the scandal. Even Schuyler Colfax, the vice president of the United States, was part of it. A congressional committee suggested that Ames be removed from the House of Representatives. However, he remained.

President Grant's administration was full of corruption in addition to the Crédit Mobilier Scandal. Secretary of War William Belknap made money by cheating American Indians living on reservations. Members of the Treasury Department had received illegal payments from the whiskey companies who wanted to avoid paying tax. Even President Grant's personal secretary was in on this Whiskey Ring Scandal, as it was called. The president, without knowing it, allowed people to make millions off the government.

Lesson 1 Review On a sheet of paper, write the answers to the following questions. Use complete sentences.

1. What is reform?

2. What was Crédit Mobilier?

3. How did Crédit Mobilier make its money illegally?

4. What government officials were part of the Crédit Mobilier Scandal?

5. How was William Belknap corrupt?

What do you think

How do you think people feel when they learn about government scandals? Explain.

It Happened in History

General Grant won many battles during the Civil War and faced tough struggles while he was president. His most courageous battle came nine years after he left the White House. Grant was financially ruined in 1884 by a business partner who mismanaged their company. Though seriously ill, Grant wanted to give his wife financial security before he died. He worked for a year to write *Personal Memoirs of U. S. Grant*. Soon after he had finished it, Grant died. The 1,231-page book sold more than 300,000 copies and earned $500,000. Ulysses S. Grant had won the last battle of his life.

Political boss

A professional politician who controls the actions of a political party

Bribe

A payment to someone to make a person act in a certain way

Mugwump

A reform group that wanted to replace the spoils system with civil service

Civil service

A system in which government employees are hired according to their qualifications

Corruption was not limited to the federal government. **Political bosses** affected many city governments. These men pretended to befriend immigrants. They offered help to poor city neighborhoods. They provided clothing, heating fuel, and food. Often they would set up social events to become known and liked among city neighborhoods. In return, they expected the people to vote for the candidates they supported.

Who Was Boss Tweed?

William Marcy Tweed was a powerful boss in New York City. Boss Tweed, as he was called, controlled a Democratic political organization known as Tammany Hall. Tweed and his friends stole millions of dollars from the city. For example, the city of New York paid one of Tweed's friends $179,729 for 30 to 40 chairs and three or four tables.

This kind of behavior made reformers angry. Newspaper stories criticized the corruption. Tweed was not concerned about the stories. He thought his supporters could not read. Tweed overlooked the power of newspaper cartoons that Thomas Nast drew. Nast pictured Tweed as a crook. Nast's cartoons eventually frightened Tweed. The public's opinion of Tweed was changing. Tweed offered Nast $500,000 to leave the country for Europe. Nast refused the **bribe.** Boss Tweed was arrested for political corruption in 1871 and convicted in 1873. He died in jail in New York City.

Who Were the Mugwumps?

Reformers in the Republican party criticized the spoils system, under which friends of politicians were given government positions. These reformers were called **Mugwumps.** The name came from an American Indian word meaning "chief." Mugwumps wanted to replace the spoils systems with **civil service.** Under civil service, people are hired for government jobs according to their qualifications.

Writing About History

Think about living in New York City in the 1880s. Write a letter to a newspaper editor about political bosses. Tell what you think should be done to fix the problem.

Rutherford B. Hayes was elected president in 1876. The Mugwumps were disappointed that Hayes won. President Hayes surprised the reformers by investigating corruption when he took office in 1877. He found that hundreds of federal workers were being paid without doing any work. He fired the people responsible and saved the country over $1 million a year.

How Did the Spoils System End?

Four years later in 1881, James Garfield became president. The new president found himself in the middle of a political fight between two Republican groups. Each group wanted Garfield to give its members government jobs. Charles Guiteau was angry because he did not get a government job. He shot President Garfield at a train station. Garfield died several weeks later from the gunshot wound.

Vice President Chester A. Arthur became president after Garfield's death. President Arthur convinced Congress to pass civil service laws. The laws made sure government jobs went to qualified people. They also prevented government workers from being fired for political reasons.

Charles Guiteau (left) killed President Garfield in 1881.

What Happened in the Election of 1884?

The Republican Party did not nominate Chester A. Arthur for a second term as president. President Arthur had made many political enemies because he promoted civil service laws. The Republicans nominated James G. Blaine instead. He was the leader of a group who wanted the president to appoint friends to government jobs. The Democrats nominated New York governor Grover Cleveland. He ran an honest campaign and would not make deals with political bosses.

The campaign was rough. The Mugwumps and the Republican reformers worked to get Cleveland elected president. He won the election by about 25,000 votes. Cleveland took office in 1885.

What Happened During President Cleveland's Term?

Like the former president, Cleveland faced difficulties dealing with people who believed in the spoils system. He agreed with the Mugwumps that people should be appointed to government positions based on their skills. His appointments angered many former supporters who had expected jobs in his administration.

During Cleveland's term in office, many in the federal government tried to change the way the nation's powerful railroad companies did business. These companies did not want the government to regulate their business. However, in 1887, Congress passed the Interstate Commerce Act. This law forced the railroads crossing state lines to charge customers the same fees for the same services.

In the election of 1888, President Cleveland lost to the Republican candidate, Benjamin Harrison. Harrison took office in 1889. Grover Cleveland was elected again in 1892.

Lesson 2 Review On a sheet of paper, write the correct word or words from the Word Bank to complete each sentence.

1. A reform group that wanted to replace the spoils system with civil service was called the _____.

2. A _____ is a professional politician who controls a party or a political machine.

3. _____ was arrested in 1873 for political corruption.

4. Mugwumps wanted to start _____.

5. _____ did not believe in the spoils system.

What do you think ?

Do you think civil service is fair? Why or why not?

Then and Now

Your bicycle in 1876 would have been the Ordinary.

Maybe your bicycle today is one of the popular mountain bikes.

You probably would have ridden the Safety bicycle in the late 1880s.

Strike

The act of stopping work to get better pay and working conditions

The need for reform spread beyond ridding the government of corruption. The treatment of American workers had become a growing concern. Labor leaders attempted to organize workers into labor unions as powerful as the big business corporations.

How Did Labor Unions Grow?

In 1869, Uriah Stevens formed the Noble Order of the Knights of Labor. This secret organization remained small until 1878, when Terrence V. Powderly became its leader. Powderly ended the secrecy and opened the union to all workers who wanted to join. Under Powderly, the union grew rapidly. Within seven years, the number of members increased from fewer than 50,000 to more than 700,000.

Samuel Gompers

A second labor union, the American Federation of Labor (AFL), began in 1886. Under the leadership of Samuel Gompers, this union wanted to organize groups of skilled workers. Each different trade such as carpentry or bricklaying would have its own small union within the larger AFL.

The two organizations had similar goals but were different in several ways. The AFL was considered to be more conservative than the Knights of Labor. Its members thought that peaceful bargaining was better than **strikes**. To strike a company means that union workers refuse to work until their demands are met. The AFL would not accept workers who were not white. The Knights of Labor, on the other hand, favored strikes and boycotts as bargaining tools. It welcomed women and blacks.

How Did Labor Unions Use Strikes?

Without its workers, a company would lose money. Successful strikes were not easy at first. Companies fought back. Sometimes they would not allow striking workers to return to work after the strike. The company hired workers who did not belong to unions to replace striking workers. These workers were called **strikebreakers.** Often fights broke out between the strikers and strikebreakers. Police were often called to stop fights.

In May 1886, a violent strike in Chicago destroyed the Knights of Labor. Seeking an eight-hour workday, almost 80,000 workers went on strike. When fights broke out on the street, police tried to break them up. Police gunfire killed several workers. A group of **anarchists,** who were against all forms of government, met at Haymarket Square to protest the workers' deaths. Someone threw a bomb that killed several police officers and one civilian. The public blamed the deaths on the Knights of Labor. Membership for the Knights of Labor decreased after the bombing.

The Chicago police fired at workers during the Haymarket Square protest.

Biography

Jane Addams: 1860–1935

A social worker and reformer, Jane Addams was committed to the relief of poverty in cities. In 1889, she founded Hull House, a settlement house in Chicago. Settlement houses offered wide-ranging services and programs to meet the needs of poor immigrants of various backgrounds. It had about 40 clubs, a day nursery, a gym, a playground, and a place to give out medicine. It also had an art gallery, a theater, a music school, and classes in cooking and sewing. Addams pressured the government for various reforms. Among them were laws to protect working women, child-labor laws, and the first juvenile court. She was against war and led the fight to give women voting rights. In 1931, she was awarded the Nobel Peace Prize.

Lesson 3 Review Choose the word or name in parentheses that best completes each sentence. Write your answers on a sheet of paper.

1. A(n) (union, strike, anarchist) is a kind of protest in which union workers refuse to work until their demands are met.

2. The (American Federation of Labor, Knights of Labor) thought peaceful bargaining was better than striking.

3. The (American Federation of Labor, Knights of Labor) liked to use strikes and boycotts.

4. (Uriah Stevens, Terrence V. Powderly, Samuel Gompers) led the American Federation of Labor.

5. A(n) (strike, anarchist, union) is a group or person against all forms of government.

What do you think ?

What problems do you think strikers and businesses face during a strike?

Prosecute

To charge with a crime

Geography Note

In 1867 in the Midwest, farmers were concerned with the high cost of producing and shipping their crops. The Grange movement grew out of this concern. It was the first group of politically active farmers. They worked together and shared resources. They defined problems in terms of economics and campaigned for political candidates who would help them. In time, the Grange spread to other parts of the country. By the 1880s, farm alliances had taken over much of this work.

Reformers had become concerned about the power of giant industries. In many cases, large companies were forcing smaller ones out of business. Small businesses were organized into trust companies. Trust companies could take away competition. The trust company became a popular way for businesses to increase their wealth. They could charge higher prices if they did not have any competition. Trusts were established in the railroad, steel, copper, sugar, coal, and meatpacking industries.

A small group of businessmen controlled large industries. Reformers believed that giving so much power to a few business leaders harmed the country. They felt the average American could not fight these powerful businesses.

How Did Congress Try to Limit Trust Companies?

Congress passed laws to correct the problem of trust companies. The Interstate Commerce Commission (ICC) was created to regulate railroads. In 1890, President Benjamin Harrison signed the Sherman Antitrust Act into law. This law made it illegal for large companies to form monopolies. The law was unsuccessful. The Sherman Antitrust Act was used more often to **prosecute** unions on strike than to prosecute big businesses. To prosecute means to charge with a crime. This outcome was the opposite of what Congress had intended.

What Did the Populist Party Stand For?

In the late 1800s, farmers were hit hard by falling crop prices. To help improve their economic condition, farmers formed political organizations called farm alliances. Membership in farm alliances grew quickly, reaching more than 1.5 million members by 1890. African American farmers formed their own group called the Colored Farmers Alliance. This organization had more than one million members in 12 states. Farmers wanted an increase in the money supply, higher crop prices, and better regulation of the railroads that carried their crops to market. The farmers' spirit of reform created a new political party called the People's, or Populist, Party. This party, organized in 1892, represented the average farmer. The Populists thought that industrial workers would also join them to fight the powerful business interest. Populists believed that American democracy was in danger of being destroyed by a few powerful businesses.

In the presidential election of 1892, James Weaver, the Populist candidate, received more than one million votes. The Republican Party began to worry about the growing power of the Populists. To gain votes, the Democratic Party began to support some Populist proposals.

How Did the 1896 Election End the Populist Party?

During the 1896 presidential campaign, the Populist Party proposed many changes for the government, including the following:

- There would be a graduated income tax plan. Taxes would increase as a person's income increased.
- The public would own the railroad, telegraph, and telephone companies.
- Senators would be elected by the people, not chosen by state legislatures.
- The government would make more money available. It was hoped this would raise prices on farm products and help the economy.

The Populists thought the best way to increase the money supply was to make silver coins again. Most business owners felt only gold should be used as money. Businesses wanted to limit the supply of money to keep prices low and make it easier for big corporations to do business. President Cleveland agreed with the business owners.

In the 1896 presidential election, the Republicans nominated William McKinley. McKinley did not care about reforms. He supported the **gold standard**. The gold standard is a system in which a basic unit of currency is equal to a certain weight of gold. The Democratic Party was split. President Cleveland wanted the gold standard. Democrats from the West and the South wanted to use silver.

One cartoon of the time called William Jennings Bryan the "Populist Paul Revere."

William Jennings Bryan, a Democrat from Nebraska, was asked to speak at his party's convention. Bryan felt that the gold standard helped only big business. It hurt American farmers, factory workers, and small business owners. Bryan said that the supporters of the gold standard could not win because "you shall not press down upon the brow of labor this crown of thorns; you shall not crucify mankind upon a cross of gold."

Bryan's "cross of gold" speech won him the Democratic nomination for president. The Populist Party nominated him too. The young man was running for president as the candidate of two political parties. He campaigned around the country. He traveled more than 18,000 miles and gave more than 600 speeches. No one before him had ever campaigned for president this way.

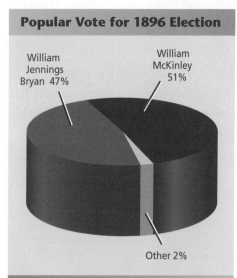

Popular Vote for 1896 Election

William Jennings Bryan 47%

William McKinley 51%

Other 2%

McKinley, on the other hand, remained in his home state of Ohio and rarely gave speeches. Railroad companies and banks gave large amounts of money to his campaign. Campaign workers gave out buttons and posters. These efforts worked, because McKinley won the election. He took office in 1897.

The Populist movement ended with the defeat of Bryan, but the spirit of reform did not end. A new group of reformers, called the Progressives, were middle-class, well-educated people from cities. Some were Democrats. Others were Republicans. They, too, wanted to make changes in American society.

What do you think ?

Why do you think so many political parties come and go as the Populist Party did?

Lesson 4 Review On a sheet of paper, write the answers to the following questions. Use complete sentences.

1. How did trust companies control the country's wealth?

2. What was the Sherman Antitrust Act and why was it not successful?

3. What was the Populist Party?

4. Which presidential candidate in 1896 supported the gold standard? Why?

5. What happened to the Populist Party?

History in Your Life

The Works of Emily Dickinson

Emily Dickinson had a reputation in Amherst, Massachusetts, as being strange for years before she died in 1886. She rarely left her house. Some said she always dressed entirely in white. After her death, friends found hundreds of poems. Dickinson had written and neatly stitched the poems into little handmade booklets. Only seven of her 1,775 poems had been published during her lifetime. Her family allowed all of them to be published after she died. Dickinson came to be thought of as one of America's greatest poets. She had an unusually brief and symbolic style. Her poems were about such topics as death, love, and faith in God. While Dickinson traveled little, her imagination seemed to span the globe. Today millions of people have read her poems. Poets like William Carlos Williams and Adrienne Rich credited Dickinson with having a major influence on their work.

Declaration of Woman's Christian Temperance Union

A small group of Ohio women began The Woman's Christian Temperance Union (WCTU) in 1874. By 1890, membership had grown to 150,000 nationwide. The group's focus was the legal forbidding of alcoholic beverages. The word temperance *refers to people controlling their own actions. These people claimed alcohol was the root of many of America's problems at the turn of the century. This passage is taken from their Declaration of 1902.*

We therefore formulate [set down] and, for ourselves, adopt the following pledge, asking our sisters and brothers of a common danger and a common hope to make common cause with us in working its reasonable and helpful precepts into the practice of everyday life:

I hereby solemnly promise . . . to abstain from all distilled, fermented, and malt liquors, including wine, beer, and cider, and to employ all proper means to discourage the use of and traffic in the same.

To conform and enforce the rationale of this pledge, we declare our purpose to educate the young; to form a better public sentiment; to reform so far as possible, by religious, ethical, and scientific means, the drinking classes; to seek the transforming power of Divine Grace for ourselves and all for whom we work, that they and we may willfully transcend no law of pure and wholesome living; and finally we pledge ourselves to labor and to pray that all of these principles . . . may be worked out into the customs of society and the laws of the land.

Document-Based Questions

1. Women began the Woman's Christian Temperance Union. Who else besides women does the first paragraph ask for help in their cause?

2. What, if any, attempt is in this statement to make using alcohol illegal?

3. What was one purpose stated in the declaration?

4. The writers said in the last paragraph they would like to form a "better public sentiment." What do you think they meant?

5. How effective do you think the WCTU's methods were in convincing people not to drink alcohol?

Source: Declaration of Woman's Christian Temperance Union, 1902.

- In 1872, the Union Pacific Railroad was found to be taking money from the government illegally. Many of the people who profited were members of Congress and business leaders. This was called the Crédit Mobilier Scandal.

- Corruption was found in federal, state, and city governments while Ulysses S. Grant was president.

- William Marcy Tweed, known as Boss Tweed, controlled an organization that stole millions of dollars from New York City's government. Thomas Nast drew political cartoons that exposed Boss Tweed. Nast's cartoons helped bring Tweed to justice.

- The Mugwumps were a group of reformers in the Republican Party. They wanted to replace the spoils system with civil service.

- Presidents Hayes, Garfield, and Arthur all worked to reform the way government jobs were performed. The civil service laws were finally passed while Arthur was president.

- During President Cleveland's first term, the government began to regulate major industries such as the railroads.

- The Interstate Commerce Act was passed in 1887. It regulated the way railroads could charge their customers.

- Labor unions changed the way workers were treated. Two of the first labor unions were the Noble Order of the Knights of Labor and the American Federation of Labor.

- The Knights of Labor thought strikes and boycotts could change working conditions. The American Federation of Labor preferred peaceful bargaining to get their demands met.

- Some unions used strikes as a way of improving working conditions. Many strikes turned violent.

- The Sherman Antitrust Act was signed in 1890. It was created to help control monopolies. The act was not successful. The outcome was the opposite of what Congress had intended.

- The Populist Party was formed to represent the average American instead of big business. The Populists proposed many changes in the government.

Chapter 21 REVIEW

Word Bank

American Federation of Labor

Boss Tweed

Chester A. Arthur

civil service

Interstate Commerce Act

Mugwumps

Sherman Antitrust Act

Thomas Nast

Whiskey Ring

William Jennings Bryan

On a sheet of paper, write the correct word or words from the Word Bank to complete each sentence.

1. _____ and his people stole millions of dollars from New York City.

2. The _____ laws required that people be qualified before they could hold a government job.

3. Samuel Gompers was one of the early leaders of the _____.

4. The _____ was one of the first laws to limit or regulate big business in America.

5. The _____ was a law to limit large business monopolies.

6. The political cartoons of _____ helped put Boss Tweed in jail.

7. A group called the _____ believed that people should be given government positions because of their skills.

8. The _____ was a major scandal of President Grant's administration involving even Grant's secretary.

9. _____ was the presidential candidate of the Populists.

10. Politicians did not like President _____ because he tried to do away with the spoils system.

On a sheet of paper, write the letter of the answer that correctly completes each sentence.

11. The Crédit Mobilier scandal involved the Union Pacific Railroad, which cheated the government by _____.

   A illegally taking government money

   B buying civil service jobs

   C giving members of Congress free train rides

   D hiring strikebreakers

12. A powerful political boss who was convicted of corruption and died in prison was _____.

    A Schuyler Colfax   **C** Chester A. Arthur

    B Mark Twain   **D** William Marcy Tweed

13. Workers who were hired to work in place of striking workers were called _____.

    A anarchists   **C** Mugwumps

    B strikebreakers   **D** political bosses

On a sheet of paper, write the answer to each question. Use complete sentences.

14. Why did the Knights of Labor lose members after the Haymarket Square bombing?

15. What were the main ideas of the Populist Party?

16. Why was the civil service system important?

17. What was the purpose of labor unions?

Critical Thinking On a sheet of paper, write your response to each question. Use complete sentences.

18. What is something that you would reform about the current government? Explain your answer.

19. If you could form a political party, what would be three of the things your party would stand for?

20. Do you think that large companies need to be regulated by the federal government? Why or why not?

Test-Taking Tip

Look for specifics in questions or directions. These may tell you in what form to give your answer. For example, some questions say to use complete sentences.

Unit 6

Using Reference Materials

Reference materials are sources for finding different kinds of information. Here are some examples of reference materials and the kind of information you can find in them:

General information almanac: Book of recent and historic facts and figures about many subjects, usually published once a year

Atlas: Book of maps of countries, states, and some cities

Encyclopedia: One book or a set of books with summaries and histories of many different subjects

Gazetteer: Dictionary of geographic place names and information

Newspaper: Daily or weekly publication with national, local, sports, and business news and regular features

Periodical index: Listing of magazine articles by subject and the publication in which they appear

Internet: Worldwide computer network with information on a wide variety of subjects. Includes online encyclopedias, newspapers, and periodicals

You could probably find the answers to all of these questions somewhere on the Internet. Name at least one other source listed above that you could use to answer these questions.

1. Where could you find the vice presidents who served between 1865 and 1900?

2. The Homestead Act of 1862 opened much western land to settlers. It did not, however, open land in Oklahoma, which was Indian Territory. On what date could settlers stake claims in Oklahoma?

3. In what year did Thomas Edison invent a safe indoor lightbulb?

4. What was the name of the first professional baseball team? In what year was the team formed?

5. There is a current dispute over fishing and hunting rights for an American Indian tribe in Minnesota. The Nelson Act of 1889 and 1890 took away rights originally granted in a treaty made in 1837. Where would you find the latest developments on this issue?

6. Where could you see a map of Montana with an enlargement of Great Falls?

7. Where would you find information about the Detroit River?

8. Where might you find an article about current methods of refining crude oil?

9. Where could you find last night's sports results for your local teams?

10. You do not remember where you recently read an article about public education in the 1870s. Where could you find the name and issue of the publication in which it appeared?

Unit 6 SUMMARY

- The Union Pacific and Central Pacific railroads finished the transcontinental railroad in 1869.

- Miners, farmers, cowhands, and homesteaders settled the West.

- Many American Indians were moved to reservations. The government promised but was unable to protect their way of life.

- Between 1864 and 1912, the nation added 13 states.

- In the second half of the 1800s, new industries began to develop. Andrew Carnegie found a method of converting iron into steel. Edwin Drake drilled the first oil well. John D. Rockefeller's Standard Oil Company of Ohio refined crude petroleum into usable oil.

- Large companies grew into corporations. Many became monopolies.

- Cornelius Vanderbilt and James J. Hill made fortunes with railroads.

- World-changing inventions marked the period.

- From 1850 to 1900, the amount of Americans living in cities grew from 15 to 40 percent.

- Many people moved to cities to find work in industry and manufacturing. Working conditions in most factories were poor.

- From 1850 to 1900, most immigrants came from Italy, Russia, Poland, and Greece. They sought their fortunes or religious freedom. Many faced prejudice because their ways were different.

- In 1884, France gave the Statue of Liberty to the United States.

- As cities grew, new developments made life better—transportation systems, department stores, museums, and concert halls.

- With rapid growth, cities had problems.

- Corruption was found in federal, state, and city governments.

- Thomas Nast's political cartoons exposed corruption in New York.

- Civil service laws were passed while Chester A. Arthur was president.

- The Interstate Commerce Act regulated the way railroads charged customers.

- Labor unions changed the way workers were treated.

- The Sherman Antitrust Act was signed in 1890 to control monopolies.

- The Populist Party represented the average American.

"Our country offers the most wonderful example of democratic government on a giant scale that the world has ever seen; and the peoples of the world are watching to see whether we succeed or fail."

~ Teddy Roosevelt, September 27, 1910

Unit 7

The Emergence of Modern America

Have you noticed as you get older that you have more and bigger responsibilities? As the United States grew and developed in the early 1900s, it took on more and bigger responsibilities. As its interests expanded, the country became concerned with the affairs of other nations. It also took responsibility for its own citizens and resources in good times and bad times.

In this unit, you will learn how America took on wider responsibilities in the world. You will learn about American involvement in smaller wars and in World War I. You will learn how America gave one-half of its citizens the right to vote. You will learn about America's economic crash after a period of great well-being.

Chapters in Unit 7

22 America Becomes a World Power

Throughout the 1800s, the United States played a limited role in world affairs. Important European nations did not think of America as a world power. This changed late in the century. Confidence as a nation, new American leaders, and new world problems brought the United States into the world picture. In this chapter, you will learn how America became a world power.

Goals for Learning

◆ To identify the reasons for the Spanish-American War

◆ To explain the outcome of the Spanish-American War

◆ To describe how America expanded in the Pacific and became a stronger nation

◆ To explain President Theodore Roosevelt's reforms and the impact of the Progressive movement

◆ To describe other accomplishments of President Roosevelt

◆ To describe achievements of President Taft and the election of Woodrow Wilson

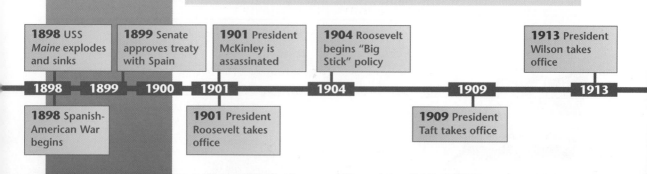

1898 USS *Maine* explodes and sinks

1899 Senate approves treaty with Spain

1901 President McKinley is assassinated

1904 Roosevelt begins "Big Stick" policy

1913 President Wilson takes office

| 1898 | 1899 | 1900 | 1901 | 1904 | 1909 | 1913 |

1898 Spanish-American War begins

1901 President Roosevelt takes office

1909 President Taft takes office

Compete

To try to win or gain something

Before the Civil War, the United States had been working on its goal of Manifest Destiny. Once it had extended its boundaries from the Atlantic Ocean to the Pacific Ocean, attention shifted to growth of industry and business. This put America in a better position to **compete** with the rest of the world. During this time, Americans became confident that they could compete with the nations of Europe.

Why Did America Go to War with Spain?

The only pieces of the former Spanish empire in North America were Cuba and nearby Puerto Rico in the West Indies. For many years, hundreds of thousands of people in Cuba had been victims of the unfair Spanish government there. Many Americans were living in Cuba, and many American businesses held important sugarcane industries there. These people felt that the United States should help Cubans become free of Spanish control.

Not eager to go to war with Spain, President McKinley offered to buy the island of Cuba. The Spanish refused. Then in January 1898, he sent the battleship USS *Maine* to Cuba to protect American lives and property. But the fighting inside Cuba continued.

The battleship *Maine* exploded on February 15, 1898, and sank into the harbor of Havana, Cuba. The explosion killed 260 American sailors. The sinking of the *Maine* shocked the nation. Newspapers blamed the Spanish government.

President McKinley demanded that Spain stop the fighting in Cuba. Meanwhile, Theodore Roosevelt, assistant secretary of the U.S. Navy, sent Admiral Dewey and a fleet of ships to the Philippine Islands in Asia. Spain controlled these islands. Roosevelt gave Admiral Dewey orders to attack the Philippines' main harbor if war broke out as a result of the *Maine* bombing.

The USS *Maine* exploded and sank in Havana Harbor in 1898.

On April 9, 1898, Spain promised that it would stop its fighting in Cuba. Spain wanted to avoid a war with the United States. Many Americans wanted to go to war. "Remember the *Maine*" was printed on posters and buttons.

President McKinley was criticized for not punishing Spain for the sailors who died on the *Maine*. On April 11, 1898, he asked Congress for permission to use the military to stop the war in Cuba. McKinley made it clear that the United States was interested in helping Cuba gain its independence, not in taking control of it. President McKinley ignored the fact that Spain, having already agreed to stop fighting, heard of McKinley's action. Spain declared war on the United States. Congress then declared war on Spain.

Word Bank

Cuba

Havana

Philippine

Puerto Rico

Spain

Lesson 1 Review On a sheet of paper, write the correct word or words from the Word Bank to complete each sentence.

1. The *Maine* was sunk in the harbor of _____, Cuba.

2. Spain controlled the _____ Islands.

3. American businesses held important sugarcane industries in _____.

4. Cuba and _____ were the last of the Spanish empire in North America.

5. _____ declared war on the United States.

What do you think ?

Why do you think it was hard for Spain to maintain its empire?

Armistice

A break in a war to talk peace

The Spanish-American War lasted four months. Admiral Dewey attacked and destroyed the Spanish navy in the Philippines. At the same time, a native Filipino group revolted on land. The Spanish quickly surrendered. Future control of the islands was left unsettled, but American troops were sent to set up bases.

The biggest battle took place in Cuba. Theodore Roosevelt left his government job to help with the war. He organized a group of soldiers called the "Rough Riders." With the help of other American groups, including the all-African American 10th Cavalry Regiment, the Rough Riders charged and captured San Juan Hill in Cuba. During this attack, the American navy under Admiral William Sampson sank all of the Spanish ships still guarding Santiago harbor.

Spain and the United States agreed to stop fighting on August 12, 1898. They discussed how to end the war. This is called an **armistice.** On December 10, 1898, Spain and the United States signed a treaty that ended the war.

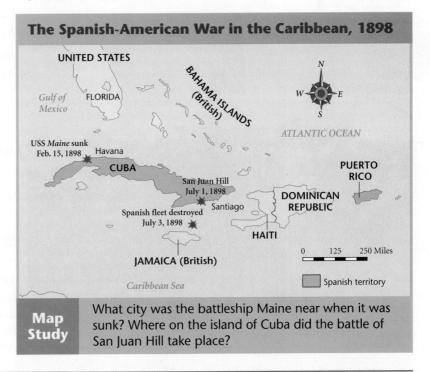

The Spanish-American War in the Caribbean, 1898

UNITED STATES

BAHAMA ISLANDS (British)

Gulf of Mexico   FLORIDA

ATLANTIC OCEAN

USS *Maine* sunk Feb. 15, 1898   Havana

CUBA

San Juan Hill July 1, 1898

Spanish fleet destroyed July 3, 1898   Santiago

PUERTO RICO

DOMINICAN REPUBLIC

HAITI

JAMAICA (British)

Caribbean Sea

0   125   250 Miles

Spanish territory

Map Study

What city was the battleship Maine near when it was sunk? Where on the island of Cuba did the battle of San Juan Hill take place?

What Were the Results of the War?

The United States Senate had to ratify the treaty with Spain. Spain agreed to give Cuba its independence. The United States gained the island of Puerto Rico in the Caribbean Sea and the Pacific islands of Guam and the Philippines.

The treaty started a debate in the Senate. Some senators did not like the idea of the United States controlling foreign territories. Other senators argued the new land would make America a stronger nation. President McKinley agreed. The Senate approved the treaty in February 1899. The United States paid $20 million to Spain for the Philippine Islands.

The people of the Philippines did not want to belong to the United States. They declared their independence. The United States sent an army to the Philippines to stop the independence movement. The United States defeated the Filipino army after three years of fighting.

The Philippine Islands provided the United States with a valuable naval base in Asia. The United States had taken the first step toward becoming a world power. Secretary of State John Hay spoke for most Americans when he said that the Spanish-American War was a "splendid little war."

Theodore Roosevelt (center, with glasses) and his Rough Riders posed at the top of San Juan Hill in Cuba.

Republic

A government in which citizens elect people to speak and act for them

Writing About History

What does it mean to be a world power? Write a short essay to explain your opinion. Describe the responsibilities and problems of a world power. Include in your essay the type of country you think usually is a world power.

What Happened to Cuba After the War?

To help the new government keep order, the United States forces remained in Cuba for four years. During this time, Cuba set up a modern educational system. New highways were built, and better sanitation was developed. Walter Reed, an American medical officer, rid the island of yellow fever, a disease that had caused problems there. In 1902, the United States withdrew from Cuba, having made an agreement with the Cuban **republic.** A republic is a government in which citizens elect people to speak and act for them. The agreement stated that America would be able to keep military bases there. It would also be able to step in if others threatened Cuba's independence.

Lesson 2 Review Choose the term in parentheses that best completes each sentence. Write your answer on a sheet of paper.

1. The Spanish-American War lasted four (weeks, months, years).

2. The biggest battle of the war took place in (the Caribbean, Cuba, the Philippines).

3. Spain and the United States called a halt to the war for peace talks. This is known as a(n) (armistice, treaty, ratification).

4. As a result of the war, (Cuba, the Philippines, Puerto Rico) received its independence.

5. After the war, an agreement with Cuba allowed the United States to (run schools, build highways, keep military bases) there.

What do you think ?

When John Hay said that the Spanish-American War was a "splendid little war," what do you think he meant?

The United States continued to increase its power in the Pacific Ocean. In 1900, the Hawaiian Islands were made an American territory. The people became American citizens. These islands, in addition to the Philippines, gave America an even stronger ability to increase trade with the Far East.

America began to focus on China. China lost its independence in the 1800s. European countries took control of several Chinese cities, using them as trading centers. Great Britain, France, Russia, and Germany established their own government and courts in China. Japan also gained new land. America had been trading with China for years. However, now American merchants were concerned that China's trade might fall under the control of a few countries.

In 1899, Secretary of State John Hay offered a new trading policy for China. This was the Open Door Policy. Hay convinced the foreign nations in China to allow open and free trade for all countries.

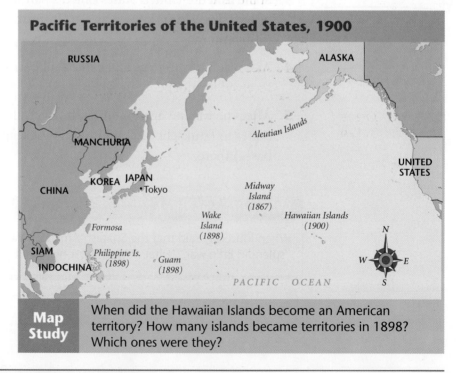

Pacific Territories of the United States, 1900

RUSSIA

ALASKA

MANCHURIA

Aleutian Islands

UNITED STATES

KOREA JAPAN
CHINA   •Tokyo

Midway Island (1867)

Wake Island (1898)

Hawaiian Islands (1900)

Formosa

N
W   E
S

SIAM   Philippine Is. (1898)   Guam (1898)
INDOCHINA

PACIFIC OCEAN

Map Study When did the Hawaiian Islands become an American territory? How many islands became territories in 1898? Which ones were they?

What Was the Boxer Rebellion?

Many Chinese were angry that parts of their country had been given to foreigners. They felt that something had to be done to stop what was happening. They formed political clubs and had secret meetings. Members discussed how to remove all foreigners from China. Each club had a different name, but they became known as "Boxers" because of the physical exercises many of them did.

The Boxers rebelled in the spring of 1900. European countries and Japan sent soldiers to stop the rebellion. The United States sent troops to protect its interests. The revolt of the Boxers threatened to destroy the Open Door Policy. The Boxer Rebellion, as it is called, did not last long. Foreign control of China was quickly brought back. Secretary of State Hay encouraged the countries to take no more Chinese territory. Instead, many countries imposed fines on the Chinese for damages done to their property and goods.

The United States returned a large part of this money to China. The money was used to allow Chinese students to attend American universities. This favor, along with other efforts by Americans to protect the land of native Chinese, helped bring friendly relations between the two countries for many years to come.

What do you think ?

Aside from improving trade with the Far East, why do you think making Hawaii a U.S. territory was important?

Lesson 3 Review Write the answers to the following questions on a sheet of paper. Use complete sentences.

1. What happened to Hawaiian people when the Hawaiian Islands became a United States territory?

2. Which countries established their own government and courts in China?

3. What was the Open Door Policy?

4. Why did the Boxer Rebellion start?

5. How did the United States gain friendly relations with China?

Lesson 4   New Leadership Brings Reforms

Imperialism

The practice of taking over land to become a stronger nation

Abroad

Throughout the world

William McKinley had become a popular president. During his administration, the United States had gained Puerto Rico. It had set up a system to protect Cuba. America was becoming an important power in Asia. The American navy had set up a base in the Philippine Islands. China had been opened to more American trade. European nations showed they respected the United States' new power. They knew America would help protect their interests in Asia.

What Happened in the Election of 1900?

McKinley had no problem winning a second term as president in 1900. For the second time, he easily defeated the Democratic candidate, William Jennings Bryan. Bryan had tried to make **imperialism** a campaign issue. Imperialism is the practice of taking over land to become a stronger nation. The Republicans avoided bringing up the issue as much as possible. McKinley chose Theodore Roosevelt as his vice president.

Less than one year after being re-elected, McKinley was assassinated. Theodore Roosevelt became the youngest president of the United States when he took office in 1901. He was 42 years old. He became a very powerful president. He believed in reforming America at home. He also wanted to strengthen the nation's power **abroad**. Roosevelt was a new, active leader for a new century.

What Reforms Did Roosevelt Support?

Roosevelt believed American society had many problems. He felt too many Americans were paid low wages. He thought that all Americans deserved equal opportunity to better their lives. American workers, said Roosevelt, should receive a "square deal."

Roosevelt wasted no time in showing that economic reforms were important to him. In 1902, Pennsylvania coal miners went on strike for higher pay. President Roosevelt agreed with their union, the United Mine Workers of America. He forced the owners to find a way to end the strike. This was the first time that the government had supported the rights of union workers.

President Roosevelt agreed that workers like these Pennsylvania coal miners deserved "a square deal."

What Political Reforms Did the Progressives Make?

Progressives believed that America should make progress by passing laws to correct the country's problems. In general, progressive economic reforms were more helpful to white workers than to African Americans. Roosevelt, however, had fought along with African American troops in Cuba. In 1903, he said that any African American who is "good enough to shed his blood for his country is good enough to be given a square deal." What a "square deal" meant for African Americans at this time was not clear. Some progressives did not support economic and social justice for African Americans.

In the same year, W. E. B. Du Bois published *The Souls of Black Folk*. A major African American leader, Du Bois argued that the "doors of opportunity" should not be closed for African Americans. In 1909, Du Bois, with other progressives, founded the National Association for the Advancement of Colored People (NAACP) to combat racial discrimination.

The Progressives believed that laws should be passed to correct America's social and political problems. Progressive reformers wanted the people to be able to choose political candidates in a **primary election**. At the time, political leaders picked the candidates. Progressives wanted to give the voters the right to approve or **reject** bills passed by state legislatures in a **referendum**. They thought that citizens should be able to suggest new laws in an **initiative**. They also believed that state and city government officials who performed poorly should be removed from office by the voters in a **recall**.

The Progressives informed the public of existing problems. Some Progressive writers, called **muckrakers**, wrote about political corruption and social problems in the early 1900s. For example, Lincoln Steffens wrote *The Shame of Cities*, describing political corruption. Upton Sinclair wrote *The Jungle*, about the terrible conditions in Chicago meatpacking plants. *The History of Standard Oil*, by Ida Tarbell, explained how John D. Rockefeller acted unfairly to create a monopoly in the oil business.

Progressives not only wrote about problems, they tried to solve them. How to help the new immigrants become part of American society became a major issue. The new immigrants came mostly from Eastern and Southern Europe. Few spoke English, and their cultural background was different from earlier immigrants. Those immigrants had come from Northern and Western Europe.

President Roosevelt said, "We must all of us be Americans, nothing but Americans." He, with many other Americans, believed that Americans could only be united by "one flag, one language, one set of national ideals." The Americanization movement promoted night school, where immigrants learned English. They could also learn about American democracy and citizenship.

Some reformers, such as Jane Addams, thought that it was more important to help the immigrants lead a better life than to try to change them. The Progressives were confident the nation was ready for reform. They had a president who believed as they did. Many business leaders feared Roosevelt.

How Did Roosevelt Control Big Business?

Although Roosevelt was in favor of economic growth, he did not want big businesses to harm society. He felt that to be fair in their business affairs, trusts should be broken into smaller companies. This would create competition and give less power to monopolies. He said that trust companies went against the Sherman Antitrust Act.

At first Congress did not respond to the president's desire to put controls on big business. However, when the president turned to the people for support, Congress started to listen. In time, many antitrust lawsuits were brought before the Supreme Court. The Department of Commerce and Labor was created to keep an eye on business dealings. People were pleased with the efforts of President Roosevelt, who came to be known as the "trustbuster."

What do you think ?

Which do you think is most important to American citizens: referendums, recalls, or initiatives? Why?

Lesson 4 Review Choose the word or name in parentheses that best completes each sentence. Write your answers on a sheet of paper.

1. (William Jennings Bryan, William McKinley) won the election of 1900.

2. (Theodore Roosevelt, William Jennings Bryan) became president after McKinley was assassinated.

3. A (referendum, initiative, primary election) is the power citizens have to suggest new laws.

4. A (primary election, referendum, recall) is voting someone from office who has performed poorly.

5. A (trustbuster, monopoly, muckraker) was a person who wrote articles and books describing corruption and problems.

Foreign policy

The plan a government follows when dealing with other nations

During Roosevelt's administration, Congress passed many laws. They protected Americans from the sale of unhealthy meat and unsafe drugs. In 1906, Congress passed the Meat Inspection Act and the Food and Drugs Act. Government officials could inspect meatpacking plants to see if they were clean. Drug companies were required to prove their drugs were safe.

What Conservation Programs Were Started?

Before 1900, the nation's natural resources seemed unlimited. America had plenty of forestland, good soil, fresh water, coal, oil, and other minerals. President Roosevelt and others worried that America would run out of these resources. Conservation was needed to protect these resources.

President Roosevelt appointed Gifford Pinchot to head the United States Forest Service. Pinchot was committed to protecting the nation's natural resources. He convinced President Roosevelt to add 150 million acres to the country's forest reserve and to preserve valuable mineral-rich lands for future use. In 1902, Congress passed a law that gave the federal government the power to build dams and to establish irrigation projects. Land was developed for five national parks. In 1908, the president called state governors to a national conference to discuss steps they could take to preserve resources within their states. Soon after the conference, many state governments set up conservation groups of their own.

What Was Roosevelt's Foreign Policy?

The plan a government follows when dealing with other nations is called **foreign policy.** The United States had three foreign policy plans. The policies involved Europe, Asia, and Latin America.

The U.S. foreign policy toward Europe had been to stay neutral and isolated from European conflicts. The policy toward Asia had more to do with settling disputes and improving trade. The United States was also concerned about Japan's increasing use of military power. In 1894, Japan invaded and defeated China.

In 1905, Roosevelt helped negotiate a peace treaty to end a war between Japan and Russia. Two years later, he negotiated a "gentlemen's agreement" with Japan that discouraged Japanese workers from coming to the United States.

The United States' position on China trade was called the Open Door Policy. China was a weak nation. European nations and Japan had taken control of China's ports and natural resources. The Open Door Policy stated that every nation, including the United States, should have an equal opportunity to trade with China. To enforce American foreign policy, Roosevelt built a powerful navy. The navy protected America's interests in Asia and the Caribbean Sea.

The policy toward Latin America had to do with the Monroe Doctrine. The Monroe Doctrine had stated that European nations could not start any new colonies in North or South America. Santo Domingo, the Dominican Republic of today, ran into trouble with foreign debts. President Roosevelt then added the Roosevelt Corollary. Under this addition to the Monroe Doctrine, the United States would come to the aid of any Latin American country. The United States took over temporary control of Santo Domingo's finances and saw to it that its debts to Europe were taken care of peacefully.

Why Was the Panama Canal Built?

The navy needed a fast way to move its warships from the Atlantic Ocean to the Pacific Ocean. Also, commercial shippers would benefit from having a direct route. To solve the problem, a canal needed to be built through Central America.

The shortest route for the canal was through Panama, a part of the Republic of Colombia. A group of Panamanians did not want the United States to build a canal, because they were afraid of losing control there. When the United States government offered the country $10 million for a strip of land through Panama, plus yearly rent, Colombia flatly refused.

Geography Note

The Panama Canal is considered one of the greatest achievements in American history. The workers faced many difficulties. All equipment and supplies had to be shipped from thousands of miles away. Thousands of workers died during construction, many from malaria or yellow fever passed on by mosquitoes.

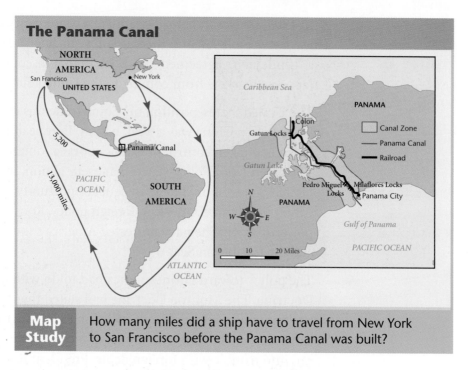

The Panama Canal

NORTH AMERICA
San Francisco
New York
UNITED STATES
5,200
13,000 miles
PACIFIC OCEAN
Panama Canal
SOUTH AMERICA
ATLANTIC OCEAN

Caribbean Sea
PANAMA
Colon
Gatun Locks
Canal Zone
Panama Canal
Railroad
Gatun Lake
Pedro Miguel Locks
Miraflores Locks
Panama City
PANAMA
Gulf of Panama
PACIFIC OCEAN
N W E S
0   10   20 Miles

Map Study How many miles did a ship have to travel from New York to San Francisco before the Panama Canal was built?

Panama revolted against Colombia in 1903. President Roosevelt sent American battleships to help Panama. The revolt was successful. That year Panama became an independent republic. The United States paid the new Republic of Panama $10 million, plus yearly rent, for a strip of land 10 miles wide. The "Big Ditch," as the canal was called, was completed in 1914. It took 10 years to build. The canal was more than 50 miles long. It cut the distance for ships traveling from New York to San Francisco by more than 7,000 miles.

The Panama Canal was a huge building project. It took 10 years to finish.

What Was Roosevelt's "Big Stick" Policy?

Many countries in Latin America had political and economic problems in 1900. They borrowed money from European countries and had difficulty repaying the loans.

The United States feared that European nations would take control of the countries that owed them money. Britain, Germany, and Italy sent battleships to Venezuela in 1902. They wanted to force Venezuela to repay its loans. Venezuela asked the United States for help. President Roosevelt convinced the European nations to let the new Hague Tribunal, or World Court, settle the dispute. The World Court is in the Netherlands.

Foreign battleships in South America worried Roosevelt. In 1904, he **revised** the Monroe Doctrine. The United States would act as a "police" power in Latin America. The United States would try to solve any political or economic problem in a Latin American country. The United States could use the military to bring back order to a Latin American country. This was called the "Big Stick" policy. The policy was called that because Roosevelt often used an African saying, "Speak softly and carry a big stick. . . ."

Then and Now

If someone offers to sell you a medicine and claims it cures anything, will you buy it? Around 1900, newspapers were full of ads for "patent" medicines. The ads claimed the medicines could cure one or more illnesses or problems. Manufacturers never tested the medicines to prove their safety or the accuracy of the claims. The medicines were often 50 percent or more alcohol. People wanted to feel better, so they believed the claims and ordered the medicines. Sellers became rich, but the medicines did not help the buyers.

Today the Food and Drug Administration (FDA) regulates medicines. Researchers must do studies to prove a medicine does what it is supposed to do. No medicine can be on the market without FDA approval. Doctors must prescribe most medicines.

Lesson 5 Review On a sheet of paper, write the answers to the following questions. Use complete sentences.

1. Which laws were passed to protect Americans from unhealthy meat and unsafe drugs?

2. What steps were taken to protect America's natural resources?

3. Why did the United States want to build the Panama Canal?

4. How did the United States gain the right to build the Panama Canal?

5. What was the "Big Stick" policy?

What do you think

Why do you think conservation of natural resources is important?

Biography

Matthew Henson: 1866–1955

Matthew Henson was a co-discoverer of the North Pole with Robert E. Peary in 1909. All the explorers on that journey received a Congressional medal in 1944. Henson was the first African American to reach the pole and the only American to accompany Peary on the last leg of his journey. Henson's association with Peary lasted more than 20 years. They made a surveying trip to Nicaragua and seven northern expeditions before they made their trek to the North Pole. Thirty-three years after his death, Matthew Henson was given a hero's burial in Arlington National Cemetery. In 2000, Henson was awarded the Hubbard Medal by the National Geographic Society.

Income tax

Tax placed on money people earn

Roosevelt enjoyed his two terms as president. He chose not to seek re-election. He said that he felt two terms as president were enough. The new president, he hoped, would continue his plan of strength abroad and reform at home. He convinced the Republican Party to nominate William Howard Taft.

What Did Taft Achieve as President?

Taft and the Republican Party had no trouble winning the presidency in 1908. The Democratic nominee, William Jennings Bryan, was defeated for the third time. President Taft took office in 1909. He did not enjoy being president. He had trouble working with Congress.

President Taft tried to fulfill promises that Roosevelt made. Taft ordered the breakup of the Standard Oil Trust. He demanded a restructuring of the American Tobacco Company, which had been operated much like a trust. While he was president, Congress passed the 16th Amendment to give the government power to collect **income taxes**. Income tax is tax placed on money people earn.

Before the amendment, it was unconstitutional to tax someone's personal income. Reformers wanted only wealthy Americans to pay taxes on their income. They thought the average worker's income was too low to tax.

Congress set up a separate Department of Labor in 1913. It also created a new Department of Commerce at this time. Laws were written to place communications companies under government control. Those who gave money to political candidates were forced to do so publicly. However, there were ongoing problems involving tariffs. At times, Taft was accused of trying to undo some of President Roosevelt's conservation plans.

What Happened in the Election of 1912?

Despite Taft's achievements, the Progressives felt he had not supported reform. They wanted Roosevelt to run against Taft for the Republican nomination in 1912. However, the Republican Party nominated Taft.

Theodore Roosevelt gestured with his hat to make a point during a campaign speech.

Roosevelt organized a new political party. The new Progressive Party nominated Roosevelt for president. Roosevelt was confident that the American people would re-elect him. People called this new political party the Bull Moose Party when Roosevelt said that he felt "as strong as a bull moose."

In 1912, the Democratic Party nominated Woodrow Wilson. The Democrats were in a good position to win, because the Republican Party was divided between Taft and Roosevelt. Wilson had a reform plan called the "New Freedom." He wanted to rid the country of all forms of trust companies, which he felt were bad for American democracy. He thought America would be a stronger nation if small companies could compete equally.

Roosevelt called his program the "New Nationalism." He believed the federal government should regulate big business. The government should be responsible for improving American society by limiting workday hours and setting a **minimum wage.** A minimum wage is the smallest amount a person can be paid to do a job. He felt that children, women, and the injured required special protection by law. Among his other wishes were an expanded conservation program and suffrage for women.

The Bull Moose Party and its candidate, Theodore Roosevelt, could not get enough support. The Democrats won the 1912 election. Woodrow Wilson took office as the 28th president in 1913.

1912 Presidential Election Results		
Candidate	Popular Votes	Electoral Votes
Woodrow Wilson	6,286,214	435
Theodore Roosevelt	4,126,020	88
William Taft	3,483,922	8

Word Bank

income tax

minimum wage

Taft

trust companies

William Jennings Bryan

Lesson 6 Review On a sheet of paper, write the correct word or words from the Word Bank to complete each sentence.

1. In the presidential election of 1908, _____ lost for the third time.

2. During Taft's presidency, Congress passed the 16th Amendment, giving government the power to collect _____.

3. During the election of 1912, the Republican Party was divided between _____ and Theodore Roosevelt.

4. Woodrow Wilson wanted to reform the country by getting rid of all forms of _____.

5. Theodore Roosevelt wanted to regulate big business by limiting workday hours and setting a(n) _____.

What do you think ?

Even though Roosevelt was not elected president in 1912, how do you think his ideas affected the future of America?

History in Your Life

Ragtime and the Music of Scott Joplin

Ragtime is a unique American style of jazz written chiefly for piano. Scott Joplin became known as "king of ragtime." The son of a former slave, Joplin left home at about age 14. For a time he played piano in saloons and honky-tonks across Missouri. He settled in Sedalia, Missouri, playing piano at the Maple Leaf Club. In 1899 he published the "Maple Leaf Rag," and the sheet music sold over a million copies. Joplin wrote or helped write more than 60 pieces of music, including the Ragtime opera *Treemonisha* (1911). Joplin's music enjoyed a revival in the 1970s. *Treemonisha* won critical acclaim for its first full-scale production in 1975. The film *The Sting* (1973) used "The Entertainer" and other Joplin rags as its background music. The Advisory Board on the Pulitzer Prize awarded Joplin a special citation in 1976, 60 years after his death.

Speech of Booker T. Washington

Booker T. Washington was born in 1856. His mother was a slave. He became a teacher and a successful founder of schools for African Americans. Washington encouraged African Americans to become skilled laborers. Because of this, many rights activists of the time thought he was promoting further enslavement to white masters. In fact, Washington desired to create peace with white people. That desire also may have separated him from his African American peers. This passage is from a speech Washington made in 1895 to white business people in Atlanta.

As we have proved our loyalty to you in the past, by nursing your children, watching by the sickbed of your mothers and fathers, and often following them with tear-dimmed eyes to their graves, so in the future, in our humble way, we shall stand by you with a devotion that no foreigner can approach, ready to lay down our lives, if need be, in defense of yours; interlacing [joining] our industrial, commercial, civil, and religious life with yours in a way that shall make the interests of both races one. In all things that are purely social we can be as separate as the fingers, yet one as the hand in all things essential to mutual progress.

Document-Based Questions

1. What are two key words Washington used to describe an African American's relationship to his or her master?

2. Who did Washington say could not approach the kind of devotion African Americans had to white masters?

3. How did Washington see the lives of whites and African Americans "interlacing"?

4. In what ways did he see their lives being separate?

5. How do you feel about the attitude and tone of Washington's speech?

Source: Speech of Booker T. Washington, 1895.

- President McKinley wanted to help Cuba and Puerto Rico free themselves from Spanish rule and to expand American interests there.

- In 1898, the USS *Maine* was sent to Cuba to protect American interests. The ship exploded in Havana harbor in February and the Spanish were blamed.

- American Admiral Dewey's ships destroyed the Spanish fleet in the Philippines. Theodore Roosevelt led soldiers to capture San Juan Hill in Cuba. The United States and Spain signed a treaty in December. The treaty gave Puerto Rico, Guam, and the Philippines to America.

- In 1899, America established its Open Door Policy with China. It allowed China to have free trade.

- The Hawaiian Islands became an American territory in 1900, and its people became American citizens.

- In 1900, the Boxer Rebellion in China failed to rid the country of foreign control. The United States established good relations with the Chinese government.

- During the first year of his second term, William McKinley was assassinated. Theodore Roosevelt then became president. Roosevelt was a reformer and pushed for both social and political change. He served two terms as president.

- The Progressive Party established political reforms such as primary elections, referendums, initiatives, and voter recalls.

- Congress passed laws such as the Meat Inspection Act and the Food and Drugs Act to protect the American people.

- Roosevelt established policies for conservation and the better use of natural resources.

- Roosevelt built a strong navy to provide defense and to show other countries America's strength.

- America financed the building of the Panama Canal, which connected the Atlantic and the Pacific oceans.

- William Howard Taft became the next president. During his presidency, Congress passed the 16th Amendment, which established an income tax. Taft's administration helped create other reforms.

- After Taft's term, Roosevelt ran again as candidate of the Bull Moose Party, but lost to Woodrow Wilson.

Chapter 22 REVIEW

Word Bank

Boxer Rebellion

conservation

Panama Canal

Progressive Party

"Remember the Maine"

Spain

"Splendid Little War"

"trustbuster"

William Howard Taft

William McKinley

On a sheet of paper, write the correct word or words from the Word Bank to complete each sentence.

1. _____ was the call to action for the Spanish-American War.

2. President _____ was assassinated during his second term.

3. The conflict with Spain was called the _____.

4. The "Big Ditch" is what some people called the _____.

5. Theodore Roosevelt encouraged wise use, or _____, of the country's natural resources.

6. _____ ordered a breakup of the Standard Oil Trust and set up the Department of Labor.

7. The _____ took place because the Chinese wanted to be rid of foreign control.

8. _____ controlled Puerto Rico, Cuba, and the Philippines before the Spanish-American War.

9. The _____ worked for political reform, especially the way voters could make choices.

10. Early in his presidency, Roosevelt became known as the _____.

On a sheet of paper, write the letter of the answer that correctly completes each sentence.

11. The United States increased its power in the Pacific Ocean by _____.

   A trading with the Philippines

   B stopping the Boxer Rebellion

   C adding Cuba as a territory

   D making Hawaii a territory

12. _____ was a president who sought reforms, began conserving resources, and held office for two terms.

   A William McKinley   **C** Howard Taft

   B Theodore Roosevelt   **D** Woodrow Wilson

13. Roosevelt used the saying "Walk softly and carry a big stick" to describe his policy about _____.

   A police power in Latin America

   B the "square deal" for workers

   C building the Panama Canal

   D breaking monopolies

On a sheet of paper, write the answers to the following questions. Use complete sentences.

14. What were two results of the Spanish-American War?

15. Who was Walter Reed and what did he do?

16. Why did some members of Congress want the United States to expand its interests in Asia?

17. What was the importance of the Panama Canal?

18. What is a primary election?

**Critical Thinking** On a sheet of paper, write your response to each question. Use complete sentences.

19. Theodore Roosevelt developed five national parks. Do you think national parks are important? Explain your answer.

20. Do you think it is important for the United States to have a strong foreign policy? Why or why not?

Test-Taking Tip

When you answer multiple choice questions, read every choice. Cross out choices you know are wrong. Choose the best answer from the remaining choices.

23 World War I

The United States had done much to become a world power in the early part of the 20th century. As President Wilson took over the presidency, it was time for the nation to learn the consequences of having this power. Tensions in Europe were high at this time. Soon a war unlike one ever seen before—World War I—would affect the United States and most of Europe. In this chapter, you will learn what caused World War I and what resulted from it.

Goals for Learning

◆ To describe major successes in Wilson's presidency and explain the events that caused World War I

◆ To explain how America stayed neutral until 1917

◆ To describe American involvement in World War I

◆ To explain President Wilson's 14 Points and the problems with the Treaty of Versailles

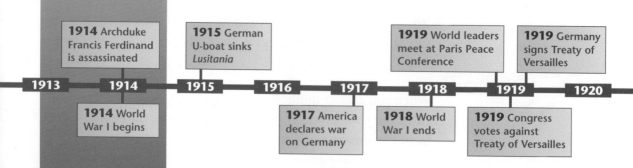

1914 Archduke Francis Ferdinand is assassinated

1915 German U-boat sinks *Lusitania*

1919 World leaders meet at Paris Peace Conference

1919 Germany signs Treaty of Versailles

1913 1914 1915 1916 1917 1918 1919 1920

1914 World War I begins

1917 America declares war on Germany

1918 World War I ends

1919 Congress votes against Treaty of Versailles

Emperor

The male ruler of an empire

President Wilson had some political experience when he became president. He had been the governor of New Jersey. During that time he was successful in fighting political bosses in that state. President Wilson was very skillful in getting Congress to pass the reform laws he wanted. These reform laws brought major changes to American society. Early in Wilson's administration, a new national banking system called the Federal Reserve System was started. This change made it easier to put money into the economy when needed. The 17th Amendment was ratified in 1913. It provided for the direct election of senators by the people of their states.

President Wilson achieved a great deal in a short period of time. Many Progressive reformers were pleased with Wilson's actions.

How Did War Start in Europe?

For many years, the countries of Europe had been competing for trade markets. At times, they had tried to control the same colonies in different parts of the world. Some nations wanted to get back parts of their lands lost in earlier wars. Some small countries wanted to gain their independence from larger ruling nations. Each nation tried to build the strongest army. Two alliances had been formed. One included Austria-Hungary, Germany, and Italy. The other united Great Britain, France, and Russia. Neither group trusted the other.

Bosnia had been a part of the Austro-Hungarian Empire since 1908. However, many people in Bosnia did not want to be part of this empire. They wanted to be included in Serbia, a neighboring country. Talks of rebellion by Bosnian groups created tension within the empire. In June 1914, the **emperor** of Austria-Hungary sent his nephew, Archduke Francis Ferdinand, to Sarajevo. An emperor is the male ruler of an empire. Sarajevo was the capital of Bosnia. The emperor wanted to improve relations between Bosnia and the government of Austria-Hungary.

As a line of government cars passed through the streets of Sarajevo, a man threw a bomb at Archduke Ferdinand's car. The bomb missed its target and exploded when another car passed. This wounded several people. Hours later, the archduke went to visit the wounded people. His car slowed near a corner. Rebel Gavrilo Princip saw the archduke, raised a pistol, and shot the archduke and his wife. The archduke was killed immediately, and his wife died soon after.

The Austro-Hungarian emperor, Francis Joseph, blamed Serbia for the death of his nephew and his nephew's wife. Francis Joseph had no proof that Serbia was responsible. However, one month later, on July 28, 1914, Austria-Hungary declared war on Serbia.

Shortly after this photo was taken, Archduke Francis Ferdinand and Archduchess Sophie were shot in Sarajevo. The killing started World War I.

Why Did Other Countries Declare War?

When Austria-Hungary declared war on Serbia, it started a **chain reaction.** Russia decided to help Serbia defend itself against Austria-Hungary. Germany decided to help Austria-Hungary defend itself against Russia. France agreed to help Russia and made plans to attack Germany. Germany then declared war on France and marched its army through Belgium to attack the French. Committed to defending Belgium and France, Great Britain declared war on Germany.

By August 14, 1914, seven European nations were at war. The **Central Powers** included Germany and Austria-Hungary and, later, Turkey (also called the Ottoman Empire) and Bulgaria. The **Allied Powers** were Great Britain, France, Serbia, Belgium, and Russia. Japan supported the Allies in hope of gaining control of Germany's Pacific colonies after the war. Italy remained neutral in the early stages of the war. Later, it broke its former alliance with Germany and Austria-Hungary to join the Allied Powers.

The war spread into most of Europe and some parts of Africa and Asia. Even most smaller European countries took part in some way. Both sides had their defeats and victories. By 1917, the Central Powers had gained an advantage over the Allied nations.

Biography

Jim Thorpe: 1888–1953

A poll of sportswriters in 1950 declared Jim Thorpe the "greatest American athlete of the first half of this century." A native of Oklahoma, he was part Sauk and Fox Indian and part Irish. Thorpe was an outstanding college football player. Then he competed in the track and field events at the 1912 Olympic Games in Sweden. He won gold medals for both the pentathlon and decathlon—the first athlete in history to do so. Thorpe later played on seven professional football teams and three major league baseball teams. He was the first president of what is now the National Football League. After his death, Thorpe was elected to the Football Hall of Fame.

Europe During World War I

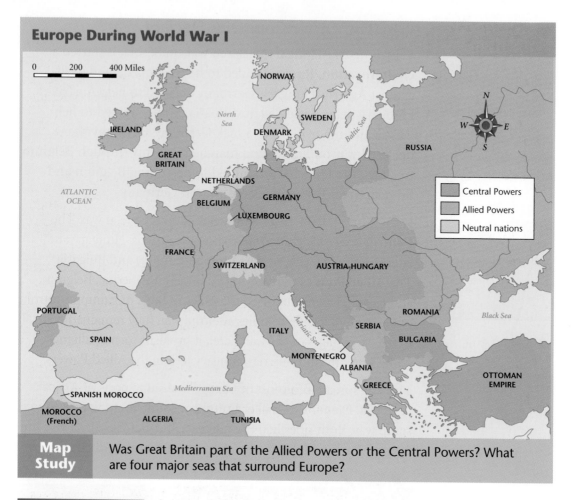

0   200   400 Miles

NORWAY

North Sea

SWEDEN

Baltic Sea

IRELAND

DENMARK

RUSSIA

GREAT BRITAIN

NETHERLANDS

ATLANTIC OCEAN

BELGIUM

GERMANY

LUXEMBOURG

FRANCE

SWITZERLAND

AUSTRIA-HUNGARY

PORTUGAL

ITALY

Adriatic Sea

SERBIA

ROMANIA

Black Sea

SPAIN

MONTENEGRO

BULGARIA

ALBANIA

SPANISH MOROCCO

Mediterranean Sea

GREECE

OTTOMAN EMPIRE

MOROCCO (French)

ALGERIA

TUNISIA

N W E S

Central Powers
Allied Powers
Neutral nations

Map Study Was Great Britain part of the Allied Powers or the Central Powers? What are four major seas that surround Europe?

What do you think ?

Why was it possible for one event to cause a war among so many countries?

Lesson 1 Review Choose the word in parentheses that best completes each sentence. Write your answers on a sheet of paper.

1. The (14th, 15th, 17th) Amendment was ratified in 1913.

2. The Federal Reserve System was a new way of (collecting taxes, banking, passing legislation).

3. Archduke (Francis Ferdinand, Gavrilo Princip, Francis Joseph) was assassinated in 1914.

4. Austria-Hungary declared war on (France, Serbia, Great Britain).

5. (Germany, Turkey, France) was part of the Allied Powers.

Submarine

A ship that can travel underwater

Torpedo

A self-powered bomb that is shot from a tube of a submarine or other ship

President Wilson said the United States would not take sides in the war. However, American companies could sell war supplies to fighting countries. Hundreds of ships from America crossed the Atlantic Ocean and carried war supplies to France and Great Britain. Germany accused the United States of not remaining neutral.

The British navy tried to prevent Americans from trading with Germany. They stopped American ships and set up "war zones" in the Atlantic Ocean. Ships from other countries were not allowed to enter the war zone. Germany also set up a war zone around the island of Great Britain. Germany thought that it could force the British out of the war by preventing them from receiving food and war supplies. Germany said that its **submarines,** called U-boats, would sink any ships found in their war zones. A submarine is a ship that can travel underwater. President Wilson felt that the war zones were illegal. He believed that all countries should be free to sail the oceans and seas of the world.

As the Central Powers appeared to be defeating the Allied nations, many Americans were concerned about Great Britain. The enemy at the time of the Revolutionary War had become a friend to them, largely because of shared democratic practices, language, and customs. France had been an ally at the time of the Revolution. Germany, on the other hand, had become cruel in the eyes of many Americans.

What Happened When the Germans Sank the *Lusitania?*

In 1915, the *Lusitania,* a large British passenger ship, was traveling from New York to England. Off the coast of Ireland, the captain of a German U-boat spotted the ship. The U-boat fired a **torpedo** that hit the *Lusitania*. A torpedo is a self-powered bomb that is shot from a tube of a submarine. The ship exploded and sank. Almost 1,200 people died; 128 were Americans.

The Lusitania *before its last voyage from New York's harbor. A German torpedo sank the ship near Ireland. Many Americans turned against Germany after the ship's sinking.*

Effective

Able to cause a desired result

Americans were shocked and upset. Some people, including Theodore Roosevelt, called on Congress to declare war on Germany. President Wilson sent a letter of protest to the German government. Germany said that the ship was carrying war supplies as well as passengers. Britain denied that any war materials were on the ship.

The sinking of the *Lusitania* turned the American public against Germany. It was becoming more difficult for the United States to remain neutral. Germany, fearing that America would enter the war, urged its U-boat captains to be more careful in selecting ships to attack. As a result, the German war zone around Britain became less **effective.** Some ships got through to Britain with goods to continue the war against Germany.

Woodrow Wilson ran for re-election in 1916 against Charles Evans Hughes. Wilson had been a good president. Democrats and many Republicans approved of his reform program.

Most Americans were pleased that the nation had stayed out of the war in Europe. The Democratic party used "He Kept Us Out of War" as Wilson's campaign slogan.

Wilson won the election. It was very close. His victory was important for the Democratic party. Woodrow Wilson was the first Democrat to be re-elected to the presidency since Andrew Jackson in 1832.

Lesson 2 Review On a sheet of paper, write the answers to the following questions. Use complete sentences.

1. What policy did President Wilson support when war broke out in Europe?

2. What did Germany do to try to prevent goods from reaching Great Britain?

3. What did the United States have in common with Great Britain?

4. What happened to the Lusitania?

5. What did Wilson do to get re-elected in 1916?

History in Your Life

The Music of Irving Berlin

Songwriter Irving Berlin was a composer who never studied music. He could not read or write musical lines on paper. He was born in Russia in 1888. His family emigrated to New York in 1893. At 14, Berlin sang in New York's saloons and worked as a singing waiter.

Early on he discovered he had a talent for making music. He contributed words and some melodies to many ragtime songs. His first big hit was "Alexander's Ragtime Band" in 1911. Berlin's first complete musical score was *Watch Your Step* in 1914. By 1919, he had his own music publishing company. Among his most successful shows were *The Ziegfeld Follies* (1919) and *Annie Get Your Gun* (1946). Berlin produced more than 1,000 songs. Many of his most popular tunes are still sung today. One example is "There's No Business Like Show Business." Many Americans regard his "God Bless America" as the second national anthem.

Standstill

Something that is not changing or improving

President Wilson gave a speech on January 22, 1917, to "the people of the countries now at war." He wanted the war to end. He did not want a winner or loser. Wilson wanted "peace without victory."

At the time of the president's speech, the war in Europe had been at a **standstill** for months. Both sides were worn down by nearly three years of fighting. Then Germany announced that its U-boats would sink any ship without warning in the war zone around Britain. The Germans thought that this action would force Britain to stop fighting. Germany knew the United States would probably declare war. Germany thought the war would be over before the United States sent an army to Europe.

During February and March 1917, German U-boats torpedoed ships flying the American flag. Tension between the United States and Germany increased. Anti-war senators argued that it would be a mistake for the United States to go to war. The United States government released to the newspapers a secret letter from Germany to Mexico. In this letter, known as the Zimmermann Note, Germany asked Mexico for help if Germany and the United States went to war. Germany told Mexico that if it helped to defeat the United States, Mexico would receive the states of Texas, New Mexico, and Arizona. Mexico had lost these lands to America in the 1800s.

How Did the United States Enter the War?

On April 2, 1917, Woodrow Wilson asked Congress to declare war on Germany. He said that America would fight for "peace and justice" and that "the world must be made safe for democracy." On April 6, Congress declared that the United States and Germany were at war. American neutrality had ended.

American factories stopped production of **consumer goods** to make war supplies. People started working longer hours to help increase the factory output. Many women joined the American workforce to replace men who had gone off to war. Other women joined the armed forces as nurses and office workers. Many others volunteered their time in other ways to support the war effort.

The war provided opportunities for African Americans as well. More than 400,000 became soldiers, although they fought in units separate from non-African Americans. Thousands of African Americans moved from the South to get jobs in northern steel mills, the meatpacking industry, and factories making war supplies. The increase in the African American population in northern cities such as Chicago, New York, and Philadelphia led to racial conflicts. Chicago's African American population increased by more than 70,000. By the end of the year, the nation experienced more than 25 race riots.

When American men went to fight in World War I, large numbers of American women joined the workforce. These women are making cannon shells.

The government increased taxes and sold bonds to raise money for the war. It asked Americans to limit their use of certain food products and fuels to conserve these items for military use. Farmers used more land for growing crops to increase food production. The United States Selective Service started to **draft** young men into the army. A draft is the selection of people to serve in the armed forces. The draft had not been used since the Civil War. In these ways, Americans were working to support their country in the Great War.

Posters like this encouraged people to join the armed forces.

American troops arrived in Europe faster than the Germans thought possible. The first American soldiers, called "doughboys," arrived in Europe by June 1917. Britain and France wanted American troops to join their military units. But American General John J. "Black Jack" Pershing argued that American soldiers should fight as a separate unit called the American Expeditionary Force (AEF). By July 1918, General Pershing commanded more than a million American troops in Europe.

American soldiers entered a war in which neither side was strong enough to defeat the other. On the Western front, both armies dug several hundred miles of trenches to protect their soldiers. The trenches were cold, wet, and unhealthy. Many soldiers died of diseases. Rapid-fire machine guns fired hundreds of bullets per minute. Huge artillery shells fired from miles away rained down deadly metal. Exploding shells released poison gas that would burn soldiers' lungs. For the first time, airplanes became weapons of war. Airplanes fought each other in the sky and dropped bombs on soldiers below.

World War I Statistics	
American soldiers killed	116,516
American soldiers wounded	204,002
Total deaths	8,528,154
Total wounded	21,189,154
Cost to United States	$32.7 billion

Large groups of American ships began to blockade German ports. They positioned **mines** to destroy enemy ships. Mines are floating bombs that explode when touched. They torpedoed many of the aggressive German U-boats that had been causing so much damage in the Atlantic.

How Did the War End?

In several battles in Europe, more than two million American soldiers under General John Pershing upset the German stronghold. By the fall of 1918, the Germans realized they could not win the war. The government of Germany asked the Allies for an armistice. The fighting stopped while both sides prepared to discuss how to end the war.

The German army officers and the officers of the Allied forces met in a private railroad car in France. The Great War, which later became known as World War I, had lasted more than four years. The war ended on the morning of the 11th day, at the 11th hour, of the 11th month—November 11, 1918. In differing ways, the war had weakened the great powers of Europe. It had, however, increased the power of the United States.

Geography Note

To protect themselves, World War I soldiers dug a network of zigzagging trenches. These trenches cut France in half from north to south along the Western Front. Front-line trenches were about six feet deep. Two soldiers could pass each other in them. Support and communications trenches ran back from the front.

Lesson 3 Review On a sheet of paper, write the letter of the answer that best completes each sentence.

1. On April 2, 1917, President Wilson asked for _____.
   A a declaration of war from Congress
   B an end to the war
   C a temporary halt to the fighting
   D the United States to remain neutral

2. In the Zimmermann Note, Germany promised land to _____ if it helped defeat the United States.
   A Texas   B Mexico   C Britain   D Europe

3. To raise money for the war effort, the government increased taxes and _____.
   A drafted young men into the army
   B closed government offices
   C sold bonds
   D traded consumer goods

4. The use of _____ by the American navy destroyed many German ships.
   A U-boats   B torpedoes   C the draft   D mines

5. The Great War became known as _____.
   A the Civil War   C World War II
   B World War I   D the European War

What do you think

Do you think it is right for a country to use a draft to get soldiers to fight in wars? Explain your answer.

Focus on Economics

World War I greatly affected the world economy. Germany was forced to pay huge war debts to other countries. This crushed the German economy. It also hurt other nations. Germany used goods and raw materials to pay for some damages. For example, Germany paid Great Britain with coal. This hurt Britain's own coal industry. After the war, the prices of goods in Britain more than doubled. The value of its money fell 258 percent.

Conference

A meeting among a large group of people

Wilson believed that if the world was to remain at peace, then the peace treaty had to be fair to all sides. In January 1918, he spoke of a plan for a lasting, or permanent, peace. This plan became known as Wilson's 14 Points.

Major Ideas of Wilson's 14 Points

- Secret treaties between nations would end.
- Any nation would be free to sail in any seas and oceans of the world.
- Nations would decrease the size of their armies and navies.
- Boundaries of nations would be changed so people with the same language and customs could live together.
- An organization called the League of Nations would be created to settle disputes between countries in a peaceful way.

What Happened at the Paris Peace Conference?

A **conference** was held in the Palace of Versailles near Paris, France, in January 1919. The purpose of the conference was to discuss and write a peace treaty that was acceptable to nations that fought in the war. President Wilson decided to go to the Paris Peace Conference. No president before Wilson had left the United States while in office. He wanted to make sure his League of Nations became a part of the treaty. Three other leaders who attended were David Lloyd George of Great Britain, Georges Clemenceau of France, and Vittorio Orlando of Italy. These political leaders became known as the "Big Four." Germany was not invited to attend until after the treaty was written.

The Treaty of Versailles changed the map of Europe. The Austro-Hungarian Empire was broken up into Austria and Hungary. Most of the rest of the empire was made into the new nations of Poland, Czechoslovakia, and Yugoslavia. Bosnia and Serbia became part of Yugoslavia.

Europe Before World War I

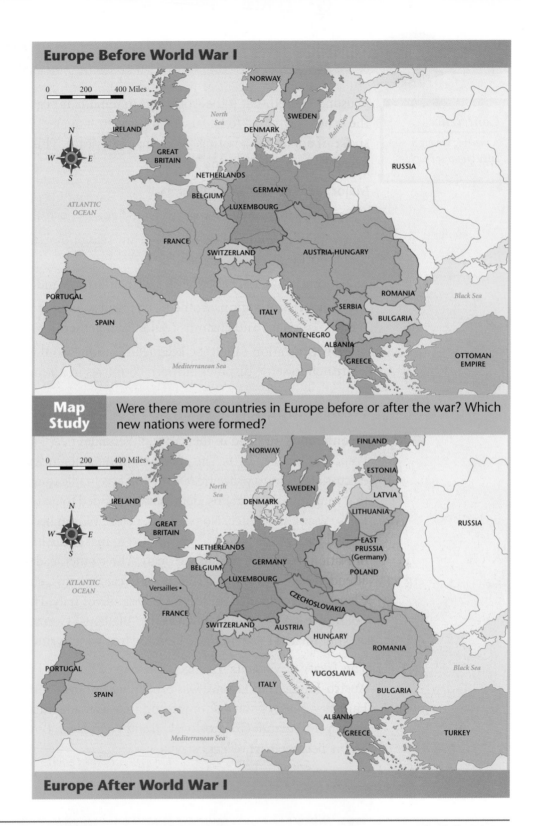

Map Study

Were there more countries in Europe before or after the war? Which new nations were formed?

Europe After World War I

President Wilson believed that the treaty did not provide the just peace he wanted. He agreed to the treaty in exchange for support of his League of Nations. Wilson thought that the league would correct the problems created by the treaty.

The treaty forced Germany to give land to France and Poland. It blamed Germany for starting the war and forced Germany to pay a huge sum of money for war damages. It took from Germany its colonies in Asia, Africa, and the North Pacific, and it demanded that the country not build a new army. The Germans were not pleased with the conditions of the treaty. However, having no other choice, Germany signed the Treaty of Versailles on July 28, 1919.

Why Didn't Congress Ratify the Treaty?

According to the Constitution, two-thirds of the Senate must approve all treaties between the United States and another nation. The Republican senators did not like the idea of a League of Nations. According to the treaty, members of the League of Nations agreed to protect the independence and territory of each member. Republican senators thought that the United States might get drawn into a number of foreign wars, perhaps without the approval of Congress. Some Republican senators were against the entire treaty, while others wanted parts of it rewritten. President Wilson would not make any major changes in the treaty.

In this cartoon, the League of Nations is trying to push the Constitution off the chair.

President Wilson toured the country to tell people about the League of Nations.

President Wilson decided to take the treaty to the American people. He set out by train to carry his message across the United States. The League of Nations, he said, was the first step in making the world safe from war. Crowds of people cheered Wilson wherever he spoke. However, the Republican senators did not change their opinion of the treaty.

Wilson became ill on September 25, 1919. He canceled the rest of the tour and returned to Washington, D.C. He had a stroke, which left him unable to move the left side of his body, but still allowed him to speak clearly. He never recovered. On November 19, 1919, the United States Senate voted on the Treaty of Versailles. The treaty did not pass. The Senate voted again in March 1920. The result was the same. It was the first time in United States history that the Senate had failed to ratify a peace treaty. The United States did not join the League of Nations. Without the United States as a member, the League of Nations was a weak organization. The Treaty of Versailles did not bring about a fair and just peace. The seeds for a second and more horrible world war had been planted. Within 20 years, the nations of the world would be at war again.

Then and Now

In 1919, President Wilson wanted to tell the American people about his plan to ensure peace after World War I. To do this, he traveled by train. He spoke to crowds of people about his plan for the League of Nations. At that time, personal appearances and newspapers were the only ways for a politician to reach a wide audience.

Now, politicians and others who need support for a cause have many choices for getting their message out. Although they still travel and talk directly to people, they also use radio and TV advertisements to spread their messages. They also understand the importance of the Internet in spreading their ideas. Many politicians now have Web sites where they spell out their views and ask for support.

Technology Connection

Rocket to the Moon

In 1920, scientist Robert H. Goddard wrote a report suggesting that a rocket could reach the moon. At the time, few people thought this would be possible. His ideas were not given much support. However, this did not stop Goddard.

He developed a rocket that used liquid fuels. His rocket weighed about 4.5 kilograms (10 pounds) and was 3.4 meters (11 feet) long. In March 1926, Goddard was ready to test his rocket. He launched the rocket at a farm in Auburn, Massachusetts. The flight lasted less than 3 seconds. The rocket soared as high as 12 meters and traveled a horizontal path of 56 meters.

Three years later, Goddard launched the first rocket that carried instruments. In this rocket were a barometer and a camera. He continued his work on rockets throughout his life and was a pioneer in rocket development. He helped set the stage for space exploration. About 50 years after Goddard's report, astronauts walked on the moon.

Word Bank

Austro-Hungarian

14 Points

League of Nations

Paris Peace Conference

Treaty of Versailles

Lesson 4 Review On a sheet of paper, write the correct word or words from the Word Bank to complete each sentence.

1. Wilson's _____ was a plan for permanent peace.

2. The _____ took place to discuss a peace treaty acceptable to all of the nations who fought in the war.

3. The _____ changed the map of Europe.

4. The _____ was part of Wilson's 14 Points.

5. The _____ Empire became Austria and Hungary.

What do you think ?

Why do you think it was so important for President Wilson to find a peace plan that would last forever?

Suffragette Letter

In 1917, women picketed in front of the White House. They were picketing for women's suffrage, or right to vote. For this action some of the women were arrested and given prison sentences. Several other groups of women had also been arrested for picketing in the 1910s. The women wrote this letter from prison to the Commissioners of the District of Columbia.

As political prisoners, we, the undersigned, refuse to work while in prison. We have taken this stand as a matter of principle after careful consideration, and from it we shall not recede.

This action is a necessary protest against an unjust sentence: In reminding President Wilson of his preelection promises toward woman suffrage, we were exercising the right of peaceful petition, guaranteed by the Constitution of the United States, which declares peaceful picketing is legal in the District of Columbia. That we are unjustly sentenced has been well recognized—when President Wilson pardoned the first group of suffragists who had been given sixty days in the workhouse, and again when Judge Mullowny suspended the sentence for the last group of picketers.

We wish to point out the inconsistency and injustice of our sentences—some of us have been given sixty days, a later group, thirty days, and another group given a suspended sentence for exactly the same action.

Conscious, therefore, of having acted in accordance with the highest standards of citizenship, we ask the commissioners of the District to grant us the rights due political prisoners.

Document-Based Questions

1. What were the women refusing to do while in prison?

2. What was the reason for their refusal?

3. The women mention two people who played a part in their dilemma. Who were they?

4. What were the women asking for?

5. How convincing do you think the women's letter was?

Source: Suffragette Letter to the Commissioners of the District of Columbia, 1917.

- Woodrow Wilson succeeded in having Congress pass many reform laws. During the early part of his administration the Federal Reserve System was established and the 17th Amendment, providing for the direct election of senators, was ratified.

- In Europe, tension mounted between two groups of allied nations. Following the assassination of Archduke Francis Ferdinand in Sarajevo in 1914, war broke out in Europe. The United States remained neutral throughout the early years of the war.

- A German U-boat sank the British passenger ship *Lusitania* in 1915. Many Americans wanted the United States to become involved in the war.

- Following the publication of the Zimmermann Note, the United States declared war on Germany on April 6, 1917. President Wilson said that the war was to make the world "safe for democracy."

- American factories immediately began to manufacture military supplies, and men were drafted to become soldiers.

- By the fall of 1918 more than two million American soldiers were fighting in Europe under General John Pershing.

- The war ended on November 11, 1918. It had weakened the great European countries but had established the United States as a major world power.

- Wilson presented his 14 Points plan for a permanent peace in Europe. In this plan he called for the formation of the League of Nations.

- The Treaty of Versailles officially ended World War I and redrew the boundary lines for many of the countries of Europe.

- Many members of Congress did not like the idea of the League of Nations in the peace treaty. Wilson struggled to get the treaty approved, but Congress never approved the Treaty of Versailles. The United States did not join the League of Nations.

Chapter 23 REVIEW

Word Bank

Allied Powers

Federal Reserve
System

Francis Ferdinand

Germany

League of Nations

submarines

Woodrow Wilson

Zimmermann
Note

On a sheet of paper, write the correct word or words from the Word Bank to complete each sentence.

1. A national banking organization called the _____ was one of President Wilson's early victories.

2. Great Britain, France, Serbia, and Russia were part of an alliance called the _____.

3. World War I began when an assassin shot Archduke _____ and his wife in Sarajevo.

4. War zones were patrolled by German _____, called U-boats, to keep supplies from reaching Great Britain.

5. _____ proposed a League of Nations as part of his plan known as the 14 Points.

6. Soon after newspapers published the _____, Congress declared war on Germany.

7. The _____ was a failure, partially because the United States refused to join.

8. _____ was not invited to attend the peace conference at the Palace of Versailles in France.

On a sheet of paper, write the letter of the answer that best answers each question.

9. When the United States entered the war, what did the government do?

   A drafted soldiers

   B lowered taxes

   C decreased factory production

   D asked the people to support the economy

10. Germany, Austria-Hungary, Bulgaria, and Turkey formed which alliance?

   A the 14 Points   **C** the Allied Powers

   B the Central Powers   **D** the League of Nations

11. What did Woodrow Wilson believe would correct the problems of an unjust peace?

   A the Treaty of Versailles

   B the Paris Peace Conference

   C the League of Nations

   D the blockade of German ports

On a sheet of paper, write the answers to the following questions. Use complete sentences.

12. What were two major events that occurred early in Woodrow Wilson's presidency?

13. What were the two European alliances and which countries belonged to each?

14. Why did sinking the *Lusitania* cause so much uproar?

15. What information was in the Zimmermann Note?

16. Why was Congress against the Treaty of Versailles?

17. What were three of the things that America did after it declared war on Germany?

18. Which four countries attended the peace conference at Versailles? Who represented each country?

Critical Thinking On a sheet of paper, write your response to each question. Use complete sentences.

19. During the early part of World War I, America remained neutral. Would it be possible for America to remain neutral today if a war broke out all over Europe? Explain.

20. World War I weakened the great powers of Europe and increased the power of the United States. In what ways was the United States' power increased?

Test-Taking Tip

Write facts and definitions on index cards. You and a partner can use them as flash cards to practice for a test.

24 The Roaring Twenties

With World War I over, Americans were ready to return to normal, or usual, times. As it turned out, however, the decade of the 1920s was anything but normal and restful. The "Roaring Twenties," as the decade was called, was an exciting time for many Americans. It was full of social and cultural changes. But near its end, the decade was also a time of hardship. It was the beginning of the worst depression in American history. In this chapter, you will learn about the changes and hardships America faced in the 1920s.

Goals for Learning

◆ To describe the presidencies of Warren G. Harding and Calvin Coolidge

◆ To explain some social developments of the period

◆ To describe some cultural developments during this time

◆ To identify social problems that developed during this period

◆ To explain the reasons for the 1929 stock market crash

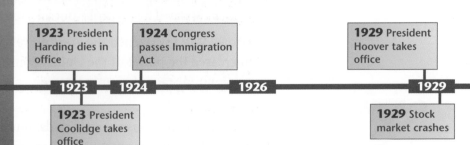

1920 19th Amendment gives women the right to vote

1923 President Harding dies in office

1924 Congress passes Immigration Act

1929 President Hoover takes office

1920   1921   1923   1924   1926   1929

1921 President Harding takes office

1923 President Coolidge takes office

1929 Stock market crashes

Decade

A period of 10 years

Landslide

A majority of votes for
one side

Heroics

Bravery well beyond
what is needed

Solution

The answer to a
problem

In 1920, the American people were tired of the tensions of reform
and war. The nation had used so much energy in the last two
decades that Americans seemed to be hoping for a rest. Average
people wished the country would return to more normal times.
They wanted the nation less involved in world affairs and more
involved in activities at home.

What Helped Americans Return to Normal Times?

Warren G. Harding, the Republican candidate, was elected
president in 1920. Harding had promised the weary voters a
"return to normalcy." The word *normalcy* fit the feelings of
the American people, and they elected him by a **landslide**.
He received more than 60 percent of the vote. This was the
greatest percentage of votes ever gained by a presidential
candidate. For the 12 years that followed this election, the
majority of Americans voted for Republican presidents.

Harding had been a senator from Ohio, while his vice president,
Calvin Coolidge, was the former governor of Massachusetts.
After the election, Harding announced that he was not interested
in "**heroics**, but healing." He was looking for quick **solutions** for
the nation's problems when he took office in 1921.

What Did Harding Do as President?

During the presidency of Warren Harding, the Emergency Quota
Act was passed. The law limited immigration to the United States.
A new tariff act was written, raising the tax on imported goods
beyond the rate set under President Wilson. In 1920, Congress
created the Veteran's Bureau to give different types of aid to ex-
soldiers and their families. Government finances were organized
as never before by the new Bureau of the Budget.

Generally, however, Harding was not an effective president. He
was a poor judge of character in appointing people to government
office. Several members of his administration were caught using
their positions to make money for themselves.

Fraud

A lie or false act to steal money or something of value

Emotion

Feelings people express

The most serious scandal began in 1921. Two oil businessmen gave Secretary of the Interior Albert B. Fall $400,000. Fall then arranged for the men to rent, at a very low price, some government oil reserves at Teapot Dome, Wyoming, and Elk Hills, California. Fall went to prison in 1929 for his crime.

Harding did not know about the dealings of the interior secretary until the Teapot Dome Scandal became public. This embarrassment was followed by charges of **fraud** and bribery against the attorney general and the head of the Veteran's Bureau. Harding would not have allowed these scandals to happen if he had known about them.

This cartoon shows officials in President Harding's administration trying to escape being crushed by the Teapot Dome scandal.

President Harding died suddenly on August 2, 1923. Millions of people expressed their sorrow for his death. Harding had once said, "I cannot hope to be one of the great presidents, but perhaps I may be remembered as one of the most loved."

What Did Coolidge Do as President?

Vice President Calvin Coolidge became the president of the United States in 1923. Coolidge was a man of few words and showed little **emotion**. One story describes how a woman told Coolidge she had bet with a friend that she could get him to say more than two words. Coolidge answered, "You lose."

Coolidge believed that "the chief business of America is business." He was a friend and supporter of the business community. He thought that government regulations to control big business were harmful to the American economy. He rejected the reform ideas of Roosevelt and Wilson. Reformers like the Progressives still fought for more government control and regulation. That fight, though, was no longer a major force in American politics.

During the election year of 1924, Coolidge seemed calm and confident about the nation's future. The economy was strong, and many people's lives were improving. Most Americans liked what they saw and voted to "keep cool with Coolidge." Coolidge was president for the next four years.

During the 1920s, the United States became a major world power. Both Harding and Coolidge promoted economic development at home and peace abroad. Both wanted less government control of business. They wanted reduced government spending and reduced corporate taxes. Political leaders thought that the success of the United States depended on peace in the world. To create a peaceful world, nations were encouraged to destroy their weapons. In 1921, during Harding's administration, the Washington Conference was held to discuss this. In 1928, Coolidge's last year as president, the United States and 14 other nations attempted to outlaw war. They signed a treaty called the Kellogg-Briand Pact. The treaty, however, had no effective way to end warfare. Most Americans, with their economy booming, were content to ignore foreign affairs.

Word Bank

Calvin Coolidge

Emergency Quota Act

Teapot Dome

Veteran's Bureau

Warren G. Harding

Lesson 1 Review On a sheet of paper, write the correct word or words from the Word Bank to complete each sentence.

1. _____ promised voters a return to normal times.

2. The _____ limited immigration to the United States.

3. The most serious scandal during President Harding's term was called _____.

4. _____ became the president of the United States in 1923.

5. A(n) _____ was established to give aid to ex-soldiers and their families.

What do you think ?

How do you know that Harding was not an effective president?

Mobile

Having the ability to travel

Geography Note

The rapid increase of auto ownership changed Americans' lives. Roads were improved for easier driving. People could find jobs farther from home. Suburbs and shopping malls developed to fill the needs of drivers. Today's cars continue to make life easier, but they also cause air pollution and other problems.

The 1920s in American society was a period of many social changes. Industry thrived across the nation. More Americans earned higher wages, so they could afford to spend more money on goods. If they did not have the cash, they could now buy things in monthly payments. Americans had more leisure time and more money to go out to movies or music clubs.

During the war, many American farmers had increased their production to meet a higher demand. After the war, farm prices fell and farmers had unwanted crops and expanding debts. Many of them started to consider other types of work in cities.

America became more **mobile** as a growing number of people were able to buy cars. Radios brought news and entertainment to American homes. Another invention now found in thousands of homes was the telephone. Communication by phone was helping to bring people closer.

What Was the First Widely Used Automobile?

During the 1920s, the Ford Model T automobile became the most popular way to travel. By 1916, a Model T cost about $400. Wealthy people owned most of the first automobiles. When the price of these cars dropped to about $250 by the mid-1920s, they became affordable for more Americans.

The assembly line made automobiles affordable for many families.

The Model T was the first mass-produced car. Henry Ford used an **assembly line** to make them. In an assembly line, a line of workers assembled the car piece by piece until it was complete. Every car was exactly alike. Henry Ford once commented that Americans could buy the Model T in "any color—as long as it's black." It had a canvas roof and no door for the driver. It had to be started with a hand crank in the front. Americans were proud to be seen in a "tin lizzie," as the Model T was nicknamed.

Owners found many different ways to use the Model T. Farmers, for example, used the car to pull plows, to run water pumps, and to haul hay. People made jokes about the rattling fenders and the parts that would fall out. But they kept buying the Model T until 1927 when Ford introduced the Model A.

The Model T put the nation on wheels. It became a necessary part of the lives of most Americans. The automobile gave people more choices for where they could work and live.

The federal government encouraged the building of modern highways to replace dirt roads. **Suburbs,** the new communities built outside of cities, grew rapidly. The automobile allowed Americans the freedom to travel from place to place.

Then and Now

If you were living in the 1920s, you might have decided to buy your first car. Although automobiles had been around for two decades, most people did not own one until the 1920s. Henry Ford's assembly line made cars affordable. Compare the features on a Model T with a modern family car.

Description	Model T	Modern Family Car
Average price	under $300	$20,000
Fastest speed	40 mph	120 mph
Speed controlled by	Lever on steering wheel	Gas pedal and cruise control
Engine	4 cylinder	4, 6, or 8 cylinder
Transmission	2 gears	3 or 4 gears
Change gears	With foot pedal	Automatic
Flat tire	Repair puncture	Change tire
Assembly	By hand	With help of computers and robots

Writing About History

Listen to a recording of an old-time radio program. Write a description of the program in your notebook. Tell how it differs from today's radio programs.

How Did Radio Change American Life?

By the mid-1920s, most middle-class Americans had a telephone, a radio, and a phonograph in their home. Silent movies had been popular since before World War I. The radio brought an unlimited source of free information and entertainment right into the home. By 1929, it was so popular that about 10 million Americans owned radios.

The first permanent commercial radio station began broadcasting in Pittsburgh in 1920. This station reported the results of the presidential election. In 1921, baseball's World Series was heard on the radio. By 1923, there were more than 500 radio stations in the United States.

Beginning in the 1920s, the radio brought information and entertainment into millions of people's homes.

Association

A group of people joined together for a common purpose

Generation

People who live in the same time period and are about the same age

What Was the 19th Amendment?

In 1869, the National Woman Suffrage **Association** had been formed. The association was led by Elizabeth Cady Stanton and Susan B. Anthony. This group wanted to amend the Constitution to give women the right to vote. Over the next 50 years, the suffrage amendment was introduced in several sessions of Congress. In August 1920, three-fourths of the states ratified the amendment. The 19th Amendment gave all American women the right to vote. The long struggle had ended in victory.

How Did Women Become More Independent?

Many young American women of the 1920s were called flappers. The name brings to mind something not tied down that flaps in the wind. These young women refused to be "tied" to the ideas, actions, and styles of an older **generation.** Flappers cut their hair short, wore skirts cut above their knees, and painted their lips bright red.

In addition to having recently won the right to vote, women gained a new independence in the 1920s. Many started to think about jobs that had been open only to men. Women began to challenge old ideas of how they should act. The changes in hair and dress styles were a clear sign that women also wanted to gain more social freedom.

Women struggled for almost 50 years to win the right to vote. They finally won that right in 1920.

Civics Connection

Women's Rights

The 19th Amendment was a great victory for women. How did votes for women change the American culture? The structure of politics did not change at all. The same political parties held the same powers. However, gradually, women's status began to change in the following ways:

- More and more women worked alongside men.
- Women formed their own political organizations.
- Women began to hold more public offices.

- More women attended college.
- More women entered professional fields.
- Women won rights to their own property and income.
- Women's health and health care improved.
- Women's earnings rose.

In 2002, women made up almost 60 percent of college graduates. U.S. women worked in larger numbers, with higher pay, and in more career fields than ever before. Yet they still did not receive equal pay for equal work.

1. Why do you think the right to vote helped women become more independent and successful?

2. Why do you think women still are not paid as well as men?

Lesson 2 Review On a sheet of paper, write the answers to the following questions. Use complete sentences.

1. Why did many farmers look for city jobs after World War I?

2. What process did Ford use to make the Model T?

3. How did radio change the American way of life?

4. What did the National Woman Suffrage Association want to do?

5. What was the purpose of the 19th Amendment?

What do you think ?

Do you think radio is as important in people's lives today as it was in the 1920s? Why or why not?

Energetic

Full of energy

Improvise

To make up as you go along

Spiritual

A religious song

Composer

One who writes music

Symphony

A long, complex musical piece

Jazz in the 1920s seemed to capture the spirit of the times. The music was "hot," **energetic,** and lively. Jazz was not played just from musical notes written on paper. Jazz songs and sounds were **improvised**.

Jazz started in the South among African American musicians. These musicians used African rhythms, work songs, and **spirituals**. A spiritual is a religious song. By mixing these styles with European-style music, the artists created a truly original American sound.

Jazz had many forms. The earliest type of jazz was Dixieland of the South. However, by the 1920s, jazz bands could be found in most northern cities. Louis Armstrong played the trumpet with his small band in Chicago and New York. Duke Ellington started writing jazz music for big bands. As jazz became more popular, classical music **composers** picked up its sound. A composer is one who writes music. Composer George Gershwin used jazz in his **symphony** "Rhapsody in Blue" (1924) and his tone poem "An American in Paris" (1928). A symphony is a long, complex musical piece. A tone poem is freer in form than a symphony.

Duke Ellington directs his big band. Ellington was a major composer and developer of jazz.

New dances like "the Charleston" also became popular. While doing the Charleston, young people moved freely around the dance floor. The dancers kicked their legs into the air and waved their arms above their heads. The faster the music was played, the faster they moved. Many older Americans were concerned about the effects jazz and the new dances were having on young people. One magazine wrote that the behavior of the young people was "shocking to their grandparents." Unlike people in past generations, these young people didn't care how much they shocked others.

Which American Writers Produced Important Works?

Some of America's greatest writers produced important works during the 1920s. Writers tried to tell the story of what was happening in America. In *The Great Gatsby*, F. Scott Fitzgerald showed the unhappy life of a wealthy, popular man who was once a poor farm boy. Sinclair Lewis wrote about small-town life in America in *Main Street* and *Babbitt*. In *A Farewell to Arms*, Ernest Hemingway told the story of the impact World War I had on the life of an American man. Edith Wharton's *The Age of Innocence* told about the foolishness of New York high society of the late 1800s. In *Three Soldiers*, John Dos Passos wrote about the sadness of men after their return from the Great War.

What Was the Harlem Renaissance?

An area in New York City called Harlem became a creative center for many African Americans. The period of the 1920s to the mid-1930s is known as the Harlem Renaissance. Writers and poets like Langston Hughes and Countee Cullen, wrote about the noble past of African Americans. They also wrote of African American dreams, disappointments, and discrimination.

History in Your Life

The Works of Langston Hughes

James Langston Hughes was one of the most productive writers of the Harlem Renaissance. Hughes brought the rhythms and styles of jazz and black speech into his poetry. In the Depression, he wrote *Not Without Laughter,* his first novel, and short stories like "The Ways of White Folks." Hughes became known as a playwright when his *Mulatto* was staged on Broadway. He founded the Harlem Suitcase Theatre in 1938. During World War II, Hughes began his weekly "Simple" column in the *Chicago Defender*. It featured an African American philosopher who talked about life, love, and race. In 1951 in his poem "Harlem," he posed a question. He asked what happens to the African American dream of equality if it continues to be put off. Would the dream, he asked, "dry up like a raisin in the sun"?

Hughes and other writers and artists of the Harlem Renaissance opened the door for many other African Americans.

Biography

Marcus Garvey: 1887–1940

Marcus Garvey was a boldly determined supporter of black nationalism. He also supported black-owned businesses. He believed blacks should have their own homeland—the entire continent of Africa. Garvey spoke out against the lynchings of blacks and urged his people to strike for freedom. In 1914, he organized the Universal Negro Improvement Association in his native Jamaica. He moved the association's headquarters to Harlem in 1916. By the 1920s, it had become the largest nonreligious association in African American history. In 1920, its first international convention brought about thousands of people from more than 20 nations. Its weekly newspaper, *Negro World,* ran for 14 years. Garvey also established a steamship line that was owned and run by African Americans. The company's ships provided transportation to Africa and helped to link black businesses worldwide.

Lesson 3 Review Choose the term in parentheses that best completes each sentence. Write your answers on a sheet of paper.

1. African Americans started the jazz movement in (Chicago, the South, Harlem).

2. Jazz music combined elements of African rhythms, work songs, and (Dixieland, European ideas, spirituals).

3. A musician who wrote jazz music for big bands was (Duke Ellington, George Gershwin, Louis Armstrong).

4. (F. Scott Fitzgerald, Ernest Hemingway, Sinclair Lewis) wrote about how World War I affected soldiers.

5. (Langston Hughes, Edith Wharton, John Dos Passos) was a voice for African Americans during the Harlem Renaissance.

What do you think ?

The older generation did not understand the younger generation in the 1920s. Why do you think this happened? Does this still happen today? Why or why not?

Communist

A person who believes in a form of government that eliminates private property and shares wealth

During the 1920s, Americans became more independent and creative. They searched for fun and the good life. Still, there were problems. Many Americans were poor. The boll weevil destroyed much of southern farmers' cotton crop. Farmers in other areas still had difficulty making a living because of the low prices for crops.

What Forms of Discrimination Were Problems?

Some Americans wanted to deny equality and freedom to people who were different from them. They wanted African Americans "kept in their place." They were fearful and suspicious of immigrants. They worried about foreigners destroying American democracy. "America First" became their slogan.

A new Ku Klux Klan was formed in the South in 1915. The last time Americans had seen the Klan was during the period of Reconstruction. The new Klan feared African Americans, Jews, Catholics, and immigrants. They wanted to define an American as white, Protestant, and native born. The ideas of the Klan spread. They gained some political power and helped elect governors in two states. In 1925, Klansmen carrying American flags marched down Pennsylvania Avenue in Washington, D.C. Behind the marchers was the symbol of American democracy, the United States capitol. Fortunately, during the last years of the 1920s, the Klan's political power declined sharply.

In 1924, Congress passed the Immigration Act. This law limited the number of immigrants allowed into the United States from southern and eastern Europe. The law was passed because some felt that these immigrants were a threat to American democracy because of their political beliefs. Americans feared that the recent **Communist** revolution in Russia would spread to the United States. Communists believed in a form of government that eliminated private property and tried to share the nation's wealth equally among its citizens.

Prohibition

The ban on making or selling alcohol

Bootlegger

Someone who made or sold alcohol illegally during Prohibition

Speakeasy

A place where liquor was sold illegally during Prohibition

Another political group Americans feared was the anarchists. Anarchists wanted to do away with all forms of government. Some anarchists were willing to use violence to achieve their political goals. A series of bombings targeting government and business leaders in the United States in 1919 led to a "Red Scare." A red flag was the symbol of the Russian Communist revolution. When the home of the attorney general of the United States, A. Mitchell Palmer, was bombed, the federal government arrested thousands of political radicals. The "Palmer Raids" often violated people's civil rights and led to the deportation of many immigrants.

What Was Prohibition?

Crime, violence, family breakups, and child abuse were all major social problems. Reformers believed that alcohol was the root of these problems. The 18th Amendment, ratified in 1919, made it illegal to sell alcohol in the United States. The ban on making and selling of alcohol was called **Prohibition**.

Because of the ban on alcohol, the 1920s also became known as "The Dry Decade." However, it really was not all that "dry." **Bootleggers** continued to make and sell liquor illegally. The public was eager to buy it. **Speakeasies,** where illegal liquor was sold, became very popular meeting places in major cities.

Many Americans ignored the law. Organized crime made millions of dollars by making and selling liquor. Reformers may have been trying to do a good thing, but Prohibition brought a rise in crime. In 1933, the 21st Amendment to the Constitution repealed the Prohibition amendment.

Word Bank

anarchists

18th

Palmer Raids

Prohibition

21st

Lesson 4 Review On a sheet of paper, write the correct word from the Word Bank to complete each sentence.

1. The _____ led to the deportation of many immigrants.
2. Many Americans feared the _____, who wanted to do away with all forms of government.
3. The _____ Amendment made it against the law to sell alcohol in the United States.
4. _____ was the name for the ban on alcohol.
5. The _____ Amendment repealed Prohibition.

What do you think

Do you think Prohibition would work if it was made a law today? Why or why not?

Solo

Done by one person

Stock market

A market for the buying and selling of company stock

Early in the morning of May 20, 1927, a small plane called the *Spirit of St. Louis* lifted off from New York. The pilot's name was Charles Lindbergh. He headed across the Atlantic Ocean for Paris, France. Up until this time, no one had made a nonstop, **solo** flight across the Atlantic Ocean. A $25,000 prize had been offered by a New York hotel owner to the first person who could do it. Lindbergh knew that he had to stay awake and fly the plane for more than 30 hours. Paris was 3,600 miles away.

Charles Lindbergh became the first person to fly a plane solo across the Atlantic Ocean.

Thirty-three hours later, "Lucky Lindy" touched his plane down in Paris. Lindbergh was a perfect symbol for the nation. Americans felt that the country was strong because it was made up of people like Lucky Lindy.

Who Won the Election of 1928?

People paid little attention to the fact that car sales and housing construction were decreasing by 1927. Too many good things were happening. Lindbergh had reached Paris. Babe Ruth hit 60 home runs. The **stock market** was going up. The stock market is a market for the buying and selling of company stock. People were making money by buying stocks. Business was good, and people believed it would get better.

Calvin Coolidge decided not to run for re-election in 1928. The Republican Party nominated Herbert Hoover. Although he had been poor as a child, Hoover worked his way through college to become a mining engineer. He was what Americans liked to call "self-made." Hoover had also been responsible for getting aid to European victims of the World War.

The Democrats nominated Al Smith, the governor of New York. Republican campaign posters said, "Let's keep what we've got . . . Hoover and happiness, or Smith and **soup houses.**" Soup houses were places where the poor could get food. In 1928, the voters picked Hoover for president. Hoover took office in 1929. The voters did not realize that they would soon get the soup houses anyway.

How Did the Stock Market Crash?

The stock market continued to rise through 1928 and most of 1929. Radio Corporation of America stock went from $94.50 a share to $505.00 in one year. People took their savings out of the bank and bought stocks. Many people even borrowed money to buy stocks. The price of many stocks was much higher than their true value. Many people did not seem to care. They were sure they could sell their stocks to someone else and make a profit.

On October 24, 1929, stock prices dropped sharply. There were more sellers than buyers. Five days later, on October 29, 1929, the stock market fell apart, or crashed. People tried to sell their stocks, but there were no buyers.

The United States was at the beginning of the worst economic depression in its history. The Roaring Twenties had come to a crashing end. The 1930s would be called the "Great Depression." It was a time of great struggle, when businesses failed and people lost their jobs.

What do you think ?

How do you think the Great Depression changed people's attitudes?

Lesson 5 Review On a sheet of paper, write the answers to the following questions. Use complete sentences.

1. Why did Americans like Charles Lindbergh?

2. What is the stock market?

3. What were soup houses?

4. What caused the stock market to crash?

5. What was the Great Depression?

James Weldon Johnson

James Weldon Johnson was an African American educator, diplomat, and writer. He was a founder of the National Association for the Advancement of Colored People. In the 1920s, he was considered a primary spokesperson and interpreter of the Harlem Renaissance. This passage is from an article written in 1928 for Harper's Magazine. *It is one of many magazine articles Johnson wrote at the time.*

All of the Negro's folk-art creations have undergone a new evaluation. His sacred music—the spirituals; his secular music— ragtime, jazz, and the work songs; his folklore—the Uncle Remus plantation tales; and his dances have received a new and higher appreciation. I dare to say that it is now more or less acknowledged that the only things artistic that have sprung from American life, and been universally recognized as American products, are the folk creations of the Negro. . . .

ut the story does not halt at this point. e Negro has done a great deal through folk-art creations to change the national titudes toward him; and now the efforts of race have been reinforced and magnified e individual Negro artist, the conscious . . .

now, is the significance of this artistic y on the part of the Negro and of its ns on the American people?

I think it is twofold. In the first place, the Negro is making some distinctive contributions to our common cultural store. I do not claim it is possible for these individual artists to produce anything comparable to the folk-art in distinctive values, but I do believe they are bringing something fresh and vital into American art, something from the store of their own racial genius—warmth, color, movement, rhythm, and abandon; depth and swiftness of emotion and the beauty of sensuousness. I believe American art will be richer because of these elements in fuller quantity.

Document-Based Questions

1. In the first sentence, what does Johnson say has happened to African Americans' folk-art creations?

2. What are three specific folk-art creations from African Americans that he names?

3. In the second paragraph, what does Johnson say changed through African Americans' folk-art creations?

4. What is one thing Johnson says African Americans' contributions are bringing to American art?

5. Identify one element of our modern culture that was an African American contribution from the Harlem Renaissance.

Harper's Magazine, *1928.*

Chapter 24 SUMMARY

- President Warren Harding faced a number of scandals during his term, including the Teapot Dome Scandal in which the secretary of the interior sold oil rights to government land.

- Calvin Coolidge became president when Harding died in office. Coolidge spoke little and showed little emotion. He was a supporter of business.

- Americans had more leisure time and earned higher wages than ever before. They were able to purchase new items such as automobiles, radios, and telephones.

- The 19th Amendment, which granted women the right to vote, was ratified in August 1920. Women gained greater independence in the 1920s. Some worked outside the home and many changed their hair and clothing styles.

- Jazz, a new style of American music, developed during this period. Louis Armstrong, Duke Ellington, and others helped make this music style popular. Along with new music came new dances like the Charleston.

- Many of America's great writers such as F. Scott Fitzgerald, Sinclair Lewis, Langston Hughes, Edith Wharton, and John Dos Passos became famous during this decade.

- There was a rebirth of pride in the African American community of Harlem in New York City. Writers, musicians, and artists were part of what became known as the Harlem Renaissance.

- African American citizens continued to face discrimination during the 1920s. Groups such as the Ku Klux Klan spread throughout the country for a brief period. Immigrants also faced discrimination.

- Prohibition, or a ban on making and selling alcoholic beverages, was in effect during this decade. There was much illegal activity because of Prohibition, including organized crime.

- In May 1927, Charles Lindbergh made the first solo transatlantic flight in his plane, the *Spirit of St. Louis*.

- After a long period of time when stock prices were overvalued, the stock market crashed on October 29, 1929. This sent the country into the Great Depression.

Chapter 24 REVIEW

Word Bank

bootleggers
Calvin Coolidge
Charles Lindbergh
Langston Hughes
Model T
presidential
    election
radio
stock market
suffrage
Warren Harding

On a sheet of paper, write the correct word or words from the Word Bank to complete each sentence.

1. Almost everyone had a _____ in their home on which they could listen to news and entertainment.

2. President _____, who had faced several scandals, died in office.

3. _____ was a president who was known for his quiet ways and unemotional manner.

4. The great _____ crash happened in October 1929.

5. The first commercial radio broadcasts covered the _____ in 1920.

6. Women earned the right to vote, or _____, when the 19th Amendment was ratified.

7. _____ made the first solo airplane flight across the Atlantic Ocean in the *Spirit of St. Louis*.

8. One of the great writers of the Harlem Renaissance was _____.

9. People who sold illegal liquor during Prohibition were called _____.

10. For only $250 you could buy a _____ and travel the bumpy streets of America.

On a sheet of paper, write the letter of the answer that best answers each question.

11. Who was elected president just before the stock market crash of 1929?
    A Al Smith   **C** Herbert Hoover
    B Calvin Coolidge   **D** Warren Harding

Unit 8

Depression and World War II

Have you noticed how hard times and difficulties can draw people together? That happened for Americans in the 1930s and 1940s. The sudden failure of the economy in 1929 resulted in very hard times for many Americans during the 1930s. Many were out of work and homeless. The government established economic and social programs to help them. Americans drew together to help each other. Then in the 1940s the United States entered another world war. Americans drew together at home and overseas to support the war effort.

In this unit, you will learn what Americans went through during the Great Depression. You will learn about programs that helped people through that difficult time. You will learn about events that brought about World War II. You also will learn how the United States pulled together to win that war.

Chapters in Unit 8

25

Depression and the New Deal

The good times of the 1920s were over when the Great Depression began. Americans spent the next decade just trying to get by. The government worked hard on plans to try to restore the country to what it had been. In this chapter, you will learn what caused the Depression, the problems and hardships people faced, and what the government did to help solve the problem.

Goals for Learning

◆ To explain the factors that contributed to the Great Depression and conditions during that time

◆ To describe Franklin Roosevelt's "New Deal" policy

◆ To explain some of the programs of the New Deal

◆ To describe some movies and well-known people of the time

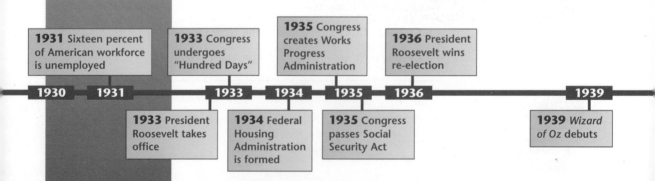

1931 Sixteen percent of American workforce is unemployed

1933 Congress undergoes "Hundred Days"

1935 Congress creates Works Progress Administration

1936 President Roosevelt wins re-election

1930 — 1931 — 1933 — 1934 — 1935 — 1936 — 1939

1933 President Roosevelt takes office

1934 Federal Housing Administration is formed

1935 Congress passes Social Security Act

1939 *Wizard of Oz* debuts

Layoff

Letting workers go because a company cannot afford to pay them

Charity

A group that helps those in need

The stock market crash of 1929 was as big a shock to President Hoover as it was to other Americans. Before the crash, the economy seemed strong. Before 1929, less than 4 percent of American workers did not have jobs. One year later, 9 percent of the workforce was unemployed.

As sales of their products decreased, American businesses were forced into **layoffs**. A layoff occurs when a company lets workers go because it cannot afford to pay them. Layoffs are often temporary. The Ford Motor Company, for example, was forced to cut its number of workers by 44 percent. By 1931, unemployment increased to 16 percent. Eight million Americans could not find work. Many people lost their life savings.

President Hoover encouraged the American people to be patient. He believed the Depression would end with time. He said the nation had seen hard times before, and each time the economy had bounced back.

Seattle's "Hooverville" was built just south of downtown Seattle.

President Hoover did not feel the federal government should have to help the unemployed. He believed state and local governments, private groups, and **charities** should help people. A charity is a group that helps those in need. According to Hoover, America was a strong democracy because Americans took responsibility for their own lives.

Although Hoover had been president for less than a year, people blamed him for causing the Depression. Bitter "Hoover jokes" became popular. Unable to make loan payments to their banks, many people lost their homes. In many cities, homeless people built cardboard and tar paper shacks. These poorly built shelters gave some protection from bad weather. But people living in them had to do without heat, lights, or running water. These slums became known as "Hoovervilles."

What Caused the Great Depression?

Several factors caused the Depression. The stock market crash was only one of the causes. Businesses had grown rapidly in the 1920s. They had produced many products quickly and often faster than consumers could buy them. This **overproduction** caused big changes in many companies. As production was slowed down, workers were laid off.

When the economy was good, people spent a lot of money. The strong economy encouraged them to buy more than they could pay for. Many people had bought things on credit. Credit is the practice of buying something and paying for it later. Then, when people lost their jobs, they could not pay their debts. Banks that "held paper" on unpaid loans went out of business.

Many foreign countries still in debt from the war were unable to buy products from America. In some cases, high tariffs were placed on American goods. The American economy might have grown much stronger during the 1920s if these countries had been able to buy more U.S. goods.

How Did the Dust Bowl Affect Farm Owners, Tenants, and Sharecroppers?

After World War I, farmers struggled with great financial difficulties. Prices for their crops continued to go down. Many farmers were barely able to support their families. In an attempt to grow more crops, many farmers plowed up the grasslands of the Great Plains that stretch from Montana to Texas. In the early 1930s, these western states were hit by drought. The lack of rain dried out the soil. When the wind swept over the Plains, it created dust storms. These weather conditions turned the Plains into a "Dust Bowl" that drove many farmers from their land. It was an economic and environmental disaster.

Breadline

A place where people could get free food

Writing About History

Research what it was like to live during the Great Depression. In your notebook, write a first-person explanation of what you think it would have been like to live during that time.

How Did Americans Lose Confidence?

During the Depression, the American people lost confidence in themselves and in their country. People lived in fear of the future. Businesses were afraid to make new investments. Workers thought they could lose their jobs at any time. Unemployed workers had little reason to believe that they would ever find other jobs.

Families stood in **breadlines** for free food. Homeless people slept in subways, parks, and old empty warehouses. Men who once worked regularly could be seen selling apples on the street. Across the country, Americans became very concerned about the nation's future.

What Impact Did the Depression Have on African Americans and Women?

As the economy declined, many African Americans lost their jobs to unemployed white workers. African American workers, like women workers, were often "last hired, first fired." Many African Americans were sharecroppers that farmed the land in the South. Thousands of sharecroppers lost their jobs as the farm owners' income declined. Before the Depression, moving north had been a major way for Southern African Americans to find higher-paying jobs. As northern factories closed, these jobs were lost. Many married women of all races lost their jobs during the Depression. Many businesses thought that it was more important that unemployed married men be employed than married women.

What do you think

Why is confidence in yourself and your country important?

Lesson 1 Review On a sheet of paper, write your answers to the following questions. Use complete sentences.

1. How did the stock market crash affect businesses?

2. Why did President Hoover not help the unemployed?

3. List three factors that helped cause the Great Depression.

4. What effects did the Depression have on the American people?

5. What were breadlines?

Surplus

An extra amount of something

Stabilize

To keep from changing

Insurance

A plan that protects against loss in return for regular payments

Moratorium

The legal act of delaying something

Crisis

An event that threatens people's well-being

The weak economy did not improve as President Hoover had believed it would. He made plans to help the economy. Hoover proposed the following:

- With the Agricultural Marketing Act, Congress approved $500 million to buy extra, or **surplus,** crops from farmers. Hoover hoped this act would **stabilize** farm prices. This plan was unsuccessful because the farm problem was too great. Farm prices continued to go down.
- The Reconstruction Finance Corporation was established in 1932. This corporation loaned emergency money to banks, railroads, and **insurance** companies. Insurance is a plan that protects against loss in return for regular payments.
- A federal public works program was established and $750 million was approved to create jobs. Some people went to work building dams, highways, and buildings. States and local communities were encouraged to establish similar programs.
- A **moratorium** was put on payments of war debts owed to the United States. This put off payments of debts until later. Hoover hoped to ease Europe's financial problems. Then, he believed, these countries would be able to buy more products from the United States.

How Did President Roosevelt Help the Nation Recover?

Hoover's proposals for improving the economy were not enough for the American people. They wanted a change in the White House. In the 1932 election, Hoover was defeated in his attempt for re-election. In a landslide victory, Democrat Franklin Delano Roosevelt became the new president. Roosevelt said he had a "new deal for the American people." He promised to act quickly to put the country back on its feet.

President Roosevelt took the oath of office on March 4, 1933. In a radio message, he told the American people that the economic **crisis** would not destroy the nation. He said with confidence that "the only thing we have to fear is fear itself."

Roosevelt promised a "New Deal" for "the forgotten man at the bottom of the economic pyramid." The plan covered three areas: relief, **recovery,** and reform. Roosevelt knew that many Americans were in need of immediate help. He had to find a way to get the economy to recover from its depression quickly. He believed that America's economic system had to be reformed. Basic changes were necessary to prevent another depression in the future.

As a young man, Roosevelt had suffered an attack of polio. He had to use a wheelchair or leg braces to walk after that. Many thought that Roosevelt's own illness made him more concerned about the problems of others.

What Actions Did Roosevelt and Congress Take?

Before he became president, Roosevelt said that he was willing to try different methods to end the Depression. "If one plan fails," he said, "admit it frankly and try another. But above all, try something."

The nation wanted action. On March 9, 1933, President Roosevelt acted boldly. He called Congress into special session. In the next 100 days, this Congress passed many important laws. Many of these early "New Deal" laws were based on ideas of progressive politicians before and during World War I. Progressives wanted more government regulation of the economy and social welfare programs. The period called the "Hundred Days" resulted in the following government actions:

- The national "bank holiday" **prohibited** people from rushing to banks and taking all of their money out. The government inspected banks before reopening them. Banks with problems could not reopen until the problems were addressed.

- The Emergency Banking Act made federal loans available to banks.

- The Federal Emergency Relief Administration loaned millions of dollars to state agencies for families who needed food, clothing, and shelter.

Recovery

The act of overcoming a problem

Prohibit

To prevent by law

- The Civilian Conservation Corps (CCC) hired people ages of 18 to 25 to plant trees, build roads, and work on flood control in rural areas.

- The Agricultural Adjustment Act (AAA) paid farmers for crops they destroyed. This would create a shortage of products that would in turn raise prices.

- The National Recovery Administration (NRA) was established to help businesses recover. It encouraged cooperation among business, labor, and government. It reduced the workweek, established a minimum wage, and ended child labor.

- The Truth-in-Securities Act controlled selling stocks and bonds.

- The Tennessee Valley Authority (TVA) employed thousands of people to work on environmental problems in the Tennessee River Basin. They constructed dams to control flooding and soil erosion and to generate hydroelectric power. For the first time, rural families in this area had electricity. In time, inexpensive electricity changed the area and provided stable jobs and a better home life.

Americans were hopeful that the new cooperation between businesses, labor, and the government would bring the Great Depression to an end. The Blue Eagle, the symbol for the NRA, began appearing in windows of small shops and gates of large factories. The NRA stood for the Roosevelt administration's first 100 days of efforts to end the Depression.

This eagle became the symbol of the NRA during the Great Depression.

What do you think

Why do you think Congress passed more laws in this period than at any other time in American history?

Lesson 2 Review Choose the best word or name in parentheses to complete each sentence. Write your answers on a sheet of paper.

1. The (Reconstruction Finance Corporation, New Deal, Agricultural Marketing Act) allowed for $500 million to buy surplus crops from farmers.

2. President (Hoover, Roosevelt) promised the New Deal to Americans.

3. The (national bank holiday, Emergency Banking Act, National Recovery Administration) prohibited people from rushing to the banks to take their money out.

4. The (Agricultural Adjustment Act, Federal Emergency Relief Administration, Civilian Conservation Corps) loaned millions of dollars to state agencies.

5. The (Emergency Banking, Truth-in-Securities, Agricultural Adjustment) Act attempted to raise farm prices by cutting back production.

Biography

Marian Anderson: 1897–1993

Philadelphia-born Marian Anderson studied classical singing in Europe. She had a wonderful homecoming in 1935 with a concert at New York's Town Hall. Anderson was praised for her glorious voice, her beauty, and her dignity. She also became a symbol for African American resistance to injustice. In 1939, she was denied permission to sing at Constitution Hall in Washington, D.C., because of her race. The Secretary of the Interior fought the injustice by asking Anderson to perform at the Lincoln Memorial. She sang there the following Easter Sunday before 75,000 people. In 1955, Marian Anderson became the first African American to sing a role in the Metropolitan Opera. Thereafter, she toured 12 nations as a performing goodwill ambassador for the United States. After retiring, Anderson supported human rights and young performers.

Mural

An artistic painting or drawing on a wall

During the first stage of the New Deal, the government focused on giving immediate relief to those most in need. These steps helped put the nation back on the road to economic recovery. The second stage, called the Second New Deal, tried to make economic reforms. These reforms changed the role of the federal government in the lives of Americans.

Which Reforms Changed the Government's Role?

In April 1935, Congress passed a $4.8 billion jobs program. It created the Works Progress Administration (WPA) to put every unemployed person to work. The WPA went on to build schools, hospitals, playgrounds, museums, and airports. Actors were hired to put on plays. Musicians were paid to give concerts. Artists were employed to paint **murals** on the walls of government buildings. Artists also produced hundreds of posters. They announced many new programs and encouraged people to travel. Eight million Americans found work with the WPA. The jobs helped restore self-respect and confidence in American workers. The restoration of the workforce helped ease the Depression. More stores opened. Factories began to hire workers as demand for their products increased.

The Works Progress Administration (WPA) offered millions of Americans jobs working on public projects. Beginning in 1936, nearly $7 billion was spent on the program. The program did much to build and repair the nation's public resources. Workers paved or repaired 280,000 miles of roads. They built 29,000 bridges and 150 airfields. They also built 4,383 new schools and repaired or added on to 30,000 others. They constructed more than 130 hospitals. The agency closed in 1943.

This poster from 1939 was for the National Park Service.

Before the time of the New Deal, the federal government usually sided with business during labor disputes. However the new National Labor Relations Act, or Wagner Act, gave workers the right to form unions. Employers could not stop workers from forming a union. The National Labor Relations Board, a government agency, made sure the vote whether to join a union was fair. For the first time, the United States government encouraged unions and employers to discuss wages and working conditions. Differences could be settled peacefully in a process of **collective bargaining**. This was a way of negotiating between groups of workers and their employers.

Many unemployed laborers found work through the Works Progress Administration.

One of the most important reforms of the New Deal was the Social Security Act of 1935. Government programs took responsibility for Americans who were elderly, unemployed, or **disabled**. Someone who is disabled faces mental or physical challenges. Many of the suggestions for this law were made by Secretary of Labor Frances Perkins. She was the first woman to become a member of a president's Cabinet.

Social Security Act of 1935

Pension Benefits for the Elderly	Unemployment Compensation	Disability Benefits
Money for the pensions came from two new taxes. One tax came from the employee's pay. An equal amount came from the employer.	The employer paid an additional tax to pay unemployed workers until they found work.	Payments were made to disabled or blind Americans.

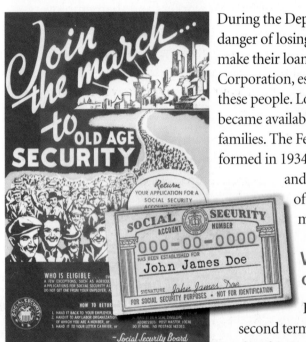

This poster from 1936 encouraged people to support Social Security programs. A Social Security card (inset) may be applied for at birth.

During the Depression, many Americans were in danger of losing their homes because they could not make their loan payments. The Home Owners Loan Corporation, established in 1933, was designed to help these people. Low-interest, long-term home loans became available to more than a million American families. The Federal Housing Administration (FHA), formed in 1934, encouraged low-cost home building and repair. It also offered banks a guarantee of repayment of loans to lower- and middle-income Americans.

Who Won the Election of 1936?

Franklin Roosevelt was elected to his second term as president in November 1936. Alf Landon, his Republican Party opponent, carried only two states—Maine and Vermont. It was a historically important election for Roosevelt and the Democratic Party. This was the first time in American history that three groups—organized labor, farmers, and African Americans—had voted in large numbers for a Democratic Party presidential candidate.

For African Americans this was a major change. Since the late 1860s, African Americans had generally voted for the Republican candidates, because they belonged to the party of Abraham Lincoln. Aid from New Deal programs convinced many African Americans to vote for Roosevelt.

How Did the Supreme Court React to Reforms?

Roosevelt and his New Deal programs ran into problems with the Supreme Court. Most of the members of the Supreme Court believed some of the New Deal legislation was unconstitutional.

The Supreme Court declared the National Recovery Act and the Agricultural Adjustment Act unconstitutional. This declaration angered President Roosevelt. He believed that the "nine old men" on the Supreme Court stood in the way of progress. Six of the justices were over 70 years old. Roosevelt decided to appoint a new justice for every justice over the age of 70.

The six new justices, Roosevelt thought, would assure that New Deal laws would not be **overturned** by the Supreme Court. Roosevelt's decision was not well accepted. Members of Congress **denounced** it as political "court-packing." Many Americans also rejected the plan.

However, as the older justices retired, Roosevelt appointed younger, more **liberal** justices. Liberals favor change. These young justices were some of the most important justices in American history—Hugo Black, William O. Douglas, and Felix Frankfurter.

How Did Labor Unions Change?

In 1881, the American Federation of Labor (AFL) had been formed. This labor union was made up of only skilled workers. Unskilled factory workers could not belong. Therefore, they had no union to represent them. The skilled workers were organized by **occupation**. Each occupation area formed its own union within the AFL. The AFL served as a governing body over all of the smaller unions.

One union leader, John L. Lewis, thought an industry-wide union was necessary. He felt that all workers, including factory workers, steelworkers, and autoworkers, should be admitted to one union.

Lewis formed a committee for industrial organizations within the AFL. However, the more **traditional** labor leaders were against this committee. Lewis broke away and established the Congress of Industrial Organizations (CIO) in 1935.

Overturn

To reverse

Denounce

To reject or show disapproval

Liberal

One who favors change

Occupation

A person's job or line of work

Traditional

The usual way of doing things

The CIO united workers from all industries into one organization. The new union used the National Labor Relations Act to increase its membership to 6 million workers by 1945. Unlike traditional unions, the CIO welcomed all workers, skilled and unskilled, including women, immigrants, and African Americans. In 1955, the American Federation of Labor and the Congress of Industrial Organizations became one organization. The new union was named the AFL-CIO.

Word Bank

American Federation

Industrial Organizations

Labor Relations

Social Security

Works Progress

Lesson 3 Review On a sheet of paper, write the correct words from the Word Bank to complete each sentence.

1. The _____ Act set up programs to help the elderly, unemployed, or disabled.

2. The National _____ Act gave workers the right to form unions.

3. The _____ Administration gave people work.

4. The _____ of Labor was made up of only skilled workers.

5. The Congress of _____ united workers from all industries.

What do you think

Why is it important to set up programs to protect the elderly, disabled, and unemployed?

Focus on Economics

Many laws passed to ease the Great Depression are still going strong today. The Federal Deposit Insurance Corporation (1933) first insured bank deposit losses up to $2,500. Today, it insures losses up to $100,000. The Fair Labor Standards Act (1938) set a minimum wage and maximum number of hours to be worked per week. In 2004, the minimum hourly wage was $5.15, with a 40-hour work week.

The best-known program carried over from the Great Depression is the Social Security Act of 1935. Originally, it provided cash to retired industry and commerce workers. Over the years, it expanded to include widows, farm workers, and state workers. Disability insurance and Medicare were included to care for lower-income and retired workers. Today, nearly every U.S. worker is part of the system.

The Great Depression affected the life of most Americans. Many people suffered great hardships. In the hard times, though, life went on. People could escape into a theater and watch a movie for five cents. The public was eager to see a world different from its own. Hollywood provided that world through movies. The movies of the 1930s gave the American public a new world of comedy, musicals, and drama.

Ginger Rogers and Fred Astaire became America's favorite dancing couple. Child star Shirley Temple usually played an orphan with a big heart and a positive outlook. Americans laughed at the crazy comedy of the Marx brothers and their humorous adventures. A favorite film among children in 1939 was *The Wizard of Oz*. A song from this film gave viewers hope that there might be a happier life "Somewhere Over the Rainbow."

Another popular movie of 1939 was *Gone With the Wind*. It told the story of Scarlett O'Hara and the destruction of her family's Georgia plantation during the Civil War. It described the American South during another period of hard times. At the end of the movie, Scarlett's world had totally changed; yet she had survived. The message of the story seemed to be one that the nation in the hard times of the 1930s wanted to hear.

Who Were Some Heroes of the 1930s?

In 1938, Joe Louis, the heavyweight champion of the world, stepped into the boxing ring. His opponent was a German boxer named Max Schmeling. The German government published harsh words that they said came from Schmeling: "I would not take this fight if I did not believe that I, a white man, can beat a Negro." Schmeling never said these words. Joe Louis had to prove that an American could defeat a representative of Germany. Two minutes and four seconds after it began, the fight was over. Louis had won. On that night, Louis became a national hero.

In 1936, over 5,000 athletes met in Berlin, Germany, to participate in the Olympic games. German leader Adolf Hitler hoped to prove that white German athletes were better than any other athletes. This hope was shattered by the performance of an African American athlete named Jesse Owens. Owens won four Olympic gold medals.

Jesse Owens (left) shattered Adolf Hitler's claim that white German athletes were the best in the world. Owens won four gold medals in the 1936 Olympics in Berlin, Germany.

In 1928, Amelia Earhart had become the first woman passenger and keeper of the logbook on a transatlantic flight. She flew from Newfoundland, Canada, to Wales in the United Kingdom. She went on to write a book about her experiences. Then, in 1932, Earhart became the first woman to fly alone over the Atlantic Ocean. She made the first solo flight from Hawaii to the United States in 1935. She gave talks to promote flying and to give women encouragement. In 1937, in an attempt to fly around the world, Earhart disappeared somewhere over the Pacific Ocean.

Amelia Earhart

What do you think

What themes do you think were present in entertainment in the 1930s?

Lesson 4 Review On a sheet of paper, write the answers to the following questions. Use complete sentences.

1. Why did people who lived during the Depression like watching movies or other entertainment?

2. Why did people like *Gone With the Wind*?

3. What did the song "Somewhere Over the Rainbow" from *The Wizard of Oz* suggest about finding a happier life?

4. What did Joe Louis do?

5. How did Jesse Owens spoil Adolf Hitler's hopes?

History in Your Life

The Development of Nylon

In the mid-1930s, Wallace H. Carothers and a team of scientists spun the first successful artificial fiber. A research chemist for Du Pont Laboratories, Carothers called the durable fiber nylon. He had experimented with fibers since the late 1920s. Using a special machine, he was able to make longer molecules than ever before. Fibers made from the compounds he used could be pulled to several times their original length. Pulling made the fibers stronger and more elastic.

Du Pont introduced the first nylon product—a toothbrush with nylon bristles—in the late 1930s. Then the first nylon stockings went on sale. Today nylon is made into powder, fibers, sheets, rods, and tubes. It is used to make parachutes, carpets, tires, clothing, fishing line, surgical thread, electrical equipment, and sporting goods. Plastic nylon panels replace steel on some automobiles. From clothes to cars, Americans enjoy the benefits of nylon every day.

Breadline

The impact of the Depression on the lives of Americans could be seen in the nation's cities. Out-of-work men gathered in breadlines to get something to eat. A few men carried signs asking for a job. This selection concerns the life of an out-of-work man in San Francisco from December 1931 to December 1933.

A wet and cold day in December, 1931, I was an active member of the breadline on Ritch Street in San Francisco. . . . I knew by bitter experience that it would be at least two hours before I could dip into a bowl of waterlogged stew. I was ravenously hungry, friendless, homeless, and far removed from the possibilities of obtaining a job.

It was four o'clock in the morning, and still pitch-dark, when our advance guard appeared and took up its position six abreast outside the municipal kitchen. . . . By six o'clock, when the actual feeding started, the line had reached as far as Folsom Street, when every moment brought its quota of semistarved, shabby, despairing men. . . .

During the daylight hours I roamed all over the city looking for work. Hatless, clad in overalls and heavy, hobnailed boots, peaked and hungry-looking, badly in need of a haircut, I must have been a sight. People didn't waste promises or interviews when I turned up. With a few exceptions they gave the cold shoulder. . . .

By the summer of 1932, I looked at least ten years older. My weight under normal conditions is about 170 pounds. After four months in the breadline I tipped the scales at 125. My ribs protruded like laths [boards], and my lusterless eyes had retreated way back into dark-ringed sockets.

I didn't beg or ransack the garbage cans; nor did I rob or steal. Instead, I walked about for hours, eyes glued to the sidewalk, looking for lost coins . . . I never found. . . .

I ate and slept in the San Francisco breadline and flophouses from the first of May to the first of December, 1933. . . . My total monthly expenses amounted to seventy cents. Thirty cents went for the purchase of a daily loaf of stale bread, at a penny a loaf, the remaining forty cents kept me in tobacco. . . .

Document-Based Questions

1. In December 1931, where did the man find himself and why was he there?

2. What did the man do during the daylight hours?

3. How did his physical appearance change?

4. By 1933, had his life improved? Why or why not?

5. By the end of 1933, what government help could this man expect?

Source: "Bread Line," The Atlantic Monthly, by Hugo Johanson, August, 1936.

Chapter 25 SUMMARY

- Following the stock market crash of 1929, the country fell into an economic slump known as the Great Depression.

- There were many reasons for the Depression. Business had expanded too rapidly. More products were made than people could buy. Businesses laid off workers. Many people bought things on credit and when they lost their jobs, they couldn't pay their debts. There were high tariffs placed on American products. Prices for farm products continued to decline.

- Many people were unemployed. Many were left homeless and had no way of buying food. People moved from place to place in search of work.

- President Hoover tried helping in several ways, but most of his plans and policies failed. Most of the American people blamed Hoover for the problems of the Depression.

- Franklin Delano Roosevelt became president in 1933. He set up a number of social and economic programs called the "New Deal." Among these were the Works Progress Administration (WPA), the Civilian Conservation Corps (CCC), and the Tennessee Valley Authority (TVA).

- The Social Security Act of 1935 set up the Social Security system to help the elderly and disabled.

- Frances Perkins, the first woman on a president's Cabinet, became secretary of labor under Roosevelt.

- The labor movement grew as John L. Lewis left the American Federation of Labor (AFL) and formed the Congress of Industrial Organizations (CIO).

- Roosevelt put new justices on the Supreme Court who would support his policies. Congress and the American people objected.

- The films of the period reflected the mood of the times by offering people an escape from their hardships.

- Roosevelt's plans and policies helped bring the United States out of the Great Depression.

Chapter 25 REVIEW

Word Bank

breadlines

Civilian Conservation Corps

Frances Perkins

Joe Louis

New Deal

overproduction

Social Security

Supreme Court

unemployment

Works Progress Administration

On a sheet of paper, write the correct word or words from the Word Bank to complete each sentence.

1. During the Depression, _____ was high because there were no jobs.

2. There were too many products and not enough people to buy them because of _____.

3. Soup kitchens and _____ helped feed people who had no money for food.

4. Roosevelt promised a "_____" for Americans.

5. _____ beat Max Schmeling in a highly publicized boxing match.

6. The _____ employed young people who planted trees, built roads, and worked on flood control.

7. The _____ Act of 1935 created programs to help the elderly, unemployed, and disabled.

8. The goal of the _____ was to put every unemployed person to work.

9. The first woman to be on a president's Cabinet was Secretary of Labor _____.

10. Roosevelt called the _____ "nine old men."

On a sheet of paper, write the letter of the answer that best completes each sentence.

11. People held Herbert Hoover responsible for _____.

   A Social Security
   B the Great Depression
   C the crash of Wall Street
   D closing charities

12. President Roosevelt felt it necessary to reform _____.

   A America's economic system
   B the Works Progress Administration
   C the Congress
   D war debts

13. By winning four Olympic gold medals in 1936, _____ defeated Hitler's plan to show German superiority.

   A Amelia Earhart   **C** Joe Louis

   B Jesse Owens   **D** Fred Astaire

On a sheet of paper, write the answer to each question. Use complete sentences.

14. What were some factors that caused the Great Depression?

15. What was life like during the Great Depression?

16. What were four programs that Roosevelt set up as part of the "New Deal?"

17. Why were the slums set up during the Depression called "Hoovervilles"?

Critical Thinking On a sheet of paper, write your response to each question. Use complete sentences.

18. Social Security was started during the Great Depression. Do you think Social Security is still important today? Explain your answer.

19. People went to the movies to escape the problems of the Depression. How does television today compare with the movies during the Depression?

20. If there were a massive depression today, do you think the government should step in and provide jobs? Why or why not?

Test-Taking Tip

When a teacher announces a test, listen carefully. Write down the topics that the teacher will include on the test. Ask if you have any questions about what the test will cover.

26 World War II

President Roosevelt's plans to bring the nation out of the Great Depression had helped. However, an even greater problem was on the horizon for the United States. After World War I, President Wilson had warned that the world might be in danger of another war in the future. As the 1930s ended, Europe was once again in trouble. A second world war, far more damaging than the first, began as Wilson had said. In this chapter, you will learn what caused World War II, how the war affected American life, and how the war ended.

Goals for Learning

◆ To describe events in Europe and Asia in the 1920s and 1930s and the reactions of the United States

◆ To explain the steps that led to World War II

◆ To describe how Germany came to control most of Europe, and why France and Great Britain declared war on Germany

◆ To describe the events at Pearl Harbor

◆ To describe life in the United States during the war

◆ To explain how American involvement affected the outcome of the war

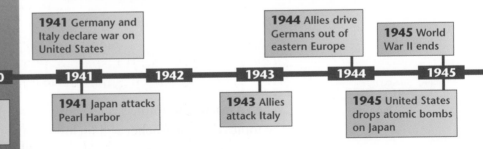

1939 World War II begins

1939 Germany Takes over several countries in Europe

1941 Germany and Italy declare war on United States

1941 Japan attacks Pearl Harbor

1943 Allies attack Italy

1944 Allies drive Germans out of eastern Europe

1943 Allies attack Italy

1945 World War II ends

1945 United States drops atomic bombs on Japan

1939 1940 1941 1942 1943 1944 1945

Fascist

One who believes that the state is more important than the individual

Inflation

A steady rise in prices of goods

Before and during the Great Depression in the United States, other countries around the world had depressions of their own. The social and economic problems of these different countries brought different outcomes. For example, Germany, Italy, and Japan fell under the control of dictators. The whole world would soon feel the effects of these dictators' beliefs that war might be a good solution to their nations' problems.

How Did Mussolini and Fascism Gain Support in Italy?

Benito Mussolini had controlled the Italian government since 1922. He believed that a strong leader must have full power to run the country. Under his dictatorship, other political parties were forbidden. Mussolini created the **Fascist** Party. Fascists believed the state was more important than the individual and rejected the idea of democracy. The Fascists believed military power and war were good for a nation. Italian Fascists used the slogan: "Believe! Obey! Fight!"

How Did Hitler and Nazism Gain Support in Germany?

The German people did not understand how they lost World War I. They were upset with the strict conditions of the peace settlement. When World War I ended, Germany removed its king and established a democracy. The new Republic of Germany tried to govern its troubled nation.

The economy in Germany fell apart in 1923. **Inflation** made German paper money nearly worthless. Inflation is a steady rise in prices of goods. Prices of goods doubled daily. Germans had to carry large bags of money just to buy food for one day. Many workers lost their jobs. The democratic government of Germany was criticized for being weak. The National Socialist German Workers' Party, or Nazi Party, opposed the German government. Adolf Hitler led the Nazis.

Chancellor

Hitler used his skills as a public speaker and organizer to increase the power of the Nazi Party. Hitler declared that democracy was weak and could not solve the nation's problems. He added that the economic crisis was not the fault of the Germans. He blamed Germany's problems on others. He told Germans that Communists and Jews were trying to destroy their government. He promised prosperity for all Germans. He preached against democracy and for hatred of the Jews.

Chancellor

The chief minister in some European countries

Citizenship

The condition of belonging to a certain country

Adolf Hitler became the **chancellor,** or chief minister, of Germany in 1933. This happened after his Nazi Party had won a majority of seats in Germany's Parliament. Within months, Hitler became a dictator. He gave himself the title "der Führer." It meant "the leader." Hitler and the Nazi Party quickly destroyed German democracy and individual freedoms.

Hitler was successful in improving the German economy. German unemployment dropped. The standard of living for most Germans rose. Hitler continued a campaign against German Jews. He called them traitors. German Jews lost their **citizenship** and their jobs. Citizenship is the condition of belonging to a certain country.

German dictator Adolf Hitler (second from right) inspects troops.

How Did Fascism Begin in Spain?

A civil war broke out in Spain in 1936. General Francisco Franco and his forces fought against anti-Fascists. The anti-Fascists wanted Spain to have a democratic government. The Spanish Civil War became a test for the Fascist governments of Germany and Italy. Italy sent troops to fight in Spain, and German planes bombed Spanish cities.

The Communist government of the Soviet Union supported the anti-Fascists. Anti-Fascist volunteers from Great Britain, France, and the United States also fought in this war. The Americans who fought did so by their own choice, not as members of the American military. The Spanish Civil War lasted three years. The Spanish Fascist forces, supported by the governments of Italy and Germany, won in 1939. Franco became the leader of a new Fascist government.

How Did Japan Establish Control in Asia?

The worldwide depression also hurt Japan, an island nation in Asia. Japanese industries needed imported coal, oil, and iron. The depression made it difficult for nations to trade with each other. Without enough raw materials, Japan found its industries threatened.

Japan relied on imported rice to help feed its people. Unable to grow enough rice on their own, many Japanese had no food. Radical military leaders, similar to those in Germany and Italy, took control of the Japanese government. The army seized Manchuria, an area rich in coal and iron, from China. In 1937, Japan invaded China again and captured several important cities. Japan had taken its first steps to control Asia and establish a Japanese empire.

Biography

Eleanor Roosevelt: 1884–1962

Eleanor Roosevelt was a diplomat and humanitarian. She became a model for women in politics and public affairs. As First Lady when her husband Franklin D. Roosevelt was president, she had a great deal of influence. She lectured and wrote a daily newspaper column that was widely published.
Active in Democratic politics, Roosevelt was a champion for the rights of women and minorities. As U.S. delegate to the United Nations, she chaired the UN's Human Rights Commission. She also took a central role in drafting the UN's Universal Declaration of Human Rights. Her uncle was President Theodore Roosevelt.

How Did America View the Problems in Europe?

Americans did not want to deal with the problems in Europe. During the 1930s, Americans had a much larger problem at home with the Great Depression. The New Deal programs took time to plan and put to use.

There was another reason Americans ignored problems in Europe. The memory of World War I was still fresh in their minds. Americans wanted no part of another foreign war. Many people felt that the United States was protected by possible attacks because of the Atlantic and Pacific oceans. Congress passed laws in 1935 and 1937 to make sure that the United States stayed neutral. These laws prevented the sale of arms or lending money to countries at war. Throughout the 1930s, Americans watched Germany, Italy, and Japan increase in military strength.

President Roosevelt was not so certain that the United States should ignore what was going on in Europe. Beginning in 1937, he tried to keep the country aware of the problems there. For that reason, some people criticized Roosevelt. They thought he wanted to start a war.

Lesson 1 Review Choose the best word or name in parentheses to complete each sentence. Write your answers on a sheet of paper.

1. (Hitler, Mussolini, Franco) started the Fascist Party in Italy.

2. (Hitler, Mussolini, Franco) became chancellor of Germany in 1933.

3. The (anti-Fascists, Fascists) in Spain wanted a democratic government.

4. The Spanish Civil War lasted (two, three, four) years.

5. Japan invaded (Italy, Spain, China) in 1937.

What do you think ?

Why do you think some countries in Europe started to have dictators as leaders?

Reich

A German empire

During the years of the Spanish Civil War, Hitler moved aggressively to expand his power in Europe. His goal was to bring the German-speaking people of Austria, Czechoslovakia, and Poland under German rule. Twice before in history, the German people had built a **reich,** or empire, in Europe. Hitler wanted to create a Third Reich.

How Did European Leaders Give in to Hitler?

Hitler took the first step in creating a German empire in March 1938. German troops marched into Austria and declared it part of the German Third Reich. Although this action went against the Treaty of Versailles, the League of Nations did nothing to stop it. Hitler's next move was to bring three million Germans living in the Sudetenland into the Third Reich. The Sudetenland was an area of Czechoslovakia. Hitler threatened to use force. To avoid war, Neville Chamberlain, the prime minister of Great Britain, suggested that the major powers of Europe meet.

European leaders met in Munich, Germany, in 1938. Among those present were (from front left) Neville Chamberlain, Edouard Daladier, Adolf Hitler, and Benito Mussolini.

Appeasement

*Doing something
to keep peace*

Synagogue

*A Jewish place of
worship*

Chamberlain, Mussolini, Hitler, and Edouard Daladier of France
met in Munich, Germany, in September 1938. Czechoslovakia
was not represented. Hitler believed that the threat of war would
frighten the leaders of Great Britain and France. He thought that
they would give in to his demands. Chamberlain and Daladier did
just that. Both leaders agreed to give Germany the Sudetenland.
They felt a policy of **appeasement** was best. Appeasement is doing
something to keep peace. Hitler agreed to make no more advances
for territory. When Chamberlain returned to Britain, he said that
the meeting in Munich had produced "peace with honor . . . peace
in our time."

*German soldiers
gathered this group of
Jewish women and
children in Warsaw,
Poland, in 1943.*

What Was the Holocaust?

On the night of November 9, 1938, Nazis set fire to Jewish
places of worship called **synagogues**. They also broke into
Jewish homes, terrorized Jewish people, and destroyed Jewish
businesses. This night of terror is called "Kristallnacht," or the
"Night of Broken Glass." Many Jews were killed or arrested.
This was only the beginning of the terror the Jews faced.

In 1939, Germany set up death camps for the Jews as a part of Hitler's "final solution." The Nazis planned to murder every Jew they could find. Jews were sent by train to the death camps. Men, women, and children were killed with gas or gunfire in these camps. Many bodies were burned in large ovens.

When it became widely known in 1945 that this **Holocaust** had occurred, the world was shocked. The government of Nazi Germany had killed nearly six million innocent European Jews. In the eyes of the Germans, the Jews were **inferior** simply because of their **ethnic heritage.** For many years after the end of World War II, Nazi war criminals were hunted and brought to justice.

Why Did Germany Attack Poland?

The Treaty of Versailles, signed at the end of World War I, had given Poland a strip of land called the Polish Corridor. On this piece of land, Poland gained access to the Baltic Sea. The Germans never liked this arrangement. The Polish Corridor isolated East Prussia and the German city of Danzig from the rest of Germany. In March 1939, Hitler demanded that Poland give back the city of Danzig in order for Germany to build a railroad through the Polish Corridor. Poland refused. Great Britain and France supported Poland. Both countries said they would go to war to defend Poland. Great Britain and France expected help from the Soviet Union in a fight against Germany.

However, Germany and the Soviet Union had signed a treaty of friendship in August 1939. The Soviet leader, Joseph Stalin, agreed not to interfere if Germany attacked Poland. In return, Germany would give the Soviet Union the eastern half of Poland. Having gained the alliance of the Soviet Union, Hitler felt confident that he could successfully seize the Polish land.

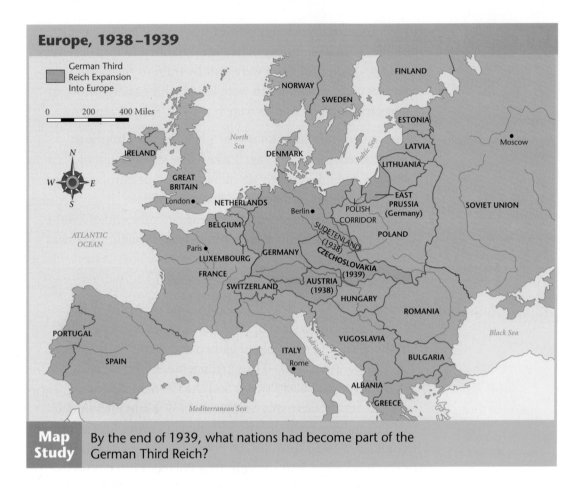

Europe, 1938–1939

☐ German Third
Reich Expansion
Into Europe

0   200   400 Miles

North Sea

Baltic Sea

ATLANTIC OCEAN

Mediterranean Sea

Adriatic Sea

Black Sea

FINLAND
NORWAY
SWEDEN
ESTONIA
LATVIA
LITHUANIA
• Moscow
IRELAND
DENMARK
GREAT BRITAIN
London •
NETHERLANDS
Berlin •
EAST PRUSSIA (Germany)
SOVIET UNION
BELGIUM
POLISH CORRIDOR
POLAND
SUDETENLAND (1938)
Paris •
LUXEMBOURG
GERMANY
CZECHOSLOVAKIA (1939)
FRANCE
SWITZERLAND
AUSTRIA (1938)
HUNGARY
ROMANIA
PORTUGAL
YUGOSLAVIA
ITALY
Rome •
BULGARIA
SPAIN
ALBANIA
GREECE

Map Study By the end of 1939, what nations had become part of the German Third Reich?

Word Bank

France

Holocaust

Soviet Union

Sudetenland

Third Reich

Lesson 2 Review On a sheet of paper, write the correct word or words from the Word Bank to complete each sentence.

1. Hitler's plan was to create a _____ by ruling other countries.

2. Chamberlain and Daladier agreed to give the _____ to Germany if Hitler would not seek more territory.

3. The murder of millions of Jews in Germany became known as the _____.

4. Hitler sought an agreement with the _____ in order to seize Poland.

5. Great Britain and _____ agreed to go to war to defend Poland from Germany.

What do you think ?

What do you think it was like to be a Jew living during the Holocaust?

Blitzkrieg
"Lightning war";
a rapid military attack

German soldiers moved rapidly into Poland by trucks on September 1, 1939. They were supported with tanks and bombing attacks by the German air force. This new method of warfare was called **blitzkrieg**, or "lightning war." This simple act of German aggression was the beginning of World War II.

Why Did France and Britain Declare War?

Troops of the Soviet Union also attacked Poland. Great Britain and France, attempting to aid Poland, declared war on Germany. While repeating his vow to remain neutral, President Roosevelt did not approve of the attack on Poland. He asked Congress to reverse its neutrality order so that the United States could sell weapons to France and Great Britain. After a long debate, the arms were made available.

A few weeks after the attack by the Soviet Union, Poland surrendered. Germany and the Soviet Union divided Poland between them. Through the winter of 1939 and 1940, there was little activity. Some people began to speak of a "phony war." The world watched and waited, however, for Hitler's next move. They remembered the Nazi phrase, "Today Germany, tomorrow the world!"

Suddenly, in April 1940, Germany attacked and defeated Denmark and Norway. The next month, Belgium, Luxembourg, and the Netherlands fell to the German army. Germany then attacked France. German soldiers broke through the French defensive line.

What Happened at Dunkirk?

More than 300,000 British, Belgian, and French soldiers were trapped between the attacking Germans and the sea. These allied troops retreated to Dunkirk, a seaport located in the north of France on the English Channel. Great Britain made a daring attempt to rescue these allied troops.

Hundreds of ships set sail from Great Britain for Dunkirk. Most of the troops were safely rescued and were in Great Britain on June 4, 1940. Six days later, Italy sided with Germany and declared war. France surrendered and requested an armistice. Hitler agreed.

What Was the Battle of Britain?

Great Britain was left alone to fight the Nazi war machine. If Great Britain was defeated, the United States would be without an ally in Europe. Prime Minister Winston Churchill spoke to the British people on June 4, 1940. He told them, "We shall defend our island, whatever the cost may be, we shall fight on the beaches . . . we shall fight in the fields and in the streets . . . we shall never surrender."

The British waited for a German invasion of their country. The German air force began around-the-clock bombing raids on Great Britain's air force bases in August 1940. The Royal Air Force (RAF) fought back. The RAF used a new **radar** system that located incoming planes. Many German bombers were destroyed. The Germans had to change their plans to invade Great Britain.

The German air force destroyed many buildings in London.

What Happened When Hitler Attacked the Soviet Union?

Hitler attacked the Soviet Union in June 1941. He ignored their friendship treaty. This decision was a major mistake for Hitler. Great Britain, Canada, Australia, the Soviet Union, and other nations joined together to fight Germany. These countries became known as the Allies. They realized that Hitler was attempting to gain control over all of Europe.

How Did America Come Closer to War?

Most Americans still did not want the United States to enter the war. However, Americans did not try to stay neutral, as in World War I. They became concerned about America's safety.

President Roosevelt told the American people that Great Britain needed help. Great Britain needed more weapons but did not have enough money to pay for the supplies. America had to be "the arsenal of democracy." Roosevelt proposed that the United States lend Great Britain military supplies. Congress passed the Lend-Lease Act in March 1941. This policy was designed to keep America out of war in Europe.

Under the Lend-Lease Act, the United States government would provide weapons to any country considered important to American **security**. These nations could buy, lease, exchange, or borrow equipment, weapons, and supplies from the United States. During World War II, the United States provided $50 billion in lend-lease aid to the Allies.

The United States began to prepare for the chance of war. Congress approved millions of dollars to strengthen the armed forces. The Selective Training and Service Act was passed in September 1940. This was the first peacetime law that drafted men into the armed forces. The last draft had been during World War I. Men between the ages of 21 and 35 were selected by a **lottery** to serve one year in the military. The lottery was a drawing of names. Later in the war, the age was lowered to 18. Men were then called to serve by age. The oldest went first.

The United States made a trade with Great Britain and loaned it 50 small warships called destroyers. In return, Great Britain leased naval and air bases to the United States in the Western Hemisphere. These bases allowed the United States to better defend itself and to keep watch over the Panama Canal.

What do you think?

How was World War II a war for democracy?

Lesson 3 Review On a sheet of paper, write the answers to the following questions. Use complete sentences.

1. What marked the beginning of World War II?

2. Which countries did Germany capture?

3. How did the British defend themselves against German attacks?

4. What was the Lend-Lease Act?

5. What was the Selective Service Act?

Civics Connection

The Selective Training and Service Act

The Selective Training and Service Act (SSA) gave Congress the right to draft young men into the armed forces. After World War II, the U.S. government stopped using the SSA. Then from 1948 until 1973, the draft was put back into effect. Tensions with the Soviet Union and Vietnam made Americans fear they would need a reserve of soldiers. Since 1973, the law has been in "standby" status. The law requires young men to register with the Selective Service at age 18. However, the draft will not resume unless there is an emergency.

Since World War II, the nature of world conflict has changed. Problems occur more quickly. American troops usually take part in small, short conflicts. If there were a large-scale conflict, the draft might have to be used again.

Some people argue that the draft robs young people of choice. They feel military service should be voluntary. They think the military should use benefits to attract volunteers. Today, because there is no draft, all members of the U.S. military are volunteers.

1. Do you think the Selective Training and Service Act is still a useful law? Explain.

2. Do you think the government should be able to draft young men for war? Explain.

Axis Powers

The alliance of Japan, Italy, and Germany in World War II

Asset

Something of worth that someone owns

The Japanese government announced that it intended to rule all of Asia, including China. That type of control went against America's Open Door Policy. The United States had established the policy so that all nations would be allowed free trade with China. America protested Japan's actions. However, Japan continued its plan to create an empire. Japan joined Germany and Italy in an alliance. These three countries became known as the **Axis Powers**.

Japan invaded the French colony of Indochina in June 1941. Indochina was just south of China. The United States became concerned that Japan was gaining too much land. America decided to stop selling oil and steel to Japan. Japan desperately needed oil to continue with its plan. The United States also offered a lend-lease program to China.

When Japan invaded Indochina, Roosevelt said Japan could not use money or investments it had in the United States. This is called freezing **assets**. Japan did the same thing to the United States. Trade between the two countries stopped.

Japan's Prime Minister Fumimaro Konoye and United States Secretary of State Cordell Hull began to negotiate. The Japanese wanted to be allowed to use their assets in the United States. They also wanted to be supplied with oil. The United States wanted Japan to withdraw from China and Southeast Asia. The negotiations failed. Hideki Tojo replaced Konoye as prime minister.

Why Did Japan Attack Pearl Harbor?

Early on December 7, 1941, a Sunday morning, 353 Japanese airplanes took off from six aircraft carriers in the Pacific Ocean. Their destination was the American naval base at Pearl Harbor, Hawaii, 220 miles away. Their mission was to destroy the American naval fleet anchored there. The Japanese thought they would be better able to conquer land in Asia if these American ships were destroyed.

Japan bombed ships in the harbor and planes on the ground. The surprise attack occurred at 7:55 A.M. Two hours later, the United States Pacific Fleet had lost many battleships, destroyers, and planes. The attack killed more than 2,000 Americans. Roosevelt said that December 7, 1941, was "a date which will live in **infamy.**" Four days later, Germany and Italy, Japan's allies, declared war on the United States.

Japan followed up its attack on Pearl Harbor by invading the Philippine Islands and other areas in the Pacific. American and Filipino troops fought the Japanese. However, they lacked planes, tanks, and ammunition. Japan gained another victory. It now controlled the Philippine Islands.

The USS West Virginia and the USS Tennessee were among the 19 American ships damaged or destroyed at Pearl Harbor.

History in Your Life

Rosie the Riveter and the Women of World War II

When America entered World War II, most healthy young men left their jobs for the armed forces. More than 4.5 million women took their place in support of the war effort. The lively song "Rosie the Riveter" was written in 1942. The title caught on as a friendly label for all women who became manufacturing workers. The song celebrated women's contributions on the homefront. Women worked in shipyards, steel mills, foundries, lumber mills, and aircraft and ammunition plants. They learned welding, electricity, mechanics, engineering, and chemistry. Women farmed, drove buses, wrote newspaper features, and played in the country's orchestras. Americans relied on female police officers, attorneys, and doctors. Thousands of American women also served in the military. These wartime changes helped break down job discrimination against women.

Japanese Expansion in Asia and the Pacific

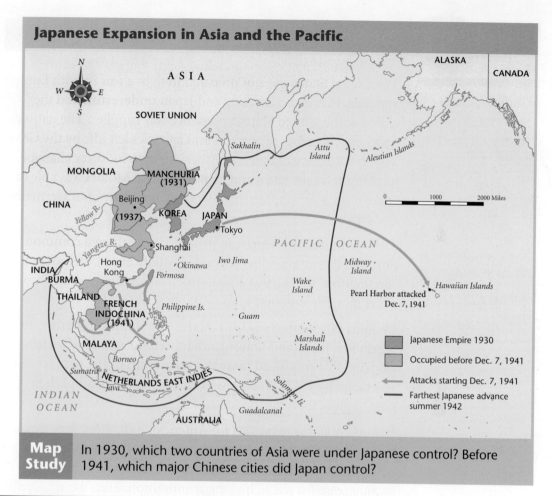

Word Bank

assets

Axis Powers

Open Door

Pearl Harbor

Philippine Islands

Lesson 4 Review On a sheet of paper, write the word or words from the Word Bank to complete each sentence.

1. The United States opposed Japan's plan to rule Asia because it went against the American _____ policy with China.

2. Japan, Italy, and Germany were the _____.

3. When Japan attacked Indochina, the United States froze Japanese _____ and stopped selling oil and steel to Japan.

4. On December 7, 1941, the Japanese air force attacked the American fleet at _____ in Hawaii.

5. Next, the Japanese attacked and defeated the _____.

What do you think

How do you think Japan's entering the war made things worse for the Allies?

Underestimate

To guess the size or importance of something as being less than it is

Civilian

One who is not in the military

Ration

To use less or limit the amount of something

Combat

Battle

The United States was not prepared to fight a war in both Europe and Asia. However, Germany and Japan **underestimated** the ability of the United States to produce war supplies. The nation had a large number of workers and factories left idle by the Great Depression. For example, the American auto industry changed its plants to make tanks and planes. General Motors was able to make more war supplies than the combined output of Germany and Japan.

The war united the American people. It gave them a common purpose. Patriotic posters reminded Americans of their duty to "do their bit" for the war effort. American **civilians** aided the war effort in many different ways.

Millions of volunteers helped increase the supply of fresh vegetables. Parks and flower gardens were turned into "victory gardens" that produced more than one-third of the nation's vegetables by 1943. This allowed farmers to use most of their land to grow food for the armed forces.

Raw materials were needed for American industries. America became a nation of collectors. Volunteers collected tons of newspapers, tin cans, and rubber tires. Housewives collected bacon grease for use in making ammunition. Even worn nylon stockings were collected to make gunpowder bags for the navy.

Many goods were in short supply during the war. The government started to **ration** materials. This limited the amount of some goods that people could buy. Ration books contained stamps used to purchase gasoline, sugar, meat, and other products. A buyer had to pay the price for the product and a certain number of ration stamps. Shortages even changed the style of clothes. Men's pants were made without cuffs and women's dresses were shortened because extra cloth was needed for military uniforms.

Women joined the armed forces in great numbers. They served in Europe and Asia in every role except **combat.** Millions of women replaced men in the workforce. Women learned to build planes and tanks as the men left for war. They now had the opportunity to prove that they were as capable as any man.

Detention

The act of holding someone against his or her will

Writing About History

In your notebook, write how you feel about how Japanese Americans were treated during the war.

How Did Minorities Gain Access to Jobs During the War?

African Americans seeking jobs in the defense industry faced discrimination. A. Philip Randolph, an African American labor leader, threatened a march on Washington to protest the job discrimination. President Roosevelt responded by prohibiting racial discrimination in defense work and creating the Fair Employment Practices Committee. Because of the war emergency and worker shortages, African Americans were needed to work in the factories and at other jobs. However, the African Americans still faced discrimination. Strikes occurred at several shipyards by white workers when African Americans were hired. African American workers also successfully used strikes to protest unfair work rules and hiring practices.

How Were Japanese Americans Treated During the War?

The United States feared that Japan would invade its west coast. Some citizens thought people of Japanese ancestry living in America would aid the Japanese. President Roosevelt ordered the army to move about 110,000 of them to **detention** camps. Detention means holding people against their will. Many Japanese Americans lost their homes and businesses. Fear, the pressure of war, and prejudice caused the nation to set aside its democratic principles. Japanese American soldiers fought bravely in Europe while their government kept their parents and relatives in detention camps.

What do you think

Did detaining Japanese Americans hurt the nation? Why or why not?

Lesson 5 Review On a sheet of paper, write the answers to the following questions. Use complete sentences.

1. How was America able to produce war supplies?

2. What were victory gardens?

3. How did Americans reuse raw materials?

4. How were women involved in the war effort?

5. Why were Japanese Americans detained?

Despite the desire for **revenge** against Japan for Pearl Harbor, the United States decided that Hitler's Germany must be defeated first. The United States had strong ties to countries already defeated by Germany. Also, Germany seemed to be a greater threat to the Western Hemisphere than Japan did.

> **Revenge**
>
> *The act of getting back at someone for some wrongdoing*

The only way to defeat Germany was through an Allied invasion of Europe. The Allies planned to hit Germany from the south through Italy and invade France from Britain. At the same time, the Soviet Union could move against the Germans from the east.

What Happened in the Invasion of Italy?

American, Canadian, and British troops invaded Italy in September 1943. They captured the island of Sicily first. As Mussolini lost the island, the Italian people, tired of war, captured and executed him. The new, rebel Italian government soon surrendered to the Allied powers.

Determined to protect Germany's southern boundary, Hitler advanced toward Italy. The Allies finally captured the city of Rome on June 4, 1944. At this time, however, the Germans occupied most of northern Italy.

Then and Now

Think how many plastic things are around you right now. You would have found far fewer plastics in 1941 than you do today. The manufacture of plastic boomed during World War II because silk and rubber were difficult to obtain. Inventors found ways to make tires, ropes, and parachutes from plastic. Electric radio cables were insulated with plastic.

Just think how many times a day plastic helps make your life easier. Today, plastic is everywhere, and its uses are growing. People predict that someday plastic will be used to build entire houses and vehicles. Medical advances with plastics are dramatic. Tiny plastic capsules one day may replace flawed or missing cells in people with progressive diseases like diabetes.

How Did the Allies Push the Germans Back?

The Nazis, who had known for some time that the United States was planning an invasion, prepared the coast of France. The beaches became death traps. The Nazis laid exploding mines in the water. They strung barbed wire all along the sandy shore.

General Dwight D. Eisenhower, commander of the Allied armies, landed his troops on the beaches of Normandy, France, on June 6, 1944. This was known as D-Day. It was a very tough battle. However, by night, the Allies occupied about 60 miles of the French coast. They could begin to move toward Germany.

By December 1944, the Allies were confident that Germany's forces were trapped. But then, suddenly, the Germans **counterattacked**. The German army pushed through the Allied line. On a map of Europe, a large bulge represented Hitler's takeover of Allied territory. Led by General George Patton, the Allies counterattacked. The Germans were pushed back. The confrontation became known as the Battle of the Bulge. It was the last offensive by the German army.

World War II in Europe

Map Study In which country was the Battle of the Bulge fought? How many major battles were fought in 1943?

What Was the Yalta Agreement?

President Roosevelt was re-elected for a fourth term in 1944. The strain of the war had taken its toll. He was able to cope with his polio, but he suffered from a number of other physical problems.

There was hope that the war against Germany would end early in 1945. Allied leaders met in February 1945 in Yalta, a small town on the Black Sea in the Soviet Union. Roosevelt, Churchill, and Stalin agreed on a plan to follow when Germany surrendered. The plan became known as the Yalta Agreement.

The plan had several points. First, the Soviet Union agreed to enter the war against Japan. Second, Germany would be divided into four zones, each controlled by one of the Allies. Third, the Soviet Union would hold democratic elections in eastern European countries under its control. Fourth, a world organization called the United Nations would be created. The Yalta Agreement seemed reasonable at the time. However, after the war ended, parts of the agreement caused political problems between the United States and the Soviet Union.

How Did the War End?

President Franklin Roosevelt died suddenly in April 1945. The nation was in shock. Vice President Harry S. Truman became president. On April 25, 1945, Adolf Hitler killed himself in a **bunker** in Berlin. A bunker is an underground shelter. Germany surrendered. The war in Europe was over.

The United States began to control the advance of the Japanese military. The Allies were led by American Army General Douglas MacArthur and Navy Admiral Chester Nimitz. Japan lost Guadalcanal, the Philippines, Iwo Jima, and Okinawa. Despite the losses, the Japanese refused to surrender. The Allies began to plan an invasion of Japan.

Why Were Atomic Bombs Dropped on Japan?

President Truman learned that the United States had developed a new weapon called the **atomic bomb,** or A-bomb. This bomb could end the war, but it would cause enormous loss of Japanese lives. Truman was advised that over a million American soldiers' lives would be lost if the United States invaded Japan on land. Such an invasion would also kill countless Japanese people.

Hiroshima (above) was in ruins after an American plane dropped an atomic bomb on the city. The mushroom cloud (on facing page) shows what happens when an atomic bomb goes off.

In an effort to avoid using the atomic bomb, the president gave one last warning to Japan. Japan, however, refused to surrender. Truman decided that he must approve the use of the atomic bomb on Japan.

On August 6, 1945, from a plane named *Enola Gay*, the atomic bomb was dropped on the city of Hiroshima. The weapon destroyed that major Japanese city and instantly killed or wounded 130,000 people. Three days later, a second atomic bomb was dropped on the city of Nagasaki, killing or wounding 75,000 people. On August 14, 1945, Japan asked for a **cease-fire**. They wanted to end the fighting. General MacArthur accepted the formal surrender of Japan on September 2, 1945. World War II, the worst war in history, was finally over.

Cease-fire

A call for an end to fighting

Lesson 6 Review On a sheet of paper, write the correct word or words from the Word Bank to complete each sentence.

Word Bank

Battle of the Bulge

D-Day

Hiroshima

Sicily

Yalta

1. Allied troops captured _____ in 1943.

2. The attack on Normandy was called _____.

3. The Germans were pushed back in the _____.

4. Allied leaders met at _____.

5. America dropped atomic bombs on _____ and Nagasaki.

What do you think ?

World War II took millions of lives and ruined much of Europe. What do you think the world learned from the war?

Roosevelt's Four Freedoms Speech

During World War II, Americans gathered around radios to hear President Franklin Roosevelt's "fireside chats." The speeches meant much to those whose loved ones defended America overseas. Roosevelt gave this speech almost a year before America entered the war.

As men do not live by bread alone, they do not fight by armaments [weapons] alone. Those who man . . . and . . . build our defenses must have . . . an unshakable belief in the manner of life which they are defending. . . .

I have called for personal sacrifice. I am assured of the willingness of almost all Americans to respond to that call.

In the future days . . . we look forward to a world founded upon four essential human freedoms.

The first is freedom of speech and expression everywhere in the world.

The second is freedom of every person to worship God in his own way, everywhere in the world.

The third is freedom from want, which . . . means economic understandings which will secure to every nation a healthy peacetime life for all its inhabitants . . . .

The fourth is freedom from fear . . . a worldwide reduction of armaments to such a point . . . that no nation will be in a position to commit an act of physical aggression against any neighbor . . . a definite basis for a kind of world attainable in our own time. . . . That kind of world is the very antithesis of the so-called new order of tyranny which the dictators seek to create. . . .

A good society is able to face schemes of world domination and foreign revolutions alike without fear.

Since the beginning of our American history we have been engaged in . . . a perpetual, peaceful revolution . . . which goes on steadily . . . without the concentration camp . . . The world order which we seek is . . . free countries, working together in a friendly, civilized society.

Document-Based Questions

1. What was Roosevelt asking of the American people?

2. When did Roosevelt feel his ideas could be accomplished?

3. What were the four freedoms he named?

4. What is the world order Roosevelt said we sought?

5. Do you think Roosevelt expected America would enter another war? Why or why not?

Source: Four Freedoms Speech, by President Franklin Roosevelt, January 6, 1941.

- Benito Mussolini controlled the government of Italy. He created the Fascist Party.

- Francisco Franco became the leader of Spain after the Spanish Civil War.

- Adolf Hitler rose to power in Germany in the 1930s. In March 1938, Germany took over Austria and the Sudetenland. In September 1939, German forces invaded Poland. Following this act, France and Great Britain declared war on Germany.

- In 1940 Germany conquered Denmark, Norway, Belgium, the Netherlands, Luxembourg, and France. Germany continued to attack Great Britain and in June 1941 began an attack on the Soviet Union. The Allies—Australia, Canada, Great Britain, the Soviet Union and other countries—joined to fight Germany.

- Japan began to invade portions of Indochina and formed an alliance with Germany and Italy. This group was known as the Axis Powers. On December 7, 1941, Japanese bombers launched a surprise attack on the American naval fleet anchored in Pearl Harbor in Hawaii. Four days later Japan's allies declared war on the United States.

- America focused its military to help its allies in Europe. The first thrust was in Italy, where Mussolini's government soon fell. Germany moved quickly into Italy and stopped the Allies in Rome.

- On D-Day, June 6, 1944, Allied troops landed in France and began an assault. Over the next months, Allied forces gained more ground against the Germans. By the end of April 1945, Germany surrendered and the war in Europe was over.

- During the period in which the Nazis were in power, over six million innocent European Jews were killed in concentration camps and death camps. This period, known as the Holocaust, lasted over seven years.

- President Roosevelt died in April 1945, and Harry Truman became president.

- Allied forces began to capture Japanese-controlled territory. The Japanese were forced back to Japan. Truman issued a final warning, but Japan refused to surrender. In an attempt to prevent the loss of American lives, Truman ordered the dropping of the first atomic bombs on Japan. Japan surrendered on September 2, 1945, soon after the second bomb was dropped.

Chapter 26 REVIEW

Word Bank

Adolf Hitler

D-Day

detention camps

Dwight D.
    Eisenhower

Kristallnacht

Lend-Lease Act

Pearl Harbor

Third Reich

Winston Churchill

Yalta

On a sheet of paper, write the correct word or words from the Word Bank to complete each sentence.

1. _____ and his Nazi party attempted to make Germany the ruler of all Europe.

2. One of the early events in the Holocaust was called _____.

3. On December 7, 1941, the Japanese attacked the American fleet anchored in _____.

4. Hitler envisioned Germany as a huge empire called the _____.

5. Prime Minister _____ led Great Britain through the worst years of World War II.

6. Congress passed the _____ to help European countries fight Germany.

7. The Allied invasion of France began on June 6, 1944, which was called _____.

8. The commander of the Allied army was _____.

9. The American government forced thousands of Japanese Americans into _____.

10. Roosevelt, Stalin, and Churchill met in _____ to form an agreement for their roles after the war.

On a sheet of paper, write the letter of the choice that correctly completes each sentence.

11. _____ was the Fascist dictator of Italy from 1922 to 1943.

   A Francisco Franco   **C** Benito Mussolini

   B Neville Chamberlain   **D** Edouard Daladier

12. Germany and Japan seriously underestimated America's ability to _____.

    A produce war supplies   **C** feed itself

    B train soldiers   **D** ration Goods

13. _____ was one country that had been friendly with Hitler and later joined the Allies.

    A Australia   **C** Italy

    B India   **D** The Soviet Union

On a sheet of paper, write the answers to the following questions. Use complete sentences.

14. Why was the German style of warfare called blitzkrieg, or "lightning war"?

15. What did people do at home to help the war effort?

16. What events led up to the attack on Pearl Harbor?

17. How did World War II begin in Europe?

Critical Thinking On a sheet of paper, write your response to each question. Use complete sentences.

18. At the beginning of World War II, the United States was neutral. Do you think the war would have ended sooner if America had gotten involved earlier? Explain your answer.

19. How can studying events like the Holocaust help prevent such things from happening again?

20. President Truman had the choice to drop the atomic bomb rather than invading Japan. If you had been president, what choice would you have made?

Test-Taking Tip

When studying for a test, go over the topics in the chapter. Think about the most important ideas. Then make up a practice test for yourself.

Unit 8

Population Growth Table

A table is an arrangement of figures or information in columns and rows. It allows you to organize information in a clear way. It also allows you to interpret information easily and quickly.

The United States takes a census, or counts the population, every 10 years. The population table below shows the figures since 1930. In addition, the table gives the percent by which the population increased.

Population of the United States: 1930–2000		
Year	Number	Increase by Percent
1930	123,202,624	16.2
1940	132,164,569	15.4
1950	151,325,798	14.5
1960	179,323,175	18.5
1970	203,302,031	13.4
1980	226,542,199	11.4
1990	248,709,873	9.8
2000	281,421,906	13.2

Use the table in the left column to answer these questions. You may need to do some math to get some of your answers.

1. What was the U.S. population in 1940?

2. What was the U.S. population in 1970?

3. By what number did the population increase from 1980 to 1990?

4. What was the percent of increase between 1980 and 1990?

5. By what number did the population increase from 1930 to 2000?

6. In what period did the U.S. population increase the most? the least?

7. Estimate the population for 1965.

8. Based on information in this table, predict what the population might be in the year 2010.

9. Why do you think the government takes a census every 10 years?

10. Write a paragraph summarizing what you learned from the table.

- The Great Depression followed the stock market crash of 1929.

- Many were unemployed and homeless. They could not buy food.

- President Hoover tried helping. Most of his plans and policies failed. Most Americans blamed Hoover for the problems of the Depression.

- Franklin Roosevelt became president in 1933. His programs helped to bring the country out of the Depression.

- The Social Security Act of 1935 set up help for the elderly and disabled.

- John L. Lewis worked to organize labor.

- Roosevelt tried to put justices on the Supreme Court who would support his policies. Congress and the American people objected.

- Films and books offered an escape from people's hardships.

- In the 1930s, Fascist Benito Mussolini ruled Italy. Francisco Franco ruled Spain's Fascist government. Nazi Adolph Hitler rose to power in Germany.

- Germany invaded Poland in 1939. France and Great Britain declared war on Germany.

- In 1940, Germany conquered Denmark, Norway, Belgium, the Netherlands, and France. It attacked Great Britain. It began attacking the Soviet Union in 1941. The Allies joined to fight Germany.

- Japan formed an alliance with Germany and Italy called the Axis Powers. On December 7, 1941, Japan bombed the U.S. naval fleet in Pearl Harbor in Hawaii. America entered World War II the next day. Four days later the Axis Powers declared war on the United States.

- America first helped the Allies in Europe. Allied forces gained ground against the Germans. By the end of April 1945, Germany surrendered. The war in Europe was over.

- The Nazis killed over six million innocent European Jews in concentration and death camps. The Holocaust lasted over seven years.

- President Roosevelt died in April 1945. Harry Truman took office.

- Allied forces began capturing Japanese-controlled territory. Japanese forces retreated to Japan. Truman ordered the first atomic bombs dropped on Japan. After the second bomb, Japan surrendered on September 2, 1945.

"We cannot seek achievement for ourselves and forget about progress and prosperity for our community. . . . Our ambitions must be broad enough to include the aspirations and needs of others, for their sakes and for our own."

~ *Cesar Chavez, 1927–1993*

Unit 9

Postwar United States

Have you ever felt uneasy even when things were going well? The United States experienced both easy and uneasy times from 1945 to 1969. The nation was uneasy about Communism's grip on many parts of the world. Even though Americans enjoyed a sense of well-being in the 1950s, a time of social unrest began at home. The unrest increased during the 1960s but ended with positive civil rights laws. America cheered its successes in outer space during this time.

In this unit, you will learn about America's efforts to stop the spread of Communism. You will learn about how the nation lived through social uneasiness. You will learn about America's involvement in other wars and its place as a world leader. You will learn about its exploration of outer space.

Chapters in Unit 9

27 A Time of Challenge and Change

orld War II was over. The Allies had defeated the Nazis and the rest of the Axis Powers. The postwar period in America and Europe was a time of recovery. New world organizations were formed to prevent such damaging wars. At the same time, a new kind of struggle between the Soviet Union and the United States was beginning. In this chapter, you will learn about this struggle and the other changes that occurred after the war.

Goals for Learning

◆ To explain changes in the economy after World War II

◆ To describe the effects of the war, formation of the United Nations, the Fair Deal program, and the election of 1948

◆ To describe the beginnings of the cold war, the Marshall Plan, and NATO

◆ To explain America's involvement in the Korean War

◆ To describe America in the 1950s, including McCarthyism, the civil rights movement, family life, and the start of the space race

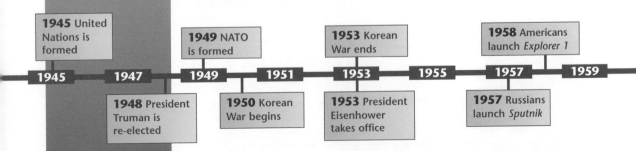

1945 United Nations is formed

1949 NATO is formed

1953 Korean War ends

1958 Americans launch *Explorer 1*

| 1945 | 1947 | 1949 | 1951 | 1953 | 1955 | 1957 | 1959 |

1948 President Truman is re-elected

1950 Korean War begins

1953 President Eisenhower takes office

1957 Russians launch *Sputnik*

Decline

Change to a lower level

White-collar

A name used to describe office workers and professionals

During World War II, the federal government focused the nation's economic resources on winning the war against Germany and Japan. When the war ended, the government faced serious economic problems at home.

How Did the Economy Change After the War?

The first problem was the fear of unemployment. The war effort had provided plenty of jobs for Americans at home. Now, 12 million men and women in the military would be "demobilized," or returned home to civilian life. Most of these people would be looking for work. In 1946, Congress passed the Full Employment Act. For the first time in American history, the federal government took responsibility for trying to help the economy provide jobs for the American people. As feared, when wartime production ended, the economy rapidly **declined**. However, this quickly changed. Americans wanted to buy cars, household products, and new homes. Few of these were produced during the war years.

What Was the GI Bill?

The GI Bill was an important law passed in 1944. Soldiers were called "GIs." After the war, this law provided former GIs with money to attend college and other benefits. Millions bought homes under the GI Bill. The GI Bill turned out to be a good economic investment. Americans became better educated. More people entered **white-collar** jobs. White-collar is a name used to describe office workers and professionals. Homes were now affordable for young families. Millions of new homes were built in areas surrounding cities, which were called suburbs. Large numbers of babies were born, creating a "baby boom." More children meant that more schools had to be built, creating more jobs for teachers. From 1946 into the 1960s, the United States was the strongest economy in the world. Two decades of economic prosperity led to the creation of a large American middle class.

How Did Farming Help the Economy?

After World War II, American farmers became the most productive in the world. Using science and technology, American farmers produced a surplus of food. The government bought much of this surplus and shipped it to Europe. Gas-powered tractors replaced horse and human labor. Scientific research developed grains that could resist disease. Using different machines, a single farmer could plow, plant, seed, and harvest various crops. A farm machine could dig up thousands of potatoes and put them in sacks in a matter of hours. Mechanical pickers harvested fruit. Modern irrigation systems assured that farmers would have enough water. Because of these improvements that saved time and labor, farming became a major part of the nation's growing economy.

What do you think?

Do you think it was a good idea for the federal government to help provide jobs? Why or why not?

Lesson 1 Review On a sheet of paper, write the answers to the following questions. Use complete sentences.

1. How did the U.S. government use the nation's economic resources during World War II?

2. Why was there a concern about unemployment after the war?

3. How did the government try to help provide jobs?

4. What did the GI Bill provide for former soldiers?

5. What was the baby boom?

Focus on Economics

GI Bill of Rights

President Franklin D. Roosevelt signed the "Servicemen's Readjustment Act of 1944" on June 22, 1944. This bill, known as the GI Bill of Rights, provided benefits and opportunities to attend college for veterans of World War II. Congress passed the bill because there were concerns about the country having enough jobs for returning war veterans. The bill allowed veterans to attend college rather than look for work immediately. The program for World War II veterans ended in 1956. Many feel that this bill was one of the best laws Congress ever passed. The modern GI Bill has continued to provide scholarships and other benefits to veterans.

Americans were happy that World War II had ended. Thousands celebrated in the streets of the nation's cities as their friends and loved ones returned home from the war. They waved flags, honked horns, cheered, and cried.

Germans cleared rubble from the streets of Berlin, Germany, after the war.

What Damages Did the War Cause?

The death and destruction caused by World War II was the worst in history. More than 55 million people died. The United States alone lost nearly 400,000 military men and women. Many millions more were seriously wounded. The bombings of Europe and Japan caused millions of civilian deaths.

The damage to cities in Europe cost well over $200 billion. Direct costs of fighting by all the countries combined was over a trillion dollars. Of that sum, America had spent $360 billion. For many years to come, the world would feel the effects of World War II.

How Did the War Change America's Role?

Americans knew that their role in the world had changed. The country could never again isolate itself from world problems. The United States was now one of the most powerful nations in the world. Not only did the nation have the power of the atomic bomb, but also it had new responsibilities in the world. In the months following the end of the war, Americans were uncertain how the country should move on. However, people did know that they wanted to develop a way to keep a lasting peace.

Why Was the United Nations Formed?

Delegates from 50 nations met in San Francisco, California, in April 1945. They created the United Nations (UN), a new world organization. Member countries of the General Assembly would come up with peaceful methods of settling international problems. They wanted to do a better job of preventing wars than the League of Nations had. The UN set up a Security Council. Eleven members (now 15) had the responsibility of keeping the peace. The United States, Great Britain, France, the Soviet Union, and China were made permanent members of the Security Council.

In response to the treatment of the Jews during World War II, the UN General Assembly declared **genocide** unlawful. Genocide is the killing of a group based on its race or political views. The assembly agreed that any country found guilty of this practice would be brought before an international court.

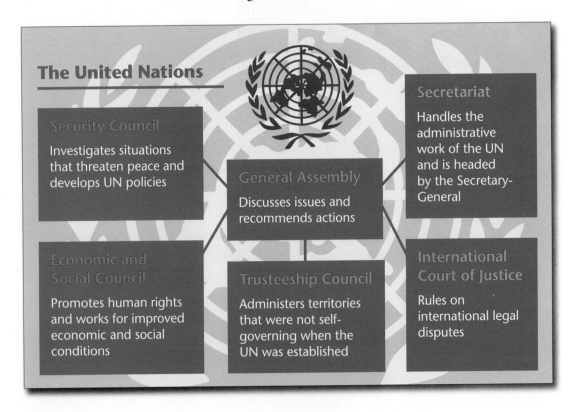

The United Nations

Security Council
Investigates situations that threaten peace and develops UN policies

General Assembly
Discusses issues and recommends actions

Secretariat
Handles the administrative work of the UN and is headed by the Secretary-General

Economic and Social Council
Promotes human rights and works for improved economic and social conditions

Trusteeship Council
Administers territories that were not self-governing when the UN was established

International Court of Justice
Rules on international legal disputes

The United Nations was soon tested with a problem in the Middle East. Palestine had been under the control of Great Britain since World War I. The Arabs and Jews who lived there wanted the British to leave. The United Nations wanted a Jewish nation and an Arab nation to be created out of Palestine. In 1948, the new nation of Israel was established. Arab nations in the Middle East objected to the creation of Israel and declared war. In 1949, the UN stopped the fighting and restored peace. The UN had passed its first test.

What Was President Truman's "Fair Deal"?

When Harry Truman became president in 1945, he had been vice president for less than three months. Although he had spent many years in the Senate, he had little experience dealing with the problems that faced the nation. Truman wanted to stabilize the country and work toward a lasting peace with other nations.

The months that followed the end of World War II were difficult for Truman. He faced many problems at home and abroad. Truman presented Congress with his own plan for improving the country. The program was called the "Fair Deal." It was based on the ideas of the New Deal. Truman wanted:

- more people included in the Social Security system;
- the minimum wage increased;
- more money for education and science; and
- public housing in cities.

The Republicans attacked the Democrats and the Fair Deal policies. They warned the American people about the power of "big government" and the growing power of labor unions. Acting on their fear, the Republican Congress ignored Truman's veto and passed the Taft-Hartley Act in 1947. This law allowed employers to hire non-union workers. Union leaders opposed this law.

Who Won the 1948 Election?

Truman won his party's nomination in 1948, but few leaders believed he could win the election. The Democratic Party was split apart over civil rights for African Americans. Truman supported civil rights. As a result, southern Democrats left the party and formed a new States' Rights "Dixiecrat" party.

Truman campaigned by train, often speaking 10 times a day. The Republican Party had nominated former New York Governor Thomas E. Dewey. Union workers supported Truman. African American voters supported his stand on civil rights. Truman defeated Dewey by more than two million votes.

Harry and Bess Truman waved from the rear platform of a train during Mr. Truman's campaign.

What do you think ?

If you were a representative of the United Nations today, what would you want to accomplish?

Lesson 2 Review Choose the word or name in parentheses that best completes each sentence. Write your answers on a sheet of paper.

1. Over (55, 65, 45) million people were killed in World War II.

2. The (League of Nations, United Nations, NATO) was set up in 1945.

3. The new nation of (Israel, Palestine) was established in 1948.

4. President Truman proposed the (Security Council, New Deal, Fair Deal).

5. (Harry Truman, Thomas E. Dewey) was elected president in 1948.

Even though the United States and the Soviet Union had been allies during the final days of World War II, a struggle between the two countries began soon after the war. Since World War I, Communists had taken control of the government of the Soviet Union. These leaders promoted the spread of Communism to other countries.

What Was the Cold War?

The United States feared that the Soviet goal was world **domination** under Communism. The Soviet Union opposed UN peacekeeping efforts. Western nations, including America, started to distrust the Soviet Union. This conflict was called the **cold war.** Its weapons were mainly economics and politics. The cold war caused each nation to stay armed just in case it became an actual war.

The Soviet Union promised to hold free elections in Eastern European countries when World War II ended. This was part of the Yalta Agreement. Early in 1946, it was clear that Joseph Stalin did not plan to keep his promise. Stalin wanted the governments in Eastern Europe and Germany to be Communist. The United States was concerned about the spread of Communism in Europe. Communism was a threat to democratic governments. Most small countries would not be able to defend themselves against Communism without the help of the United States.

Winston Churchill, wartime leader of Great Britain, told an audience at a college in Missouri that "an Iron Curtain has **descended** across the continent" of Europe. He said Communist dictators controlled the people of Eastern Europe. These dictators were supported by the powerful Soviet Union. The "Iron Curtain" stood for the military weapons that the Soviet Union used to keep control of these nations. Churchill challenged the United States. He believed that the United States had the power to stop the spread of Communism before the democratic governments of Europe were threatened.

Domination

Complete control

Cold war

The disagreements between Communist and non-Communist nations over economics and politics following World War II

Descend

To come down on

What Was the Containment Policy?

The United States believed it needed a policy to fight the spread of Communism. It developed a new policy called the Truman Doctrine. The spread of Communism was compared to water. Water flows wherever there is no resistance to it. The Soviet expansion was thought of in this way. Water can be contained by dams. Perhaps Communism could be contained by applying American force wherever the Soviet Union tried to gain influence.

President Truman (left) and Winston Churchill believed the spread of Communism should be stopped.

The new policy of containment was tested in 1947. Turkey and Greece had serious political and economic problems after World War II. The Soviet Union wanted part of Turkey's territory. Civil war had broken out in Greece. Communist forces tried to gain power in each country. In March 1947, President Truman asked Congress for $400 million to help these countries. He said that "it must be the policy of the United States to support free peoples who are resisting . . . outside pressures. . . . If we falter in our leadership, we may endanger the peace of the world." Congress approved. Greece and Turkey were able to defeat those countries that wanted to overthrow their governments. The Truman Doctrine, now called the **containment policy,** had passed its first test.

What Was the Marshall Plan?

Secretary of State George C. Marshall knew that the United States had to help Europe after the war. European cities had to be rebuilt and weak economies had to be made stronger. Marshall hoped to help Europeans avoid Communist takeovers. He asked the leaders of Europe to find out how much money they needed to rebuild their countries. A four-year, multibillion-dollar plan was proposed. Congress agreed to fund the European Recovery Program, or the Marshall Plan as it came to be known. The Soviet Union opposed the program.

Cold War Divides Europe

ICELAND

0   200   400 Miles

NATO countries in Europe
Communist countries in Europe

FINLAND

NORWAY
SWEDEN

North
Sea

DENMARK

★ Moscow

IRELAND

GREAT
BRITAIN

ATLANTIC
OCEAN

London ★

Baltic Sea

SOVIET UNION

NETH.

Berlin
★

BELG.

EAST
GERMANY

POLAND

WEST
GERMANY

Paris ★
LUXEMBOURG

CZECHOSLOVAKIA

FRANCE

SWITZ.

AUSTRIA

HUNGARY

PORTUGAL

SPAIN

ITALY

★ Rome

YUGOSLAVIA

ROMANIA

BULGARIA

Black Sea

ALBANIA

TURKEY

Mediterranean Sea

GREECE

Map Study Which Communist countries are shown in the above map?
Which Communist countries are shown below?

Black
Sea

SOVIET UNION

TURKEY

JAPAN

Caspian Sea

MONGOLIA

NORTH
KOREA

IRAQ

SOUTH
KOREA

IRAN

AFGHANISTAN

CHINA

PACIFIC
OCEAN

SAUDI
ARABIA

WEST
PAKISTAN

NEPAL

BHUTAN

TAIWAN

INDIA

BURMA

LAOS

NORTH VIETNAM

PHILIPPINES

EAST
PAKISTAN

THAILAND

SOUTH
VIETNAM

Non-Communist countries in Asia
Communist countries in Asia

Bay of Bengal

CEYLON

CAMBODIA

Cold War Divides Asia

What Was the Berlin Blockade and Airlift?

When World War II ended, Germany was divided among the four Allies—the United States, the Soviet Union, Great Britain, and France. France, Great Britain, and the United States agreed to combine their sections of West Germany into one nation. It was called the Federal Republic of Germany. The Soviet Union objected. To show their anger, the Soviets set up a blockade in 1948. This cut off road and train traffic into Berlin.

The German city of Berlin, capital of Germany before 1945, was located in East Germany. The Soviet Union controlled East Germany. The city of Berlin was supposed to be open to France, Great Britain, and the United States. Because the Soviet Union closed off the city, Berlin was not able to get supplies from Western Europe. Three days after the blockade was set up, President Truman ordered an **airlift** of supplies to Berlin. For more than a year, planes carried tons of supplies to Berlin. Finally, the Soviet Union gave in. West Berlin remained a free, democratic city.

Why Was NATO Formed?

The Berlin blockade made Congress think that the United States should join Canada and 10 European nations for the protection of one another. In 1949, the countries formed the North Atlantic Treaty Organization (NATO). This group's treaty said that an attack on one member would be considered an attack on all members. NATO would have its own military troops sent by the member nations. General Dwight D. Eisenhower was the first head of the NATO force. The United States volunteered 350,000 troops.

Lesson 3 Review On a sheet of paper, write the correct word or words from the Word Bank to complete each sentence.

1. Democratic countries tried to limit Communism during the _____.

2. _____ considers an attack on one member of its organization to be an attack on all members.

3. The _____ was a Communist country.

4. The _____ was an attempt to keep Communism from spreading in areas where there was little resistance.

5. The _____ was a plan to help Europe after the war.

What do you think ?

What do you think are the dangers of a cold war?

Then and Now

Do you have a computer in your home or use one at school? The computer you use is a lot smaller than a computer was in the 1950s. One computer then filled an entire room. The room had to be kept cool and clean. People punched information onto cards and fed the cards into the computer. Only large businesses could afford a computer. Businesses used computers mainly to keep records and to print customers' bills and employees' paychecks.

Today businesses and schools have many computers. Many people have home computers. You may have learned how to use a computer in school. In the 1950s, you would have used a manual typewriter to prepare a report. Now you use a computer and maybe the Internet to do your homework. Maybe you send letters over e-mail. People with portable laptop computers carry them to the library, a business meeting, or even the park. Computer uses are endless.

Communism in Asia also presented a problem for the United States and its allies. Since the 1920s, a civil war had been waged between two Chinese political groups. Those groups were the Chinese Communist Party and the Nationalist Party, which controlled the Chinese government. During World War II, the parties joined together to fight the invading Japanese. With the defeat of Japan, these rival political groups began to fight each other again. The United States supported the Nationalist Party. In 1949, the Communist Party, led by Mao Zedong, defeated the Nationalist Party. The Truman administration opposed the new Chinese Communist government, but there was little that they could do about it. The Communist Chinese revolution caused bitter political debates in the United States over who had "lost China."

The peninsula of Korea is located between China and Japan. During World War II, the Japanese conquered Korea. After the war, the country was divided into two parts. The Soviet Union occupied the northern section. The United States controlled South Korea. In 1948, the democratic Republic of Korea was formed in the south. America withdrew its troops from the south and provided economic aid to the new country. The Soviet Union created a Communist government in North Korea called the Democratic People's Republic.

From the beginning, there was tension between North and South Korea. On June 25, 1950, North Korea invaded South Korea. Two days later, the United Nations Security Council declared that North Korea was wrong. The Security Council asked the UN to help South Korea. The Soviets had been boycotting the UN, so they were unable to veto this plan of action. With UN backing, President Truman ordered American troops to support the South Koreans.

How Did Fighting Begin?

Fifteen other nations agreed to help South Korea. Still, the defense of South Korea was mainly an American responsibility. President Truman refused to call the fighting in Korea a war. Instead, Truman called it a "police action." The goal was to force North Korean troops to return to their own territory.

Armed with many modern tanks and weapons supplied by the Soviet Union and China, North Korea captured Seoul, the South Korean capital. General Douglas MacArthur, commander of the American troops, was not prepared to fight an **offensive** war. Soon only a small area in the southeast remained under UN control.

MacArthur set up a defensive line at the southern port of Pusan. Then, with the aid of 50,000 more American troops, the UN forces were able to stop the North Koreans and take the offensive. MacArthur and his troops were able to push the North Korean army past their own capital city toward the Chinese province of Manchuria.

Communist China had warned the UN that it would become involved if troops moved any closer to Manchuria. MacArthur told Truman that China would not enter the war. However, on November 26, 1950, about 300,000 Chinese soldiers attacked the American army in North Korea. The American troops were pushed back into South Korea. Fortunately, by the following spring, they were able to set up a new defensive line there.

General MacArthur asked President Truman for permission to bomb China. Truman feared that bombing would bring the Soviet Union into the war. When Truman refused, MacArthur asked Congress for permission. This action angered Truman. General MacArthur was challenging the power of the president. Truman fired MacArthur in April 1951.

How Did the Korean War End?

Peace talks began in July 1951. The two sides disagreed on the problem of prisoner exchange. The Communists wanted all prisoners returned to their homeland. The United Nations wanted to give the prisoners a choice. The negotiations continued for two years. An agreement was reached in July 1953. Prisoners had their choice. North and South Korea became two separate nations.

North and South Korea each withdrew 1.25 miles from the final battle line. This formed a 2.5 mile neutral zone between them. The North Koreans and Chinese who opposed the Communists in North Korea were allowed to stay in South Korea. To provide protection from any future attacks, American troops stayed in South Korea. The United States also gave further economic aid.

Lesson 4 Review On a sheet of paper, write the word or words in parentheses that best complete each sentence.

1. (North Korea, The Soviet Union, Manchuria) invaded South Korea in 1950.

2. Most of the UN troops that fought in the Korean War were supplied by (the United States, Japan, Manchuria).

3. President Truman called the fighting in Korea a (war, police action, disagreement).

4. President Truman fired General MacArthur because the general (attacked Manchuria, failed to conquer North Korea, challenged the president's power).

5. After the war, the United States continued to help South Korea with troops and (tanks, economic aid, trade).

What do you think ?

Do you think the United States is right to provide economic aid to poor countries? Why or why not?

Nuclear war

War that uses atomic weapons

The Republicans argued that the Democratic Party had become filled with corruption. They claimed that the Truman administration had handled the Korean War badly. "It is time for a change," the Republicans said.

General Dwight D. Eisenhower, the Republican candidate, was elected president in 1952. He won in a landslide victory over Adlai Stevenson. Known as "Ike," Eisenhower was a hero of World War II. He took office in 1953 and became a popular president.

The nation's economy was doing well during most of the years Eisenhower held office. Soldiers who had returned from fighting in World War II and Korea had started families. New home construction soared, as did the need for more and better American products. During this time, the lives of most Americans improved.

This "family model" bomb shelter shows an escape opening at the top and an entrance that attached to a cellar. This kind of shelter was placed underground.

The fear of Communism and the Soviet Union still existed. The Soviet Union developed an atomic bomb. Americans were worried about a war using atomic weapons, or **nuclear war.** People built bomb shelters in their backyards. Cities set up air raid warning signals. Schoolchildren were taught to get under their desks or go to a certain place quickly when they heard air raid sirens.

What Was McCarthyism?

In 1947, President Truman and other political leaders feared that Communists were working within the United States government. Truman issued an order creating a loyalty-security program for federal employees. During the Truman and Eisenhower administrations, nearly 7,000 federal workers suspected of being "security risks" were either fired or forced to resign.

Americans feared Communism, and Senator Joseph McCarthy used this fear for his own political gain. He kept saying that traitors were trying to destroy the country. McCarthy became one of the most feared members of the Senate. Many American educators, journalists, and entertainers lost their jobs as a result of his **accusations.** Others had their **reputations** ruined. For a long time, few politicians were willing to challenge McCarthy.

McCarthy began to investigate army officials. The Senate held televised hearings for 36 days in 1954. When television audiences saw McCarthy as a lying bully, they demanded an investigation. A special Senate committee found that most of McCarthy's charges were untrue. With the help of television, the American people were able to take away much of McCarthy's power. The campaign he had used to make his accusations soon became known as **McCarthyism.**

How Did the Civil Rights Movement Begin?

African Americans had fought for democracy in two world wars. Yet when they returned from those wars, they were still denied basic political and social rights. In the 1950s, many African Americans decided that the members of their race could no longer be victims.

The civil rights movement was sparked by a 1954 decision of the Supreme Court, *Brown v. the Board of Education of Topeka, Kansas.* A young African American girl was denied the right to attend a white school. Her father sued the school board.

NAACP lawyers, including Thurgood Marshall, worked very hard on this case. Marshall later became the first African American appointed to the Supreme Court. In the decision, the Supreme Court ruled that separate schools for whites and African Americans were unconstitutional. In 1954, Chief Justice Earl Warren wrote that separate can never be equal. Local school boards were ordered to end school segregation.

In December 1955, Rosa Parks, a 42-year-old African American woman, got on a bus in Montgomery, Alabama. She found a seat near the middle of the bus. The bus driver asked Parks to

Rosa Parks

give up her seat to a white person. Parks would not. Police were called and she was arrested. Parks had not planned to challenge the law on that day. Parks said, "I felt it was just something that I had to do." Her decision not to move from her seat on a bus was the quiet beginning of a national civil rights movement.

History in Your Life

The Advent of Credit Cards

Credit allows a person to make purchases without cash. In America, credit plans grew quickly between 1850 and 1900. The plans allowed buyers to pay for purchases over time.

Modern credit cards began with the formation of Diners Club in 1950. Card holders used the same card to buy from many merchants. In 1951, Franklin National Bank of New York was the first bank to offer a card. By 1958, several other companies offered credit cards. In the 1980s, credit card companies had huge growth. Now nearly every American family has at least one major credit card. They use a card to buy groceries, vacations, and more.

A 26-year-old minister named Martin Luther King Jr. led a boycott of the buses in Montgomery in 1956. He helped to organize car pools to help African Americans travel around the city. He was arrested for his actions. One year later the Supreme Court ruled that segregation on public transportation was unconstitutional.

King went on to become the most visible person in the civil rights movement. He urged his supporters to use non-violent protest to gain equal rights. His speeches moved many to action and drew attention to racial discrimination that affected African Americans.

A new civil rights law was passed in August 1957. This law made it illegal to use force to stop someone from voting. This was the first civil rights law since Reconstruction. Progress was continually challenged. The governor of Arkansas tried to prevent nine African American children from attending an all-

Martin Luther King Jr.

white school in Little Rock. The state's **National Guard** was ordered to protect this school. A national guard is a state's military force. President Eisenhower sent federal troops to help the African American children. The governor finally backed down.

It Happened in History

Martin Luther King Jr. gave one of his most famous speeches, called "I Have a Dream," in 1963. This speech is considered to be a cornerstone of the civil rights movement. It can be found at www.stanford.edu/group/King/publications/speechesFrame.htm. (Click on *A Call to Conscience: The Landmark Speeches of Martin Luther King Jr.*) You can also visit The King Center Web site at www.thekingcenter.com/tkc/index.asp to learn more about Dr. King.

What Was Life Like in the 1950s?

American society experienced many changes in the 1950s. Jobs were available for most Americans. With the development of **automation,** factories employed thousands of people to produce countless new products. Advances in science and technology offered Americans better health and a higher standard of living than ever before.

The family and the home became popular symbols of American life. The image of women as "housewives" and husbands as "breadwinners" were commonly found in magazine advertising and TV commercials. In the late 1950s, many middle class families had both husbands and wives working outside the home. Most women did not hold "career" jobs like their husbands. In general, jobs held by married women were seen as temporary until children arrived. But unlike their mothers, many women thought that being a homemaker or a temporary employee was not their only choice. Women began to question the narrow role assigned to them in society. Early in the 1960s, the first steps of the women's movement were taken. The purpose of the women's movement was to seek social and economic equality for American women.

Most television programs were black and white in the 1950s.

Geography Note

In 1959, Alaska and Hawaii joined the United States. They were the first states added to the nation since the admission of Arizona in 1912. Alaska was the 49th state; Hawaii was the 50th.

In 1956, the federal government started a huge program to build interstate highways. The highways would connect most cities with populations over 50,000. As the roads were built, suburbs attracted more home builders.

New cars had large "fins" on their rear fenders. Some young people drove hot rods, or cars that had been adjusted to go faster. Crew cuts were a common hairstyle for boys. Girls wore their hair in ponytails. Television was only black and white. Young children watched a puppet named Howdy Doody and his friend, Buffalo Bob. Rock and roll music was new, and young people loved it. The term UFO (unidentified flying object) entered the vocabulary of many Americans.

How Was Eisenhower Re-elected?

In the election of 1956, Eisenhower was elected by an even greater landslide than in the previous election. The Democrats, however, took control of Congress. Although many Republicans considered the president to be too liberal, Americans seemed to be happy with him.

Biography

Margaret Chase Smith: 1897–1995

A Republican from Maine, Margaret Chase Smith was the first woman elected to each of the houses of Congress. She completed her husband's term in the House of Representatives after his death in 1940. Then Smith was elected to four more two-year terms. She next served in the Senate for 25 years—longer than any other woman. During the early 1950s, she spoke out against the methods of Senator Joseph McCarthy. In 1964, Smith campaigned for the Republican presidential nomination. She was the first woman ever to campaign for the presidential nomination in a major party. Smith wrote the book *Gallant Women* in 1968. The book documented the lives of independent women in American public life.

How Did the Space Race Begin?

Artificial satellite

An object made by humans that travels in outer space and sends signals back to Earth

The United States was taken by surprise when the Soviet Union launched *Sputnik* on October 4, 1957. *Sputnik* was an **artificial satellite** that traveled in outer space and sent radio signals back to Earth. Everyone was concerned that a foreign country knew how to do something that the Americans did not.

The United States was developing space technology, but the Russians raced ahead. *Sputnik 2*, carrying a dog, was launched before the United States could get into space. A new battle had been added to the cold war.

On January 31, 1958, the U.S. army put the first American satellite, *Explorer 1*, into orbit. This was three months after the launch of *Sputnik 2*. The following October, the United States created the National Aeronautics and Space Administration (NASA).

Lesson 5 Review On a sheet of paper, write the answers to the following questions. Use complete sentences.

1. How did Americans prepare for a nuclear war?

2. What was McCarthyism?

3. How did Rosa Parks help begin the civil rights movement?

4. How did roads improve in the 1950s?

5. How did the Russians start the space race?

What do you think ?

Do you think you would have liked living in the 1950s? Why or why not?

The Crisis at Central High School

In 1954, the Supreme Court declared school segregation unconstitutional. In 1957, Central High School in Little Rock, Arkansas, was going to admit African American students for the first time. Governor Orval Faubus said he could not maintain order if African American students tried to enter. Elizabeth Eckford was one of nine African American students who tried to integrate the school. Here are the viewpoints of Governor Faubus and Elizabeth Eckford.

The question at issue . . . is not integration versus segregation. . . . The question now is whether . . . the head of a sovereign state can exercise his constitutional powers and discretion in maintaining peace and good order within his jurisdiction, being accountable to his own conscience and to his own people. . . .

The situation in Little Rock and Arkansas grows more explosive by the hour. This is caused for the most part by the misunderstanding of our problem by a federal judge who decreed 'immediate integration' of the public schools . . . without hearing any evidence . . . as to the conditions . . . in the community. . . .

I saw a large crowd of people standing across the street from the soldiers guarding Central. As I walked on, the crowd suddenly got very quiet. Superintendent Blossom had told us to enter by the front door. . . .

When I got right in front of the school, I went up to a guard . . . he just looked straight ahead and didn't move to let me pass him. . . . I walked until I was right in front of the path to the front door.

I stood looking at the school—it looked so big! Just then the guards let some white students go through.

The crowd was quiet . . . waiting to see what was going to happen. When I was able to steady my knees, I walked up to the guard who had let the white students in. He . . . didn't move. When I tried to squeeze past him, he raised his bayonet . . . the other guards closed in and . . . raised their bayonets. . . .

I was very frightened and didn't know what to do. I turned around and the crowd came toward me. They moved closer and closer. Somebody started yelling, "Lynch her!"

Document-Based Questions

1. Why did Governor Faubus oppose admitting African American students?

2. Who did Faubus think caused the crisis?

3. What did Elizabeth Eckford see when she arrived at the school?

4. How did some white guards treat her?

5. Why do you think Elizabeth Eckford risked her safety to attend a high school?

Source: A message from Governor Faubus to President Eisenhower, September 4, 1957.

Source: Long Shadow of Little Rock, by Daisy Bates, 1962.

- Congress passed the GI Bill in 1944 and the Full Employment Act in 1946 to help Americans.

- Improvements in farming methods helped farmers produce more food.

- The United Nations was created in San Francisco, California in April 1945. The UN was established as an international organization with the responsibility of keeping peace among its member countries.

- Distrust developed between Communist and non-Communist countries. The United States did not want Communism to spread beyond the countries where it was already established. The United States fought Communism by supporting governments that were opposed to Communism.

- The Marshall Plan provided American aid to European countries that had suffered damage during the war.

- The United States, France, and Great Britain flew supplies to West Berlin during a period when the Soviet Union cut off ground transportation to the city. The Berlin airlift lasted until the Soviets reopened the railroads and highways.

- In 1950, North Korea invaded South Korea. The United States was among 16 countries that sent troops to help South Korea. After three years of fighting, the Communist North Koreans agreed to peace talks.

- General Dwight D. Eisenhower, a hero of World War II, was elected president in 1952.

- Fear of Communism was widespread. Senator Joseph McCarthy used this fear to accuse hundreds of Americans of being Communists or Communist sympathizers. Because of McCarthy, many people lost their jobs.

- The civil rights movement grew in strength in the 1950s. The Supreme Court ruled that separate schools for whites and African Americans were unconstitutional. Martin Luther King Jr. led a boycott of buses in Montgomery, Alabama. Congress passed a civil rights law in 1957.

- During the 1950s, jobs were available for most Americans. People had money to purchase such items as televisions and new cars. Because of interstate highways, people built homes in suburbs.

- America launched its first successful satellite into orbit in 1958.

Chapter 27 REVIEW

Word Bank

General Douglas
MacArthur

Fair Deal

Iron Curtain

Israel

Joseph Stalin

Rosa Parks

Sputnik

Taft-Hartley Act

United Nations

West Berlin

On a sheet of paper, write the correct word or words from the Word Bank to complete each sentence.

1. The United Nations established the country of _____ in the Middle East.

2. President Truman's economic plan was called the _____.

3. An international organization called the _____ was created in San Francisco in 1946.

4. Under the rules of the _____, employers could hire nonunion workers.

5. Winston Churchill used the term _____ to describe the division between Eastern and Western Europe.

6. _____ was the leader of the Soviet Union.

7. Truman helped establish an airlift to provide supplies to _____.

8. Truman fired _____ because he went to Congress and challenged the power of the president.

9. By refusing to give up her seat on the bus, _____ helped begin the civil rights movement.

10. In 1957, the Soviet Union launched _____, an artificial satellite.

On a sheet of paper, write the letter of the answer that correctly completes each sentence.

11. In 1954, the Supreme Court ruled that schools must end _____.

   A McCarthyism   C segregation

   B discrimination   D containment

12. Joseph McCarthy became powerful by playing to Americans' fear of _____.

   A Communism   **C** integration

   B nuclear war   **D** space war

13. The United States became involved in a police action when North Korea invaded _____.

   A Manchuria   **C** Japan

   B South Korea   **D** China

On a sheet of paper, write the answers to the following questions. Use complete sentences.

14. What were some of the early events of the civil rights movement?

15. What were three results of World War II?

16. What was the United States like in the 1950s?

17. How was the United States involved in the Korean War?

18. Why was America involved in the cold war?

Critical Thinking On a sheet of paper, write your response to each question. Use complete sentences.

19. Senator McCarthy used Americans' fear of Communism to accuse many people falsely. Do you think something like this could happen today? Why or why not?

20. Television had a major effect on American life in the 1950s. Do you think new Internet technology will have a major effect on life in America? Why or why not?

Test-Taking Tip

As you study for a test, look over maps, graphs, and other visuals in the chapter. Figure out how they fit in with the chapter's important ideas. Summarize the meaning of each graphic in your own words.

28

Support for Freedom

The 1960s was a time of protest in America. There were still many problems at home that needed to be addressed. Individual freedoms became important as never before in the nation. Yet another war—the Vietnam War—caused many of these protests. African Americans, Hispanic Americans, American Indians, and women sought to increase their rights. In this chapter, you will learn how the United States worked to gain freedom for all its citizens during the 1960s.

Goals for Learning

◆ To describe the beginning of U.S. space exploration and the election of 1960

◆ To explain the United States' involvement in world events

◆ To describe the start of the civil rights movement and the achievements and assassination of President Kennedy

◆ To describe Lyndon Johnson's presidency and the increasing U.S. involvement in Vietnam

◆ To explain the civil rights movement, the women's movement, and concerns of Hispanics and young people

◆ To describe the events of the 1968 election and the assassinations of Martin Luther King Jr. and Robert Kennedy

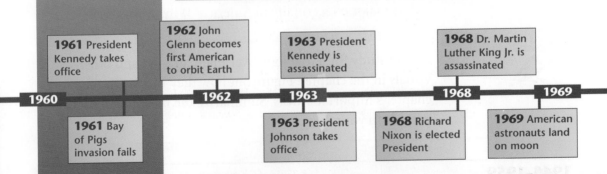

1961 President Kennedy takes office

1962 John Glenn becomes first American to orbit Earth

1963 President Kennedy is assassinated

1968 Dr. Martin Luther King Jr. is assassinated

1960 | 1962 | 1963 | 1968 | 1969

1961 Bay of Pigs invasion fails

1963 President Johnson takes office

1968 Richard Nixon is elected President

1969 American astronauts land on moon

Suborbital

Not out of Earth's atmosphere

Atmosphere

The layer of gases covering Earth

The United States launched six Mercury spacecraft with people aboard between 1961 and 1963. On May 5, 1961, Alan B. Shepard Jr. piloted *Mercury-Redstone 3 (Freedom 7)* on a 15.5 minute **suborbital** flight. This means that the flight did not make it out of Earth's **atmosphere** and into orbit. John Glenn made history when he became the first American to orbit the earth.

On February 20, 1962, Glenn orbited the earth three times in *Friendship 7*.

Project Gemini was the code name for the United States program to launch two astronauts in a spacecraft capable of orbiting for a long time. The first two-person mission of Project Gemini took place in 1965. In the years that followed, there were nine additional Gemini flights.

John Glenn was the first American to orbit the earth.

Technology Connection

1960s Space Exploration

The 1960s was a busy time for the space program in the United States. As the technology improved, scientists were able to gather more information from space. In addition to the missions noted above, here are some other explorations of this decade:

1962 *Ranger 4* First U.S. spacecraft to land on the moon
Mariner 2 Flew past Venus

1964 *Ranger 7* Took close-up photos of the moon
Mariner 4 Took close-up photos of the surface of Mars; detected a weak magnetic field on Mars

1967 *Pioneer 8* Transmitted data from a solar probe

1968 *Apollo 7* Transmitted first live television pictures from space

Who Won the 1960 Election?

The cold war briefly "thawed" in the late 1950s. Soviet Premier Nikita Khrushchev visited the United States in 1959 and invited President Eisenhower to visit the Soviet Union. However, Khrushchev quickly withdrew the invitation after the Soviets captured an American pilot flying far inside Soviet borders.

The 1960 presidential election grew in importance. The Republican Party had controlled the White House for eight years. The 22nd Amendment to the Constitution, ratified in 1951, said that a president could not serve more than two terms. Therefore, Eisenhower was **ineligible** for a third term in office. The Republicans chose Richard Nixon as their candidate. The Democrats nominated a 43-year-old senator from Massachusetts—John F. Kennedy.

Known as a tough opponent of Communist expansion, Nixon had gained experience in world affairs during his eight years as Eisenhower's vice president. Kennedy had been a member of Congress since 1946.

Kennedy and Nixon held a series of debates. For the first time, presidential debates were on national television. According to many political observers, the debates played a major role in the outcome of the election. Kennedy was young and handsome, and he remained cool under the pressure of the televised debate.

The election was very close. Kennedy narrowly won the popular vote. He was the youngest man ever to be elected president. Kennedy was also the first president who was a Roman Catholic.

Kennedy took the presidential oath of office on January 20, 1961. In his inaugural address, he called on Americans to work for the good of the nation and freedom around the world. His domestic and foreign policy goals were called the "New Frontier." The symbol of a New Frontier recalled America's past challenges. It linked them to the nation's struggles at home and the threat from Communism abroad. Kennedy's youth, confidence, and **enthusiasm** motivated many young people to help others.

Richard Nixon (left) and John F. Kennedy took part in debates on national television.

Lesson 1 Review Choose the best word or name in parentheses to complete each sentence. Write your answers on a sheet of paper.

1. (Alan B. Shepard, John Glenn) was the first American to orbit the earth.

2. (Project Gemini, *Friendship 7*, Project Mercury) was the code name for the U.S. program to launch astronauts into space for long flights.

3. The (20th, 21st, 22nd) Amendment said a president could not be elected for more than two terms.

4. The (Republicans, Democrats) chose Richard Nixon as their candidate for president.

5. (John F. Kennedy, Dwight D. Eisenhower, Richard Nixon) won the election of 1960.

What do you think ?

Do you think presidential debates help determine the outcome of an election? Explain your answer.

Refugee

A person who flees his or her home country to seek protection

Geography Note

The Berlin Wall was built to stop Germans from leaving East Berlin and emigrating to West Berlin. The barrier consisted of concrete slabs, guard dogs, guard towers, trenches, barbed wire, and land mines. Eventually, about 110 miles of barriers completely surrounded West Berlin. The wall was was torn down in 1989.

The Communist government in Cuba was of major concern to the United States. Fidel Castro, the head of the Cuban government since 1959, had originally won support from the United States for leading a revolt against Cuba's dictator. Then, he surprised America by declaring that he was a Communist. He requested help from the Soviets and received it. Cuba was only 90 miles from the Florida coastline.

The Castro government seized property in Cuba owned by Americans and people from other countries. The Eisenhower administration stopped all trade with Cuba except food and medicine. It encouraged anti-Castro Cuban **refugees** to invade their homeland and overthrow the government.

When Kennedy became president, he was asked to approve an invasion plan. Kennedy approved the plan but would not allow American troops to take part. The United States did, however, train and arm the Cuban rebels.

In April 1961, American-supported Cubans invaded Cuba at the Bay of Pigs. The invaders thought that the Cuban people and the Cuban army would support them. They were wrong. The invasion was a complete failure. Within three days, most of the invaders were killed or captured. President Kennedy took full responsibility for the failure.

Why Was the Berlin Wall Built?

President Kennedy and the Soviet leader, Nikita Khrushchev, met in Vienna, Austria, in June 1961. Khrushchev believed that Kennedy was too young and inexperienced to be a strong leader. Khrushchev thought that it was time to force the United States out of West Berlin. President Kennedy said that the United States would not leave the city. The Soviet Union responded by building a wall dividing the city of Berlin. The wall was between Communist East Berlin and democratic West Berlin.

The Berlin Wall prevented East Berliners from leaving their section of the city.

What Was the Cuban Missile Crisis?

One of the most serious events of the cold war occurred in October 1962. The Cuban **missile** crisis almost caused a war between the United States and the Soviet Union. A missile is a self-driven bomb. The United States discovered that Cuba was secretly building missile bases. Kennedy ordered the navy to stop Soviet ships from carrying missiles to Cuba. The world watched nervously as two powerful nations challenged each other to back down. Radio and television news kept the American people informed of the situation. War appeared very possible.

Suddenly, on October 26, the Soviet ships turned around. They headed back to the Soviet Union. The tension was broken.

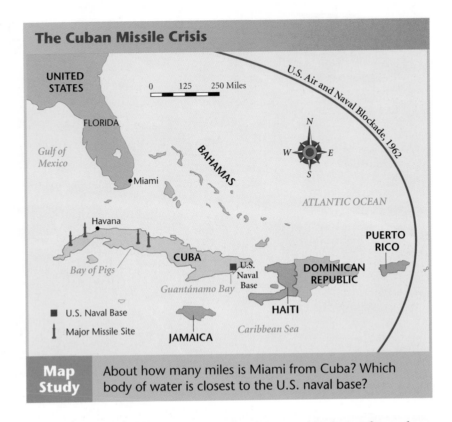

The Cuban Missile Crisis

Map Study About how many miles is Miami from Cuba? Which body of water is closest to the U.S. naval base?

On the same day, President Kennedy received a letter from the Soviet premier. Khrushchev said that he would remove the missiles from Cuba if Kennedy would promise not to invade Cuba. The Cuban missile crisis was over. President Kennedy was praised for his tough stand.

Lesson 2 Review On a sheet of paper, write the answers to the following questions. Use complete sentences.

1. How far is Cuba from the United States?

2. How did Kennedy try to help the Cubans?

3. What did the Soviet Union do to Berlin?

4. How did the Cuban missile crisis almost turn into a war?

5. How did people view Kennedy after the Cuban missile crisis?

What do you think?

How would you feel if you knew there were enemy missile bases so close to the United States? Explain your answer.

Fulfill

To carry out or put into effect

Riot

A violent public disturbance

In the 1960s, the struggle for African American equality moved from the courts to the streets. Segregation was still the law of the land in many parts of the country. Many African Americans were denied the right to vote. Some progress had been made during the 1950s. Yet African Americans were still treated as second-class citizens in many parts of the country.

In June 1963, President Kennedy said, "The time has come for this nation to **fulfill** its promise . . . for equality. . . . Those who do nothing are inviting shame as well as violence." The federal government tried to help end inequality and segregation for African Americans.

How Did Groups Attack Segregation?

A group of African Americans and whites called "freedom riders" boarded buses and headed south. Their plan was to draw attention to segregation in the southern states. The group was led by James Farmer of the Congress of Racial Equality (CORE).

Following the example set by Martin Luther King Jr., the freedom riders believed in peaceful protests. Yet some of their buses were burned. Many people were beaten. Television cameras brought the shame of segregation into the living rooms of the American people.

During 1962 and 1963, the civil rights movement caught the attention of the nation. **Riots** broke out at the University of Mississippi. A riot is a violent public disturbance. James Meredith was not allowed to attend because he was African American. A court ordered the university to admit him. The governor of the state said that he would keep Meredith out. Meredith's life was threatened. Mobs of white people protested his admission. Local police failed to keep the peace. President Kennedy sent federal troops to the university to protect Meredith. Meredith became the first African American to attend the University of Mississippi.

How Was President Kennedy Assassinated?

President Kennedy began to turn his thoughts toward being re-elected. He flew to Texas to begin his campaign. On Friday, November 22, 1963, President Kennedy rode through the streets of Dallas, Texas. Riding with him were his wife and Governor John Connally of Texas and Connally's wife. The **motorcade** was moving through the streets of downtown Dallas when shots were fired.

Governor Connally was seriously wounded. President Kennedy, who had been shot in the head and neck, was dead. A few hours later, Vice President Johnson took the presidential oath of office. Lee Harvey Oswald was arrested and accused of killing the president. Two days later on live television, Jack Ruby shot and killed Oswald. The nation was shocked that Kennedy had been assassinated.

President Kennedy (rear seat to left) rode through Dallas, Texas, before he was assassinated.

What Had Kennedy Achieved as President?

During President Kennedy's brief time in office, he did many things that had lasting effects. In 1961, the Peace Corps was established to work in **developing countries**. A developing country is a nation that is slowly improving its industry and economy. The first Peace Corps volunteers were sent as teachers to the African nation of Ghana. Five years later, more than 10,000 Americans were serving in 52 countries.

When Communists threatened Southeast Asia, Kennedy allowed the transport of troops and equipment to aid them. Under Kennedy, the United States, Britain, and the Soviet Union signed the Limited Test Ban Treaty. The treaty made above-ground nuclear tests illegal. One of his strongest moves was allocating $20 billion to NASA with a challenge to put an American on the moon by 1970.

The first Peace Corps volunteers provided help to nations in Africa.

What do you think ?

Why do you think it is important to protest peacefully?

Lesson 3 Review Choose the term in parentheses that best completes each sentence. Write your answer on a sheet of paper.

1. The Congress of Racial Equality was led by (James Farmer, President Kennedy, Martin Luther King Jr.).

2. James Meredith's struggle drew the nation's attention to (Washington, Los Angeles, the University of Mississippi).

3. A peaceful march for civil rights was held on (June 25, 1961; August 28, 1963; November 22, 1963) in Washington, D.C.

4. The Civil Rights Act of 1964 called for an end to (segregation, sit-ins, protests).

5. President John F. Kennedy was assassinated by (John Connally, Lee Harvey Oswald, Jack Ruby).

Conservative

One who is cautious about change

President Lyndon Johnson's vision for the future of America was similar to that of John Kennedy. Johnson challenged America to wage a "War on Poverty." The country, he felt, must provide good education for every child and at least minimum health care for all Americans. Certainly it must bring an end to racial injustice. In May 1964, he gave his vision a name. He challenged the nation to build a "Great Society."

Who Won the Election of 1964?

Robert Weaver (left) was the first African American to serve in a president's Cabinet.

In 1964, the Democratic Party nominated Lyndon Johnson for president. The Republican Party nominated Senator Barry Goldwater of Arizona. There were great differences between the views of the two candidates.

Johnson felt federal programs needed to be created to improve the quality of life for every American. Goldwater, on the other hand, was very **conservative**. He felt individual states should have the final say in their policies. The federal government should not interfere.

Johnson easily won the election. He received more votes than any president before him. This election also gave the Democratic Party a stronger control of Congress.

What New Laws Did Johnson Help Pass?

President Johnson acted quickly to get Congress to pass laws to create programs for his "Great Society." A Medicare plan was passed to provide health insurance for the elderly. The Elementary and Secondary School Act provided more than $1 billion in federal funds to school districts with needy students.

Maintain

To keep in good condition

Divisive

Dividing or separating in a damaging way

Other laws attacked problems of **maintaining** clean air and water. The Housing Act encouraged the building of low-cost housing for low-income families. President Johnson appointed Robert Weaver to head the new Department of Housing and Urban Development. He was the first African American to become a member of a president's Cabinet.

For four decades, the effectiveness of these programs has been debated. Although the Great Society programs did not end poverty, the rate of poverty dropped four percent from 1965 to 1978. It was at the same level in the year 2000. Great Society programs still try to help people escape poverty. Medicare continues to provide medical care for elderly citizens. Low-cost housing is still being built. Federal funds are still provided to improve the education of elementary and secondary students from low-income families.

In 1965, President Johnson decided to expand America's role in a small country in Asia called South Vietnam. The Vietnam War became the most **divisive** conflict in the United States since the Civil War.

What Caused the Vietnam War?

After World War II, the former French colony of Vietnam was divided into two parts. North Vietnam was controlled by a Communist government. South Vietnam was non-Communist. America first became involved in this area of Southeast Asia in the 1950s.

President Johnson continued the policy set forth by previous presidents. Eisenhower had provided military weapons and economic aid to South Vietnam. Kennedy had sent military advisors. Johnson at first sent only noncombat troops to Vietnam.

Total American Troops in Vietnam by Year	
1963	15,000
1965	183,300
1967	475,000
1969	543,000

American soldiers in Vietnam had to bear harsh fighting conditions.

In August 1964, there were reports that two American ships were attacked off the coast of North Vietnam. President Johnson asked Congress for the right "to take all necessary measures" to protect American forces in the area. This vote of Congress was called the Tonkin Gulf Resolution. Congress never declared war against North Vietnam. Johnson used the Tonkin Gulf Resolution as authority to increase American involvement in South Vietnam.

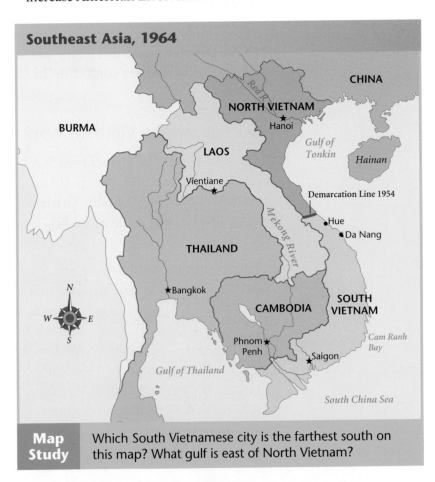

Southeast Asia, 1964

| **Map Study** | Which South Vietnamese city is the farthest south on this map? What gulf is east of North Vietnam? |

The Communist North Vietnamese continued to hold on to rural sections of South Vietnam. Even though many Vietcong groups were destroyed, they were quickly **replenished** by North Vietnamese. By the start of 1968, it was clear that the United States was not winning the war.

President Johnson set up a meeting with North and South Vietnam, the United States, and the Vietcong. The 1969 meeting was held in Paris, France, just after Johnson's presidency ended. Unfortunately, this meeting had little effect on ending the fighting.

Lesson 4 Review On a sheet of paper, write the correct word or words from the Word Bank to complete each sentence.

Word Bank

Barry Goldwater

Housing Act

Lyndon Johnson

Medicare

Tonkin Gulf Resolution

1. _____ won the 1964 election for president.

2. The Republican Party nominated _____ for the 1964 election.

3. The _____ encouraged people to build low-cost housing.

4. The _____ Plan provided health insurance to the elderly.

5. Congress passed the _____ to protect American forces near North Vietnam.

What do you think

Why is it important to have low-cost housing available?

It Happened in History

In 1900, the United States government began to protect the nation's natural environment. In that year, President William McKinley signed a law to prevent birds from being killed for their feathers. This law was the beginning of the nation's first conservation movement to protect wildlife.

Sixty years later, birds were seen dropping from the sky. In 1962, Rachel Carson published *Silent Spring.* Carson argued in her book that a chemical (DDT) created to kill insects was killing birds. Something had to be done to protect wildlife and the environment. The first Clean Air Act was passed in 1963. The National Wilderness Preservation System became law in 1964. The Endangered Species Preservation Act was passed in 1966. President John F. Kennedy wrote in 1963, "The history of America has been the story of Americans seizing, using, squandering and belatedly protecting their natural heritage."

Feminist

A person who seeks equal rights for women

Liberation

Equal social or economic rights

The 1960s was a time when many Americans were committed to changing their society. The civil rights movement started a movement for Black Power. **Feminists** called for the **liberation** of women. Hispanic Americans made their problems known to the nation. The American Indian Movement (AIM) demanded better opportunities for American Indians. College students wanted more control of what they studied. Antiwar protesters wanted to end America's involvement in the war in Vietnam. Young people challenged the basic social rules of an older generation.

Many Americans protested the Vietnam War.

Who Led the Civil Rights Movement?

Martin Luther King Jr. was awarded the Nobel Peace Prize in 1964. This award recognized the work of Dr. King in the civil rights movement. Under his leadership, progress had been made in increasing equality for African Americans. The civil rights movement tried to end segregation.

Some leaders called for a new direction for African Americans. Malcolm X, a Black Muslim, encouraged African Americans to develop their own power and separate from white Americans who treated them unequally. He believed that African Americans should start their own businesses. He wanted them to begin to control their own communities.

Stokely Carmichael, an African American leader, said African Americans needed "Black Power." He wanted them to have more than economic and political power. The Black Power movement encouraged African Americans to become interested in their history and culture. They developed a pride in their ethnic heritage.

Under the forceful leadership of President Johnson and members of Congress, the Civil Rights Act of 1964 was passed. The law prohibited discrimination in public places, such as stores, transportation facilities, and restaurants. In addition, this law prohibited those that receive federal funds from discriminating against anyone on the basis of their race, sex, religion or national origin. The Voting Rights Act of 1965 gave federal government the power to protect the right of every citizen to vote. In a few years, voter registration by African Americans in southern states increased by more than 50 percent.

What Was the Women's Movement?

In 1960, leaders of a new feminist, or women's, movement said that women should have the same social and economic rights as men. They believed women should be able to work in any job, including jobs that men usually held. Feminists wanted equal pay for equal jobs. The women's movement tried to gain full equality for women through the Equal Rights Amendment (ERA). The leaders of the movement wanted this amendment added to the Constitution. The Equal Rights Amendment was passed by many states but not enough to make it part of the Constitution.

Biography

Cesar Chavez: 1927–1993

Labor leader Cesar Chavez devoted his time to unionizing poor migrant farm workers. Chavez was born into a Mexican American family who became migrant farm laborers when he was 10 years old. As a child, Chavez worked in the fields as he moved with his family. In 1962, he established the National Farm Workers Association. Migrant farm workers lived at the mercy of their employers and without protection of federal law. He organized strikes and picket lines to gain support for their cause. Chavez also organized peaceful sit-ins and marches. His efforts included a long, bitter strike against California grape growers. One of the strategies of the strike was a nationwide refusal to buy California grapes. The strike's startling success in 1970 led to the organization of farm workers' unions in different states.

Migrant

A worker who travels from place to place to work

Baby boom

The millions of babies born after World War II

What Problems Did Hispanic Americans Face?

Americans whose parents or ancestors came from Spanish-speaking countries are called Hispanic Americans. Hispanic culture—food, music, dress, and language—had had a major influence on American life. Still, in the 1960s, many Hispanic Americans were poor and had little education. Many were discriminated against. Hispanic leaders brought these problems to the nation's attention. One such leader was Cesar Chavez. He led a movement to organize Mexican American **migrants**. These are workers who move from place to place to find work. Chavez organized the National Farm Workers Association to help Hispanic farm workers.

What Was the Youth Movement?

After World War II, millions of children were born. This was known as the **baby boom**. These children grew up during the cold war, yet they were raised in a nation with a growing economy. America held great opportunity for them.

In the 1960s, the baby boom generation reached their late teens and early 20s. Many challenged the values and views of their parents. The main challenge involved the Vietnam War. Unlike their parents who had lived through World War II, many baby boomers had trouble viewing the war as a patriotic effort.

What Was the Counterculture?

In the 1960s, many young people started creating a **counterculture**. It was very different from American society at the time. Long hair, casual clothes, beads, and headbands were the accepted styles of the counterculture. Rock music became their voice. Freedom from America's social rules was one theme of the youth movement. The phrase "doing your own thing" became popular. The most extreme members of the youth culture were called **hippies**.

Many youths got very involved with their communities. They worked to clean up their environment. They became interested in politics. Many young people joined the antiwar movement. They organized protest marches to bring attention to their causes.

Then and Now

On July 20, 1969, American Astronauts Neil Armstrong and Edwin Aldrin Jr. landed their spacecraft, the *Eagle,* on the moon. This mission, called *Apollo 11,* put the first astronauts on the moon. About 6 hours after landing, Armstrong took his first steps on the moon. He said, "That's one small step for a man, one giant leap for mankind." Armstrong and Aldrin put the American flag on the moon and collected rock and soil samples.

Since that first step on the moon, our knowledge of space has grown enormously. Satellites, rovers, and space stations—as well as crews and scientists—have continued to uncover new information about the solar system. For example, in June and July 2003, twin rovers were sent to Mars. Those rovers—named *Spirit* and *Opportunity*—landed on Mars in January 2004. There they explored the rocks and craters. They found evidence that liquid water had been there in the past. An expert at NASA predicted that humans could be on Mars by the year 2030.

What Was Woodstock?

On a weekend in August 1969, a rock concert took place on a 600-acre farm in upstate New York. About 400,000 people attended the concert, which was billed as the Woodstock Music and Arts Fair. There were shortages of water and food. People shared what little they had and the crowd remained peaceful. Woodstock became national news; it was hailed for its peacefulness. Many young people hoped that Woodstock was the beginning of a new and better America.

Lesson 5 Review On a sheet of paper, write the answers to the following questions. Use complete sentences.

1. What was the goal of feminists?

2. What did Malcolm X encourage?

3. What happened to the Equal Rights Amendment?

4. How did Cesar Chavez help Mexican American farm workers?

5. What is a counterculture?

What do you think?

How is the counterculture of the 1960s like youth today?

It Happened in History

The role of the Supreme Court is to interpret the Constitution. It tells the nation what the Constitution means because it is not always clear to everyone. Interpreting the Constitution can be difficult, because it was written more than 200 years ago. For example, the First Amendment states: "Congress shall make no law respecting an establishment of religion or prohibiting the free exercise thereof. . . . "

How does the Supreme Court determine what the words "respecting an establishment of religion" mean? What does the "free exercise" of religion mean? The Supreme Court looks at the "plain meaning" of the words and what the original writers of the Constitution meant. In 1963, the Supreme Court considered whether a state could require Bible reading in the public schools. The court ruled that the government must be neutral about religion. The court created a test: Laws must have a non-religious purpose that neither harms nor helps the free exercise of religious beliefs.

Ironic

The opposite of what is expected

Throughout the 1960s, the Vietnam War grew to be a major concern for Americans. Questions arose about why the United States was involved. Americans were unsure who was winning the war. One day, the United States would announce a major victory in Vietnam. The next day, news reports would announce heavy losses of American troops. The public did not know what to believe. Television brought the horrors of the war directly into American homes.

Why Did Johnson Decide Not to Run for Re-election?

President Johnson was concerned about the political election. He saw the nation becoming divided into two groups—the hawks and the doves. The hawks favored war and wanted to win at all costs. The doves did not want the United States to be involved with the war.

Johnson tried to please both sides. He increased the bombing to please the hawks. At the same time, he helped start peace talks to make the doves happy.

On March 31, 1968, President Johnson spoke to the nation on television. He began with a routine talk about the war. He announced that he was going to reduce the bombings in North Vietnam. He ended his speech with the announcement that he would not seek the Democratic nomination for president.

What Happened to Martin Luther King Jr.?

Four days later, on April 4, 1968, Martin Luther King Jr. was shot to death. He had traveled to Memphis, Tennessee, to support a strike by African American city workers. It was **ironic** that a man who had preached and practiced nonviolence died as the victim of a violent act. It was also ironic that the anger that many African Americans felt at his murder led to riots and to acts of violence. Military troops were needed to control riots in many cities.

What Happened to Robert Kennedy?

Robert Kennedy's campaign for the Democratic nomination for president had been gaining strength. On June 4, 1968, Robert Kennedy won the California primary. That night, he was shot by a young Jordanian Arab who did not like Kennedy's support for Israel. Two days after he was shot, Robert F. Kennedy died.

Who Won the Election of 1968?

The Democratic Party nominated Vice President Hubert Humphrey as its candidate for president. The Democratic convention was held in August in Chicago, Illinois. Thousands of people held antiwar protests outside of the convention site. Police broke up the protests by beating protesters with clubs. Inside the convention hall, delegates shouted angry words at each other. The Democratic Party was divided and confused. Many people felt that Humphrey would continue Johnson's **controversial** policies in Vietnam.

The Republican Party nominated Richard M. Nixon for president. Nixon's campaign theme was "Bring Us Together." He called for "law and order" and said he had a plan to end the war in Vietnam. He wanted "peace with honor."

George Wallace entered the presidential race as a candidate of the newly formed American Independent Party. He was a former Democratic governor from Alabama who had supported segregation. Wallace appealed to southern **blue-collar** workers. Many of these people had worked their way up without help from the federal government. They were not supportive of many federal programs.

The election was very close. Nixon received 31.8 million votes to Humphrey's 31.3 million votes. Wallace received almost 10 million votes. Nixon won the election, but he received less than 50 percent of the popular vote.

Word Bank

Lyndon B. Johnson

Martin Luther
  King Jr.

Hubert Humphrey

Richard M. Nixon

Vietnam

Lesson 6 Review Choose the name in the Word Bank that best completes each sentence. Write your answers on a sheet of paper.

1. President Johnson tried to please both the hawks who wanted victory in _____ and the doves who wanted out of the war.

2. On March 31, 1968, President _____ announced that he would not run for re-election.

3. An act of violence ended the life of _____, who preached nonviolence.

4. The Democratic Party nominated _____ to run for president in 1968.

5. Republican candidate _____ won the election with less than 50 percent of the vote.

What do you think ?

Why do you think there was so much political violence in the 1960s?

History in Your Life

Salk and the Polio Vaccine

In 1943, the most well-known person with polio was President Franklin D. Roosevelt. In 1943, polio caused 1,151 deaths. Still more people became crippled with polio that year.

A viral infection causes polio, which is short for poliomyelitis. In severe form, polio destroys nerve cells that control skeletal muscles. It paralyzes the legs, arms, or trunk. Swallowing, talking, breathing, and heart functions can be affected. Polio occurs most often in children.

In 1953, Jonas E. Salk developed a polio vaccine. After intense laboratory tests, he vaccinated Pittsburgh schoolchildren. That same year, the vaccine was tested in schools in 44 states. It was the largest field test in history. In 1956, Salk announced that before long polio would be wiped out. He was right—1969 was the first year in recorded American medical history that no one died from polio.

John F. Kennedy's Inaugural Address

On January 20, 1961, John Fitzgerald Kennedy became the 35th president of the United States. Before becoming president, Kennedy served in the House of Representatives and the Senate from Massachusetts.

As president, Kennedy wanted to gather support for his plans for the country, especially in foreign affairs. The following passages are from his inaugural address, which inspired many Americans.

We observe today not a victory of party, but a celebration of freedom—symbolizing an end, as well as a beginning—signifying renewal as well as change. . . .

Let the word go forth from this time and place, to friend and foe alike, that the torch has been passed to a new generation of Americans—born in this century, tempered by war, disciplined by a hard and bitter peace, proud of our ancient heritage—and unwilling to witness or permit the slow undoing of those human rights to which this nation has always been committed, and to which we are committed today at home and around the world.

Let every nation know, whether it wishes us well or ill, that we shall pay any price, bear any burden, meet any hardship, support any friend, oppose any foe, in order to assure the survival and success of liberty. This much we pledge—and more. . . .

Finally, to those nations who would make themselves our adversary [enemy], we offer not a pledge but a request: that both sides begin anew the quest for peace. . . .

And so, my fellow Americans: ask not what your country can do for you—ask what you can do for your country.

My fellow citizens of the world: ask not what America will do for you, but what together we can do for the freedom of man.

Finally, whether you are citizens of America or citizens of the world, ask of us here the same high standards of strength and sacrifice which we ask of you. With a good conscience our only sure reward, with history the final judge of our deeds, let us go forth to lead the land we love. . . .

Document-Based Questions

1. What did Kennedy mean when he said, "the torch has been passed to a new generation"?

2. What did Kennedy pledge Americans would do on behalf of liberty?

3. What did the president offer to enemies?

4. What did Kennedy ask Americans and world citizens to ask themselves?

5. According to Kennedy, what is the final judge of citizens?

Source: President John F. Kennedy's Inaugural Address, 1961.

- In 1961, the first of many space flights with people on board began with the Mercury and Gemini space programs.

- John F. Kennedy became president in 1961. He approved a plan developed under President Eisenhower to support an invasion of Cuba by Cuban rebels to overthrow the Castro government. The invasion at the Bay of Pigs was a complete failure.

- In 1961 the Soviets built the Berlin Wall that divided East and West Berlin.

- The Soviet Union was providing supplies for missile bases in Cuba. U.S. ships prevented Soviet ships from reaching Cuba. Later, a deal was struck between America and the Soviet Union that ended the Cuban missile crisis.

- African Americans and whites joined together to help end segregation. Hundreds of protest marches, sit-ins, and demonstrations were staged. In 1963, an immense march on Washington was held to urge passage of civil rights legislation.

- During his presidency, Kennedy had created the Peace Corps and NASA and had proposed funding to help many people in poverty. President Kennedy was assassinated in Dallas on November 22, 1963. Lyndon Johnson became president.

- President Johnson wanted to build a "Great Society." He wanted to provide education and health care for all Americans. At his urging, Congress passed legislation that created Medicare, provided federal funds for schools, and encouraged low-cost housing.

- In 1964, Congress passed the Tonkin Gulf Resolution, which allowed Johnson to send American combat troops to Vietnam.

- Among the social developments of the 1960s were the feminist movement, the Black Power movement, the antiwar movement, the organization of Hispanic migrants, and the youth movement.

- Civil rights leader Martin Luther King Jr. was assassinated on April 4, 1968.

- Richard Nixon was elected president in November 1968.

Chapter 28 REVIEW

Word Bank

baby boom

Cesar Chavez

Cuban missile crisis

Great Society

John F. Kennedy

Peace Corps

Robert Weaver

Tonkin Gulf
   Resolution

On a sheet of paper, write the correct words from the Word Bank to complete each sentence.

1. President _____ ordered American ships to prevent Soviet ships from reaching Cuba.

2. The _____ was what President Johnson called his plan for the country.

3. President Kennedy started the _____, which sent American volunteers overseas to help underdeveloped nations.

4. America's population grew after World War II because of the _____.

5. _____ was the first African American to be on a president's Cabinet.

6. _____ organized a union for farm workers in California.

7. The _____ showed that President Kennedy could stand up to the Soviet Union.

8. The _____ allowed President Johnson to send combat troops to Vietnam.

On a sheet of paper, write the letter of the answer that correctly completes each sentence.

9. The Civil Rights Act passed in 1964 granted the government power to _____.

A organize boycotts

B increase segregation of public areas

C use violence against peaceful protesters

D speed up school desegregation

10. _____ were an important factor in deciding the presidential election of 1960.

A African American votes   **C** cold war fears

B televised debates   **D** scandals

11. The _____ was a failed invasion of Cuba supported by President Kennedy.

    A Cuban missile crisis   **C** *Sputnik*

    B Bay of Pigs   **D** Berlin Wall

12. _____ was a strong leader for African American civil rights.

    A Cesar Chavez   **C** Martin Luther King Jr.

    B John Glenn   **D** Robert Weaver

On a sheet of paper, write the answers to the following questions. Use complete sentences.

13. What were three of the federal social programs that were passed during the 1960s?

14. Why were the Bay of Pigs invasion and the Cuban missile crisis major events in the Kennedy presidency?

15. What were three developments in the civil rights movement during this period?

16. Why did America become involved in Vietnam?

17. How did the Vietnam War cause a division in the American people?

18. Who were the "freedom riders" and what did they do?

Critical Thinking On a sheet of paper, write your response to each question. Use complete sentences.

19. During the 1960s, young people listened to music that spoke about their society and their concerns. Is there anything similar to this today? Explain your answer.

20. Before the space program, people had never flown in space. Today space shuttles make regular flights. Would you like to go into space? Why or why not?

Test-Taking Tip

Directions for a test may include examples. Read the examples thoroughly. Try to understand why the example is done as shown. If it is unclear to you, try reading the directions again.

Political Cartoons

Political cartoons are funny drawings about political events. The purpose of a cartoon is to make people laugh. However, cartoons also express a viewpoint about a political issue or topic. Cartoons encourage people to think about current issues. Cartoonists reveal various opinions in a drawing. They can persuade others to support their opinion through the cartoon.

Cartoons often use symbols, or objects that stand for something else. The elephant has long been a symbol of the Republican Party. The donkey is the symbol of the Democratic Party. These two animals often show up in political cartoons.

Cartoonists add labels or captions to help readers interpret the drawing. The cartoon here has three labels. They are "1964," "L.B.J.," and "Old Smoky Sauce." This cartoon was published in 1964, a presidential election year. The label "1964" is on top of a bed of hot coals. "L.B.J." is Lyndon Baines Johnson, the 36th president. LBJ was a Democrat from Texas who was campaigning for president in 1964. His opponent was Senator Barry Goldwater, a Republican from Arizona. "Old Smoky Sauce" is barbecue sauce. The cartoon shows LBJ painting Old Smoky Sauce on an elephant. He is pictured as getting ready to barbecue the Republicans in the 1964 election.

"Hang Around Till Next Fall . . . We're Planning a Big, Texas-Style Barbecue"

Study the cartoon. Then answer these questions. Use complete sentences.

1. Why is the fire labeled "1964"?

2. Why did the cartoonist dress LBJ as a cowboy?

3. What does the elephant symbolize?

4. What is the meaning of the cartoon?

5. Find a current political cartoon in your newspaper. Write what you think it means.

- The United Nations was created in San Francisco, California, in April 1945.

- Distrust developed between Communist and non-Communist countries. America supported anti-Communist governments.

- The Berlin airlift lasted until the Soviets reopened railroads and highways.

- In 1950, North Korea invaded South Korea. America sent troops to South Korea. After three years, the war ended.

- World War II hero Dwight D. Eisenhower was elected president in 1952.

- Senator Joseph McCarthy used fear of Communism to accuse people of Communism or Communist sympathy.

- The civil rights movement grew in the 1950s. Congress passed the Civil Rights Law in 1957.

- During the 1950s, America was prosperous.

- America launched its first successful satellite in 1958. The first space flights with people on board began in 1961.

- John F. Kennedy became president in 1961. His plan to invade Cuba and overthrow the Castro government failed.

- The Soviets built the Berlin Wall in 1961.

- The Soviets supplied Cuban missile bases. U.S. ships kept Soviet ships from Cuba. A deal between America and the Soviets ended the crisis.

- African Americans and whites joined to help end segregation. In 1963, the March on Washington was held to urge civil rights legislation.

- President Kennedy was killed in Dallas on November 22, 1963. Lyndon Johnson became president.

- At Johnson's urging, Congress passed laws for Medicare, school funds, and low-cost housing.

- In 1964, the Tonkin Gulf Resolution allowed Johnson to send American troops to Vietnam.

- The 1960s had many social movements that changed society.

- Martin Luther King Jr. was murdered on April 4, 1968.

- Richard Nixon was elected president in 1968.

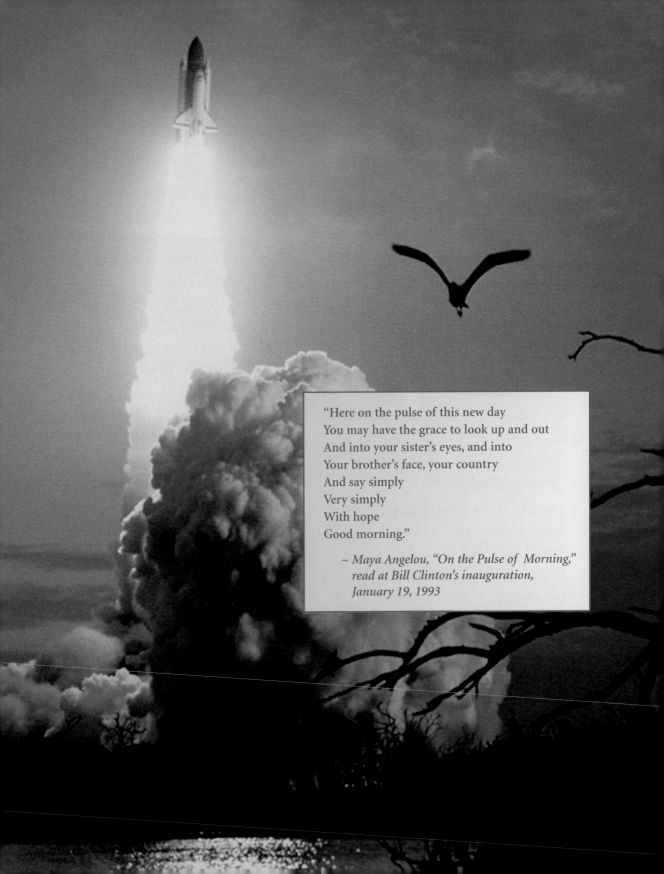

"Here on the pulse of this new day
You may have the grace to look up and out
And into your sister's eyes, and into
Your brother's face, your country
And say simply
Very simply
With hope
Good morning."

~ *Maya Angelou, "On the Pulse of Morning,"*
read at Bill Clinton's inauguration,
January 19, 1993

Unit 10

Contemporary United States

Perhaps you know how good it feels to be a peacemaker or a peacekeeper. The United States has experienced that feeling. America celebrated its 200th birthday in 1976 with the wisdom of age. Then in the 1980s and 1990s it played a role as peacemaker or peacekeeper in the troubled Middle East. America signed agreements to limit nuclear weapons. It helped other countries defend their freedom. At home, the country attempted to resolve its own social and economic struggles.

Contemporary refers to modern times. In this unit, you will learn about America's roles as an international peacemaker and peacekeeper since 1970. You will learn how the nation handled economic and social situations at home. You will learn about America's place in the world following the terrorist attacks of September 11, 2001.

Chapters in Unit 10

29 America in a Changing World

The nation had been in turmoil during much of the 1960s. The Vietnam War was one of the reasons. Americans were ready to see the war end. As the nation moved into the 1970s, scandals in the presidency provided a new problem at home. International issues also challenged the nation's foreign policy. In this chapter, you will learn more about the Vietnam War, about presidential scandal, and about American involvement in international issues.

Goals for Learning

◆ To explain how the Vietnam War ended and the results of the war

◆ To describe how the United States improved relations with China and the Soviet Union

◆ To describe the events of the Watergate scandal

◆ To list the problems President Ford faced

◆ To list national and international problems President Carter faced

◆ To describe the hostage crisis and problems with the Soviet Union

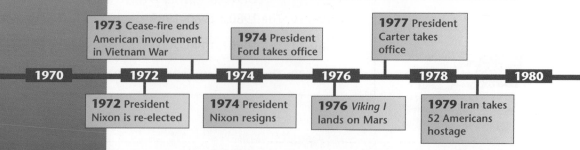

1973 Cease-fire ends American involvement in Vietnam War

1974 President Ford takes office

1977 President Carter takes office

| 1970 | 1972 | 1974 | 1976 | 1978 | 1980 |

1972 President Nixon is re-elected

1974 President Nixon resigns

1976 *Viking I* lands on Mars

1979 Iran takes 52 Americans hostage

Collapse

Breakdown or ruin

Richard Nixon had promised to bring the troubled country together again. This was not a simple task. The first problem he faced when he took office in 1969 was to try to end the Vietnam War.

How Did Problems Continue in Vietnam?

Nixon announced a plan to turn the defense of South Vietnam over to the South Vietnamese during the next three years. Americans, however, had grown impatient waiting for an end to the war.

Cambodia is along the western border of South Vietnam. It tried very hard to remain neutral. However, its government could not prevent the Vietcong and the North Vietnamese from setting up bases on the South Vietnam border. The Communists used these bases to set up attacks against the Americans and South Vietnamese. In 1970, President Nixon allowed American troops to destroy the enemy supplies in Cambodia.

The North Vietnamese and Vietcong seized control of the northeastern section of Cambodia. Some Cambodians joined forces with these armies and spread out westward and southward. They were moving toward the capital of Phnom Penh. The United States wanted to prevent the complete **collapse** of the Cambodian government. It sent Cambodia large amounts of military supplies. American bombers gave air support to the Cambodian army.

What Happened at Kent State University?

The news of the American involvement in Cambodia caused large antiwar protests in cities around the country. Many protests took place at colleges. Feeling that these protesters were a small minority, Nixon asked for support from the "silent majority."

On May 2, 1970, a protest by students at Kent State University in Ohio ended with the burning of a school building. The governor ordered the National Guard to the university. On May 4, some students threw rocks at National Guard soldiers. The soldiers began shooting at the protesters, killing four students. This caused the Senate to end financial and military support for Cambodia.

How Did the Vietnam War End?

Nixon was re-elected president in 1972. He ran against Senator George McGovern of South Dakota. McGovern wanted to withdraw from Vietnam immediately. Many Democrats refused to support such a policy and voted for Nixon. Others voted for Nixon because he was trying to remove troops from Vietnam gradually.

In 1973 in Paris, France, North Vietnam and the United States signed a cease-fire agreement. The Paris Peace Accords stated

that the United States would remove all troops from South Vietnam but continue to give the country military and economic aid. North Vietnam agreed to release American prisoners of war, or POWs. This agreement was only partly successful. In 1975, North Vietnam invaded South Vietnam. Without American military support, the South Vietnamese government could not survive. Their army soon fell apart. In April 1975, the army of North Vietnam captured Saigon, the capital of South Vietnam.

The Vietnam War Memorial in Washington, D.C., was designed by Maya Lin. It was built in 1982 to honor American soldiers killed or missing in Vietnam.

Helicopters from the roof of the American Embassy rescued American officials and some South Vietnamese. After a decade of fighting, the Vietnam War ended. More than one million Vietnamese on both sides died in the war. More than 50,000 American soldiers were killed.

Summary of the Vietnam War

- It was the longest war in United States history.
- About 58,000 Americans were killed; about 300,000 were wounded.
- The total cost to the United States was $150 billion.
- The war caused confusion about the nation's role in world affairs.
- The War Powers Act was passed, requiring the president to explain to Congress within 48 hours whenever American troops were to be sent into a foreign country.

Lesson 1 Review On a sheet of paper, write the answers to the following questions. Use complete sentences.

1. What was President Nixon's plan for Vietnam?

2. Why did the United States want to help Cambodia?

3. Why did violence break out at Kent State University?

4. What was the purpose of the Paris Peace Accords?

5. What became of South Vietnam once the United States stopped helping it?

What do you think ?

Do you think President Nixon was right to withdraw troops from Vietnam? Why or why not?

Rival

A well-matched opponent

In the early 1950s, Chinese and American troops were enemies in the Korean War. For 20 years afterward, the relations between China and the United States had remained weak. Americans did not trade with or travel to China. The United States refused to recognize the government of the People's Republic of China. Instead, they called the Taiwan government the legal government of China.

Nixon wanted to relax the tensions of the cold war. The goal was called *détente,* a French word meaning relaxation. He hoped to improve relations with China and the Soviet Union. He waited until he thought these two countries would be open to his ideas. The Soviet Union and China were never close allies. Now their relationship was weakening, and they were becoming **rivals**. Nixon saw this as a good time for new negotiations.

What Did Nixon Do in China?

Henry Kissinger, Nixon's top foreign policy adviser, secretly went to China in 1971. He met with Chinese Premier Chou En-lai. Afterward, Chou En-lai invited Nixon to come to China. When Nixon announced to the American public that he intended to visit China, many were shocked. The Soviet Union was not pleased.

Nixon went to China in February 1972. Nixon and Chou En-lai made many efforts to settle their differences. After eight days of meetings, the two leaders announced that they agreed:

- to open up trade;
- to improve scientific and cultural relations;
- that neither country would try to dominate the Pacific;
- that the United States would recognize Taiwan as belonging to the People's Republic of China.

What Did Nixon Do in the Soviet Union?

The Soviet Union was concerned about the new relationship between the United States and China. The Soviets feared that these two countries might become allied against them. Three months after the successful meeting in China, Nixon went to Moscow. This was the first time a United States president had visited the Soviet Union in peacetime.

Nixon and Soviet President Leonid Brezhnev discussed the arms race between the two countries. They agreed to sign a treaty limiting the number of **strategic** weapons each country could have. It was called the Strategic Arms Limitation Talks (SALT). They also agreed to increase trade between the two countries and to cooperate in space exploration.

President Nixon (center, holding papers) and President Brezhnev enjoyed a light moment in Moscow. Henry Kissinger (seated) signed an agreement between the United States and the Soviet Union.

It Happened in History

Government and the Environment

During the Nixon and Ford administrations, laws were passed to clean the nation's waterways and polluted air. Laws to protect endangered species and national forests were also passed. The environment gained further protection during the Carter administration. The Clean Air Act and Clean Water Act were strengthened. More land was set aside as national parks and wilderness areas. During the Carter administration, more land came under environmental protection than under any previous president.

The Endangered Species Act passed in 1973 prohibited the federal government from changing the land if the change would harm the animals that lived there. Today there are more than 500 threatened and endangered animal species in the United States.

The Environmental Protection Agency protects against air pollution such as this.

Word Bank

China

Chou En-lai

détente

Leonid Brezhnev

trade

What do you think ?

Why do you think it was important for President Nixon to meet with the Chinese and the Soviets?

Lesson 2 Review On a sheet of paper, write the correct word or words from the Word Bank to complete each sentence.

1. The word _____ was used to describe President Nixon's attempt to relax tensions of the cold war.

2. Nixon visited China and met with Chinese Premier _____.

3. Next, Nixon was asked to visit the Soviet Union and meet with its president _____.

4. The United States reached agreements with both _____ and the Soviet Union.

5. These meetings resulted in increased _____ and limited strategic weapons.

Wiretap

A device used to listen in on phone conversations

Conspiracy

A joint act of breaking the law

Guilty

Having done wrong; deserving blame

Aide

One who assists

Even though Nixon was re-elected president in 1972, he was no longer in office when the fighting in Vietnam finally stopped in 1975. The political scandal known as Watergate ended his presidency.

Former Attorney General John Mitchell was chairman of Nixon's Committee to Re-elect the President (CREEP). In March 1972, Mitchell accepted a proposal from a former FBI agent named Gordon Liddy. Liddy wanted to spy on the Democrats. On June 17, 1972, five burglars broke into the Democratic Party main office in the Watergate building in Washington, D.C. The burglars wanted to photograph documents and place devices called **wiretaps** that could be used to listen in on telephone conversations. A night watchman became suspicious and called the police, who arrested the five burglars. A White House spokesman called the break-in just a "third-rate burglary."

How Was the Watergate Scandal Exposed?

The five burglars were convicted of **conspiracy,** burglary, and wiretapping in January 1973. A conspiracy is a joint act of breaking the law. Later, the judge received a letter from one of the men he had convicted. This man, James McCord, admitted that he lied under oath. He said that he was pressured by the Nixon administration to plead **guilty** and to remain silent about others who were involved in the spying. During the next several months, Nixon's top **aides** and advisers H. R. Haldeman and John Ehrlichman resigned. Another aide, John Dean, was fired.

In a televised speech on April 30, 1973, President Nixon announced the resignations of his aides and the firing of Dean. He later gave permission to Attorney General Elliot Richardson to appoint Archibald Cox as special prosecutor to investigate Watergate. Meanwhile, the Senate had formed its own committee to question members of Nixon's staff. These televised hearings lasted three months.

John Dean told the Senate committee that Nixon approved paying the burglars to keep quiet. The president had committed a crime by hiding the truth. Nixon denied Dean's charges. It was one man's word against the other. During the Senate hearings, it was learned that tape recordings of White House meetings could prove whether Nixon or Dean was telling the truth. Nixon refused to give either the committee or Cox these tapes. A court order, or **subpoena,** was issued for the tapes. Nixon still refused to turn them over.

Why Did the Vice President Resign?

An unrelated scandal went on about the same time as Watergate. It involved Vice President Spiro Agnew. He was under investigation for bribery, **extortion,** and **tax evasion** during his time as Maryland governor, and while he was vice president. Extortion is stealing money by using some kind of threat. Tax evasion is failing to pay one's taxes. On October 10, 1973, Agnew resigned. Nixon nominated Congressman Gerald R. Ford of Michigan to be the new vice president.

What Happened to President Nixon?

On a Saturday, 10 days after Agnew's resignation, Nixon ordered Archibald Cox to be fired. Attorney General Richardson resigned in protest because Nixon had not kept his promise of an investigation of Watergate. Nixon later fired Richardson's deputy, William Ruckelshaus. These events became known as the "Saturday Night Massacre."

The White House was flooded with phone calls and telegrams protesting Nixon's actions, while newspapers demanded that he resign. In response, Nixon handed over the subpoenaed tapes. One tape had an 18-minute gap. Apparently, a section of the tape had been erased. Some of the tapes Nixon promised to turn over could not be found. Meanwhile, the House Judiciary Committee was gathering **evidence** that might prove that the president should be impeached. Evidence is something that furnishes proof.

Gerald Ford was sworn in as president after President Nixon resigned.

President Nixon made another important speech on television in April 1974. He calmly explained that stacks of notebooks on a table beside him contained typed pages of what was said on the missing tapes. The president hoped everyone would believe that he had nothing to hide.

In May, Nixon refused when asked to turn over the disputed tapes. He knew the tapes contained evidence against him. By the end of July, the House Judiciary Committee had facts that were grounds for impeachment. In response, Nixon handed over the typed records of what was included on the tapes. These records revealed the president had been involved with the Watergate cover-up from the beginning.

The only way Nixon could avoid being impeached was to resign. On August 9, 1974, Nixon resigned from office. No president in United States history had ever resigned. While he did not admit guilt, Nixon said that some of his **judgments** were "wrong."

How Did Watergate Test the Constitution?

Several people in the Nixon administration were convicted of illegal acts in the Watergate scandal. The Constitution was tested as all three branches of government met up with a constitutional crisis. How well had the system worked? Gerald Ford said on the day that he became the 38th president, "My fellow Americans, our long national nightmare is over. Our Constitution works. Our great republic is a government of laws and not of men. Here, the people rule."

Then and Now

For many years, TV viewers were limited to programs on three big television networks. Then, cable TV came along. The basic appeal of cable TV is simple. The broadcast networks must provide programs that a large general audience will watch. The cable networks, on the other hand, can offer movies without commercials, music videos, or non-stop sports 24 hours a day. The broadcast networks cannot offer such specialized programming.

During the 1970s, cable TV expanded. Along with satellite delivery systems, it allowed people to choose from dozens of entertainment and information channels. As a result, cable TV has given everyone more control over what they see and hear.

Lesson 3 Review Choose the word or name in parentheses that best completes each sentence. Write your answers on a sheet of paper.

1. Five burglars broke into the Democratic Party main office in the (Watergate, White House, Senate) building.

2. (H. R. Haldeman, John Ehrlichman, Archibald Cox) was a special prosecutor for the Watergate investigation.

3. Vice President (Spiro Agnew, John Dean, Gerald R. Ford) resigned from office.

4. President Nixon left office when he (resigned, was impeached, was put in jail).

5. (Archibald Cox, Spiro Agnew, Gerald R. Ford) replaced President Nixon.

What do you think ?

You have learned about several scandals in presidencies in addition to the Watergate scandal. Why do you think there are so many scandals in presidencies?

Embargo

A government action that prevents certain goods from leaving a country

Crude oil

Oil in its natural state, before being processed

President Ford brought a very different atmosphere to the White House. Ford was direct and good-natured. He had been a popular and hard-working member of Congress.

In September 1974, President Ford surprised the nation by pardoning Nixon. Ford said Nixon had suffered enough punishment. He felt the nation had to forget Watergate and move on to other matters. However, Ford was criticized for this action.

What Problems Did Ford Face?

The Ford administration was left with several problems. Inflation and unemployment were very high. People were also unhappy with the government after the Vietnam War. Ford went forward cautiously.

A new conflict broke out between Israel and its Arab neighbors in October 1973. The United States and other countries were giving aid to Israel. Because of this aid, some Arab states put an **embargo** on oil shipments to these countries. An embargo is a government action that prevents certain goods from leaving a country. This resulted in a gas shortage. People had to wait in long lines at gas stations. There was a shortage of home heating oil. Americans were shocked at how dependent they were on other countries.

The Organization of Petroleum Exporting Countries (OPEC) began to control prices. OPEC included several nations in the Middle East, Africa, and South America. OPEC countries raised the price of **crude oil**. This action drove up the price of gasoline and heating oil in the United States.

U.S. Gasoline Prices (cents per gallon)

Year	Leaded Regular	Unleaded Regular
1973	38.8	—
1974	53.2	—
1975	56.7	—
1976	59.0	61.4
1977	62.2	65.6
1978	62.6	67.0

How Did America Celebrate Its Bicentennial?

In 1776, America declared its independence from Great Britain. The document was dated July 4, 1776. On July 4, 1976, Americans celebrated the fact that the Declaration of Independence was 200 years old. This celebration is called a **bicentennial**.

The celebration lasted for several months. More than 200 large sailing ships, called "tall ships," came from 30 nations. The ships docked in many East Coast harbors. Queen Elizabeth of Great Britain helped celebrate the independence that had been declared against King George III, her great-great-great grandfather. She presented a six-ton bell as a gift to the nation. In the nation's capital, 33 tons of fireworks lit the sky around the Washington Monument.

Although America's history was being celebrated in 1976, the nation seemed happy to forget its recent past for the moment. The nation's last 13 years had been difficult. A president and two national leaders were assassinated. A war was fought. A president and vice president resigned.

Biography

An Wang: 1920–1990

While at Harvard Computer Laboratory in 1948, physicist An Wang invented a magnetic core memory for computers. That invention was the most common early device for storing computer data. It revolutionized the computer industry before the microchip was invented. In 1951, he founded Wang Laboratories in Boston. The company produced specialty electronic devices, including desktop calculators. It was one of the largest, most successful high-tech companies in the United States in the 1970s. Wang held more than 35 patents related to computer technology. In addition, he was a board member and trustee of many institutions, including the Museum of Science of Boston. A native of Shanghai, China, Wang became a naturalized American citizen in 1954.

Fireworks celebrated America's bicentennial.

On July 4, 1976, it seemed that Americans were ready to celebrate a proud past and hope for a promising future. Two weeks later, on July 20, 1976, *Viking I* successfully landed on the surface of Mars. This was a perfect example of how far America had come in 200 years.

What do you think ?

Why is it important to celebrate the nation's meaningful dates such as the bicentennial?

Lesson 4 Review On a sheet of paper, write the answers to the following questions. Use complete sentences.

1. Why did President Ford pardon Nixon?

2. What problems did President Ford face when he took office?

3. What problems did OPEC cause for America?

4. What is a bicentennial?

5. How did Americans celebrate the bicentennial?

Focus on Economics

When OPEC changes the price of crude oil, the world economy is immediately affected. The United States depends on foreign countries for more than 50 percent of its oil needs. Higher oil prices mean higher prices for gasoline and other petroleum products. When people pay more for these products, they have less to spend elsewhere. Dependence on foreign oil leaves Americans with little control over oil prices. This is one reason many Americans want to find other energy sources.

Morality

Good behavior; knowing the difference between right and wrong

July 1976 was also the month the Democratic Party held its political convention. The Democrats nominated the little-known Jimmy Carter, former governor of Georgia, for their presidential candidate. Carter campaigned very hard to get his name and ideas known to the American people. He stressed honesty, openness, trust, and **morality** in his speeches. People responded positively to his promise to restore morality in the government.

People liked Carter because he was an outsider. He was not part of the established political groups in Washington, D.C. When he accepted the nomination, he said that "1976 will not be a year of politics as usual." He said that there was a "new mood in America" in people looking for "new voices, new ideas, and new leaders." Carter promised to give the government back to the people. Senator Walter Mondale, of Minnesota, was Carter's running mate.

President Ford and Ronald Reagan, the former governor of California, ran against one another for the Republican presidential nomination. Ford won a narrow victory over Reagan at the Republican National Convention. Ford selected Senator Robert Dole, of Kansas, as his running mate.

Who Won the Election of 1976?

The 1976 presidential election focused on such issues as the economy, the reputation of the candidates, and the desire for change. The election was extremely close. Carter won a narrow victory over Ford. Ford actually carried more states than Carter, but Carter's states had more electoral votes. Carter was the first person from the Deep South to be elected president since before the Civil War.

Writing About History

List five ways you could help save energy by conserving gasoline, heating oil, or natural gas. Make a chart to keep track of your efforts.

What Changes Did President Carter Make?

Jimmy Carter wanted to bring a different style to the office of president. He wanted the American people to see him as someone like them. He wore a plain business suit to his inauguration in 1977. His goal was to restore the people's confidence in their government. He was concerned with more than just style. President Carter wanted the government to provide better service at a lower cost. He reorganized the executive branch. He added two new departments—the Department of Energy in 1977 and the Department of Education in 1979.

The United States uses large amounts of energy. In the 1970s, Americans made up six percent of the world's population but used 33 percent of the world's energy. Millions of barrels of oil were imported from the Middle East. Before Carter became president, countries in the Middle East increased the price of oil and produced less of it. President Carter said that energy was a major problem for the nation. In 1978, Congress passed an energy bill that lowered the taxes for businesses that used less energy. Automotive companies were encouraged to produce smaller cars.

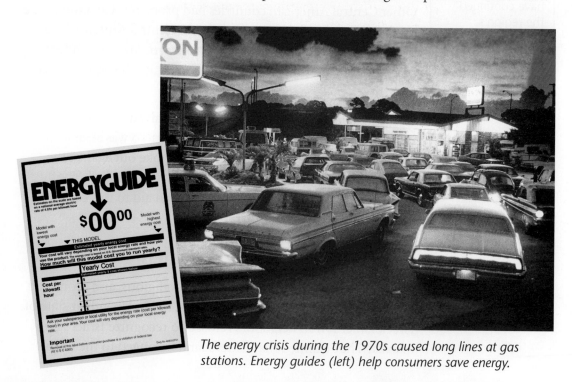

The energy crisis during the 1970s caused long lines at gas stations. Energy guides (left) help consumers save energy.

Geography Note

The term *Middle East* describes an area of northeast Africa, southeast Europe, and southwest Asia. The landscape varies from mountains to deserts to seacoasts. From ancient times, the Middle East has been a crossroads of competing empires and nearly constant warfare. Islam is the major religion of the region's many ethnic groups. Oil discoveries have continued the region's importance in world politics.

President Carter wanted to improve the American economy. The energy crisis made it difficult for him to do that. In 1978, inflation became a serious problem. As prices went up, workers demanded higher wages. Higher wages increased the cost of doing business. Businesses had to raise prices to cover their costs. By 1979, inflation was just over 11 percent. Normal inflation was three to five percent per year.

What Problems Developed in Central America?

Central America became a troubled area for American foreign policy at this time. The government of Panama was not happy over American ownership of the Panama Canal. President Carter signed two treaties with the government of Panama in 1977. The treaties promised to give control of the Panama Canal to Panama in the year 2000. One treaty gave the United States the right to defend the canal against any attack. Not all Americans agreed that the United States should give up control of the Panama Canal. However, the treaties created a warmer relationship between the two countries.

Other Central American countries had problems. Civil war broke out in Nicaragua, the largest country in Central America. The dictator, Anastasio Somoza, was overthrown. An independent government was established. The United States recognized this government.

Political violence broke out in 1980 in El Salvador, a tiny country in Central America. Archbishop Oscar Romero was assassinated. Romero had been a popular figure who spoke out against the military. Later, in December, six Americans were killed. The Carter administration took away American aid to this country until an investigation was completed.

What Problems Developed with Israel?

The Middle East had had many ethnic, religious, and economic problems. The United States supported the independent state of Israel. Israel's Arab neighbors refused to recognize Israel's right to exist. They claimed that Israel's land belonged to the Arabs.

From left, Anwar Sadat, President Carter, and Menachem Begin shook hands after signing the peace treaty at Camp David.

Throughout the years, the Arab countries were supported by Egypt in any conflicts in which they were involved. In November 1977, Egypt's president, Anwar Sadat, attempted to make peace with Israel's government.

President Carter wanted to encourage peace between these two nations. He invited Sadat and Prime Minister Menachem Begin of Israel to Camp David, the presidential retreat in Maryland. A peace treaty was signed in March 1979. Egypt finally recognized Israel as an independent state.

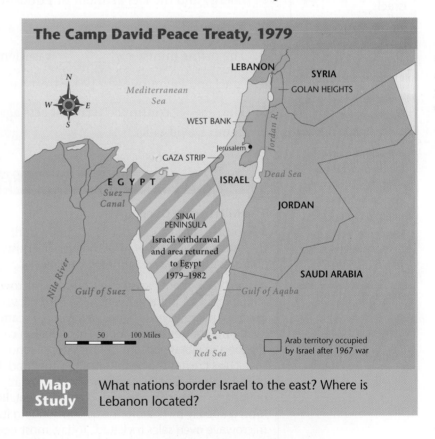

The Camp David Peace Treaty, 1979

LEBANON
SYRIA
GOLAN HEIGHTS
Mediterranean Sea
WEST BANK
Jerusalem
Jordan R.
GAZA STRIP
EGYPT
ISRAEL
Dead Sea
Suez Canal
JORDAN
SINAI PENINSULA
Israeli withdrawal and area returned to Egypt 1979–1982
Nile River
SAUDI ARABIA
Gulf of Suez
Gulf of Aqaba
0   50   100 Miles
Red Sea
Arab territory occupied by Israel after 1967 war

Map Study What nations border Israel to the east? Where is Lebanon located?

Arab nations felt **betrayed** by Sadat. The treaty did not deal with Jerusalem or Palestine. These lands had been taken over by Israel during earlier wars. The Palestine Liberation Organization (PLO) continued **terrorist** acts against Israel. Terrorists are groups or individuals who use violence to make others give in to their demands. Lebanon, Israel's neighbor, was caught in the middle of this tension. Many members of the PLO were located in Lebanon. Israel bombed Lebanon several times. The United States continued to support Israel and worked hard to find a solution to the Palestinian problem.

Word Bank

Anwar Sadat

Camp David

Israel

Jimmy Carter

PLO

Lesson 5 Review On a sheet of paper, write the correct word or words from the Word Bank to complete each sentence.

1. _____ added two new departments—the Department of Energy and the Department of Education.

2. The president of Egypt was _____.

3. The prime minister of _____ was Menachem Begin.

4. Israel and Egypt signed a peace treaty at _____.

5. The _____ continued terrorist acts against Israel after the Camp David talks.

What do you think

President Carter tried to work out disputes other countries were facing. Do you think it is America's responsibility to settle disputes?

History in Your Life

The Microwave Oven

Microwaves first caught public attention during World War II with the use of radar. Shortly after the war, scientists were able to "harness" microwaves for home cooking.

In the 1950s, manufacturers introduced microwave ovens called "radar ranges." In these ovens, an electronic vacuum tube produces bursts of microwaves. The microwaves are scattered around the oven until they enter the food. The radiation causes molecules in the food to vibrate billions of times per second. Friction among the molecules creates the heat that cooks the food. Microwave cooking produces heat directly inside the food. It greatly reduces the time needed to thaw frozen food and cook a meal. Regular ovens cook food gradually by heating the air surrounding it. In the 1970s, microwave oven sales rocketed. Today, most homes have a microwave oven.

Hostage

A person being held against his or her will by someone who wants certain demands to be met

The nation of Iran is an important oil-producing country in the Middle East. The United States depended on Iran's government to protect the flow of oil from the Middle East. The leader of Iran, Mohammad Reza Pahlavi, was called the shah. He allowed his country to adopt Western ways. As shah, he wanted Iran to be a modern nation. This went against the Islamic religious beliefs of some of his people.

In 1978, the shah began to lose his power. Public violence in the capital city of Tehran killed hundreds of people. Iranian students in the United States organized protests. The United States ordered any Americans living in Iran to leave the country.

A Muslim religious leader, the Ayatollah (meaning "reflection of God") Ruhollah Khomeini came to power in Iran. He established an Islamic republic to replace the shah in 1979.

What Was the Hostage Crisis?

In October 1979, President Carter allowed the shah to come to the United States for medical treatment. This act made some Iranians angry. On November 4, hundreds of Iranians took control of the American embassy in Iran. Sixty-six Americans were taken as **hostages**. A hostage is a person being held against his or her will by someone who wants certain demands to be met. Most of the women and all African Americans were soon released. The Iranians refused to release 52 remaining Americans until the United States returned the shah and the shah's wealth to Iran. They claimed that the shah stole money from Iran with the help of the United States.

The United States refused to return the shah. President Carter sent naval ships to the area. He ordered all oil imports from Iran stopped. Still, the Iranians refused to release the hostages. Americans paid close attention to the hostage crisis in the news.

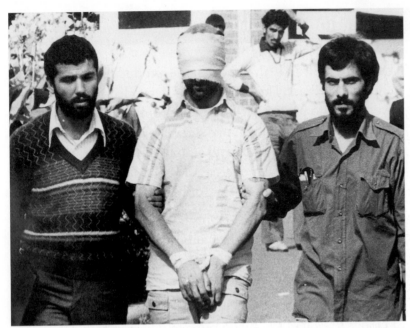

In April 1980, President Carter sent a small group of soldiers to rescue the hostages. The mission failed. Eight soldiers died in the desert when their helicopter crashed. President Carter spent many hours trying to find a way to bring the hostages home safely. He could not find a way to do it.

Two Iranians posed with this American hostage in Tehran, Iran.

Why Did the Soviets Invade Afghanistan?

On December 27, 1979, the Middle East suffered another crisis. Soviet troop transport planes landed in Kabul, the capital of Afghanistan, in support of government groups. Two days after the invasion, President Amin of Afghanistan and his family were executed. The new president, Babrak Karmal, was friendly toward the Soviet Union.

It is believed the Soviets invaded Afghanistan because the religious unrest in the Islamic world had made its way into the Soviet Union. Invading was one way to stop this problem. President Carter protested this invasion strongly. The United States boycotted the 1980 Olympics in the Soviet Union to show disapproval of the Soviet actions. Many other countries followed the United States' decision. The United States also stopped sending wheat and corn to the Soviet Union. The protests didn't stop the invasion. It took 10 years for the Soviets to end the fighting with Afghanistan.

What Was the SALT II Treaty?

Seven years after the SALT treaty was agreed to with the Soviet Union, President Carter met with Soviet Premier Leonid Brezhnev in Vienna, Austria. In 1979, they agreed to another treaty called SALT II. This treaty was never ratified by the United States Senate. Members of the Senate felt the treaty put the United States at a military disadvantage.

President Carter shook hands with Leonid Brezhnev after agreeing to the SALT II treaty.

What do you think ?

Some people in the Middle East do not like Americans. Why do you think this is so?

Lesson 6 Review Choose the term in parentheses that best completes each sentence. Write your answers on a sheet of paper.

1. The shah of Iran lost power because he allowed (Islamic, Western, violent) ways.

2. Iran took American hostages to protest when (the shah, the Ayatollah, President Carter) came to the United States for medical treatment.

3. Soviet troops invaded (Iran, Afghanistan, Austria) in 1979.

4. The United States and other countries did not attend the (1980 Olympics, SALT II talks, annual trade conference) in the Soviet Union.

5. The United States also stopped sending (oil, money, grain) to the Soviet Union in protest.

This Is the America We Want

In 1976, Jimmy Carter had been nominated as the Democratic candidate for president. He was full of hope and confidence. In this part of his acceptance speech for the nomination, he describes his vision for America in 1976.

Nineteen seventy-six will not be a year of politics as usual. It can be a year of inspiration and hope, and it will be a year of concern, of quiet and sober reassessment of our nation's character and purpose . . . a year when voters have confounded the experts. And I guarantee you that it will be the year when we give the government of this country back to the people of this country.

There is a new mood in America. We have been shaken by a tragic war abroad and by scandals and broken promises at home. Our people are searching for new voices and new ideas and new leaders. . . . There is a fear that our best years are behind us. But I say to you that our nation's best is still ahead.

Our country has lived through a time of torment. It is now a time for healing. We want to have faith again. We want to be proud again. We just want the truth again. It is time for the people to run the government, and not the other way around.

It is the time to honor and strengthen our families and our neighborhoods and our diverse cultures and customs.

I have never had more faith in America than I do today. We have an America that . . . is busy being born, not busy dying. . . . I see an America on the move again, united, a diverse and vital and tolerant nation, entering our third century with pride and confidence, an America that lives up to the majesty of our Constitution and the simple decency of our people.

This is the America we want. This is the America that we will have.

Document-Based Questions

1. According to President Carter, how was 1976 different from past election years?

2. What did Carter say had shaken America?

3. What three things did Carter say that the American people wanted?

4. What kind of America did Carter say the nation could be?

5. In your opinion, has President Carter's vision of America taken place?

Source: Jimmy Carter's acceptance speech, July 15, 1976.

- In 1969 when President Nixon took office, he announced a plan for Vietnam. This plan would end American involvement in the Vietnam War and give the South Vietnamese the responsibility of defending themselves. American forces left Vietnam in 1973. The war cost many American lives. North Vietnam took over South Vietnam by 1975.

- President Nixon traveled to China and the Soviet Union in 1972. This improved American relations with these countries.

- In 1974, President Nixon resigned from office to avoid being impeached because of the Watergate scandal. Evidence had been found that he had been involved in a conspiracy to spy on the Democratic party in the Watergate building.

- President Ford was met with high inflation, unemployment, and a Middle East oil embargo when he took office in 1974.

- America celebrated its 200th birthday, or bicentennial, in 1976.

- President Carter took office in 1977. People liked him because he seemed to be like them. He dealt with an energy crisis and problems in the Middle East and Central America during the early years of his presidency. Iran took 52 Americans hostage in 1979. Carter was unable to find a way to get the hostages released.

- The United States protested the Soviet Union's invasion of Afghanistan in 1979.

- President Carter agreed to the SALT II treaty with Soviet Premier Leonid Brezhnev in Vienna, Austria, in 1979. The U.S. Senate refused to ratify the treaty.

Chapter 29 REVIEW

Word Bank

Afghanistan

bicentennial

embargo

Gerald Ford

Iran

Jimmy Carter

Richard Nixon

resigned

SALT II

Watergate

On a sheet of paper, write the correct word or words from the Word Bank to complete each sentence.

1. _____ became president in 1977.

2. _____ met with President Brezhnev of the Soviet Union in 1972.

3. The _____ scandal involved a break-in at the Democratic party's main office.

4. Richard Nixon _____ from office to avoid being impeached.

5. _____ took over as president after Nixon left office.

6. America celebrated its _____ in 1976.

7. _____ held 52 Americans hostage.

8. Some Arab states set up an oil _____ because the United States and other countries were giving aid to Israel.

9. The Soviets invaded _____ in 1979.

10. President Carter agreed to the _____ treaty with the Soviet Union in 1979.

On a sheet of paper, write the letter of the answer that correctly completes each sentence.

11. The U.S. invasion of _____ led to angry protests and four student deaths.

A North Vietnam   **C** South Vietnam

B Kent State   **D** Cambodia

12. The vice president who resigned over charges of wrongdoing was _____.

A Spiro Agnew   **C** John Dean

B John Mitchell   **D** Richard Nixon

13. Countries that belonged to _____ raised oil prices in 1973.

A OPEC   **C** the PLO

B the Arab-Israeli alliance   **D** Ayatollah

On a sheet of paper, write the answer to each question. Use complete sentences.

14. What were the effects of the Vietnam War on the American people?

15. How did President Nixon improve relations with the Soviet Union and China?

16. Why did President Nixon refuse at first to give tape recordings to the Senate committee?

17. How did an energy problem develop when Gerald Ford became president?

18. What problems did President Carter face with the Middle East?

Critical Thinking On a sheet of paper, write your response to each question. Use complete sentences.

19. Many Americans protested the Vietnam War. If a similar war broke out today, would you protest? Why or why not?

20. If you had been an Olympic athlete in 1980, how would you have felt about the boycott of the Olympic games?

Test-Taking Tip

When taking a true-false test, read each statement carefully. Write *true* only when the statement is totally true. Write *false* if part or all of the statement is false. After each item, ask yourself, "Is this entire item true?" If not, mark it false.

The 1980s

International problems continued in the 1980s. The Reagan and Bush administrations, the next two American presidencies, faced these problems and made sweeping changes at home. During this time, the nation experienced social problems, the successes and failures of the space program, and the end of the cold war. In this chapter, you will learn about these and other important events that took place in the 1980s.

Goals for Learning

◆ To identify important national events that the Reagan administration faced

◆ To explain important foreign events facing the Reagan administration

◆ To describe events at the start of the Bush administration

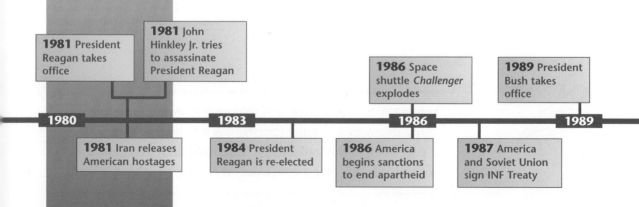

1981 President Reagan takes office

1981 John Hinkley Jr. tries to assassinate President Reagan

1986 Space shuttle *Challenger* explodes

1989 President Bush takes office

1980   **1983**   **1986**   **1989**

1981 Iran releases American hostages

1984 President Reagan is re-elected

1986 America begins sanctions to end apartheid

1987 America and Soviet Union sign INF Treaty

Surge

To rise swiftly

Dependent

Relying on others for one's needs

Budget

A plan that shows how much money is available and how the money will be spent

The Iranian hostage crisis caused the American people to question President Carter as a leader. He lost the 1980 election to Ronald Reagan. On January 20, 1981, the same day Ronald Reagan became president, Iran released the 52 American hostages.

Reagan was the oldest person ever to become president. He was 69 years old when he took office. He was well known to the American people. Reagan had been in movies and had appeared on television. He also had served as governor of California.

President Reagan wanted to return confidence to the American people. In his inaugural address, Reagan said that the country's biggest problem was inflation. He wanted to lower taxes and decrease the power of the federal government.

How Was Reagan Almost Assassinated?

President Reagan made a speech in Washington, D.C., on his 70th day in office. It was March 30, 1981. He included in his speech the remark, "Violent crime has **surged** 10 percent." Shortly thereafter, Reagan was walking toward his car when several shots were fired by a young man named John Hinkley Jr. The president, two of his aides, and a policeman were shot. Hinkley was immediately captured. President Reagan was rushed to a hospital, seriously wounded. His courage, confidence, and good humor calmed the nation. He was back in the White House full time in a month.

What Was Reagan's "New Federalism"?

President Reagan thought that many federal programs made people too **dependent** on the government. He believed that people should take responsibility for their own lives. Community problems, he said, should be solved by volunteer groups.

In 1981, Reagan announced that he wanted to cut the 1982 federal **budget** by $33 billion. He limited the amount of money spent on social programs. The only department not affected by the budget cuts was the Department of Defense. President Reagan called his plan to decrease the power of the federal government the "New Federalism."

What Was "Reaganomics"?

Literally

Taken exactly as something is stated, written, or directed

In an effort to get the country out of the "worst economic mess since the Great Depression," Reagan suggested tax and budget cuts. He believed these cuts would improve the economy and decrease the size of the federal government and the expansion of social programs. Congress passed the Economic Recovery Tax Act in 1981.

President Reagan's economic plan became known as "Reaganomics." This plan was based on a theory called "supply-side economics," which included these ideas: 1) When companies grow, they supply the economy with more jobs. 2) If companies spend less on paying government taxes, they will have more to invest in expanding their businesses. 3) The federal government collects too much money in taxes. 4) Paying fewer taxes and cutting government spending would eventually create more jobs.

Following this economic plan, the Reagan administration cut personal income taxes by 25 percent over a three-year period. They lowered business taxes and cut federal spending for education and the environment. Government spending on urban, social, cultural, and health problems was reduced. Critics of Reaganomics argued that cutting these programs seriously hurt the poor and middle class.

Who Did Reagan Appoint to the Supreme Court?

Justice Sandra Day O'Connor was the first woman to serve on the Supreme Court.

Reagan had promised that if a position opened on the Supreme Court, he would fill the opening with a woman. A position opened several months after Reagan took office. He appointed Sandra Day O'Connor from Arizona. She became the first woman to serve on the Supreme Court.

Reagan wanted to make the Supreme Court more conservative. Justice O'Connor was his first conservative appointment to the court. Conservatives interpret the Constitution **literally**. Conservatives have charged that liberal justices found new rights in the Constitution that were not intended when it was written.

Biography

Geraldine Ferraro: 1935–

Geraldine Ferraro is a native of New York. While she was working as a second-grade teacher, she went to school at night to earn a law degree. She practiced law and then worked as an assistant district attorney in New York. She served three terms in the House of Representatives.

She was working with the Democratic Party when Walter Mondale, who was running for president in 1984, chose her as his running mate. She was the first woman nominated to run for vice president by a major political party. Although the Mondale-Ferraro ticket lost the 1984 election, she changed ideas about women in politics. She went on to serve on the UN Human Rights Commission.

Career

A permanent job or line of work

What Did Americans Think of Reagan?

Reagan's style as a leader was criticized. He worked a normal eight-hour business day. He gave much of the responsibility of making decisions to members of his Cabinet and staff. In spite of the criticism, Reagan proved to be a popular president. He was re-elected in 1984. He defeated Walter Mondale, Carter's vice president. Mondale chose Congresswoman Geraldine Ferraro to run as his vice president.

What Happened to the Space Shuttle *Challenger*?

Before January 28, 1986, everyone thought of the space shuttle as a wonder of technology. The shuttle blasted into space and back successfully 24 times. People were confident that space travel was safe.

Much had been expected of the shuttle *Challenger*. Among the crew was a high school teacher named Christa McAuliffe. She planned to teach lessons from space and help with scientific experiments. After the flight, she would serve as a spokesperson for NASA about scientific **careers**.

Crew members of the Space Shuttle Challenger *are (left to right, front row). Michael J. Smith, Francis R. (Dick) Scobee, Ronald E. McNair; and (back row) Ellison S. Onizuka, Christa McAuliffe, Gregory Jarvis, and Judith A. Resnik.*

The *Challenger* takeoff seemed normal. However, two rubber "O-rings" failed as a result of cold temperatures. Millions of viewers across the world watched as the *Challenger* exploded into flames just 73 seconds into the flight. All seven members of the crew were killed. It was the worst disaster in 25 years of space flight. This loss and a series of rocket failures in 1986 set back the U.S. space program for two years.

Lesson 1 Review On a sheet of paper, write the correct word or words from the Word Bank to complete each sentence.

1. The first woman on the Supreme Court was _____.

2. _____ was the first woman to be nominated for vice president by a major political party.

3. President Reagan's plan to decrease the power of the federal government was known as _____.

4. _____ was President Reagan's plan to cut taxes and spending on education and the environment.

5. The crew of the space shuttle *Challenger* included _____, a high school teacher.

Word Bank

Christa McAuliffe

Geraldine Ferraro

New Federalism

Reaganomics

Sandra Day O'Connor

What do you think ?

Ronald Reagan was the oldest person ever to become president. Do you think this was an advantage or a disadvantage for him? Explain your answer.

At the end of World War II, political leaders divided the world into three parts. The first group of nations were the Western democracies. The second group were Communist countries. The nations that were not part of either group were called the Third World. Today we refer to them as developing countries. Most of these countries continue to struggle. They are not industrialized and have little power in world affairs.

The United States was concerned with problems in the developing countries. The Middle East continued to be a troubled area. In Central America, Nicaragua had a Communist government. The policies of South Africa troubled many Americans.

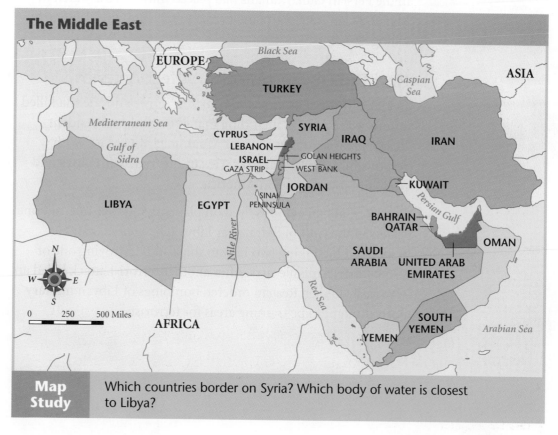

The Middle East

Map Study

Which countries border on Syria? Which body of water is closest to Libya?

What Problems Occurred in the Middle East?

President Anwar Sadat of Egypt was assassinated in 1981. Israeli troops moved into the nation of Lebanon in 1982 to destroy the bases of the Palestine Liberation Organization (PLO). The PLO wanted a homeland for the Palestinians. The Israelis accused the PLO of being a terrorist organization.

The United States wanted a peaceful settlement and sent marines as a peacekeeping force. In October 1983, a terrorist drove a truck loaded with **explosives** into the marine base. The truck exploded. Over 200 American soldiers died. Reagan did not remove American troops from Lebanon until February 1984, but the situation was still not settled. A war between Iran and Iraq began in 1980. The United States Navy began to protect shipping lanes in the Persian Gulf. Iranians had placed mines in the water. In May 1987, an Iraqi warplane fired a missile into the USS *Stark*, killing 37 sailors.

How Did Libyan Terrorism Affect America?

In 1985, terrorist attacks at airports in Rome and Vienna killed a number of people, including many Americans. President Reagan charged Libyan leader Muammar al-Gadhafi with responsibility for the attacks. He cut off trade with Libya and froze all Libyan assets in America.

In 1986, Gadhafi's troops fired on planes flying over international waters in the Gulf of Sidra, near Libya. The United States responded by sinking two Libyan ships and destroying one of that country's missile sites. After another terrorist attack killed an American soldier, Reagan ordered bombings of Libyan military posts thought to be training areas for terrorists.

In 1980, Mount Saint Helens erupted violently, leaving a huge crater. Volcanic ash shot 15 miles into the sky, killing crops and animals. Damage from the blast included floods, forest fires, and mudslides. Sixty-two people died. In late 2004, the mountain again erupted, though less violently than in 1980. Scientists were delighted at the opportunity to learn more about volcanoes.

What Was the Contra Scandal?

A Communist government took power in the Central American nation of Nicaragua in 1979. The United States feared that Communists would gain power in other Central American nations. In fact, Nicaragua supplied military aid to Communist groups in other countries. The Reagan administration's policy was to fund a Nicaraguan group called the contras. The contras wanted to overthrow the Communist government of Nicaragua. Funding the contras was controversial. Members of Congress disagreed with the White House and voted to cut off funds to the contras.

In November 1986, a magazine in the Middle East reported that officials in the Reagan administration had secretly sold weapons to Iranian officials. Weapons were being exchanged for the release of American hostages. The hostages were thought to be held in Lebanon by terrorists, yet the Reagan administration had a policy of never dealing with terrorists. Later it was discovered that some of the money that paid for the weapons was sent to the contras in Nicaragua. Members of Congress were shocked at President Reagan's actions. He denied that he knew anything about it. However, several officials were charged with attempting to cheat the government.

How Did Relations Improve with the Soviet Union?

Tensions had increased between the Soviet Union and the United States during the Carter administration. The cold war appeared to be growing worse. President Reagan called the Soviet Union the "evil empire." He said the Soviets could not be trusted. The United States began the largest military buildup ever in peacetime. Critics said the United States should be trying to decrease its amount of military weapons. The Reagan administration argued that the nation had to be strong before any serious talks could take place.

President Reagan spoke with Mikhail Gorbachev in front of St. Basil's Cathedral in Moscow in 1988.

Mikhail Gorbachev became the new leader of the Soviet Union in 1985. He wanted to make changes to improve Soviet society. He spoke of a new "openness" that allowed more criticism of Soviet society. By 1987, the relations between the Soviet Union and the United States seemed to be improving.

Gorbachev and Reagan signed a treaty to decrease the amount of nuclear weapons on December 8, 1987. Both countries agreed to destroy medium-range nuclear weapons.

This new arms control agreement was called the Intermediate Nuclear Forces (INF) Treaty. Both nations agreed to allow government officials to inspect weapons factories to make sure that the terms of the treaty were being carried out. President Reagan said, "We can only hope that this history-making agreement will not be an end in itself but the beginning of a working relationship. . . ." In 1988, President Reagan visited the Soviet Union.

Apartheid

The South African policy of racial segregation

How Did America React to Apartheid?

The white government of South Africa had denied equal political and civil rights to its black population. Blacks made up over 70 percent of South Africa's population. The South African policy of racial segregation was called **apartheid**.

During the 1980s, there were protests in the United States against the policies of South Africa. Those against apartheid argued that the United States should pressure South Africa to change its policy. Others argued that the United States should not interfere in South Africa's problems.

Sanction

An action taken to force a country to do something

In an effort to end apartheid in South Africa, Congress proposed a bill imposing economic **sanctions** on the country. A sanction is an action taken to force a country to do something. Under this bill, South African imports would no longer be allowed into the United States. American exports to South Africa would be stopped. Also, Americans would no longer be able to invest in new South African businesses. The bill also canceled landing rights in America for all South African airlines.

Believing that the sanctions would do too much damage to the South African economy, President Reagan vetoed the bill. However, Congress overrode his veto. The sanctions bill became law in 1986.

Writing About History

Choose a developing country and research it. Write a report in your notebook about the country as if you are a citizen of the country.

How Did NASA Return to Space?

For two and a half years, NASA did not send any astronauts into space. NASA spent a lot of time making sure that the shuttle would be safe. On September 29, 1988, the space shuttle *Discovery* lifted safely into space at 11:37 A.M. It carried five astronauts and the future of America's space program. The four-day flight was, above all, a test of the shuttle itself. The shuttle worked just fine. America's first step back into space was a success.

Then and Now

You probably know that AIDS is an incurable disease caused by the virus called HIV. You probably also know that one way the virus is spread is through HIV-infected blood. The first cases to be identified as AIDS in the United States surfaced in 1981. It was 1983 before American and French researchers discovered the virus. It took until 1985 to develop the first blood test for HIV. Before 1985, one way people got AIDS was through blood transfusions. Without the test, health workers had no way to identify blood donors with HIV. There was no way to ensure the safety of blood supplied for transfusion.

If you need a transfusion today, you can be assured that the blood has been tested for HIV. People in the United States no longer get AIDS through blood transfusions. However, blood transfusions in other parts of the world are not always safe. This is one reason that AIDS has become an epidemic in poor countries throughout the world.

History in Your Life

Political Polls

Political polls are surveys of public opinion. They are especially important in election campaigns. The first political opinion poll was conducted in Pennsylvania in 1824. Early polls were simple. The person taking the poll, or pollster, went out and asked people their opinion on political issues.

Scientific polling began in the 1930s. Depending on a poll's purpose, between 500 and 2,000 people will be questioned. This small sample allows pollsters to guess accurately about a much larger population. Over time, polls have become more accurate. Still, notable failures in public opinion polls have occurred during national elections. The most famous occurred in the presidential election of 1948. Major polls predicted Thomas Dewey would defeat Harry S. Truman. Truman, however, won in a major landslide.

Some people believe polls not only record public opinion but also help shape it. For example, an exit poll may clearly show one candidate far ahead of a second. The supporters of the second candidate might decide not to vote at all if they believe their candidate will lose anyway.

What do you think ?

How do you think apartheid was similar to problems African Americans have faced in America?

Lesson 2 Review Choose the best word or name in parentheses to complete each sentence. Write your answers on a sheet of paper.

1. Over 200 American soldiers died after a bombing in (Iran, Iraq, Lebanon).

2. To make sure Communism would not spread to Central American countries, the Reagan administration funded a group called the (Libyans, contras, Palestinians).

3. America bombed (Iran, Libya, Nicaragua) in 1986.

4. America and (the Soviet Union, Iran, China) signed the Intermediate Nuclear Forces (INF) Treaty in 1987.

5. Racial segregation in South Africa was called (contra, apartheid, PLO).

Deficit

Debt; spending more than what is taken in

Scourge

Widespread pain or distress

In the election of 1988, the Republican Party chose Vice President George H. W. Bush as its candidate. The Reverend Jesse Jackson was the first African American to run for president. He ran for president in the 1984 and 1988 elections. His efforts received much media attention. Massachusetts Governor Michael Dukakis eventually won the Democratic nomination in 1988, but Jackson's efforts were not forgotten.

On November 8, 1988, George H. W. Bush was elected president. Bush won 54 percent of the popular vote and 426 electoral votes. Dukakis won 112 electoral votes. On January 20, 1989, George H. W. Bush became the 41st president of the United States.

What Problems Did President Bush Face?

By January 1989, the United States had experienced six straight years of economic growth. This was the longest economic growth period in American history. Still, many problems faced the new Bush administration. The nation's banking industry was in deep trouble. The federal government had a large budget debt, or **deficit**. Many social problems challenged the United States.

Homelessness was a common sight in the 1980s.

What Social Problems Did Bush Face?

The budget was not the only problem facing the nation. The "quality of life" in America was a major concern. President Bush called the problem of crime and drug abuse a **"scourge."** Some people blamed the crime and drug problems on the fact that not all Americans were part of the 1980s economic boom. Several major American cities were in poor economic shape. Low-cost housing was in short supply throughout the nation.

American cities also experienced a growing problem of homelessness. People who had no homes lived in the streets and parks of many cities. Soup kitchens increased in many American cities. These places fed hundreds of hungry people daily.

How Did Women Affect the Workforce?

By the end of the 1980s, more women had entered the workforce than at any other time in American history. Because men's wages declined in the 1970s and 1980s, the two-income family became very common. Many women worked because they were the only economic support for their family. Increasing numbers of women graduated from college. Women workers became a very important part of the American economy. Working and raising a family put additional strain on most women. In 1980, about half of married women with children worked outside the home. Most married women reported that they still did more than half of the household chores. They also had more responsibility than their husband for their children.

What "Firsts" Did African Americans Achieve?

Jesse Jackson ran for president in the 1984 and 1988 elections. He was the first African American to run for president.

In 1989 and 1990, several African Americans reached positions of power never before held by an African American. General Colin Powell was appointed by President Bush to be the Chairman of the Joint Chiefs of Staff. This position made General Powell the nation's top military officer.

In Virginia, Douglas Wilder was elected the first African American governor of a state since Reconstruction. David Dinkins was elected the first African American mayor of New York City. The cities of Seattle, Washington; Durham, North Carolina; and New Haven, Connecticut, all elected their first African American mayors.

How Did Communism Begin to Fall?

In 1989, the cold war seemed to be ending. Communism was beginning to fall. During much of the 1980s, the Soviet Union had been experiencing economic problems. The Communist system had failed to provide the Soviet people with enough food. Soviet citizens demanded a more democratic voice in their government.

Communism began to show signs of falling in Europe as well. Eastern European countries under Communist rule, such as Hungary, Poland, Czechoslovakia, and East Germany, began to protest Communist rule. President Bush reacted to the situation in 1989 by saying, "The cold war began with the division of Europe. It can only end when Europe is whole."

In November 1989, the East German government announced for the first time that its citizens could leave their country if they wished. East Germany opened its borders to the west and allowed thousands of its citizens to pass through the Berlin Wall. In time, the wall was removed completely. This was only one of many changes Communist nations would see in the next few years.

What do you think

What do you think should be done about the problem of homelessness?

Lesson 3 Review On a sheet of paper, write the answers to the following questions. Use complete sentences.

1. Why was it significant that Jesse Jackson ran for president in 1988?

2. What financial problems in America did the Bush administration face?

3. What were two social problems in America that the Bush administration faced?

4. What was happening to the Soviet Union in the 1980s?

5. What happened in East Germany in 1989?

"Women Shooting for the Stars"

Stella Guerra was the Acting Deputy Assistant Secretary of the Air Force in the 1980s. She gave this speech as a tribute and encouragement to women in the armed forces. Her comments address American women even today.

Dating back to our forebears who first stepped foot on American soil, [women] have been a part of our nation's progress. In what some have called the 'toddler years' of our country—the 1800s, we helped America take its first steps toward world prominence. We moved west, we worked in the fields tilling the soil and in the factories to produce the food and goods that our country needed to grow and prosper. . . . In the 1900s, during . . . the 'Rosie the Riveter' period, working in shipyards and steel mills, we helped our nation meet labor shortages in a time of national crisis. Afterwards, many . . . who had entered the workforce returned home—but not for long. By the midpoint of the 20th century, virtually no aspect of American society had been untouched by our eager rush into the labor force. . . .

We began to stretch, to grow, and expand our horizons. In . . . less than 50 years, our numbers in the labor force doubled. . . . In the second half of the 1970s, more of us were enrolled in college than ever before, and we began to move rapidly into business, industry, the federal sector, the teaching fields and other professions such as law and medicine. . . .

As our visions were broadened, women began to move into nontraditional areas. . . . It serves as a glistening example that in the past and in the present our hopes and dreams are interwoven into the very fiber of America. . . .

As we enter America's early adulthood we find that our hopes and dreams have been uplifted toward achievement. . . . The future holds exciting changes, challenges, and opportunities that will tax our abilities, test our skills, and require a total commitment from you and me. . . .

To meet the challenges ahead and . . . to progress, we must continue to take charge of our destinies and take responsibility for our own self-development. [No factor is more] important to our self-development . . . than self-esteem. Self-esteem comes in different doses and different degrees, and its potential is limitless.

Document-Based Questions

1. What is one contribution Guerra says women have made to America's success?

2. What years were the "toddler years"?

3. What was the "Rosie the Riveter" period?

4. What does Guerra say is most important to women's self-development?

5. How does Guerra suggest women meet the challenges ahead?

Source: "Women in America Shooting for the Stars: As We See Ourselves So Do We Act," by Stella Guerra.

- Ronald Reagan took office as president in 1981. Reagan introduced a plan to limit money to all departments except defense. Large budget and tax cuts were meant to strengthen the economy.

- Reagan appointed Sandra Day O'Connor, a conservative, as a Supreme Court justice. She was the first female justice.

- Reagan became a popular president and was re-elected in 1984.

- In January 1986, the space shuttle *Challenger* exploded, killing everyone on board. The disaster started a slump in the space program.

- Tensions eased between America and the Soviet Union when Mikhail Gorbachev and Reagan signed the INF Treaty in 1987 to reduce nuclear weapons.

- In October 1983, American marines were in Lebanon as a peacekeeping force in the Middle East conflict between Israel and the PLO. A terrorist attack killed 200 marines. The situation was unsettled when troops left in February 1984.

- Fearing the spread of Communism from Nicaragua throughout Central America, Reagan's administration funded the contras. Congress later cut off the controversial funds.

- Reagan's administration secretly sold weapons to Iran in 1986 in exchange for American hostages in Lebanon. The weapons money was used to fund the Nicaraguan contras, angering Congress after it had cut off funds.

- Several Libyan terrorist attacks killed Americans in 1985. Reagan cut off trade with Libya and froze their assets. When Libya fired on American planes and made more terrorist attacks in 1986, Reagan approved bombing Libyan military posts.

- The space program started up again in September 1988, when the space shuttle *Discovery* successfully lifted off.

- Vice President George H. W. Bush won the 1988 presidential election.

- Crime, drug abuse, and homelessness were social problems Bush faced. The Soviet Union and other Communist countries began to challenge Communism in the late 1980s.

Chapter 30 REVIEW

Word Bank

apartheid

conservative

contras

deficit

economic

federal
    government

INF Treaty

Libya

sanctions

On a sheet of paper, write the correct word or words from the Word Bank to complete each sentence.

1. Reagan cut funds and limited spending to make people less dependent on the _____.

2. Reagan approved bombing military sites in _____ because of that country's terrorist attacks.

3. Mikhail Gorbachev and Reagan signed the _____ to limit nuclear weapons.

4. Sandra Day O'Connor was appointed a Supreme Court justice to make the court more _____.

5. Funds were given to the _____ because they wanted to overthrow Communism in Nicaragua.

6. The United States was against South Africa's policy of _____.

7. Congress overrode Reagan's veto of the bill to impose economic _____ on South Africa.

8. A large budget _____ faced President Bush at the start of his term.

9. Severe _____ problems in the Soviet Union led the Soviet people to begin to question Communism.

On a sheet of paper, write the letter of the answer that correctly completes each sentence.

10. An arms buildup was part of Reagan's hard line against the _____.

   A conservatives   **C** Soviet Union

   B contras   **D** Libyans

11. President Reagan's plan to decrease the power of the federal government was called _____.

   A Reaganomics   **C** apartheid

   B New Federalism   **D** the Economic Recovery Tax

12. In the election of 1988, the Republican Party chose _____ as its candidate.

A Jesse Jackson

C Sandra Day O'Connor

B Michael Dukakis

D George H. W. Bush

On a sheet of paper, write the answers to the following questions. Use complete sentences.

13. What were two social problems that challenged President Bush?

14. What were some "firsts" that happened for African Americans during the 1980s?

15. How did President Reagan want to solve problems with the economy?

16. What did the United States and the Soviet Union agree to do in the treaty they made in 1987?

17. What are developing countries?

18. Why did NASA wait to continue the space shuttle program after the *Challenger* exploded in 1986?

Critical Thinking On a sheet of paper, write your response to each question. Use complete sentences.

19. President Reagan wanted community problems to be solved by more volunteer efforts. In what ways do you think volunteers' efforts can be effective in solving community problems?

20. People demonstrated in the United States against South Africa's policies. How effective do you think demonstrations are in bringing about change? Explain.

Test-Taking Tip

If you are asked to compare and contrast things, be sure to tell how they are alike (compare) and how they are different (contrast).

The 1990s

Worwith affairs continued to affect America in the 1990s. Communism in the Soviet Union ended, marking the true end of the Cold War. At the same time, the Bush administration faced a new conflict in the Middle East with the nation of Iraq. This was the beginning of several conflicts America faced throughout the decade. In this chapter, you will learn about the 1990s.

Goals for Learning

◆ To explain how Communist rule in the Soviet Union ended

◆ To describe the Persian Gulf War

◆ To describe the policies and attempts at reform by the Clinton administration

◆ To explain the world conflicts involving America in the 1990s

◆ To list the problems and changes that took place in America during the 1990s

◆ To describe the beginning of the new millennium and the election of 2000

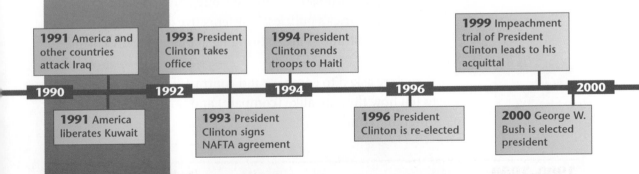

1991 America and other countries attack Iraq

1993 President Clinton takes office

1994 President Clinton sends troops to Haiti

1999 Impeachment trial of President Clinton leads to his acquittal

| 1990 | 1992 | 1994 | 1996 | 2000 |

1991 America liberates Kuwait

1993 President Clinton signs NAFTA agreement

1996 President Clinton is re-elected

2000 George W. Bush is elected president

Reunification

Joining together as one country again

Conventional

Something that is traditional or commonly used

Summit

A meeting held between or among world leaders

In early 1990, East Germany held free elections. The new government was able to come to terms with West Germany. The four World War II nations (Australia, Canada, Great Britain, and the Soviet Union) agreed to free up their ties to either half of Berlin. After several meetings, East and West Germany agreed on **reunification**. This means they were joined into one nation again. This was made official October 3, 1990. By mid-1991, Berlin had been re-established as the capital of Germany.

What Was Done to Reduce Arms?

In the fall of 1990, the United States, the Soviet Union, and 20 other nations signed an agreement to decrease **conventional** military forces. It was known as the Conventional Forces in Europe (CFE) Treaty. The agreement set limits on military vehicles and arms in Europe.

President Bush and Soviet Premier Gorbachev held a **summit** in Moscow in 1991. A summit is a meeting held between or among world leaders. Each country agreed to reduce its store of intercontinental missiles. The Strategic Arms Reduction Treaty (START) called for 30 percent fewer missile systems within seven years of the treaty. This treaty became effective in 1994.

How Did Communism End in the Soviet Union?

Since 1949, the Soviet Union, also called the USSR, had kept economic control of many Eastern European countries. In 1991, these countries made an effort to cut their economic ties to the USSR. They looked to the West for new partnerships and financial help.

President Gorbachev of Russia tried to begin changes during the 1980s with his policies of **glasnost** and **perestroika**. Glasnost was open discussion of political and social issues. Perestroika was economic and government reform. However, citizens grew more and more dissatisfied. Newspapers began to run articles criticizing the government. All across the land, voters replaced many of the Communist leaders.

A group of Communists tried to overthrow Gorbachev in 1990. They held him hostage while they tried to capture Boris Yeltsin. Yeltsin was president of the Russian republic and an anti-Communist. However, thousands of citizens who assembled in Moscow in protest forced the rebels to give up. Shortly after that, Gorbachev resigned as general secretary of the Communist Party. However, he remained president of Russia.

In December 1991, three former Soviet republics—Russia, Ukraine, and Belarus—formed the Commonwealth of Independent States. A **commonwealth** is a group of self-governing states.

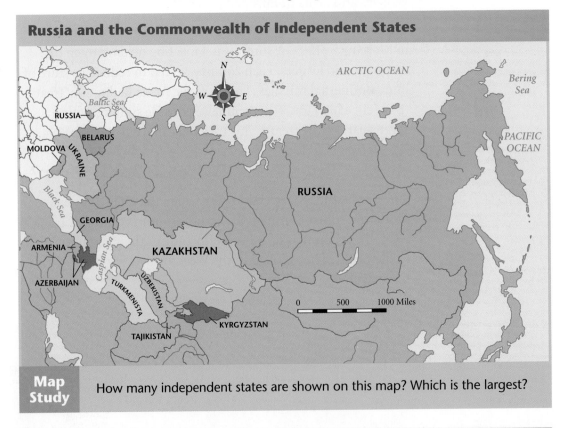

Russia and the Commonwealth of Independent States

Map Study   How many independent states are shown on this map? Which is the largest?

Former Soviet-Influenced Countries

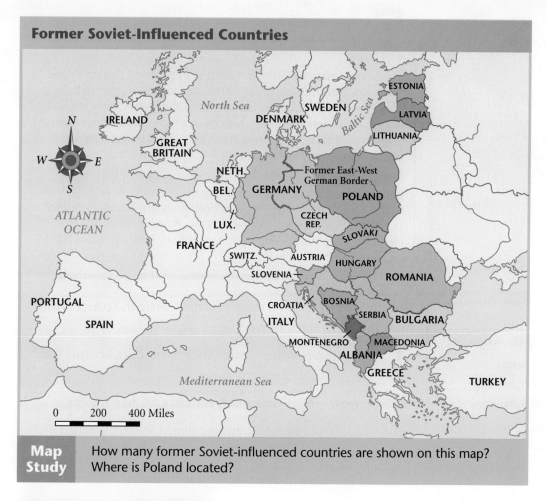

Map Study How many former Soviet-influenced countries are shown on this map? Where is Poland located?

Vladimir Putin

The end of the USSR was made final by the resignation of Gorbachev as its president. President Yeltsin remained leader of the new Russian Federation. All but three of the former republics of the Soviet Union joined the commonwealth by 1995. These republics are Estonia, Latvia, and Lithuania. They are called the Baltic States.

Countries under Soviet control began to break away in the late 1980s and early 1990s. These included Hungary, Poland, and Czechoslovakia.

On December 31, 1999, Boris Yeltsin resigned as president of Russia. In March 2000, the Russian people elected Vladimir Putin president.

Then and Now

The Soviet Union (USSR) was founded in violence. During World War I, the Communists under Lenin staged a revolution in Russia. They overthrew and killed the tsar and other rulers. They then waged a civil war for power, executing thousands of other Russians. Over the decades, the Communists continued to use violence to add other countries to their territory.

In the early 1990s, the Soviet Union began to fall apart. Many people feared it would end as it began: violently. After the breakup of the Soviet Union in 1991, a period of violence and confusion occurred. However, in 2000 and 2004, Russia held its first free elections since the USSR began. Since then, Russia has moved more or less peacefully forward.

Word Bank

Commonwealth

glasnost

perestroika

reunification

summit

Lesson 1 Review On a sheet of paper, write the correct word from the Word Bank to complete each sentence.

1. All but three of the former Soviet republics became the _____ of Independent States.

2. German _____ was made official October 3, 1990.

3. A meeting between or among world leaders is called a _____.

4. _____ allowed open discussion of political and social issues.

5. _____ called for economic and government reform.

What do you think ❓

How do you think America was affected by the collapse of Communism in the Soviet Union?

In July 1990, a conflict developed in the Middle East between the nation of Iraq and its small neighbor, Kuwait. President Saddam Hussein of Iraq accused Kuwait of trying to keep oil prices low and of stealing oil from Iraq's wells.

Iraq threatened Kuwait by sending more than 100,000 troops to its border. Kuwait had only 20,000 soldiers. By the end of July, many oil-producing nations in the Persian Gulf agreed to raise the price of oil. Saddam Hussein seemed satisfied and said that he would not invade Kuwait.

What Happened When Iraq Invaded Kuwait?

On August 2, 1990, the Iraqi army invaded Kuwait. President Bush and other officials questioned whether Iraq should be allowed to conquer Kuwait. Kuwait was an independent country and member of the United Nations. In addition, they feared that Iraq might conquer oil-rich Saudi Arabia. Many nations, including the United States, were concerned about one nation controlling so much of an important natural resource.

On August 6, 1990, the United States and other members of the United Nations agreed to stop trading with Iraq in protest of the invasion. The UN said that the Iraqi army should leave Kuwait. The next day, President Bush sent American troops to protect Saudi Arabia. The military called it "Operation Desert Shield."

On November 29, the UN Security Council voted 12-2 to give Iraq until January 15, 1991, to pull out of Kuwait. If Iraq failed to meet this deadline, the United States and its UN allies could use armed force.

What Was "Operation Desert Storm"?

Diplomat

One skilled in negotiating between nations

Casualty

A person who is wounded, killed, or lost in action

Diplomats from several nations tried to get Iraq to leave Kuwait. A diplomat is a person skilled in negotiating between nations. The diplomats failed. On January 17, 1991, the United States, Great Britain, France, Saudi Arabia, Kuwait, and others launched an air attack against Iraq. "Operation Desert Shield" had become "Operation Desert Storm."

For five weeks, planes rained bombs on Iraq and Iraqi forces in Kuwait. Iraq launched missiles into Israel. Saddam Hussein wanted to draw Israel into the war. He hoped to force the Arab nations to join him in a fight with Israel. Although hit with many missiles, Israel did not enter the war.

Saddam Hussein received a final deadline to remove his army from Kuwait. When this deadline passed, the United States and its allies launched a large ground and air attack against Iraq. The ground war lasted only four days. Many Iraqi soldiers were killed; thousands surrendered to the allies. Many Iraqi civilians also died as a result of the war. The American and allied combat **casualties** during the war were about 370. A casualty is a person who is wounded, killed, or lost in action. Norman Schwarzkopf, commander of the allied forces, called it "miraculous" that there were not more allied troops killed. On February 27, 1991, President Bush announced to the nation, "Kuwait is liberated."

The United States and its allies used tanks and other vehicles to attack the Iraqi army.

During the Persian Gulf War, Arab and Western nations cooperated against a common enemy. President Bush felt that this cooperative spirit could help to bring a lasting peace to the Middle East. In March 1991, the president sent Secretary of State James Baker to the Middle East to meet with leaders. President Bush felt that the United States should help to build a "new world order" where the nations of the world seek to solve their conflicts peacefully.

Even though Saddam Hussein's army was defeated, Hussein remained in power. Problems in the Middle East remained in spite of Desert Storm.

Lesson 2 Review On a sheet of paper, write the answers to the following questions. Use complete sentences.

1. Why did Iraq invade Kuwait in 1990?

2. Why did Saddam Hussein want to draw Israel into the war?

3. Who was the commander of the allied forces?

4. Why was the United States concerned about one nation controlling so much oil?

5. Why did the UN Security Council give Iraq a deadline to pull out of Kuwait?

What do you think ?

The Persian Gulf War was caused in part over oil. Do you think it is necessary for America to be protective of oil? Why or why not?

Republicans backed the George H. W. Bush-Dan Quayle ticket for re-election in 1992. The Democrats chose Governor Bill Clinton of Arkansas as their presidential candidate. Senator Al Gore of Tennessee was Clinton's choice for vice president. Texas billionaire Ross Perot ran as an independent. Although the American people were pleased with the way President Bush handled the Persian Gulf War, many Americans were concerned about the economy. The unemployment rate was at an eight-year high and many families lived in poverty.

Clinton, who stressed the need for an improved economy, won the election. He took office in 1993. Perot had the best showing for a third-party candidate since Theodore Roosevelt ran for president in 1912.

The Democrats kept control of Congress, but more new people were elected to Congress in 1992 than in any year since 1948. Many longtime senators and representatives had not sought re-election. Many more women, African Americans, and

President Clinton took the oath of office in 1993. His daughter, Chelsea, (left) and his wife, Hillary Rodham Clinton, (right) were present for the ceremony.

Carol Mosely-Braun

Hispanic Americans had been elected. Carol Mosely-Braun of Illinois became the first African American woman to be elected to the Senate.

What Was NAFTA?

In December 1992, the governments of the United States, Mexico, and Canada approved the North American Free Trade Agreement (NAFTA).

Under this agreement, limits on investments, trade, and services among the three North American countries would be stopped over a 15 year period. The three countries now formed a giant market of goods and services. Mexico, a major importer of American goods and agricultural services, would stop its huge tariffs. The United States would also free Mexican imports of duties. The NAFTA agreement was signed into law by President Clinton in late 1993 and went into effect in January 1994. The NAFTA agreement led to more U.S. exports to both Canada and Mexico.

What Reforms Did President Clinton Attempt?

President Clinton proposed lowering the federal deficit by $496 billion over five years. After some changes, the bill passed in 1993. It included plans for both tax increases and budget cuts.

The Brady Bill was passed in 1993. It was named for James Brady, who was shot and permanently injured during the assassination attempt on President Reagan in 1981. This bill set a five-day waiting period for the purchase of a handgun. It also set up a national computer network to check on the criminal record and age of a person who wanted to buy a gun.

Congress passed the Omnibus Violent Crime Control and Prevention Act in 1994. The word *omnibus* means it contains many things at once. Under this act, local governments would be given power to hire 100,000 new police officers. It also called for new state prisons and crime-prevention programs. This bill also banned certain weapons and increased the number of crimes punishable by death.

Largely aided by First Lady Hillary Rodham Clinton, the president proposed huge changes in the nation's health care system to provide less expensive medical care for all Americans. Under this system, employers would have to pay most of their employees' insurance costs. After many attempts at a compromise between supporters and opponents of the plan, Congress rejected it.

Lesson 3 Review On a sheet of paper, write the answers to the following questions. Use complete sentences.

1. What was the focus of the 1992 presidential election?

2. How did the makeup of Congress change in 1992?

3. What was the NAFTA agreement?

4. What was the Brady Bill?

5. What was the Omnibus Violent Crime Control and Prevention Act?

What do you think ?

Do you think the government should find a way to give all people health care? Why or why not?

Famine
Widespread starvation

During the first years of his administration, President Clinton became involved in changes affecting many other countries. Although the United States was not directly involved in many of these, it helped to promote peace or to provide aid to these other countries.

What Happened in Somalia?

Civil war, drought, and **famine** cost thousands of lives and threatened many more in the African nation of Somalia by 1992. America and the UN sent troops to Somalia in 1992 to bring food to Somalia's starving people. However, severe American casualties led the United States to pull out the troops by 1994. The UN pulled out its troops by 1995. While the efforts had saved millions of Somalians from starvation, the problems in that country remained.

What Middle East Peace Treaty Was Signed?

In 1993, President Clinton hosted an important summit between Israel's Prime Minister Yitzhak Rabin and Yasir Arafat of the Palestine Liberation Organization (PLO). There he witnessed the signing of a peace agreement between those two leaders that ended their 46-year war. However, tensions remain between Israel and the PLO.

What Deal Was Made with Russia and the Ukraine?

President Clinton and Russian President Yeltsin met in Moscow in January 1994 to discuss further ways to curb the threat of nuclear war. They agreed that neither would aim strategic weapons at the other country. Clinton also convinced Ukraine President Kravchuk to take down that country's nuclear arsenal. Ukraine did so in exchange for $1 billion in U.S. aid and a promise of American protection in case of attack.

> **Writing About History**
>
> Find a newspaper or magazine article about a country that is experiencing famine. Write a paragraph about the hardships the people face and the reasons for the famine, if that information is available.

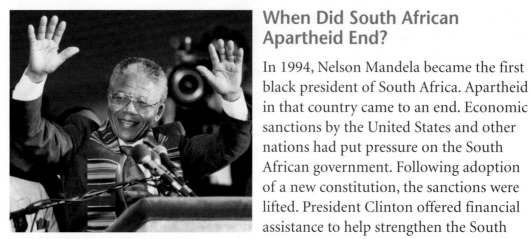

Nelson Mandela

When Did South African Apartheid End?

In 1994, Nelson Mandela became the first black president of South Africa. Apartheid in that country came to an end. Economic sanctions by the United States and other nations had put pressure on the South African government. Following adoption of a new constitution, the sanctions were lifted. President Clinton offered financial assistance to help strengthen the South African economy.

How Did Relations Improve with Vietnam?

Persecute

To treat someone poorly or violently because of his or her religious beliefs or ethnic background

More than 20 years after the Vietnam War, many Americans were still missing in action from the war. However, in 1995 President Clinton announced that there would be full diplomatic relations with Vietnam. Since then, Vietnam has released information about missing soldiers.

What Occurred in Bosnia-Herzegovina?

America became involved in a conflict in Bosnia-Herzegovina, part of the former Yugoslavia. Three-way fighting broke out between Croats, Bosnian Serbs, and Muslims in 1992. In 1993, America parachuted food and medicines to Muslims being **persecuted** by Serbs. Fighting continued even after a cease-fire was called in 1994. NATO began a series of air strikes against Bosnian Serbs, and UN peacekeepers were sent to the area. Bosnian Serbs took more than 350 UN peacekeepers hostage to discourage air strikes.

By 1995, the warring parties agreed to a cease-fire. A peace agreement sponsored by the United States in 1995 ended fighting by 1996. However, the war left many people homeless. In 1997, the International Criminal Tribunal tried a number of Bosnian leaders for war crimes. Human rights continue to be a big issue in this area of the world.

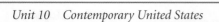

What Problems Developed with Haiti and Cuba?

President Clinton had met with removed Haitian President Jean-Bertrand Aristide in 1993. Clinton appealed to the UN for help in restoring Aristide to power. In September 1994, President Clinton sent out 23 warships and 20,000 troops to restore the Aristide government.

Thousands of Cubans, wanting to escape unpleasant living conditions in their homeland, fled to the United States. In the fall of 1994, after negotiations with Cuba, the United States agreed to allow 20,000 Cubans per year to enter this country. Cuban officials promised to encourage citizens to remain in their homeland.

Biography

Trevor Ferrell: 1972–

A cold December night in 1983 changed Trevor Ferrell's life forever. Trevor, who lived near Philadelphia, was only 11 years old at the time. He heard a news story about shelters for homeless people. The story shocked him. He talked his parents into driving downtown. There, the family gave blankets to the homeless. Soon the family took food and clothing downtown every night. People heard about Trevor's work and offered much support. A TV drama was made about Trevor, and President Reagan also honored him.

Trevor and his family started Trevor's Place, a homeless shelter. At age 18, Trevor left his organization, Trevor's Campaign. He did not like the public attention. Today, Trevor continues to help the less fortunate. He runs a thrift shop, and sometimes he gives speeches. "For me, it's a selfish thing. I've always enjoyed being around people, real people. It's what I've liked to do since I was 11 years old."

Lesson 4 Review Choose the best word in parentheses to complete each sentence. Write your answers on a sheet of paper.

1. America and the UN sent troops to (Bosnia, Somalia, Haiti) in 1992 to bring food to that country's starving people.

2. President Clinton met with Russian President (Rabin, Yeltsin, Aristide) in Moscow to discuss further ways to curb the threat of nuclear harm.

3. Apartheid ended in 1994 in (South Africa, Vietnam, Haiti).

4. A peace agreement sponsored by the United States ended fighting in (Haiti, Russia, Bosnia-Herzegovina) by 1996.

5. President Clinton sent 23 warships and 20,000 troops to restore the Aristide government in (Haiti, Vietnam, South Africa) in 1994.

What do you think ?

Do you think it is America's responsibility to feed starving people in other countries? Why or why not?

Technology Connection

E-mail

E-mail might seem a complicated system, but it really is simple. Businesses called Internet service providers (ISPs) provide e-mail addresses. An address with an "@" symbol is needed to send or receive messages. The address acts as an address in the same way an address for regular mail does. It directs messages to the correct mailbox. ISP software lets users read, compose, and send images and attachments.

The problem of spam has grown with e-mail's popularity. Spam is annoying "junk e-mail." Spammers send these unwanted advertisements to thousands, or even millions, of people at once. Processing so many messages slows the efficiency of ISPs and frustrates e-mail users. Some countries have created laws to discourage the use of spam. Despite this problem, e-mail will most likely continue to fill an important role in daily life.

In 1994, the Republicans gained control of both houses of Congress for the first time since 1954. A new Republican plan called the "Contract with America" had been introduced. It was intended to balance the budget. Representative Newt Gingrich of Georgia introduced the plan. He became speaker of the House in 1995.

Congress proposed a bill calling for a constitutional amendment for a balanced federal budget by the year 2002. The bill passed the House, but it was rejected by the Senate. A second bill that called for term limits for members of Congress was defeated in the House of Representatives. A third bill, however, was passed and signed into law by President Clinton. It said that the federal government could not make demands on states unless the government provided federal money for the cost of carrying out those demands.

What Was the Whitewater Affair?

Beginning in 1993, President Clinton and First Lady Hillary Rodham Clinton faced accusations in what became known as the Whitewater Affair. The Clintons were part owners of a company called the Whitewater Development Corporation in the 1970s. The company was backed by Madison Savings and Loan. A federal investigation found illegal political campaign contributions, income tax fraud, and other wrongdoings to be linked to Whitewater and Madison Savings and Loan. The Clintons denied that they took part in the illegal acts. Despite what seemed to be a scandal, Congressional hearings in 1995 found nothing to prove the Clintons took part in anything illegal.

What Terrorism Occurred on American Soil?

Buildings on American soil were targets of major acts of **terrorism** in the 1990s. In 1993, a bomb exploded in the parking garage of the World Trade Center in New York City. Six people were killed and more than 1,000 were injured. The next year four men were found guilty of charges connected with that bombing.

In 1995, a car bomb exploded next to the Murrah Federal Building in Oklahoma City, Oklahoma killing 168 people, including 19 children. This was the worst terrorist bombing that had taken place on American soil. In 1997 Timothy McVeigh was found guilty of the bombing and executed.

In 1996, President Clinton signed antiterrorism legislation. This included stiffer penalties for terrorist actions and new methods to prevent terrorism.

A car bomb destroyed much of Oklahoma City's Murrah Federal Building in 1995.

What Was the Million Man March?

In October 1995, hundreds of thousands of African American men took part in the Million Man March in Washington, D.C. The purpose of the march was to show a sense of responsibility toward family and community. President Clinton praised the objectives of the people who participated in the rally.

What Reform Legislation Was Approved?

A number of bills first introduced in Congress right after Clinton took office were passed. A welfare reform bill passed in 1996 reduced federal help to the poor. The bill gave more responsibility for dealing with poverty to the states. Under this bill, direct federal government payments to the poor were replaced by block grants to states. These grants were to be used for the poor under federal guidelines.

A health care reform bill was passed. Under this bill, an American worker could keep health insurance after leaving the company that provided it. It also became illegal for insurance companies to drop customers because of a medical condition.

Upon signing a minimum wage bill in 1996, President Clinton claimed that it would enable "10 million workers to raise stronger families." The minimum wage was raised 90 cents an hour to $5.15.

What Racial Terrorism Took Place?

In the mid-1990s, arsonists began to burn churches because of hate and racism. **Arson** is setting fire to something on purpose. Most of these church burnings took place in the southern and midwestern states. Between 1990 and January 1999, arsonists set on fire 829 churches in the United States. Of these, 376, or 45 percent, were African American churches. People in the communities, many of them white, worked together to rebuild the burnt-out churches.

Who Won the 1996 Election?

In 1996, Republicans nominated Senator Robert Dole of Kansas as their presidential candidate. Former congressman Jack Kemp was his running mate. Again, Ross Perot ran as the candidate of the independent Reform Party. The **incumbent** ticket of Bill Clinton and Al Gore was the Democratic Party's choice. An incumbent is a person who currently holds a certain position or office. President Clinton was re-elected by a wide margin.

Arson

The act of purposely setting fire to something

Incumbent

A person who currently holds a certain position or office

On December 19, 1998, the U.S. House of Representatives approved two articles of impeachment against President Clinton. They accused him of lying under oath and of obstructing justice in an effort to conceal an extramarital affair with Monica Lewinsky. She had been an intern at the White House.

On February 12, 1999, the Senate acquitted the president. He had been only the second president to be impeached. (Andrew Johnson was the first, in 1868. He, too, was acquitted.)

Lesson 5 Review Choose the word or name in parentheses that best completes each sentence.

1. In 1994, the (Democratic, Republican, Independent Reform) Party gained control of both houses of Congress for the first time since 1954.

2. In 1997, (Timothy McVeigh, Newt Gingrich, Robert Dole) was found guilty of bombing the Federal Building in Oklahoma City, Oklahoma.

3. (Ross Perot, Jack Kemp, Bill Clinton) was elected president in 1996.

4. President Clinton was the (first, second, third) president to be impeached.

5. Ross Perot represented the (Democratic, Republican, Independent Reform) Party in the election of 1996.

What do you think ?

In 1996, Ross Perot ran for president as the candidate of the Reform Party. Do you think that such "third party" candidates help or hurt the campaign and election process? Explain your answer.

Millennium

A period of 1,000 years

Geography Note

The world is more of a global village than ever before. Countries and regions are linked closely. For example, the United States imports most of the oil it needs to produce its goods. The oil comes from many foreign countries. American goods are shipped to many countries, including the countries from which the United States bought the oil to begin with.

How Did the World Celebrate the New Millennium?

As the year 2000 approached, nations around the world prepared to celebrate the ending of the second **millennium**. (A millennium represents 1,000 years.) The world began to celebrate on December 31, 1999, and continued until January 1, 2001. That date marked the beginning of the third millennium.

Some people feared that many computers had not been programmed to move from the 1900s to the year 2000. People called this problem "the Y2K Bug." (In metric measurements, *K* stands for 1,000.) Some people stockpiled food and water. They bought guns in case Y2K brought riots. However, December 31, 1999, easily turned into January 1, 2000.

One concern in the year 2000 was the rising price of gasoline. Many Americans blamed the Organization of Petroleum Exporting Countries (OPEC) for not increasing their production of oil. Around the country, people also worried about the rising price of heating oil and natural gas.

What Happened in the 2000 Election?

In 2000, Republicans nominated Texas Governor George W. Bush as their presidential candidate. He is the son of George H. W. Bush, president from 1989 to 1993. Dick Cheney, a former secretary of defense, was the Republican running mate. Pat Buchanan was the Reform Party candidate. Ralph Nader was nominated by the Green Party.

The Democrats nominated Al Gore as their presidential candidate. Gore had served as vice president during the eight years that Bill Clinton was president. Joseph Lieberman, a U.S. senator from Connecticut, was the Democratic running mate.

During the fall of 2000, the candidates for president debated their differences on the use of the budget surplus and how to handle Social Security. They argued over education and the military.

Democratic candidate Al Gore won the popular vote nationally, but did not win the presidency. The popular vote is the total number of votes cast in a presidential election. George W. Bush, the Republican candidate, won the electoral vote and the presidency. This is not the first time a presidential candidate has won the popular vote but not the electoral vote.

The Electoral College system was set up by the Constitution. It gives each state a number of electoral votes equal to the number of U.S. Senators plus the number of its U.S. Representatives. If a state has two senators and eight representatives, that state will have 10 electoral votes. There are a total of 538 electoral votes. A presidential candidate needs 270 electoral votes to win the election. Citizens vote for the president and vice president by name, but they are actually voting for an elector. The electors will vote for that president and vice president when the Electoral College meets following the election.

Florida became the deciding state in the 2000 election. The vote was too close to call. Without the Florida electoral votes, Al Gore had 266 electoral votes and George W. Bush had 246 electoral votes. Both candidates needed the 25 electoral votes from Florida to win.

George W. Bush received several hundred more votes than Al Gore. When a vote is this close, a recount is required. Many problems occurred during the recount. The United States Supreme Court ordered the recount stopped. It then heard the lawyers for both sides argue their case. On December 12, the United States Supreme Court ruled that the recount process in Florida could not continue. Al Gore conceded the election. George W. Bush became the 43rd president of the United States in January 2001.

Civics Connection

Conflicts Outside the United States

The United States Constitution protects the rights and freedoms of American citizens. It is the basis for democracy. However, not all nations are democracies. Some governments are controlled by dictators who have absolute power. They use the military to keep control. They may abuse human rights or try to take other lands by force. Conflicts result, and they can threaten an entire region.

For much of its history, the United States tried to avoid conflicts with other countries. Protecting the American people from war was important. Today, however, the United States has a more global view. Nations are connected in many ways. Conflicts in other parts of the world affect the United States. In addition, nuclear weapons have changed the security of the world. Nuclear weapons give nations the power to destroy other nations. Future wars might involve their use. This must be avoided. Therefore, it is important to solve world conflicts quickly and at a local level.

1. Do you think American soldiers should be sent to fight in other countries? Explain.
2. How do you think local governments can help solve world conflicts?

Lesson 6 Review On a sheet of paper, write the correct word or words from the Word Bank to complete each sentence.

Word Bank

Al Gore

Florida

George W. Bush

oil prices

millennium

1. The Republican presidential candidate in 2000 was _____.
2. The Democratic presidential candidate in 2000 was _____.
3. The deciding state in the 2000 election was _____.
4. The year 2001 began the third _____.
5. One of the challenges facing the United States and the world in 2000 was _____.

What do you think ?

From what you know of the Electoral College, what do you think should happen for future elections?

"Favor Positive Themes"

Luis Morales is a former president of the Public Relations Society of America. In April 1996, he gave a speech entitled "Favor Positive Themes." Although he was speaking to business people, his message applies to all Americans.

"It seems to me that lost in the noise of political issues, lost in the . . . self-serving groups, is one issue that transcends everything else. . . . 'citizenship.'

Perhaps my own ethnic background makes me more conscious of this than most, but it does seem to me that the most pervasive issue facing us is the decline of America's traditional values. . . . We are rude, uncivil to one another, selfish to a fault, and uninterested or ignorant of our history. . . .

It is entirely within our field . . . to encourage respect and respectability and a sense of community. . . .

What can we do [to make change?] . . .

First, we can inform ourselves. Broaden our reading habits. Besides the major . . . periodicals, read some thoughtful books. . . .

We can expose ourselves to the thinking and ideas of others. . . . When we address the issues of diversity and multiculturalism, we will do so evenhandedly. We will become more aware and appreciative of the value and richness [of] a diverse society and workforce. . . .

We . . . can . . . promote a positive view of America. . . .

But we desperately need to recover our moral balance. . . . I urge you to join me in . . . regaining a sense of community, rebuilding our self-respect by respecting others. . . ."

Document-Based Questions

1. What is the issue that Morales says has gotten lost?

2. According to Morales, what is the largest overall issue facing Americans?

3. What is one thing he suggests people can do to make change?

4. What does Morales say we need to regain and rebuild?

5. How does Morales's view of citizenship agree or disagree with your view of it?

Source: Speech by Luis W. Morales, Vital Speeches, July 15, 1996.

- East and West Germany were reunified in 1990.

- In 1990, Iraq invaded Kuwait. In response, "Operation Desert Shield" sent American troops to protect Saudi Arabia from the Iraqi army. In 1991, America and its allies liberated Kuwait and caused severe casualties to the Iraqi army.

- Communism collapsed in the Soviet Union in 1991. All but three of the former Soviet republics joined to form the Commonwealth of Independent States by 1995.

- President Clinton took office in 1993. He signed the NAFTA agreement in 1993 to reduce restrictions on trade with Canada and Mexico.

- President Clinton sent a number of proposals to Congress and proposed huge changes to the health care system. Congress rejected Clinton's initial health care plans.

- Beginning in 1992, America experienced much foreign involvement. America improved relations with Russia, the Ukraine, South Africa, and Vietnam, and worked with Israeli and Arab leaders to form a peace agreement. It was also involved militarily in Somalia, Bosnia-Herzegovina, and Haiti.

- Beginning in 1993, the Clintons were investigated for wrongdoings in what became known as the Whitewater Affair.

- In 1994, Republicans gained control of Congress and implemented their plan called the "Contract with America." Among the ideas of this plan was to balance the federal budget by 2002.

- Terrorism began to occur on American soil in 1993.

- Welfare reform and minimum wage bills were passed in 1996.

- In 1995, the Million Man March took place in Washington, D.C. It focused on the responsibilities of African American men toward family and community.

- In 1998, the U.S. House of Representatives approved two articles of impeachment against President Clinton. In early 1999, the U.S. Senate held an impeachment trial. The Senate acquitted President Clinton.

- George W. Bush, governor of Texas, became president in January 2001.

Chapter 31 REVIEW

Word Bank

Al Gore

Bill Clinton

Boris Yeltsin

Brady Bill

Commonwealth of Independent States

Desert Storm

Kuwait

millennium

Million Man March

NAFTA

Newt Gingrich

Saddam Hussein

On a sheet of paper, write the word or words from the Word Bank to complete each sentence.

1. All but three of the Soviet republics formed the _____.

2. _____ was the president of Russia in 1994.

3. Iraq attacked _____ in 1990.

4. The American ground attack on Iraq was called Operation _____.

5. The _____ agreement reduced limits on trade among Canada, America, and Mexico.

6. The leader of Iraq during the Persian Gulf War was _____.

7. The _____ focused on the responsibilities of African American men.

8. _____ took office as president in 1993.

9. The _____ put more controls on guns in America.

10. _____ and the Republican Congress proposed the "Contract with America."

11. During the year 2000, people celebrated the start of the third _____, which began on January 1, 2001.

12. The Democratic candidate in the 2000 election was _____.

On a sheet of paper, write the letter of the answer that correctly completes each sentence.

13. The organization that decides how much oil to produce is called _____.

   A NAFTA   **C** OPEC

   B Desert Shield   **D** the Electoral College

14. The Strategic Arms Reduction Treaty called for 30 percent fewer _____ within seven years.

   A political parties   **C** petroleum exports

   B missile systems   **D** candidates

15. In 1995, America sponsored a peace agreement to end fighting in _____.

   A Bosnia-Herzegovina   **C** South Africa

   B Somalia   **D** Cuba

On a sheet of paper, write the answer to each question. Use complete sentences.

16. What became of the Soviet Union?

17. What was the purpose of the Contract with America?

18. There were many changes throughout the world in the 1990s. What were two of them?

Critical Thinking On a sheet of paper, write your response to each question. Use complete sentences.

19. Are events such as the Million Man March helpful in making positive changes in the United States? Explain your answer.

20. Do you think it is the responsibility of the United States to help developing countries? Explain your answer.

Test-Taking Tip

Avoid waiting until the night before a test to study. Plan your time so that you can get a good night's sleep the night before a test.

32 The 21st Century Begins

As the 21st century began, the people and leaders of America had many fears. Some were concerned about the economy and health care. Others were troubled by global issues like war, poverty, and the environment.

Sadly, the new century began with tragedy. On September 11, 2001, terrorists attacked the United States. These attacks killed many Americans and others from around the world. The attacks also changed the lives of all American citizens. In this chapter, you will learn about these attacks and the events that followed. You will also learn about other political, social and scientific concerns of this time.

Goals for Learning

◆ To describe the terrorist attacks of September 11, 2001

◆ To describe the wars in Afghanistan and Iraq

◆ To list the events following the war in Iraq

◆ To describe the presidential election of 2004

◆ To describe life in the United States at the beginning of the 21st century

September 2001 Terrorists attack New York City and Washington, D.C.

October 2001 Patriot Act is signed into law

November 2002 Department of Homeland Security is created

May 2003 President Bush declares that major fighting is over in Iraq

November 2004 President George W. Bush is re-elected

2001   2002   2003   2004

October 2001 United States and Great Britain attack Afghanistan

March 2003 United States and Great Britain invade Iraq

December 2003 Saddam Hussein is captured

Who Are Terrorists?

Al Qaeda

The terrorist group that attacked New York City and Washington, D.C., on September 11, 2001

9/11

The shortened name for the terrorist attacks on September 11, 2001

Terrorists use violence to frighten people and leaders. They hope this fear will allow their demands to be met. There are many kinds of terrorists. National terrorists want to change the government or create their own nation on land controlled by someone else. Religious terrorists want to force people to follow their religious beliefs. Environmental terrorists want to bring attention to the destruction of the natural environment.

What Terrorism Took Place in 2001?

In January 2001, George W. Bush became president of the United States. As the former governor of Texas, he had little experience

with world problems. President Bush was more concerned with solving problems at home. The president and American citizens were not prepared for terrorism. Americans had experienced terrorism before, but nothing like what happened on September 11, 2001. On that day, terrorists attacked New York City and Washington, D.C.

A terrorist group headed by a man named Osama bin Laden planned these attacks. The terrorist group is called **Al Qaeda**. On that day in September, 19 Al Qaeda terrorists, in three groups, crashed airplanes into buildings in New York City and Washington, D.C. For Americans, the day came to be known simply as **9/11**.

On September 11, 2001, terrorists flew an airplane into each of the twin towers of the World Trade Center in New York City.

Both World Trade Center towers fell to the ground after the terrorist attacks.

Hijack

To steal an occupied vehicle by use of force

The first attack struck the two towers of the World Trade Center in New York City. Terrorists **hijacked** two passenger planes, meaning they took over the planes by use of force. The terrorists flew a plane into each of the World Trade Center's twin buildings. The jet fuel in the crashing planes started a huge fire. Hundreds of people were trapped inside each tower.

The fire soon weakened the buildings, and they came crashing to the ground. Almost 2,800 people died. Hundreds more were injured.

The second attack was aimed at the Pentagon building outside Washington, D.C. The Pentagon is the huge, five-sided headquarters for the U.S. Department of Defense. As they did with the Trade Center, the terrorists crashed a passenger plane into the Pentagon. At the Pentagon, 189 people were killed and many were injured.

The terrorists wanted to attack a third target. This target was thought to be the White House or the Capitol building in Washington, D.C. These buildings were never attacked because the fourth hijacked plane crashed in a field in Pennsylvania.

The passengers and crew decided to fight the hijackers and take control of the plane. Some of the passengers had learned about the attacks on New York City and Washington, D.C., by using their cell phones. Their heroic actions prevented another terrorist attack. Unfortunately, the crash killed all 40 people on board.

How Did the American People and Government React to the Terrorist Attacks?

The terrorist attacks on the United States shocked Americans. But in spite of this horrible event, thousands of Americans acted very bravely. **Patriotism,** or pride in one's own country, increased. Suddenly American flags were flying everywhere. Patriotic songs were playing on radio and television and sung at public gatherings.

In New York City, hundreds of firefighters and police officers died trying to save people trapped in the World Trade Center towers before their collapse. The attacks created many heroes. Rudy Giuliani, the mayor of New York City, was widely praised for the way he handled the crisis in his city.

President Bush announced that the "war on terrorism . . . will be the focus of my administration from now on." To protect the nation from future terrorist attacks, the president created the Department of Homeland Security. Congress passed a new law called the Patriot Act in October 2001.

Many Americans gathered together to remember those killed in the terrorist attacks.

Writing About History

Many people remember exactly what they were doing when they heard of the crashes at the World Trade Center, at the Pentagon, and in rural Pennsylvania. In a notebook, write what you were doing and how you felt. Write how your feelings have changed since 2001.

What Is the Purpose of the Patriot Act?

The Patriot Act gave the government new powers to fight terrorism. It allowed the government to get court approval to secretly search the homes and businesses of suspected terrorists without showing a search warrant. It also allowed the government to use a court order to get information about e-mail and Internet usage of suspected terrorists. Business, medical, library, and bookstore records of suspected terrorists could also be seized, if there was court approval. Some people believed the Patriot Act gave too much power to the executive branch of government. They feared that the constitutional rights of American citizens would be violated.

What Is the Department of Homeland Security?

President Bush created the new Office of Homeland Security in October 2001. It became the Department of Homeland Security in November 2002. It is responsible for seeing that more than 22 federal agencies work together to protect American citizens. State law enforcement agencies are also involved in homeland security. The federal government took more control over airport and seaport security.

Why Was the United States Attacked?

The buildings that were attacked are well-known symbols of American economic and political power. The World Trade Center was a symbol of America's economic power. The Pentagon is a symbol of America's military power. The White House and the Capitol building are symbols of America's democracy.

Osama bin Laden hated the United States for many reasons. He did not like that the United States supported the country of Israel. He wanted the United States to remove its troops from the Middle East. He believed that American economic and political power were changing traditional ways of life in the Middle East. Osama bin Laden wanted to show that the United States could be a successful target of terrorism. He wanted to prove that his terrorist group could destroy important symbols of American power. By doing this he hoped to get other terrorists to attack Americans at home and abroad.

What do you think ?

Do you think the Patriot Act restricts the rights of Americans? Do you think it was necessary? Explain.

Lesson 1 Review On a sheet of paper, write the answers to the following questions. Use complete sentences.

1. What is terrorism?

2. What terrorism occurred on September 11, 2001?

3. Why were the World Trade Center and the Pentagon buildings attacked?

4. What is the purpose of the Patriot Act?

5. What is the purpose of the Department of Homeland Security?

Biography

Colin Powell: 1937–

Colin Powell was born April 5, 1937, in New York City. His parents emigrated from Jamaica, an island country southeast of the United States. After graduating from the City College of New York, Powell attended military school. Beginning as an army lieutenant, Powell rose through the ranks. He served in Vietnam starting in 1962, then again from 1968 to 1969. At his retirement, Powell was a general in the U.S. Army. He earned a master of business administration degree, held several government posts, and directed the first Gulf War in 1991. Beginning in 2001, Powell served as the secretary of state to George W. Bush. He has received many awards for his military and nonmilitary service. Powell is widely admired around the world.

Taliban

The group that controlled the government of Afghanistan

Al Qaeda had headquarters in Afghanistan. Because of this, the war on terror started there in October 2001. President Bush called America's response to 9/11 "the war on terror."

How Did the War on Terror Begin?

A group called the **Taliban** controlled the government of Afghanistan. Under Taliban rule, females could not go to school or work outside the home. Television was banned. Harsh punishment was given to anyone who disobeyed their rules. Osama bin Laden and Al Qaeda were allowed to train in Afghanistan. The United States and the United Nations warned the Taliban to turn over Osama bin Laden and other terrorists or face war.

After repeated warnings, the United States and Great Britain began bombing Afghanistan on October 7, 2001. Some Afghan soldiers had been fighting the Taliban for years. With the help of these troops and bombings, the Taliban soon fell apart, but Osama bin Laden was not found.

The people of Afghanistan were very poor before the war started. After the war, the United States and other nations helped Afghanistan rebuild. In June 2002, Hamid Karzai became the president of Afghanistan. A new government was formed with the goal of creating a democracy.

The Afghanistan war destroyed most of the training camps and headquarters of Al Qaeda. It also removed the Taliban from power. More than three years after the attacks on the United States, Osama bin Laden still has not been captured. Many Al Qaeda leaders have not been found. Al Qaeda appeared to still be active.

Geography Note

Iraq borders the Persian Gulf between the countries of Iran, Turkey, Syria, Jordan, Saudi Arabia, and Kuwait. Most of the land is desert, but there are mountains in northern Iraq. The country is about twice the size of the state of Idaho and is home to about 25 million people. Desertification, or the destruction of good soil to form a desert, is a major problem, and there is a shortage of water.

Why Did the United States Believe Saddam Hussein Was a Threat?

In the fall of 2002, the United States turned its attention to Iraq and its leader, Saddam Hussein. The United States thought that Hussein was a threat to them and to other nations of the world.

In 1991, the United States had led a military force that defeated the Iraqi army. This followed Hussein's invasion of Kuwait, a neighboring country. After this war, called the Persian Gulf War, it was thought that Hussein was hiding **weapons of mass destruction**. These are weapons that cause death on a large scale. Hussein was told to destroy these weapons in 1991. By 2000, some believed that he was trying to create nuclear weapons. They believed he would give them to terrorist groups.

What Caused the Invasion of Iraq?

By fall 2002, United States leaders believed that it did not matter whether Iraq and Al Qaeda were linked. President Bush said, "You can't distinguish between Al Qaeda and Saddam when you talk about the war on terror."

The United Nations Security Council warned Iraq that it would face "serious consequences" if it did not cooperate with the United Nations inspectors searching for weapons of mass destruction. France, Germany, and other countries in the United Nations argued that Iraq should be given more time to cooperate. The United States and Great Britain disagreed. On March 19, 2003, the United States and Great Britain invaded Iraq.

How Long Did the Iraq War Last?

American and British troops moved quickly into the country from the south. In three weeks, the capital city of Baghdad was under the control of the United States and Great Britain. On April 15, President Bush said that the government of Saddam Hussein no longer existed. In early May 2003, Bush declared that the war was over. However, American soldiers continued to die.

The Life-Changing Attacks of September 11

Many people have said that the attacks of September 11, 2001, changed life in the United States. Short-term changes included stopping all U.S. air traffic for a brief period, a shutdown of the stock markets, and other measures.

Long-term changes will be felt for many years to come. Several government agencies responsible for the safety of the United States were combined into the Department of Homeland Security. Airports and public buildings saw increased security. Economically, the U.S. had been in a recession, and the attacks sharply increased the effects. Unemployment climbed. Several major airlines suffered financial problems because travelers were afraid to travel on airplanes.

Lesson 2 Review On a sheet of paper, write the answers to the following questions. Use complete sentences.

1. Why did the war on terror begin in Afghanistan?

2. What was the Taliban?

3. What freedoms did the Taliban deny its people?

4. What was it believed that Saddam Hussein was hiding?

5. Why did President Bush say in May 2003 that the war in Iraq was over?

What do you think ?

Do you think the United States and Great Britain had the right to attack Afghanistan? Explain your answer.

Saddam Hussein

After the main fighting ended in Iraq, the United States and allied forces remained there. Soldiers searched for weapons of mass destruction. They also wanted to find Saddam Hussein and to change Iraq into a new democratic nation.

Were Weapons of Mass Destruction Found?

By the end of 2003, no weapons of mass destruction had been found. But the graves of thousands of people murdered by Hussein's government were found. On December 13, 2003, Saddam Hussein was captured by American soldiers. President Bush said Hussein would face justice.

What Was Iraq Like After the War?

Nearly 130,000 American and British soldiers remained in Iraq. The United States and Great Britain wanted to create a new democratic Iraq. That was not an easy goal. In the 1980s, Iraq had fought a long war with Iran. This had left Iraq a poor country. Hussein's government had done little to improve the lives of its citizens.

The Iraqi economy had to be rebuilt. After the invasion, Iraq had no army. It had no police force. Looting and robbery increased. Water and electrical systems had been damaged. The United States and Great Britain hoped that Iraq's huge supply of oil would help pay for its reconstruction. However, Iraq's oil wells needed many costly repairs.

At first the American government said that it did not need support from the United Nations to remain in Iraq. But that changed after American soldiers began dying in terrorist attacks. It was hoped that soldiers from other countries would help American and British troops. The cost of rebuilding Iraq would be billions of dollars. By September 2003, the U.S. and Great Britain sought more military and financial help for Iraq from United Nations members. President Bush asked Congress for $87 billion to pay for the reconstruction of Iraq and Afghanistan.

American forces remained in Iraq after President Bush said the war had ended.

Some believe that the United States and other countries will have to stay in Iraq for many years. How long it will take to make Iraq a democratic country controlled by its own people is unknown. However, there are plans in place for elections to be held in 2005. Between March 2003 and the end of November 2004, the number of U.S. service members killed was 1,256.

What do you think ?

What do you think needs to happen before Iraq can become a democratic country? Explain.

Lesson 3 Review On a sheet of paper, write the answers to the following questions. Use complete sentences.

1. Why did U.S. military forces remain in Iraq?

2. What happened to Saddam Hussein?

3. What problems did Iraq have after the war?

4. How did the United States and Great Britain hope to pay for rebuilding Iraq?

5. Why did the United States ask the United Nations for help?

President George W. Bush campaigned for a second term as president.

Massachusetts Senator John Kerry was the Democratic candidate for president.

As the presidential election of 2004 approached, people were considering many issues. Terrorism, the war in Iraq, education, healthcare, prescription drug costs, the environment, and the economy were all concerns.

Republican George W. Bush hoped to win a second term in the White House. Bush's running mate was Vice President Dick Cheney. His challenger, Democratic Senator John Kerry from Massachusetts, thought he could do a better job as president. Kerry's running mate was Senator John Edwards of North Carolina. Four debates on TV between the candidates made their positions clearer. But few people said they changed their minds because of the debates.

The war in Iraq proved to be an issue that divided people. President Bush thought that the war was going in the right direction and that Iraq would soon have democratic elections. Kerry wanted to fight the war differently and bring home troops sooner. He thought that the United States should have allowed more time for UN sanctions to work before attacking Iraq.

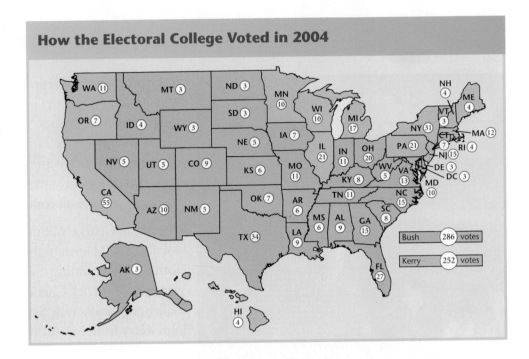

How the Electoral College Voted in 2004

WA 11 · MT 3 · ND 3 · MN 10 · WI 10 · MI 17 · NH 4 · ME 4

OR 7 · ID 4 · WY 3 · SD 3 · IA 7 · NY 31 · VT 3

NV 5 · UT 5 · CO 9 · NE 5 · IL 21 · IN 11 · OH 20 · PA 21 · CT 7 · MA 12 · RI 4

CA 55 · KS 6 · MO 11 · KY 8 · WV 5 · VA 13 · NJ 15 · DE 3 · DC 3 · MD

AZ 10 · NM 5 · OK 7 · AR 6 · TN 11 · NC 15

TX 34 · LA 9 · MS 6 · AL 9 · GA 15 · SC 8

AK 3 · FL 27 · HI 4

| Bush | 286 votes |
| Kerry | 252 votes |

On November 2, 2004, the election was held. The number of electoral votes needed to win the presidency is 270. Bush ended up with 286 electoral votes and Kerry with 252 electoral votes. The map above shows how the Electoral College voted. California, with 55, has the most electoral votes. Alaska, Montana, North Dakota, South Dakota, Delaware, Vermont, Washington, D.C., and Wyoming have three votes each. Bush won 31 states and 51 percent of the popular vote. Kerry won 19 states plus the District of Columbia, and 48 percent of the popular vote. George W. Bush began his second term in January 2005.

What do you think 🅟

What do you think was the most important issue in the election of 2004? Why?

Lesson 4 Review On a sheet of paper, answer each of the following questions. Use complete sentences.

1. Who was George W. Bush's running mate?

2. Who was John Kerry's running mate?

3. Why do you think that the debates did not make many people change their minds?

4. Why do you think that people had strong opinions about the war in Iraq?

5. How many electoral votes are needed to win the presidency?

How Has Space Exploration Continued?

The United States has experienced both disaster and success in the opening years of the century. On the morning of Saturday, February 1, 2003, the space shuttle *Columbia* exploded shortly before it was scheduled to land. All seven members of the crew were killed. The crew included two women and five men, one of whom was Israel's first astronaut.

A piece of foam came off the shuttle during takeoff and hit the left wing. The damage to the wing was thought to be the cause of the disaster. Flights of space shuttles came to a halt while NASA continued to investigate the tragedy. *Columbia,* which was on its 28th mission, was the oldest of the shuttles at NASA.

The International Space Station

The International Space Station celebrated its fourth year in existence in November 2004. Russian cosmonauts and American astronauts at the space station maintain the craft and conduct experiments. When the space station is completed, possibly in 2010, it will be the third-brightest object in the night sky. Only the moon and the planet Venus will be brighter.

Can New Technology Help or Harm Us?

In the early part of the 20th century, people predicted that technology would solve many of the world's problems. Electricity would provide the energy for many labor-saving machines. People would work only a few hours a week. Everyone would have an automobile. Airplanes would fill the sky.

Today, people around the world share ideas, art, music, and different ways of living. Technology has helped to create global connections. What happens in one country affects every other country. Satellites, computers, and **telecommunications** have led to a higher living standard in industrialized nations like the United States.

New technology has been behind many advances in medicine. Doctors are now able to remove a person's heart and fix it. They replace livers and hips. They sew fingers, arms, and legs onto a person who has lost them in an accident. Technology makes all this possible.

However, some people think that we are losing our freedom. Every time we use a credit card, a computer files the information away. Computers also contain information about medicines we take. The government collects information about us and stores it on computers. This leads to a loss of privacy.

But who will decide how to use all this information? How can we control what people know about us? If technology can cause harm, should we limit its development? Who will decide what that limit is? These important questions have no easy answers.

What Are Some Concerns About the Environment?

In the 1960s, astronauts went into space. They took pictures that showed Earth as a beautiful, blue planet. But today, satellite pictures show polluted air and water.

Air pollution affects our health, and it may change our climate. The burning of coal, oil, and natural gas causes most air pollution. We also have water pollution. Farming and industry have poisoned lakes and rivers.

Farmers around the world use fertilizers to make crops grow and pesticides to kill bugs. Rain makes these chemicals run off into rivers, lakes, and oceans. Then they end up in the bodies of fish and other animals. People who eat these animals or drink the water get sick. The problem is most serious in developing countries where many people cannot get clean water.

Since the 1980s, scientists have warned us about **global warming**. They believe that gases from cars and factories are heating up the earth. Burning wood, coal, oil, or natural gas releases carbon monoxide. Trees remove this gas from the air and release oxygen into the air for us to breathe. But overpopulated countries are now cutting down forests and jungles to provide farmland and firewood.

Many people fear that this will increase the carbon dioxide in the air and raise the earth's temperature. This might change rainfall patterns around the world. Too much rain would cause floods; too little rain would cause droughts and famine. Scientists also believe that the polar ice caps are melting. This will raise the sea levels and flood cities like New York, which are on the coast. If this happens, two billion people around the world would have to move inland.

Do All People Receive Equal Treatment?

Generally, women's organizations shared several important goals over the last three decades. These include equal opportunity for women in higher education, equal access to professional careers, and equal pay for equal work. Although equal opportunity for women in education and professions is a reality, the "pay gap" continues. Women now earn 77 cents for every dollar a man earns.

As the nation enters the 21st century, racial and ethnic minorities still have real concerns about protection of their rights. In a poll taken in 2000, more than 40 percent of African Americans felt that police stopped them because of the color of their skin. This is called **racial profiling**. More than 80 percent of African Americans polled felt that racial profiling was widespread. Just over 50 percent of white Americans agreed. In a democracy there will always be differences of opinion. With the Constitution as a foundation, the nation has addressed the concerns of minorities and expanded the Constitutional rights and protections to all the citizens of the United States.

Where Do We Live?

Beginning in the 1960s, America's older industrial cities in the Northeast and Midwest began to grow slowly or lose population. These cities, such as Philadelphia, Baltimore, Cleveland, and Detroit, were named the "Rust Belt." Suburbs surrounding these cities gained population. Also, many people moved from the colder climates in the North to the warmer climates of southwestern states. These warmer states were named the "Sun Belt."

What Other Changes Are Happening?

By 2000, globalization, or the knitting together of all the world's economies, had changed the world. Like many other nations, the United States has begun to trade without barriers between countries.

What Does the "Aging of America" Mean?

During the 1960s, 17 million Americans were 65 years or older. By 2003 that number had more than doubled. Older Americans now make up almost 13 percent of the population. Many of them will live past age 80. Many plan to continue to work, even if only part-time. Others look forward to volunteering in their communities. As the first of the "baby boomers" become senior citizens, their skills, experience, and energy will be a new resource for the nation.

What Is the United States Population?

In 1900, the United States population was around 76 million. In 1990, the total U.S. population was around 249 million. The 2000 U.S. Census results, released in January 2001, showed the population at 281,421,906. Thirteen percent of United States citizens are African Americans, and 12 percent are Hispanics. Four percent of the U.S. population are Asian or from the Pacific Islands. Around 1 percent are American Indian or Alaskan Inuit. Over 70 percent of the population are non-Hispanic caucasians. Around 92 percent of the population were born in the United States, and 8 percent were born in other countries.

Then and Now

Do you realize how rapidly the world's population is growing? The number of people living on Earth is exploding. Some scientists blame overpopulation for problems like pollution, famine, and global warming. The world's population is expected to increase by one billion people every 12 years. Many people think overcrowding will be the major problem in the future. They are concerned with being able to feed so many people. Look at the world population figures and estimates in the chart at the right.

Year	Approximate Number of People
1800	1 billion
1930	2 billion
1968	3.5 billion
1990	5.3 billion
2002	6.3 billion
2014	7.1 billion

In the last 100 years, nearly 40 million people have emigrated to the United States. The largest number of immigrants today are from Cuba, Mexico, and other Latin American countries. Within 50 years, it is predicted that Hispanics will make up 20 percent of the United States population.

What do you think ?

What do you think will be the most difficult problem facing the United States in the future? Why?

Lesson 5 Review On a sheet of paper, write the answers to the following questions. Use complete sentences.

1. What was the cause of the space shuttle *Columbia* disaster?

2. What are some ways that technology helps us? What are some concerns about technology?

3. Which environmental problem do you think is most important? Why?

4. In what part of the country is the Rust Belt? the Sun Belt?

5. What is the "aging of America"?

George W. Bush's Speech on Terrorism

On September 20, 2001, President George W. Bush addressed the U.S. Congress. He thanked the world for its support, and then outlined his war on terror. In the following paragraphs, President Bush describes Al Qaeda and the Taliban, who ruled Afghanistan until October 2001.

[Al Qaeda] and its leader—a person named Osama bin Laden—are linked to many other organizations in different countries . . . They are recruited from their own nations and neighborhoods and brought to camps in places like Afghanistan, where they are trained in the tactics of terror. They are sent back to their homes or sent to hide in countries around the world to plot evil and destruction.

The leadership of Al Qaeda has great influence in Afghanistan and supports the Taliban regime in controlling most of that country. In Afghanistan, we see Al Qaeda's vision for the world.

Afghanistan's people have been brutalized—many are starving and many have fled. Women are not allowed to attend school. You can be jailed for owning a television. Religion can be practiced only as their leaders dictate. A man can be jailed in Afghanistan if his beard is not long enough. . . .

And tonight, the United States of America makes the following demands on the Taliban: Deliver to United States authorities all the leaders of Al Qaeda who hide in your land. Release all foreign nationals, including American citizens, you have unjustly imprisoned. Protect foreign journalists, diplomats and aid workers in your country. Close immediately and permanently every terrorist training camp in Afghanistan, and hand over every terrorist, and every person in their support structure, to appropriate authorities. Give the United States full access to terrorist training camps, so we can make sure they are no longer operating.

These demands are not open to negotiation or discussion. The Taliban must act, and act immediately. They will hand over the terrorists, or they will share in their fate. . . .

Document-Based Questions

1. What does President Bush say is Al Qaeda's goal?

2. According to President Bush, who is Al Qaeda's leader?

3. Why does the president say Al Qaeda's vision can be seen in Afghanistan?

4. What does President Bush mean when he says the Taliban might share the terrorists' fate?

5. Why do you think the president says Al Qaeda plots "evil and destruction"?

Source: "Address to a Joint Session of Congress and the American People," The White House,
http://www.whitehouse.gov/news/releases/2001/09/20010920-8.html.

Chapter 32 SUMMARY

- Terrorism is planned violence by individuals or groups against civilians for political reasons. Terrorists hope to frighten people in order to get what they want.

- On September 11, 2001, a terrorist group named Al Qaeda attacked the United States. The leader of Al Qaeda is Osama bin Laden. Terrorists crashed two passenger planes into the World Trade Center and one into the Pentagon. Another attack with a passenger plane, planned for either the White House or the Capitol building, failed.

- Americans were shocked by the terrorist attacks. Many Americans acted bravely. Patriotism increased.

- The American government responded to the attacks by passing the Patriot Act. Signed in October 2001, it gave government officials new powers to prevent terrorism. The Department of Homeland Security was made official in November 2002. It combines the efforts of more than 22 federal agencies to protect American citizens.

- The war on terrorism began in Afghanistan. Al Qaeda headquarters were based there. The Taliban controlled the government of Afghanistan.

- The United States and Great Britain attacked Afghanistan in October 2001. The Taliban government fell apart in November 2001. Osama bin Laden was not found. The United States and many other nations gave money to help rebuild Afghanistan.

- By the fall of 2002, the United States focused on Iraq and Saddam Hussein. Some feared that he had weapons of mass destruction. When Hussein would not cooperate with weapons inspectors, American and British troops invaded Iraq in March 2003. President Bush said in May 2003 that the fighting was over.

- After the main fighting ended in Iraq, American and allied forces remained. Their task was to search for weapons of mass destruction, find Saddam Hussein and other Iraqi leaders, help rebuild the economy, and help Iraq become a democracy. No weapons of mass destruction were found in Iraq.

- Saddam Hussein was captured in December 2003.

- George W. Bush won a second term as president on November 2, 2004. He beat his Democratic challenger, John Kerry.

- Terrorism, the economy, the environment, and healthcare were concerns of many people in the first years of the 21st century.

Chapter 32 REVIEW

Word Bank

9/11
Afghanistan
Al Qaeda
George W. Bush
hijacked
Iraq
Osama bin Laden
Saddam Hussein
Taliban
terrorism
weapons of mass
destruction

On a sheet of paper, write the correct word or words from the Word Bank to complete each sentence.

1. Planned violence by individuals or groups against civilians for political reasons is called _____.

2. _____ became president of the U.S. in January 2001.

3. The terrorist group that attacked the United States on September 11, 2001, is called _____.

4. The leader of the terrorist group that attacked the United States is named _____.

5. Terrorists _____ passenger planes and crashed them into buildings in Washington, D.C., and New York City.

6. The attacks on September 11, 2001, are known as _____.

7. The _____ controlled the government of Afghanistan.

8. The war on terror began in the nation of _____.

9. The leader of Iraq was _____.

10. Some people believed that Saddam Hussein had _____.

11. American and British forces invaded _____ on March 19, 2003.

On a sheet of paper, write the letter of the answer that correctly completes each sentence.

12. Cities in the Northeast and Midwest, such as Philadelphia and Detroit, are called the _____.

    A Sun Belt   **C** Population Belt

    B Rust Belt   **D** Technology Belt

13. The state of _____, with 55, has the most electoral votes.

    A Vermont   **B** Alaska   **C** California   **D** New York

14. The number of _____ votes needed to win the presidency is 270.

    A Democratic   **C** popular

    B Republican   **D** electoral

15. Cities in the southwestern states are called the _____.

    A Sun Belt   **C** Population Belt

    B Rust Belt   **D** Technology Belt

16. Every state in the United States has at least _____ electoral votes.

    A 3   **B** 13   **C** 30   **D** 300

17. The knitting together of all the world's economies is called _____.

    A global warming   **C** the aging of America

    B racial profiling   **D** globalization

On a sheet of paper, write the answers to the following questions. Use complete sentences.

18. How did the United States respond to the terrorist attacks?

19. What is the Patriot Act?

20. What does the Department of Homeland Security do?

21. Why did American and British forces attack Afghanistan?

22. Why did American and British forces invade Iraq?

23. What happened after President Bush said the war had ended in Iraq?

Critical Thinking On a sheet of paper, write your response to each question. Use complete sentences.

24. Do you think the United States took the correct course of action after the September 11 attacks? Why or why not?

25. Do you think that the United States should have stopped exploring space after the *Columbia* space shuttle tragedy? Explain your answer.

Test-Taking Tip

Decide which questions you will do first and last. Limit your time on each question accordingly.

Voting

As U.S. citizens, we vote to elect leaders and decide certain issues. As voters, we can do several things to inform ourselves about different candidates and issues. We can read newspapers and listen to political debates on radio and TV. We can read articles about candidates in news magazines. We can become informed by reading flyers delivered to our door. We may attend political rallies at which candidates speak. We can get information from the political party of our choice. Studying a voting record on issues can show the positions of a candidate already holding office.

Voter Registration Application

Qualified voters 18 and older must first register at a city or county clerk's office. In some states they also can register at the polls on election day. The polls are usually open from 7 A.M. to 8 P.M. Each voter is assigned a polling place in his or her district. The local newspaper usually tells people where to vote. Voters also can call the city or county clerk's office to learn their polling place. Voters who will be out of town on election day can request an absentee ballot in person or by mail. They can mark and turn in the absentee ballot ahead of the election.

At the polls, voters fill out a ballot. Election judges instruct voters on how to fill out the ballot. Different districts use various methods. Voters might have to mark Xs or complete arrows with a pen, punch holes, or pull a lever. To ensure privacy, voters make their selections in a private booth.

Election judges at each polling place count the votes at the end of election day. They deliver the count to the city or county clerk's office. Television, radio, and newspapers give election results. When all votes are counted, a winner is declared.

Before you can vote, you need to know several things. Find out the answer to these questions.

1. How long must I live in my state and district before I can vote?

2. Where do I register to vote?

3. How do I register to vote?

4. Where do I vote?

5. Where do I get an absentee ballot?

6. How do I decide who to vote for?

7. How do I fill out the ballot?

8. How are the votes counted?

9. Why do you think it is important to vote in elections?

10. Identify the day, month, and year when you can vote in a national election for the first time.

- In 1973, signing of the Paris Peace Accords ended U.S. involvement in the Vietnam War.

- President Nixon resigned in 1974, and Gerald Ford became president.

- America celebrated its 200th birthday in 1976.

- Jimmy Carter became president in 1977. He signed the SALT II treaty with Leonid Brezhnev in 1979.

- Ronald Reagan became president in 1981. He wanted to make people less dependent on the government.

- Sandra Day O'Connor became the first female Supreme Court justice.

- Reagan was re-elected in 1984.

- In 1986, the space shuttle *Challenger* exploded.

- Mikhail Gorbachev and Reagan signed the INF Treaty in 1987.

- In October 1983, a terrorist attack killed 200 U.S. marines in Lebanon.

- Libya made terrorist attacks in 1985 and 1986. U.S. planes bombed Libyan military posts.

- The space program resumed in September 1988.

- George H.W. Bush became president in 1989. A growing budget deficit, crime, drug abuse, and homeless people were problems he faced.

- East and West Germany were reunified in 1990.

- In 1990, Iraq invaded Kuwait. U.S. and UN forces freed Kuwait and caused severe Iraqi casualties.

- Communism fell in the Soviet Union in 1991.

- William Clinton became president in 1993. He was re-elected in 1996.

- In 1993, the NAFTA agreement opened trade with Canada and Mexico. In 2000, the Senate passed a bill to open more trading with China.

- In April 2000, Israeli Prime Minister Barak asked the United States to help negotiate peace talks between the Israelis and the Palestinians.

- In 2000, George W. Bush was elected to the presidency. The election was so close that the outcome was not announced until five weeks after the election.

- Given current immigration, Hispanics will represent one in five Americans within 50 years.

- The 21st century offers many challenges to the United States. One of the most pressing is global warming.

- The worst terrorist attacks ever on American soil occurred on September 11, 2001, in New York City and Washington, D.C.

- George W. Bush won a second term as president in November 2004.

The Declaration of Independence

Adopted in Congress July 4, 1776
The Unanimous Declaration of the
Thirteen United States of America

When, in the course of human events, it becomes necessary for one people to dissolve the political bands which have connected them with another, and to assume among the powers of the earth, the separate and equal station to which the laws of nature and of nature's God entitle them, a decent respect to the opinions of mankind requires that they should declare the causes which impel them to the separation.

We hold these truths to be self-evident, that all men are created equal, that they are endowed by their Creator with certain unalienable rights, that among these are life, liberty, and the pursuit of happiness. That to secure these rights, governments are instituted among men, deriving their just powers from the consent of the governed. That whenever any form of government becomes destructive of these ends, it is the right of the people to alter or to abolish it, and to institute new government, laying its foundation on such principles and organizing its powers in such form, as to them shall seem most likely to effect their safety and happiness. Prudence, indeed, will dictate that governments long established should not be changed for light and transient causes; and accordingly all experience hath shown that mankind are more disposed to suffer, while evils are sufferable, than to right themselves by abolishing the forms to which they are accustomed. But when a long train of abuses and usurpations, pursuing invariably the same object evinces a design to reduce them under absolute despotism, it is their right, it is their duty, to throw off such government, and to provide new guards for their future security.

Such has been the patient sufferance of these colonies; and such is now the necessity which constrains them to alter their former systems of government. The history of the present King of Great Britain is a history of repeated injuries and usurpations, all having in direct object the establishment of an absolute tyranny over these states. To prove this, let facts be submitted to a candid world.

He has refused his assent to laws, the most wholesome and necessary for the public good.

He has forbidden his governors to pass laws of immediate and pressing importance, unless suspended in their operation till his assent should be obtained; and when so suspended, he has utterly neglected to attend to them.

He has refused to pass other laws for the accommodation of large districts of people, unless those people would relinquish the right of representation in the legislature, a right inestimable to them and formidable to tyrants only.

He has called together legislative bodies at places unusual, uncomfortable, and distant from the depository of their public records, for the sole purpose of fatiguing them into compliance with his measures.

He has dissolved representative houses repeatedly, for opposing with manly firmness his invasions on the rights of the people.

He has refused for a long time, after such dissolutions, to cause others to be elected; whereby the legislative powers, incapable of annihilation, have returned to the people at large for their exercise; the state remaining in the mean time exposed to all the dangers of invasion from without, and convulsions within.

He has endeavored to prevent the population of these states; for that purpose obstructing the laws for naturalization of foreigners; refusing to pass others to encourage their migrations hither, and raising the conditions of new appropriations of lands.

He has obstructed the administration of justice, by refusing his assent to laws for establishing judiciary powers.

He has made judges dependent on his will alone, for the tenure of their offices, and the amount and payment of their salaries.

He has erected a multitude of new offices, and sent hither swarms of officers to harass our people, and eat out their substance.

He has kept among us, in times of peace, standing armies without the consent of our legislatures.

He has affected to render the military independent of and superior to the civil power.

He has combined with others to subject us to a jurisdiction foreign to our constitution, and unacknowledged by our laws; giving his assent to their acts of pretended legislation:

For quartering large bodies of armed troops among us:

For protecting them, by a mock trial, from punishment for any murders which they should commit on the inhabitants of these states:

For cutting off our trade with all parts of the world:

For imposing taxes on us without our consent:

For depriving us in many cases, of the benefits of trial by jury:

For transporting us beyond seas to be tried for pretended offenses:

For abolishing the free system of English laws in a neighboring province, establishing therein an arbitrary government, and enlarging its boundaries so as to render it at once an example and fit instrument for introducing the same absolute rule into these colonies:

For taking away our charters, abolishing our most valuable laws, and altering fundamentally the forms of our governments:

For suspending our own legislatures, and declaring themselves invested with power to legislate for us in all cases whatsoever.

He has abdicated government here, by declaring us out of his protection and waging war against us.

He has plundered our seas, ravaged our coasts, burned our towns, and destroyed the lives of our people.

He is at this time transporting large armies of foreign mercenaries to complete the works of death, desolation and tyranny, already begun with circumstances of cruelty and perfidy scarcely paralleled in the most barbarous ages, and totally unworthy the head of a civilized nation.

He has constrained our fellow citizens taken captive on the high seas to bear arms against their country, to become the executioners of their friends and brethren, or to fall themselves by their hands.

He has excited domestic insurrections amongst us, and has endeavored to bring on the inhabitants of our frontiers, the merciless Indian savages, whose known rule of warfare, is an undistinguished destruction of all ages, sexes, and conditions.

In every stage of these oppressions we have petitioned for redress in the most humble terms: our repeated petitions have been answered only by repeated injury. A prince, whose character is thus marked by every act which may define a tyrant, is unfit to be the ruler of a free people.

Nor have we been wanting in attentions to our British brethren. We have warned them from time to time of attempts by their legislature to extend an unwarrantable jurisdiction over us. We have reminded them of the circumstances of our emigration and settlement here. We have appealed to their native justice and magnanimity, and we have conjured them by the ties of our common kindred to disavow these usurpations, which would inevitably interrupt our connections and correspondence. They too have been deaf to the voice of justice and of consanguinity. We must, therefore, acquiesce in the necessity, which denounces our separation, and hold them, as we hold the rest of mankind, enemies in war, in peace friends.

We, therefore, the representatives of the United States of America, in General Congress, assembled, appealing to the Supreme Judge of the world for the rectitude of our intentions, do, in the name, and by authority of the good people of these colonies, solemnly publish and declare, that these united colonies are, and of right ought to be free and independent states; that they are absolved from all allegiance to the British Crown, and that all political connection between them and the state of Great Britain, is and ought to be totally dissolved; and that as free and independent states, they have full power to levy war, conclude peace, contract alliances, establish commerce, and to do all other acts and things which independent states may of right do. And for the support of this declaration, with a firm reliance on the protection of Divine Providence, we mutually pledge to each other our lives, our fortunes, and our sacred honor.

Signed by John Hancock of Massachusetts as President of the Congress and by the fifty-five other Representatives of the thirteen United States of America:

New Hampshire
Josiah Bartlett
William Whipple
Matthew Thornton

Connecticut
Roger Sherman
Samuel Huntington
William Williams
Oliver Wolcott

Massachusetts Bay
Samuel Adams
John Adams
Robert Treat Paine
Elbridge Gerry

Rhode Island
Stephen Hopkins
William Ellery

Pennsylvania
Robert Morris
Benjamin Rush
Benjamin Franklin
John Morton
George Clymer
James Smith
George Taylor
James Wilson
George Ross

Delaware
Caesar Rodney
George Read
Thomas M'Kean

New York
William Floyd
Philip Livingston
Francis Lewis
Lewis Morris

Virginia
George Wythe
Richard Henry Lee
Thomas Jefferson
Benjamin Harrison
Thomas Nelson, Jr.
Francis Lightfoot Lee
Carter Braxton

North Carolina
William Hooper
Joseph Hewes
John Penn

South Carolina
Edward Rutledge
Thomas Heyward, Jr.
Thomas Lynch, Jr.
Arthur Middleton

Georgia
Button Gwinnett
Lyman Hall
George Walton

Maryland
Samuel Chase
William Paca
Thomas Stone
Charles Carroll of
    Carrollton

New Jersey
Richard Stockton
John Witherspoon
Francis Hopkinson
John Hart
Abraham Clark

The Constitution of the United States

Preamble

We the people of the United States, in order to form a more perfect Union, establish justice, insure domestic tranquility, provide for the common defense, promote the general welfare, and secure the blessings of liberty to ourselves and our posterity, do ordain and establish this Constitution for the United States of America.

Article I
The Legislative Branch*

Congress

Section 1 All legislative powers herein granted shall be vested in a Congress of the United States, which shall consist of a Senate and House of Representatives.

The House of Representatives

Section 2 (1) The House of Representatives shall be composed of members chosen every second year by the people of the several states, and the electors in each state shall have the qualifications requisite for electors of the most numerous branch of the state legislature.

(2) No person shall be a representative who shall not have attained to the age of twenty-five years, and been seven years a citizen of the United States, and who shall not, when elected, be an inhabitant of that state in which he shall be chosen.

(3) Representatives and direct taxes shall be apportioned among the several states which may be included within this Union, according to their respective numbers, [which shall be determined by adding to the whole number of free persons, including those bound to service for a term of years, and excluding Indians not taxed, three-fifths of all other persons]. The actual enumeration shall be made within three years after the first meeting of the Congress of the United States, and within every subsequent term of ten years, in such manner as they shall by law direct. The number of representatives shall not exceed one for every thirty thousand, but each state shall have at least one representative; [and until such enumeration shall be made, the state of New Hampshire shall be entitled to choose 3, Massachusetts 8, Rhode Island and Providence Plantations 1, Connecticut 5, New York 6, New Jersey 4, Pennsylvania 8, Delaware 1, Maryland 6, Virginia 10, North Carolina 5, South Carolina 5, and Georgia 3].

* Headings and paragraph numbers have been added to help the reader. The original Constitution has only the article and section numbers.

(4) When vacancies happen in the representation from any state, the executive authority thereof shall issue writs of election to fill such vacancies.

(5) The House of Representatives shall choose their speaker and other officers; and shall have the sole power of impeachment.

The Senate

Section 3 **(1)** The Senate of the United States shall be composed of two senators from each state, [chosen by the legislature thereof,] for six years; and each senator shall have one vote.

(2) Immediately after they shall be assembled in consequence of the first election, they shall be divided as equally as may be into three classes. The seats of the senators of the first class shall be vacated at the expiration of the second year, of the second class at the expiration of the fourth year, and of the third class at the expiration of the sixth year, so that one-third may be chosen every second year; [and if vacancies happen by resignation, or otherwise, during the recess of the legislature of any state, the executive thereof may make temporary appointments until the next meeting of the legislature, which shall then fill such vacancies].

(3) No person shall be a senator who shall not have attained to the age of thirty years, and been nine years a citizen of the United States, and who shall not, when elected, be an inhabitant of that state for which he shall be chosen.

(4) The Vice President of the United States shall be president of the Senate, but shall have no vote, unless they be equally divided.

(5) The Senate shall choose their other officers, and also a president pro tempore, in the absence of the Vice President, or when he shall exercise the office of President of the United States.

(6) The Senate shall have the sole power to try all impeachments. When sitting for that purpose, they shall be on oath or affirmation. When the President of the United States is tried, the Chief Justice shall preside: and no person shall be convicted without the concurrence of two-thirds of the members present.

(7) Judgment in cases of impeachment shall not extend further than to removal from office, and disqualification to hold and enjoy any office of honor, trust, or profit under the United States: but the party convicted shall nevertheless be liable and subject to indictment, trial, judgment, and punishment, according to law.

Organization of Congress

Section 4 **(1)** The times, places, and manner of holding elections for senators and representatives, shall be prescribed in each state by the legislature thereof; but the Congress may at any time by law make or alter such regulations, [except as to the places of choosing senators].

(2) The Congress shall assemble at least once in every year, [and such meeting shall be on the first Monday in December,] unless they shall by law appoint a different day.

Rules and Procedures
Section 5 (1) Each house shall be the judge of the elections, returns and qualifications of its own members, and a majority of each shall constitute a quorum to do business; but a smaller number may adjourn from day to day, and may be authorized to compel the attendance of absent members, in such manner, and under such penalties as each house may provide.

(2) Each house may determine the rules of its proceedings, punish its members for disorderly behavior, and, with the concurrence of two-thirds, expel a member.

(3) Each house shall keep a journal of its proceedings, and from time to time publish the same, excepting such parts as may in their judgment require secrecy; and the yeas and nays of the members of either house on any question shall, at the desire of one-fifth of those present, be entered on the journal.

(4) Neither house, during the session of Congress, shall, without the consent of the other, adjourn for more than three days, nor to any other place than that in which the two houses shall be sitting.

Payment and Privileges
Section 6 (1) The senators and representatives shall receive a compensation for their services, to be ascertained by law, and paid out of the treasury of the United States. They shall in all cases, except treason, felony, and breach of the peace, be privileged from arrest during their attendance at the session of their respective houses, and in going to and returning from the same; and for any speech or debate in either house, they shall not be questioned in any other place.

(2) No senator or representative shall, during the time for which he was elected, be appointed to any civil office under the authority of the United States, which shall have been created, or the emoluments whereof shall have been increased during such time; and no person holding any office under the United States, shall be a member of either house during his continuance in office.

How a Bill Becomes a Law
Section 7 (1) All bills for raising revenue shall originate in the House of Representatives; but the Senate may propose or concur with amendments as on other bills.

(2) Every bill which shall have passed the House of Representatives and the Senate, shall, before it becomes a law, be presented to the President of the United States; if he approve he shall sign it, but if not he shall return it, with his

objections to that house in which it shall have originated, who shall enter the objections at large on their journal, and proceed to reconsider it. If after such reconsideration two-thirds of that house shall agree to pass the bill, it shall be sent, together with the objections, to the other house, by which it shall likewise be reconsidered, and if approved by two-thirds of that house, it shall become a law. But in all such cases the votes of both houses shall be determined by yeas and nays, and the names of the persons voting for and against the bill shall be entered on the journal of each house, respectively. If any bill shall not be returned by the President within ten days (Sundays excepted) after it shall have been presented to him, the same shall be a law, in like manner as if he had signed it, unless the Congress by their adjournment prevent its return, in which case it shall not be a law.

(3) Every order, resolution, or vote to which the concurrence of the Senate and House of Representatives may be necessary (except on a question of adjournment) shall be presented to the President of the United States; and before the same shall take effect, shall be approved by him, or being disapproved by him, shall be repassed by two-thirds of the Senate and House of Representatives, according to the rules and limitations prescribed in the case of a bill.

Powers Granted to Congress

Section 8 The Congress shall have power:

(1) To lay and collect taxes, duties, imposts, and excises, to pay the debts and provide for the common defense and general welfare of the United States; but all duties, imposts, and excises shall be uniform throughout the United States;

(2) To borrow money on the credit of the United States;

(3) To regulate commerce with foreign nations, and among the several states, and with the Indian tribes;

(4) To establish a uniform rule of naturalization, and uniform laws on the subject of bankruptcies throughout the United States;

(5) To coin money, regulate the value thereof, and of foreign coin, and fix the standard of weights and measures;

(6) To provide for the punishment of counterfeiting the securities and current coin of the United States;

(7) To establish post offices and post roads;

(8) To promote the progress of science and useful arts, by securing for limited times to authors and inventors the exclusive right to their respective writings and discoveries;

(9) To constitute tribunals inferior to the Supreme Court;

(10) To define and punish piracies and felonies committed on the high seas, and offenses against the law of nations;

(11) To declare war, grant letters of marque and reprisal, and make rules concerning captures on land and water;

(12) To raise and support armies, but no appropriation of money to that use shall be for a longer term than two years;

(13) To provide and maintain a navy;

(14) To make rules for the government and regulation of the land and naval forces;

(15) To provide for calling forth the militia to execute the laws of the Union, suppress insurrections and repel invasions;

(16) To provide for organizing, arming, and disciplining, the militia, and for governing such part of them as may be employed in the service of the United States, reserving to the states respectively, the appointment of the officers, and the authority of training the militia according to the discipline prescribed by Congress;

(17) To exercise exclusive legislation in all cases whatsoever, over such district (not exceeding ten miles square) as may, by cession of particular states, and the acceptance of Congress, become the seat of the government of the United States, and to exercise like authority over all places purchased by the consent of the legislature of the state in which the same shall be, for the erection of forts, magazines, arsenals, dockyards, and other needful buildings; —And

(18) To make all laws which shall be necessary and proper for carrying into execution the foregoing powers, and all other powers vested by this Constitution in the government of the United States, or in any department or officer thereof.

Powers Denied Congress

Section 9 (1) The migration or importation of such persons as any of the states now existing shall think proper to admit, shall not be prohibited by the Congress prior to the year one thousand eight hundred and eight, but a tax or duty may be imposed on such importation, not exceeding ten dollars for each person.

(2) The privilege of the writ of habeas corpus shall not be suspended, unless when in cases of rebellion or invasion the public safety may require it.

(3) No bill of attainder or ex post facto law shall be passed.

(4) No capitation, [or other direct,] tax shall be laid, unless in proportion to the census or enumeration herein before directed to be taken.

(5) No tax or duty shall be laid on articles exported from any state.

(6) No preference shall be given by any regulation of commerce or revenue to the ports of one state over those of another: nor shall vessels bound to, or from, one state, be obliged to enter, clear, or pay duties in another.

(7) No money shall be drawn from the treasury, but in consequence of appropriations made by law; and a regular statement and account of the receipts and expenditures of all public money shall be published from time to time.

(8) No title of nobility shall be granted by the United States: And no person holding any office of profit or trust under them, shall, without the consent of the Congress, accept of any present, emolument, office, or title, of any kind whatever, from any king, prince, or foreign state.

Powers Denied the States
Section 10 (1) No state shall enter into any treaty, alliance, or confederation; grant letters of marque and reprisal; coin money; emit bills of credit; make anything but gold and silver coin a tender in payment of debts; pass any bill of attainder, ex post facto law, or law impairing the obligation of contracts, or grant any title of nobility.

(2) No state shall, without the consent of the Congress, lay any imposts or duties on imports or exports, except what may be absolutely necessary for executing its inspection laws: and the net produce of all duties and imposts, laid by any state on imports or exports, shall be for the use of the treasury of the United States; and all such laws shall be subject to the revision and control of the Congress.

(3) No state shall, without the consent of Congress, lay any duty of tonnage, keep troops, or ships of war in time of peace, enter into any agreement or compact with another state, or with a foreign power, or engage in war, unless actually invaded, or in such imminent danger as will not admit of delay.

ARTICLE II
The Executive Branch

The President
Section 1 (1) The executive power shall be vested in a President of the United States of America. He shall hold his office during the term of four years, and, together with the Vice President, chosen for the same term, be elected, as follows:

(2) Each state shall appoint, in such manner as the legislature thereof may direct, a number of electors, equal to the whole number of senators and representatives to which the state may be entitled in the Congress: but no senator or representative, or person holding an office of trust or profit under the United States, shall be appointed an elector.

[The electors shall meet in their respective states, and vote by ballot for two persons, of whom one at least shall not be an inhabitant of the same state with themselves. And they shall make a list of all the persons voted for, and of the number of votes for each; which list they shall sign and certify, and transmit sealed to the seat of the government of the United States, directed to the president of the Senate. The president of the Senate shall, in the presence of the Senate and House of Representatives, open all the certificates, and the votes shall then be counted. The person having the greatest number of votes shall be the President, if such number be a majority of the whole number of electors appointed; and if there be more than one who have such majority, and have an equal number of votes, then the House of Representatives shall immediately choose by ballot one of them for President; and if no person have a majority, then from the five highest on the list the said House shall in like manner choose the President. But in choosing the President, the votes shall be taken by states, the representation from each state having one vote; a quorum for this purpose shall consist of a member or members from two-thirds of the states, and a majority of all the states shall be necessary to a choice. In every case, after the choice of the President, the person having the greatest number of votes of the electors shall be the Vice President. But if there should remain two or more who have equal votes, the Senate shall choose from them by ballot the Vice President.]

(3) The Congress may determine the time of choosing the electors, and the day on which they shall give their votes; which day shall be the same throughout the United States.

(4) No person except a natural-born citizen, or a citizen of the United States at the time of the adoption of this Constitution, shall be eligible to the office of President; neither shall any person be eligible to that office who shall not have attained to the age of thirty-five years, and been fourteen years a resident within the United States.

(5) In case of the removal of the President from office, or of his death, resignation, or inability to discharge the powers and duties of the said office, the same shall devolve on the Vice President, and the Congress may by law provide for the case of removal, death, or resignation or inability, both of the President and Vice President, declaring what officer shall then act as President, and such officer shall act accordingly, until the disability be removed, or a President shall be elected.

(6) The President shall, at stated times, receive for his services, a compensation, which shall neither be increased or diminished during the period for which he shall have been elected, and he shall not receive within that period any other emolument from the United States, or any of them.

(7) Before he enter on the execution of his office, he shall take the following oath or affirmation: —"I do solemnly swear (or affirm) that I will faithfully execute the office of President of the United States, and will to the best of my ability, preserve, protect, and defend the Constitution of the United States."

Powers of the President

Section 2 (1) The President shall be commander in chief of the Army and Navy of the United States, and of the militia of the several states, when called into the actual service of the United States; he may require the opinion, in writing, of the principal officer in each of the executive departments, upon any subject relating to the duties of their respective offices, and he shall have power to grant reprieves and pardons for offenses against the United States, except in cases of impeachment.

(2) He shall have power, by and with the advice and consent of the Senate, to make treaties, provided two-thirds of the senators present concur; and he shall nominate, and by and with the advice and consent of the Senate, shall appoint ambassadors, other public ministers and consuls, judges of the Supreme Court, and all other officers of the United States, whose appointments are not herein otherwise provided for, and which shall be established by law: but the Congress may by law vest the appointment of such inferior officers, as they think proper, in the President alone, in the courts of law, or in the heads of departments.

(3) The President shall have power to fill up all vacancies that may happen during the recess of the Senate, by granting commissions which shall expire at the end of their next session.

Duties of the President

Section 3 He shall from time to time give to the Congress information of the state of the Union, and recommend to their consideration such measures as he shall judge necessary and expedient; he may, on extraordinary occasions, convene both houses, or either of them, and in case of disagreement between them, with respect to the time of adjournment, he may adjourn them to such time as he shall think proper; he shall receive ambassadors and other public ministers; he shall take care that the laws be faithfully executed, and shall commission all the officers of the United States.

Impeachment

Section 4 The President, Vice President, and all civil officers of the United States, shall be removed from office on impeachment for, and conviction of, treason, bribery, or other high crimes and misdemeanors.

ARTICLE III
The Judicial Branch

Federal Courts and Judges
Section 1 The judicial power of the United States, shall be vested in one Supreme Court, and in such inferior courts as the Congress may from time to time ordain and establish. The judges, both of the Supreme and inferior courts, shall hold their offices during good behavior, and shall, at stated times, receive for their services, a compensation, which shall not be diminished during their continuance in office.

Jurisdiction of United States Courts
Section 2 (1) The judicial power shall extend to all cases, in law and equity, arising under this Constitution, the laws of the United States, and treaties made, or which shall be made, under their authority; — to all cases affecting ambassadors, other public ministers and consuls; — to all cases of admiralty and maritime jurisdiction; — to controversies to which the United States shall be a party; — to controversies between two or more states; — [between a state and citizens of another state;] — between citizens of different states; — between citizens of the same state claiming lands under grants of different states, and between a state, or the citizens thereof, and foreign states, [citizens or subjects].

(2) In all cases affecting ambassadors, other public ministers and consuls, and those in which a state shall be party, the Supreme Court shall have original jurisdiction. In all the other cases before mentioned, the Supreme Court shall have appellate jurisdiction, both as to law and fact, with such exceptions, and under such regulations as the Congress shall make.

(3) The trial of all crimes, except in cases of impeachment, shall be by jury; and such trial shall be held in the state where the said crimes shall have been committed; but when not committed within any state, the trial shall be at such place or places as the Congress may by law have directed.

Treason
Section 3 (1) Treason against the United States, shall consist only in levying war against them, or in adhering to their enemies, giving them aid and comfort. No person shall be convicted of treason unless on the testimony of two witnesses to the same overt act, or on confession in open court.

(2) The Congress shall have power to declare the punishment of treason, but no attainder of treason shall work corruption of blood, or forfeiture except during the life of the person attainted.

ARTICLE IV
The States and the Federal Government

State Acts and Records
Section 1 Full faith and credit shall be given in each state to the public acts, records, and judicial proceedings of every other state. And the Congress may by general laws prescribe the manner in which such acts, records, and proceedings shall be proved, and the effect thereof.

Rights of Citizens
Section 2 (1) The citizens of each state shall be entitled to all privileges and immunities of citizens in the several states.

(2) A person charged in any state with treason, felony, or other crime, who shall flee from justice, and be found in another state, shall on demand of the executive authority of the state from which he fled, be delivered up, to be removed to the state having jurisdiction of the crime.

(3) [No person held to service or labor in one state, under the laws thereof, escaping into another, shall, in consequence of any law or regulation therein, be discharged from such service or labor, but shall be delivered up on claim of the party to whom such service or labor may be due.]

New States and Territories
Section 3 (1) New states may be admitted by the Congress into this Union; but no new state shall be formed or erected within the jurisdiction of any other state; nor any state be formed by the junction of two or more states, or parts of states, without the consent of the legislatures of the states concerned as well as of the Congress.

(2) The Congress shall have power to dispose of and make all needful rules and regulations respecting the territory or other property belonging to the United States; and nothing in this Constitution shall be so construed as to prejudice any claims of the United States, or of any particular state.

Protection of States Guaranteed
Section 4 The United States shall guarantee to every state in this Union a republican form of government, and shall protect each of them against invasion; and on application of the legislature, or of the executive (when the legislature cannot be convened) against domestic violence.

ARTICLE V
Amending the Constitution

The Congress, whenever two-thirds of both houses shall deem it necessary, shall propose amendments to this Constitution, or, on the application of the legislatures of two-thirds of the several states, shall call a convention for proposing amendments, which, in either case, shall be valid to all intents and purposes, as part of this Constitution, when ratified by the legislatures of three-fourths of the several states, or by conventions in three-fourths thereof, as the one or the other mode of ratification may be proposed by the Congress; provided [that no amendment which may be made prior to the year one thousand eight hundred and eight shall in any manner affect the first and fourth clauses in the ninth section of the first article; and] that no state, without its consent, shall be deprived of its equal suffrage in the Senate.

ARTICLE VI
General Provisions

(1) All debts contracted and engagements entered into, before the adoption of this Constitution, shall be as valid against the United States under this Constitution, as under the Confederation.

(2) This Constitution, and the laws of the United States which shall be made in pursuance thereof; and all treaties made, or which shall be made, under the authority of the United States, shall be the supreme law of the land; and the judges in every state shall be bound thereby, anything in the constitution or laws of any state to the contrary notwithstanding.

(3) The senators and representatives before mentioned, and the members of the several state legislatures, and all executive and judicial officers, both of the United States and of the several states, shall be bound by oath or affirmation, to support this Constitution; but no religious test shall ever be required as a qualification to any office or public trust under the United States.

ARTICLE VII
Ratifying the Constitution

The ratification of the conventions of nine states shall be sufficient for the establishment of this Constitution between the states so ratifying the same.

Done in convention by the unanimous consent of the states present the seventeenth day of September in the year of our Lord one thousand seven hundred and eighty-seven and of the independence of the United States of America the twelfth. In witness thereof we have hereunto subscribed our names.

George Washington —
*President and deputy from
Virginia*

Delaware
George Read
Gunning Bedford, Jr.
John Dickinson
Richard Bassett
Jacob Broom

Maryland
James McHenry
Dan of St. Thomas Jenifer
Daniel Carroll

Virginia
John Blair
James Madison, Jr.

North Carolina
William Blount
Richard Dobbs Spaight
Hugh Williamson

South Carolina
John Rutledge
Charles Cotesworth
   Pinckney
Charles Pinckney
Pierce Butler

Georgia
William Few
Abraham Baldwin

New Hampshire
John Langdon
Nicholas Gilman

Massachusetts
Nathaniel Gorham
Rufus King

Connecticut
William Samuel Johnson
Roger Sherman

New York
Alexander Hamilton

New Jersey
William Livingston
David Brearley
William Paterson
Jonathan Dayton

Pennsylvania
Benjamin Franklin
Thomas Mifflin
Robert Morris
George Clymer
Thomas FitzSimons
Jared Ingersoll
James Wilson
Gouverneur Morris

Attest:
William Jackson,
Secretary

Amendments to the Constitution

The Bill of Rights

AMENDMENT 1
Religious and Political Freedoms (1791)

Congress shall make no law respecting an establishment of religion, or prohibiting the free exercise thereof; or abridging the freedom of speech, or of the press; or the right of the people peaceably to assemble, and to petition the government for a redress of grievances.

AMENDMENT 2
Right to Bear Arms (1791)

A well-regulated militia, being necessary to the security of a free state, the right of the people to keep and bear arms shall not be infringed.

AMENDMENT 3
Housing of Soldiers (1791)

No soldier shall, in time of peace be quartered in any house, without the consent of the owner, nor in time of war, but in a manner to be prescribed by law.

AMENDMENT 4
Search and Arrest Warrants (1791)

The right of the people to be secure in their persons, houses, papers, and effects, against unreasonable searches and seizures, shall not be violated, and no warrants shall issue, but upon probable cause, supported by oath or affirmation, and particularly describing the place to be searched, and the persons or things to be seized.

AMENDMENT 5
Rights in Criminal Cases (1791)

No person shall be held to answer for a capital, or otherwise infamous crime, unless on a presentment or indictment of a grand jury, except in cases arising in the land or naval forces, or in the militia, when in actual service in time of war or public danger; nor shall any person be subject for the same offense to be twice put in jeopardy of life or limb; nor shall be compelled in any criminal case to be a witness against himself, nor be deprived of life, liberty, or property, without due process of law; nor shall private property be taken for public use, without just compensation.

AMENDMENT 6
Rights to a Fair Trial (1791)

In all criminal prosecutions, the accused shall enjoy the right to a speedy and public trial, by an impartial jury of the state and district wherein the crime shall have been committed, which district shall have been previously ascertained by law, and to be informed of the nature and cause of the accusation; to be confronted with the witnesses against him; to have compulsory process for obtaining witnesses in his favor, and to have the assistance of counsel for his defense.

AMENDMENT 7
Rights in Civil Cases (1791)

In suits at common law, where the value in controversy shall exceed twenty dollars, the right of trial by jury shall be preserved, and no fact tried by a jury, shall be otherwise re-examined in any court of the United States, than according to the rules of the common law.

AMENDMENT 8
Bails, Fines, and Punishments (1791)

Excessive bail shall not be required, nor excessive fines imposed, nor cruel and unusual punishments inflicted.

AMENDMENT 9
Rights Retained by the People (1791)

The enumeration in the Constitution, of certain rights, shall not be construed to deny or disparage others retained by the people.

AMENDMENT 10
Powers Retained by the States and the People (1791)

The powers not delegated to the United States by the Constitution, nor prohibited by it to the states, are reserved to the states respectively, or to the people.

AMENDMENT 11
Lawsuits Against States (1795)

The judicial power of the United States shall not be construed to extend to any suit in law or equity, commenced or prosecuted against one of the United States by citizens of another state, or by citizens or subjects of any foreign state.

AMENDMENT 12
Election of the President and Vice President (1804)

The electors shall meet in their respective states and vote by ballot for President and Vice President, one of whom, at least, shall not be an inhabitant of the same state with themselves; they shall name in their ballots the person voted for as President, and in distinct ballots the person voted for as Vice President, and they shall make distinct lists of all persons voted for as President, and of all persons voted for as Vice President, and of the number of votes for each, which lists they shall sign and certify, and transmit sealed to the seat of the government of the United States, directed to the president of the Senate; — the president of the Senate shall, in the presence of the Senate and House of Representatives, open all the certificates and the votes shall then be counted; — the person having the greatest number of votes for President, shall be the President, if such number be a majority of the whole number of electors appointed; and if no person have such majority, then from the persons having the highest numbers not exceeding three on the list of those voted for as President, the House of Representatives shall choose immediately, by ballot, the President. But in choosing the President, the votes shall be taken by states, the representation from each state having one vote; a quorum for this purpose shall consist of a member or members from two-thirds of the states, and a majority of all the states shall be necessary to a choice. And if the House of Representatives shall not choose a President whenever the right of choice shall devolve upon them, [before the fourth day of March next following,] then the Vice President shall act as President, as in the case of the death or other constitutional disability of the President.

The person having the greatest number of votes as Vice President, shall be the Vice President, if such number be a majority of the whole number of electors appointed, and if no person have a majority, then from the two highest numbers on the list, the Senate shall choose the Vice President; a quorum for the purpose shall consist of two-thirds of the whole number of senators, and a majority of the whole number shall be necessary to a choice. But no person constitutionally ineligible to the office of President shall be eligible to that of Vice President of the United States.

AMENDMENT 13
Abolition of Slavery (1865)

Section 1 Neither slavery nor involuntary servitude, except as a punishment for crime whereof the party shall have been duly convicted, shall exist within the United States, or any place subject to their jurisdiction.

Section 2 Congress shall have power to enforce this article by appropriate legislation.

AMENDMENT 14
Civil Rights (1868)

Section 1 All persons born or naturalized in the United States, and subject to the jurisdiction thereof, are citizens of the United States and of the state wherein they reside. No state shall make or enforce any law which shall abridge the privileges or immunities of citizens of the United States; nor shall any state deprive any person of life, liberty, or property, without due process of law; nor deny to any person within its jurisdiction the equal protection of the laws.

Section 2 Representatives shall be apportioned among the several states according to their respective numbers, counting the whole number of persons in each state, [excluding Indians not taxed]. But when the right to vote at any election for the choice of electors for President and Vice President of the United States, representatives in Congress, the executive and judicial officers of a state, or the members of the legislature thereof, is denied to any of the male inhabitants of such state, being twenty-one years of age, and citizens of the United States, or in any way abridged, except for participation in rebellion, or other crime, the basis of representation therein shall be reduced in the proportion which the number of such male citizens shall bear to the whole number of male citizens twenty-one years of age in such state.

Section 3 No person shall be a senator or representative in Congress, or elector of President and Vice President, or hold any office, civil or military, under the United States, or under any state, who, having previously taken an oath, as a member of Congress, or as an officer of the United States, or as a member of any state legislature, or as an executive or judicial officer of any state, to support the Constitution of the United States, shall have engaged in insurrection or rebellion against the same, or given aid or comfort to the enemies thereof. But Congress may by a vote of two-thirds of each House, remove such disability.

Section 4 The validity of the public debt of the United States, authorized by law, including debts incurred for payment of pensions and bounties for services in suppressing insurrection or rebellion, shall not be questioned. But neither the United States nor any state shall assume or pay any debt or obligation incurred in aid of insurrection or rebellion against the United States, or any claim for the loss or emancipation of any slave; but all such debts, obligations, and claims shall be held illegal and void.

Section 5 The Congress shall have power to enforce, by appropriate legislation, the provisions of this article.

AMENDMENT 15
Right to Vote (1870)

Section 1 The right of citizens of the United States to vote shall not be denied or abridged by the United States or by any state on account of race, color, or previous condition of servitude.

Section 2 The Congress shall have power to enforce this article by appropriate legislation.

AMENDMENT 16
Income Taxes (1913)

The Congress shall have power to lay and collect taxes on incomes, from whatever source derived, without apportionment among the several states, and without regard to any census or enumeration.

AMENDMENT 17
Direct Election of Senators (1913)

(1) The Senate of the United States shall be composed of two senators from each state, elected by the people thereof for six years; and each senator shall have one vote. The electors in each state shall have the qualifications requisite for electors of the most numerous branch of the state legislatures.

(2) When vacancies happen in the representation of any state in the Senate, the executive authority of such state shall issue writs of election to fill such vacancies: provided, that the legislature of any state may empower the executive thereof to make temporary appointments until the people fill the vacancies by election as the legislature may direct.

(3) This amendment shall not be so construed as to affect the election or term of any senator chosen before it becomes valid as part of the Constitution.

AMENDMENT 18
Prohibition of Liquor (1919)

Section 1 After one year from the ratification of this article the manufacture, sale, or transportation of intoxicating liquors within, the importation thereof into, or the exportation thereof from the United States and all territory subject to the jurisdiction thereof for beverage purposes is hereby prohibited.

Section 2 The Congress and the several states shall have concurrent power to enforce this article by appropriate legislation.

Section 3 This article shall be inoperative unless it shall have been ratified as an amendment to the Constitution by the legislatures of the several states, as provided in the Constitution, within seven years from the date of the submission hereof to the states by the Congress.

AMENDMENT 19
Women's Suffrage (1920)

Section 1 The right of citizens of the United States to vote shall not be denied or abridged by the United States or by any state on account of sex.

Section 2 Congress shall have power to enforce this article by appropriate legislation.

AMENDMENT 20
Terms of the President and Congress (1933)

Section 1 The terms of the President and Vice President shall end at noon on the 20th day of January, and the terms of senators and representatives at noon on the third day of January, of the years in which such terms would have ended if this article had not been ratified; and the terms of their successors shall then begin.

Section 2 The Congress shall assemble at least once in every year, and such meeting shall begin at noon on the third day of January, unless they shall by law appoint a different day.

Section 3 If, at the time fixed for the beginning of the term of the President, the President elect shall have died, the Vice President elect shall become President. If a President shall not have been chosen before the time fixed for the beginning of his term, of if the President elect shall have failed to qualify, then the Vice President elect shall act as President until a President shall have qualified; and the Congress may by law provide for the case wherein neither a President elect nor a Vice President elect shall have qualified, declaring who shall then act as President, or the manner in which one who is to act shall be selected, and such person shall act accordingly until a President or Vice President shall have qualified.

Section 4 The Congress may by law provide for the case of the death of any of the persons from whom the House of Representatives may choose a President whenever the right of choice shall have devolved upon them, and for the case of the death of any of the persons from whom the Senate may choose a Vice President whenever the right of choice shall have devolved upon them.

Section 5 Sections 1 and 2 shall take effect on the 15th day of October following the ratification of this article.

Thereafter, when the President transmits to the president pro tempore of the Senate and the speaker of the House of Representatives his written declaration that no inability exists, he shall resume the powers and duties of his office unless the Vice President and a majority of either the principal officers of the executive department or of such other body as Congress may by law provide, transmit within four days to the president pro tempore of the Senate and the Speaker of the House of Representatives their written declaration that the President is unable to discharge the powers and duties of his office. Thereupon Congress shall decide the issue, assembling within forty-eight hours for that purpose if not in session. If the Congress, within twenty-one days after receipt of the latter written declaration, or, if Congress is not in session, within twenty-one days after Congress is required to assemble, determines by two-thirds vote of both houses that the President is unable to discharge the powers and duties of his office, the Vice President shall continue to discharge the same as acting President; otherwise, the President shall resume the powers and duties of his office.

AMENDMENT 26
Suffrage for 18-Year-Olds (1971)

Section 1 The right of citizens of the United States, who are eighteen years of age or older, to vote shall not be denied or abridged by the United States or by any state on account of age.

Section 2 The Congress shall have power to enforce this article by appropriate legislation.

AMENDMENT 27
Congressional Pay (1992)

No law, varying the compensation for the services of the senators and representatives, shall take effect, until an election of representatives shall have intervened.

Presidents of the United States

1. George Washington

Term of Office: 1789-1797
Elected From: Virginia
Party: None
Born: 1732   Died: 1799

2. John Adams

Term of Office: 1797-1801
Elected From: Massachusetts
Party: Federalist
Born: 1735   Died: 1826

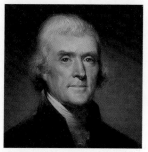

3. Thomas Jefferson

Term of Office: 1801-1809
Elected From: Virginia
Party: Democratic-Republican
Born: 1743   Died: 1826

4. James Madison

Term of Office: 1809-1817
Elected From: Virginia
Party: Democratic-Republican
Born: 1751   Died: 1836

5. James Monroe

Term of Office: 1817-1825
Elected From: Virginia
Party: Democratic-Republican
Born: 1758   Died: 1831

6. John Quincy Adams

Term of Office: 1825-1829
Elected From: Massachusetts
Party: None
Born: 1767   Died: 1848

7. Andrew Jackson

Term of Office: 1829-1837
Elected From: Tennessee
Party: Democratic
Born: 1767   Died: 1845

8. Martin Van Buren

Term of Office: 1837-1841
Elected From: New York
Party: Democratic
Born: 1782   Died: 1862

9. William H. Harrison

Term of Office: 1841
Elected From: Virginia
Party: Whig
Born: 1773   Died: 1841

10. John Tyler
Term of Office: 1841-1845
Elected From: Virginia
Party: Whig
Born: 1790   Died: 1862

11. James K. Polk
Term of Office: 1845-1849
Elected From: Tennessee
Party: Democratic
Born: 1795   Died: 1849

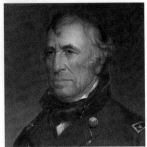

12. Zachary Taylor
Term of Office: 1849-1850
Elected From: Virginia
Party: Whig
Born: 1784   Died: 1850

13. Millard Fillmore
Term of Office: 1850-1853
Elected From: New York
Party: Whig
Born: 1800   Died: 1874

14. Franklin Pierce
Term of Office: 1853-1857
Elected From: New Hampshire
Party: Democratic
Born: 1804   Died: 1869

15. James Buchanan
Term of Office: 1857-1861
Elected From: Pennsylvania
Party: Democratic
Born: 1791   Died: 1868

16. Abraham Lincoln
Term of Office: 1861-1865
Elected From: Illinois
Party: Republican
Born: 1809   Died: 1865

17. Andrew Johnson
Term of Office: 1865-1869
Elected From: Tennessee
Party: Democratic
Born: 1808   Died: 1875

18. Ulysses S. Grant
Term of Office: 1869-1877
Elected From: Ohio
Party: Republican
Born: 1822   Died: 1885

19. Rutherford B. Hayes
Term of Office: 1877-1881
Elected From: Ohio
Party: Republican
Born: 1822   Died: 1893

20. James A. Garfield
Term of Office: 1881
Elected From: Ohio
Party: Republican
Born: 1831   Died: 1881

21. Chester A. Arthur
Term of Office: 1881-1885
Elected From: New York
Party: Republican
Born: 1830   Died: 1886

22., 24. Grover Cleveland
Term of Office: 1885-1889,
   1893-1897
Elected From: New York
Party: Democratic
Born: 1837   Died: 1908

23. Benjamin Harrison
Term of Office: 1889-1893
Elected From: Indiana
Party: Republican
Born: 1833   Died: 1901

25. William McKinley
Term of Office: 1897-1901
Elected From: Ohio
Party: Republican
Born: 1843   Died: 1901

26. Theodore Roosevelt
Term of Office: 1901-1909
Elected From: New York
Party: Republican
Born: 1858   Died: 1919

27. William H. Taft
Term of Office: 1909-1913
Elected From: Ohio
Party: Republican
Born: 1857   Died: 1930

28. Woodrow Wilson
Term of Office: 1913-1921
Elected From: New Jersey
Party: Democratic
Born: 1856   Died: 1924

29. Warren G. Harding

Term of Office: 1921-1923
Elected From: Ohio
Party: Republican
Born: 1865   Died: 1923

30. Calvin Coolidge

Term of Office: 1923-1929
Elected From: Massachusetts
Party: Republican
Born: 1872   Died: 1933

31. Herbert Hoover

Term of Office: 1929-1933
Elected From: California
Party: Republican
Born: 1874   Died: 1964

32. Franklin D. Roosevelt

Term of Office: 1933-1945
Elected From: New York
Party: Democratic
Born: 1882   Died: 1945

33. Harry S. Truman

Term of Office: 1945-1953
Elected From: Missouri
Party: Democratic
Born: 1884   Died: 1972

34. Dwight D. Eisenhower

Term of Office: 1953-1961
Elected From: Kansas
Party: Republican
Born: 1890   Died: 1969

35. John F. Kennedy

Term of Office: 1961-1963
Elected From: Massachusetts
Party: Democratic
Born: 1917   Died: 1963

36. Lyndon B. Johnson

Term of Office: 1963-1969
Elected From: Texas
Party: Democratic
Born: 1908   Died: 1973

37. Richard M. Nixon

Term of Office: 1969-1974
Elected From: California
Party: Republican
Born: 1913   Died: 1994

38. Gerald R. Ford

Term of Office: 1974-1977
Elected From: Michigan
Party: Republican
Born: 1913

39. James E. Carter

Term of Office: 1977-1981
Elected From: Georgia
Party: Democratic
Born: 1924

40. Ronald W. Reagan

Term of Office: 1981-1989
Elected From: California
Party: Republican
Born: 1911   Died: 2004

41. George H.W. Bush

Term of Office: 1989-1993
Elected From: Texas
Party: Republican
Born: 1924

42. William J. Clinton

Term of Office: 1993-2001
Elected From: Arkansas
Party: Democratic
Born: 1946

43. George W. Bush

Term of Office: 2001–2009
Elected From: Texas
Party: Republican
Born: 1946

Articles of the 1999 Presidential Impeachment

On December 19, 1998, the U.S. House of Representatives approved two articles of impeachment. These accused President Bill Clinton of obstruction of justice and perjury in connection with his relationship to Monica Lewinsky. Lewinsky was a White House intern during Clinton's presidency. The U.S. Constitution required that the Senate try the president on the two articles of impeachment.

The last time the Senate had conducted a presidential impeachment trial was in 1867. The House impeached Andrew Johnson for firing his secretary of war against the wishes of Congress. However, after a two-month trial, the Senate failed to remove him from office by one vote.

The impeachment trial of President Clinton began on January 7, 1999. As chief justice of the United States, William Rehnquist presided over the proceedings. He administered an oath to the 100 senators who served as the jury in the trial.

The House Judiciary Committee acted as the prosecutors. Henry Hyde, Republican representative from Illinois, served as the committee chairman. In addition to Hyde, twelve other House Republican members served on the committee.

The Senate first heard opening arguments from the House prosecutors and from President Clinton's lawyers. Then they questioned the two sides. After that the senators subpoenaed three witnesses. These witnesses responded with a closed-door, videotaped deposition.

While the impeachment trial was proceeding, the senators discussed three ways of dealing with the alleged conduct of the president. Some wanted to censure, or condemn, him and impose a fine. Many, however, questioned whether that was constitutional.

Others wanted to adopt a "finding of fact." That option would punish the president without removing him from office. However, many senators maintained that only one constitutional option was open to them. They could acquit the president or convict him and remove him from office.

On February 12, 1999, in an open Senate session, the 100 senators voted on each of the two articles of impeachment. Conviction required a two-thirds majority vote of all the senators present. All 100 were present on that day, so conviction meant 67 guilty votes. With a strong partisan vote, the Senate acquitted the president of perjury and obstruction of justice.

The senators rejected Article 1, the charge of perjury, by a vote of 55-45. They voted 50-50 on Article 2, the charge of obstruction of justice. One hundred senators, 45 Democrats and 55 Republicans, voted. All the Democrats voted not guilty on both articles. Of the 55 Republicans, 45 voted guilty on both articles; 5 voted not guilty on both articles; and 5 voted not guilty on Article 1. The same five Republicans voted guilty on Article 2.

The 50 United States

State population ranks are from 2003 population figures.

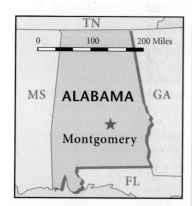

Alabama

Capital: Montgomery
Organized as a territory: March 3, 1817
Entered Union: December 14, 1819
Order of entry: 22nd state
Motto: We dare defend our rights.
Geographic region: South
Nicknames: Yellowhammer State, The Heart of Dixie
Origin of name Alabama: May come from a Choctaw word, meaning "thicket clearers" or "vegetation gatherers"
State flower: Camellia
State bird: Yellowhammer
Largest city: Birmingham
Land area: 50,750 square miles
Land area rank: 28th largest state
Population: 4,500,752
Population rank: 23rd largest state
Postal abbreviation: AL

Alaska

Capital: Juneau
Organized as a territory: 1912
Entered Union: January 3, 1959
Order of entry: 49th state
Motto: North to the future.
Geographic region: West
Nicknames: The Last Frontier, Land of the Midnight Sun
Origin of name Alaska: Misinterpreted Aleut word, meaning "great land" or "that which the sea breaks against"
State flower: Forget-me-not
State bird: Willow ptarmigan
Largest city: Anchorage
Land area: 570,374 square miles
Land area rank: Largest state
Population: 648,818
Population rank: 47th largest state
Postal abbreviation: AK

Arizona

Capital: Phoenix
Organized as a territory: February 24, 1863
Entered Union: February 14, 1912
Order of entry: 48th state
Motto: God enriches.
Geographic region: West
Nickname: Grand Canyon State
Origin of name Arizona: From the Indian word Arizonac, meaning "little spring" or "young spring"

State flower: Saguaro cactus flower
State bird: Cactus wren
Largest city: Phoenix
Land area: 114,000 square miles
Land area rank: 6th largest state
Population: 5,580,811
Population rank: 18th largest state
Postal abbreviation: AZ

Arkansas

Capital: Little Rock
Organized as a territory: March 2, 1819
Entered Union: June 15, 1836
Order of entry: 25th state
Motto: The people rule.
Geographic region: South
Nickname: Land of Opportunity
Origin of name Arkansas: From the Quapaw Indians

State flower: Apple blossom
State bird: Mockingbird
Largest city: Little Rock
Land area: 52,075 square miles
Land area rank: 27th largest state
Population: 2,725,714
Population rank: 32nd largest state
Postal abbreviation: AR

California

Capital: Sacramento
Organized as a territory: 1847
Entered Union: September 9, 1850
Order of entry: 31st state
Motto: I have found it.
Geographic region: West
Nickname: Golden State
Origin of name California: From a book, *Las Sergas de Esplandián,* by Garcia Ordóñez de Montalvo, written about 1500

State flower: Golden poppy
State bird: California valley quail
Largest city: Los Angeles
Land area: 155,973 square miles
Land area rank: 3rd largest state
Population: 35,484,453
Population rank: Largest state
Postal abbreviation: CA

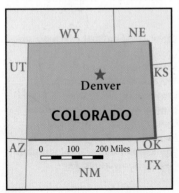

Colorado

Capital: Denver
Organized as a territory: February 28, 1861
Entered Union: August 1, 1876
Order of entry: 38th state
Motto: Nothing without Providence.
Geographic region: West
Nickname: Centennial State
Origin of name Colorado: From Spanish, meaning "ruddy" or "red"

State flower: Rocky Mountain columbine
State bird: Lark bunting
Largest city: Denver
Land area: 103,730 square miles
Land area rank: 8th largest state
Population: 4,550,688
Population rank: 22nd largest state
Postal abbreviation: CO

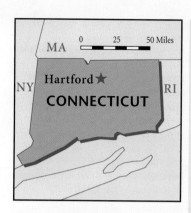

Connecticut

Capital: Hartford
Became a colony: 1662
Entered Union: January 9, 1788
Order of entry: 5th state
Motto: He who transplanted still sustains.
Geographic region: Northeast
Nicknames: Nutmeg State, Constitution State
Origin of name Connecticut: From the Indian word *Quinnehtukqut*, meaning "beside the long tidal river"
State flower: Mountain laurel
State bird: American robin
Largest city: Bridgeport
Land area: 4,845 square miles
Land area rank: 48th largest state
Population: 3,483,372
Population rank: 29th largest state
Postal abbreviation: CT

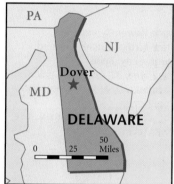

Delaware

Capital: Dover
Became a colony: 1682
Entered Union: December 7, 1787
Order of entry: First state
Motto: Liberty and independence.
Geographic region: Northeast
Nicknames: Diamond State, First State, Small Wonder
Origin of name Delaware: From Delaware River and Bay, which were named for Sir Thomas West, Lord De La Warr
State flower: Peach blossom
State bird: Blue hen chicken
Largest city: Wilmington
Land area: 1,982 square miles
Land area rank: 49th largest state
Population: 817,491
Population rank: 45th largest state
Postal abbreviation: DE

Florida

Capital: Tallahassee
Organized as a territory: March 20, 1822
Entered Union: March 3, 1845
Order of entry: 27th state
Motto: In God we trust.
Geographic region: South
Nickname: Sunshine State
Origin of name Florida: From the Spanish, meaning "feast of flowers"
State flower: Orange blossom
State bird: Mockingbird
Largest city: Jacksonville
Land area: 53,997 square miles
Land area rank: 26th largest state
Population: 17,019,068
Population rank: 4th largest state
Postal abbreviation: FL

Georgia

Capital: Atlanta
Became a colony: 1733
Entered Union: January 2, 1788
Order of entry: 4th state
Motto: Wisdom, justice, and moderation.
Geographic region: South
Nicknames: Peach State, Empire State of the South
Origin of name Georgia: In honor of King George II of England
State flower: Cherokee rose
State bird: Brown thrasher
Largest city: Atlanta
Land area: 57,919 square miles
Land area rank: 21st largest state
Population: 8,684,715
Population rank: 9th largest state
Postal abbreviation: GA

Hawaii

Capital: Honolulu
Organized as a territory: 1900
Entered Union: August 21, 1959
Order of entry: 50th state
Motto: The life of the land is perpetuated in righteousness.
Geographic region: West
Nickname: Aloha State
Origin of name Hawaii: Islands may have been named by Hawaii Loa, their traditional discoverer; may have been named after Hawaii or Hawaiki, the traditional home of the Polynesians
State flower: Yellow hibiscus
State bird: Nene (hawaiian goose)
Largest city: Honolulu
Land area: 6,423.4 square miles
Land area rank: 47th largest state
Population: 1,257,608
Population rank: 42nd largest state
Postal abbreviation: HI

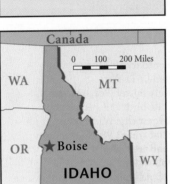

Idaho

Capital: Boise
Organized as a territory: March 3, 1863
Entered Union: July 3, 1890
Order of entry: 43rd state
Motto: It is forever.
Geographic region: West
Nicknames: Gem State, Spud State, Panhandle State
Origin of name Idaho: An invented name of unknown meaning
State flower: Syringa
State bird: Mountain bluebird
Largest city: Boise
Land area: 82,751 square miles
Land area rank: 11th largest state
Population: 1,366,332
Population rank: 39th largest state
Postal abbreviation: ID

Illinois

Capital: Springfield
Organized as a territory: February 3, 1809
Entered Union: December 3, 1818
Order of entry: 21st state
Motto: State sovereignty, national union.
Geographic region: Midwest
Nickname: Prairie State
Origin of name Illinois: From an Indian word and French suffix, meaning "tribe of superior men"
State flower: Violet
State bird: Cardinal
Largest city: Chicago
Land area: 55,593 square miles
Land area rank: 24th largest state
Population: 12,653,544
Population rank: 5th largest state
Postal abbreviation: IL

Indiana

Capital: Indianapolis
Organized as a territory: May 7, 1800
Entered Union: December 11, 1816
Order of entry: 19th state
Motto: The crossroads of America.
Geographic region: Midwest
Nickname: Hoosier State
Origin of name Indiana: Meaning "land of Indians"
State flower: Peony
State bird: Cardinal
Largest city: Indianapolis
Land area: 35,870 square miles
Land area rank: 38th largest state
Population: 6,195,643
Population rank: 14th largest state
Postal abbreviation: IN

Iowa

Capital: Des Moines
Organized as a territory: June 12, 1838
Entered Union: December 28, 1846
Order of entry: 29th state
Motto: Our liberties we prize and our rights we will maintain.
Geographic region: Midwest
Nickname: Hawkeye State
Origin of name Iowa: Probably from an Indian word meaning "I-o-wa, this is the place," or "the beautiful land"
State flower: Wild rose
State bird: Eastern goldfinch
Largest city: Des Moines
Land area: 55,875 square miles
Land area rank: 23rd largest state
Population: 2,944,062
Population rank: 30th largest state
Postal abbreviation: IA

Kansas

Capital: Topeka
Organized as a territory: May 30, 1854
Entered Union: January 29, 1861
Order of entry: 34th state
Motto: To the stars through difficulties.
Geographic region: Midwest
Nicknames: Sunflower State, Jayhawk State
Origin of name Kansas: From a Sioux word, meaning "people of the south wind"
State flower: Sunflower
State bird: Western meadowlark
Largest city: Wichita
Land area: 81,823 square miles
Land area rank: 13th largest state
Population: 2,723,507
Population rank: 33rd state
Postal abbreviation: KS

Kentucky

Capital: Frankfort
Became a colony: 1607, as part of Virginia
Entered Union: June 1, 1792
Order of entry: 15th state
Motto: United we stand, divided we fall.
Geographic region: South
Nickname: Bluegrass State
Origin of name Kentucky: From the Iroquoian word *Ken-tah-ten*, meaning "land of tomorrow"
State flower: Goldenrod
State bird: Kentucky cardinal
Largest city: Louisville
Land area: 39,732 square miles
Land area rank: 36th largest state
Population: 4,117,827
Population rank: 26th largest state
Postal abbreviation: KY

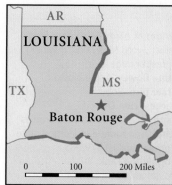

Louisiana

Capital: Baton Rouge
Organized as a territory: March 26, 1804
Entered Union: April 30, 1812
Order of entry: 18th state
Motto: Union, justice, and confidence.
Geographic region: South
Nicknames: Pelican State, Sportsman's Paradise, Creole State, Sugar State
Origin of name Louisiana: In honor of King Louis XIV of France
State flower: Magnolia
State bird: Pelican
Largest city: New Orleans
Land area: 43,566 square miles
Land area rank: 33rd largest state
Population: 4,496,334
Population rank: 24th largest state
Postal abbreviation: LA

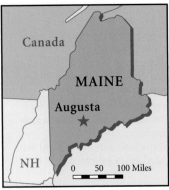

Maine

Capital: Augusta
Became a colony:
1620, as part of Massachusetts
Entered Union: March 15, 1820
Order of entry: 23rd state
Motto: I lead.
Geographic region: Northeast
Nickname: Pine Tree State
Origin of name Maine: It has been considered a compliment to Henrietta Maria, wife of King Charles I of England, who was said to have owned the province of Mayne in France.
State flower: White pine cone and tassel
State bird: Chickadee
Largest city: Portland
Land area: 30,865 square miles
Land area rank: 39th largest state
Population: 1,305,728
Population rank: 40th largest state
Postal abbreviation: ME

Maryland

Capital: Annapolis
Became a colony: 1632
Entered Union: April 28, 1788
Order of entry: 7th state
Motto: Manly deeds, womanly words.
Geographic region: Northeast
Nicknames: Free State, Old Line State
Origin of name Maryland: In honor of Henrietta Maria, wife of King Charles I of England
State flower: Black-eyed susan
State bird: Baltimore oriole
Largest city: Baltimore
Land area: 9,775 square miles
Land area rank: 42nd largest state
Population: 5,508,909
Population rank: 19th largest state
Postal abbreviation: MD

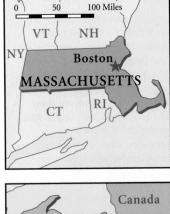

Massachusetts

Capital: Boston
Became a colony: 1620
Entered Union: February 6, 1788
Order of entry: 6th state
Motto: By the sword we seek peace, but peace only under liberty.
Geographic region: Northeast
Nicknames: Bay State, Old Colony State
Origin of name Massachusetts: From two Indian words, meaning "great mountain place"
State flower: Mayflower
State bird: Chickadee
Largest city: Boston
Land area: 7,838 square miles
Land area rank: 45th largest state
Population: 6,433,422
Population rank: 13th largest state
Postal abbreviation: MA

Michigan

Capital: Lansing
Organized as a territory: January 11, 1805
Entered Union: January 26, 1837
Order of entry: 26th state
Motto: If you seek a pleasant peninsula, look around you.
Geographic region: Midwest
Nickname: Wolverine State
Origin of name Michigan: From Indian word *Michigana*, meaning "great or large lake"
State flower: Apple blossom
State bird: Robin
Largest city: Detroit
Land area: 56,809.2 square miles
Land area rank: 22nd largest state
Population: 10,079,985
Population rank: 8th largest state
Postal abbreviation: MI

Minnesota

Capital: St. Paul
Organized as a territory: March 3, 1849
Entered Union: May 11, 1858
Order of entry: 32nd state
Motto: The North Star.
Geographic region: Midwest
Nicknames: North Star State, Gopher State, Land of 10,000 Lakes

Origin of name Minnesota: From a Dakota Indian word, meaning "sky-tinted water"
State flower: Showy lady slipper
State bird: Common loon
Largest city: Minneapolis
Land area: 79,617 square miles
Land area rank: 14th largest state
Population: 5,059,375
Population rank: 21st largest state
Postal abbreviation: MN

Mississippi

Capital: Jackson
Organized as a territory: April 7, 1798
Entered Union: December 10, 1817
Order of entry: 20th state
Motto: By valor and arms.
Geographic region: South
Nickname: Magnolia State
Origin of name Mississippi: From an Indian word, meaning "Father of Waters"

State flower: Flower of the magnolia or evergreen magnolia
State bird: Mockingbird
Largest city: Jackson
Land area: 46,914 square miles
Land area rank: 31st largest state
Population: 2,881,281
Population rank: 31st largest state
Postal abbreviation: MS

Missouri

Capital: Jefferson City
Organized as a territory: June 4, 1812
Entered Union: August 10, 1821
Order of entry: 24th state
Motto: The welfare of the people shall be the supreme law.
Geographic region: Midwest
Nickname: Show-Me State

Origin of name Missouri: Named after Missouri Indians; *Missouri* means "town of the large canoes"
State flower: Hawthorn
State bird: Bluebird
Largest city: Kansas City
Land area: 68,945 square miles
Land area rank: 18th largest state
Population: 5,704,484
Population rank: 17th largest state
Postal abbreviation: MO

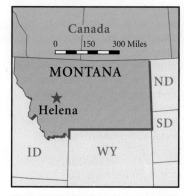

Montana

Capital: Helena
Organized as a territory: May 26, 1864
Entered Union: November 8, 1889
Order of entry: 41st state
Motto: Gold and silver.
Geographic region: West
Nickname: Treasure State
Origin of name Montana: Latinized Spanish word, meaning "mountainous"

State flower: Bitterroot
State bird: Western meadowlark
Largest city: Billings
Land area: 145,556 square miles
Land area rank: 4th largest state
Population: 917,621
Population rank: 44th largest state
Postal abbreviation: MT

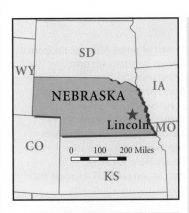

Nebraska

Capital: Lincoln
Organized as a territory: May 30, 1854
Entered Union: March 1, 1867
Order of entry: 37th state
Motto: Equality before the law.
Geographic region: Midwest
Nicknames: Cornhusker State, Beef State, Tree Planter State

Origin of name Nebraska: From an Oto Indian word, meaning "flat water"
State flower: Goldenrod
State bird: Western meadowlark
Largest city: Omaha
Land area: 76,878 square miles
Land area rank: 15th largest state
Population: 1,739,291
Population rank: 38th largest state
Postal abbreviation: NE

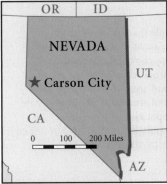

Nevada

Capital: Carson City
Organized as a territory: March 2, 1861
Entered Union: October 31, 1864
Order of entry: 36th state
Motto: All for our country.
Geographic region: West
Nicknames: Sagebrush State, Silver State, Battle Born State
Origin of name Nevada: Spanish word, meaning "snowcapped"

State flower: Sagebrush
State bird: Mountain bluebird
Largest city: Las Vegas
Land area: 109,806 square miles
Land area rank: 7th largest state
Population: 2,241,154
Population rank: 35th largest state
Postal abbreviation: NV

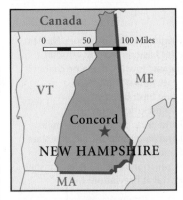

New Hampshire

Capital: Concord
Became a colony: 1623
Entered Union: June 21, 1788
Order of entry: 9th state
Motto: Live free or die.
Geographic region: Northeast
Nickname: Granite State
Origin of name New Hampshire: From the English county of Hampshire

State flower: Purple lilac
State bird: Purple finch
Largest city: Manchester
Land area: 8,969 square miles
Land area rank: 44th largest state
Population: 1,287,687
Population rank: 41st largest state
Postal abbreviation: NH

New Jersey

Capital: Trenton
Became a colony: 1702
Entered Union: December 18, 1787
Order of entry: 3rd state
Motto: Liberty and prosperity.
Geographic region: Northeast
Nickname: Garden State
Origin of name New Jersey: From the Channel Isle of Jersey

State flower: Purple violet
State bird: Eastern goldfinch
Largest city: Newark
Land area: 7,419 square miles
Land area rank: 46th largest state
Population: 8,638,396
Population rank: 10th largest state
Postal abbreviation: NJ

New Mexico

Capital: Santa Fe
Organized as a territory: September 9, 1850
Entered Union: January 6, 1912
Order of entry: 47th state
Motto: It grows as it goes.
Geographic region: West
Nicknames: Land of Enchantment, Sunshine State

Origin of name New Mexico: From the country of Mexico
State flower: Yucca
State bird: Roadrunner
Largest city: Albuquerque
Land area: 121,635 square miles
Land area rank: 5th largest state
Population: 1,874,614
Population rank: 36th largest state
Postal abbreviation: NM

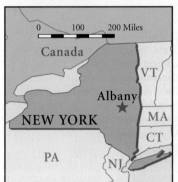

New York

Capital: Albany
Became a colony: 1609 as a Dutch colony, 1664 as an English colony
Entered Union: July 26, 1788
Order of entry: 11th state
Motto: Ever upward.
Geographic region: Northeast
Nickname: Empire State
Origin of name New York: In honor of the English Duke of York

State flower: Rose
State bird: Bluebird
Largest city: New York City
Land area: 47,224 square miles
Land area rank: 30th largest state
Population: 19,190,115
Population rank: 3rd largest state
Postal abbreviation: NY

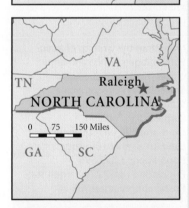

North Carolina

Capital: Raleigh
Became a colony: 1663
Entered Union: November 21, 1789
Order of entry: 12th state
Motto: To be rather than to seem.
Geographic region: South
Nickname: Tar Heel State
Origin of name Carolina: In honor of King Charles I of England

State flower: Dogwood
State bird: Cardinal
Largest city: Charlotte
Land area: 48,718 square miles
Land area rank: 29th largest state
Population: 8,407,248
Population rank: 11th largest state
Postal abbreviation: NC

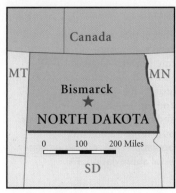

North Dakota

Capital: Bismarck
Organized as a territory: March 2, 1861
Entered Union: November 2, 1889
Order of entry: 39th state
Motto: Liberty and union, now and forever, one and inseparable.
Geographic region: Midwest
Nicknames: Sioux State, Flickertail State, Peace Garden State

Origin of name Dakota: From the Sioux tribe, meaning "allies"
State flower: Wild prairie rose
State bird: Western meadowlark
Largest city: Fargo
Land area: 68,994 square miles
Land area rank: 17th largest state
Population: 633,837
Population rank: 48th largest state
Postal abbreviation: ND

Ohio

Capital: Columbus
Organized as a territory: 1783
Entered Union: March 1, 1803
Order of entry: 17th state
Motto: With God, all things are possible.
Geographic region: Midwest
Nickname: Buckeye State
Origin of name Ohio: From an Iroquoian word, meaning "great river"

State flower: Scarlet carnation
State bird: Cardinal
Largest city: Columbus
Land area: 40,953 square miles
Land area rank: 35th largest state
Population: 11,435,798
Population rank: 7th largest state
Postal abbreviation: OH

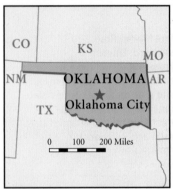

Oklahoma

Capital: Oklahoma City
Organized as a territory: May 2, 1890
Entered Union: November 16, 1907
Order of entry: 46th state
Motto: Labor conquers all things.
Geographic region: West
Nickname: Sooner State
Origin of name Oklahoma: From two Choctaw Indian words, meaning "red people"

State flower: Mistletoe
State bird: Scissor-tailed flycatcher
Largest city: Oklahoma City
Land area: 68,679 square miles
Land area rank: 19th largest state
Population: 3,511,532
Population rank: 28th largest state
Postal abbreviation: OK

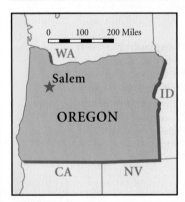

Oregon

Capital: Salem
Organized as a territory: August 14, 1848
Entered Union: February 14, 1859
Order of entry: 33rd state
Motto: She flies with her own wings.
Geographic region: West
Nickname: Beaver State
Origin of name Oregon: Unknown, but generally accepted to have been taken from the writings of Major Robert Rogers, an English army officer
State flower: Oregon grape
State bird: Western meadowlark
Largest city: Portland
Land area: 96,003 square miles
Land area rank: 10th largest state
Population: 3,559,596
Population rank: 27th largest state
Postal abbreviation: OR

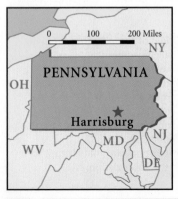

Pennsylvania

Capital: Harrisburg
Became a colony: 1681
Entered Union: December 12, 1787
Order of entry: 2nd state
Motto: Virtue, liberty, and independence.
Geographic region: Northeast
Nickname: Keystone State
Origin of name Pennsylvania: In honor of Admiral Sir William Penn, father of William Penn, meaning "Penn's woodland"
State flower: Mountain laurel
State bird: Ruffed grouse
Largest city: Philadelphia
Land area: 44,820 square miles
Land area rank: 32nd largest state
Population: 12,365,455
Population rank: 6th largest state
Postal abbreviation: PA

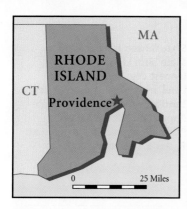

Rhode Island

Capital: Providence
Became a colony: 1636
Entered Union: May 29, 1790
Order of entry: 13th state
Motto: Hope.
Geographic region: Northeast
Nickname: The Ocean State
Origin of name Rhode Island:
From the Greek island of Rhodes

State flower: Violet
State bird: Rhode Island Red
Largest city: Providence
Land area: 1,045 square miles
Land area rank: Smallest state
Population: 1,076,164
Population rank: 43rd largest state
Postal abbreviation: RI

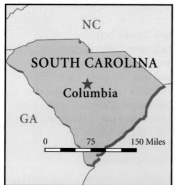

South Carolina

Capital: Columbia
Became a colony: 1663
Entered Union: May 23, 1788
Order of entry: 8th state
Mottoes: Prepared in mind and resources. While I breathe, I hope.
Geographic region: South
Nickname: Palmetto State
Origin of name Carolina:
In honor of King Charles I of England

State flower: Carolina yellow jessamine
State bird: Carolina wren
Largest city: Columbia
Land area: 30,111 square miles
Land area rank: 40th largest state
Population: 4,147,152
Population rank: 25th largest state
Postal abbreviation: SC

South Dakota

Capital: Pierre
Organized as a territory: March 2, 1861
Entered Union: November 2, 1889
Order of entry: 40th state
Motto: Under God the people rule.
Geographic region: Midwest
Nicknames: Mount Rushmore State, Coyote State
Origin of name Dakota: From the Sioux Indians, meaning "allies"

State flower: American pasqueflower
State bird: Ring-necked pheasant
Largest city: Sioux Falls
Land area: 75,898 square miles
Land area rank: 16th largest state
Population: 764,309
Population rank: 46th largest state
Postal abbreviation: SD

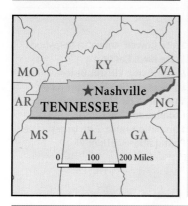

Tennessee

Capital: Nashville
Organized as a territory: 1790
Entered Union: June 1, 1796
Order of entry: 16th state
Motto: Agriculture and commerce.
Geographic region: South
Nickname: Volunteer State
Origin of name Tennessee:
Cherokee word of unknown meaning

State flower: Iris
State bird: Mockingbird
Largest city: Memphis
Land area: 41,220 square miles
Land area rank: 34th largest state
Population: 5,841,748
Population rank: 16th largest state
Postal abbreviation: TN

Texas

Capital: Austin
Became an independent republic: 1836
Entered Union: December 29, 1845
Order of entry: 28th state
Motto: Friendship.
Geographic region: West
Nickname: Lone Star State
Origin of name Texas: From an Indian word, meaning "friends"

State flower: Bluebonnet
State bird: Mockingbird
Largest city: Houston
Land area: 261,914 square miles
Land area rank: 2nd largest state
Population: 22,118,509
Population rank: 2nd largest state
Postal abbreviation: TX

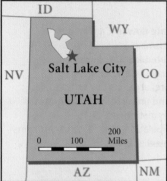

Utah

Capital: Salt Lake City
Organized as a territory: September 9, 1850
Entered Union: January 4, 1896
Order of entry: 45th state
Motto: Industry.
Geographic region: West
Nickname: Beehive State
Origin of name Utah: From the Ute Indians, meaning "people of the mountains"

State flower: Sego lily
State bird: California gull
Largest city: Salt Lake City
Land area: 82,168 square miles
Land area rank: 12th largest state
Population: 2,351,467
Population rank: 34th largest state
Postal abbreviation: UT

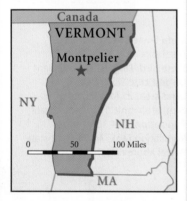

Vermont

Capital: Montpelier
Became a colony: 1623, as part of New Hampshire
Entered Union: March 4, 1791
Order of entry: 14th state
Motto: Vermont, freedom, and unity.
Geographic region: Northeast
Nickname: Green Mountain State
Origin of name Vermont: From the French words *vert mont,* meaning "green mountain"

State flower: Red clover
State bird: Hermit thrush
Largest city: Burlington
Land area: 9,249 square miles
Land area rank: 43rd largest state
Population: 619,107
Population rank: 49th largest state
Postal abbreviation: VT

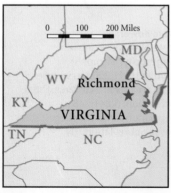

Virginia

Capital: Richmond
Became a colony: 1607
Entered Union: June 25, 1788
Order of entry: 10th state
Motto: Thus always to tyrants.
Geographic region: South
Nicknames: The Old Dominion, Mother of Presidents
Origin of name Virginia: In honor of Elizabeth I, "Virgin Queen" of England

State flower: American dogwood
State bird: Cardinal
Largest city: Virginia Beach
Land area: 39,598 square miles
Land area rank: 37th largest state
Population: 7,386,330
Population rank: 12th largest state
Postal abbreviation: VA

Washington

Capital: Olympia
Organized as a territory: March 2, 1853
Entered Union: November 11, 1889
Order of entry: 42nd state
Motto: Al-Ki (Indian word, meaning "by and by").
Geographic region: West
Nicknames: Evergreen State, Chinook State

Origin of name Washington: In honor of George Washington.
State flower: Coast rhododendron
State bird: Willow goldfinch
Largest city: Seattle
Land area: 66,582 square miles
Land area rank: 20th largest state
Population: 6,131,445
Population rank: 15th largest state
Postal abbreviation: WA

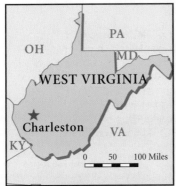

West Virginia

Capital: Charleston
Became a colony: 1607, as part of Virginia colony
Entered Union: June 20, 1863
Order of entry: 35th state
Motto: Mountaineers are always free.
Geographic region: South
Nickname: Mountain State
Origin of name Virginia: In honor

of Elizabeth I, "Virgin Queen" of England
State flower: Rhododendron
State bird: Cardinal
Largest city: Charleston
Land area: 24,087 square miles
Land area rank: 41st largest state
Population: 1,810,354
Population rank: 37th largest state
Postal abbreviation: WV

Wisconsin

Capital: Madison
Organized as a territory: July 4, 1836
Entered Union: May 29, 1848
Order of entry: 30th state
Motto: Forward.
Geographic region: Midwest
Nickname: Badger State
Origin of name Wisconsin: French misinterpretation of an Indian word whose meaning is disputed

State flower: Wood violet
State bird: Robin
Largest city: Milwaukee
Land area: 54,314 square miles
Land area rank: 25th largest state
Population: 5,472,299
Population rank: 20th largest state
Postal abbreviation: WI

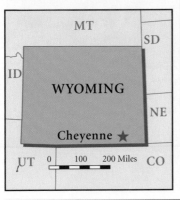

Wyoming

Capital: Cheyenne
Organized as a territory: May 19, 1869
Entered Union: July 10, 1890
Order of entry: 44th state
Motto: Equal rights.
Geographic region: West
Nickname: Equality State
Origin of name Wyoming: From the Delaware Indian word, meaning "mountains and valleys alternating"

State flower: Indian paintbrush
State bird: Meadowlark
Largest city: Cheyenne
Land area: 97,105 square miles
Land area rank: 9th largest state
Population: 501,242
Population rank: Smallest state
Postal abbreviation: WY

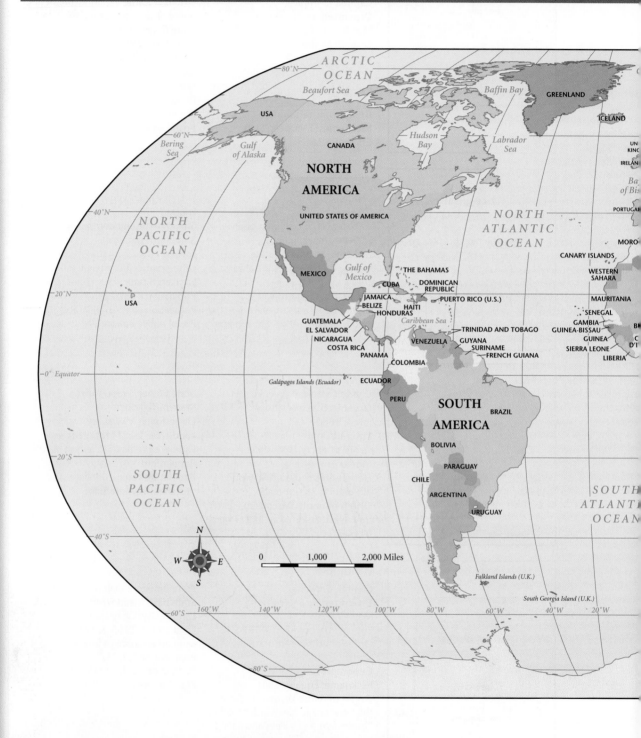

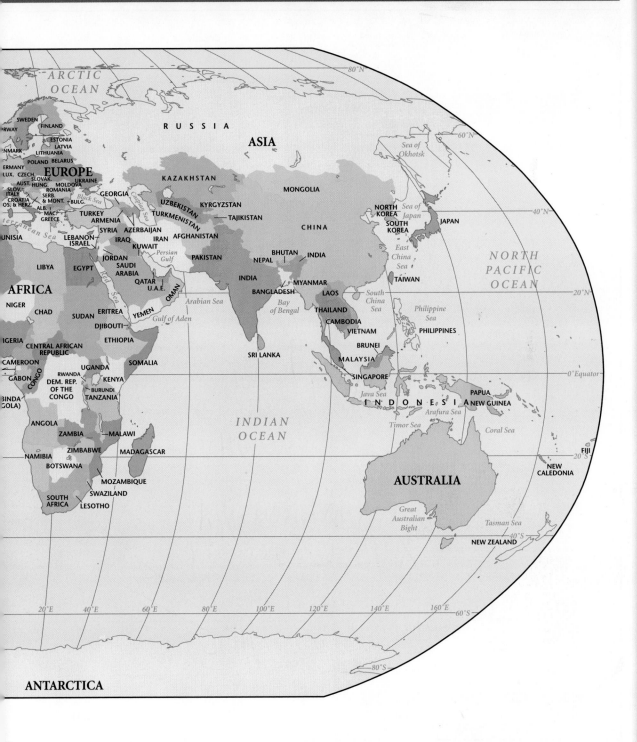

United States of America

CANADA

Ft. Albany

Sept-Iles

Gulf of St. Lawrence

Quebec

Fredericton

NOVA SCOTIA

Halifax

Thunder Bay

Lake Superior

Sault Ste. Marie

Montreal

MAINE

Augusta

Duluth

MINNESOTA

Lake Huron

Ottawa

Montpelier

VT

NH

Concord

60°W

St. Paul

Minneapolis

WISCONSIN

MICHIGAN

Lansing

Lake Michigan

Toronto

L. Ontario

Albany

MA

Boston

Madison

NEW YORK

Hartford

RI Providence

Milwaukee

Detroit

Lake Erie

Buffalo

CT

Waterloo

Chicago

Cleveland

PENNSYLVANIA

Newark

New York City

IOWA

Davenport

Gary

Ft. Wayne

Harrisburg

Philadelphia

Trenton

NJ

Atlantic City

Des Moines

ILLINOIS

Peoria

OHIO

Columbus

Pittsburgh

MD

Dover

ATLANTIC
OCEAN

Indianapolis

Springfield

INDIANA

Cincinnati

Washington, D.C.

WEST
VIRGINIA

DE
Annapolis

Kansas City

St. Louis

Frankfort

Charleston

Richmond

Jefferson City

Louisville

VIRGINIA

Norfolk

MISSOURI

KENTUCKY

Durham

Raleigh

Springfield

Knoxville

NORTH
CAROLINA

Nashville

Charlotte

Fort Smith

TENNESSEE

Greenville

Wilmington

ARKANSAS

Memphis

Columbia

City

Little Rock

Birmingham

Atlanta

SOUTH
CAROLINA

Greenville

Augusta

Charleston

MISSISSIPPI

ALABAMA

GEORGIA

Savannah

Shreveport

Jackson

Montgomery

LOUISIANA

Albany

Mobile

Baton Rouge

Tallahassee

Jacksonville

New Orleans

65°W

ston

FLORIDA

Tampa

Gulf of Mexico

Miami

THE
BAHAMAS

70°W

United States
of America

★ National Capital

★ State Capital

• City

0   200   400 km

0   200   400 Miles

Havana

CUBA

95°W   90°W   85°W   80°W   75°W

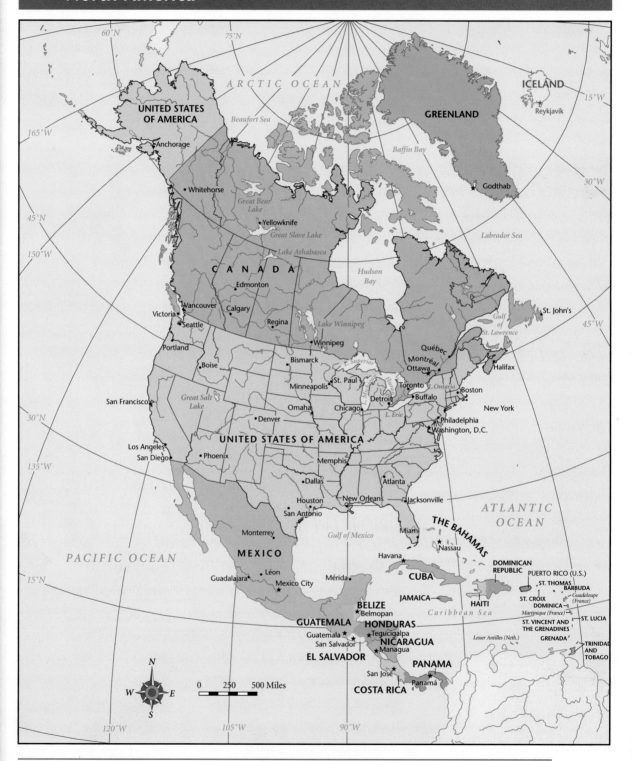

Caribbean Sea

Managua

Barranquilla

San José

Panama

Caracas

TRINIDAD AND TOBAGO

Valencia

VENEZUELA

Cúcuta

Georgetown

Medellín

GUYANA

Paramaribo

Bogotá

SURINAME

Cayenne

COLOMBIA

FRENCH GUIANA

Mitú

Quito

Manaus

Belém

ECUADOR

Guayaquil

Galápagos Islands (Ecuador)

Talara

PERU

Fortaleza

Trujillo

Pôrto Velho

BRAZIL

Recife

Huánuco

Lima

Salvador

Ica

Cuzco

BOLIVIA

La Paz

Brásilia

Santa Cruz

Goiânia

Sucre

Iquique

PARAGUAY

Rio de Janeiro

Antofagasta

São Paulo

CHILE

Asunción

Córdoba

URUGUAY

Santiago

Rosario

Buenos Aires

Montevideo

Concepción

ARGENTINA

ATLANTIC OCEAN

Valdivia

Puerto Montt

PACIFIC OCEAN

N
W   E
S

Comodoro Rivadavia

0   250   500 Miles

Falkland Islands (U.K.)

South Georgia Island (U.K.)

10°N

0°

10°S

20°S

30°S

40°S

50°S

90°W   80°W   70°W   60°W   50°W   40°W

Europe

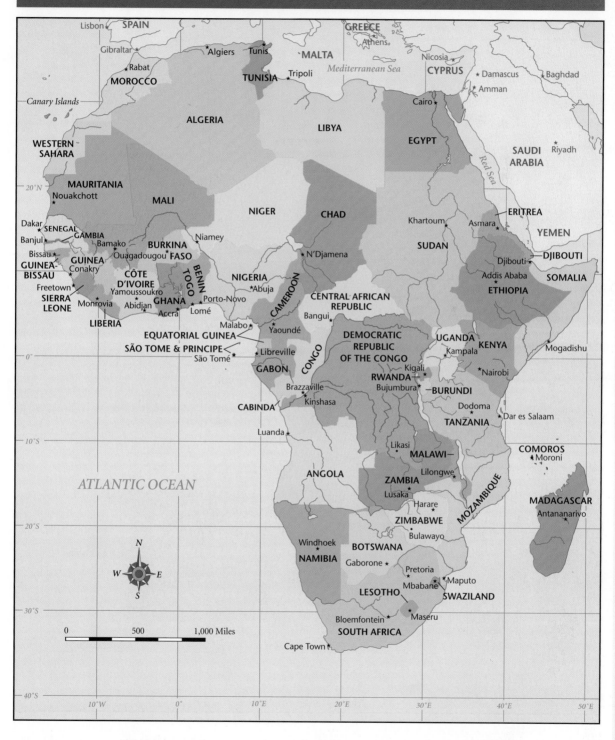

Africa map

ATLANTIC OCEAN

N
W   E
S

0   500   1,000 Miles

Asia and Australia

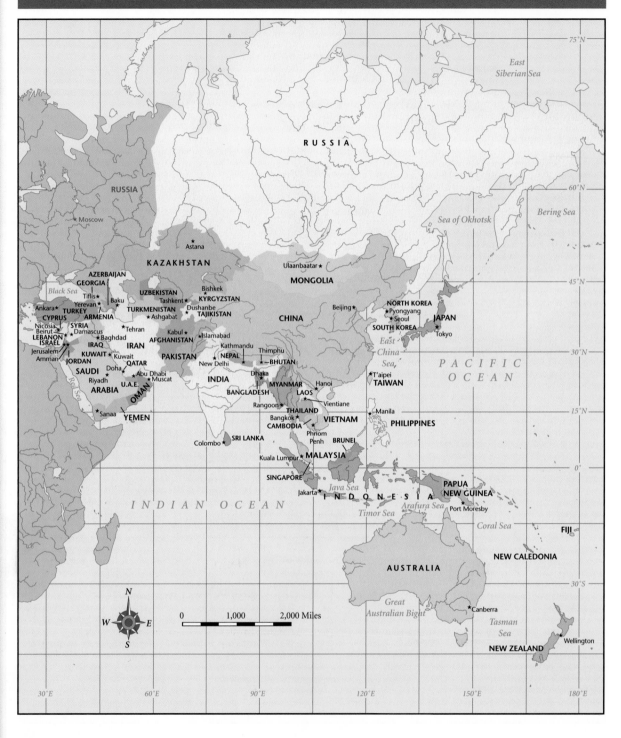

Time Zones of the United States

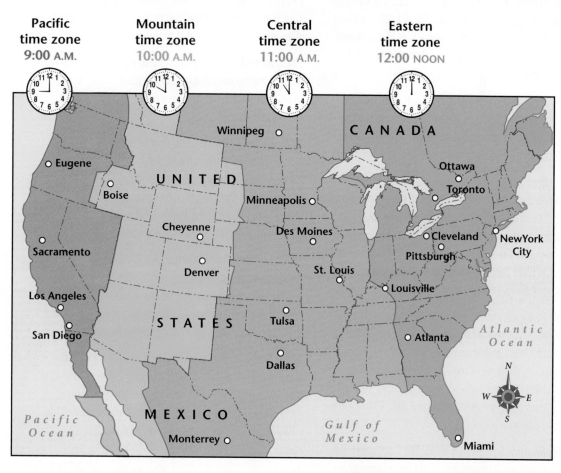

Pacific time zone
9:00 A.M.

Mountain time zone
10:00 A.M.

Central time zone
11:00 A.M.

Eastern time zone
12:00 NOON

Winnipeg

CANADA

Eugene

UNITED

Ottawa

Boise

Toronto

Minneapolis

Cheyenne

Des Moines

Cleveland

Pittsburgh

New York City

Sacramento

Denver

St. Louis

Louisville

Los Angeles

STATES

Tulsa

Atlanta

Atlantic Ocean

San Diego

Dallas

Pacific Ocean

MEXICO

Monterrey

Gulf of Mexico

Miami

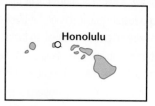

Hawaii-Aleutian
time zone
7:00 A.M.

Honolulu

Alaska
time zone
8:00 A.M.

Juneau

Appendix H

Selected Landmark Decisions of the U.S. Supreme Court

1803: *Marbury v. Madison.* The Court ruled that Congress exceeded its power in the Judiciary Act of 1789; the Court thus established its power to review acts of Congress and declare invalid those it found in conflict with the Constitution.

1819: *McCulloch v. Maryland.* The Court ruled that Congress had the authority to charter a national bank, under the Constitution's granting of the power to enact all laws "necessary and proper" to responsibilities of government.

1857: *Dred Scott v. Sanford.* The Court declared unconstitutional the already-repealed Missouri Compromise of 1820 because it deprived a person of his or her property—a slave—without due process of law. The Court also ruled that slaves were not citizens of any state nor of the U.S. (The latter part of the decision was overturned by ratification of the 14th Amendment in 1868.)

1896: *Plessy v. Ferguson.* The Court ruled that a state law requiring federal railroad trains to provide separate but equal facilities for black and white passengers neither infringed upon federal authority to regulate interstate commerce nor violated the 13th and 14th Amendments. (The "separate but equal" doctrine remained effective until the 1954 *Brown v. Board of Education* decision.)

1904: *Northern Securities Co. v. U.S.* The Court ruled that a holding company formed solely to eliminate competition between two railroad lines was a combination in restraint of trade, violating the federal antitrust act.

1908: *Muller v. Oregon.* The Court upheld a state law limiting the working hours of women. (Instead of presenting legal arguments, Louis D. Brandeis, counsel for the state, brought forth evidence from social workers, physicians, and factory inspectors that the number of hours women worked affected their health and morals.)

1911: *Standard Oil Co. of New Jersey et al. v. U.S.* The Court ruled that the Standard Oil Trust must be dissolved because of its unreasonable restraint of trade.

1919: *Schenck v. U.S.* The Court sustained the Espionage Act of 1917, maintaining that freedom of speech and press could be constrained if "the words used . . . create a clear and present danger. . ."

1925: *Gitlow v. New York.* The Court ruled that the First Amendment prohibition against government abridgment of the freedom of speech applied to the states as well as to the federal government. The decision was the first of a number of rulings holding that the 14th Amendment extended the guarantees of the Bill of Rights to state action.

1935: *Schechter Poultry Corp. v. U.S.* The Court ruled that Congress exceeded its authority to delegate legislative powers and to regulate interstate commerce when it enacted the National Industrial Recovery Act, which afforded the U.S. president too much discretionary power.

1951: *Dennis et al. v. U.S.* The Court upheld convictions under the Smith Act of 1940 for invoking Communist theory that advocated the forcible overthrow of the government. (In the *1957 Yates v. U.S.* decision, the Court moderated this ruling by allowing such advocacy in the abstract, if not connected to action to achieve the goal.)

1954: *Brown v. Board of Education of Topeka.* The Court ruled that separate public schools for black and white students were inherently unequal, so that state-sanctioned segregation in public schools violated the equal protection guarantee of the 14th Amendment. And in *Bolling v. Sharpe* the Court ruled that the congressionally mandated segregated public school system in the District of Columbia violated the 5th Amendment's due process guarantee of personal liberty. (The *Brown* ruling also led to abolition of state-sponsored segregation in other public facilities.)

1961: *Mapp v. Ohio.* The Court ruled that evidence obtained in violation of the 4th Amendment guarantee against unreasonable search and seizure must be excluded from use at state as well as federal trials.

1962: *Engel v. Vitale.* The Court held that public schools could not require pupils to recite a state-composed prayer, even if nondenominational and voluntary, because this would be an unconstitutional attempt to establish religion.

1962: *Baker v. Carr.* The Court held that the constitutional challenges to the unequal distribution of voters among legislative districts could be resolved by federal courts, rejecting its own *1946* precedent.

1963: *Gideon v. Wainwright.* The Court ruled that state and federal defendants charged with serious crimes must have access to an attorney, at state expense if necessary.

1964: *New York Times Co. v. Sullivan.* The Court ruled that the First Amendment guarantee of freedom of the press protected the press from libel suits for defamatory reports on public officials unless it was proved that the reports were made from malice, i.e., "with knowledge that [the defamatory statement] was false or with reckless disregard of whether it was false or not."

1966: *Miranda v. Arizona.* The Court ruled that, under the guarantee of due process, suspects in custody, before being questioned, must be informed that they have the right to remain silent, that anything they say may be used against them, and that they have the right to counsel.

1974: *U.S. v. Nixon.* The Court ruled that neither the separation of powers nor the need to preserve the confidentiality of presidential communications could alone justify an absolute executive privilege of immunity from judicial demands for evidence to be used in a criminal trial.

1976: *Gregg v. Georgia, Profitt v. Fla., Jurek v. Texas.* The Court held that death, as a punishment for persons convicted of first degree murder, was not in and of itself cruel and unusual punishment in violation of the 8th Amendment. But the Court ruled that the sentencing judge and jury must consider the individual character of the offender and the circumstances of the particular crime.

1978: *Regents of Univ. of Calif. v. Bakke.* The Court ruled that a special admissions program for a state medical school, under which a set number of places were reserved for minorities, violated the 1964 Civil Rights Act, which forbids excluding anyone, because of race, from a federally funded program. However, the Court ruled that race could be considered as one of a complex of factors.

1995: *Adarand Constructors v. Peña.* The Court held that federal programs that classify people by race, unless "narrowly tailored" to accomplish a "compelling governmental interest," may violate the right to equal protection.

1995: *U.S. Term Limits Inc. v. Thornton.* The Court ruled that neither states nor Congress could limit terms of members of Congress, since the Constitution reserves to the people the right to choose federal lawmakers.

1998: *Clinton v. City of New York.* The Court struck down the Line-Item Veto Act (1996), holding that it unconstitutionally gave the president "the unilateral power to change the text of duly enacted statutes."

2000: *Bush v. Gore.* The Court ruled that manual recounts of presidential ballots in the Nov. 2000 election could not proceed because inconsistent evaluation standards in different counties violated the equal protection clause. In effect, the ruling meant existing official results leaving George W. Bush as narrow winner of the election would prevail.

2003: *Ewing v. California* and *Lockyer v. Andrade.* The court, in two 5-4 rulings, held that California's "three-strikes" law, which dramatically increased penalties for those convicted of a third felony offense, did not constitute cruel and unusual punishment.

2003: *Georgia v. Ashcroft.* The justices ruled, 5-4, that the 1965 Voting Rights Act allowed Southern states to redraw legislative districts to reduce the number of districts in which blacks and other minorities formed large voting majorities, as long as the intent was to widen their political influence, not dilute it.

The Emancipation Proclamation

January 1, 1863

Abraham Lincoln

Whereas, on the twenty-second day of September, in the year of our Lord one thousand eight hundred and sixty-two, a proclamation was issued by the President of the United States, containing, among other things, the following, to wit:

"That on the first day of January, in the year of our Lord one thousand eight hundred and sixty-three, all persons held as slaves within any State or designated part of a State, the people whereof shall then be in rebellion against the United States, shall be then, thenceforward, and forever free; and the Executive Government of the United States, including the military and naval authority thereof, will recognize and maintain the freedom of such persons, and will do no act or acts to repress such persons, or any of them, in any efforts they may make for their actual freedom. . . .

Now, therefore I, Abraham Lincoln, President of the United States . . . order and designate as the States and parts of States wherein the people thereof respectively, are this day in rebellion against the United States, the following, to wit: Arkansas, Texas, Louisiana . . . Mississippi, Alabama, Florida, Georgia, South Carolina, North Carolina, and Virginia. . . .

And by virtue of the power, and for the purpose aforesaid, I do order and declare that all persons held as slaves within said designated States, and parts of States, are, and henceforward shall be free; and that the Executive government of the United States, including the military and naval authorities thereof, will recognize and maintain the freedom of said persons.

For the full text of this document, go to the following web site and click on "Transcript of the Proclamation"
www.archives.gov/exhibit_hall/featured_documents/emancipation_proclamation/

"Common Sense"

Author Thomas Paine met Benjamin Franklin in London in 1774. At Franklin's encouragement, Paine traveled to America where he began writing and publishing. His writings helped to move the colonists toward declaring independence from Britain. Here is a selection from Paine's pamphlet called "Common Sense."

"It is repugnant to reason . . . that this continent can longer remain subject to any external power. . . . The utmost stretch of human wisdom cannot, at this time, compass a plan short of separation, which can promise the continent even a year's security. Reconciliation is now a fallacious dream.

As to government matters, it is not in the power of Britain to do this continent justice: The business of it will soon be too weighty, and intricate, to be managed with any tolerable degree of convenience by a power so distant from us, and so very ignorant of us; for if they cannot conquer us, they cannot govern us. To be always running three or four thousand miles with a tale or a petition, waiting four or five months for an answer, which when obtained requires five or six more to explain it in, will in a few years be looked upon as folly and childishness—There was a time when it was proper, and there is a proper time for it to cease. . . .

To talk of friendship with those in whom our reason forbids us to have faith . . . is madness and folly. Every day wears out the little remains of a kindred between us and them, and can there be any reason to hope, that as the relationship expires, the affection will increase, or that we shall agree better, when we have ten times more and greater concerns to quarrel over than ever? . . .

O ye that love mankind! Ye that dare oppose, not only the tyranny but the tyrant, stand forth! Every spot of the old world is overrun with oppression. Freedom hath been hunted round the globe. Asia and Africa have long expelled her—Europe regards her like a stranger, and England hath given her warning to depart. O! Receive the fugitive, and prepare in time an asylum for mankind."

Source: "Common Sense," 1776, by Thomas Paine.

Glossary

A

Abolitionist (ab ə lish´ə nist) A person who wanted slavery stopped (p. 250)

Abroad (ə bròd´) Throughout the world (p. 444)

Access (ak´ses) The ability to obtain or make use of something (p. 57)

Accusation (ak yə zā´ shən) A charge of wrongdoing (p. 572)

Acquire (ə kwīr´) To gain something by purchasing or taking it (p. 168)

Administration (ad min ə strā´ shən) The period of time a president is in office (p. 347)

Advertise (ad´ vər tīz) To announce publicly (p. 401)

Adviser (ad vī´zər) A person who gives information, advice, or help (p. 142)

Affairs (ə fārz´) The day-to-day business of a person or group (p. 158)

Agency (ā´ jən sē) An organization set up by the federal government (p. 336)

Aggressive (ə gres´ iv) Forceful (p. 179)

Agreement (ə grē´ mənt) An arrangement between people or countries as to the course of action (p. 208)

Agricultural (ag´ rə kul chər əl) Having to do with raising crops or animals for food or profit (p. 210)

Aide (ād) One who assists (p. 621)

Airlift (âr´ lift) Using planes to deliver food and supplies (p. 566)

Alien (ā´ lyən) Someone who lives in one country but is a citizen of another (p.163)

Alliance (ə lī´ əns) An agreement that joins groups of people or countries together (p. 75)

Allied Powers (ə līd´ pou´ ərz) A group of allied nations that included Great Britian, France, Serbia, Belgium, and Russia (p. 463)

Al Qaeda (al kī´ dəh) The terrorist group that attacked New York City and Washington, D.C., on September 11, 2001 (p. 685)

Ambassador (am bas´ ə dər) A representative from a country who works out problems with another country (p. 168)

Amendment (ə mend´ mənt) A change (p. 147)

Ammunition (am yə nish´ ən) Bullets, gunpowder, and other things used with guns or other weapons (p. 297)

Amnesty (am´ nə stē) A pardon granted by the government (p. 333)

Anarchist (an´ ər kist) A person or group against all forms of government (p. 422)

Anthem (an´ thəm) A song or hymn of praise or gladness (p. 186)

Anti-Federalist (an´ tē fed´ ər ə list) One who felt that the Constitution gave the central government too much power (p. 145)

Apartheid (ə pärt´ hāt) The South African policy of racial segregation (p. 648)

Appeasement (ə pēz´ mənt) Doing something to keep peace (p. 532)

Appoint (ə point´) To name or choose a person to do something (p. 77)

Approval (ə prüv´ l) An acceptance or agreement(p. 132)

Archaeologist (är kē ol´ ə jist) A person who studies the remains of past human life (p. 3)

Architect (är´ kə tekt) A person skilled in designing buildings (p. 6)

Armada (är mä´ da) A fleet of warships (p. 34)

Armistice (är´ mə stis) A break in a war to talk peace (p. 439)

Arrogant (ar´ ə gənt) Showing a feeling of being better than others (p. 162)

Arsenal (är´ sə nəl) A place used to make or store military weapons (p. 297)

Arson (är ´sən) The act of purposely setting fire to something (p. 675)

Artificial satellite (är tə fish´ əl sat´ l īt) An object made by humans that travels in outer space and sends signals back to Earth (p. 577)

Artisan (är´ tə zən) A skilled worker (p. 8)

Assassination (ə sas´ ən ā shən) The killing of a politically important person (p. 333)

Assemble (ə sem´bəl) To gather together (p. 149)

Assembly line (ə sem´ blē līn) A process by which a line of workers assemble something piece by piece until it is complete (p. 487)

Asset (as´ et) Something of worth that someone owns (p. 539)

Association (ə sō sē ā´ shən) A group of people joined together for a common purpose (p. 489)

Astronomy (ə stron´ ə mē) The study of space and the planets (p. 6)

Atmosphere (at´ mə sfir) The layer of gases covering Earth (p. 583)

Atomic bomb (ə tom´ ik bom) A bomb with great destructive powers (p. 546)

Authorities (ə thôr´ ə tēz) Persons in command of something (p. 206)

Automation (ȯ tə mā´ shən) The use of machines to do work (p. 575)

Axis Powers (ak´ sis pou´ərz) The alliance of Japan, Italy, and Germany in World War II (p. 539)

B

Baby boom (bā´ bē büm) The millions of babies born after World War II (p. 600)

Ban (ban) To disallow something (p. 99)

Belittling (bi lit´ tling) Insulting (p. 293)

Beringia (bə rin´ gyə) A land bridge a thousand miles wide that connected Siberia to Alaska (p. 3)

Betray (bi trā´) To go against someone's trust (p. 632)

Bicentennial (bī sən ten´ ē əl) A 200th year celebration (p. 626)

Bill (bil) A proposal for a new law (p. 141)

Billboard (bil´ bôrd) A large sign used to advertise something (p. 257)

Black Codes (blak kōds) Laws that prevented African Americans from owning certain land, voting, and working certain skilled jobs (p. 335)

Blitzkrieg (blitz´ krēg) "Lightning war"; a rapid military attack (p. 535)

Blockade (blo kād´) Something that prevents goods or people from entering a country (p. 172)

Blockhouse (blok´hous) A building used for protection from attack; fort (p. 48)

Blue-collar (blü kol´ ər) A name used to describe workers in jobs that require little training (p. 604)

Bond (bond) A document that is proof of money owed (p. 156)

Bootlegger (büt´ leg ər) Someone who made or sold alcohol illegally during Prohibition (p. 495)

Boundary (boun´ dər ē) A real or imaginary marker that shows what land a person owns (p. 55)

Boycott (boi´ kot) To refuse to have dealings with a person, country, or group (p. 92)

Bravery (brā´ vər ē) The ability not to be afraid when facing danger (p. 248)

Breadline (bred līn) A place where people could get free food (p. 509)

Bribe (brīb) A payment to someone to make a person act in a certain way (p. 417)

Budget (buj´ it) A plan that shows how much money is available and how the money will be spent (p. 641)

Bunker (bung´ kər) An underground shelter (p. 546)

Burial (bər´ ē əl) The act of burying the dead (p. 11)

By-product (bī´ prod əkt) Something produced in the process of making something else (p. 387)

C

Cabinet (kab´ ə nit) A group of advisers to the president (p. 155)

Campaign (kam pān´) A group of activities connected to getting elected to office (p. 217)

Canal (kə nal´) A waterway made by humans (p. 8)

Candidate (kan´ də dāt) A person who has been selected to run for a political office (p. 161)

Capable (kā´ pə bəl) Having the ability for a task (p. 217)

a	hat	e	let	ī	ice	ȯ	order	u̇	put	sh	she	ə {	a in about
ā	age	ē	equal	o	hot	oi	oil	ü	rule	th	thin		e in taken
ä	far	ėr	term	ō	open	ou	out	ch	child	ᴛʜ	then		i in pencil
â	care	i	it	ȯ	saw	u	cup	ng	long	zh	measure		o in lemon
													u in circus

Capital (kap´ ə təl) Money used for investments (p. 385)

Career (kə rir´) A permanent job or line of work (p. 643)

Cargo (kär´ gō) Objects or goods carried in a ship or some other form of transportation (p. 98)

Caribou (kar´ ə bü) A large deer that lives in arctic regions (p. 3)

Carpetbagger (kär´ pit bag ər) A Northerner elected to political office in the South who took advantage of people; carried belongings in carpetbags (p. 341)

Cash crop (kash krop) A crop that can be sold (p. 181)

Casualty (kazh´ ü əl tē) A person who is wounded, killed, or lost in action (p. 664)

Cease-fire (sēs fīr´) A call for an end to fighting (p. 547)

Centennial (sen ten´ ē əl) A 100th-year celebration (p. 348)

Central Powers (sen´ trəl pou´ ərz) A group of allied nations that included Germany, Austria-Hungary, and later Turkey and Bulgaria (p. 463)

Chain reaction (chān rē ak´ shən) A series of events linked to one another (p. 463)

Chancellor (chan´ sə lər) The chief minister in some European countries (p. 528)

Charity (châr´ ə tē) A group that helps those in need (p. 507)

Charter (chär´ tər) A written agreement granting power in the name of a state or country (p. 34)

Chattel slavery (chat´ l sla´ vər ē) Slavery in which the enslaved person was legally owned by his or her master (p. 61)

Circulate (sėr´ kyə lāt) To pass something from person to person or place to place (p. 145)

Citizenship (sit´ ə zən ship) The condition of belonging to a certain country (p. 528)

Civics (siv´ iks) The study of the duties, rights, and priviledges of citizens

Civilian (sə vil´ yən) One who is not in the military (p. 542)

Civilization (siv ə lə zā´ shən) A high level of cultural development (p. 6)

Civil lawsuit (siv´ əl lȯ´ süt) A court case involving private rights (p. 149)

Civil rights (siv´ əl rītz) Basic human rights belonging to all people (p. 337)

Civil service (siv´ əl sėr´ vis) A system in which government employees are hired according to their qualifications (p. 417)

Civil war (siv´ əl wôr) A war between groups within the same country (p. 308)

Classic (klas´ ik) A book that has lasting value or meaning (p. 248)

Clause (klȯz) A certain section of a document (p. 115)

Clergy (klėr´ jē) A person given the power by the church to perform religious tasks (p. 55)

Clovis point (klō´ vis point) A finely flaked stone spearhead (p. 4)

Coercion (kō ėr´ shən) Pressure on a person or group to do something (p. 172)

Cold war (kōld wôr) The disagreements between Communist and non-Communist nations over economics and politics that caused tensions following World War II (p. 563)

Collapse (kə laps´) Breakdown or ruin (p. 615)

Collective bargaining (kə lek´ tiv bär´ gən ing) A way of negotiating between groups of workers and employers (p. 515)

Colony (kol´ ə nē) A group of people living in a new area under rule of their native land (p. 34)

Combat (kəm´ bat) Battle (p. 542)

Commander (kə man´ dər) Someone who controls an army or some other military group (p. 111)

Commerce (kom´ ərs) Having to do with buying or selling goods (p. 240)

Commercial (kə mėr´ shəl) Something linked to business or buying and selling (p. 135)

Commission (kə mish´ ən) To appoint a person or group to do something (p. 30)

Commonwealth (kom´ən welth) A group of self-governing states (p. 660)

Communication (kə myü nə kā´ shən) The act of sending and receiving information (p. 240)

Communist (kom´ yə nist) A person who believes in a form of government that eliminates private property and shares wealth (p. 494)

Compass (kum´ pəs) A device used to show direction (p. 25)

Compete (kəm pēt´) To try to win or gain something (p. 437)

Competitor (kəm pet´ ə tər) A company that sells or buys the same goods or services as another company (p. 98)

Complex (kəm pleks´) Having many details or parts (p. 70)

Composer (kəm pō´ zər) One who writes music (p. 491)

Compromise (kom´ prə mīz) A settlement of differences in which each side gives up some of its demands (p. 120)

Conductor (kən duk´ tər) A person who helped free slaves by using the Underground Railroad (p. 281)

Confederacy (kən fed´ ər ə sē) A group that has formed an alliance; the Confederate States of America (p. 182)

Conference (kon´ fər əns) A meeting among a large group of people (p. 473)

Conflict (kon´ flikt) A fight, battle, or war (p. 179)

Confusion (kən fyü´ zhən) The state of being mixed up (p. 188)

Congress (kong´ gris) The body of government that makes laws, consisting of the House of Representatives and the Senate (p. 139)

Conquer (kong´ kər) To gain something by force; defeat (p. 30)

Conservation (kon sər vā´ shən) The act of protecting or limiting the use of natural resources (p. 390)

Conservative (kən sər´ və tiv) One who is cautious about change (p. 594)

Conspiracy (kən spir´ ə sē) A joint act of breaking the law (p. 621)

Constitutional (kon stə tü´ shə nəl) Something that follows the ideas set forth in the Constitution (p. 164)

Consumer goods (kən sü´ mər gudz) Objects or things the average person buys and uses (p. 469)

Containment policy (kən tān´ mənt pol´ ə sē) The policy of using strength or threat of force to prevent the spread of Communism (p. 564)

Continent (kon´ tə nənt) A large land mass on Earth; for example, North America or Africa (p. 27)

Contract (kon´ trakt) A work agreement between at least two groups (p. 415)

Contribute (kən trib´ yüt) To add to or take part in something (p. 160)

Controversial (kon trə vėr´ shəl) Causing much debate and disagreement (p. 604)

Convention (kən ven´ shən) A formal meeting called for a special purpose (p. 101)

Conventional (kən ven´ shə nəl) Something that is traditional or commonly used (p. 659)

Convict (kən vikt´) To find someone guilty of a crime (p. 123)

Corporation (kôr pə rā´ shən) A large, organized company owned by stockholders (p. 384)

Corruption (kə rup´ shən) Using wrong or unlawful ways for financial gain (p. 341)

Counterattack (koun´ tər ə tak) To fight back following an attack (p. 545)

Counterculture (koun´ tər kul´ chər) A culture or lifestyle that goes against the common culture (p. 601)

Cowhand (kou´ hand) A person who tends cattle (p. 362)

Crisis (krī´ sis) An event that threatens people's well-being (p. 508)

Criticize (krit´ ə sīz) To show disapproval (p. 384)

Crude oil (krüd oil) Oil in its natural state, before being processed (p. 625)

Cultivate (kul´ tə vāt) To grow crops (p. 6)

Cultural (kul´ cher əl) Having to do with the arts (p. 69)

Culture (kul´ chər) The values, attitudes, and customs of a group (p. 3)

Customhouse (kus´ təm hous) A building where taxes are paid on imports and exports (p. 308)

a	hat	e	let	ī	ice	ô	order	ù	put	sh	she	ə	a in about
ā	age	ē	equal	o	hot	oi	oil	ü	rule	th	thin		e in taken
ä	far	ėr	term	ō	open	ou	out	ch	child	ᵺ	then		i in pencil
â	care	i	it	ò	saw	u	cup	ng	long	zh	measure		o in lemon
													u in circus

Fraud (frȯd) A lie or false act to steal money or something of value (p. 484)

Free state (frē stāt) A state that did not allow the practice of slavery (p. 205)

Freedmen (frēd′ mən) Former slaves (p. 335)

Frontier (frun tir′) A region with little population (p. 74)

Fugitive (fyü′ jə tiv) One who is fleeing from danger or from being kept against one's will (p. 278)

Fulfill (fu̇l fil′) To carry out or put into effect (p. 589)

G

General assembly (jen′ ər əl ə sem′ blē) A group that makes laws for a larger group (p. 49)

Generation (jen ə rā′ shən) People who live in the same time period and are about the same age (p. 489)

Genocide (jen′ ə sīd) The killing of a group based on its race or political views (p. 560)

Gilded (gil′did) Covered with a thin coating of gold (p. 415)

Glacier (glā′ shər) A large body of ice (p. 4)

Glasnost (glaz′ nost) The Soviet policy of open discussion of political and social issues (p. 660)

Global warming (glō′ bəl wȯrm′ing) A rise in the earth's temperature (p. 699)

Globe (glōb) A model of the earth (p. 25)

Gold standard (gōld stan′ dərd) A system in which a basic unit of currency is equal to a certain weight of gold (p. 426)

Governor (guv′ ər nər) A person chosen to lead a group of people within a given area, such as a colony or a state (p. 48)

Grandfather clause (grand′ fä thər klȯz) A clause that stated that any adult African American male could vote if his grandfather was a registered voter on January 1, 1867 (p. 346)

Growing season (grō′ ing sē′ zn) The length of time a crop is given to grow (p. 200)

Guarantee (gar ən tē′) An agreement to protect something, such as property (p. 139)

Guidance (gīd′ ns) Direction or leading (p. 55)

Guilty (gil′ tē) Having done wrong; deserving blame (p. 621)

Gunboat (gun′ bōt) An armed ship used for battle (p. 314)

H

Heroics (hi rō′ iks) Bravery well beyond what is needed (p. 483)

Hessian (hesh′ ən) A soldier paid by the British to fight the Americans (p. 118)

Hieroglyphic (hī ər ə glif′ ik) A system of writing that uses picturelike symbols (p. 6)

Hijack (hī′ jak) To steal an occupied vehicle by use of force (p. 686)

Hippie (hip′ ē) An extreme member of the youth culture in the 1960s (p. 601)

Holocaust (hol′ ə kȯst) The mass murder of European Jews during World War II (p. 533)

Homeland (hōm′ land) Land that a person or group came from originally (p. 224)

Homesteader (hōm′ sted ər) A pioneer who owned land under the Homestead Act (p. 365)

Horizontal combination (hȯr ə zon′ tl kom bə nā′ shən) A kind of business organization that joins two or more businesses that are in the same industry (p. 385)

Host (hōst) A person or group who provides a place for guests to do something (p. 136)

Hostage (hos′ tij) A person being held against his or her will by someone who wants certain demands to be met (p. 633)

I

Ice Age (īs āg) A period of time when much of Earth and Earth's water was frozen (p. 3)

Immigrant (im′ ə grənt) A person who comes to live in a new country (p. 163)

Impeach (im pēch′) To charge a president with misconduct (p. 339)

Imperialism (im pir′ ē ə liz əm) The practice of taking over land to become a stronger nation (p. 444)

Import (im′ pȯrt) A good brought in from a foreign country (p. 132)

Impose (im pōz′) To establish a rule or law, such as a tax, on a group with less power (p. 98)

Improvise (im′ prə vīz) To make up as you go along (p. 491)

Inaugural address (in ȯ′ gyər əl ə dres′) A speech a president gives to accept the presidency (p. 167)

Inaugurate (in ȯ′ gyər āt) To swear someone into office (p. 167)

Income (in´ kum) Money earned (p. 406)

Income tax (in´ kum taks) Tax placed on money people earn (p. 453)

Incumbent (in kum´ bənt) A person who currently holds a certain position or office (p. 675)

Indentured servant (in den´ chərd sėr´ vənt) A person who came to the colonies under a contract to work without pay for a certain time (p. 61)

Independence (in di pen´ dəns) Ability to take care of oneself (p. 69)

Indigo (in´ də gō) A plant used to make dye (p. 62)

Industry (in´ də strē) Related to business and manufacturing (p. 157)

Ineligible (in el´ ə jə bəl) Not able to do something because it is against rules (p. 584)

Infamy (in´ fə mē) Disgraceful or lacking honor (p. 540)

Inferior (in fir´ ē ər) Less advanced or lower in position (p. 533)

Inflation (in flā´ shən) A steady rise in prices of goods (p. 527)

Influence (in´ flü əns) The ability to convince someone of something (p. 179)

Initiative (i nish´ ə tiv) The power citizens have to suggest new laws (p. 446)

Inland (in´ lənd) A region of land that is far away from the coast (p. 124)

Insult (in´ sult) An action that upsets others (p. 262)

Insurance (in shür´ əns) A plan that protects against loss in return for regular payments (p. 510)

Interchangeable parts (in tər chān´ jə bəl pärts) Parts of a machine that can be used with other machines (p. 236)

Interest (in´ tər ist) Money paid to someone who lends money (p. 156)

Interfere (in tər fir´) To enter into or take part in other people's business (p. 111)

Interpret (in tėr´ prit) To explain or tell the meaning of something (p. 142)

Interstate (in´ tər stāt) An action that occurs between two states, such as trade (p. 133)

Invade (in vād´) To attack or take over something (p. 114)

Investigate (in ves´ tə gāt) To look into something to solve a problem or to answer a question (p. 416)

Investor (in ves´ tor) A person who lends money to a company; the investor hopes to receive more money back when the company makes money (p. 50)

Ironclad (ī´ ərn klad) A military ship covered in iron plates (p. 314)

Ironic (ī ron´ ik) The opposite of what is expected (p. 603)

Irrigation (ir ə gā´ shən) A system of watering crops that uses canals or ditches of water (p. 10)

Isolate (ī´ sə lāt) To set apart from others (p. 120)

Issue (ish´ ü) A topic of discussion or debate (p. 223)

J

Jim Crow Laws (jim krō´ lȯz) Laws that separated African Americans and whites in public places (p. 402)

Joint declaration (joint dek lə rā´ shən) To declare something as a group (p. 208)

Judgment (juj´ mənt) The ability a person has to decide and act on something (p. 623)

Judicial branch (jü dish´ əl branch) The branch of government that interprets laws (p. 142)

Justice (jus´ tis) A judge who serves on the Supreme Court (p. 142)

K

Kachina (kə chē´ nə) The spirit of an ancestor (p. 12)

Kerosene (ker´ ə sēn) A fuel used in lamps (p. 384)

Kiva (kē´ və) A large underground room used for ceremonies (p. 10)

Ku Klux Klan (kü´ kluks klan´) A secret group against people who were not white (p. 347)

a	hat	e	let	ī	ice	ȯ	order	u̇	put	sh	she	ə	a	in about
ā	age	ē	equal	o	hot	oi	oil	ü	rule	th	thin		e	in taken
ä	far	ėr	term	ō	open	ou	out	ch	child	ᴛʜ	then		i	in pencil
â	care	i	it	ȯ	saw	u	cup	ng	long	zh	measure		o	in lemon
													u	in circus

L

Labor union (lā′ ber yü′ nyən) A group of workers trying to bring about change in working conditions (p. 235)

Landslide (land′ slīd) A majority of votes for one side (p. 483)

Lawsuit (lȯ′ süt) A case brought before a court of law (p. 336)

Layoff (lā′ ȯf) Letting workers go because a company cannot afford to pay them (p. 507)

Legal (lē′ gəl) Having to do with law (p. 92)

Legislative branch (lej′ ə slā tiv branch) The branch of government that makes laws (p. 141)

Legislature (lej′ə slā chər) A group of people elected to make laws (p. 69)

Leisure (lē′ zhər) Something that is done for amusement (p. 405)

Liability (lī ə bil′ ə tē) A risk (p. 385)

Liberal (lib′ ər əl) One who favors change (p. 517)

Liberation (lib ə rā′ shən) Equal social or economic rights (p. 598)

Literally (lit′ ər ə lē) Taken exactly as something is stated, written, or directed (p. 642)

Livestock (līv′stok) Animals used for food or profit (p. 324)

Loan (lōn) Money lent to someone (p. 200)

Location (lō kā′ shən) The place where something is positioned (p. 114)

Locomotive (lō kə mō′ tiv) A vehicle that rides on rails and has an engine for pulling railroad cars (p. 240)

Loot (lüt) To take or damage things by use of force (p. 34)

Lottery (lot′ ər ē) Drawing names to decide who is drafted into the military (p. 537)

Lowland (lō′ land) A low or level piece of land (p. 200)

Loyalist (loi′ ə list) An American who supported the king of Great Britain (p. 114)

Loyalty (loi′əl tē) The act of being faithful to someone (p. 111)

Lure (lùr) To draw in someone or something by hinting of gain (p. 124)

M

Mainland (mān′ land) The main part of a continent (p. 39)

Maintain (mān tān′) To keep in good condition (p. 595)

Majority (mə jôr′ ə tē) A number greater than half of the total (p. 51)

Manifest Destiny (man′ ə fest des′ tə nē) A belief something is meant to happen, especially that America would own land from coast to coast (p. 260)

Manufacturer (man yə fak′ chər ər) A company that makes something to sell to the public or to other companies (p. 132)

Massacre (mas′ ə kər) The act of killing a large number of people in a cruel way (p. 95)

Mass-produce (mas prə düs′) To make great amounts of product very fast (p. 236)

McCarthyism (mə kär′ thē iz əm) An attempt to gain power by attacking the patriotism of others (p. 572)

Mechanic (mə kan′ ik) Someone skilled in working with machines (p. 236)

Melting pot (melt′ ing pot) A nation where several groups of people belonging to different races or cultures live together (p. 244)

Memorize (mem′ ə rīz) To remember what has been learned (p. 236)

Mercantilism (mėr′ kən ti liz əm) The practice of regulating colonial trade for the profit of the home country (p. 70)

Merchant (mėr′ chənt) A buyer and seller of goods (p. 25)

Mesa (mā′ sə) A flat-topped height (p. 10)

Mesoamerica (mes ō ə mer′ ə kə) The area of land that includes what is now Mexico and other countries south through Costa Rica (p. 6)

Method (meth′ ‚əd) A way of doing something (p. 379)

Migrant (mī′ grənt) A worker who travels from place to place to work (p. 600)

Military (mil′ ə ter ē) Having to do with armed forces (p. 8)

Militia (mə lish′ ə) An organized group of citizens who serve as soldiers in times of war (p. 109)

Millennium (məl len′ ē um) A period of 1,000 years (p. 677)

Mine (mīn) A bomb that floats in water and explodes when touched (p. 471)

Minimum wage (min´ ə mem wāj) The smallest amount a person can be paid to do a job (p. 454)

Minority (mə nôr´ ə tē) A group of people that is a smaller part of a population (p. 60)

Minutemen (min´ it men) A group of men trained to be soldiers and who agreed to gather at a minute's notice (p. 102)

Misconduct (mis kon´ dukt) Wrongdoing by someone holding a political or business position(p. 339)

Missile (mis´ əl) A self-driven bomb or rocket (p. 587)

Mission (mish´ ən) A church (p. 225)

Misunderstanding (mis un dər stan´ ding) Failure to understand (p. 370)

Mobile (mō´ bəl) Having the ability to travel (p. 486)

Monarch (mon´ ərk) A person who rules a kingdom or territory (p. 25)

Monopoly (mə nop´ ə lē) A corporation that has little competition (p. 384)

Morality (mə ral´ə tē) Good behavior; knowing the difference between right and wrong (p. 628)

Moratorium (môr ə tôr´ ē əm) The legal act of delaying something (p. 510)

Motorcade (mō´ tər kād) A parade of cars (p. 592)

Movement (müv´ mənt) A series of actions carried out to work toward a certain goal (p. 205)

Muckraker (muk´ rā kər) A person who wrote articles and books describing corruption and problems (p. 446)

Mugwump (mug´ wump) A reform group that wanted to replace the spoils system with civil service (p. 417)

Mural (myûr´ əl) An artistic painting or drawing on a wall (p. 514)

N

National Guard (nash´ ə nəl gärd) A state's military force (p. 574)

Nationalism (nash´ ə nə liz əm) A sense of loyalty to one's country (p. 189)

Nativist (nā´ tiv ist) A person who believes that people born in a country should have more rights than immigrants (245)

Natural resources (nach´ ər əl ri sors´ ez) Raw materials from nature, such as water and soil (p. 390)

Navigation (nav ə gā´ shən) Travel by water (p. 159)

Negotiate (ni gō´ shē āt) To work out a deal (p. 168)

Network (net´ wèrk) A system that is linked together in some way (p. 281)

Neutral (nü´ trəl) Not siding with any particular person or group (p. 158)

9/11 (nīn i lev´ ən) The shortened name for the terrorist attacks on September 11, 2001 (p. 685)

Noble (nō´ bəl) Someone who is part of a society's upper or ruling class (p. 25)

Nomads (nō´ madz) People who do not live in one place p. 3)

Nominate (nom´ ə nāt) To choose someone to do something, such as run for office (p. 218)

Nuclear war (nü´ klē ər wôr) War that uses atomic weapons (p. 571)

O

Oath (ōth) A pledge that promises loyalty to a government or other cause (p. 333)

Occupation (ok yə pā´shən) A person's job or line of work (p. 517)

Occupy (ok´ yə pī) To take control of a place (p. 124)

Offensive (ə fen´ siv) Attacking rather than defending (p. 569)

Opponent (ə pō´ nent) A person who takes an opposite position in an event such as a debate or contest(p. 296)

Oppression (ə presh´ ən) Unfair or cruel actions by one group against another group with less power (p. 219)

a	hat	e	let	ī	ice	ò	order	ù	put	sh	she	⎧a	in about
ā	age	ē	equal	o	hot	oi	oil	ü	rule	th	thin	⎧e	in taken
ä	far	èr	term	ō	open	ou	out	ch	child	ᴛH	then	ə⎨i	in pencil
â	care	i	it	ȯ	saw	u	cup	ng	long	zh	measure	⎩o	in lemon
												⎩u	in circus

Optimistic (op tə mis´ tik) Having good feelings toward what may happen in the future (p. 294)

Orator (ôr´ ə tər) One who is good at public speaking (p. 114)

Organize (ôr´ gə nīz) To put together in some kind of order (p. 182)

Outmaneuver (out mə nü´ vər) To move more quickly or better than an enemy (p. 185)

Outnumber (out num´ bər) To have more people than an opponent in a battle (p. 315)

Outrage (out´ rāj) Anger (p. 99)

Overproduction (ō vər prə duk´ shən) Producing too many goods (p. 508)

Override (ō vər rīd´) To reject or not accept (p. 338)

Overturn (ō vər tėrn´) To reverse (p. 517)

Ownership (ō´ nər ship) The state of owning something, such as land or a house (p. 131)

P

Pardon (pärd´ n) An official statement forgiving someone of something (p. 111)

Parliament (pär´ lə mənt) A group in England that makes laws (p. 52)

Pastor (pas´ tər) A member of the clergy (p. 55)

Patriot (pā´ trē ət) Someone who loves his or her own country (p. 101)

Patriotism (pā´ trē ə tiz əm) Pride in one's country (p. 687)

Patroon (pə trün´) A Dutch landowner (p. 56)

Perestroika (per ə stroi´ kə) The Soviet policy of economic and government reform (p. 660)

Permanent (pėr´ mə nənt) Meant to last for a long time (p. 35)

Persecute (pėr´ sə kyüt) To treat someone poorly or violently because of his or her religious beliefs or ethnic background (p. 670)

Petition (pə tish´ ən) A written paper asking for a right or benefit from someone in power (p. 110)

Petroleum (pə trō´ lē əm) A liquid that can be made into fuel (p. 379)

Philosophy (fe los´ ə fē) A person's beliefs or way of understanding something (p. 167)

Phonograph (fō´ nə graf) A machine used to reproduce sound (p. 388)

Pioneer (pī ə nir´) One of the first persons to settle in a territory (p. 131)

Plantation (plan tā´ shən) A large farm that grows huge amounts of a certain crop (p. 48)

Platform (plat´fôrm) A statement of ideas, policies, and beliefs of a political party in an election (p. 300)

Plea (plē) An urgent request (p. 111)

Policy (pol´ ə sē) A set of rules or an action plan set forth by a person or group (p. 56)

Political (pə lit´ ə kəl) Relating to government or the way it runs (p. 36)

Political boss (pə lit´ ə kəl bȯs) A professional politician who controls the actions of a political party (p. 417)

Political party (pə lit´ ə kəl pär´ tē) A group that represents a certain political belief (p. 158)

Poll (pōl) A method of predicting the winner of an election by asking people who they plan to vote for; a method of gathering information (p. 632)

Pollution (pə lü´ shən) Anything added to the environment that is harmful to living things (p. 390)

Popular sovereignty (pop´ yə lər sov´ rən tē) The power of the people to decide something, especially whether to become a free state or a slave state (p. 284)

Possession (pə zesh´ ən) An object belonging to someone (p. 188)

Postmaster (pōst´ mas tər) A person who runs the post office (p. 111)

Prejudice (prej´ə dis) A belief or action against someone because of race, sex, religion, or age (p. 402)

Primary election (prī´ mer ē i lek´ shən) An election in which the people choose candidates (p. 446)

Prime minister (prīm min´ ə stər) The main official in some countries, such as Great Britain and Canada (p. 124)

Proclamation (prok lə mā´ shən) An official public announcement (p. 209)

Produce (prō´ düs) Fruits or vegetables (p. 283)

Professional (prə fesh´ ə nəl) A person who is skilled or trained to do a task (p. 266)

Profitable (prof´ ə tə bəl) Able to bring in money above operating costs (p. 201)

Progressives (prə gres´ ivz) People who believed that America should pass laws to correct America's social and political problems (p. 445)

Prohibit (prō hib´ it) To prevent by law (p. 511)

Prohibition (prō ə bish´ ən) The ban on making or selling alcohol (p. 495)

Proposal (prə pō´ zəl) A suggestion for others to consider (p. 120)

Proprietor (prə prī´ə tər) One who owns a colony (p. 55)

Prose (prōz) The ordinary form of spoken or written language (p. 249)

Prosecute (pros´ ə kyüt) To charge with a crime (p. 424)

Prospector (pros´pek tər) A person who searches an area for gold, silver, or other minerals (p. 362)

Prosper (pros´ pər) To succeed (p. 189)

Province (prov´ əns) A part of a country or region (p. 100)

Provisions (prə vizh´ ənz) Supplies needed for a trip or voyage (p. 53)

Public service (pub´ lik sėr´ vis) Any job or effort done for the good of the people, such as a government job (p. 159)

Publish (pub´ lish) To print something, such as a book, newspaper, or magazine (p. 25)

Purify (pyu̇r´ ə fī) To make something pure (p. 379)

Q

Qualified (kwäl´ ə fīd) Fit for a given purpose (p. 210)

R

Racial profiling (rā´ shəl prō´ fīl ing) The practice of stopping and searching cars based only on the race of the driver (p. 699)

Radar (rā´ där) A system used to locate objects such as planes (p. 536)

Radical (rad´ ə kəl) Very great; more than usual (p. 291)

Ratify (rat´ ə fī) To approve something (p. 145)

Ration (rash´ ən) To use less or limit the amount of something (p. 542)

Rebellion (ri bel´ yən) A group fighting another group that is in power (p. 73)

Rebuild (rē bild´) To build something again (p. 326)

Recall (rē´ kȯl) The act of voting someone who has performed poorly out of office (p. 446)

Reconstruction (rē kən struk´ shən) Rebuilding of the South after the Civil War (p. 334)

Recovery (ri kuv´ ər ē) The act of overcoming a problem (p. 511)

Recruit (ri krüt´) To get new members for a group (p. 76)

Redeem (ri dēm´) To release from blame for something by doing something else better (p. 124)

Reference book (ref´ ər əns bu̇k) A book, such as a dictionary, used to find information (p. 247)

Referendum (ref ə ren´dem) The practice of giving voters the right to approve or not approve bills (p. 446)

Refinery (ri fī´ nər ē) A place where a good is made pure or made into other products (p. 383)

Reform (ri fôrm´) A change intended to make something better (p. 415)

Refuge (ref´ yüj) Protection or shelter (p. 60)

Refugee (ref yə jē´) A person who flees his or her home country to seek protection (p. 586)

Regiment (rej´ ə mənt) A large group of soldiers (p. 77)

Regular army (reg´ yə lər är´ mē) A state or country's permanent army (p. 182)

Regulate (reg´ yə lāt) To govern, or direct, according to a rule (p. 70)

Reich (rīk) A German empire (p. 531)

Reinforcements (rē in fôrs´ mənts) Additional soldiers used to back up an army (p. 80)

Reject (ri jekt´) To refuse to accept (p. 446)

Relationship (ri lā´ shən ship) Two or more things or groups connected in some way (p. 91)

Religious (ri lij´ əs) Relating to a belief in a higher being (p. 11)

a	hat	e	let	ī	ice	ȯ	order	u̇	put	sh	she		ə	{ a in about
ā	age	ē	equal	o	hot	oi	oil	ü	rule	th	thin			e in taken
ä	far	ėr	term	ō	open	ou	out	ch	child	₮H	then			i in pencil
â	care	i	it	ȯ	saw	u	cup	ng	long	zh	measure			o in lemon
														u in circus

Renew (ri nü´) To make something new again, such as a charter that has come to an end (p. 222)

Repeal (ri pēl´) To remove something, especially a law (p. 93)

Replenish (ri plen´ish) To make full or complete again (p. 597)

Representative (rep ri zen´ tə tiv) A person who is given power to act for others; a government with officials elected by the people (p. 49)

Reproduce (rē prə düs´) To copy or duplicate (p. 388)

Republic (ri pub´ lik) A government in which citizens elect people to speak and act for them (p. 441)

Reputation (rep yə tā´ shən) How a person is judged by others (p. 572)

Request (ri kwest´) The act of asking for something (p. 308)

Reservation (rez ər vā´ shən) Land set aside by the government for the American Indians (p. 368)

Reservoir (rez´ ər vwär) A large place used to store water (p. 12)

Resign (ri zīn´) To give up an office or job (p. 110)

Resistance (re zis´ təns) The act of opposing something (p. 99)

Resolution (rez ə lü´ shən) An expression of opinion or intent voted on by a group (p. 164)

Resolve (ri zolv´) To settle a difference (p. 294)

Resource (rē´ sôrs) A thing of value, often found in nature, that can be used to do or make something (p. 169)

Respond (ri spond´) To do or say something in return (p. 99)

Responsibility (ri spon sə bil´ ə tē) The need to complete duties or tasks (p. 69)

Restore (ri stôr´) To put something back or give something back to its owner (p. 188)

Restriction (ri strik´ shən) An act of limiting or preventing something (p. 179)

Retail (rē´ tāl) Relating to the buying and selling of goods (p. 405)

Reunification (rē yü nə fə kā´ shən) Joining together as one country again (p. 659)

Revenge (ri venj´) The act of getting back at someone for some wrongdoing (p. 544)

Revenue (rev´ ə nü) Money gained from something (p. 94)

Revise (ri vīz´) To make changes, especially to a document (p. 451)

Revolt (ri vōlt´) A rebellion (p. 206)

Revolution (rev ə lü´ shən) The act of overthrowing and replacing a government (p. 117)

Riot (rī´ ət) A violent public disturbance (p. 589)

Ritual (rich´ ü əl) An action that takes place during a ceremony (p. 10)

Rival (rī´ vəl) A well-matched opponent (p. 618)

Romantic (rō man´ tik) Glorified (p. 505)

Ruling (rü´ ling) A decision of a court case (p. 294)

Runaway (run´ ə wā) Someone who is trying to escape (p. 141)

Running mate (run´ing māt) A candidate who runs for office with another candidate who is running for a different position (p. 164)

Rural (rür´ əl) Relating to places well outside of cities (p. 235)

S

Saloon (sə lün´) A public building where people gathered to drink or gamble (p. 364)

Sanction (sangk´ shən) An action taken to force a country to do something (p. 649)

Sanitation (san ə tā´ shən) The act of disposing of waste and keeping areas clean (p. 407)

Scalawag (skal´ ə wag) A white Southerner who controlled the new politicians who had little government knowledge (p. 341)

Scandal (skan´ dl) A disgraceful event (p. 347)

Scourge (skėrj) Widespread pain or distress (p. 651)

Secede (si sēd´) To leave a group or organization (p. 301)

Secrecy (sē´ krə sē) The act of keeping something private (p. 137)

Sectional (sek´ shə nəl) Related to the interests of a region (p. 203)

Security (si kyür´ ə tē) Safety (p. 537)

Segregate (seg´ rə gāt) To separate by race (p. 344)

Self-sufficient (self sə fish´ ənt) Able to do something without help (p. 189)

Session (sesh´ ən) A meeting or a series of meetings (p. 137)

Settlement (set´ l mənt) A place or region newly settled (p. 6)

Share (shâr) A certificate bought from a stock company that represents a certain part of ownership of the company (p. 50)

Sharecropper (shâr´ krop ər) A farmer who pays some of his or her crop to a landowner as rent (p. 342)

Sharpshooting (shärp´ shü ting) The ability to shoot a gun with great success (p. 124)

Siege (sēj) An event in which an army prevents people in a fort or city from leaving; this is done in an attempt to capture the fort or city (p. 118)

Skyscraper (skī´ skrā pər) A tall building (p. 380)

Slaughter (slȯ´ tər) To kill animals for food and other products (p. 387)

Slavery (slā´vər ē) Forcing a person or group to work without pay or rights (p. 30)

Slave state (slāv stāt) A state that allowed the practice of slavery (p. 205)

Slogan (slō´ gən) A word or phrase used to explain a stand or goal (p. 257)

Slum (slum) A run-down urban area often without electricity or indoor plumbing (p. 407)

Sod (sod) Thickly matted grass and roots (p. 237)

Solo (sō´ lō) Done by one person (p. 496)

Solution (sə lü´ shən) The answer to a problem (p. 483)

Soup house (süp hous) A place where the poor could get food (p. 497)

Speakeasy (spēk´ ē zē) A place where liquor was sold illegally during Prohibition (p. 495)

Speaker of the House (spē´ kər ov thə hous) Leader of the House of Representatives (p. 181)

Specialize (spesh´ ə līz) To make and sell goods or services in one or two areas of business (p. 397)

Spectator (spek´ tā tər) One who watches an event (p. 406)

Spiritual (spir´ ə chü əl) A religious song (p. 491)

Spoils system (spoilz sis´ təm) The practice of giving government jobs to loyal supporters (p. 218)

Stabilize (stā´ bə līz) To keep from changing (p. 510)

Stagecoach (stāj´ kōch) A horse-drawn coach that was used for transporting people or mail (p. 359)

Stampede (stam pēd´) A wild rush of animals (p. 364)

Standards (stan´ derdz) Guidelines that a person or group must follow; a generally accepted way of doing something (p. 246)

Standstill (stand´ stil) Something that is not changing or improving (p. 468)

Starvation (stär vā´ shən) Suffering from lack of food (p. 244)

Statehood (stāt´ hu̇d) The condition of being a state (p. 206)

Statesman (stāts´ mən) Someone who knows and practices government ideas (p. 114)

Steerage (stir´ ij) A part of a ship for passengers paying the lowest fare (p. 400)

Stock company (stok kum´ pə nē) A company that is owned by people who own the company's stock (p. 50)

Stock market (stok mär´ kit) A market for the buying and selling of company stock (p. 496)

Strategic (strə tē´ jik) Important or helpful in carrying out a plan (p. 619)

Streetcar (strēt´ kär) A horse-drawn or electric carriage that rides on rails and is used for transportation (p. 405)

Strike (strīk) The act of stopping work to get better pay and working conditions (p. 421)

Strikebreaker (strīk´ brā kər) A worker used to replace a striking union worker (p. 422)

a	hat	e	let	ī	ice	ȯ	order	u̇	put	sh	she	ə	a	in about
ā	age	ē	equal	o	hot	oi	oil	ü	rule	th	thin		e	in taken
ä	far	ėr	term	ō	open	ou	out	ch	child	ᴛʜ	then		i	in pencil
â	care	i	it	ȯ	saw	u	cup	ng	long	zh	measure		o	in lemon
													u	in circus

Stronghold (strȯng´ hōld) A place, such as a military base, that is well-protected from attack (p. 80)

Submarine (sub´mə rēn) A ship that can travel underwater (p. 465)

Submission (səb mish´ ən) The act of giving up on something (p. 101)

Suborbital (sub ȯr´ bə təl) Not out of Earth's atmosphere (p. 583)

Subpeona (sə pē´ nə) A court order (p. 622)

Suburb (sub´ ėrb) A community built outside of a city (p. 487)

Sue (sü) To bring legal action against a person to settle a difference (p. 295)

Suffrage (suf´ rij) The right to vote (p. 163)

Summit (sum´it) A meeting held between or among world leaders (p. 659)

Supreme (sə prēm´) To the highest degree (p. 145)

Surge (sėrj) To rise swiftly (p. 641)

Surplus (sėr´ pləs) An extra amount of something (p. 510)

Survivor (sər vī´ vər) Someone who has lived through a dangerous event (p. 78)

Suspension bridge (sə spen´ shən brij) A large bridge supported by wires or chains attached to tall towers (p. 380)

Symphony (sim´ fə nē) A long, complex musical piece (p. 491)

Synagogue (sin´ ə gȯg) A Jewish place of worship (p. 532)

T

Tactic (tak´ tik) A method of doing something (p. 590)

Taliban (tal´ i ban) The group that controlled the government of Afghanistan (p. 690)

Tar and feather (tär and feth´ ər) To cover persons with tar and then with feathers in order to punish them (p. 92)

Tariff (tar´ if) A tax on goods leaving or entering some place (p. 133)

Taxation (tak sā´ shən) The act of taxing, or charging people for public and government sevices (p. 92)

Tax evasion (taks i vā´ zhən) Failing to pay one's taxes (p. 622)

Technology (tek nol´ ə jē) The use of science to create new machines or other advances

Telecommunications (tel´ ə kə myü nə kā´ shən) The transfer of information over long distances using such things as telephone lines, radio waves, or satellites (p. 698)

Telegraph (tel´ ə graf) A device that uses coded signals to send communications over a wire (p. 240)

Temporary (tem´ pə rer ē) Lasting only a short time (p. 131)

Tenant farmer (ten´ ənt fär´ mər) A farmer who pays rent to a landowner for use of the land (p. 342)

Tenement (ten´ ə mənt) A cheaply made building divided into apartments (p. 407)

Tension (ten´ shən) Uncomfortable feelings toward another person or group (p. 284)

Territory (ter´ə tôr ē) Land belonging to a country or government(p. 25)

Terrorism (ter´ ə riz əm) Planned violence by individuals or groups against civilians for political reasons; people who commit terrorism are called terrorists (p. 674)

Terrorist (ter´ ər ist) A group or individual who uses violence to make others give in to its demands (p. 632)

Textile (tek´ stil) Fabric or cloth (p. 236)

Theory (thē´ər ē) A best guess (p. 3)

Three-pronged attack (thrē prȯngd a tak´) An attack in three separate places against an enemy (p. 120)

Tobacco (tə bak´ ō) A plant that some people smoke or chew (p. 14)

Tolerate (tol´ ə rāt) To allow something to happen (p. 92)

Torpedo (tôr pē´ dō) A self-powered bomb that is shot from a tube of a submarine or other ship (p. 465)

Totem pole (tō´ təm pōl) A tall, colorful carved object with a certain religious meaning (p. 19)

Traditional (trə dish´ ə nəl) The usual way of doing things (p. 517)

Traitor (trā´ tər) Someone who turns against his or her own country (p. 123)

Transatlantic (tran sət lan´ tik) Crossing the Atlantic Ocean (p. 240)

Transcontinental (tran skon tə nen′ tl) Extending across a continent (p. 359)

Treason (trē′zn) A crime involving an attempt to overthrow the government (p. 298)

Treasury (trezh′ ər ē) A place where money is stored; the government department that handles money (p. 155)

Treaty (trē′ tē) An agreement to end fighting (p. 80)

Triangular trade (tri ang′gyə lər trād) Trade between Africa, the West Indies, and New England (p. 72)

Trolley (trol′ ē) A carriage that rides on rails and is used for transportation (p. 405)

Trust company (trust kum′ pə nē) A large, powerful company that often is a monopoly (p. 386)

Turnpike (tėrn′ pīk) A road that travelers pay to use (p. 238)

Tutor (tü′ tər) A person who has been paid to teach another person (p. 246)

Typesetting (tīp′ set ing) The methods used to prepare type to be printed (p. 389)

U

Unanimous (yü nan′ ə məs) When all sides agree (p. 147)

Underestimate (un dər es′ tə māt) To guess the size or importance of something as being less than it is (p. 542)

Unemployment (un em ploi′ mənt) The state of not having work (p. 228)

Unify (yü′ nə fī) To join together as a group or whole (p. 101)

Union (yü′ nyən) Territories joining together under one government (p. 75)

Unite (yü nīt′) To join together as a single unit (p. 72)

Urban (ėr′ bən) Related to the city (p. 397)

Urbanization (ėr bə nīz ā′ shən) The process of taking on the ways of city life (244)

V

Ventilation (ven tə lā′ shən) The process of circulating fresh air in an enclosed area (p. 408)

Vertical combination (vėr′ tə kəl kom bi nā′ shən) A kind of business organization that controls each step in making something (p. 385)

Veteran (vet′ ər ən) An experienced or former member of the armed forces (p. 314)

Veto (vē′ tō) The power given to the president to turn down a bill (p. 222)

Violence (vī′ ə ləns) Rough or harmful action (p. 245)

Vow (vou) To promise to do something (p. 296)

Voyage (voi′ ij) A trip, especially by sea (p. 26)

W

Wagon train (wag′ ən trān) A large number of wagons traveling together (p. 359)

Weapons of mass destruction (wep′ əns ov mas di struk′ shən) Weapons that cause death on a large scale (p. 9)

Western Hemisphere (wes′ tərn hem′ ə sfir) The land and oceans around North and South America (p. 209)

White-collar (wīt kol′ ər) A name used to describe office workers and professionals (p. 557)

Windmill (wind′ mil) A wind-powered device used to pump water from a well (p. 366)

Wiretap (wīr′ tap) A device used to listen in on phone conversations (p. 621)

a	hat	e	let	ī	ice	ȯ	order	u̇	put	sh	she	ə	a in about
ā	age	ē	equal	o	hot	oi	oil	ü	rule	th	thin		e in taken
ä	far	ėr	term	ō	open	ou	out	ch	child	ᴛʜ	then		i in pencil
â	care	i	it	ȯ	saw	u	cup	ng	long	zh	measure		o in lemon
													u in circus

Index

Bridges, 379–82, 393–94

British. *See* Great Britain and British

British Parliament. *See* Parliament

Brooklyn Bridge, 380–82

Brooks, Preston, 293, 295

Brown, John, 290–91, 297–99, 303–05, 355

Brown v. the Board of Education of Topeka, Kansas, 572–573

Bruce, Blanche, 410

Bryan, William Jennings, 426–27, 430, 444, 453, 455

Buchanan, James, 294–95, 303–04, 307–09

Buchanan, Pat, 677

Budget defined, 641

Buena Vista, 263–65

Buffalo, 367, 371

Bulgaria, 463, 480

Bulge, Battle of the, 545, 547

Bull Moose Party, 454, 457

Bull Run, 313, 316–17

Bunker Hill, 112–13, 127

Bunkers defined, 546

Bureau of the Budget, 483

Burgoyne, John, 120

Burial
    defined, 11
    grounds, 16
    mounds, 14–15, 18, 21–22

Burnside, Ambrose, 316–17, 329

Burr, Aaron, 164–66, 175

Bush, George H. W., 640, 651–53, 655–57, 659, 663–66

Bush, George W., 677–79, 681, 685, 687–96, 702–3

Bushnell, David, 112

Butler, Andrew, 293

Butler, Richard, 344

By-product defined, 387

C

Cabeza de Vaca, Álvar Núñez, 38

Cabinet, 155, 157, 175–76
    defined, 155

Cable television, 624

Cabot, John, 29, 39, 43

Cahokia, 17, 19, 22

Calhoun, John C., 181, 191, 203, 220, 278

California, 241, 253, 256, 262–67, 269–71, 273, 277–79, 283, 287–89, 359, 363, 600

Calvert, George, 55, 87

Calvert, Lord Cecilius, 55, 59, 65–66

Cambodia, 615–16, 617, 638

Cameras, 389, 393–94

Campaign, 217–18, 256, 426–27, 650
    defined, 217
    posters, 497

Camp David, 631–32

Canada, 76, 80, 114, 120, 125, 127, 181–82, 184–85, 191, 259, 261, 281, 287, 369, 520, 537, 549, 566, 681–82

Canal, 8, 10, 13, 21, 239, 253
    defined, 8

Candidate defined, 161

Cape Cod, 51, 65

Capital defined, 385

Capitol building, 686, 688, 703

Carbon monoxide, 699

Cargo defined, 98

Caribbean Sea, 440, 441

Carmichael, Stokely, 599

Carnegie, Andrew, 379–82, 384–86, 393–95, 433

Carnegie Steel, 385–86

Carolina, 56, 59, 65–66, 87. *See also* North Carolina; South Carolina

Carothers, Wallace H., 521

Carpenter's Hall, 101

Carpetbaggers, 341, 345, 347, 351
    defined, 341

Carson, Rachel, 597

Carter, Jimmy, 614, 620, 628–38, 641

Cartier, Jacques, 31, 36, 39–40, 43

Carver, George Washington, 388

Carver, John, 51, 54

Cash crop defined, 181

Cass, Lewis, 265–66

Castro, Fidel, 586, 607, 611

Casualty defined, 664

Catlin, George, 372

Cattle ranching, 362–64, 366–67, 375–76, 387, 391

Cayuga, 17

Cease-fire, 547, 616
    defined, 547

Centennial defined, 348

Centennial Exposition, 353

Central America, 449–50, 630, 645

Central High School, 578

Central Pacific Railroad, 359–61, 375–76, 433

Central Powers, 463, 465
    defined, 463

Chacoan Anasazi, 11

Chaco Canyon, 11

Challenger, 643–44, 655, 657

Chamberlain, Neville, 531–32, 534

Champlain, Lake, 185, 192

Champlain, Samuel de, 36

Chancellor defined, 528

Chancellorsville, 319, 322

Charles I, 55

Charles II, 56–57, 65–66

Charleston (South Carolina), 99, 114, 124, 206, 244

Charleston (dance), 491, 499

Charter defined, 34

Chattel slavery defined, 61

Chavez, Cesar, 600, 602, 608

Checks and balances, 173

Cheney, Dick, 677, 695

Cherokees, 17, 204, 209, 224, 227, 231

Chesapeake Bay, 55, 65, 124

Cheyenne, 367, 369, 375

Chicago (Illinois), 363, 366, 397, 406, 422, 469

Chickasaws, 224

Chief justice, 142, 173

Child labor, 237, 391, 398–99, 512

China and Chinese, 25, 29, 442–43, 448–49, 457, 503, 560, 614, 618–20, 637, 639
    immigrants, 374, 401
    Revolution, 568–69
    working in America, 360, 362, 376, 401, 518
    World War II and, 529, 539, 541

Chinampas, 8

Chinese Communist Party, 568

Chiricahua Apaches, 370

Chisholm Trail, 364

Choctaws, 224, 231

Chou En-lai, 618, 620

Chouteau, Auguste, 78

Churchill, Winston, 536, 546, 550, 563, 580

Church of England, 50

Cincinnati (Ohio), 239

Citizenship, 403, 528
    defined, 528

City of Brotherly Love, 57

Civics Connection, 33, 71, 138, 242, 339, 403, 490, 591, 679

Civilian Conservation Corps (CCC), 512, 523–24

Civilian defined, 542

Civilizations, 2, 6–9, 21, 23, 43. *See also* Names of individual civilizations
    defined, 6

Civil lawsuits defined, 149

Civil Rights Act, 336, 351–52, 402, 590, 593, 599, 608

Civil rights defined, 337

Civil Rights Law, 611

Civil rights movement, 556, 572–574, 578, 579, 580, 582, 589–91, 598–600, 607, 609, 611

Civil service, 417, 429–31
    defined, 417

Civil War, 306–31
    defined, 308

Clark, George Rogers, 122, 128

Clark, William, 171, 173, 175, 177

Classes, 61

Clause defined, 115

Clay, Henry, 179, 181, 191, 200, 203, 206, 210–11, 214, 223–24, 227, 260, 278

Clean Air Act, 597, 620

Reagan, Ronald, 628, 640–50, 655–57, 667
Reaper, 237
Rebellion, 216. *See also* Boxer Rebellion; Shays's Rebellion; Turner, Nat
defined, 73
Rebels, 586, 607
Rebuild defined, 326
Recall, 446, 447, 457
defined, 446
Reconstruction Act, 338–41, 345, 351–52, 355
Reconstruction defined, 334
Reconstruction Finance Corporation, 510
Recovery defined, 511
Recovery Program. *See* Marshall Plan
Recruit defined, 76
Red Cloud, Chief, 370
Redeem defined, 124
Red Scare, 495
Reed, Ezekiel, 119
Reed, Walter, 441, 459
Reference book defined, 247
Referendum, 446, 457
defined, 446
Reform, 357, 414–33, 479, 503, 511
defined, 415
Bill Clinton's, 667–68, 675
Franklin Roosevelt's, 510–18
Theodore Roosevelt's, 436, 444–47
Reformers, 417–20, 424–27, 429, 453, 461, 495. *See also* Progressive Party
Reform Party, 677
Refuge defined, 60
Refugee defined, 586
Regiment, 77
African American, 319
defined, 77
Regular Army defined, 182
Regulate
defined, 70
trade, 71–73, 83, 133, 141
Reich defined, 531
Reinforcements defined, 80
Relationship defined, 91
Repeal, 93, 95, 105, 173
defined, 93
Representative defined, 49
Republican National Convention, 628
Republican Party, 166, 284–85, 300–01, 347, 417–19, 429, 483
Republic defined, 441
Republic of Columbia, 449–50
Republic of Korea, 568
Republic of Panama, 450
Republic of Texas, 226, 231
Reservations, 337, 368–69, 370, 375–76
defined, 368
Reservoir defined, 12

Resistance, 99, 337
defined, 99
Resolution defined, 164
Resource defined, 169
Responsibility, 69, 83, 87
defined, 69
Retail defined, 405
Reunification defined, 659
Revenue, 94, 98, 182
defined, 94
Revere, Paul, 102–03
Revise defined, 451
Revolt, 206–07, 213, 216, 219, 231–33, 273, 297, 303, 449–50
defined, 206
Revolutionary War. *See* American Revolutionary War
Revolution defined, 117
Rhode Island, 55, 62, 65–66, 87, 147, 247
Rice, 343, 529
Rich, Adrienne, 427
Richardson, Elliot, 621–22
Richmond (Virginia), 310–12, 314–15, 323, 325
Riis, Jacob, 408
Rio Grande River, 262–63, 269
Riots, 469, 589, 591, 603, 677
defined, 589
Ritual defined, 10
Rival defined, 618
Roads, 200, 213, 344
Roanoke (North Carolina), 34–35, 37, 39, 41
Roaring Twenties, 482–503
Rockefeller, John D., 379, 384–86, 393–95, 433, 446
Rockets, 477
Rocky Mountains, 171, 359, 362, 375–77
Roebling, Emily and John, 381
Rolfe, John, 48
Rome (Italy), 544, 549, 646
Romero, Oscar, Archbishop, 630
Roosevelt, Eleanor, 529
Roosevelt, Franklin Delano, 506, 510–13, 516–17, 523–25, 526, 529–30, 535, 537, 539–40, 543, 545–46, 548–50, 553, 558, 605
Roosevelt, Theodore, 390, 434, 436, 437, 439, 444–55, 457–59, 466, 484, 503
Roosevelt Corollary, 449
"Rosie the Riveter," 540
Ross, John, 204
Rough Riders, 439, 440
Rovers, 601
Royal Air Force (RAF), 536
Ruby, Jack, 592
Ruckelshaus, William, 622
Ruling defined, 294
Runaway defined, 141. *See also* Slaves and slavery

Running mate defined, 164
Rural, 235, 512
defined, 235
Russia and Russians, 449, 577, 660–62, 669, 672, 681–82. *See also* Soviet Union
Communism and, 494–95
immigrants, 400, 411, 433
World War I and, 461, 463, 480
Russian Federation, 661
Rust Belt, 700–01
Ruth, Babe, 496

S

Sacajawea, 171
Sacramento (California), 359, 361
Sadat, Anwar, 631–32, 646
Saigon (South Vietnam), 616–17
St. Lawrence River, 31, 36, 39, 43
St. Leger, Barry, 120
St. Louis (Missouri), 239, 359
St. Marks (Florida), 204, 213
St. Marys City (Maryland), 55, 65
Salem (Massachusetts), 244
Salk, Jonas E., 605
Salt Lake City (Utah), 397
Salvation Army, 408, 411
Sampson, William, 439
San Antonio (Texas), 225, 230, 364
Sanction defined, 649
San Francisco (California), 266, 397, 450, 522, 560, 579–80, 611
Sanitation, 407, 411–12
defined, 407
San Jacinto River, 226
San Juan Hill, 439, 457
Santa Anna, Antonio López de, 225–26, 230, 262
Santa María, 26
Santiago harbor, 439
Santo Domingo, 449
Sarajevo, 461–62, 479, 480
Saratoga, 108, 120, 122–23, 127, 129
Satellites, 312, 577, 579–80, 601, 611, 698
Saturday Night Massacre, 622
Saudi Arabia, 663–64, 681
Sauk and Fox, 224, 463
Savannah (Georgia), 58, 65–66, 124–25, 324
Scalawag, 341, 345, 347, 351
defined, 341
Scandal, 347, 484, 499–500, 503. *See also* Contra Scandal; Crédit Mobilier Scandal; Teapot Dome; Watergate Scandal; Whiskey Ring Scandal
defined, 347
Scarlet Letter, The, 249, 254
Schmeling, Max, 519, 524
Schwarzkopf, Norman, 664

Tilden, Samuel J., 348
Timber resources, 363
Tin can, 189
Tippecanoe, 257, 270
Titusville (Pennsylvania), 383–84, 393
Tlingit, 19, 21
Tobacco, 14, 48–49, 343
  defined, 14
Tojo, Hideki, 539
Tolerate, defined, 92
Toleration Act, 55
Toltecs, 7, 9
Tom Thumb, 240
Tonkin Gulf Resolution, 596–97, 607–08,
  611
Torpedo, 465, 471
  defined, 465
Totem pole, 19, 23
  defined, 19
Townshend, Charles, 94, 97
Townshend Acts, 94–97, 105–06
Trade, 157, 202, 213. *See also* Open Door
  Policy; Regulate trade
  American Indian, 15, 17–18, 76
  Arab, 25
  colonial, 68, 70–73, 83, 87
  international, 70, 83, 179, 182, 191
  problems, 132, 141
Traditional defined, 517
Trail of Tears, 204, 216, 223–24
Traitor, 123, 125, 128, 572
  defined, 123
Transatlantic, 240, 243, 253, 496, 499,
  503, 520
  defined, 240
Transcendentalism, 251
Transcontinental
  defined, 359
  railroad, 358–61, 375–77, 415, 433
Transportation, 234, 238–42. *See also*
  Automobiles; Highways; Railroads;
  Roads; Trolleys
  water, 239
  public, 200, 240–42, 253
Travel, 487, 514. *See also* Automobiles
Travis, William Barrett, 225–26, 230
Treason, 298, 303
  defined, 298
Treasury, 155, 157
  defined, 155
Treaty. *See also* Jay's Treaty
  defined, 80
  of 1846, 261
  of Ghent, 188–89, 191, 193, 195
  of Guadalupe Hidalgo, 263, 269
  of Paris, 80–81, 83–85, 87, 91, 125,
    127, 130, 132, 195
  of Versailles, 460, 475–77, 479, 481,
    503, 531, 533
  Reconstruction, 337
  with American Indians, 368, 370

Trenches, 470, 471
Trenton (New Jersey), 118–19, 127
Trevor's Campaign, 671
Triangular trade, 68, 72–73, 83–84, 87
Trist, Nicholas P., 263
Trolley defined, 405
Truman, Harry S., 546–47, 549, 553,
  561–62, 566, 568–72, 580
Truman Doctrine, 564
Trust company, 386, 424, 427, 453–55
  defined, 386
Truth, Sojourner, 281–82, 287
Truth-in-Securities Act, 512
Tsimshian, 19, 21
Tubman, Harriet, 281, 285, 287–88
Turkey, 463, 480, 564
Turner, Nat, 216, 219, 221, 231–33, 273
Turnpikes defined, 238
Tuscarora, 17
Tuskegee Institute, 388
Twain, Mark, 342, 415
Tweed, William Marcy, 417, 420, 429–30
12th Amendment, 165, 175
21st Amendment, 495
22nd Amendment, 584–85
Tyler, John, 257–58, 270

U

Ukraine, 660, 669, 681
Unanimous defined, 147
Uncle Tom's Cabin, 250–51
Underground Railroad, 276, 280–82,
  285, 287–88
Unemployment, 228, 334, 505, 507, 509,
  514–15, 518, 523–24, 553, 557–58,
  625, 637, 666
  defined, 228
Unify defined, 101
Union defined, 75. *See also* Labor unions
Union Pacific Railroad, 359–61, 375–76,
  415–16, 429–30, 433
Unite, 72, 115
  defined, 72
United Mine Workers of America, 445
United Nations, 33, 529, 546, 556,
  560–62, 569–70, 579–80, 611, 663,
  669, 671–72, 690, 693–94
  Human Rights Commission, 529,
    643
  Security Council, 568, 663, 665, 691
United States
  Army, 182
  Bureau of the Census, 146
  Department of Defense, 641, 686
  Forest Service, 448
  Military Academy, 167
  Navy, 123, 162, 175, 182–83, 471–72,
    646
  Postal Service, 241–42

Universal Declaration of Human Rights,
  529
Universal Negro Improvement
  Association, 493
University of Mississippi, 589, 593
Urbanization defined, 244. *See also*
  Urban living
Urban living
  areas, 245, 253, 433
  benefits of, 405–06
  defined, 397
  growth, 357, 396–409, 411–13, 433
  problems of, 407–09
Utah, 278, 362

V

Vaccinations, 160, 605
Valley Forge, 121–22
Van Buren, Martin, 216–17, 227–29, 231,
  257, 265, 273
Vanderbilt, Cornelius, 387, 393–94, 433
Venezuela, 451
Vermont, 109, 516
Verrazano, Giovanni da, 31, 39, 43
Vertical combination defined, 385
Vesey, Denmark, 206–7, 213–14
Vespucci, Amerigo, 29, 39–40, 43
Veteran defined, 314
Veteran's Bureau, 483, 485
Veto, 222, 224, 231
  defined, 222
Vicksburg (Mississippi), 239, 323, 327,
  330
Victory gardens, 542–43
Vietcong, 597, 615
Vietnam, 582, 603–05, 609, 611, 614–17,
  637, 639, 681
Vietnam War, 582, 603–05, 609, 611,
  614–17, 637, 639
Viking I, 627
Violence, 245, 293, 298, 347, 349, 433,
  589–93, 603–05, 607
  defined, 245
Virginia, 36, 47–49, 62, 66, 109–10,
  135–36, 146–47, 199, 323
  Company, 36, 39, 43, 48–49
  Plan, 130, 139–41, 151
Voting rights
  Act, 599
  of African Americans, 222, 335–37,
    346, 351, 355, 589
  of women, 162–63, 200, 262, 346,
    362, 423, 478, 489–90, 499–500, 503
Voyage defined, 26

W

Wages, 398–99, 412. *See also* Minimum
  wage

Acknowledgments

Acknowledgment is made for permission to reprint and record the following copyrighted material.

Page 38: Excerpt reprinted with permission of Scribner, an imprint of Simon & Schuster Adult Publishing Group, from *Cabeza de Vaca's Adventures in the Unknown Interior of America,* translated and annotated by Cyclone Covey. Copyright © 1961 by Macmillan Publishing Company.

Page 374: Excerpt from *China Men* copyright © 1977 by Maxine Hong Kingston. Alfred A. Knopf. Reprinted and digitalized by permissin of the author and the Sandra Dijkstra Literary Agency.

Page 498: Excerpt from "Race Prejudice and the Negro Artist" by James Weldon Johnson. Permission by Dr. Sondra Kathryn Wilson, Executor of the Estate of Trace and James Weldon Johnson.

Page 522: Excerpt from "Bread Lines," by Hugo Johanson, *The Atlantic Monthly,* 1936. Reproduced with permission of *The Atlantic Monthly.*

Page 554: TM/© 2005 the Cesar E. Chavez Foundation. www.chavezfoundation.org. Used by permission.

Page 578: Excerpt from *The Long Shadow of Little Rock* by Daisy Bates. Reprinted by permission of The University of Arkansas Press. Copyright © 1987 by Daisy Bates.

Page 612: From poem "On the Pulse of Morning" by Maya Angelou, copyright © 1993 by Maya Angelou. Used by permission of Random House, Inc.

Page 654: Excerpt from *Vital Speeches of the Day,* "Women in America Shooting for the Stars: As We See Ourselves So Do We Act" by Stella Guerra, September 15, 1986.

Page 680: Excerpt from *Vital Speeches of the Day,* "Favor Positive Themes" by Luis W. Morales, July 15, 1996.

Other Acknowledgments

Page xxx: Excerpt from Stephen R. Lilley, *The Conquest of Mexico.* San Diego: Lucent Books, 1997, p. 19. (Fair Use)

Page 20: Excerpt from *The Omaha Tribe,* trans. by Alice Fletcher and Francis LaFlesche, 1905–1906. (Public Domain)

Page 44: Quote from Virginia Company Broadside, in *The Genesis of the United States* edited by Alexander Brown, 1890, Vol. 1, pp. 248-9. (Public Domain)

Page 762-763: From *The World Almanac and Book of Facts 2005,* pages 43, 571-572; © 2005 World Almanac Education Group, a WRC Media Inc. company.

Page 196: Quote from *My Antonia* by Willa Cather, 1918. (Public Domain)

Page 350: Excerpt from W. E. B. DuBois letter to student, 1905, as appeared in *A Documentary History of the Negro People in the United States,* by Herbert Aptheker. (Public Domain)

Page 392: Excerpt from *History of the Later Years of the Hawaiian Monarchy,* by W. D. Alexander, 1896. (Public Domain)

Image Credits

Page viii, 309, © Library of Congress

Unit 1 Opener
© Dan Budnik/Woodfin Camp & Associates

Chapter 1
Page 5, © Mercyhurst Archaeological Institute; Page 7, © Richard A. Cooke, III; Page 9, © Stephen Alvarez/ National Geographic Image Collection; Page 11, © Nancy Carter/ North Wind Picture Archives; Page 12, © Ray Manley, SuperStock; Page14, © Richard A. Cooke, III; Page 17, © Michael S. Lewis/ Corbis; Page 19, © Anne B. Keiser/National Geographic Image Collection

Chapter 2
Pages 26, 29, 30, 34, 35, 36, 37, © The Granger Collection, New York

Unit 2 Opener
© The Granger Collection, New York

Chapter 3
Pages 47, 51, 52, © The Granger Collection, New York; Page 53, © New York Historical Society, New York, USA/Bridgeman Art Library; Page 57, © Francis G. Mayer/Corbis; Page 58, © Judy King

Chapter 4
Page 70, © Bettmann/Corbis; Pages 73, 76, 80, 82, © The Granger Collection, New York

Unit 3 Opener
© The Granger Collection, New York

Chapter 5
Pages 91, 93, © The Granger Collection, New York; Pages 95, 97, © Bettmann/Corbis; Page 99, © The Granger Collection, New York; Page 102 (both), © The Granger Collection, New York

Chapter 6
Page 112, © Bettmann/Corbis; Page 115 (top), © The Granger Collection, New York; Page 115 (bottom), © John McGrail Photography; Page 118, © Courtesy of Putnam County Historian; Page 121, © The Granger Collection, New York

Chapter 7
Page 131, © North Wind Picture Archives; Page 133 © The Granger Collection, New York; Page 134, © Massachusetts Historical Society; Pages 136, 143, © The Granger Collection, New York; Page 144, © North Wind Picture Archives

Chapter 8
Pages 155, 156, 157, © The Granger Collection, New York; Page 158, © Francis G. Mayer/Corbis; Pages 162, 164, 171, 173, © The Granger Collection, New York

Chapter 9
Page 179, © Corbis; Page 182, © The Granger Collection, New York; Page 183, © Bettmann/ Corbis; Page 184, © The Granger Collection, New York; Page 186, © Bettmann/ Corbis

Unit 4 Opener
© Newberry Library, Chicago/SuperStock

Chapter 10
Page 201, 202, 204, © The Granger Collection, New York; Page 205, © Corbis; Page 209 (top), © The Granger Collection, New York; Page 209 (bottom), © Burstein Collection/Corbis; New York

Chapter 11
Pages 217, 219, 222, © The Granger Collection, New York; Page 223, © Woolaroc Museum; Pages 225, 228, © The Granger Collection, New York

Chapter 12
Page 237 (top), © The Granger Collection, New York; Page 237 (bottom), © Graphic Arts Collection, National Museum of American History, Smithsonian Institution, Photograph number 86-6161; Pages 240, 241, © Brown Brothers; Page 246, © Francis G. Mayer/Corbis; Pages 247, 248, 252, © The Granger Collection, New York

Chapter 13
Page 257, © The Granger Collection, New York; Page 258 (left), © Bettmann/Corbis; Page 258 (right), © The Huntington Library, Art Collections, and Botanical Gardens, San Marino, California/SuperStock; Page 261, © The Granger Collection, New York; Page 262, © Bettmann/ Corbis; Pages 263, 266, © Brown Brothers

Unit 5 Opener
© The Granger Collection, New York

Chapter 14
Page 281 (top), © The Granger Collection, New York; Page 281 (middle), © Brown Brothers; Page 281 (bottom), © The Granger Collection, New York; Page 285, © Culver Pictures

Chapter 15
Page 292, © Culver Pictures; Pages 293, 294, 296, © The Granger Collection, New York; Page 297, © Brown Brothers

Chapter 16
Page 307, © Brown Brothers; Page 308, © Bettmann/Corbis; Page 310, © The Granger Collection, New York; Page 311, © Bettmann/Corbis; Page 313, © Brown Brothers; Page 315, © The Granger Collection, New York; Page 316, © Bettmann/ Corbis; Page 318, © The Granger Collection, New York; Page 319, © Bettmann/Corbis; Page 321, © The Granger Collection, New York; Page 323, © Burstein Collection/ Corbis; Pages 324, 326, © The Granger Collection, New York; Page 327, © Brown Brothers

Chapter 17
Page 333, © Bettmann/Corbis; Pages 334, 338, © The Granger Collection, New York; Page 341, © Bettmann/ Corbis; Page 344, © Underwood Photo Archives; Page 345, © J.C. Coovert/Library of Congress; Page 346, © Library of Congress; Page 347, © The Granger Collection, New York; Page 350, © Brown Brothers